Freud, Biologist of the Mind

FRANK J. SULLOWAY is a Harvard-trained historian of science who wrote this book while a Junior Fellow in the Harvard Society of Fellows and, more recently, as a member of the Institute for Advanced Study at Princeton. He is currently a Miller Institute postdoctoral fellow in psychology at the University of California, Berkeley.

Sigmund Freud in 1922 (age 66).

Freud, Biologist of the Mind

BEYOND THE PSYCHOANALYTIC LEGEND

Frank J. Sulloway

FONTANA PAPERBACKS

First published in Great Britain by
Burnett Books Ltd in association with
André Deutsch Ltd 1979

First issued in Fontana Paperbacks 1980

Copyright © Basic Books Inc. 1979

Made and printed in Great Britain by
Richard Clay (The Chaucer Press) Ltd,
Bungay, Suffolk

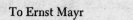

To Ernst Mayr

CONTENTS

PART TWO
PSYCHOANALYSIS:
THE BIRTH OF A GENETIC PSYCHOBIOLOGY

PART THREE
IDEOLOGY, MYTH, AND HISTORY IN THE
ORIGINS OF PSYCHOANALYSIS

PREFACE AND GUIDE TO THE READER

This book, a comprehensive intellectual biography of Sigmund Freud, seeks to bring both Freud and the history of psychoanalysis within the professional boundaries of the history of science. Hitherto, Freud scholarship has been a largely internal affair dominated by Freud, the Freud family, psychoanalysts-turned-historians, and former patients. Over the years, these psychoanalytic devotees have cultivated a complex and politically expedient mythology about their collective past, a mythology that ranks as a fascinating accomplishment in its own right. The present work is by no means the first publication to challenge the Freud legend. Dissident historical voices have been calling for a substantial reinterpretation of Freud and his achievements for many years, and such voices were heard even while Freud's able lieutenant Ernest Jones (1953–57) was in the midst of his monumental three-volume biography of Freud. But the Freud legend, together with the historical scenario that purports to legitimate it, has proved difficult indeed to supplant; and there are strong reasons why this is so and why, except to the historical specialist, this may always be so. If in this intellectual biography I have aspired to mark a watershed in the history of Freud studies, I have not underestimated either the resilience of the Freud legend or the powerful historical credibility of such a sophisticated mythology. On the contrary, I have dedicated the third and concluding part of this book to elucidating the brilliant political strategy embodied in the Freud legend, and I have particularly emphasized this legend's numerous affinities with the classical myth of the hero.

I have aimed a number of chapters at a general audience of scholars and laymen, who, independently of their interest in Freud, will, I hope, value this book for the various psychological, sociological, and historical issues it raises. Thus, each chapter has been carefully designed so that it may be read apart from the whole. Additionally, each chapter ends with a summary and concluding section—easily located through the table of contents—to facilitate access both to the book's general contents and to the broader context of each chapter.

As a further help, I offer here a brief guide to the reader. This work consists of three parts, of which the first two (Chapters 1–11) represent the intellectual biography proper, and the third (Chapters 12–14) forms a theoretical commentary on the Freud legend as a whole. In the specific context of Freud studies, Chapter 5 ("Wilhelm Fliess and the Mathematics of Human Sexual Biology") and Chapter 6 ("Freud's Psychoanalytic Transformation of the Fliessian Id") constitute perhaps the most original aspects of this revisionist interpretation of Freud. In treating the origins of psychoanalysis as a genetic psychobiology during the period of Freud's most creative intellectual achievements, these two chapters introduce an entirely new historical interpretation of Freud and his theories; they also credit the long-neglected Wilhelm Fliess—the "father of biorhythms theory"—with a significant and long-suppressed part in this story. Chapters 7–8 and 10–11 extend this historical conception, independently of Fliess, to encompass the whole of Freud's doctrines seen in the wider context of nineteenth-century psychobiological theory. Chapter 9 ("Dreams and the Psychopathology of Everyday Life") presents a comprehensive review of Freud's theories of dreaming and the normal mind and illustrates these conceptions through various clinical examples drawn from his works. This chapter may be read as a convenient introduction to Freud's theory of the mind.

In addition to the Introduction and the Epilogue, four chapters possess a more general scope than the rest. Chapter 7 ("The Darwinian Revolution's Legacy to Psychology and Psychoanalysis") and Chapter 8 ("Freud and the Sexologists") treat the pervasive influence exerted by Charles Darwin and evolutionary theory upon Freud and his scientific generation. Darwin's influence on Freud—a conceptual bond that unites two of the most important revolutionaries in the history of scientific thought—has long received formal lip service from traditional Freud scholarship. Ultimately, however, this source of inspiration is in fundamental conflict with the Freud legend, so that what has emerged in Freud studies is a classic "compromise formation" in which the real influence of Darwin and evolutionary theory has gone unrecognized. The relationship between Freud and the contemporary sexology movement led by Richard von Krafft-Ebing, Havelock Ellis, Albert Moll, and others (Chapter 8) is a particularly fascinating and little-documented aspect of this whole Darwinian influence. For it was largely through the sexologists, among whom we must include Wilhelm Fliess, that Freud was prompted to substitute an evolutionary and phylogenetic conception of psychosexuality for the physicochemical one with which he and Josef Breuer began their pioneering studies of the neuroses.

Two other chapters—Chapter 12 ("Freud as Crypto-Biologist") and Chapter 13 ("The Myth of the Hero in the Psychoanalytic Movement")— place Freud and his followers in the even more general context of the sociology of knowledge. These chapters seek to illustrate the political power of historical knowledge by analyzing the psychosociological determinants of how people—in this case psychoanalysts—choose to remember their past. Here I explain how the Freud legend arose and what inspired this legend's major features. In this context, Freud and his movement are presented as a particularly cogent case study of man's pervasive need to shape historical consciousness in ways that legitimate the here and now. Above all, what I have sought to achieve in Part Three is a social psychology of myth and legend, especially as it pertains to scientific revolutions and revolutionary ideology.

Finally, I see that one of the major achievements of this work is the construction of a natural history of history itself—a natural history that, however crude and incomplete in its present outlines, may nevertheless prove useful to future students of science, myth, and ideology; for the sociology of knowledge is still, in spite of its already venerable history, a field of the future. I hope this book will be appreciated both as a unified conceptual history and, more generally, as a contribution to the problem of how human beings—for whom recollection is always an active reconstruction—respond to their past.

ACKNOWLEDGMENTS

I could not have written this book without access to the splendid resources of three great libraries: Widener Library, Harvard University; Countway Library, Harvard Medical School; and the University Library, Cambridge, England. I am particularly indebted to the Widener Interlibrary Loan Staff, headed by Barbara Dames, for many years of tireless assistance in procuring rare publications.

Dr. Anna Freud kindly allowed me to examine that portion of her father's personal library retained by him when he immigrated to London in 1938. I am especially grateful to Dr. Freud and to her housekeeper, Paula Fichtl, for their gracious hospitality during my several visits to the Freud home. My access to the Library of the New York State Psychiatric Institute, where another major portion of Freud's personal library was housed prior to June 1978, was facilitated by James W. Montgomery and John B. Harrison.

This book was written largely during my tenure as a Junior Fellow in the Harvard Society of Fellows (1974–77). To the society I extend my warmest appreciation for the unusual opportunity that was afforded to me. I am also grateful to the School of Social Sciences at the Institute for Advanced Study, where I spent a year as a visiting member during 1977–78.

I am indebted to my several mentors at Harvard University for their considerable advice and encouragement in connection with this project: most notably, to Stephen J. Gould, Everett Mendelsohn, Barbara Rosenkrantz, and Edward O. Wilson. I owe a special debt of gratitude to I. Bernard Cohen, Donald Fleming, Nathan G. Hale, Jr., Robert R. Holt, Jerome Kagan, Ernst Mayr, Carl Pletsch, Shirley Roe, and Alvah W. Sulloway for reading the manuscript in its entirety and for offering detailed criticisms regarding style and content. With Professors Kagan and Mayr I shared my emerging ideas and drew in the process upon their own numerous thoughts and reactions. Their influence has been far greater than may be judged from my references to them in the text.

Gretel Mayr, Teresa Decker, and Karl Kaussen were kind enough to check a number of my translations from the German. John Lupo did most of the photographic work, and always with superb technical skill. The manuscript was typed in its entirety by Susan Learned-

Driscoll, who suggested many improvements in the text and whose accuracy as a typist continually bordered on the unbelievable. Finally, I am grateful to Phoebe Hoss and Julia Strand for their splendid skills and painstaking professionalism in the editing of my manuscript.

Grateful acknowledgment is made to the following for permission to reprint previously published material:

Basic Books, Inc., and The Hogarth Press Ltd.: Excerpts from *The Life and Work of Sigmund Freud* by Ernest Jones. Copyright © 1953 by Ernest Jones. Excerpts from *Studies on Hysteria* by Sigmund Freud and Josef Breuer, translated and edited by James Strachey in collaboration with Anna Freud. Published in the United States by Basic Books, Inc., by arrangement with the Hogarth Press Ltd.

Basic Books, Inc., The Hogarth Press Ltd., and Sigmund Freud Copyrights Ltd.: Excerpts from *The Origins of Psycho-Analysis, Letters to Wilhelm Fliess, Drafts and Notes: 1887–1902,* by Sigmund Freud, edited by Marie Bonaparte, Anna Freud, and Ernst Kris, translated by Eric Mosbacher and James Strachey. Copyright © 1954 by Basic Books, Inc. Excerpts from *Three Essays on the Theory of Sexuality* by Sigmund Freud, translated and edited by James Strachey. Copyright © 1962 by Sigmund Freud Copyrights Ltd. and Basic Books, Inc. Excerpts from *The Letters of Sigmund Freud, 1873–1939,* selected and edited by Ernst L. Freud, translated by James and Tania Stern. Copyright © 1960 by Sigmund Freud Copyrights Ltd. and Basic Books, Inc.

Basic Books, Inc., and George Allen & Unwin Ltd.: Excerpts from *The Interpretation of Dreams* by Sigmund Freud, translated and edited by James Strachey. Published in the United States by Basic Books, Inc., by arrangement with George Allen & Unwin Ltd. and The Hogarth Press Ltd.

W. W. Norton & Company, Inc., and The Hogarth Press Ltd.: Excerpts from *An Autobiographical Study* by Sigmund Freud, translated by James Strachey. Copyright © 1952 by W. W. Norton & Company, Inc., and renewed 1963 by James Strachey. Excerpts from *Beyond the Pleasure Principle* by Sigmund Freud, translated and edited by James Strachey. Copyright © 1961 by James Strachey. Reprinted by arrangement with Liveright Publishing Corporation.

W. W. Norton & Company, Inc., and George Allen & Unwin Ltd.: Excerpts from *Introductory Lectures on Psycho-Analysis* by Sigmund Freud, translated and edited by James Strachey. Copyright © 1920, 1935 by Edward L. Bernays, © 1963, 1964, 1965 by James Strachey, © 1966 by W. W. Norton & Company, Inc.

International Universities Press, Inc.: Excerpts from *The Minutes of the Vienna Psychoanalytic Society,* edited by Herman Nunberg and Ernst Federn. Vol. 1: Copyright © 1962 by Herman Nunberg and Ernst Federn; Vol. 2: © 1967 by Herman Nunberg and Ernst Federn; Vol. 3: © 1974 by International Universities Press, Inc.; Vol. 4: © 1975 by International Universities Press, Inc.

W. W. Norton & Company, Inc., The Hogarth Press Ltd., Sigmund Freud Copyrights Ltd., and The Institute of Psycho-Analysis.: Excerpts from *The Standard Edition of the Complete Psychological Works of Sigmund Freud,* translated and edited by James Strachey. Copyright © 1957, 1958, 1959, 1960, 1962, 1964 by James Strachey, The Hogarth Press Ltd., and W. W. Norton & Company, Inc.

ABBREVIATIONS

Anfänge

Freud (1950a [1887–1902]), *Aus den Anfängen der Psychoanalyse: Briefe an Wilhelm Fliess, Abhandlungen und Notizen aus den Jahren 1887–1902.* Introduction by Ernst Kris. Edited by Marie Bonaparte, Anna Freud, and Ernst Kris. London: Imago Publishing Co.

Autobiography

Freud (1925d [1924]), *An Autobiographical Study.* In *Standard Edition,* 20:3–70.

C.W.

Jung (1953—), *The Collected Works of C. G. Jung.* Edited by Gerhard Adler, Michael Fordham, and Herbert Read. William McGuire, Executive Editor. Translated by R. F. C. Hull, Bollingen Series XX. Vols. 1, 3–5, 7–12, and 15–17, New York: Pantheon Books, 1953–66; vols. 2, 6, 13–14, and 18, Princeton: Princeton University Press, 1967–76; London: Routledge & Kegan Paul.

Freud/Abraham Letters

Freud (1965b), *A Psycho-Analytic Dialogue: The Letters of Sigmund Freud and Karl Abraham 1907–1926.* Edited by Hilda C. Abraham and Ernst L. Freud. Translated by Bernard Marsh and Hilda C. Abraham. New York: Basic Books; London: Hogarth Press and The Institute of Psycho-Analysis.

Freud/Andreas-Salomé Letters

Freud (1972a), *Sigmund Freud and Lou Andreas-Salomé: Letters.* Edited by Ernst Pfeiffer. Translated by William and Elaine Robson-Scott. New York: Harcourt Brace Jovanovich; London: Hogarth Press and The Institute of Psycho-Analysis.

Freud/Jung Letters

Freud (1974b), *The Freud/Jung Letters: The Correspondence between Sigmund Freud and C. G. Jung.* Edited by William McGuire. Translated by Ralph Manheim and R. F. C. Hull. Bollingen Series XCIV. Princeton: Princeton University Press; London: Routledge & Kegan Paul.

Freud library, London

That part of Freud's original library now in the possession of Anna Freud. For a partial catalogue, see Trosman and Simmons (1973).

Freud library, New York

That part of Freud's original library now in the possession of the Health Sciences Library, Columbia University, 701 W. 168th Street, New York, N.Y. For a catalogue, see Lewis and Landis (1957).

Freud/Pfister Letters

Freud (1963*b*), *Psycho-Analysis and Faith: The Letters of Sigmund Freud and Oskar Pfister*. Edited by Ernst L. Freud and Heinrich Meng. Translated by Eric Mosbacher. New York: Basic Books; London: Hogarth Press and The Institute of Psycho-Analysis.

G.W.

Freud (1940–68), *Gesammelte Werke*. 18 vols. Edited by Anna Freud with the collaboration of Marie Bonaparte (and others). Vols. 1–17, London: Imago Publishing Co., 1940–52; vol. 18, Frankfurt am Main: S. Fischer, 1968.

Jones archives

The papers of Ernest Jones now in the possession of the Institute of Psycho-Analysis, 63 New Cavendish St., London W1.

Letters

Freud (1960*b*), *Letters of Sigmund Freud*. Selected and edited by Ernst L. Freud. Translated by Tania and James Stern. New York: Basic Books; London: Hogarth Press, 1961.

Minutes

Nunberg and Federn, eds. (1962–75), *Minutes of the Vienna Psychoanalytic Society*. 4 vols. Translated by M. Nunberg in collaboration with Harold Collins. New York: International Universities Press.

Origins

Freud (1954*e*), *The Origins of Psycho-Analysis, Letters to Wilhelm Fliess, Drafts and Notes: 1887–1902*. Introduction by Ernst Kris. Edited by Marie Bonaparte, Anna Freud, and Ernst Kris. Translated by Eric Mosbacher and James Strachey. New York: Basic Books; London: Imago Publishing Co.

S.E.

Freud (1953–74), *The Standard Edition of the Complete Psychological Works of Sigmund Freud*. 24 vols. Translated from the German under the General Editorship of James Strachey. In collaboration with Anna Freud. Assisted by Alix Strachey and Alan Tyson. London: Hogarth Press and The Institute of Psycho-Analysis.

ILLUSTRATIONS

FIGURES

Freud, Biologist
of the Mind

It is making severe demands on the unity of the personality to try and make me identify myself with the author of the paper on the spinal ganglia of the petromyzon [Freud 1878a]. Nevertheless I must be he, and I think I was happier about that discovery than about others since.

Sigmund Freud to Karl Abraham,
21 September 1924

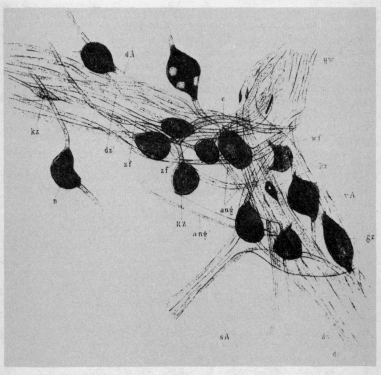

The spinal ganglia of *Ammocoetes* (*Petromyzon planeri*), a primitive form of fish, as drawn by Freud. (From 1878a: Plate 1, Fig. 1.)

Introduction

Few individuals, if any, have exerted more influence upon the twentieth century than Sigmund Freud (1856–1939). By teaching us that what "appears to be" in the life of the mind is but a tiny and often misleading reflection of the overall psychical forces that govern our lives, Freud revolutionized our thinking about ourselves. Yet in spite of his enormous influence, Freud himself remains one of the most misunderstood thinkers in the history of Western thought. This book offers a comprehensive reinterpretation of the meaning and conceptual roots of Freudian psychoanalysis. In form an intellectual biography, it elucidates Freud's scientific career; it describes the intellectual generation from which he emerged; it outlines the heritage of ideas that he absorbed from this generation; and it delineates the manner in which this conceptual legacy and other background influences in turn contributed to his brilliant scientific accomplishments. This is equally a work about Freud as a person, about his personality (and its intimate relationship to his "scientific temperament"), his ambitions, and his strengths and weaknesses.

FREUD AS CRYPTO-BIOLOGIST

At the same time, this is an intellectual biography with a particular thesis. A central message is that Freud, through the years, has become a crypto-, or covert, biologist, and that psychoanalysis has become, accordingly, a crypto-biology. It is my contention that the hidden biological roots of Freudian psychoanalytic thought must first be understood if one is to comprehend fully many of Freud's most extraordinary and controversial claims about the human mind. Significantly, these biological roots of Freudian thought were not originally as cryptic as they are today. It is only with the growth of a formidable bio-

graphical tradition in Freud studies that these roots have become so
obscured. As long ago as 1917, William Morton Wheeler, a Harvard
biologist and student of social insects, expressed his high satisfaction
with the sort of biological psychology that psychoanalysis seemed to
be pioneering in the study of man. Comparing the writings of Freud,
Jung, Adler, Jones, Ferenczi, and other psychoanalysts with the more
traditional and philosophically oriented psychologies of the times,
Wheeler saw the ties between biology and psychoanalysis as the revolutionary core of Freud's new system of ideas:

> After perusing during the past twenty years a small library of rose-water
> psychologies of the academic type and noticing how their authors ignore
> or merely hint at the existence of such stupendous and fundamental
> biological phenomena as those of hunger, sex and fear, I should not
> disagree with, let us say, an imaginary critic recently arrived from
> Mars, who should express the opinion that many of these works read
> as if they had been composed by beings that had been born and bred
> in a belfry, castrated in early infancy and fed continually for fifty years
> through a tube with a stream of liquid nutriment of constant chemical
> composition. . . .
>   Now I believe that the psychoanalysts are getting down to brass
> tacks. . . . They have had the courage to dig up the subconscious, that
> hotbed of all the egotism, greed, lust, pugnacity, cowardice, sloth, hate,
> and envy *which every single one of us carries about as his inheritance
> from the animal world*. (1920–21 [1917]:316; italics added)

As Wheeler plainly recognized, any truly meaningful theory of human
psychology must be, at the same time, a partly *biological* theory.

Likewise, Freud himself shared the deepest possible commitment
as a psychoanalyst to such a fundamental point of view about mind.
Having begun his own scientific career as a biologist, he owed his
basic scientific views to his studies with the foremost Viennese
luminaries in the fields of zoology, anatomy, and physiology. During
his crucial years of discovery as a psychoanalyst (1890–1905), Freud
therefore found it perfectly natural to place man as a biological entity
at the very heart of his psychoanalytic system. But he was also
highly ambivalent about admitting the true extent of his intellectual
debt to the field of biology. Indeed, once he had finally achieved his
revolutionary synthesis of psychology and biology, Freud actively
sought to camouflage the biological side of this creative union.

Ernest Jones (1879–1958), whose monumental three-volume study
of Freud has deservedly remained the definitive and indispensable biographical source about him since its publication in the mid-1950s, is
also among those who initially grasped Freud's work in a "psychobiological" sense. It was Jones (1913:xii) who bestowed upon Freud
the highly appropriate title, "Darwin of the mind." "If psychology is
regarded as part of biology, and surely it must be," Jones expanded
upon this theme in 1930, "then it is possible to maintain that Freud's
work, that is, the creation of psycho-analysis, signifies a contribution

to biology comparable in importance only with that of Darwin's"
(1930:601). Ironically, Ernest Jones was later to play a key role, along
with other Freudians, in establishing Freud's subsequent identity as a
"pure psychologist." For Jones, as for Freud himself, it was one
matter to recognize methodological affinities with, and psychoanalytic
contributions to, biological theory—that is, as extensions of Freud's
psychoanalytic thinking to .be ranked alongside his contributions to
literary criticism, art, history, and so forth. It was entirely another
matter for Jones and fellow analysts to admit that psychoanalysis
might owe many of its most fundamental *theoretical inspirations* to
biological sources. Psychoanalysis has therefore remained a theory of
purely psychological methodology and origins for the orthodox members of the psychoanalytic movement.

In contrast to this approach, it is my contention that many, if not
most, of Freud's fundamental conceptions were biological by *inspiration* as well as by implication. In my historical appraisal, Freud stands
squarely within an intellectual lineage where he is, at once, a principal
scientific heir of Charles Darwin and other evolutionary thinkers in
the nineteenth century and a major forerunner of the ethologists and
sociobiologists of the twentieth century. From this historical perspective, Freud's theories reveal an otherwise hidden rationality, as
well as certain limitations, that few students of his ideas have ever
really understood. In developing this particular point of view about
Freud, I am building upon a minority—but nonetheless long-standing—
voice in previous Freud scholarship.

THE MYTH OF THE HERO IN PSYCHOANALYTIC HISTORY

At yet another level, this book is a case study in the psychology and
the sociology of intellectual revolution, especially insofar as psychosociological forces contribute to distortion in history. Seen in this
context, the insufficient recognition of Freud's debt to biology stems
from an even greater source of historical misunderstanding about
Freud. I am speaking of the truly mythical proportions that Freud's
life and achievements have assumed within the subsequent biographical and historical traditions in psychoanalysis. After more than
half a century since publication of the first biography of Freud (Wittels
1924a), the mythical bubble surrounding Freud's life and achievements is finally beginning to show signs of rupture and gradual defla-
tion. With the recent progress of Freud studies, these myths can not
only be identified and set apart from historical fact but, more important, they can now be understood in their own right as an integral and
fascinating part of the historical process.

Henri Ellenberger, in his impressively erudite if also much-
disputed *Discovery of the Unconscious* (1970), has done more than

any other student of Freud's life to question these myths in a systematic matter and to sketch out their general proportions. According
to Ellenberger, the Freud legend has two main attributes: "The
first is the theme of the solitary hero struggling against a host of
enemies, suffering 'the slings and arrows of outrageous fortune' but
triumphing in the end. The legend considerably exaggerates the extent and role of anti-Semitism, of the hostility of the academic world,
and of alleged Victorian prejudices. The second feature of the Freudian legend is the blotting out of the greatest part of the scientific
and cultural context in which psychoanalysis developed, hence the
theme of the absolute originality of the achievements, in which the
hero is credited with the achievements of his predecessors, associates, disciples, rivals, and contemporaries" (1970:547).

The Freud legend undoubtedly owes its truly majestic proportions to a unique circumstance in the history of science. Psychoanalysis is the first major scientific theory of which an integral part
has been a historical vision of precisely how that theory *should have
arisen* in its author's own mind. Much has therefore been at stake in
psychoanalytic historiography vis-à-vis the truth of psychoanalytic
theory as a whole. To question the Freud legend is often to question
the foundations of Freudian thought, a possibility that Freud's more
orthodox followers have rarely been willing to entertain.

A great deal in this Freud legend is pertinent to the formation of
myths in general; and therein lies the exceptional interest of this legend to us, particularly since the myths surrounding Freud's life have
patterned themselves after "origins" and "hero" myths with a universal content. One of my major purposes has been to extract from
the study of Freud's life what may be useful to a broader understanding of legendary distortion in history and of the purposes that
such distortion generally serves in great intellectual movements. Why
is the history of intellectual revolution so often the history of conscious and unconscious attempts by the participants to obscure the
true nature and roots of their own revolutionary activity? A partial
answer to this question is that such revolutionary minds frequently
seek to deny history in order to re-create it in their own ideological
image. We are quite accustomed to this phenomenon in such overtly
political contexts as the founding of religious movements or the
overthrow of one political regime by another. It is only natural for
such movements to deify their heroes, to vilify their enemies, and to
institutionalize their moral propaganda through history. An extreme
example of this phenomenon is George Orwell's negative utopia *Nineteen Eighty-Four*, in which Big Brother and his regime systematically
rewrite history to suit their own political purposes, throwing old and
potentially embarrassing historical facts down the "memory hole."
"Who controls the past," Big Brother's Party slogan runs, "controls
the future: who controls the present controls the past" (Orwell
1949:37).

In regard to Freud, we have the rare opportunity to divine the myth-making forces at work in the biography of an intellectual who paradoxically dedicated his own career to unmasking the myths by which the rest of us live. Of course, the objective aims of the scientific investigator should not be allowed to obscure the essentially human methods by which these aims are inevitably carried out. Moreover, in science and intellectual life there generally exists a powerful underlying tension between the forward-looking orientation of the would-be discoverer and the backward-looking orientation of the historian. As a scientist, Freud might well be expected to have possessed an excellent sense of history, since his psychoanalytic methodology was essentially historical in nature. And yet when it came to himself, Freud allowed the forward-looking propensities of the scientist to interfere radically with the past, thus complicating the task of his later biographers.

What seems even more remarkable is that Freud took steps to deny history well before he had assured himself a place of lasting fame in its graces. Twice in his life, in 1885 and again in 1907, he completely destroyed all his manuscripts, private diaries, notes, and correspondence. He described the first of these two occasions, which occurred when he was only twenty-eight, in a fascinating letter of confession to his fiancée:

> One intention . . . I have almost finished carrying out, an intention which a number of as yet unborn and unfortunate people will one day resent. Since you won't guess what kind of people I am referring to, I will tell you at once: they are my biographers. I have destroyed all my notes of the past fourteen years, as well as letters, scientific excerpts, and the manuscripts of my papers. As for letters, only those from the family have been spared. Yours, my darling, were never in danger. In doing so all old friendships and relationships presented themselves once again and then silently received the *coup de grâce* (my imagination is still living in Russian history); all my thoughts and feelings about the world in general and about myself in particular have been found unworthy of further existence. They will now have to be thought all over again, and I certainly had accumulated some scribbling. But that stuff settles around me like sand drifts round the Sphinx; soon nothing but my nostrils would have been visible above the paper; I couldn't have matured or died without worrying about who would get hold of those old papers. Everything, moreover, that lies beyond the great turning point in my life, beyond our love and my choice of profession, died long ago and must not be deprived of a worthy funeral. As for the biographers, let them worry, we have no desire to make it too easy for them. Each one of them will be right in his opinion of "The Development of the Hero," and I am already looking forward to seeing them go astray. (*Letters*, pp. 140–41)

Hence Freud actively sought to cultivate the unknown about himself to ensure that he, as intellectual hero, would not be devalued by an overly detailed understanding of his genius. Even in his own lifetime this strategy had its benefits. To remain inscrutable, even if only in part, was to preserve an atmosphere of mystery about himself that in turn promoted awe and respect among those who joined his movement.

A major result of Freud's systematic destruction of his past was that, until relatively recently, psychoanalysis appeared even to his closest followers to have sprung full-blown from his own head "like Athena from the head of Zeus" (Erikson 1957:80). This circumstance, more than any other, has permitted the heroic myth of Freud's "self-analytic" path of discovery to reinforce the long-entrenched claims for psychoanalysis as a "pure psychology." In actual fact, Freud extracted many conclusions from his analyses, both of himself and of his patients, that he had already become convinced of from other, and now obliterated, sources of evidence. Biology, as a key source of these hypothetico-deductive inspirations, subsequently became a special target of analytic obliteration.

Thus, Sigmund Freud, the ruthless critic of Victorian myth and ideology, is now the subject (and, in part, the victim) of his own powerful and equally obscurantist ideology. Indeed, so caught up were Freud and his followers by the legends they helped to create that they came to live many of these legends as psychological reality. Fact and legend were continually blending during the rise of the psychoanalytic movement. It is hardly surprising, then, that the history of psychoanalysis proves to be such a paradigm of "history remembered, recovered, and invented"—to borrow the felicitous phrase of Bernard Lewis (1975). To understand Freud as "psychobiologist," one must extricate historical fact from fiction and examine them side by side. It is to this end that I have devoted this book.

PART ONE

FREUD AND NINETEENTH-CENTURY PSYCHOPHYSICS

1

The Nature and Origins
of Psychoanalysis

THE NATURE OF FREUD'S ACHIEVEMENT

Psychoanalysis may be conveniently introduced in terms of three interdependent achievements by Freud: (1) a method, (2) a theory of the neuroses, and (3) a theory of the normal mind.

At a practical and clinical level, psychoanalysis is an *original method* of psychological investigation. Briefly, this method attempts to elucidate repressed and therefore unconscious mental impulses in a patient. Most commonly, this end is achieved by requiring the patient to lie on a couch and to report—without fail—everything that comes to mind (the "fundamental rule" of psychoanalysis). The analyst then interprets these reports and other relevant psychoanalytic material (e.g., symptoms, dreams, slips of the tongue, etc.) according to psychoanalytic theory. If properly done—and here the analyst must be on the lookout for *resistances* and take advantage, when possible, of the phenomenon of *transference*—such material should provide an insight into the ultimate psychological nature of the patient's repressions, which may include infantile sexual traumas, the Oedipus complex, guilt over childhood masturbation, and so forth. Optimally the psychoanalytic method, by also revealing *to the patient* his own repressions, then becomes a method of therapy as well.

As a *theory of the neuroses*, psychoanalysis has two closely connected subsidiary theories—one of psychopathological symptom formation and one of overall normal and abnormal psychosexual development, of personality, and of human behavior in general. These theories of Freud's serve to integrate the purely empirical results of analysis within a theoretical-developmental superstructure of instincts and their psychobiological manifestations in man.

Finally, psychoanalysis provides a comprehensive *theory of the normal mind,* based upon the crucial assumption that normal and abnormal mental functioning stand in a continuous relationship to one another. Thus the psychoanalyst believes that healthy mental activity, together with the basic instinctual drives that underlie it, offers us a simpler and relatively conflict-free parallel to psychopathology. Moreover, in certain psychical states, notably dreaming, the basic principles of normal and neurotic mental functioning are held to be identical.

Although this distinction between normal and abnormal in Freudian theory is commonly made by students of psychoanalysis, it is appropriate to minimize it when looking at Freud's theories from a historical point of view. Such a formal antithesis was continually bridged by Freud himself on many disparate fronts throughout his career. He completely transcended such categorizations in his various writings on dreams, psychosexual development, the psychopathology of everyday life, wit and jokes, character formation, and so forth. What is more, Freud eventually extended certain key implications from the psychopathological side of his psychoanalytic theorizing into various sociological and cultural-historical spheres, in such works as *Totem and Taboo* (1912–13), *Group Psychology and the Analysis of the Ego* (1921c), *The Future of an Illusion* (1927c), *Civilization and Its Discontents* (1930a), and *Moses and Monotheism* (1939a).

Consequently, while the "normal" and the "psychopathological" indeed are the chief poles of Freud's theoretical vision, this dichotomy should not obscure either the essential unity of that vision or, especially, the fact that logically as well as historically these poles are directly related. To wit, the pathological served, to begin with at least, as the principal conceptual model for Freud's theory of the normal. As he himself once expressed it, "there is no reason for surprise that psycho-analysis, which was originally no more than an attempt at explaining pathological mental phenomena, should have developed into a psychology of normal mental life. The justification for this arose with the discovery that dreams and mistakes ['parapraxes,' such as slips of the tongue, etc.] of normal men have the same mechanism as neurotic symptoms" (1926f, S.E., 20:266–67). According to Freud's own testimony, then, his theory of the neuroses provided him with a fundamental "psychological window" into the workings of the normal mind, and this theory stands at the very focal point of both his intellectual development as a psychoanalyst and his peculiar logic about human behavior. "An introduction to psycho-analysis," he once insisted, "is provided by the study of parapraxes and dreams; *the theory of the neuroses is psycho-analysis itself*" (1916–17, S.E., 16:379; italics added).

THE ORIGINS OF PSYCHOANALYSIS

Freud as Biologist

Over the years, two dominant traditions have developed among intellectual historians, as well as psychoanalysts, about the origins and the subsequent development of Freud's most fundamental insights. The first of these traditions I may appropriately characterize as "biological"; the second, as "psychological." [1] Owing to their antithetical nature, these two points of view have aroused considerable debate among Freud scholars. We are told either that psychoanalysis was largely derived from Freud's prior physicalist-physiological training within the Helmholtz school of medicine; or, in contrast, that Freud's most original achievements only became possible when he finally rejected this same biological orientation in favor of an independent and purely psychological science of mind.

The first of these two dominant traditions—and one that I will at once describe as the less accepted—claims that many of the most important and most controversial concepts of psychoanalysis can only be fully understood and evaluated when considered within the general background of late-nineteenth-century biological thought from which Freud drew so much of his scientific inspiration. From the very outset, one has good intuitive reason to believe that many of the crucial components of Freud's psychology were influenced by biological assumptions. Freud scholars have long pointed out, in this regard, that Freud's decision to practice medicine interrupted a promising career as a research biologist. During his last years at the Gymnasium in the early 1870s, still undecided as to a career, Freud had come under the spell of Darwinism. As he later recalled in his *Autobiography*, "the theories of Darwin, which were then of topical interest, strongly attracted me, for they held out hopes of an extraordinary advance in our understanding of the world . . ." (1925*d*, *S.E.*, 20:8). Freud enrolled in the University of Vienna as a medical student in the autumn of 1873 (taking as an elective that first year Professor Carl Claus's

---

1. This is, of course, something of a historical simplification. David Bakan (1958), who has specifically emphasized the importance of the Jewish mystical tradition as an influence upon Freud's achievements, has also provided a more expansive summary of past and present historical viewpoints on Freud's intellectual development. In addition to the two historical positions I have cited as the dominant ones, Bakan also mentions the following four variants of the "psychological" tradition: (1) that psychoanalysis owes its origins to idiosyncrasies in Freud's personal life—for example, his unusual childhood family constellation (pp. 10–11); (2) that Freud's theories came to him as a sudden "flash" or "revelation" (p. 11); (3) that Freud was simply a genius whose intellectual gifts must remain "inscrutable" (p. 12); and (4) that psychoanalysis arose because "germinal ideas" (e.g., from Charcot, Breuer, and others) fell upon the extremely fruitful intellectual territory of Freud's own mind (pp. 13–18). See also Rapaport (1960*a*:11–15), whose own careful survey of various historical influences upon Freud likewise encompasses examples of what I have called the biological and the psychological traditions.

Ernst Brücke in 1867 (age 48).

"General Biology and Darwinism") and finally settled down during his third year in the Physiological Institute of Ernst Brücke (1819–92).

A renowned Viennese physiologist, Brücke, along with Émil du Bois-Reymond, Hermann Helmholtz, and Carl Ludwig, had succeeded in revolutionizing German physiology during the preceding quarter century. As youthful students of that science in the early 1840s, the first three of these four men had banded together and pledged their mutual dedication to overthrowing the then-dominant position of vitalistic biologists like Johannes Müller—their common teacher; Ludwig, who was not a Müller student, joined the movement in 1847. The basic goals of the program launched by these four men may be summarized by the statement Émil du Bois-Reymond made in 1842 in a letter to a friend:

> Brücke and I pledged a solemn oath to put into power this truth: no other forces than the common physical-chemical ones are active within the organism. In those cases which cannot at the time be explained by these forces one has either to find the specific way or form of their action by means of the physical-mathematical method, or to assume new forces equal in dignity to the chemical-physical forces inherent in matter, reducible to the force of attraction and repulsion. (1918:108; trans. Bernfeld 1944:348)

Young Freud thus acquired his first scientific training within what has often been referred to, after its most famous member, as the "Helmholtz school of medicine."

Under the joint tutelage of Claus and, particularly, Brücke, Freud published five scientific papers during the next six years (1876–82): two on the neuroanatomy of *Ammocoetes (Petromyzon planeri)*—a primitive form of fish (Freud 1877a and 1878a); one on the gonadal structure of the eel (1877b); an announcement of a new chemical method for preparing nerve tissues for microscopic examination (1879a); and a study of the nerve cells of the crayfish (1882a). This record of publication was sufficient to establish the general expectation within Brücke's institute that to Freud would undoubtedly fall the next available post of assistant to Brücke himself.

Only two such assistantships to Brücke, however, were then extant at the Physiological Institute, and both were held by relatively young men —Sigmund Exner (1846–1926) and Ernst Fleischl von Marxow (1846–91), who, in their mid-thirties, were ten years older than Freud. Having little native desire to practice medicine, Freud seems to have done his best to overlook the limited future of his own situation in Brücke's laboratory. It was only when Brücke himself, in 1882, sensibly pointed out to Freud the inevitable financial difficulties that the latter would have to face if he were to continue with a research career in biology that he finally— and reluctantly—turned to the practice of medicine (*Autobiography*, 1925d, S.E., 20:10).

Brücke subsequently played a key role in winning for Freud, three years later, an invaluable opportunity for a fellowship to study with Jean-Martin Charcot in Paris (Jones 1953:60). Brücke's continued high regard for Freud was matched by Freud's lifelong esteem for his famous teacher. Freud subsequently named his third son after Brücke and later wrote of him that he had "carried more weight with me than any one else in my whole life" (1927a, S.E., 20:253).

In spite of Freud's decision in 1882 not to continue with a research career in biology, he spent the next fifteen years of his life working on highly related topics of scientific investigation. As he himself recounts in his *Autobiography*: "In a certain sense I nevertheless remained faithful to the line of work upon which I had originally started. The subject which Brücke had proposed for my investigations had been the spinal cord of one of the lowest of the fishes (*Ammocoetes Petromyzon*); and I now passed on to the human central nervous system" (1925d, S.E., 20:10). During this period he devised and published reports, in both German and English, on a second new histological method for staining nerve tracts (1884b, 1884c, and 1884d); he wrote three papers on the structure of the medulla oblongata, describing therein a relatively novel embryological technique for tracing nerve-fiber origins (1885d, 1886b, and 1886c); he conducted a series of pioneering, as well as controversial, investigations into the medicinal properties of cocaine (1884e, 1885a, 1885b, 1885e, 1885f, and 1887d);

Slide projection of a human brain in the lecture hall of Salomon Stricker. At the University of Vienna, Freud took two courses from Stricker, including one on the general pathology of the nervous system (spring semester 1878).

and he established himself as a specialist on the subject of cerebral paralyses in children (1888a, 1891a, and 1893b). Additionally, a published lecture by Freud on "The Structure of the Elements of the Nervous System" (1884f [1882]) has been considered by at least three prominent historians of psychoanalysis to contain a clear anticipation of the later neurone theory, whose first formulation is usually associated with Wilhelm Waldeyer's introduction of the term neurone in 1891 (Brun 1936; Jelliffe 1937; and Jones 1953:49–50).

Slightly later, Freud contributed a series of articles to Villaret's Handwörterbuch der gesamten Medizin, an encyclopedia in which he was personally allotted the subjects of brain structure, hysteria, and aphasia (1888b). Freud's interest in the last of these, aphasia, culminated three years later in a highly insightful monograph (1891b). Even while engaged during the next few years in writing Studies on Hysteria with Josef Breuer (1895d), Freud confessed to his close friend Wilhelm Fliess that he hoped soon "to return to my old pursuit and do a little anatomy; after all, that is the only satisfying thing" (quoted in Jones 1953:299).

Freud's last major publication from this neuroanatomical phase of his career appeared in 1897, the crucial year when he, then aged forty-one, discovered infantile sexuality and the Oedipus complex. This particular neurological work, 327 pages in length, set forth Freud's most comprehensive treatment of childhood cerebral paralyses. As late as 1936 the Swiss neurologist Rudolf Brun commented upon the unrivaled status of this monograph, calling it "the most thorough and complete that has yet been written on the cerebral paralyses of children. . . . One gets an idea of the superb command of the vast clinical material here brought together and critically digested if one considers that the bibliography alone occupies fourteen and a half pages. . . . [It] was a brilliant achievement, which alone would suffice to assure Freud's name a permanent place in clinical neurology" (1936:205). Right up to the turn of the century, Freud continued to provide yearly summaries of the literature on this particular medical specialty for the *Jahresbericht über die Leistungen und Fortschritte auf dem Gebiete der Neurologie und Psychiatrie* (Annual Report on the Achievements and Developments in the Fields of Neurology and Psychiatry), a journal of which he was coeditor (Freud 1898c, 1899b, 1900b).

Thus, Freud's psychoanalytic career began comparatively late in life. He himself once commented that psychoanalysis "was born in 1895 or 1900 or in between" (Jones 1957:462). These two dates mark the period between publication of *Studies on Hysteria* (1895d) and *The Interpretation of Dreams* (1900a), Freud's most celebrated psychoanalytic work. Freud was therefore between thirty-nine and forty-four years of age when, according to his own assessment, he finally began to develop the core of psychoanalytic theory; and it is not unreasonable to expect that his subsequent thinking as a psychoanalyst bore a substantial imprint of what was already a distinguished record of intellectual achievement as a biological and, especially, neuroanatomical specialist on the human nervous system. Of Freud's neurological education under Ernst Brücke and others, Ramzy proclaims: "The later Freudian theories derive their roots from this work not only in fundamentals but also in detail. The impact of these intensive . . . years cannot be overemphasized . . ." (1956:118).

This is not to say, of course, that Freud's pioneering development of psychoanalysis may not have also involved a considerable departure from this earlier tradition. Robert Holt, one of the most ardent spokesmen for the biological derivation of Freud's psychoanalytic ideas, has expressed this historical rationale in the following words: "In many respects Freud seems to have undergone a profound reorientation as he turned from being a neuroanatomical researcher to a clinical neurologist who experimented with psychotherapy, finally becoming the first psychoanalyst. We would be poor psychologists, however, if we imagined that there was not at least as much continuity as change in this development. Twenty years of passionate investment in the study of the nervous system were not easily tossed aside by Freud's decision to become a psychologist instead and to work with a purely abstract, hypothetical model" (1965a:101).

Freud as Psychologist

On the other hand, those commentators who are more friendly to orthodox Freudian theory have argued that the very essence of

Freud's psychoanalytic innovations—namely, his dynamic psychological approach to human behavior—transformed his later thinking
about mind into an independent, *psychological* science. The birth of
psychoanalysis, they accordingly insist, was coincident with Freud's
radical break from all of his earlier attempts at physiological *reductionism*.[2] As Ernst Kris has declared in arguing just this position, the
debate over supposed biological premises in psychoanalysis actually
rests upon an unfortunate *linguistic* misunderstanding: that is,
Freud's retention of considerable prepsychoanalytic, neurological
terminology in his later psychoanalytic writings has simply misled
people into assuming that his *conceptual* thinking never really underwent such a revolutionary transformation. Furthermore, it is especially important, Kris insists, to accentuate the purely linguistic nature
of this continuity in Freud's intellectual career, because of the frequent objection to which this misunderstanding has given rise: "This
objection maintains that since the terminology used by Freud derives
in part from the neurophysiology of the nineteenth century, the concepts of psycho-analysis are antiquated. We readily grant that historical
overtones may make psycho-analytic terminology confusing to some
students in the field, but the problem is one that concerns the terms
only and not the concepts" (1905*a*:116). "The question of the origin
of the terminology and fundamental assumptions of psycho-analysis,"
Kris concludes in another publication, "is therefore of only historical
interest; it has nothing whatever to do with the question of the
value of those assumptions and that terminology for psycho-analysis
as a science" (1954:47).

Exemplifying this tradition among psychoanalyst-historians is
the equally widespread conclusion that Freud discovered the existence
of spontaneous sexual impulses in children, along with many other
fundamental psychoanalytic insights, through his famous "self-
analysis" in the summer and fall of 1897.[3] Thus, only by first overcoming his own infantile sexual repressions was Freud then able to
elucidate the truly dynamic nature of the unconscious mental life that
is common to all human beings. Furthermore, this major fruit of
Freud's self-analysis—particularly his contemporaneous discovery of
the Oedipus complex—also paved the way for the hostile reception
of psychoanalysis by an outraged and indignant world (Jones 1955:12).

2. The term *reductionism* denotes the process of reducing complex data to
simpler levels of scientific explanation. Within biology, *reductionism* has the further
specific meaning of assigning the phenomena of life to the explanatory categories
of physics and chemistry. It is in this specific biological sense (the organism as "reducible to the force[s] of attraction and repulsion") that du Bois-Reymond made his
famous reductionistic pledge with Brücke in 1842 (see p. 14). A *psychological* reductionist is one who seeks to reduce the phenomena of psychology to the explanatory categories of biology, which may themselves be further reduced.
3. The hypothesis that Freud's self-analysis played a crucial role in his discovery of infantile sexuality was first suggested by Fritz Wittels (1924*b*:107) in
Freud's own lifetime. Ernst Kris (1950*a*:113–14; 1954:33), Ernest Jones (1953:320,
325), and numerous other students of Freud's life have subsequently endorsed this
view. See, for example, Natenberg 1955:117–47; Anzieu 1959:59–65; Wells 1960:193;
Fine 1963:68, 218; Lauzon 1963:49; Bailey 1965:20; Robert 1966:102; Costigan
1967:49–50; Stewart 1967:22, 43; Balogh 1971:40–41; and Duke 1972:29.

All in all, Freud's self-analysis has come to be recognized by most Freud scholars as a milestone not only in his own intellectual development but also in the wider context of the general history of science. "Copernicus and Darwin dared much in facing the unwelcome truths of outer reality," Ernest Jones wrote shortly after Freud's death, "but to face those of inner reality, costs something that only the rarest of mortals would unaided be able to give" (1940a:5). Kurt Eissler has said much the same thing in comparing Freud's achievements with those of another great pioneer in science: "His findings had to be wrested in the face of his own extreme resistances—the self-analysis being comparable, in terms of the danger involved, to Benjamin Franklin's flying a kite in a thunderstorm in 1752, in order to investigate the laws of electricity. The next two persons who tried to repeat his experiment were both killed" (1971:307).

Above all, Freud's self-analysis stands at the very focal point of the psychological account these commentators have provided for the origins of psychoanalytic theory. Reuben Fine, who has compared the "revolutionary" nature of Freud's self-analysis with the momentous achievements of Darwin and Einstein, has spoken for most other traditional Freud scholars in asserting that Freud's self-analysis finally precipitated "the decisive change in his interest from neurology to psychology, and [thus] created a whole new science, psycho-analysis" (1963:31).

Thus, Ernst Kris, Ernest Jones, and, indeed, the vast majority of Freud scholars, by portraying Freud's ideas as fundamentally *alien* to their times and as the product of unique personal experiences (e.g., Freud's self-analysis), have created a tradition of a man whose ideas were so without precedent that only a psychological explanation can account for them.

What of Freud himself? His own attitude toward possible biological presuppositions in psychoanalysis remained rather contradictory. For instance, while acknowledging the virtual impossibility of avoiding certain terms and concepts common to the biological sciences, Freud nevertheless insisted that "We have found it necessary to hold aloof from biological considerations during our psycho-analytic work and to refrain from using them for heuristic purposes, so that we may not be misled in our impartial judgement of the psycho-analytic facts before us" (1913j, S.E., 13:181–82). Similarly, he maintained elsewhere in equally categorical language that "psycho-analysis must keep itself free from any hypothesis that is alien to it, whether of an anatomical, chemical or physiological kind, and must operate entirely with purely psychological auxiliary ideas . . ." (1916–17, S.E., 15:21; also quoted by Jones [1953:395] as evidence for the purely psychological nature of Freud's later theories).

Yet Freud did occasionally admit to certain biological assumptions in psychoanalysis, especially in his writings after 1920; but, in doing so, he unfortunately tended to express himself rather diffusely, as in "Analysis Terminable and Interminable," where he tersely commented that "for the psychical field, the biological field does in fact play the part of the underlying bedrock" (1937c, S.E., 23:252).[4]

Thus, Freud's various autobiographical references to the possible impact of biological concepts upon psychoanalysis can inevitably be cited in contradictory ways; and he is—unfortunately—an ambiguous and unreliable guide in any attempt to assess the overall merits of the biological camp. A further complication stems from the fact that Freud himself undoubtedly meant different things at different times whenever he referred to "biological premises" in psychoanalysis—a circumstance that has a great deal to do with the subsequent historical disagreement on this whole issue.

Of course, neither Freud nor later students of his writings have ever denied that his psychological discoveries also constitute a partly biological theory of human behavior—one of instincts and their psychobiological transformations in mental life; but they insist that the *contents* of this theory ought not to be confused with the essential *means* by which Freud made his revolutionary discoveries. Hartmann and Kris have aptly expressed this point in a discussion of Freud's brilliant insight into the sequence of oral, anal, and phallic stages of libidinal development: "It will remain an astonishing document in the history of science that from material so far removed from direct observation of the child as that of the analysis of adult neurotics, phenomena of high regularity in biological development could have been so accurately reconstructed" (1954:23; see also Stewart 1967:24). Erik Erikson has underscored this historical point of view with his own comparison of the major sources of scientific inspiration for Freud, "the psychological discoverer," with those of the great Charles Darwin. "What was Freud's Galapagos . . . ?" Erikson rhetorically asks. The "neurologist's office" and "hysterical ladies" is his reply (1957:82–83).

Prospects and Conclusions

Unfortunately, whatever the merits of the biological and psychological positions, this rigid dichotomy has effectively obscured one crucial point: that Freud's approach to human behavior was itself closely allied with certain unmistakably biological but definitely nonphysiological points of view. That is to say, Freud's increasingly genetic approach to human motivation and behavior after 1895 drew heavily upon contemporary hypotheses stemming from developmental and evolutionary biology as well.

That Freud was influenced by current evolutionary ideas is not

4. See also 1914d, S.E., 14:17; 1920a, S.E., 18:171; 1920g, S.E., 18:60; and 1925d, S.E., 20:57–58.

by any means a new insight; [5] but that he, as well as many of his most influential contemporaries, was inspired in the specific manner that I shall describe in the course of this book is by no means sufficiently appreciated, either by Freud scholars in general or by those outspoken proponents of the two opposing historical camps whose positions I have just reviewed.

5. See, for example, Jones 1957:302–33; Rapaport 1960a:12, 22–23; and Ritvo 1965, 1972, 1974.

2

Sigmund Freud and Josef Breuer: Toward a Psychophysical Theory of Hysteria (1880-95)

It was not until March 1881, fully seven and a half years after having enrolled in the University of Vienna medical curriculum, that Freud finally submitted himself for his qualifying examinations and took his medical degree. The following May, he was appointed to the post of demonstrator at Ernst Brücke's Physiological Institute, a position that carried with it a slight salary and commensurate teaching responsibilities. During his free time at the institute, Freud applied himself to finishing up what Brücke later praised as a "very important" paper on the structure of the nerve cells in the crayfish (Freud 1882a; for Brücke's appraisal, see Bernfeld 1951:215).

As I have already mentioned, Freud's prospects for advancement at Brücke's institute were at best far distant, promising an impecunious future, owing to the relative youth of Brücke's two assistants, Fleischl von Marxow and Exner. The turning point came in June of 1882, after Freud's third semester as demonstrator at the Physiological Institute, when Ernst Brücke finally took it upon himself to advise Freud to think more seriously about the practice of medicine.

Another important reason, besides the professionally expedient one

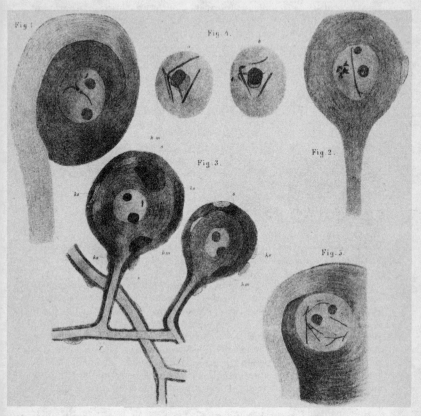

Nerve cells of the crayfish, as drawn by Freud (1882a: Plate 1).

expressed in Brücke's friendly advice, greatly reinforced Freud's decision to prepare himself for the practice of medicine at this time. In the spring of that same year, he had fallen in love with Martha Bernays (1861–1951); and if he was to marry without an extended engagement, possibly lasting the better part of a decade, then he needed an income considerably more substantial than whatever a research career in theoretical biology could generate.

Thus, from the first of July 1882, Freud spent three years acquiring clinical experience in medicine by arduously working his way through the various departments of the Vienna General Hospital—three months in Billroth's Department of Surgery; six months in Nothnagel's Clinic for Internal Medicine; five months (at the elevated rank of *Sekundararzt*) in Meynert's Psychiatric Clinic; three months in Zeissl's

Department of Dermatology; fourteen months in Scholz's Department of Nervous Diseases; and finally, beginning in March 1885, three months in the Department of Ophthalmology. After his appointment to the rank of *Sekundararzt* on 1 May 1883, Freud was required to take up residency at the hospital, the first occasion in his life that he had left home for more than a short period of time.

Besides rounding out Freud's medical knowledge, this hospital training introduced him to many of the stellar representatives of contemporary Viennese medical science. The great brain anatomist and professor of psychiatry Theodor Meynert (1833–92), whom Freud, as a medical student, had previously admired from afar after hearing him lecture, now made a particularly strong personal impression. Meynert soon invited Freud to work in his Laboratory for Cerebral Anatomy, which Freud did from 1883 to 1886. At some point during these three years, Meynert went so far as to propose that Freud take over his university lectures on brain anatomy, but the latter declined, feeling he was not up to the task (*Autobiography*, 1925d, *S.E.*, 20:11). Freud always judged Meynert, in spite of their subsequent estrangement in the late 1880s, as perhaps the most brilliant man he had ever met, and years later he wrote in *The Interpretation of Dreams* of "the great Meynert, in whose footsteps I had trodden with such deep veneration" (1900a, *S.E.*, 5:437).

It was also while working as *Sekundararzt* in Meynert's Psychiatric Clinic that Freud finally decided, in September 1883, to become a neurologist. The immediate inspiration for this decision was the tragic suicide of Nathan Weiss, an extremely brilliant and eccentric young neurologist whom Freud hoped to succeed in the medical community. At the same time, this decision followed naturally from Freud's previous professional experience, given both Freud's neuroanatomical background and various irreparable gaps that he had come to recognize in his overall medical training. As Freud complained five years later to a close friend, he had unfortunately learned far too little medicine, owing to his previous research interests, ever to aspire to the more lucrative career of general practitioner: "I was able to learn just enough to become a neuropathologist" (*Origins*, p. 57).

As a neuropathologist, however, he soon became famous for his pinpoint diagnoses. In his *Autobiography* he recalled with considerable pride how in postmortems he was able, from his detailed knowledge of the nervous system's structure and function and from a description of a given patient's symptoms, "to localize the site of a lesion in the medulla oblongata so accurately that the pathological anatomist had no further information to add" (1925d, *S.E.*, 20:12). Freud's continued predilection for the more "exact" field of neuroanatomy stood in marked contrast at this time to his contemptuous remarks about "unfruitful psychiatry" following five months' residency in Meynert's clinic (see Jones 1953:68).

By the spring of 1885, Freud's record of publication, which now included a clinical paper on a case of cerebral hemorrhage (1884a) and another on the medicinal uses of cocaine (1884e), was sufficiently impressive to justify his nomination by Ernst Brücke, seconded by Meynert and Nothnagel, for the coveted position of *Privatdozent*. This prospective rank entitled Freud to offer lectures on his medical specialty, diseases of the nervous system; and these he accordingly proposed to undertake, as he detailed in his application for *Privatdozent*, from a combined anatomical, physiological, and clinical point of view (Bernfeld 1951:215). His nomination was approved by the faculty, with the strong backing of his three supporters, in July of that year. The appointment was confirmed by the Ministry of Education the following September.

During the three years of his internship at the Vienna General Hospital, Freud was continually preoccupied with the hope of making an important scientific discovery—one that would bring him early fame and the promise of a large private practice, and thus allow him to marry without having to wait another five to ten years. He at first held high hopes that his gold chloride method of tissue staining would suffice to bring him this early fame; but the technique proved to be too variable in its effects upon neurological preparations and was never widely adopted by histologists. Freud's other great hope of this period rested upon his pioneering researches with cocaine. This brings us to what has generally become known in Freud's life as "the cocaine episode" (Bernfeld 1953; Jones 1953:78–97).

The Cocaine Episode

In the spring of 1884, Freud began to experiment with the alkaloid of cocaine after hearing of the German Army doctor Theodor Aschenbrandt's (1883) results with the drug in enhancing endurance among soldiers. After taking repeated small doses of the narcotic, Freud found that it was able to relieve depression as well as to stimulate his capacity for concentrated work; it also appeared to have no harmful side effects. He thereupon published an article in which he recommended cocaine's potential use as a stimulant, as a local anesthetic, as a cure for vomiting and indigestion, and as a means of withdrawal from morphine addiction ("On Coca," 1884e).[1] The last of these recommendations was based upon Freud's personal administration of the drug to his friend Fleischl von Marxow, who had years before been the victim of a poorly performed amputation of the thumb and had taken heavily to morphine in desperation over the growth of painful neuromas.

Meanwhile, Freud had suggested to two ophthalmologist friends, Leopold Königstein and Carl Koller, that cocaine might be used as an analgesic in treating certain conditions of the skin and mucous membranes. In support of this idea, Freud had demonstrated to both col-

1. Freud's six papers on cocaine (1884e, 1885a, 1885b, 1885e, 1885f, and 1887d) have been translated into English under the title *Cocaine Papers* (Freud 1974a). Bernfeld's (1953) valuable study, together with extracts from Freud's letters, dreams, and recollections on the subject of cocaine, have also been reprinted in this volume.

leagues the drug's general anesthetizing properties, by administering a solution to a fellow intern suffering from acute abdominal pains (Eissler 1971:157). Freud also suggested to Königstein that cocaine might be useful in treating eye complaints. In July 1884, Freud departed Vienna for his summer holidays, and on his return, he and Königstein jointly experimented on a dog's eye. During the interval, however, the more secretive Koller had performed a similiar experiment and had managed to have a "Preliminary Communication" of his results read on 15 September before the Ophthalmological Congress in Heidelberg. Koller's communication caused a sensation. Almost overnight he achieved worldwide fame for the revolution he brought about in the field of eye surgery. Freud, at first quite pleased with his pivotal role in this discovery, later came to regret that he had not taken more initiative himself and had thus lost the "lion's share" of the credit to Koller's final demonstration.[2]

But the disappointments of "the cocaine episode" were not yet over, for Koller's demonstration of cocaine's value in eye surgery proved to be one of the very few safe uses for this narcotic. By mid-1885, Freud, who had attracted considerable notoriety in Vienna with his various lectures and articles on the marvelous powers of cocaine (the "magical substance," as he dubbed it), was also coming under heavy attack, as repeated instances of cocaine addiction were reported from all over the world. Cocaine, it should be noted, has an addictive effect upon some individuals but not upon others; Freud, for one, never became addicted to the drug even though he used it for more than a decade.[3]

Albrecht Erlenmeyer, perhaps Freud's most vocal opponent, went so far as to label cocaine "the third scourge of humanity"—after alcohol and morphine (Erlenmeyer 1885). Freud, whose vain literary defense (1887d) against such medical "skeptics" was not particularly well taken, as Jones points out, soon came to regret both his involvement in the whole episode and, more especially, the "grave reproaches" from his medical colleagues that followed in its wake. It is not true, though, as Jones mistakenly recounts (1953:94), that one of Freud's patients died from an overdose of cocaine prescribed and injected by Freud himself. The patient succumbed, in fact, to a dose of sulphonal, then widely used by neurologists as a sedative and generally presumed safe.[4]

On the other hand, Freud's good friend Fleischl, to whom Freud *had* prescribed cocaine, soon became severely addicted to the drug—an addiction that apparently hastened his death in 1891 (*Interpretation of Dreams*, 1900a, S.E., 4:111). Although it should not be forgotten that Fleischl was probably no worse off as a cocaine addict than he had previously been, before Freud's well-intentioned intervention, as an addict of morphine, Fleischl's tragic fate nevertheless became a lingering

---

2. Unpublished letter to Minna Bernays, 29 October 1884; cited by Jones 1953:89; see also Freud's *Autobiography*, 1925d, S.E., 20:14–15.

3. See, for example, his reference to cocaine in the famous dream of "Irma's injection" (*The Interpretation of Dreams*, 1900a, S.E., 4:111).

4. See *The Interpretation of Dreams*, 1900a, S.E., 4:111, for a reference to this unfortunate incident.

Freud and his future wife, Martha Bernays, September 1885.

personal reminder to Freud of his premature therapeutic recommendation of cocaine.

The whole cocaine affair remains an ironic one in Freud's life. It brought him to the very brink of world fame at the early age of twenty-eight and then left him, for all his troubles, with a tarnished medical reputation. At the same time, this episode reveals the first distinct sign of the spirited advocacy Freud was soon to bring to his development of psychoanalytic theory.

Paris and Charcot (Winter 1885/86)

It was a decisive moment in Freud's life when he applied for and won a government-sponsored traveling fellowship open to the junior *Sekundarärzte* at the Vienna General Hospital. The fellowship, which was allotted to him in June of 1885 by the university's Faculty of Medicine, carried with it an automatic six-month leave of absence from his post at the hospital. In his proposal, Freud had announced his intention to study with Charcot in Paris. His narrow victory over his sole rival candidate—by thirteen votes to eight—was accomplished, so his friend Fleischl later told him, only upon "Brücke's passionate intercession, which had caused a general sensation." [5] Freud was in Paris from 13 October 1885 to 28 February 1886, and he spent seventeen of these twenty weeks in attendance at Charcot's clinic.

Jean-Martin Charcot (1825–93) was then at the height of the varied medical career that had led him to the study of neurology, and his stature in French medicine was equaled only by that of the great Louis Pasteur.[6] Son of a carriage builder, Charcot had become by the 1880s a consulting physician to the most prominent royal families in Europe. And from all over the world ordinary patients and physicians flocked to the Salpêtrière in Paris in order to seek his medical advice. Charcot was charismatic and authoritarian and enjoyed a legendary reputation even in his own lifetime. He was especially famed for the miraculous cures in which the power of his commandment alone repeatedly enabled paralytic individuals (no doubt largely hysterics) to throw off their crutches and walk.

Also a highly cultured man, Charcot was particularly at home with art and literature. He read widely in the English, German, Spanish, and Italian languages and enjoyed quoting Shakespeare and Dante, his two favorite authors, in their native tongues. In social circles he was also well known for the spectacular receptions and parties at his palatial

---

5. Unpublished letter to Martha Bernays, 23 June 1885; cited by Jones 1953:76.
6. With the possible exception of Guillain (1955, trans. 1959), no adequate biographical treatment of Charcot yet exists. This surprising lacuna in the history of medicine is perhaps related to the sharp reversal of medical opinion after Charcot's death regarding the reliability of his famous researches on hypnotism and hysteria. The following account of his life and work relies heavily upon Ellenberger (1970:89–101), who has composed a brief but multifaceted portrait of Charcot on the basis of many scattered recollections by contemporaries who knew and worked with him. See also Jones (1953:185–86, 207–8, 226–29) for a more anecdotal account, based largely upon Freud's letters to his fiancée, Martha Bernays, written during his stay in Paris; and *Letters*, pp. 171–211.

home on the Boulevard Saint-Germain, where Freud himself was several times a guest (*Letters*, pp. 194–96, 206–8).

Almost every prominent French neurologist in the late nineteenth century studied at one time or another under Charcot at the famous Salpêtrière. This huge medical complex included some forty-odd buildings devoted largely to the care of older women. There Charcot had gradually built up numerous research laboratories in the various major medical disciplines. He had also created the necessary teaching facilities for instructing medical students about the many unique neurological disorders then common among the Salpêtrière's several thousand patients. It is perhaps worth noting that Freud found the laboratory conditions at the Salpêtrière rather unsatisfactory for his own neuroanatomical needs—compared at least with what he was used to—and he eventually gave up, on this account, his plans to pursue anatomical studies of infantile brains while in Paris (Jones 1953:210–11).

Like Freud, hundreds of other foreigners came yearly to visit this "Mecca of neurology" and to attend Charcot's famous Tuesday and Friday lectures on the subject of nervous diseases. The Tuesday lectures were extemporaneous and consisted of Charcot's on-the-spot diagnoses of ailing patients brought to him without prior consultation from the well-stocked wards of the Salpêtrière. It was an unforgettable performance about which Freud, in speaking of "the magic" of Charcot's great personality, later warmly reminisced in his Preface to the German translation of these lectures (Freud 1892–94, *S.E.*, 1:135–36). In contrast to the Tuesday lectures, those given on Fridays were models of highly organized learning and lucidity; and Charcot rarely failed to keep his packed audience spellbound throughout the two hours that he customarily devoted to each major neurological disease.

Charcot had begun his medical career in pathological anatomy. As a young intern at the Salpêtrière, where he had served for a short time in the course of his medical training, he had been fascinated by the many strange and seemingly incurable neurological afflictions he had encountered there. He had vowed to himself then and there that he would someday return to study in more detail this neglected world of medical treasures; and in 1862, at the age of thirty-seven, he finally honored that vow, coming back to the Salpêtrière as head of one of its major divisions.

By 1870, Charcot was concentrating on the problem of how to distinguish hysterical from epileptic convulsions. With his disciple and assistant Paul Richer, he succeeded in providing a formal clinical description of the stages that, in his view, characterized the "hysterical crisis" (*grande hystérie*). His approach, while extremely important in the scientific understanding of hysteria, was also symptomatic of the dubious "type" concept of disease then popular in French medicine. Although the type concept had formerly proved useful in Charcot's anatomically based neurological work, it later brought him into considerable discredit when he attempted to apply it to the more problematic phenomena of hysteria.

By 1878, Charcot had taken up the study of hypnotism—a bold

step in his medical career, since in France, as elsewhere, the whole subject had been in considerable scientific disrepute for almost a century (ever since the debates over mesmerism in the 1780s). Four years later, in 1882, Charcot delivered a paper on hypnotism at the *Académie des Sciences* in which he personally endorsed the phenomenon of hypnotism as genuine and provided a detailed description of the hypnotic trance as occurring in three sequential stages ("lethargy," "catalepsy," and "somnambulism"). Charcot's paper created a sensation. It also brought about a complete reversal within France of the negative attitude in official science toward mesmerism or "animal magnetism"—a subject that the *Académie des Sciences* itself had twice formally condemned.[7]

By the mid-1880s, when Freud went to Paris to study with Charcot, the latter had just begun his famous researches on the subject of traumatic paralyses. In 1884 and 1885, Charcot had shown that these traumatic paralyses were distinct symptomatically from organic ones, and he had succeeded in *artificially* reproducing such nonorganic paralyses with the use of hypnosis. He subsequently established a similar medical distinction between traumatic and organic amnesia. Before his death in 1893, Charcot's interests in the psychopathology of disease even caused him to consider the psychological mechanism of faith healing (Charcot 1893). It is no wonder, then, that the neurologist whose work on hypnotism and hysteria in the 1880s enthralled both the French medical community and a generation of novelists and playwrights eventually received the nickname "Napoleon of Neuroses" (Ellenberger 1970:95).

Charcot exerted an immediate and profound influence upon Freud, who later named his eldest son after this important figure in his life. His first personal impression of Charcot, whom Freud met a week after reaching Paris, readily conveys his fascination:

> At ten o'clock M. Charcot arrived, a tall man of fifty-eight [in fact, only a month shy of sixty], wearing a top hat, with dark, strangely soft eyes (or rather, one is; the other is expressionless and has an inward cast), long wisps of hair stuck behind his ears, clean shaven, very expressive features with full protruding lips—in short, like a worldly priest from whom one expects a ready wit and an appreciation of good living. . . . I was very much impressed by his brilliant diagnosis and the lively interest he took in everything, so unlike what we are accustomed to from our great men with their veneer of distinguished superficiality. (*Letters*, p. 175)

By the end of November (a month later), Freud was even more ecstatic in singing the praises of Charcot. "I think I am changing a great deal," he wrote to his future bride. "Charcot, who is one of the greatest physicians and a man whose common sense borders on genius, is simply

---

7. See Ellenberger (1970:57–85) and Darnton (1968) for informative treatments of the life of Franz Anton Mesmer and the subsequent history of the mesmerism and hypnotism movements.

Charcot in the autopsy room at the Salpêtrière, examining a brain. From a sketch by E. Brissaud in 1875. Henry Meige, one of Charcot's pupils, wrote of this portrait: "Nothing is more typical than this sketch made with a few strokes of the pen on hospital paper. It brings to mind a daily spectacle which cannot be forgotten by those who frequented the Salpêtrière at that time: Charcot in the ampitheater, his hat on his head, an apron tied around his middle, his feet encased in big goloshes, examining a brain, while standing motionless in silence" (quoted in Guillain 1959:51 n.).

wrecking all my aims and opinions. I sometimes come out of his lectures as from out of Notre Dame, with an entirely new idea about perfection. . . . Whether the seed will ever bear fruit, I don't know; but what I do know is that no other human being has ever affected me in the same way" (*Letters*, pp. 184–85).

It is nevertheless odd that, by the beginning of December, Freud was at the point of returning to Vienna, as Jones (1953:208) has reported on the basis of an unpublished letter to Martha Bernays. Freud's reasons seem to have been twofold: his inability to carry out his planned work on the anatomy of the brain and his disappointment over a lack of personal contact with Charcot, to whom Freud was just another face in a large crowd of foreign visitors. But fortunately the idea occurred to Freud at about this time of offering his services to Charcot as German translator for the third volume of Charcot's *Leçons sur les mal-*

adies du système nerveux (1887). In a formal letter of request to Charcot, Freud humorously commented, "Concerning my capacity for this undertaking it must be said that I only have motor aphasia in French but not sensory aphasia" (quoted in Jones 1953:209).

Charcot received Freud's proposal warmly. Thanks to the latter's proficiency as a translator, the German volume was published only seven months later—even before the French original—under the title *Neue Vorlesungen über die Krankheiten des Nervensystems insbesondere über Hysterie* (New Lectures on the Diseases of the Nervous System, Particularly on Hysteria, 1886). Charcot rewarded Freud's labors by giving him a complete leather-bound set of his works inscribed "*À Monsieur le Docteur Freud, excellents souvenirs de la Salpêtrière. Charcot*" (Freud library, New York). Finally, as a result of this translation arrangement, Freud entered into a much closer relationship with Charcot and his circle of personal friends and was soon invited to attend the splendid parties given by Charcot at his home.

It was, of course, Charcot's demonstrations concerning hysteria and hypnotism—many of which, Freud later recalled, had initially provoked in him and others "a sense of astonishment and an inclination to scepticism"—that really captured Freud's imagination during his four-and-a-half-month stay in Paris (*Autobiography*, 1925d, S.E., 20:13). These dramatic demonstrations—particularly those of hypnotism—first revealed to Freud the remarkable circumstance that multiple states of consciousness could simultaneously coexist in one and the same individual without either state apparently having knowledge of the other. Charcot and his disciples had used such demonstrations not only for illustrating the psychogenic nature of hysterical paralyses but also as an aid to understanding the phenomenon of "split personality" (or *double conscience*). As Freud later commented about such hypnotic experiments: "I received the profoundest impression of the possibility that there could be powerful mental processes which nevertheless remained hidden from the consciousness of men" (*Autobiography*, 1925d, S.E., 20:17; see also 1893f, S.E., 3:22).

With regard to the specific problem of hysteria, Charcot, who seems to have believed that the theory of *organic* nervous diseases was virtually complete, had accordingly begun full-time work upon this long-puzzling malady in the period immediately preceding Freud's visit to the Salpêtrière. Later, on the occasion of Charcot's death in 1893, Freud described what was known about this disease before Charcot's medical intervention, with the following words: "This, the most enigmatic of all nervous diseases, for the evaluation of which medicine had not yet found a serviceable angle of approach, had just then fallen into thorough discredit; and this discredit extended not only to the patients but to the physicians who concerned themselves with the neurosis. It was held that in hysteria anything was possible, and no credence was given to a hysteric about anything." Charcot's personal achievement in elucidating this protean disease, Freud added, was comparable to, but on a somewhat smaller scale than, Philippe Pinel's (1745–1826) famous liberation of the madmen from their chains at the Salpêtrière almost a

Charcot, giving a lecture on hysteria at the Salpêtrière (1885). A. Brouillet's famous painting captures an important flaw in Charcot's technique: his verbal commentary and the picture on the wall have already suggested to the patient the "crisis" she is beginning to undergo.

century before. "The first thing that Charcot's work did," Freud said in summing up Charcot's medical revolution, "was to restore its dignity to the topic. Little by little, people gave up the scornful smile with which the patient could at that time feel certain of being met. She was no longer necessarily a malingerer, for Charcot had thrown the whole weight of his own authority on the side of the genuineness and objectivity of hysterical phenomena" ("Charcot," 1893f, S.E., 3:19).

A series of more specific medical discoveries had also soon emerged from Charcot's intensive work on hysteria. Three of these, in particular, Freud later stressed as having profoundly affected his own thinking on the problem that, in many ways, launched him into his psychoanalytic career.

To begin with, Charcot had shown how the peculiar mechanism of traumatic-hysterical dysfunctions was to be understood from the remarkable fact that identical symptoms could be *induced artificially* by means of suggestions given to hysterical patients during a state of hypnosis. Furthermore, the analogy of hypnotically induced paralysis was all the more convincing as a key to such hysterical dysfunctions when one learned that these impairments were not always manifested immediately. Rather, the patient might return home apparently unharmed by a frightening experience, only to suffer a severe dysfunction several days or even weeks later.

In a like manner, Charcot had persuasively demonstrated that "hysterically prone" individuals could be put into a hypnotic trance and, without any suggestion at all, be induced to simulate paralytic dysfunctions after receiving a light blow to an arm or a leg. Charcot and his assistants explained this phenomenon by assuming that, in these patients, the power of external suggestion had simply been replaced by that of *auto*suggestion. All such subconscious hypnotic suggestions, Charcot believed, were dependent upon an idea or a series of ideas somehow isolated psychically from normal waking consciousness— the ego—and yet firmly planted within a second region of the mind in what he described as "the fashion of parasites" (Charcot 1887:335–37). Freud concluded: "[Charcot] succeeded in proving, by an unbroken chain of argument, that these paralyses were the result of ideas which had dominated the patient's brain at moments of a special disposition" (1893f, S.E., 3:22). In other words, Charcot was the first to understand the hitherto hidden *mechanism* of hysterical phenomena, and he did so, moreover, in proto-Freudian terms.

Implicit in Charcot's first major medical generalization about hysteria was his second—namely, the *psychogenic nature of hysterical symptoms*. "M. Charcot was the first to teach us that to explain hysterical neurosis we must apply to psychology" (Freud 1893c, S.E., 1: 171); and Freud also commented on how foreign Charcot's clinical and psychological approach to neurological problems had at first seemed to a physician like himself, trained in the Germanic tradition, with its emphasis on a physiological interpretation of symptoms.[8] At the same time, Freud encountered in Charcot's clinical emphasis a refreshing subordination of theory to medical facts. In one of his favorite anecdotes about Charcot, Freud tells how he once dared to contradict the master on some medical point with the remark: "But that can't be true, it contradicts the Young-Helmholtz theory"—to which Charcot unhesitatingly replied, *"La théorie, c'est bon, mais ça n'empêche pas d'exister* ['Theory is good; but it doesn't prevent things from existing']" (Freud 1893f, S.E., 3:13).

Freud deemed Charcot's third and last major contribution to the scientific understanding of hysteria to be his emphatic *rejection of the common notion that this disease is always caused by the female hysteric's disturbed sexual organization*. In his 1888 article "Hysteria" for Villaret's *Handwörterbuch der gesamten Medizin* (Encyclopedic Handbook of Medicine), Freud later exhibited the ironic imprint of Charcot's influence by giving as his principal argument against the sexual etiology of hysteria Charcot's own insistence that this disease could be found in children *before the onset of puberty* (a denial of infantile sexuality) and that severe cases were unquestionably found in the male sex. (Charcot had further fixed the ratio of male to female hysteria at roughly 1:20. See Freud 1888b, S.E., 1:50–51.)

In addition to working on his translation of Charcot's lectures while in Paris, Freud began an ingenious study on the psychogenic nature of traumatic hysterical paralyses. He later credited Charcot with the basic

8. Preface to Freud's translation of Charcot's *Tuesday Lectures* (1892–94), S.E., 1:134–35.

idea, but as Jones (1953:233) rightly points out, other contemporary evidence indicates that the major inspiration, although implied in Charcot's overall teachings, was really Freud's own. Freud's idea was to show, using clinical material available to him at the Salpêtrière, that *hysterical* paralyses are largely independent of the regular anatomical distributions governing known instances of *organic* paralysis. For example, he observed that organic cerebral paralyses regularly affected a distal segment (the hand) more than they did a proximal one (the shoulder), but that in hysterical paralysis this was not always true (1893c, *S.E.*, *1*:162–63). In short, the functional lesions of hysterical paralysis appeared to follow a layman's notion of paralysis, not the laws of neuroanatomy. Hysteria, Freud concluded, *"behaves as though anatomy did not exist or as though it had no knowledge of it"* (*S.E.*, *1*:169).

Return to Vienna: Charcot's Missionary to the Viennese

Freud left Paris and Charcot, whom he never saw again, on 28 February 1886 and returned to Vienna on 4 April after spending a month in Berlin studying childhood diseases at Adolf Baginsky's clinic. On his return, Freud became director of the new neurological section in Max Kassowitz's private Institute for Children's Diseases—a job that had been offered to, and accepted by, Freud before he left for Paris. He was also invited by Theodor Meynert to make full use of the latter's laboratory at the University of Vienna in order to continue his anatomical studies. Freud had yet to make public his support of hypnotic therapy —which to Meynert was an absolute bête noire—and Meynert, who was then still on friendly terms with Freud, seems to have held high hopes for the latter's future achievements in neuroanatomy. "Meynert has just been making me a grand speech," Freud had earlier reported to his fiancée, "about the thanks the Institute owes me for enriching it with so many valuable preparations, for the technical mastery peculiar to me, and for the promises my researches hold. That naturally pleased me a little, but I don't really like him in that extravagant mood. When he is honest he is uncommonly sparing in his praise. Still it probably doesn't signify anything bad" (quoted in Jones 1953:237).

At the end of April 1886, Freud sent out notices announcing the opening of his own private medical practice. The following month, he delivered two papers on the subject of hypnotism at the Physiological Club and at the Society for Psychiatry and Neurology, respectively. Finally, with his financial situation now stable, it became possible for him to marry Martha Bernays in September 1886, after an engagement of more than four years. With his scientific work, his *Privatdozent* lecturing duties at the university, his private practice, his work at the Kassowitz Institute, and his marriage, Freud was truly a much occupied man at this point in his life. He still found time, however, to involve himself almost immediately in several major scientific controversies.

The first of these embattled episodes in Freud's post-Paris medical career arose in connection with an event that Siegfried and Suzanne Bernfeld, among the earliest of the systematic students of Freud's life, have rightly termed a "far-reaching influence on his future" (1952:39). On 15 October 1886, Freud gave a paper entitled "On Male Hysteria" before the Viennese Gesellschaft der Ärzte (Society of Physicians). This paper constituted a report on his activities in Paris, and in it Freud enthusiastically endorsed Charcot's general teachings on hysteria. More specifically, as the title indicates, Freud took the opportunity to present Charcot's views on the existence of hysteria in the male sex. As his main clinical example, Freud described the case of a man whom he had personally seen at the Salpêtrière and who had developed the symptoms of a traumatic hysteria following a fall from a scaffold.

According to the traditional story of this event, Freud's exposition was met with almost complete incredulity. Nearly forty years later in his *Autobiography,* Freud recalled at some length—and with lingering signs of bitterness—details of the "bad reception" his paper had received. "Persons of authority, such as the chairman (Bamberger, the physician), declared that what I said was incredible." Meynert, Freud reported, challenged him to find such a case of male hysteria and to present it before the membership of the society. This Freud promptly attempted to do; but he was greeted by further resistance from the senior physicians at the Vienna General Hospital, some of whom refused to allow him to examine, much less to exhibit, the most likely prospects in their wards. "One of them, an old surgeon," Freud added, "actually broke out with the exclamation: 'But, my dear sir, how can you talk such nonsense? *Hysteron* (*sic*) means the uterus. So how can a man be hysterical?'" (1925*d, S.E.,* 20:15). Outside the hospital, Freud was eventually able to find a case of male hysteria apparently triggered by a traumatic experience, and he presented his case before the society a month later (1886*d*). This time he was applauded, but no further interest was taken in his work on this subject. "The impression that the high authorities had rejected my innovations," Freud concluded his account of the incident, "remained unshaken; and, with my hysteria in men and my production of hysterical paralyses by suggestion, I found myself forced into the Opposition. As I was soon afterwards excluded [by Theodor Meynert] from the laboratory of cerebral anatomy and for terms on end had nowhere to deliver my lectures, I withdrew from academic life and ceased to attend the learned societies. It is a whole generation since I have visited the 'Gesellschaft der Aerzte'" (1925*d, S.E.,* 20:15–16).

Although this account is compelling, depicting as it apparently does Freud's first taste of the hostile and irrational reception that was to characterize a lifetime of psychoanalytic innovations in science,[9] it

<hr/>

9. Siegfried and Suzanne Bernfeld hardly depart from Freud's own account when they ask of Freud's superiors in this controversy: "What motivated their hasty, non-scientific judgements? What emotions could have interfered with reason?" (1952:42). Even Ernest Jones, who, as we shall see, presents a much more balanced account of this incident, is still inclined to portray it within a largely psychological framework, where he takes Freud to task for his youthful overzealousness, for his sensitivity to criticism, and for a certain degree of tactlessness, while he accuses Freud's opponents of exhibiting a basic "lack of imagination" (1953:230). Robert (1966:77) also follows the traditional account.

is largely a myth. Not only has this account given rise to considerable misunderstanding and oversimplification in the history of psychoanalysis; but it has also become the prototype for similar legends about Freud's life (see Chapter 13). For these reasons I shall examine this incident in some detail.

To begin with, the real source of the cool reception given Freud's paper of 15 October 1886 was by no means his attempt to support the supposedly controversial existence of male hysteria.[10] In the decade preceding this paper, passenger travel by railway had significantly increased. Occasional accidents naturally led to insurance claims against the railroads; and the critical problem soon arose, for both physicians and insurance companies, of distinguishing purely traumatic (that is, nonorganic) instances of so-called railway brain and railway spine from similar symptomologies involving true physical injury to the nervous system. In England the physician Herbert Page (1883) had recently claimed that many such instances of railway spine were indeed the product of psychological shock alone. He had further argued that cases like these, which often displayed symptoms like *hemianesthesia* (half-sided paralyses), so characteristic of hysteria, were essentially hysterical. Dr. Page's viewpoint had subsequently received the support of a number of prominent American physicians, including G. L. Walton (1883, 1884) and James Jackson Putnam (1883).

A spirited controversy soon developed when Robert Thomsen and Hermann Oppenheim (1884), two Berlin neurologists, drew special attention to the fact that hemianesthesia was by no means restricted to hysteria as a neurological disorder. Moreover, they showed that the precise forms of railway hemianesthesia and other common railway-accident symptomologies possessed significantly different characteristics from purely hysterical instances of these disorders. (In particular, the symptoms of railway-accident victims were generally more severe and far less amenable to therapy.) For these reasons, Thomsen and Oppenheim had set aside such instances of railway spine as a separate clinical entity under the more general medical category of "traumatic neurosis." Charcot, who seems to have recognized the peculiar nature of certain of the railway-accident stigmata described by Thomsen and Oppenheim, nevertheless opposed this separate clinical status, believing that he had

10. This conclusion was first recognized clearly by Ernest Jones (1953:229–32), who, following the earlier and less critical historical researches of Siegfried and Suzanne Bernfeld (1952) on this topic, compares Freud's later recollections of the incident with three contemporaneous accounts of the Society of Physicians meeting of 15 October, published shortly thereafter in the local medical press. (As the most prestigious of the many medical societies in Vienna, the Society of Physicians usually received detailed press coverage both of the papers presented to its members and of the discussions that generally followed.) Even more recently, this episode has been set in its proper historical context through the researches of Ilse Bry and Alfred Rifkin (1962:9–12) and Henri Ellenberger (1970:437–42). The latter, in particular, presents the most complete historical account to date and places the entire incident within a framework of more than a century of pre-Freudian neurological research on the subject of hysteria (including hysteria *in the male*). Ellenberger's conclusions have been disputed by Eissler (1971:351–54), although not convincingly. See note 14, this chapter.

demonstrated the validity of his own views by successfully inducing such hemianesthesias, as well as other hysterical symptoms, through hypnotic suggestion.

When Freud finally visited Paris, the whole issue was still very alive. Its current focus was whether what was thought to be a predominantly *hereditary*, often chronic, but also frequently curable disease like hysteria (male or female) was now to be equated with the purely *acquired* but often permanent dysfunctions of these accident victims. Inasmuch as these victims were mostly males, also involved was the issue of whether they were being overhastily and erroneously stigmatized as male hysterics.

Freud, for his own part, was not unaware of this aspect of the debate over traumatic paralyses. And in Berlin, on his way back to Vienna from Paris, he had paid a personal visit to Thomsen and Oppenheim in order to examine those male patients in their wards who seemed to confirm such a separate clinical picture. (Unfortunately, when Freud arrived these cases were no longer in residence at the Berlin Charité. See Freud 1956a [1886], S.E., 1:12–13.) Thus, the existence of male hysteria per se (as a nontraumatic clinical entity) was by no means a controversial medical issue of this period, but had long been accepted, in fact, by most European and American physicians. Finally, if one is to understand the reception given Freud's paper, one must also appreciate that the Society of Physicians had a long-standing tradition that papers delivered before its members should contain something original. Freud's paper, while it provoked controversy, contained little that was new to his superiors.

The recorded response to Freud's paper fully substantiates the preceding interpretation of the historical facts.[11] The first physician to speak, the neurologist Moritz Rosenthal, declared that he had published an article on two such cases of male hysteria sixteen years earlier (Rosenthal 1870; 2nd ed., 1875); to this assertion he added that male hysteria, although certainly far less common than hysteria in the female, was nevertheless well known.

Theodor Meynert, whose clinic had published the details of a particularly unusual case of male hysteria only a month before (see Luzenberger 1886), remarked that he had many times witnessed instances of epileptic seizures and other symptoms of disturbed mental consciousness following traumatic accidents. Meynert suggested that it would be interesting to see if any such cases exhibited the exact symptoms described by Freud, and he offered to put at Freud's disposal any appropriate material in his clinic, so that a more exact demonstration could be arranged.

11. Ellenberger (1970:439, 554) has pointed out the existence of half a dozen contemporary reports of the 15 October 1886 Society of Physicians meeting. All six reports appeared shortly thereafter in different Viennese and German medical journals, and they follow one another closely in both the substance and the specific wording of the discussions that accompanied Freud's paper. See further: *Anzeiger der K. K. Gesellschaft der Aerzte in Wien*, no. 25 (1886):149–52; *Wiener medizinische Wochenschrift*, 36 (1886):1445–47; Schnitzler 1886:1407–9; Frank 1886:506–7; *Wiener medizinische Blätter*, 9 (1886):1292–94; and *Münchener medicinische Wochenschrift*, 33 (1886):768.

The chairman of the meeting, Heinrich von Bamberger (one of the four professors on the committee that awarded Freud his traveling stipend), responded to Freud's presentation with the words: "In spite of my great admiration for Charcot and my high interest for the subject, I was unable to find anything new in the report of Dr. Freud because all that has been said has already long been known" (Schnitzler 1886: 1409). Male hysteria was common knowledge, he said, as had the others. As for railway spine, his own clinical experience made him inclined to consider it all too premature to equate this affliction with hysteria—despite the undeniable similitude of the symptoms.[12] In any event, Bamberger felt that the one case of Charcot's cited by Freud was clearly indecisive, given the possibility of a "hereditary disposition." Bamberger then went on to question Charcot's characterization of *grande hystérie* and noted that some of the most extreme cases of this disease failed to conform to Charcot's typological specifications. In particular, the convulsive attacks that Charcot considered so typical of this affliction were not always observed. As an example, Bamberger mentioned the case of a girl of two who had developed paralysis of the legs, contractures of the extremities, and paralysis of the bladder (all without convulsions)—an extremely pronounced case of hysteria that nevertheless failed to agree with Charcot's "type" of the disease.

Professor Leidesdorf, the last commentator on Freud's paper, followed Bamberger's remarks with similar clinical criticisms of Charcot's claims about traumatic hysteria. Although Leidesdorf was not personally opposed to the idea that hysteria might occasionally result from a psychic trauma induced by a railway accident, he also warned against the conclusion that the trauma itself was the *real* cause of the hysteria. One did not always know, Leidesdorf elaborated, the extent of possible *organic* lesions in such cases.

Discussion of Freud's paper was followed by Professor Latschenberger's presentation, entitled "On the Presence of Bile in Tissues and Fluids during Grave Illnesses of Animals," which provoked a sharp controversy between Bamberger and Latschenberger. As Ellenberger observes, the "critical" reception of Freud's own paper was clearly a routine affair amidst such a learned society of medical experts (1970:440).

Three points of interest emerge from a survey of the responses to Freud's paper. First, Freud was apparently unaware, before he delivered his paper, of just how well known Charcot's ideas already were to his own superiors in Vienna. Freud thus failed to fulfill one of the most important expectations of his listeners: that he would present something new.

Second, Freud obviously returned from Paris with an idealized picture of Charcot; he had remained at the Salpêtrière too briefly to form a critical attitude toward certain of Charcot's teachings and clinical pro-

---

12. Curiously, in his report to the ministry, written some six months earlier, Freud had reached the same conclusion as Bamberger on this subject. There Freud, too, commented that the cases examined by Thomsen and Oppenheim were probably more complicated than those seen by Charcot, and that the whole issue was, as he put it, "not ripe for decision" (1956a [1886], S.E., 1:12).

cedures. It is now generally recognized that Charcot formulated his theories of hypnotism and hysteria on the basis of experiments performed repeatedly with a few dozen subjects, most of whom lived on the wards of the Salpêtrière, and many of whom, unknown to Charcot, had been rehearsed beforehand in the various responses expected of them. Such deceitful practices were encouraged not only by certain of Charcot's enemies but also by his most loyal disciples, who stood in awe of his authoritarian personality and accordingly sought to please him with ever more remarkable examples of the "types." Patients at the Salpêtrière responded most obligingly to this atmosphere of suggestion and mutual self-deception; and indeed, they vied with one another in their display of "classic" symptoms for the high honor of being the center of attention at one of Charcot's public demonstrations. One patient, Blanche Wittmann, earned herself the title "Queen of the Hysterics" for her ability to produce both the three stages of hypnosis and a complete hysterical crisis à la Charcot. After leaving the Salpêtrière, Blanche Wittmann revealed to Jules Janet, Pierre Janet's brother, that even in a state of hypnosis she had all the while been conscious of her "act" when serving as Charcot's prize model (J. Janet 1888; Ellenberger 1970:98).

Not all of Charcot's visitors were as captivated by his teachings as was Sigmund Freud. The Belgian physician Joseph Delboeuf, who visited Paris contemporaneously with Freud, was appalled by the laxity of Charcot's experimental procedures and, upon returning home, issued a highly critical account of them (Delboeuf 1886). Thus, while many prominent figures in the Viennese medical community, like Bamberger, Leidesdorf, Benedikt, and others, were openly avowed admirers of Charcot, their simultaneous doubts about certain aspects of his recent work, particularly the classification of *grande hystérie* and *grande hypnotisme* as real clinical types, were not without foundation.

The third and last point about this incident is Freud's tactical blunder in attributing as unique to Charcot certain ideas and discoveries that were common medical knowledge in Vienna at the time. Freud's student contemporary and acquaintance, the psychiatrist and subsequent Nobel Prize laureate Julius Wagner-Jauregg (1847–1940), was also present at this meeting, and he later recorded in his autobiography how Freud had affronted his superiors when he "spoke only of Charcot and praised him in the highest fashion. This, however, the Viennese celebrities did not tolerate well" (1950:78). In addition to Meynert, Bamberger, and Rosenthal, who had all explicitly recognized the existence of male hysteria, Moritz Benedikt had described cases of male hysteria as many as twenty years earlier in his textbook on electrotherapy (1868:413–45). (It was Benedikt, a close friend of Charcot's, who provided Freud with a letter of introduction to the great French savant before Freud departed for Paris.)

As for Charcot's supposed refutation of hysteria as a disease of the uterus, this turns out to have been an achievement that he had taken over from his Parisian predecessor Pierre Briquet, who had published a classic study on this subject in 1859 under the title *Traité de l'hys-*

térie.[13] By 1885, the year before Freud delivered his talk on male hysteria at the Society of Physicians, the *Index Catalogue* of the Surgeon-General's Library in Washington had already amassed a hundred or so references under the specific heading "Hysteria *in the male*" (Bry and Rifkin 1962:10). Freud was the only one at the Society of Physicians meeting even to bring up the old uterine theory of hysteria, which only a handful of physicians (particularly gynecologists) took seriously any longer; and from Freud's autobiographical report about the extreme difficulty he later had in finding clinical material to back up his talk, it is clear that it was an *old* surgeon who had raised the antiquated etymological objection that *hysteria* is derived from the Greek word for *womb*.

All in all, the reception of Freud's paper tells us more about his ambitious expectations as a young man of science (and about his overly sensitive attitude toward criticism) than it does about the supposedly backward state of affairs in Viennese medical circles in 1886. Ernest Jones has himself given ample recognition to this conclusion:

> When an enthusiastic, perhaps over-enthusiastic, young man sets out to announce to his seniors (mostly his former teachers) that they have a lot to learn and that he is prepared to enlighten them, the inevitable response is defensive, usually taking the form of minimizing the novelty of the information and damping the exaltation of the speaker. A critical comment on the incident might lay stress on the naiveté of the youthful mentor, and perhaps upon his sensitiveness, as much as on the obvious lack of imagination on the part of his seniors. (1953:230)

Although we do not know the precise tone of voice in which Meynert, Bamberger, and others expressed their critical reserve about Freud's enthusiasm for Charcot's ideas, the published records of this meeting most certainly indicate a far more rational and sophisticated debate than Freud himself was to depict from personal memory almost forty years later.[14]

13. Briquet's *Traité* presented the results of over 400 investigations of hysterical patients. On the basis of these researches, which required approximately ten years to complete, he was able to dismiss altogether the prevailing notions that hysteria was related to unsatisfied sexual impulses (he found that prostitutes suffered more than nuns), to disturbances of the womb, or to an exclusive etiology in the female sex. Briquet estimated twenty cases of female hysteria for every male case, the same ratio later reported by both Charcot and Freud. Briquet personally attributed this disease to the effects of overpowering emotions connected with various major conflicts and disappointments in life. He also stressed the role of hereditary predisposition. See Ellenberger (1970:142) for a more detailed summary of Briquet's views.

14. It seems likely that the tone of the meeting was indeed more negative than the published record suggests. Wagner-Jauregg, who was there, records in his *Lebenserinnerungen* that "Bamberger and Meynert rejected Freud harshly in the discussion, and with this he had fallen into disgrace, so to speak, with the faculty. He was thus a neurological practitioner without patients" (1950:72). Eissler (1971: 354) places considerable weight upon Wagner-Jauregg's recollections and disagrees on this basis with the conclusion of Jones (1953:230) and Ellenberger (1970:441) that Freud was both naïve and oversensitive in connection with his talk. No doubt Freud's superiors firmly rebuffed him. But Eissler's specific suggestion that Freud

Further, it is not true that Freud ceased on this account to attend the various local medical societies, as he also claims in his *Autobiography*. Records exist of his having attended the Society of Physicians twice in 1887 and again a year later (Jones 1953:232; *Origins*, p. 55). On 16 February 1887, Freud's name was proposed for membership in that society. A month later—and a year and a half after his ill-fated talk—he was duly elected to the society's membership! He remained a member in good standing until he was forced by the Nazis to leave Vienna in 1938.[15] Finally, as Ernest Jones (1953:232) and others have pointed out, Freud attended other medical societies, either speaking or reading papers, until about 1904—by which date the earliest members of the group that later became the Vienna Psychoanalytic Society had already begun their weekly meetings at Freud's home.

The Debates over Hypnotism

In the wake of his personally inspiring visit to Paris, Freud also became actively involved in the debates over hypnotism that had been rekindled by Charcot's endorsement of this subject. Freud's involvement in these general debates soon led him into a more specialized controversy that arose at this time between the school of Charcot at the Salpêtrière in Paris and that of Hippolyte Bernheim in Nancy.

The first and more polemical of these two intellectual episodes in Freud's early neurological career was precipitated by his head-on confrontation with his former teacher Theodor Meynert. Soon after Freud's return to Vienna, Meynert had begun to take a dim view of Freud's new allegiance to the views of Charcot, apparently considering it to be disloyal both to himself and to his own more somatically oriented views of disease.

Meynert had personally sought to stigmatize hypnotism as "an experimentally produced psychosis" (Freud 1888–89, *S.E.*, *1*:75–76). Among the specific reasons that he advanced for his opposition to hypnosis was the claim that in the hypnotic state "a human being is reduced to a creature without will or reason, and his nervous and mental degeneration is only hastened by it" (Meynert 1889*a*:687; see also 1889*b*). He even went so far as to label the growing hypnotism movement a "psychical epidemic among doctors"—precisely the same epithet

---

was arguing in his talk for an "approximately equal" ratio between male and female hysteria, and that he was therefore saying something quite new and worthy of notice from his colleagues, is a claim not borne out by Freud's later views. See Freud's article "Hysteria," where he endorses Charcot's 1:20 ratio of male to female hysteria (1888*b*, *S.E.*, *1*:51).

15. In addition, Freud was on sufficiently good terms with the Society of Physicians to donate a presentation copy of his *Studies on Hysteria* (coauthored with Josef Breuer) to its library in the winter of 1896/97. More than a decade later, he gave the society copies of *The Psychopathology of Everyday Life* and his *Shorter Writings on the Theory of the Neuroses from the Years 1893–1906*. In 1931 Freud was made an honorary member of the society. See Sablik (1968), who searched through the society's records in documenting most of the facts cited above regarding Freud's continuing relationship to the Society of Physicians.

Theodor Meynert (1833–92).

used twenty years later by a critic of the nascent psychoanalytic move-ment (Jones 1953:235–36). Finally, Meynert firmly believed that most hypnotic "cures" were the result either of fraudulence or of self-delu-sion on the part of doctors and patients.

Such views about hypnotism seem strange to us today, given the widespread therapeutic use of hypnotism in everything from dental work and smoking cures to occasional major surgery. There is no rea-son to believe, however, that Meynert's opinions were not sincere. Fur-thermore, his apprehensions were shared by many prominent physi-cians of this period and must therefore be understood in their specific historical context.

To begin with, criticisms of Charcot's and others' hypnotic re-searches were the culmination of a long history of similar efforts in Europe and America to separate fact from fiction in hypnotic psycho-therapy. What *was* new in the 1880s was that a stellar representative of official medicine like Jean-Martin Charcot had taken up hypnotism at a time when it was once again out of general favor. More particularly, one must appreciate the contemporary objections to hypnosis, advanced by Meynert and others, in terms of the specific theories of hypnotism and hysteria that Charcot himself had formulated since 1878. Hypnosis, Charcot had concluded, was nothing more than an artificially induced morbid condition, a neurosis of sorts—one peculiar to neuropaths and especially to the hysterics with whom he worked at the Salpêtrière. Hypnotizability, therefore, appeared to depend on the neuropathic subject, not on the hypnotic suggestions provided by the hypnotist. Charcot accordingly believed that hypnotizability must be a fairly rare phenomenon, like hysteria itself, and that suggestibility in normal waking life was different from the sort of pathological suggestibility found in hypnosis.[16] Finally, all these medical opinions were further linked to Charcot's conclusion that it was potentially dangerous to induce hypnosis in healthy individuals, who might thereby be made hysterical (Charcot 1887–89, 2:247–56; see also Ellenberger 1970:119, 751). Thus, Theodor Meynert, in objecting to the use of hypnosis in suggestion therapy, was merely expressing his concern over a possible danger (the similitude of hypnotic and hysterical phenomena) already pointed out by Charcot himself.

One further objection by Meynert to the use of hypnosis is also worth mentioning briefly. He believed that much of the basis of the hypnotic trance was sexual. By inhibiting the subject's higher cortical activity (and thus his conscious control over his own body), hypnosis encouraged, Meynert argued, the involuntary release of sexual impulses in the subcortex. He therefore considered this method to be improper for general medical use. Meynert cited in this connection the experiences of one candid physician who confessed that he had more than once experienced involuntary pollutions after having been placed in a state of hypnosis. To this same subcortical liberation of sexual impulses, Meynert was also inclined to ascribe the well-known state of "euphoria" so often experienced by subjects under hypnosis (Meynert 1889c:490; 1890:197).

It was only after several years of utilizing hypnosis that Freud discovered the important psychoanalytic kernel of truth embedded in Meynert's last objection. In his *Autobiography*, Freud describes how one of the major factors leading to his abandonment of the hypnotic technique was an untoward incident in which a particularly amenable female subject, upon being awakened from a hypnotic trance, suddenly threw her arms around his neck in embrace. The unexpected entrance of a servant spared Freud a painful discussion of the matter with his patient; but from this point on, there was "a tacit understanding" between them that hypnosis would no longer be used. And it was also then that Freud finally glimpsed "the mysterious [erotic] element that was at work behind hypnotism," and that apparently provided the essential key to the hypnotist's therapeutic effectiveness (1925d, S.E., 20:27). Years later, the closely derivative psychoanalytic phenomenon of *transference* became for Freud one of the most "irrefragable" proofs in favor of his controversial sexual etiology of the neuroses (1914d, S.E., 14:12).

Similarly, Meynert's implicit cortical/subcortical model of the mind parallels Freud's subsequent division of mental functioning into *primary* ("wish-fulfillment") and *secondary* (i.e., more "inhibitory") processes and undoubtedly had something to do with Freud's later conceptualization (cf. Jones 1953:281, 376).

In Vienna, Freud's early support for hypnotic psychotherapy played a significant part in hastening the general acceptance of this predominantly French medical development. Freud was later cited in this connection by two other major pioneers in the use of hypnotism and suggestion therapy—Albert Moll (1890:13) and A. W. van Renterghem (1898:133), who also mentioned Josef Breuer as Freud's Viennese collaborator. Championing hypnotism with his "characteristic ardor" (Jones 1953:236), Freud found it very difficult to restrain himself in his replies to Theodor Meynert's uninformed diatribes against the hypnotists. "Because the attitude of all my friends demanded it," Freud reported to his friend Wilhelm Fliess in August 1888, "I had to be moderate in my criticism of Meynert, who in his usual impudent-malicious manner had delivered himself authoritatively on a subject of which he knew nothing. Even so, they think I have gone too far. I have belled the cat" (*Origins,* pp. 58–59). "It is difficult for most people to suppose," Freud wrote in one such public reply to Meynert, "that a scientist who has had great experience in certain regions of neuropathology, and has given proof of much acumen, should have no qualification for being quoted as an authority on other problems; . . . But . . . [respect for intellectual greatness] should yield to respect for the facts" (1889a, S.E., 1:92–93).

Meynert's exclusion of Freud from his anatomical laboratory in the wake of this controversy lends credence to Jones's (1953:237) conjecture that personal jealousy and petty ambitions were behind Meynert's opposition to Freud.[17] Among other circumstances, Freud's support of hypnotism had made him an ally of Leidesdorf, the hypnotizing superintendent of Obersteiner's sanatorium, with whom Meynert was involved in yet another personal feud.

One last story remains to be told about Freud's relationship to Meynert. Freud recounts in *The Interpretation of Dreams* (1900a, S.E., 5:438) how he visited his old teacher during Meynert's last illness in 1892, and how, to Freud's combined satisfaction and astonishment, Meynert confessed that he had always known himself to be a classic case of male hysteria! To psychoanalysts, Meynert's reputed confession has always seemed pregnant with meaning—so much so that they have never wondered at the oddity of such an admission. To under-

---

17. Meynert's reputation as a difficult and polemical man with an overly narrow, somatic orientation to nervous disease was not undeserved. Freud's contemporary at the University of Vienna, Julius Wagner-Jauregg, later wrote of Freud's adversary: "With Meynert, the guilt was usually on Meynert's side" (1950:71). Meynert's stubborn refusal to consider nonsomatic methods of psychotherapy is exemplified by one of his comments about Freud: "I find his defense of the suggestion therapy all the more remarkable inasmuch as he left Vienna [for Paris] a physician with an exact training in physiology" (1889b:501 n.). See also Lesky 1965:373–74; Ellenberger 1970:434; Eissler 1971:351–58; and Stockert-Meynert's (1930) biography of Meynert.

stand this episode, whose authenticity is not being disputed,[18] one must bear in mind that Meynert's personal disenchantment with Freud at no time revolved around Freud's belief in the existence of male hysteria per se (a misconception later reinforced by Freud in his *Autobiography*, 1925d, S.E., 20:15; see also Wittels 1924b:32). Meynert simply disagreed with Freud about equating male hysteria, a hereditary disease, with instances of traumatic neurosis resulting from shock. Meynert therefore had no real reason to regard his self-diagnosis as a "confession," and his remark would have meant something completely different to him than it evidently did to Freud.

More revealing about Freud's early conception of the mind than the dispute with Meynert is the position he took in a second and more theoretical aspect of the hypnotism debates. In the mid-1880s, Hippolyte Bernheim (1840–1919) and his rival Nancy school had issued a major challenge to Charcot's theory of hypnotic phenomena. Charcot had seen in hypnotism a primarily physiological process: that is, it was an innately predisposed reaction on the part of neuropaths to stroking, fixations of the sensory apparatus, and various other means of hypnotic induction. As Freud later wrote, "it is the great authority of Charcot which supports this exclusively somatic view of hypnosis" (1889a, S.E., 1:97).

In 1884, in opposition to Charcot, Bernheim lent his influential support to a more psychological theory of hypnosis, according to which the results of hypnotism, as well as the whole process of hypnotic induction itself, were all to be explained *ideogenically* in terms of the effects of conscious "suggestions" upon the hypnotized subject. Bernheim, in adopting such views, was following the earlier and much-neglected teachings of his elderly mentor Ambroise Auguste Liébeault (1823–1904), whose own theories on this subject had been published almost twenty years earlier in *Du Sommeil et des états analogues* (Of Sleep and Similar States, 1866). Until Bernheim brought him belated fame, Liébeault had been viewed by his medical contemporaries as a quack—because he dared to hypnotize openly—and as a fool—because he offered to treat skeptics free of charge and made payment of fees voluntary for others (Ellenberger 1970:85–87).

Bernheim's 1884 revival of Liébeault's suggestion therapy was subsequently expanded in 1886 into a larger textbook (*De la Suggestion et de ses applications à la thérapeutique*), which Freud himself had presumably read by the end of December 1887, since he was already under contract by that date, as he informed his friend Fliess, to translate this work into German (*Origins*, p. 53). In this textbook, Bernheim reiterated his basic theme that hypnotizability, or simple "suggestibility" as he preferred to call it, was a capacity shared by *all* human beings, not just hysterics and neuropaths. Bernheim was equally staunch in his rejection of Charcot's three stages of *grande hypnotisme*,

18. Henri Ellenberger (1970:556, n. 151), on the other hand, has been inclined to doubt the authenticity of this particular anecdote: after all, one does not easily hide a classic case of hysteria from one's neurological colleagues.

which he believed to be artifacts of the hysterical patients with whom Charcot had foolishly worked.

Freud, in his Preface to the German translation of Bernheim's book, warmly welcomed the latter's psychological approach to the subject. Freud especially praised Bernheim's attempt to link hypnotism with the more familiar phenomenon of sleep.[19] At the same time, Freud felt that Bernheim's theoretical views had introduced certain new contradictions and had, as it were, gone to the opposite extreme—that of a psychology without physiology. In a contemporary letter to his friend Fliess, Freud succinctly conveyed the judgment of his translator's Preface (1888–89) with the words: "I do not share Bernheim's views, which seem to me one-sided, and I have tried to stand up for Charcot in the introduction—I do not know how skillfully . . ." (*Origins*, p. 58).

The main problem with Bernheim's theory was as follows: If hypnotism were indeed *purely* the effect of suggestion, then the "type" of *grande* (hysterical) *hypnotisme,* which Charcot had described as being characterized by contractures, neuromuscular spasms, and other symptoms of *grande hystérie,* was simply not genuine. And if it were not genuine, Freud realized, then serious doubt was cast upon the whole of Charcot's attempt to show that hysterical phenomena are governed by regular laws (*S.E., 1*:77–78). But this last possibility Freud was unwilling to admit. Indeed, it was the identical physiological nature of certain "core" symptoms or stigmata in both hysteria and *grande hypnotisme*—symptoms seemingly independent of any *ideogenic* content—that underlay Freud's qualified support for Charcot's somatic theory of hypnosis.[20] "Thus physiological phenomena do occur," Freud insisted, "at all events in hysterical major hypnosis" (*S.E., 1*:80). He therefore remained confident that, despite Bernheim's repeated doubts, Charcot's three stages of *grande hypnotisme* could be successfully shown to exist in hysterical patients brought newly to the Salpêtrière and then hypnotized under the most scrupulous of conditions.[21]

What, then, *was* the essential mechanism of hypnosis if it was not, as Bernheim claimed, purely a consequence of psychological sugges-

19. Freud later used the Nancy school's analogy between hypnosis and sleep to strike back at Theodor Meynert's alarmist tactics regarding the dangerous "euphoretic" (i.e., uncontrolled subcortical) aspects of the hypnotic trance. As Freud pointed out, the similarly reduced cortical activity of sleep had hardly convinced people that they should give up sleeping on this account (1889a, *S.E., 1*:93–94).

20. Freud (1888–89, *S.E., 1*:78–80). This was a position that Freud later reiterated with equal conviction in *Studies on Hysteria* (1895d) when he frankly confessed his medical opinion that certain of Charcot's (1887:255) "permanent symptoms" of hysteria might well persist, at least for a while, even after completion of a successful treatment of all the ideogenic symptoms by the Breuer-Freud cathartic method (*S.E., 2*:265; see also Freud 1896c, *S.E., 3*:192–93).

21. As it has turned out, Bernheim was right, and Freud, who later retracted his support for Charcot on this point, was wrong. One might say, in this regard, that Freud had reached a psychoanalytically fruitful conclusion (the lawful nature of hysteria) for the wrong reasons (presumed physiological phenomena that no one but Charcot could ever replicate). One assiduous critic of Charcot's hypnotic theory, Otto Wetterstrand, later claimed to have hypnotized over 3,500 persons without finding a single instance of Charcot's three stages of *grande hypnotisme* (see Moll 1890:59).

tion? This particular problem could be resolved, Freud thought, by recognizing certain basic psychophysical ambiguities implicit in the use of words like "suggestion" and "consciousness." A successful (direct) hypnotic suggestion, he argued, is also an "indirect" or "auto-" suggestion at the same time. Successful autosuggestions could be described "equally as physiological or as psychical phenomena," he contended, since every autosuggestion plays upon a natural physiological capacity in human beings that links our conscious mental states with purely neurophysiological processes. An example of this linking process in autosuggestion is when closing the eyes leads naturally to sleep (1888–89, *S.E.*, *1*:84).

Similarly, Freud urged, one had to avoid Bernheim's apparent equation of "psychical" with what is accessible to consciousness, and "physiological" with what is not accessible to it. Many mental processes are, on the contrary, both psychical and unconscious. In short, as a convinced psychophysical *dualist* on the subject of mental processes, Freud concluded: "there are both psychical and physiological phenomena in hypnotism, and hypnosis itself can be brought about in the one manner or the other" (*S.E.*, *1*:81).

In the hope of perfecting his hypnotic technique, Freud journeyed to Nancy in the summer of 1889 and spent several weeks with Bernheim and old Liébeault. Personal contact with these two physicians seems to have mollified Freud's earlier criticisms of Bernheim's hypnotic theory. Freud later arranged with Bernheim to translate a second book on hypnosis into German (Bernheim 1891; Freud 1892*a*).

Resolution of the Hypnotism Debates (1888–93)

The period between 1888 and 1893 was one of prodigious and unabated research on the subjects of hypnotic induction and therapy. Max Dessoir's *Bibliographie des modernen Hypnotismus* (1888) carried references to 801 recent publications; two years later that list had been augmented by nearly 400 new titles. This literature quickly confirmed the basic thrust of Bernheim's point of view—namely, that hypnotic suggestibility was independent of a hysterical or neuropathic disposition. Simultaneously, Charcot's phenomenon of *grande hypnotisme*, with its classic three stages, was widely pronounced a chimera. Thus, it is not surprising that Freud, when he wrote his obituary notice of Charcot in 1893, took a considerably more critical stand on his teacher's theory of hypnotism than he had initially done some five years before:

> . . . the exclusively nosographical approach adopted at the School of the Salpêtrière was not suitable for a purely psychological subject. The restriction of the study of hypnosis to hysterical patients, the differentiation between major and minor hypnotism, the hypothesis of three stages of "major hypnosis," and their characterization by somatic phenomena— all this sank in the estimation of Charcot's contemporaries when Liébeault's pupil, Bernheim, set about constructing the theory of hypnotism

on a more comprehensive psychological foundation and making suggestion the central point of hypnosis. (1893f, S.E., 3:22–23)

In short, by 1893 the work of Bernheim and others had succeeded in
convincing Freud that much of Charcot's evidence for the *physiological*
nature of hypnosis was completely bogus.

FREUD'S POSITIONS ON HYPNOTISM AND MENTAL PROCESSES

The Controversy with Meynert

Freud's disputes with Theodor Meynert over hypnotic psychotherapy and the psychogenic nature of hysteria might easily be—and
often have been—taken as the first major signs of a far-reaching new
trend in Freud's intellectual development. And it was this same trend, so
continues this historical argument, that culminated in Freud's final
abandonment of neurophysiological for "purely psychological" modes
of thought.[22]
While it is true that Charcot's influence introduced the young
Viennese brain anatomist to a number of new and important psychological insights about psychoneurosis, one must also be careful not to
read more into this influence than was there at the time. To begin
with, any suggestion that Freud's return from Paris somehow signaled
his incipient emancipation from neurophysiology tends to ignore the
important fact that he was already interested in psychological approaches to the mental apparatus long before he ever set foot in Paris.
Not only did he take three and one-half years of elective courses with
the psychologist-philosopher Franz Brentano while a medical student
at the University of Vienna, but Freud is even known to have kept
private notebooks of his dreams in the early part of his life (Jones
1953:351). Similarly, Freud's systematic and graphic analysis of the
reasons for neurologist Nathan Weiss's suicide in 1883 ranks as a mas-
terful psychological study in its own right (Jones 1953:166; *Letters*, pp.
59–66). Hence, it would be fair to say that, while in Paris, Freud found
Charcot's ideas on hypnotism and hysteria as fascinating as he did precisely because they appealed to a long-standing personal interest in the
subject of psychology.
On the other hand, one of Freud's major post-Paris projects, mentioned repeatedly in his letters to Wilhelm Fliess during 1887 and 1888,
was the writing of a major book on the anatomy of the brain. (Only a
much-abridged remnant of this project ever appeared in print: namely,
what Freud later described, with some annoyance, as his "severely cut"
article on the brain for Villaret's *Handwörterbuch der gesamten Medizin*;

22. Jones (1953:211–12, 236), for example, hints more than once at such a
trend in Freud's post-Paris thinking; see also Strachey's Editor's Note to Freud
1956a [1886], S.E., 1:3.

see *Origins*, p. 59; Freud 1888*b*.) More to the point, Freud's enthusiastic support of Charcot's theories—albeit to critics like Theodor Meynert a seeming repudiation of somatically sound medicine—was fully
consistent with Freud's contemporaneous ambition of establishing a
combined psychophysiological basis for both hypnotic and hysterical
phenomena. Indeed, it was primarily the *physiological* side to Charcot's findings that initially had impressed Freud, according to his own
testimony, with the genuinely lawful nature of these phenomena
(1888–89, *S.E.*, *1*:77–85). In sum, Freud's post-Paris positions on the
problems of hypnosis and hysteria were well balanced and dualist—a
conclusion borne out more fully by his involvement in the Charcot-
Bernheim controversy.

Charcot vs. Bernheim: Freud's Dualist Alternative

Freud's views on the nature of hypnosis evolved through two overlapping stages. In the first, he took a stand against what he considered
to be Bernheim's "one-sided" views, but not wholly with those of Charcot (*Origins*, p. 58); while in the second and later stage—following the
eventual discrediting of Charcot's hypnotic researches by other workers
in the field—Freud shifted his allegiance toward Bernheim. "[O]ver the
question of hypnosis," Freud later wrote about this second position, "I
sided against Charcot, even if not entirely with Bernheim . . ." (*Letters*,
p. 394).[23]

Notwithstanding Freud's various modifications of his views on hypnotism, each of his two principal positions over the years reflects a common and lasting preference for a dualist approach; that is to say, his
views on hypnotism always allowed for both neurophysiological and
psychological levels of explanation. Freud therefore never wavered
from his initial pronouncement in 1888 on the general problems of
hypnosis and psychophysical parallelism—namely, that "it would be
just as one-sided to consider only the psychological side of the process
as to attribute the whole responsibility for the phenomena of hypnosis
to the vascular innervation" (1888–89, *S.E.*, *1*: 84).

Three years later, in his monograph *On Aphasia* (1891*b*), Freud
reiterated this dualist position on the mind-body problem within the
more general context of his support for J. Hughlings Jackson's doctrine of the "dependent concomitant" relationship between psychical
and physiological events. "The relationship between the chain of physiological events in the nervous system and the mental processes,"
Freud wrote, "is probably not one of [literal] cause and effect. The
former do not cease when the latter set in; they tend to continue but,
from a certain moment, a mental phenomenon corresponds to each
part of the chain, or to several parts. The psychic is, therefore, a process parallel to the physiological, 'a dependent concomitant'" (1891*b*;

23. Many years later, Freud's final or *phylogenetic* theory of hypnotic induction marked a return to the earlier of his two positions. For his last theory, as he
himself admitted in 1921, led him to reaffirm his support for the sort of "innate
disposition" conception originally advanced by Charcot (Freud 1921*c*, *S.E.*, *18*:128 n.).

trans. 1953a:55). Freud's precise intent in this passage is made clearer by his further citation of the following specific warning on Jackson's part: "In all our studies of diseases of the nervous system we must be on our guard against the fallacy that what are physical states in lower centres fine away *into* psychical states in higher centres; that, for example, vibrations of sensory nerves *become* sensations, or that somehow or other an idea produces a movement" (Freud 1891b; trans. 1953a:56; quoted from Jackson 1879:306).

Thus, just as Freud did not seek to reduce all hysterical phenomena to physiology in these early years (despite his strong background of medical training in anatomy and neurophysiology), neither did he ever subscribe before 1900 to a purely psychological theory of mental disease. In sum, his interest in phenomena like hypnosis and hysteria was accompanied from the first by a balanced concern for the intricacies of the age-old mind-body problem and, consequently, by a considered attempt to avoid an overly simplified stand on those fascinating medical issues (see also Stewart 1967:25–32). I will consider in later chapters the broader issue of whether Freud, after 1900 or so, ever abandoned this early stand in favor of a purely psychological science of mind.

THE BREUER PERIOD

If Jean-Martin Charcot was the first of the two momentous personal influences that started Freud on the pathway to psychoanalytic theory, the second was Josef Breuer (1842–1925). Breuer was the son of a religious teacher of modest but respected attainment within the Viennese Jewish community (Breuer's mother died when he was a young child). He later described his father, whom he greatly revered, as having "belonged to that generation of Jews who were the first to emerge from the intellectual ghetto into the free atmosphere of Western civilization" (Breuer [1925]; trans. Oberndorf 1953:65).

Like Freud, Breuer did his principal training as a Vienna University medical student under Ernst Brücke. He received his medical degree in 1867 at the age of twenty-five. Although largely known today for his close personal and scientific association with Sigmund Freud, Breuer was an accomplished physiologist in his own right. Moreover, Breuer's physiological researches provided a conceptual foundation for the pioneering theory of hysteria that he and Freud later proposed.

Prior to coming in contact with Freud, Breuer had made two important physiological discoveries. The first involved his successful unraveling—while still working as a medical student under Ewald Hering—of the self-regulating mechanism of breathing as controlled by the vagus nerve (the so-called Hering-Breuer reflex). Breuer (1868) made this particular discovery by means of an elegant piece of experimental research, and his demonstration furnished conclusive evidence

Josef Breuer in 1877, about the time he first encountered Freud in Brücke's Physiological Institute.

for one of the first biological feedback mechanisms to be documented in mammals.[24]

Breuer's second major contribution to physiology was his discovery in 1873, essentially simultaneously with the great Ernst Mach and the Edinburgh chemist A. Crum Brown, of the function played by the semicircular canals in the ear. The inner ear is a double organ—for both hearing and balance. Breuer, in his own work on this problem, skillfully elucidated the delicate series of reflex mechanisms by which the sensory receptors within the inner-ear labyrinth succeed in regulating posture, equilibrium, and movement (Breuer 1874, 1875). He also called attention to the importance of the more obscure otolith system, an aspect of the problem that had been overlooked by Mach and Brown.[25]

24. See Cranefield (1970a:446) and Hirschmüller (1978), whose excellent reviews of Breuer's scientific career I have largely followed here; also Meyer 1928; Jones 1953:221–67; and Ackerknecht 1963.

25. The first Austrian Nobel Laureate, Robert Bárány, won the Physiology and Medicine Prize in 1914 for his work on the equilibrium organs of the inner ear. In 1916 he was denied academic advancement by the Senate of the University of Vienna because he had given insufficient credit to prior researchers on this subject, principally Josef Breuer. Although Bárány indeed admitted to having forgotten Breuer's 1874 paper, Breuer himself made light of the whole episode and actually came to Bárány's defense in the priority proceedings (Hirshmüller 1978:105–7).

On the strength of these early and impressive findings in physiology, Breuer was appointed in 1875 to the rank of *Privatdozent* at the University of Vienna. Subsequent difficulties in gaining patients for teaching purposes apparently caused him to resign his position ten years later. At this time he also refused the offer of Theodor Billroth, the famous surgeon, to propose him for the title "Extraordinary Professor," retiring instead into the full-time private practice that became his principal medical devotion.

The caliber of Breuer's continued scientific reputation is nevertheless well illustrated by the fact that he was elected to the Viennese Academy of Sciences in 1894 upon the nominations of Ernst Mach, Ewald Hering, and Sigmund Exner, three of that body's most accomplished and internationally known members. Although it is often assumed that Breuer published relatively little in his lifetime, a bibliography of his purely physiological publications includes nearly twenty articles totaling some five hundred printed pages of meticulously conducted and carefully described research (Cranefield 1970a:447). Among Breuer's many patients were the families of Brücke, Exner, Billroth, Chrobak, and many other prominent members of the Viennese scientific community.

All who knew Breuer intimately are agreed that he was a fascinating and highly cultured personality. He was a particularly superb conversationalist, and on literary and philosophical questions his opinions were often sought by the most brilliant Viennese minds of his

Josef Breuer's technique for dissecting the canals of the inner ear, illustrated with a young pigeon (1875:96).

generation. Breuer maintained an extensive correspondence with the philosopher-psychologist Franz Brentano as well as with the poetess Marie von Ebner-Eschenbach. In spite of his well-deserved reputation for a sharp and critical mind, Breuer was also widely esteemed as an unusually selfless and warm-hearted individual (see Ellenberger [1970:432] for a collection of such testimonials). As witness to this side of Breuer's personality, Freud, in the 1880s, referred to him in letters to his fiancée as "the ever-loyal Breuer" (Jones 1953:223).

Freud first encountered Breuer while both men were pursuing their respective anatomical-physiological researches at Brücke's Physiological Institute during the late 1870s. "Our relations soon became more intimate," Freud later recounted in his *Autobiography*, "and he became my friend and helper in my difficult circumstances. We grew accustomed to share all our scientific interests with each other. In this relationship the gain was naturally mine" (1925d, S.E., 20:19). In 1881, Breuer's tutelage included regular monthly loans, and Freud's financial debt to him eventually was substantial—a debt that became a sore burden to Freud a decade later, when Breuer tried to refuse its repayment during the period when the two men were growing estranged. Following Freud's marriage in 1886, however, the two families were on the closest of social terms; and Freud dedicated his monograph *On Aphasia* (1891b) to Breuer and named his eldest daughter Mathilde, born in 1887, after Breuer's wife.

The Case of Anna O.

In his *Autobiography*, Freud mentions that his clinical work with hypnotism had been carried out from the very first in "*another* manner" than that of simply making therapeutic suggestions to his patients (1925d, S.E., 20:19). By this statement, Freud meant that he had also begun employing hypnotism during the late 1880s as a means of helping hysterical patients to recall the precise circumstances surrounding onset of their symptoms. This alternative use of hypnotism Freud had learned from Josef Breuer as a result of the latter's singular experience some seven or eight years earlier with his famous patient known as "Anna O."

Fräulein Anna O., whose real identity as Bertha Pappenheim (1859–1936) was revealed by Ernest Jones in 1953, was twenty-one years of age when she began in the fall of 1880 to show signs of severe psychological disturbance. The immediate occasion for Anna O.'s illness was her mental and physical exhaustion after nursing her ailing father for several months. The latter, to whom Anna O. was devoted, eventually succumbed the following spring to an incurable peripleuritic abscess.

Breuer treated Anna O. from December 1880, when she took to her bed, until June 1882. During this period, she displayed the most remarkable series of symptoms, including rigid paralysis and loss of sensation in the extremities on the right side of her body, similar (but more occasional) paralytic dysfunctions on the left side of her body, severely disturbed ocular movements and power of vision, sporadic deafness, difficulties with the posture of her head, a nervous cough, and aversion to nourishment and even liquids (at one point she lived for several weeks upon oranges alone). Anna O. was also afflicted by suicidal impulses, by the loss of her ability to speak the German language (although she retained a perfect command of English—the language in which Breuer had to conduct much of his treatment of her), and finally by *absences* or "secondary" states of confused delirium, accompanied by alterations of her entire personality. During the daytime, these *absences* (a French term) would mount with increasing frequency into somnolence, and, after sunset, they would give way to a state of autohypnosis, which the patient referred to as her period of "clouds." In the course of these *absences*, the patient became totally dissociated from her normal waking self and, upon finally recovering her mental stability, exhibited little or no memory of these previous hallucinatory phases.

Breuer immediately recognized the case as one of hysterical double personality. He discovered at one point that, merely by showing her an orange, he could induce a transition from Anna O.'s normal personality to what she called her "bad self." More remarkable still, at the height of her illness, the patient regularly hallucinated the various events in her life that had actually taken place 365 days earlier. Breuer documented this aspect of the case history from a diary of the illness kept by Anna O.'s mother.

In the course of treating this unusual patient, Breuer made another curious discovery. He found that if he repeated to his patient each evening, when she entered a state of autohypnosis, the frightened words she had uttered during her daytime *absences*, she was able to recall the forgotten details of her terrifying hallucinations. Therapeutically this process relieved both her symptoms and her often agitated state of mind by the end of each day. Anna O. dubbed this therapeutic procedure— in English—her "talking cure" and, jokingly, "chimney sweeping."

Gradually the patient, to whom Breuer began to devote several hours each day, evolved the methodical routine of informing him, in reverse chronological order, about each and every past appearance of a given symptom. She proceeded in this manner until she reached the very first moment of each symptom's appearance—at which point, to Breuer's amazement, the symptom disappeared. This was the method of "catharsis" (Breuer's term). By applying this laborious procedure, which Breuer supplemented with daytime hypnotic sessions, to each of her symptoms, he was eventually able to restore his patient to a fairly normal life. Each of Anna O.'s symptoms proved to be rooted in certain psychical conflicts, moments of fright, and so forth, first experienced during the period of her nursing duties. The very last of Anna O.'s symptoms, paralysis of the right arm, was finally relieved after she reported a previous hallucination of a large black snake while sitting by her father's bedside. In her attempt to ward off the snake with her right arm, as she recalled under Breuer's ministrations, the arm had been unable

Anna O. (Bertha Pappenheim)
in 1882.

to move, at which point an English-language prayer had been the only thing that she could think of in her fright. With this final confession, the paralysis of the arm was cured, and the patient's native German tongue was suddenly restored to her.

The medical cure was nothing short of stupendous, given the almost unheard-of time and patience Breuer spent in treating this one patient. According to Breuer, he listened to stories of the circumstances, people, places, and often *exact* dates (for Anna O. had a remarkable memory) associated with 303 separate instances in which the patient had previously experienced dysfunctions in her hearing alone (*S.E.*, 2: 36). The systematic Breuer carefully recorded them all and even managed to group them under seven different contextual subheadings!

The evolution of the cathartic technique appears to be linked to another contemporary development. Juan Dalma (1963, 1964) has pointed out that Jacob Bernays, the uncle of Freud's future wife, had long been concerned with the Aristotelian concept of dramatic catharsis (Bernays 1857, 1880). In Vienna, as elsewhere, this whole subject was much discussed among scholars and in the salons and even assumed for a time the proportions of a craze. According to Hirschmüller (1978: 207 n.), by 1880 Bernays's ideas had inspired some seventy German-language publications on catharsis, a number that more than doubled by 1890. It seems very possible that an intelligent girl like Anna O. might have been acquainted with the subject and have unconsciously incorporated this knowledge into the dramatic plot of her illness. And the connection between catharsis in its theatrical and medical senses was certainly not lost upon Bernays and others.[26] It is not known whether Breuer and Freud were acquainted with Bernays's ideas while they were developing their theory of hysteria. Still, it is extremely difficult to believe they were not; and a year after *Studies on Hysteria* (1895d) appeared in print, Breuer, who had a special interest in Greek drama, discussed Bernays's views in a letter to Theodor Gomperz (Hirschmüller 1978:210–11).

According to Ernest Jones, Anna O.'s cure was by no means as successful as Breuer himself suggested in *Studies on Hysteria* (1895d). In fact, the patient apparently had many relapses and was eventually institutionalized. Breuer even expressed the hope, a year after he discontinued personal treatment of the case, that his patient might die and so be released from her suffering.[27] As long as five years after Breuer's contact with her had ceased, Anna O. was still liable—according to the testimony of Freud's wife, who encountered the patient then—to occasional hallucinations whenever evening approached.

Eventually she recovered, and in later life Anna O., as Bertha Pappenheim, became an important pioneer in the women's movement. In the late 1880s, she took up social work. She spent twelve years as director of an orphanage in Frankfurt (1895–1907); she founded a League of Jewish Women in 1904 and a home for unwed mothers in 1907; and she traveled widely in Russia, Poland, and Rumania in order to help orphaned children and to investigate the widespread problems of prostitution and white slavery (Edinger 1963). Bertha Pappenheim published a great deal on these various topics, including short stories and dramatic works, and she once wrote, "If there is any justice in the next life, women will make the laws and men will bear the children." [28] In 1954 the West German government issued a commemorative postage stamp in her honor.

Bertha Pappenheim's attitude toward psychoanalysis remained cool. She never spoke to anyone of her experience with Breuer, and she later refused to allow the girls under her care to be psychoanalyzed (Johnston 1972:236). "Psychoanalysis," she remarked in the 1920s, "is in the hand of the physician what the confessional is in the hand of the Catholic clergyman; it depends upon the person applying it and the [specific] application whether it is a good instrument or a double-edged sword" (quoted in Edinger 1963:12–13).

26. See, for example, Berger (1897), who specifically cited *Studies on Hysteria* in this connection.
27. See Jones (1953:225), who supplies this detail from the evidence of an unpublished letter of Freud's to Martha Bernays, dated 5 August 1883.
28. Cited by Jones 1953:224 n.; see also Ellenberger 1970:480–81.

Breuer apparently told Freud about the details of his unusual case as early as 18 November 1882, according to an unpublished letter written by Freud to Martha Bernays the following day (Jones 1953:226). Freud was fascinated by the strange case history; and he repeatedly discussed it with Breuer, who also obliged Freud's interest by reading to him many extracts from his own careful notes on the course of Anna O.'s illness. When Freud visited Paris in the winter of 1885/86, he informed Charcot about this remarkable case history. "But the great man showed no interest in my first outline of the subject, so that I never returned to it and allowed it to pass from my mind," Freud later recalled in his *Autobiography* (1925d, S.E., 20:19–20).

Freud was slow to apply Breuer's new therapeutic technique himself after returning from Paris, probably because his initial clientele presented him with many strictly neurological disorders and, as a specialist in neurology, his own interests were still largely focused upon physiological aspects of the neuroses. During the first year and one-half of private practice, he seems to have relied exclusively upon the standard neurologist's repertory of hydrotherapy, electrical treatments, massage, and rest cures (Strachey, Introduction to Freud 1895d, S.E., 2:xi). Freud did not systematically apply the cathartic method until May 1889.[29] The case was that of a highly hysterical woman, Frau Emmy von N., whom he decided to treat with the cathartic method after discovering that she could easily be put into a deep state of hypnotic somnambulism (S.E., 2:48). Freud attended this patient for about seven weeks in 1889 and then, a year later, for about eight weeks.

Of the three other medical histories that ultimately made up the bulk of Freud's own clinical contribution to *Studies on Hysteria*, Fräulein Elisabeth von R., treated by him in the autumn of 1892, represents his first full-length analysis of a case of hysteria using Breuer's method. Miss Lucy R. was likewise treated toward the end of 1892; while one other undated case history, that of Katharina, rounds out this group of four and dates from some time in the early 1890s. Occasional details of three other named, and eleven unnamed, case histories were also mentioned by Freud in the *Studies*. Especially important among these was the "most instructive" case, studied jointly with Breuer, of Frau Cäcile M. Unfortunately this patient's illness could not be discussed more fully, owing to professional discretion.

Following Freud's repeated confirmation of Breuer's experience with Anna O., Breuer, who had been reluctant to publish his results based solely upon a single, and possibly atypical, case history of hysteria, finally agreed to a joint publication with Freud. The collective results of their investigations were first issued as a "Preliminary Communication" in January of 1893 and then published in much expanded form in

29. The evidence for the precise date of this first cathartic treatment, referred to inconsistently by Freud as in 1888 and 1889, is provided by Ellenberger (1977). Drawing upon the unpublished researches of Ola Andersson, Ellenberger has also revealed the patient's true identity as Fanny Moser, the wife of a wealthy Swiss industrialist, and has provided a fascinating psychological portrait of the Moser family over three generations.

May of 1895 as *Studies on Hysteria* (1895*d*). To the latter work, in which the jointly authored "Preliminary Communication" (1893*a*) was reprinted as the introductory chapter, Josef Breuer contributed the first case history, that of Anna O., and the "Theoretical" chapter. Freud supplied four clinical chapters and a final, general chapter on "The Psychotherapy of Hysteria."

Freud's Clinical Contributions to Studies on Hysteria

The mysterious clinical diminution of hysteria in the course of the twentieth century makes Breuer and Freud's *Studies on Hysteria* (1895*d*) an unusual book in the history of science; for while it marks a turning point in psychiatric theory, it deals with a disease many present-day neurological specialists see only once or twice in a lifetime of medical practice. Yet this affliction was sufficiently widespread in Freud's day to provide him with an important source of financial support for his family and with a revolutionary stepping-stone toward a new science of the human mind.[30] Reading the case histories recorded by Breuer and Freud in *Studies on Hysteria* is therefore to reenter a lost world of incredible and often bizarre behavior which is preserved for us only through the printed word. More fascinating still is the engrossing detective-story nature of these case histories—a point on which Freud himself felt compelled to comment in the *Studies*:

> I have not always been a psychotherapist. Like other neuropathologists, I was trained to employ local diagnoses and electro-prognosis, and it still strikes me myself as strange that the case histories I write should read like short stories and that, as one might say, they lack the serious stamp of science. I must console myself with the reflection that the nature of the subject is evidently responsible for this, rather than any preference of my own. The fact is that local diagnosis and electrical reactions lead nowhere in the study of hysteria, whereas a detailed description of mental processes such as we are accustomed to find in the works of imaginative writers enables me, with the use of a few psychological formulas, to obtain at least some kind of insight into the course of that affection. (*S.E.*, 2:160–61)

The case of Frau Emmy von N., the first of Freud's four clinical contributions, describes his initial attempt at using the cathartic method. Frau Emmy was a highly intelligent woman of about forty, whose apparently hysterical illness had begun fourteen years earlier, shortly after the death of her husband. She came to Freud suffering

30. Although no one has succeeded in satisfactorily explaining why hysterical afflictions have become as rare as they have in Europe and America, an interesting discussion of this problem from a social historian's point of view has been provided by Carroll Smith-Rosenberg (1972). In a quasi-Adlerian analysis of the problem, Smith-Rosenberg has tentatively related the passing of this primarily female affliction to the increased opportunity that women have in modern life to control their own destinies, especially when faced with the sort of oppressive or intolerable circumstances that formerly allowed only one principal form of escape—flight into illness (and the role of the invalid).

from loss of appetite, from fits of delirium, and from convulsive tic-like twitches of the facial and neck muscles. She had also acquired the involuntary habit of emitting strange clacking sounds; she stammered spastically; and she was constantly terrified by a cobweb of recurrent hallucinations and phobias, particularly animal phantasies.[31] Whenever these horrifying hallucinations interrupted Frau Emmy's normal consciousness, they were met with a protective verbal formula: "Keep still!—Don't say anything!—Don't touch me!" (*S.E.*, 2:49).

Freud succeeded in tracing most of Frau Emmy's symptoms back to a series of traumatic experiences that had plagued her in the course of her sad life. The case history provided Freud with his first insight into the role of memory in the etiology of the neuroses, for Frau Emmy's symptoms proved to be closely tied to her extremely active and accurate capacity for recollection. It was this circumstance that not only served to remind her constantly of her unhappy past but also enabled her to associate, in a systematic manner, virtually every current unpleasantness with some related incident in her past life (*S.E.*, 2:90, 102). Frau Emmy's animal phobias, for example, dated back to childhood when one of her brothers had thrown a dead toad at her, inducing her first attack of hysterical spasms. Her disgust toward food was also determined in childhood when she was once forced to eat cold meat that had repelled her. Later, in adulthood, these feelings of disgust were reinforced at a time when she was sharing her meals with her two brothers, both of whom were afflicted with contagious diseases (*S.E.*, 2:82, 87, 89). The patient was partially cured of her various symptoms by Freud's cathartic treatment, but later relapsed.

The therapeutic outcome of the case of Miss Lucy R., a young English governess, was considerably more successful. Freud was able to cure her of two recurrent olfactory hallucinations (the smells of burnt pudding and of cigar smoke) by relating them back to the moments when they had originally been experienced—two separate incidents during which Miss Lucy's secret love for her widowed employer had received a severe rebuff. The patient was cured when she finally acknowledged that her amorous aspirations toward her employer were unrealistic, and that the latter did not return her love.

Freud's third case history, that of Katharina, chronicles the story of a hysterical girl of eighteen who was troubled by frequent attacks of anxiety and shortness of breath. Freud traced these symptoms back to

31. *Phantasy* vs. *fantasy*. James Strachey (*S.E.*, *1*:xxiv), whose spelling I have followed, adopts the "ph" form of this word for the English translation of Freud's technical term *Phantasie*. In this connection, Strachey cites the *Oxford English Dictionary* (under "Fantasy"), which reads in part: "In modern use *fantasy* and *phantasy*, in spite of their identity in sound and in ultimate etymology, tend to be apprehended as separate words, the predominant sense of the former being 'caprice, whim, fanciful imagination,' while that of the latter is 'imagination, visionary notion.'" *Webster's Third International Dictionary* includes a similar etymological discussion and states that *phantasy* "applies more to the psychological image-making power in general or its product, often also standing as a clearer antonym of *truth* or *reality*." Like Strachey, I have occasionally used the word *fantasy* in its appropriate sense.

a series of sexual traumas, including an uncle's attempted seduction when she was fourteen. (The "uncle" turns out to have been the patient's father, as was later revealed by Freud in the 1925 edition of the *Studies*.) The effect of Freud's analysis remains unknown, since he treated the young lady only once, during a brief stay at a summer resort, and never saw her again.

Freud's fourth and last case history, that of Fräulein Elisabeth von R., deals with a sad and lonely girl of twenty-four who was afflicted by pains and weakness in her legs and was able to walk only with the upper part of her body bent noticeably forward. Fräulein Elisabeth's symptoms proved to be associated with a number of recent family misfortunes: with the death of her father, whom she, like Anna O., had nursed for eighteen months; with the mother's subsequent illness; with her concern over her family's general sense of lost happiness; and, most especially, with a painful psychical conflict in her emotional life, stemming from her repressed love for her deceased sister's husband. Both the patient's leg pains and her contracted manner of walking were cured by Freud through cathartic treatment of her repressed conflicts. Analysis resulted in the patient's recovering the traumatic memory of arriving at her ailing sister's bedside, only to learn that her sister had just died, and having suddenly flash through her mind the dreadful thought: "Now he is free again and I can be his wife" (*S.E.*, 2:156). Freud's account ends with the patient's reluctant but ultimately successful struggle to accept the painful truth revealed to her by the cathartic cure.

Freud's chapter "The Psychotherapy of Hysteria" brings *Studies on Hysteria* to a close with a discussion of the application and the limitations of the cathartic method. The ultimate goal in the psychotherapy of hysteria, Freud declares, is that of transforming "hysterical misery into common unhappiness" (*S.E.*, 2:305).

The Breuer–Freud Theory of Hysteria

"*Hysterics suffer mainly from reminiscences.*" This was the fundamental clinical message of Breuer and Freud's joint theory of hysteria (1893a, *S.E.*, 2:7). The general theoretical assumptions underlying this clinical model were predominantly psychophysicalist; that is to say, according to their model, the human mind works by virtue of mental "forces" and "energies" following patterns of investment and displacement similar to those in a complicated electrical apparatus. Perhaps the clearest statement of their psychophysicalist presuppositions is Freud's conclusion to his 1894 paper "The Neuro-Psychoses of Defence":

> I should like, finally, to dwell for a moment on the working hypothesis which I have made use of in this exposition of the neuroses of defence. I refer to the concept that in mental functions something is to be dis-

tinguished—a quota of affect or a sum of excitation—which possesses all the characteristics of a quantity (though we have no means of measuring it), which is capable of increase, diminution, displacement and discharge, and which is spread over the memory-traces of ideas somewhat as an electric charge is spread over the surface of a body.

This hypothesis, which, incidentally, already underlies our theory of "abreaction" in our "Preliminary Communication" (1893a), can be applied in the same sense as physicists apply the hypothesis of a flow of electric fluid. It is provisionally justified by its utility in co-ordinating and explaining a great variety of psychical states. (1894a, S.E., 3:60–61)

Within this general physicalist framework, hysteria became equated with a "short circuit" in the normal flow of electric fluid (S.E., 2:207 n.).

What Freud called a "working hypothesis" in the preceding passage includes a series of assumptions that James Strachey, in a valuable editorial commentary on the theoretical underpinnings of psychoanalysis, has felicitously termed Freud's most "fundamental hypotheses" (Appendix to Freud 1894a, S.E., 3:62–68). These "fundamental hypotheses" may be conveniently separated, following Freud's own metapsychological schema, according to their *economic, dynamic,* and *topographical* aspects (e.g., Freud 1915e, S.E., 14:181).

The Economic Aspect

The economic aspect is embodied in Breuer and Freud's theoretical attribution of hysterical symptoms to a certain "quantity" of excitation, affect, or mental energy. In healthy individuals, this quantity is dissipated along the nervous pathways of everyday mental and physical activity. But in hysteria, Breuer and Freud believed, a certain quota of affect succeeds in becoming pathologically "converted" into inappropriate somatic channels (S.E., 2:206).

Under this first general, economic point of view falls a psychoanalytic hypothesis which holds that the mental apparatus seeks to maintain a constant (low) level of psychic energy. Although this subsidiary hypothesis is not explicit in the "Preliminary Communication," it is clearly expressed in an even earlier manuscript draft of that paper, written in Freud's own hand (dated "End of November, 1892"), in a passage he italicized: *"The nervous system endeavours to keep constant something in its functional relations that we may describe as the 'sum of excitation.' It puts this precondition of health into effect by disposing associatively of every sensible accretion of excitation or by discharging it by an appropriate motor reaction"* (1940d, S.E., 1:153–54). It was by means of this neurophysiological hypothesis (the *principle of constancy*), which Freud further describes as having "far-reaching consequences," that one of the most fundamental characteristics of the hysterical attack was ultimately understood in the Breuer-Freud theory: that is to say, its function as an outlet for innervations that have failed to achieve normal discharge.

The principle of constancy in turn provided the economic underpinnings for the closely related *pleasure-unpleasure principle*: unpleasure is seen as mechanically equivalent to a sudden rise in the level of excitation within the nervous system, and pleasure as mechanically equivalent to its discharge through the appropriate reflex mechanism (cf. the sexual act as the paradigm of this latter phenomenon). Both Breuer, in his "Theoretical" chapter (*S.E.*, 2:197), and Freud, in his later writings on this subject, claim that the pleasure principle is logically *prior* to the principle of constancy. Freud makes this point in *Beyond the Pleasure Principle*, where he also argues that the two principles of constancy and pleasure-unpleasure represent, so to speak, two sides of the same coin: "for if the work of the mental apparatus is directed towards keeping the quantity of excitation low, then anything that is calculated to increase that quantity is bound to be felt as adverse to the functioning of the apparatus, that is as unpleasurable. The pleasure principle follows from the principle of constancy: actually the latter principle was inferred from the facts which forced us to adopt the pleasure principle" (1920*g*, *S.E.*, *18*:9).

In purely economic terms, the goal of cathartic therapy was to facilitate the nervous system's normal, but occasionally thwarted, tendency to obey the principles of *constancy* and *pleasure*. The therapist accomplished this aim by uncovering major sources of "strangulated affect" within the unconscious and by "abreacting" them along more normal (and conscious) nervous pathways (*S.E.*, 2:8). Elsewhere Freud describes the essential aim of successful psychotherapy in such economic terms, when he speaks of reducing the "total load" within the nervous system below that particular threshold that separates good health from the neuroses (Freud 1895*f*, *S.E.*, 3:130).

The Dynamic Aspect

The principles of constancy and pleasure already imply, in their general self-regulatory capacities, the rudiments of the second or dynamic metapsychological aspect of the Breuer-Freud theory, which conceives mental phenomena in terms of the play of their psychical forces —forces that may conflict, inhibit one another, combine, and so forth. Fundamentally, this dynamic standpoint aims to explain how a pathological "damming up" of affect can occur within a portion of the mind that is inaccessible to normal waking consciousness. Three different mechanisms were suggested by Breuer and Freud to account for these "strangulations of affect": (1) when a strong affect (for example, fright) is experienced by an individual during either involuntary or self-induced "hypnoid states" (like those peculiar to Anna O.'s hallucinatory *absences*); (2) when a strong affect is not permitted immediate or adequate conscious discharge—as with known clinical instances of hysteria arising from severe insults endured in silence or from excessive and inexpressible grief over the loss of a loved one (so-called retention hysterias); and finally (3) in connection with psychic defense against ideas intolerable to the ego (as with incompatible sexual ideas).

By the middle of 1895, Freud's own clinical findings had led him to ascribe primary etiological importance to the second and especially the third of these three independent dynamic mechanisms. The specific diagnosis of "defence hysteria" was particularly important in Freud's treatment of Fräulein Elisabeth von R., whose illness had been precipitated by her repeated attempts to deny her love for her brother-in-law.

The Topographical Aspect

The last or topographical aspect of the Breuer-Freud theory of hysteria inheres in the hypothesis of an "unconscious" portion of the mind. The first published instance of the term *das Unbewusste* ("the unconscious") by either Breuer or Freud occurs in Breuer's discussion of the case history of Anna O. (*S.E.*, 2:45). Breuer also coined the expression "inadmissible to consciousness" (*Bewusstseinsunfähig*), which was adopted and used frequently by Freud in his later psychoanalytic writings (*S.E.*, 2:225).

The existence of several earlier drafts of the theories of abreaction and conversion in Freud's own hand, together with various subsequent autobiographical statements by both collaborators, allow us to conclude with a fair degree of certainty who contributed precisely what to this joint intellectual effort.[32] Breuer, by his unusual diligence, perspicacity, and extreme patience as a physician, provided the initial discoveries that hysterical symptoms can arise from unconscious ideas and that they can be made to disappear if they are brought back into consciousness. Breuer later endorsed such an assessment of his own role (Cranefield 1958:319). He also coined the term *catharsis* and possibly the term *abreaction* and was responsible for the notions of hypnoid hysteria and retention hysteria.

Freud was responsible, first and foremost, for reviving Breuer's dormant interest in his famous patient and for greatly extending Breuer's clinical findings in general support of this initial discovery. Freud subsequently added to Breuer's new clinical procedure the psychoanalytically distinct "free association" technique, and gradually dispensed with hypnosis (see also Chapter 3). Freud was specifically credited by Breuer with having contributed the principle of constancy and the notion of conversion, although Freud himself later qualified this last attribution by saying that only the term was actually original with him— the idea having apparently occurred to both of them simultaneously (1895d, *S.E.*, 2:197, 206; 1914d, *S.E.*, 14:8–9). A similar qualification is perhaps justified for the principle of constancy, whose congruence

32. Freud, "Letter to Josef Breuer," dated 29 June 1892 (1941a, *S.E.*, 1:147-48); the manuscript fragment of Section III of the "Preliminary Communication" (1893a; 1941b, *S.E.*, 1:149-50); "On the Theory of Hysterical Attacks" (1940d [1892], *S.E.*, 1:151-54); "On the History of the Psycho-Analytic Movement" (1914d, *S.E.*, 14:7-11); *Autobiography* (1925d, *S.E.*, 20:19-23); and Josef Breuer to August Forel, 21 November 1907, in Cranefield 1958:319-20; see also the Editor's Introduction to *Studies on Hysteria* (1895d, *S.E.*, 2:xxi-xxviii).

with the various self-regulatory devices previously discovered by Breuer
in his physiological work has been pointed out by Cranefield (1970a:
448). Finally, it was Freud's assiduous clinical work that led to the
further discovery that defense against distressing ideas could induce
a "splitting of the mind" independently of Breuer's mechanism of hypnoid states. *Uluve is not of unconsciour from ?*

HISTORICAL ROOTS OF THE BREUER–FREUD THEORY

In developing their theory of hysteria, Breuer and Freud were influenced by at least four points of view beyond their immediate clinical
experience: (1) the so-called Helmholtz school of medicine; (2) the writings of Gustav Theodor Fechner; (3) the writings of Johann Friedrich
Herbart; and (4) a number of contemporary students of hysteria who
were actively publishing their own findings in the period from about
1888 to 1894.

The Helmholtz School of Medicine: Fact and Fiction

It has often been said that the basic metapsychological principles
in the Breuer-Freud theory of hysteria (particularly the economic ones)
are among the most essential derivatives in psychoanalysis of Freud's
training within the Helmholtz school of medicine.[33] While this claim
certainly has some substance, it has nevertheless tended to create an unfortunate historical misconception within Freud studies, as Cranefield
(1966a, 1966b, 1970b) has repeatedly pointed out.[34] "According to the
extreme form of this particular myth," Cranefield writes (1966b:35),
"Freud was subjected to two conflicting forces, namely his allegiance to
mechanistic and molecular explanation [i.e., the Helmholtz school's in-
fluence] and his desire to forge a new way of looking at the mind, a
psychological way free from the entanglements of narrow and naïve
materialism." We have already encountered this mythical scenario in
connection with the debates over hypnotism and male hysteria. It is
the dragonlike specter of the Helmholtz school, however, that most
typifies this mythical conflict of allegiance from which psychoanalysis
(a "pure psychology") supposedly emerged.

In the first place, Helmholtz himself was by no means ever considered to be the head of a "school" in medicine, even among the original group of four—du Bois-Reymond (the group's real leader), Brücke,
Ludwig, and Helmholtz himself—who together initiated what Cranefield has more appropriately termed "the 1847 biophysics program."
(The year 1847 was when Ludwig joined the group.) Furthermore, Helm-

33. See, for example, Bernfeld (1944, 1949), who coined the phrase "the
School of Helmholtz"; also Jones 1953:passim; Amacher 1965; and Holt 1965a.
34. See also Shakow and Rapaport (1964:33-35, 41-46), who independently
reached a similar conclusion.

holtz was actually an isolated figure in science compared with the other three; he had few students or close associates, even within the fields of mathematics and physics where he did his major and most valuable scientific work. Secondly, the members of this movement were at no time typical, as both Bernfeld (1944) and Jones (1953:43) have implied, of the extreme brand of nineteenth-century mechanism-materialism that was espoused by men like Karl Vogt and Ludwig Büchner. Carl Ludwig, for example, treated the subject of dreams in his *Lehrbuch der Physiologie des Menschen* (1852–56, 1:456–58) in what is certainly the language of psychology; and Brücke, du Bois-Reymond, and Helmholtz all showed a sophisticated, and far from purely "mechanical," interest in higher mental functioning (Cranefield 1966a).

Finally, by the time Freud began his medical training in the 1870s, the 1847 biophysics program had been in manifest retreat for many years. Indeed, by the 1870s, most of the movement's original members had frankly acknowledged the prematurity of their initial vision that physiology was soon to become nothing but physics and chemistry. As Adolf Fick (1829–1901), one of Carl Ludwig's more prominent pupils, confessed a quarter century later, "The absolute dominance of the mechanistic-mathematical orientation in physiology has proved to be an Icarus flight" (1874:390–91).

Gustav Theodor Fechner's Psychophysics

On the other hand, the mechanistic thrust of Helmholtz and his biophysics confreres *did* enter psychoanalysis indirectly from the field of psychology through Gustav Theodor Fechner (1801–87). It was Fechner who not only introduced into psychology the principle of the conservation of energy (formulated in 1842 by the physician Robert Mayer and further developed by Helmholtz in 1845), but also derived a sophisticated equivalent of Freud's pleasure-unpleasure principle from this notion (Fechner 1873:94–95).

It is not known exactly when Sigmund Freud first came upon Fechner's psychophysical ideas. In his *Autobiography*, Freud later acknowledged Fechner's general intellectual influence: "I was always open to the ideas of G. T. Fechner and have followed that thinker upon many important points" (1925d, S.E., 20:59).[35] Freud was certainly reading Fechner's psychological works in the late 1890s in connection with his theory of dreams (*Origins*, p. 244); and Fechner's famous law describing the mathematical relationship between the intensity of stimulation and the resultant sensation is mentioned by Freud three years earlier in the *Project for a Scientific Psychology* (*Origins*, p. 376). It seems almost

---

35. Without claiming a direct intellectual lineage, Freud also notes in *Beyond the Pleasure Principle* that Fechner's 1873 derivation of the pleasure principle from the principle of constancy (or "stability," to use Fechner's own term) was indeed a complete anticipation of his own psychoanalytic thinking on this subject (1920g, S.E., 18:8–9). Henri Ellenberger (1956; 1970:217–18) has further traced certain aspects of Freud's topographical conception of the mind, as well as his later "principle of repetition," back to Fechner's writings.

certain, however, that Fechner's ideas were already known to both Breuer and Freud when they developed their theory of hysteria in the early 1890s. Josef Breuer, for his own part, greatly admired Fechner, who, along with Goethe, was one of his two favorite authors (Jones 1953:223). Fechner likewise exerted considerable influence upon Freud's teacher Theodor Meynert (Dorer 1932:158–59).

Thus, perhaps most *directly*, the Breuer-Freud theory of hysteria reflects the "Fechnerian school" of psychophysics far more than it does the long-since defunct "Helmholtz school" of biophysics.

Johann Friedrich Herbart and the Dynamic Psychological Tradition

Certain of the dynamic and topographical features of the Breuer-Freud theory of hysteria have manifest historical roots in the psychological writings of Johann Friedrich Herbart (1776–1841). Like Freud, Herbart was a psychological dualist. He developed his own dynamic theory of unconscious mental processes, wrote of ideas being "repressed" (*verdrängt*) from consciousness by other opposing ideas, and conceived of mental operations in terms of "forces" possessing specific "quantities." In spite of his dream of a quasi-mathematical science of mind, Herbart always ranked the phenomena of psychology ahead of those of physiology in this ultimate goal (Dorer 1932:71–106; see also Jones 1953:371–74).

In his last year at the Gymnasium, Freud is known to have read a textbook of psychology that was based almost exclusively upon the teachings of the Herbart school (Lindner 1858; see Jones 1953:374). Herbart's influence may also be traced in the psychological writings of Fechner, as well as in those of the psychiatrist Wilhelm Griesinger (1817–69), both of whose ideas were in turn important sources of inspiration to Freud's teacher Theodor Meynert (Dorer 1932:158–70).

Contemporary Researches on Hysteria (1888–94)

Studies on Hysteria was just one of a series of similar contributions on the problem of hysteria to appear around 1890. This literature had occasionally discussed both the dynamic, ideogenic nature of hysterical symptom formation and specific examples of catharsislike cures. It was in the light of this expanding literature that Breuer himself went so far as to disavow, in 1895, any substantial originality to the Breuer-Freud theory (*S.E.*, 2:186). In the course of his "Theoretical" contribution to the *Studies*, Breuer specifically cited the works of men like Paul Möbius (1888, 1894), Adolf von Strümpell (1892), Pierre Janet (1889, 1893a, 1894), Joseph Delboeuf (1889), and Moritz Benedikt (1894) for their many anticipations of, as well as general agreement with, the basic ideas advocated by himself and Freud.

Although the Frenchman Pierre Janet's researches are now perhaps the best known of this group of psychotherapists, Viennese neurologist Moritz Benedikt's views were the closest to those of Breuer and Freud. As early as 1868, Benedikt had insisted, in opposition to Charcot's predecessor Pierre Briquet, that hysteria often depends upon functional disorders of the libido. In subsequent publications, he continued to elaborate this doctrine on the basis of clinical evidence suggesting that most hysterics fall ill owing to their excessive preoccupation with a "secret life" of phantasies or frustrated desires, frequently of a sexual nature (Benedikt 1889, 1894; see also Ellenberger 1970: 301, 536). Benedikt reported many instances of catharsislike cures in cases where he had been successful in bringing these pathogenic secrets out into the open.

To conclude, what perhaps serves most of all to distinguish the work of Breuer and Freud from that of their many contemporaries in the scientific study of hysteria is their unusually detailed clinical documentation of case histories, their synthetic-psychophysicalist theoretical approach to the whole problem, and their evolution of a formal therapeutic method (see also Chapter 3).

SUMMARY AND CONCLUSION

The Breuer-Freud theory of hysteria—that "hysterics suffer mainly from reminiscences" and that these reminiscences are invariably linked to unconscious psychical traumas—had three major historical sources. *First,* the theory grew naturally out of Josef Breuer's persistent study of the remarkable case of Anna O. (1880–82), the patient who invented the cathartic method.

Second, Sigmund Freud then revived Breuer's therapeutic procedure in 1889 and demonstrated that the psychical mechanisms discovered by Breuer nearly ten years before were of general application. In this achievement, Freud was indebted to Charcot, who had convinced Freud during his stay in Paris (1885/86) that the hysteric is not a malingerer and that hysterical phenomena, being genuine, must therefore obey lawful principles.

Third, the Breuer-Freud theory was a natural outgrowth of the common scientific background of these two men. In particular, their strong mutual interest in psychological as well as physiological processes underlay the implicit *dualism* of their theory of hysteria, with its respect for the language of psychology and its simultaneous positing of a bold psychophysicalist model to account for the key phenomena of strangulated affect, abreaction, and catharsis. And in its most fundamental respects, the theory itself was a transposition to mind of a paradigm of self-regulatory behavior previously entertained by Breuer in all his physiological researches. Finally, the implicit dualism of their theory of hysteria exhibits the same general orientation toward mind taken earlier by Freud himself in the debates over hypnotism.

For Freud, the fifteen-year period from 1880 to 1895 was one of exceptionally eclectic scientific achievement. He worked simultaneously on the study of brain anatomy (1884*f*, 1886*b*, 1886*c*, 1888*b*), cocaine (1884*e*, 1887*d*), hypnosis (1889*a*, 1892–93), aphasia (1891*b*), cathartic psychotherapy, childhood cerebral paralyses (1888*a*, 1891*a*, 1891*c*, 1893*b*), and the translation of two books each by Charcot and Bernheim—to give just a partial listing. This formative period also witnessed Freud's increasing specialization in the problem of the neuroses. And having finally "hit on the neuroses," as Freud expressed himself to his friend Fliess in 1895, the subject of psychology likewise began to loom as his "consuming passion" (*Origins*, p. 119).

3

Sexuality and the Etiology of Neurosis: The Estrangement of Breuer and Freud

The Estrangement

When Freud first announced to his friend Wilhelm Fliess, in December 1892, that the theory of hysteria was finally to be published as a brief "Preliminary Communication" (1893a), he was also obliged to confess that this arrangement had cost him "a long battle with my collaborator" (*Origins*, p. 64). This was just the beginning of Freud's various complaints about his deteriorating relationship with Breuer. By mid-1894, differences of scientific opinion between the two had reached a point where Freud felt personally compelled to "dissociate" himself in advance from the "Theoretical" chapter that Breuer had been assigned to write for *Studies on Hysteria* (*Origins*, p. 95). A year later, when the *Studies* finally appeared in print, it included a formal prefatory acknowledgment of the theoretical differences between the two investigators.

Freud and Freud scholars have pointed to three principal causes both of the "long battle" that accompanied Freud's efforts to get his and Breuer's theory into print and of their ensuing personal and intellectual estrangement:

1. Freud's insistence that the splitting of the mind associated with hysterical symptom formation is exclusively caused by psychical defense rather

than by Breuer's more physiological mechanism of hypnoid states. This source of intellectual friction is most strongly emphasized by Ernst Kris (*Origins*, p. 64, n. 1).

2. Breuer's personal reluctance to accept both the frequency and the fundamental importance of sexuality in the etiology of hysteria.[1]

3. Breuer's apparent dismay over the poor reception of *Studies on Hysteria*, especially his reaction to a rather harsh review by the eminent German neurologist Adolf von Strümpell (1896).[2]

Although most psychoanalytic historians have considered the first and the last of these causes as subsidiary to the estrangement, they have considered the second, the issue of sexuality, as essential to it (Jones 1953:253), and all three as arising from a common root. That is to say, these causes were equally symptomatic of Breuer's reluctance to accept the full implications of his joint researches with Freud.

It is also significant that Freud's own contributions to *Studies on Hysteria* (1895d) reflected two basic points of divergence from the earlier views he and Breuer had jointly endorsed in the "Preliminary Communication" (1893a). The first of these involved an important series of modifications in clinico-investigatory *technique*. The second came as a result of various clinical *discoveries* that were in turn largely derived from Freud's modified technique. Both of Freud's emendations had given a substantially new cast to his and Breuer's original theory of hysteria. And it is for this last reason that Ernest Jones (1953:145), in a frankly psychoanalytic vein, was inclined to suspect that the unbelieving Breuer harbored a "fatherly" jealously toward Freud's increasing emancipation from his long-standing tutelage.

However valid this last supposition, there can be no doubt that Freud's new clinical findings concerning the delicate issue of sexuality eventually provoked the estrangement between the two collaborators; but the real story of the estrangement is by no means so simple as it is often made out to be. Behind this traditional oversimplification there lies a fascinating and little-appreciated chapter in the development of psychoanalytic thought. In order to evaluate properly both the estrangement and the controversial psychoanalytic developments that accompanied it, I shall review the crucial technical innovations that made possible Freud's psychoanalytic discoveries between 1893 and mid-1895.

Freud's Technical Innovations and Their Psychoanalytic Consequences

To appreciate why Freud began to modify Breuer's original form of cathartic therapy during the early 1890s, we must go back even farther in time and briefly review Freud's earliest experiences with general

1. See Freud, "On the History of the Psycho-Analytic Movement," 1914d, *S.E.*, 14:12–13; *Autobiography*, 1925d, *S.E.*, 20:26–27; Jones 1953:224–25, 248–50, 253; Kris 1954:12.

2. See, for example, Freud's *Autobiography*, where he comments that Breuer's "self-confidence and powers of resistance were not developed so fully as the rest of his mental organization" (1925d, *S.E.*, 20:23); also Jones 1953:252–53.

Sigmund Freud in 1891 (age 35).

hypnotic psychotherapy. To begin with, he had employed hypnotic treatments merely as an adjunct to various other techniques currently used by nerve specialists—for example, electrotherapy, massage, hydrotherapy, and the Weir Mitchell rest cure (Strachey, Editor's Introduction to *Studies on Hysteria*, S.E., 2:xi–xii). By December 1887, however, he had started to rely more exclusively upon hypnotic therapy. "During the last few weeks," he wrote to Fliess in a letter that same month, "I have plunged into hypnotism, and have had all sorts of small but peculiar successes" (*Origins*, p. 53). Freud subsequently published an account of one particularly successful case of hypnotic treatment, that of a woman who had complained of nausea when attempting to breast-feed her child (Freud 1892–93).

Nevertheless, hypnotism soon proved to have drawbacks. Freud found that some of his patients were totally unhypnotizable and that many others were not sufficiently *deeply* hypnotizable to allow the methods of suggestion or catharsis to operate with much success. In this connection, we should remember that Breuer's famous patient Anna O. was a highly gifted hysteric who had largely effected her own cures under the influence of autohypnosis. (Her autohypnotic ability had also predisposed Breuer to consider sporadic hypnoid states as the principal cause of her hysterical splitting of the mind.)

In 1889, after wrestling with this problem unsuccessfully, Freud persuaded one particularly suitable case for cathartic treatment—a female patient whom he had up to that time been unable to place in a deep enough state of hypnosis to effect a proper therapy—to journey with him to Nancy. There he sought the assistance of Bernheim and Liébeault, who by then, as perhaps the two reigning doyens of hypnotism in Europe, had hypnotized some ten to twenty thousand individuals with better than 90 percent success (Bramwell 1896:461). But even Bernheim proved unable to hypnotize Freud's patient—or at least to bring her to the stage of somnambulism with amnesia, which Freud believed at that time to be a prerequisite for hypnotic cures. Moreover, Bernheim frankly admitted to Freud on this occasion that his own therapeutic success was almost entirely limited to his hospital practice and did not include many of his private patients (*Autobiography*, 1925d, S.E., 20:18).

On the other hand, Bernheim did impart a piece of information that ultimately became the basis for Freud's whole change in technique. Bernheim had many times demonstrated to Freud the remarkable fact that patients who have been hypnotized to a state of somnambulism with amnesia can nevertheless be *made* to remember in a subsequent waking state what they are otherwise totally unable to recollect. Bernheim effected this recall in his patients upon their awakening by firmly commanding them to remember and by simultaneously placing his hand upon the patient's forehead and exerting pressure. This latter technique was apparently intended to help the patient tap the forgotten state of consciousness. Freud therefore surmised that his own unhypnotizable patients *also* knew the seemingly forgotten traumas that had originally determined their hysterical symptoms, and he resolved to extract this information, without hypnosis, following Bernheim's example in overcoming posthypnotic amnesia. And so arose the "concentration" and "pressure" techniques that Freud used independently of hypnosis in the wake of his visit to Nancy (*Studies*, 1895*d*, *S.E.*, 2:108–10, 268–72; *Autobiography*, 1925*d*, *S.E.*, 20:28).

The better-known psychoanalytic method of free association was already in partial use as early as 1889 or 1890 in the treatment of Frau Emmy von N., who spontaneously used this technique as a supplement to her hypnotic treatments. One day in late 1892 during treatment, Fräulein Elisabeth von R. permanently established the free association technique when she sternly reproved Freud for unnecessarily interrupting her train of thought (*Studies*, 1895*d*, *S.E.*, 2:56 n.; Jones 1953: 243–44).[3]

Along with Freud's dissatisfaction with the limited applicability of hypnosis, the subsequent evolution of his psychoanalytic technique reflects his growing doubt that patients could really be *permanently* cured by means of hypnotic suggestions. For, even when successful, suggestion merely seemed to rid his patients of highly specific symptoms, which were often replaced by others. As Freud dryly remarked at about this time in a footnote to his German translation of Charcot's famous *Tuesday Lectures*, "In the long run neither the doctor nor the patient can tolerate the contradiction between the decided denial of the ailment in the [hypnotic] suggestion and the necessary recognition of it outside the suggestion" (1892–94, *S.E.*, 1:141; see also 1891*d*, *S.E.*, 1:113).

With the abandonment of both hypnotism and suggestion therapy, and with the replacement of these two techniques by free association, concentration, and pressure, the basic features of psychoanalysis as a peculiarly Freudian clinical procedure had begun to emerge. The term *psychoanalysis* was used by Freud for the first time with reference to this new method in two papers he drafted almost simultaneously just nine months after *Studies on Hysteria* (1895*d*) appeared in print (1896*a* and 1896*b*).

After Freud decided to abandon the use of hypnosis, he began to unveil what he later referred to as a new "interplay of forces" within the human mind (*Autobiography*, 1925*d*, *S.E.*, 20:29). What is more, he now realized that the greater degree of psychical work required on his part to refresh his patients' forgotten memories without the aid of hypnosis was itself closely related to this new interplay of psychical forces. For if hysterics could remember the traumatic causes of their symptoms in spite of all their initial protestations to the contrary, then it was only reasonable to infer, as Freud himself now explained it, that "*by means of my psychical work I had to overcome a psychical force in the patients which was opposed to the pathogenic ideas becoming conscious (being remembered)*" (*Studies*, *S.E.*, 2:268; Freud's italics). "From all this

---

3. We should not forget that Fräulein Elisabeth von R. and certain other intelligent patients spontaneously contributed a great deal to the development of psychoanalysis as a method of therapy.

there arose, as it were automatically, the thought of *defence*" (*S.E.*, 2:269). More than thirty years later, Freud was to judge the innovation entailed in this new concept of defense (or "repression," as it increasingly came to be called) as a major turning point in the history of psychoanalysis. "I named this process *repression*; it was a novelty, and nothing like it had ever before been recognized in mental life" (*Autobiography*, 1925d, *S.E.*, 20:30). Although Freud's claim of complete novelty in the concept of repression can be challenged historically (for example, by the writings of Herbart—see Chapter 2), there is no denying that this concept was indeed integral to the originality of psychoanalysis as a dynamic science of mind. Perhaps the most immediate psychoanalytic derivative of Freud's concepts of defense and repression was his disagreement with Breuer over the importance of hypnoid states in hysterical symptom formation.

Hypnoid States vs. the Theory of Defense

I can now return to the main theme of this chapter, namely, to the overall scientific discord between Breuer and Freud that came to a head in *Studies on Hysteria* (1895d). Oddly enough, as James Strachey comments in his Editorial Introduction to the *Studies*, the book itself yields surprisingly few signs of the apparent divergence of scientific opinions so prominently announced in the Preface (*S.E.*, 2:xxi). Take, for example, the issue of Breuer's support for the theory of hypnoid states as opposed to Freud's growing preference for the theory of defense. Even in *Studies on Hysteria*, a careful reader can discern that Freud himself was still apparently treating their respective theories on hysterical splitting of the mind as more complementary than his later recollections suggest. In his own final chapter on the psychotherapy of hysteria, Freud even acknowledged that in the remarkable case of Anna O., who had herself spontaneously sought to reveal to Breuer the causes of her symptoms, the patient exhibited little or no active defense. "I regard this distinction as so important," wrote Freud, commenting on Anna O.'s complete lack of resistance to treatment, "that, on the strength of it, I willingly adhere to this hypothesis of there being a hypnoid hysteria" (*S.E.*, 2:286). (He nevertheless added that he himself had yet to meet with such a case in his own clinical practice.) Nor was his concession in this regard an isolated statement, for he reiterated the same general point much earlier in the book (*S.E.*, 2:167 n.).

Thus, at this stage in his thinking Freud seems to have believed in the existence of a complementary relationship between the two theories —with most, but apparently not all, instances of autohypnoidal splitting of mind being considered the product of a *prior* attempt at defense (the case of Anna O. notably excepted). "In short," he concluded, "I am unable to suppress a suspicion that somewhere or other the roots of hypnoid and defence hysteria come together, and that there the primary factor is defence. But I can say nothing about this" (*S.E.*, 2:286).

In fact it was not until a year later, in his paper on the etiology of hysteria (1896c), that Freud finally rejected any possible cooperation between the two theories. By then his views on the etiology of hysteria had been considerably recast in terms of his infantile-seduction theory, which completely did away with his previous indecision on the matter of hypnoid states.

In any case, we have it on Freud's own testimony that this particular difference between his views and Breuer's was definitely not the decisive factor in their breach of relations (1914d, S.E., 14:11; 1925d, S.E., 20:22–23). Rather, as Freud later emphasized, the breach had "deeper causes"—that is, Breuer's great dismay about the sexual motives that Freud had ascribed to hysterical defense.

Freud's mounting emphasis upon sexuality's importance in the neuropsychoses of defense was already apparent in his first general paper on that topic, published in January 1894. "In all the cases I have analyzed," he insisted of his clinical findings to date, "it was the subject's *sexual life* that had given rise to a distressing affect. . . . Moreover, it is easy to see that it is precisely sexual life which brings with it the most copious occasions for the emergence of incompatible ideas" (1894a, S.E., 3:52).

The realization that such clinical findings had cost him his personal and scientific association with Breuer came, Freud later commented, as something of a surprise. For even before Freud's journey to Paris to study with Charcot, Breuer himself had once remarked privately, in connection with the behavior of one of his female patients, that neurotic complaints were almost always tied up with secrets of the marriage bed. Freud, who at that time was astonished by Breuer's remark, also recalled that both Charcot and the famous gynecologist Chrobak later made similar pronouncements to him, and that Breuer and Chrobak, upon being reminded of these private observations years afterward, jointly denied ever having made such statements! Charcot, Freud added, would likely have denied his own statement, too, if Freud had ever had the opportunity to question him again on this point (1914d, S.E., 14:13–14). At all events, Breuer's momentarily unguarded understanding of his patients' nervous problems was a far cry, Freud discovered, from a public willingness to endorse such a heterodox point of view. To marry an idea, as Freud liked to say, was quite a different matter from recognizing it in passing.

Thus, in spite of Breuer's pivotal role in *Studies on Hysteria*, it soon became clear to Freud that Breuer, too, "shrank from recognizing the sexual aetiology of the neuroses" (*Autobiography*, 1925d, S.E., 20: 26). Breuer was in fact the first, Freud later recalled more psychoanalytically, "to show the reaction of distaste and repudiation which was later to become so familiar to me, but which at that time I had not yet learnt to recognize as my inevitable fate" (1914d, S.E., 14:12).

Even more puzzling to Freud was Breuer's failure to put forth his clinical observations in the case of Anna O.—about whom Breuer had remarked in the *Studies* that "the element of sexuality was astonishingly underdeveloped in her" (*S.E.*, 2:21)—as a definitive *refutation* of

Anna O.
(Bertha Pappenheim)
about 1890.

Freud's views. Gradually Freud began to surmise that Breuer's treatment of Anna O.—the termination of which had remained obscure in
Breuer's discussions—must have ended in a condition of "transference
love," and that the unfortunate Breuer, failing to connect this disconcerting development with his patient's illness, had not understood it
(*Autobiography, S.E.,* 20:26).

As Ernest Jones (1953:224–25) subsequently reported in his biography of Freud, Breuer had apparently become aware of his patient's
unhealthy attachment to him and decided to cut short the therapy one
day—only to be called back that same evening to discover that his patient had suffered a severe relapse and was in the throes of a hysterical childbirth! The meaning of this "phantom pregnancy" was all
too clear to Breuer, Jones recounts.[4] Deeply disturbed, Breuer hypnotized his patient, "fled the house in a cold sweat," and, the very next
day, departed Vienna for Venice on a second honeymoon with his wife

4. According to Freud's later testimony, Breuer asked his patient what was
wrong with her, to which she replied, "Now Dr. B.'s child is coming!" (*Letters,* p.
413, Freud to Stefen Zweig, 2 June 1932). The issue of Breuer's possible counter-
transference toward his famous patient has been discussed by George Pollock (1968,
1972), a psychoanalyst. Pollock points out that Breuer's mother, who died when
Breuer was between three and four, possessed the same first name as Bertha Pappenheim. Breuer's eldest daughter was also named Bertha. Did Breuer's sympathetic
treatment of his patient, whose illness was associated with her father's death, re-
kindle the unresolved conflicts of Breuer's own childhood object loss? Pollock's intriguing hypothesis, which has led him to endorse Ernest Jones's account of the
whole affair, need not be totally discounted in the reappraisal that follows.

—an occasion for rapprochement between his jealous spouse and himself that led to the conception of a daughter named Dora. Although Freud later explained to Breuer, Jones adds, the general "transference" nature of such an attachment, Breuer's subsequent cooperation in their two joint publications was ensured only with the strict understanding that "the theme of sexuality was to be kept in the background" (1953:250).

THE ESTRANGEMENT RECONSIDERED

Breuer's Views on the Role of Sexuality in Neurosis   ‒ Acceptance 5b

In spite of the manifest sincerity with which Freud, Ernest Jones, and most subsequent biographers of Freud have insisted upon this colorful scenario of Breuer's growing rift with Freud, it is largely a myth. In fact, Breuer was quite outspoken on the importance that he believed should be accorded to the sexual factor in hysteria as well as in other nervous disorders. In his "Theoretical" contribution to *Studies on Hysteria*, he even cited the argument about the marriage bed as the source of most neurotic complaints that Freud, thirty years later, alleged was a purely private remark subsequently "disavowed" by Breuer. "I do not think I am exaggerating," Breuer wrote, "when I assert that *the great majority of severe neuroses in women have their origin in the marriage bed*" (*S.E.*, 2:246; Breuer's italics). To this particular statement Breuer appended a footnote in which he deplored his medical colleagues' customary silence on sexuality, "one of the most important of all the pathogenic factors." And he likewise chided these same colleagues for their regrettable failure to communicate this medical knowledge to their juniors, "who as a rule," he claimed, "blindly overlook sexuality."

Nor was this discussion an isolated exception within the overall context of Breuer's "Theoretical" contribution to the *Studies*. Breuer went on to make it clear, for instance, that his various clinical remarks about sexuality were in full accord with the theoretical model of hysterical symptom formation he and Freud proposed in this same work. "The sexual instinct is undoubtedly the most powerful source of persisting increases of excitation (and consequently of neuroses)," Breuer succinctly proclaimed (*S.E.*, 2:200). In further amplification of this "economic" assertion, he cited the regular outbreak of hysteria after puberty and the physiological onset of sexual maturity at that age. "In saying this we are already recognizing sexuality as one of the major components of hysteria," he reemphasized. To this same statement he apposed, "We shall see that the part it [sexuality] plays in it [hysteria] is very much greater still and that it contributes in the most various ways to the constitution of the illness" (*S.E.*, 2:244).

Breuer then proceeded to discuss the harmful effects of "perverse

demands" and "unnatural [sexual] practices" perpetrated by husbands
upon their wives (p. 246); he had already joined with Freud in the
Preface to the *Studies* in regretting that their most convincing case
materials could not be made public precisely because of such intimate
sexual details. One case that Breuer *did* make public relates his successful cathartic treatment, independently of Freud, of a twelve-year-
old boy whose hysterical symptoms (vomiting, loss of appetite) were
brought on by a frankly described homosexual trauma (*S.E.*, 2:211–12).
Once again it was Breuer who compared (p. 248) the "wealth of affect"
and "restriction of consciousness" at the very height of sexual orgasm
to the similarly hypothesized mechanism of hysterical symptom formation during moments of hypnoid states. Finally, not only did Breuer
publicly endorse sexuality as one of the most important factors in hysteria, but he also endorsed Freud's integrally related notion that *in
such cases* the hysterical symptoms arise from psychical defense
against the traumatic demands of sexuality rather than from any hyp-
noidal tendencies per se (p. 247).

Obviously, then, Freud's memory was faulty, to say the least, for
in his *Autobiography*, when leading up to Breuer's supposed refusal to
accept the sexual factor in hysteria, he wrote: "It would have been
difficult to guess from the *Studies on Hysteria* what an importance
sexuality has in the aetiology of the neuroses" (1925d, *S.E.*, 20:22).
Freud's inconsistent recollection of the facts may also be seen in his
characterization of Breuer (*Origins*, p. 121), shortly after reading the
latter's "Theoretical" chapter for the *Studies* in May 1895, as "fully
converted to my theory of sexuality."

As for Ernest Jones's later reconstruction of Breuer's relationship
with Anna O., Henri Ellenberger, who has carefully researched both the
life of Bertha Pappenheim and the remarkable course of her illness,
describes this particular account as "fraught with impossibilities"
(1970:483).[5] Breuer's last daughter Dora, for example—supposedly con-

5. It is to Ellenberger's (1972) even more recent and detectivelike research
efforts that we owe the unexpected rediscovery of a contemporaneous, twenty-one-
page case history of Bertha Pappenheim prepared by Josef Breuer in 1882 for the
Sanatorium Bellevue, Kreuzlingen, Switzerland (where Anna O. was transferred in
July of that year). Ellenberger also uncovered a brief follow-up report written by
one of the physicians at the Sanatorium Bellevue for the period of Anna O.'s three-
and-a-half-month sojourn there. Although these documents contribute nothing star-
tlingly new about the course of Anna O.'s illness as it was later recounted by Breuer
in *Studies on Hysteria* (1895d), Breuer's original notes on the case provide us with
a richer picture of Anna O.'s family life, particularly her extreme devotion to her
father. We learn as well that the patient was not completely cured by Breuer, as
Freud later admitted to Jung, who reported this fact in a seminar given in Zurich
in 1925 (Jones 1953:225), and that none other than Richard von Krafft-Ebing was
at one time called in on the case as a special consultant. Albrecht Hirschmüller
(1978), who has published the German texts of the various documents discovered
by Ellenberger, has found other equally relevant materials at the Sanatorium Bellevue. These new documents show that Breuer treated at least seven other patients
for psychical disorders, six of them after Anna O. Moreover, several of these cases
involved clear-cut sexual etiologies according to Breuer's handwritten diagnoses. So
much for the myth about "timid" Breuer, retreating from the distasteful implications of his own momentous discoveries! These newly disclosed case histories, some
of which have been published as appendices to Hirschmüller's book, probably represent only a small portion of the mental patients that Breuer continued to see after
his treatment of Anna O.

ceived on Breuer's second honeymoon with his wife in June of 1882 (when Breuer's treatment of Anna O. ended)—was in fact born on 11 March 1882. Furthermore, it was the patient herself, not Breuer, who determined to end her treatment in June of 1882 on account of her desire to be cured by the anniversary of the day on which she had been moved to a country house outside of Vienna (Studies, S.E., 2:40).

Nor did Anna O.'s phantom pregnancy cause Breuer to react to Freud's later discoveries in quite the way Freud himself was later to suppose. In 1895 both Breuer *and* Freud earnestly believed the Anna O. case to be nonsexual—and nondefensive—in nature on account of her remarkable efforts to cure herself by recalling the origins of each of her symptoms. Breuer, for his own part, simply failed to connect his patient's growing personal attachment to him, as suddenly revealed at the termination of treatment, with the causes of her illness.[6] This conclusion is borne out by his response in 1907 to an inquiry from the famous Swiss psychiatrist, August Forel, about his early relationship to Freud. In his reply Breuer reiterated once again his belief in the preponderant role of sexuality in neurotic complaints, but he also noted: "The case of Anna O., which was the germ-cell of the whole of psycho-analysis, proves that a fairly severe case of hysteria can develop, flourish, and be resolved without having a sexual basis" (trans. Cranefield 1958:320). At any event, even the delicate problem of Anna O.'s misunderstood transference relationship with Breuer did not stop him from openly supporting the sexual etiology of hysteria in subsequent cases whenever sexuality proved itself more obviously linked to the initial outbreak of the illness. As Breuer summed up his position to Forel in 1907, "I confess that plunging into sexuality in theory and practice is not to my taste. But what have my taste and feeling about what is seemly and what is unseemly to do with the question of what is true?" (trans. Cranefield 1958:320).

Thus, in conclusion, whatever the causes of the growing estrangement between Breuer and Freud, neither the etiological importance of sexuality in hysteria nor Breuer's response to Anna O.'s hysterical pregnancy provides a really convincing explanation for the termination of their collaboration.

The Reception of Studies on Hysteria

As for the claim that Studies on Hysteria met with a poor reception—the last of the three traditional explanations for Breuer's decision

6. Nor was this connection made until much later by Freud, to whom Breuer had told the story of Anna O.'s phantom pregnancy long before they began collaborating in the late 1880s on other cases (Letters, p. 413, Freud to Stefan Zweig, 2 June 1932). As Freud reveals in this letter to Zweig, he had forgotten this aspect of the case, which Breuer never repeated, and only recalled it several decades later when writing his "History of the Psycho-Analytic Movement" (1914d). By then the sexual nature of Anna O.'s symptoms (the hallucinated snakes, the "stiffening" in her extremities) as well as their origin (nursing her father) had become evident to Freud in the light of other psychoanalytic discoveries. Freud accordingly seized upon this "reinterpreted" case history after 1914 to explain Breuer's desertion from "the cause" (see S.E., 14:11–12).

to terminate his collaboration with Freud—this, too, is a myth, as Henri Ellenberger (1970) has convincingly shown. A careful survey of the contemporary literature reveals that the reviews of both the "Preliminary Communication" and the later *Studies* combined the highest praise and respect for the unusual medical achievement documented in these two publications, with reasonable questions concerning the practical application and efficacy of the cathartic method. Generally favorable comments were forthcoming from Pierre Janet (1893b:252–57) in France; from Clarke (1896), Myers (1897), and Ellis (1898b) in England; from Obersteiner (1893:44), Bleuler (1896), Bressler (1896–97), Berger (1896), and others in German-speaking countries; and from Runkle (1899) in America. Bleuler, for instance, judged the *Studies* to be one of the most significant publications of the last few years; while Janet wrote, "I am happy to see that the results of my already old findings have been recently confirmed by two German authors, Breuer and Freud." [7]

Critical notices were definitely in the minority, with Krafft-Ebing (1896; 1897–99, 3:193–211), Benedikt (1894:64–65), and Strümpell (1896) voicing the most serious reservations—such as Krafft-Ebing's doubt, based upon detailed clinical experience with hysterics, whether abreaction of a trauma always suffices to cure the patient.

Even the review by Adolf von Strümpell (1896), which Jones (1953:252) characterizes as "very antagonistic," was hardly less appreciative of Breuer and Freud's work than was what Jones describes as the "full and favorable review" by J. Michell Clarke (1896). As Henri Ellenberger (1970:772) has commented in this connection, both reviewers gave "the same praise and the same criticism, though differently phrased." Strümpell lauded the *Studies* as "a gratifying proof that the conception of the psychogenic nature of hysterical symptoms is more and more finding diffusion and recognition among physicians." Concerning Breuer and Freud's specific innovations, Strümpell added: "Both authors have sought, with much skill and psychological acumen, to attain a deeper insight into the emotional condition of hysterics, and their explanations offer many a point of interest and stimulation" (1896:159).

True, Strümpell did have certain personal doubts about the advisability of a method of investigation that "often intrudes into the most minute details of the private relations and experiences of the patient" (p. 160). He questioned whether this sort of inquiry was "equally permissible in every circumstance," especially inasmuch as sexual matters were often concerned. (Strümpell, I should emphasize, did not disagree with Breuer and Freud on the predominant sexual causes of hysteria.) Finally, Strümpell voiced his concern about whether what emerges during investigation of a patient under hypnosis always corresponds to reality—that is to say, whether patients might not "give leave to their phantasies under such circumstances" and thus put many a physician in the unwitting position of giving advice based upon totally false

7. See Ellenberger (1970:768, 771–73) for other representative extracts from these reviews.

premises (p. 160). Thus, while the method of catharsis had clearly achieved remarkable therapeutic results in the "skillful hands of Messrs. Breuer and Freud," Strümpell doubted that many physicians could so successfully duplicate their painstaking and delicate procedures.

Strümpell's various reservations about the cathartic method were just as seriously entertained by J. Michell Clarke in his supposedly laudatory review of the *Studies*. "Into the question of the advisability," Clarke wrote, "of penetrating so intimately into the most private thoughts and concerns of a patient I do not enter; it would seem likely that the patients would, in many cases at least, strongly resent it." As for the problem of clinical reliability, Clarke concluded: "The necessity of bearing in mind, in studying hysterical patients, the great readiness with which they respond to suggestions, may be reiterated, [inasmuch] as the weak point in the method of investigation may perhaps be found here. The danger being that in such confessions the patient would be liable to make statements in accordance with the slightest suggestion given to them, [and] it might be quite unconsciously given to them, by the investigator" (1896:414).

Both of the two major difficulties raised by Strümpell and Clarke —that of applying the cathartic method and that of distinguishing the hysteric's phantasies from reality—were hardly unreasonable issues in an informed review of *Studies on Hysteria*. Years later, when Freud's ideas were beginning to gain a favorable hearing in America from early advocates of psychoanalysis like Adolf Meyer, James Jackson Putnam, and G. Stanley Hall, these early sympathizers were among the first to speak of the extreme importance of the therapist's "individual temperament" for the successful employment of either the cathartic or the psychoanalytic method.[8] As for the danger of confusing hysterics' phantasies with reality, Freud himself was currently on the verge of succumbing to it by accepting as truth his female patients' phantasized confessions of having been sexually seduced as young children by their fathers (see Chapter 4).

At all events, even the more reserved attitude displayed by certain (and, nota bene, generally more clinically experienced) reviewers toward *Studies on Hysteria* could hardly have been a major cause of Breuer's disillusionment with his previous working relationship with Freud. Breuer, who had undoubtedly pondered many of these problems himself, was simply not as sensitive to criticism as Freud would have us believe.[9] Furthermore, Breuer's scientific collaboration with Freud had ceased for all practical purposes, according to Freud, by mid-1894

8. For the views of Putnam and Meyer on this subject, see Meyer 1906; for those of Hall, see Ross 1972:393.

9. Breuer *was* apparently bothered, however, by one specific criticism of *Studies on Hysteria*—that of Adolf von Strümpell (1896). (See Freud's *Autobiography*, 1925d, S.E., 20:23; and *Origins*, pp. 156–57, Freud to Fliess, 6 and 13 February 1896.) The bulk of Strümpell's critical remarks were devoted to Breuer's "Theoretical" contribution and highlighted his inconsistent philosophical stand on the mind-body problem. In my view, neither Strümpell's specific rebuke nor Breuer's dismay at it was unjustified. See further Appendix B, where I treat this whole issue in more detail and present other extracts from Strümpell's review.

—that is, well before most of the reviews, especially the mixed ones, were even out (*Origins*, p. 95).

Individual Temperament and Scientific Style

If Breuer did not shrink from publicly proclaiming the dominant role of sexuality in hysteria, what exactly did come between him and Freud? To answer this question properly, it is essential to recouch this whole estrangement issue in terms that neither Freud nor Breuer ever clearly articulated themselves. That from the very outset of their acquaintance there were potentially incompatible and irreconcilable differences between these two men, both personal and intellectual, is my principal message. Indeed, their friendship was initially based upon an attraction of opposites.[10] Let us take another close look at the much-misunderstood Josef Breuer.

One of the most striking features of Breuer's brief autobiography is his repeated lionization of those men who had honored him in life by their personal contact and esteem. The list begins with his father, who provided him with his early education, and goes on to include his teachers at the University of Vienna; figures like Billroth and Brücke, who later adopted him as their family physician; and, finally, the three great scientists—Mach, Hering, and Exner—who sponsored his successful candidacy for election to the Vienna Academy of Sciences (Breuer [1925]).

Breuer's attitude toward his Judaic heritage also reveals his generous and even-tempered nature. Where Sigmund Freud was sensitive to the typical anti-Semitism of his times, Breuer believed such feelings of persecution to be more frequently imagined than real among the generally upwardly mobile Jews of his generation (Ellenberger 1970:464). In short, Breuer's unassuming, but not unworldly, personality exhibited little or no trace of the pent-up frustrations and the associated capacity for fanaticism that are so often at the root of a revolutionary disposition in intellectual life.[11]

As for Breuer's long-unpublished thoughts on hysteria, they were by no means out of keeping with his more general approach to matters scientific. In his painstaking work on the semicircular canals of the inner ear, Breuer did not stop until he had generalized his findings to fish, reptiles, birds, and mammals. If, prior to Freud's confirmation of Breuer's initial findings, the latter was reluctant to publish his dis-

10. Galdston (1956:493–94), Cranefield (1958), Ackerknecht (1963:129), and Walter Stewart (1967:17–19) have previously recognized many of these important temperamental differences and have also related them, as I do here, to the estrangement issue. Ackerknecht sums up these differences: "Breuer was an eclectic. Freud was a dogmatic person. Breuer was cautious, peace-loving, and harmonious (Jones calls him 'normal' in the best sense of the word), Freud was revolutionary" (1963: 129). See also Gedo et al. (1964) and Schlessinger et al. (1967), though one must read with extreme caution their arguments about Breuer's "scientific style" as seriously lacking in "reality-testing" ability.

11. On fanatic disposition and its psychosociological antecedents, see Eric Hoffer's classic *The True Believer* (1951); and Darnton 1968:165.

coveries in the case of Anna O., this was simply because he did not believe that the isolated and possibly atypical results in this one case were grounds for formal (theoretical) publication on a subject of such complexity.[12] I therefore concur with Cranefield's refreshing historical judgment in challenging the traditional image of Breuer's failings as a psychopathologist. "It has been suggested," Cranefield asserts, "that Breuer was in some ways less scientific in his psychoanalytic reporting than in his physiological research, but the same sort of active observation, active accumulation of facts, and active suspension of final judgment until the facts arranged themselves into meaningful patterns is entirely characteristic of his investigations of psychopathology" (1970a:447).

Nor was Breuer, a family physician with a large practice, able to use the cathartic method after his discovery of it. "Thus at that time," he wrote to August Forel in 1907, recalling his experiences with Anna O., "I learned a very great deal: much that was of scientific value, but something of practical importance as well—namely, that it was impossible for a 'general practitioner' to treat a case of that kind without bringing his activities and mode of life completely to an end. I vowed at the time that I would *not* go through such an ordeal again" (trans. Cranefield 1958:319). Hence it was that Sigmund Freud, a specialist in neurology, became Breuer's clinically active collaborator.

In sharp contrast to Breuer, however, Freud saw far less need for copious replications of the cathartic procedure before making it known to the medical world. "The state of things which he [Breuer] had discovered," Freud recalled in his *Autobiography*, "seemed to me to be of so fundamental a nature that I could not believe it could fail to be present in any case of hysteria if it had been proved to occur in a single one" (1925d, S.E., 20:21).[13]

Only after Freud encountered what he later described as the "most instructive" case of Frau Cäcilie M., with its remarkable patterns of

12. How many other potentially interested physicians, I wonder, did Breuer informally tell about Anna O.? Certainly Breuer's written notes on the case—a copy of which was made available to physicians at the Sanatorium Bellevue in Kreuzlingen, Switzerland—were kept with an eye to possible scientific communication. It is difficult to believe that Breuer, who was well acquainted with many prominent Viennese physicians and scientists, told *only* Freud about this case.

At the same time, one must not forget that Breuer probably weighed the merits of publishing this particular case history against the considerable difficulty of preserving the patient's anonymity. Not only was the patient still living in Vienna until 1888, but she had yet to recover from her illness. During this period she was re-institutionalized three times at the Sanatorium Bellevue in Kreuzlingen (from 30 July 1883 to 17 January 1884, from 4 March to 2 July 1885, and from 30 June to 18 July 1887). Even as late as 1895, when Breuer and Freud finally published *Studies on Hysteria*, Bertha Pappenheim's identity as "Anna O." became immediately evident to many Viennese readers of that book (Hirschmüller 1978:156–57, 204).

13. Freud's attitude in this respect was characteristic of his whole approach to science, as Jones has commented in connection with his earlier work on cocaine: "His great strength, though sometimes also his weakness, was the quite extraordinary respect he had for the *singular fact*. . . . That is the way Freud's mind worked. When he got hold of a simple but significant fact he would feel, and know, that it was an example of something general or universal, and the idea of collecting statistics on the matter was quite alien to him" (1953:96–97).

symptom formation through symbolic association, was he finally able to persuade the cautious Breuer to agree to joint publication of their theory (*Studies*, 1895*d*, *S.E.*, 2:178). It was therefore Breuer's relative caution in matters scientific—not his supposed reluctance to accept the sexual etiology of hysteria—that prompted the "long battle" preceding joint publication of the Breuer-Freud "Preliminary Communication" in 1893 (*Origins*, p. 64).[14]

On the other hand, sexuality certainly did become a major source of later disagreement between Breuer and Freud. But what Breuer found impossible to accept on this subject was the theory that the *essential* cause of *every* hysteria was *sexual*—a theory that Freud himself had begun to endorse, both privately and in print, following publication of the "Preliminary Communication" (1893*a*).[15] In 1907, twelve years after publication of *Studies on Hysteria*, Breuer gave just this explanation to August Forel in recalling his increasing divergence from Freud's own scientific views on hysteria:

> Freud is a man given to absolute and exclusive formulations: this is a psychical need which, in my opinion, leads to excessive generalization. There may in addition be a desire *d'épâter le bourgeois* [*sic*, "to shock the old fogies"]. In the main, however, his views on the question [of sexuality] are derived, as I have said, simply from experience; and anything that goes beyond it is merely fulfilling the law of the swing of the pendulum, which governs all [intellectual] development. In earlier times all hysteria was sexual; afterwards we felt we were insulting our patients if we included any sexual feeling in their aetiology; and now that the true state of things has once more come to light, the pendulum swings to the other side. (Trans. Cranefield 1958:320)[16]

To sum up, Breuer's collaboration with Freud came to an end when Freud began to insist that sexuality was the essential cause of *every* hysteria as well as of most other neuroses (see also Chapter 4).

14. In further confirmation of the fact that the issue of sexuality did not provoke this "long battle," Freud was later forced to confess that he himself had unfortunately overlooked the factor of sexuality in the majority of early cases that formed the basis of the "Preliminary Communication" (1893*a*). See *Studies*, 1895*d*, *S.E.*, 2:259–60.

15. For Freud's more extreme claims to this effect, see *Origins*, pp. 84–85 (Freud to Fliess, 21 May 1894), pp. 86–88 (Draft D); and *Studies*, 1895*d*, *S.E.*, 2:257–61. Between 1893 and 1895, Freud had also begun to posit an exclusively libidinal origin to various other neuroses, including anxiety neurosis, neurasthenia, obsessional neurosis, and paranoia (see Chapter 4).

Ernest Jones's (1953:254) claim in this connection that Breuer particularly "baulked at" Freud's views on the incestuous seduction of children is untenable and is derived from an erroneous dating of Freud's seduction theory (Stewart 1967: 17–18).

16. Compare this passage with Breuer's similar statement in *Studies on Hysteria*: "It is self-evident and also sufficiently proved by our observations that the non-sexual affects of fright, anxiety and anger lead to the development of hysterical phenomena. But it is perhaps worth while insisting again and again that the sexual factor is by far the most important and the most productive of pathological results. The unsophisticated observations of our predecessors, the residue of which is preserved in the term 'hysteria' [derived from the Greek word for 'uterus'], came nearer to the truth than the more recent view which puts sexuality almost last, in order to save the patients from moral reproaches" (1895*d*, *S.E.*, 2:246–47).

To return to the two men's contrasting temperaments, we see in Freud a radically different sort of scientific personality from that of the even-tempered Breuer. The following observation, which Freud made in a letter to his fiancée in 1886, captures better than perhaps any other the side of his nature upon which he based his hopes for possible fame in life:

> One would hardly guess it from looking at me, and yet even at school I was always the *bold oppositionist,* always on hand when an extreme had to be defended and usually ready to atone for it. . . . You know what Breuer told me one evening? . . . He told me he had discovered that hidden under the surface of timidity there lay in me an extremely daring and fearless human being. . . . I have often felt as though I had inherited all the defiance and all the passions with which our ancestors defended their Temple and could gladly sacrifice my life for one great moment in history. (*Letters,* pp. 202–3; italics added)

No sooner had he returned from his studies with Charcot in Paris than Freud began, as we have seen, to channel this previously latent capacity for playing the "bold oppositionist" into a series of highly concrete medical disputations. As Ernest Jones succinctly describes the post-Paris Freud, "He felt he was leading a crusade of revolution against the accepted conventions of medicine, or at all events his seniors in Vienna, and he accepted his mission wholeheartedly" (1953:249).

The issue of sexuality's role in hysteria and other neuroses was made to order for the crusade-seeking Freud. "I am pretty well alone here in tackling the neuroses," he informed his friend Fliess in a letter of 21 May 1894. "They regard me rather as a monomaniac, while I have the distinct feeling that I have touched on one of the great secrets of nature [the importance of sexuality]" (*Origins,* p. 83). Sexuality was "the key that unlocks everything" in Freud's conception of the neuroses (*Origins,* p. 75). If Freud seemed to others, including Breuer, to be indulging too freely or too dramatically in extremist and speculative (sexual) hypotheses, this was all simply part of Freud's more visionary style of practicing science. As he wrote in 1895 to his comrade-in-arms Fliess, "We cannot do without men with the courage to think new things before they can demonstrate them" (*Origins,* p. 137; slightly retranslated).

Nor did Freud want any unnecessary delays in publication of his ideas to result in *his* being scooped by others, as Breuer had been.[17] Thus, while Freud, in 1895, showed understandable displeasure at Heinrich Sachs for what he believed to be "almost a plagiarism" of his

17. By the time Breuer finally consented to joint publication of his researches with Freud, these researches had already lost a considerable part of their claim to scientific originality owing to the recent publications on hysteria in France by Charcot and his school—e.g., Binet, Richer, and particularly Janet (see Chapter 2). Freud later emphasized this point in his obituary notice of Breuer (1925*g,* *S.E.,* 19:280). Breuer's delay also made it later seem as if both he and Freud might have owed their initial insights into the problem of hysteria to the French, a possibility that subsequently gave rise to unfortunate polemics about scientific priority between Pierre Janet and later psychoanalysts. See Janet 1914–15; Jones 1914–15; and Freud, *Autobiography, S.E.,* 20:30–31.

own published ideas on hysterical paralyses, even "more painful" to him, he remarked to Fliess, was "Sachs's [independently] putting forward the principle of the constancy of psychological energy" (*Origins*, p. 135). Similarly, Freud described Paul Möbius to Fliess about this same time as "the best mind among the neurologists," to which judgment Freud added that "fortunately he is not on the track of sexuality" (*Origins*, p. 101). In a word, Freud feared mediocrity and others' anticipation of his ideas more than he feared error in science, and he fully accepted the risks inherent in this particular choice of values.[18] Breuer, on the other hand, placed exactitude and humility above all else. As Freud bitterly summed up their temperamental differences on the eve of their estrangement in early 1896, "I believe he has never forgiven me for having lured him into writing the *Studies* with me and so committed him to something definite, when he always knows three candidates for *one* truth and abominates every generalization as a piece of arrogance." [19]

All the same, one must give Breuer considerable credit for his personal efforts after the publication of *Studies on Hysteria* to see that Freud's heterodox views received a full and fair hearing before their Viennese medical colleagues.[20] Freud at first seems to have taken such efforts as indicating Breuer's unqualified support; and when Freud later discovered that this was not the case, he seems to have felt even more frustrated over what he now considered his colleague's vacillation. It is in this light that one must carefully weigh Freud's testimony about Breuer's supposedly two-faced attitude toward Freud's theories after publication of the *Studies*.[21]

Breuer's position is plain enough from several subsequently published accounts detailing his 4 November 1895 public defense of Freud's views before the Wiener medicinisches Doctorencollegium (Vienna College of Physicians).[22] Freud had given three lectures on hysteria (1895*g*) before this society on the evenings of 14, 21, and 28 October 1895. The following week, Freud's lectures were discussed.

Paul Mittler began by insisting that although, in investigating a case of hysteria, a physician should always consider the likelihood of sexual factors, it was impossible to refer *every* hysteria, as Freud seemed inclined to do, to this one cause. Even though he, too, agreed with the valuable truth implicit in the ancient Greek etymological derivation of the word *hysteria*, Mittler reemphasized that fright, anxiety, and other strong affects could just as easily be the root of a hysterical

---

18. A youthful letter of 16 June 1873 to Emil Fluss, written by Freud at the age of seventeen, is revealing of his early fear of possible mediocrity in life: "You take my 'worries about the future' too lightly. People [like me] who fear nothing but mediocrity, you say, are safe. Safe from what? I ask. Surely not safe and secure from being mediocre? What does it matter whether we fear something or not? Isn't the main question whether what we fear exists?" (*Letters*, p. 5).

19. Unpublished Fliess correspondence, letter of 1 March 1896; cited by Jones 1953:312.

20. See Freud, *Autobiography*, 1925*d*, *S.E.*, 20:26; and Appendix A.

21. E.g., *Origins*, p. 134, letter of 8 November 1895.

22. Two such accounts of Breuer's remarks have been translated in full in Appendix A.

illness. Grossmann followed Mittler with much more specific comments on diagnosing hysterical disturbances of the larynx and vocal chords— a topic Freud had touched upon in his lectures.

Breuer then spoke, and his remarks were received with "lively applause." He noted that the theory of repression was "essentially Freud's property," and that he himself had not witnessed the genesis of this new theory "without some opposition." He was now, however, "a convert" to it and therefore proclaimed himself in a unique position to refute various objections to it before the members of the College of Physicians. Stressing the "great quantity of observations" in Freud's lectures, Breuer flatly rejected the idea that Freud's results might be the product of suggestions conveyed to the patient. Breuer was particularly adamant about the medical profession's consistent underestimation of the sexual factor in young women: "We find ourselves in the state of a hysteria with regard to this matter; we repress this feeling which is unpleasant to us. We simply know nothing about the sexuality of young girls and women. No physician has any idea what sort of symptoms an erection calls forth in women, because the young women refuse to speak of the matter and the old ones have already forgotten about it" (1895b).

In spite of this endorsement, Breuer clearly questioned, with Mittler, Freud's more extreme theoretical emphasis upon the role of sexuality in hysteria: "One point on which the speaker is not in agreement with Freud is the [theoretical] overvaluation of sexuality. Freud probably did not intend to say that every hysterical symptom has a sexual background, but rather that the original root of hysteria is sexual." Only the future, Breuer added, would be able to confirm this latter claim. In the meantime, physicians should be thankful to Freud, Breuer declared, for his valuable "theoretical hints" on the whole problem. Characteristically, Breuer closed his remarks by stressing "that we have provisional conclusions before us and that every theory is a temporary structure" (1895b).[23]

When Freud later thanked Breuer for announcing himself as "a convert" to Freud's own views before the College of Physicians, Breuer

23. Discussion of Freud's lectures at the College of Physicians continued the following week (11 November). Teleky (1895) welcomed the beginnings of "a rational psychotherapy" for hysteria. The sexual origins of hysteria were well known to the ancients, he added. He seemed doubtful, however, whether psychical treatment would bring cures in all such cases, and he pointed out that extirpation of the ovaries and other somatic procedures were also accompanied by success (!) in many instances. Heinrich Weiss (1895), the only other discussant on 11 November, was more critical of Freud's views. He refused to accept Freud's claim that neurasthenia has an exclusively sexual basis (see Chapter 4), and he insisted that "the struggle for existence" in modern culture was also a relevant factor in this neurosis. In addition, Weiss was opposed to the separation of anxiety neurosis from neurasthenia in Freud's own etiological scheme (see Chapter 4). He likewise dismissed the idea that hysteria is exclusively a sexual disorder, although he agreed with Freud and his predecessor Moritz Benedikt that sexual secrets could create what Benedikt (1894) had previously described as a "second life" within the mind and thus could induce a hysterical condition. Finally, Weiss believed that Freud's methods might hold certain dangers for the patient unless they were pursued with extreme care— as he admitted Freud had done.

Josef Breuer in 1897
(age 55).

disappointed him with the reply, "But all the same I don't believe it." [24]
But what Breuer still refused to accept in late 1895 was simply Freud's
claim that every hysterical symptom—Charcot's nonpsychogenic "stigmata" excluded—has a purely sexual etiology (1896a, S.E., 3:149; and
1896c, S.E., 3:199). Even so, it would have been difficult to find many
physicians in Vienna who concurred with Freud as much as Breuer did
at this time on the general importance of sex in psychopathology. Thus,
Breuer's inability to follow Freud completely on this issue is simply a
measure of Freud's own growing fanaticism about it.

FREUD'S PHILOSOPHY OF SCIENCE; OR, WHY SEX?

To rest content with a purely subjective explanation of Freud's views on
sexuality—as Josef Breuer seems to have done with his later pronouncement about Freud's penchant for shocking the old fogies—

24. "*Ich glaub' es ja doch nicht*" (*Origins*, p. 134; *Anfänge*, p. 144, letter of
8 November 1895).

would be to disregard the formidable scientific logic that Freud himself believed underlay his position on this controversial issue. Indeed, Freud would have indignantly rejected, and rightly so, the accusation that his views on sexuality were simply a reflection of his own personality. In order to delineate Freud's philosophy of science insofar as it proves directly relevant to his views on sexuality, I shall consider four separate aspects of his psychoanalytic thinking: (1) the notion of sexuality as "the indispensable 'organic foundation'" for a reductionist-biological explanation of mental illness; (2) Freud's fundamental physicalist hypotheses, with their economic and dynamic approaches to neurotic symptom formation; (3) the relationship between heredity and environment in the etiology of mental illness, including Freud's Lamarckian convictions; and (4) his unflagging faith in the strict determinism of all psychical processes.

Sexuality as "the Indispensable 'Organic Foundation'"

As both Jones (1953:272, 280) and Kris (1954:25) have acknowledged, Freud's initial fascination with establishing sexuality's omnipresent part in neuroses was inspired by his highly ambitious vision in the 1890s "of transforming psychology into a biological or even physiological discipline" (Jones 1953:272). Even after he had long abandoned that reductionist dream as scientifically premature, the biological foundations of sexuality continued to prove fundamental to his psychoanalytic system of ideas. This biological substratum provided Freud with his best defense against a common physiological objection to his later theories—namely, that, as purely psychological constructs, they were "ipso facto incapable of solving a pathological problem." Such criticisms, Freud replied in 1905, made the fundamental mistake of confusing his psychoanalytic methodology with his theoretical premises. "It is the therapeutic technique alone," he argued, "that is purely psychological. . . . No one, probably, will be inclined to deny the sexual function the character of an organic factor, and it is the sexual function that I look upon as the foundation of hysteria and of the psychoneuroses in general" (1905e, S.E., 7:113).

Just how sincerely committed Freud continued to be in later years to this sexual-organic aspect of his psychopathology is revealed even more explicitly by a comment he made in 1908, at the age of fifty-one, to his newly acquired disciple Carl Jung: "I am rather annoyed with Bleuler [Jung's chief] for his willingness to accept a psychology without sexuality, which leaves everything hanging in mid-air. In the sexual processes we have the indispensable 'organic foundation' without which a medical man can only feel ill at ease in the life of the psyche" (Freud/Jung Letters, pp. 140–41).

Freud's abiding allegiance to "the indispensable 'organic foundation'" of every neurosis was not without subsequent divisive repercussions within the psychoanalytic movement. In 1912, during a debate held by the members of the Vienna Psychoanalytic Society over the etiological effects of childhood masturbation, Freud adamantly rejected his younger follower Wilhelm Stekel's attempt to reduce the pathological effects of masturbation to purely psychological causes—for example, guilt. Stekel, Freud insisted, was trying to "overstretch psychogenicity" by ignoring the purely toxicological basis of masturbatory neuroses (1912f, S.E., 12:248). Writing in his *Autobiography* some years later, Freud aptly summed up this sexual-organic legacy to psychoanalytic theory by referring to it as part of his "medical conscience" (1925d, S.E., 20:25). *Ontological commitment.*

Freud's "Fundamental Hypotheses"

As I explained in Chapter 2, Freud's fundamental hypothesis of a displaceable "quota of affect" undergoing "discharge" and obeying the law of psychic "constancy" formed the core of his economic and dynamic metapsychology. Of special interest here is the way in which these fundamental physicalist hypotheses allowed Freud to assume with high confidence in the 1890s—in spite of his still limited clinical evidence—that *nonsexual* forms of neurosis would simply never be encountered by him or by anyone else. In "The Aetiology of Hysteria" (1896c), Freud made no secret of the fact that his clinical material was limited at that time to only eighteen fully analyzed cases of hysteria. The nineteenth and twentieth cases would not disappoint his theory, he predicted. "Besides," he forthrightly added, "I am influenced by another motive as well, which for the moment is of merely subjective value. In the sole attempt to explain the *physiological* and *psychical mechanism* of hysteria which I have been able to make in order to correlate my observations, I have come to regard the participation of sexual motive forces as an indispensable premiss" (S.E., 3:200; italics added).[25] In a word, sexuality provided Freud with the constant source for the quota of affect and abreactive discharge that he deemed necessary to fulfill the economic and dynamic components of his theory of psychoneurosis. In subsequent years, Freud's psychoanalytic thinking never departed from the ready theoretical connection between sex and psychopathology originally provided by this quantitative point of view about libido.[26]

Nature vs. Nurture: Freud's "Etiological Equation"

Any theory of causation in mental pathology must take account of the straightforward medical consideration that disease can have only

---

25. Freud clearly took his reductionist metapsychology literally when it came to the phenomenon of sex. Breuer, on the other hand, was inclined to be more cautious in generalizing the various mechanical analogies in their model of hysteria. In *Studies on Hysteria* he treated this model as a psychological heuristic and thus saw no need to make sexuality any more "indispensable" to hysterical symptom formation than affects like fright or anger. I treat this issue of Breuer's and Freud's contrasting metapsychologies in more detail in Appendix B.

26. E.g., Freud 1940a [1938], S.E., 23:145, 157, 172, 181–84.

two logical sources, acting singly or together: (1) harmful experiences and/or agents originating in the external environment; and (2) endogenous (generally hereditary) factors. Ultimately, however, medical science must also seek to explain what contributes to disease-prone heredity, either in terms of inherited residues of noxious, ancestral experiences—the now-discredited Lamarckian position that Freud himself endorsed—or in terms of some other form of genetic anomaly.

In the causality of disease, Freud naturally accepted just such a logical dichotomy between the innate and the acquired. But in response to various mid-1890s critics of his sexual-etiological schemes, he expanded this basic dichotomy into a considerably more sophisticated, fourfold analysis of the causes of disease. Together these four causal factors comprised what Freud referred to as an "etiological equation" —that is to say, an exhaustive logical formula for describing the acquisition of every neurosis. The terms of this equation were as follows: (1) precondition, (2) specific cause, (3) concurrent cause, and (4) precipitating or releasing cause (1895f, S.E., 3:135–36). In general, each of the terms of this formula had to be satisfied, Freud believed, before a neurosis could finally manifest itself in a given individual.

Freud considered the precondition of a neurosis to be a "disposition," either innate or acquired, to subsequent illness. Such preconditions are present in every neurosis, he maintained, although they are usually insufficient in themselves to trigger the final emergence of psychopathology from a previously latent state. An instance of a precondition to neurosis would be having a syphilitic father (e.g., Freud 1905d, S.E., 7:236).

Specific causes were in turn assumed by Freud to determine the specific form of a given neurosis. For example, to cite the logic of Freud's later seduction theory, specific modes of childhood sexual assault result in specific neurotic symptoms in adulthood. A specific cause of neurosis is simultaneously an "acquired" precondition of that illness.

Freud considered a concurrent cause as ineffectual, like the precondition, in causing a neurosis on its own but nevertheless as instrumental in weakening the overall psychosexual constitution through, for example, overwork, exhaustion, or certain traumatic emotions such as fright and anxiety. Finally, the precipitating cause of neurosis is simply that cause which makes its appearance last in the etiological equation.[27]

What particularly concerns us here is how effectively Freud used this formal causal analysis of disease to ward off criticisms by those

27. Freud's four-part logic of disease brings to mind Aristotle's well-known and similar fourfold analysis of causality into material, efficient, formal, and final causes. Thus, it is of particular interest that, at the University of Vienna, Freud took five separate courses in philosophy with Franz Brentano, a specialist on Aristotle who also emphasized that Greek philosopher's relevance to modern psychology. Two of Freud's five courses with Brentano were devoted to Aristotle and to logic, respectively. See Bernfeld (1951:216) and, especially, Ramzy (1956:118–21), who discusses a number of more general parallels between the doctrines of Aristotle and Freud.

contemporary neurologists who sought to challenge his claims about
the exclusively sexual etiology of the neuroses. In a nutshell, Freud
argued that all possible clinical evidence pointing to the importance
of nonsexual pathogens as either concurrent or precipitating causes of
neurosis did not disprove his contention that sexual influences were
ultimately the preconditioning and especially the specific causes of
every neurosis (1895f). And only through the laborious procedure of
psychoanalysis, Freud further claimed, could the physician really distinguish the specific—and true—determinants of neurosis from the
preconditioning and auxiliary, or "stock," causes.

Ultimately, of course, Freud judged the preconditioning and especially the specific (sexual) causes of neurosis to be the invariable, *true*
causes on account of his other philosophical considerations—that
is, sex as an "indispensable 'organic foundation' " and the fundamental
economic and dynamic hypotheses premised upon this organic foundation. To Carl Jung, Freud conceded just such an inferential logic as
late as 1907: "I regard (for the present) the role of sexual complexes in
hysteria merely as a *theoretical necessity* and do not infer it from
their frequency and intensity. Proof, I believe, is not yet possible. When
we see people made ill by their work, etc., that is not conclusive [of a
nonsexual etiology], for the sexual (in the male, homosexual) component can easily be demonstrated in analysis" (*Freud/Jung Letters*,
p. 80; italics added.) In short, Freud did not so much reject his
critics on the issue of nonsexual etiology as he simply went beyond
them in his own causal analysis of mental disease.

Freud's etiological equation served another extremely useful function in his sexual theory when he combined it with the Lamarckian
notion of the inheritance of acquired characteristics. In espousing a
sexual theory of neurosis during the 1890s, Freud increasingly found
himself in direct opposition to his personal bête noire in neurology—
the doctrine of "hereditary degeneration" (see Stewart 1976). What
bothered him most about this common medical diagnosis was the fact
that its extreme overuse by Charcot and others had "left no room
for the acquisition of nervous illness" (1893f, *S.E.*, 3:23). Logically, the
problem of disease *acquisition* had to come before that of "pathogenic
heredity" for Freud. But if all acquired neuroses were really sexual in
nature, was it not also possible, he began to ask himself in the early
1890s, that hereditary degeneration was merely an acquired (Lamarckian) heritage of previous sexual disturbance?

Freud was thinking along such Lamarckian lines as early as manuscript Draft B (8 February 1893) in his correspondence with Wilhelm
Fliess. In this draft Freud declared that society's continued failure to
provide its members with an innocuous method of contraception would
eventually "destroy the marriage relation and bring hereditary ruin on
the whole coming generation." He likewise spoke of "the most far-
reaching speculations" that might follow upon the proof that acquired
sexual neuroses could be passed on by "pure heredity" (*Origins*, p. 72).

By mid-1894 Freud had apparently collected all the additional proof he needed to support such "far-reaching speculations" as medical actuality. "The core and mainstay of the whole business," he summed up his thinking on neurotic etiology in a 21 May 1894 letter to Fliess, "remains, of course, the fact that even healthy people can acquire the different forms of neurosis if they are subject to special sexual noxae. *And the bridge to the more generalized view is provided by the fact that, where a neurosis develops* without *a sexual noxa, a similar [hereditary] disturbance of the sexual affects can be shown to have been present from the first*" (*Origins*, p. 85; italics added).[28]

In sum, sexual disturbances, unlike the vague conception of hereditary degeneration which they ultimately replaced in Freud's Lamarckian-psychoanalytic scheme, provided Freud with suitable explanations for acquired (*preconditioning* and *specific*) causes of neurosis. The priority that he placed upon understanding the first acquisition of neurosis also explains why he immediately proclaimed his theory of seduction, developed in the fall in 1895, as "the discovery of a *caput Nili* ['source of the Nile'] in neuropathology" (1896c, S.E., 3:203). "If this [seduction theory] is so," Freud insisted at that time, "the prospect is opened up that what has hitherto had to be laid at the door of still unexplained hereditary predisposition may be accounted for as having been acquired at an early age" (S.E., 3:202).

Freud as Psychological Determinist

We must not envision Freud's philosophical and metapsychological assumptions as being removed from his day-to-day clinical work. Freud's conviction of *psychic determinism* provides a particularly cogent example of such an interconnection. Not only did this conviction shape his development of the psychoanalytic method, but it also facilitated the remarkable skill with which he applied that method in his practice.

Freud's entire life's work in science was characterized by an abiding faith in the notion that all vital phenomena, including psychical ones, are rigidly and lawfully determined by the principle of cause and effect. Cranefield (1966b:39) has rightly traced this conviction back to the influence of Freud's teachers and, more generally, to the 1847 biophysics program. Together with the belief that dreams have meaning and can therefore be interpreted, the extreme prominence Freud

28. Lamarckian theory also helped Freud envision every symptom of neurosis as somehow tied up with sexuality. In the Lamarckian organism, external influences must ultimately impress themselves upon the reproducing germ plasm if they are to be passed on to future generations. Throughout the late nineteenth century, numerous biologists, including Darwin (1868), had sought to explain such Lamarckian transmissions of acquired characteristics in terms of "gemmules" and other hypothetical hereditary particles supposedly thrown off by each cell into the blood, whence they were assumed to migrate to the gonads. That Freud evidently believed in some such scheme is revealed by a remark he made in 1913 before the Vienna Psychoanalytic Society: "In patients who are suffering from walking disturbances (abasias), muscle activity is an exquisitely sexual act. Moreover, it is probable that the processes in any organism exercise an influence on sexual production; that is what makes [Lamarckian] heredity possible" (*Minutes*, 4:160–61).

gave to the free association technique in his clinical work is perhaps the most explicit derivative of this philosophical legacy. "I am bound to say that it is sometimes most useful to have prejudices," he remarked when describing how this deterministic philosophy had led him to seize upon the free association technique (1910a, S.E., 11:29). The standard English expression "free association" is a misleading approximation of Freud's own choice of the German words *freier Einfall* for his technique. Freud's term conveys much more of the intended impression of an uncontrollable "intrusion" (*Einfall*) of preconscious ideas upon conscious thinking, a process that his fundamental rule of analysis—that the patient should report everything that comes to mind— was further designed to lay bare to the physician. Clearly, Freud himself did not believe that anything at all was truly "free" in the life of the mind.

As a clinician in the 1890s, Freud was not just a passive observer of his patients' free associations—that is, according to the popular, and not always unjustified, conception of the professional analyst's silent demeanor. Rather, what proved decisive in his psychoanalytic program of research was his ability to push each of his current psychoanalytic hypotheses to the very limits of his exploratory powers during the analytic session. Freud achieved this end only by skillful and persistent questioning of his patients, and he guided all his patients' "free associations" according to his theoretical concerns of the moment. In *Studies on Hysteria*, for instance, he openly admitted that much of his early clinical work on the problem of hysteria was of little value to his more recent sexual theory of neurosis. He had unfortunately failed, he conceded, to take this particular hypothesis into account when questioning these earlier patients (1895d, S.E., 2:259–60).

Once he realized his previous oversight, Freud was quick to see that his patients' undirected free associations were often merely decoys to help conceal the real, sexual cause of neurosis from both patient and physician. Freud as psychoanalyst accordingly became Freud the prosecuting attorney within his own clinical court of psychoanalytic law. In the case of an extremely pious woman's attempt to offer a nonsexual explanation for the origins of her illness, Freud describes in *Studies on Hysteria* the strategy that he was often compelled to assume with such patients: "I naturally rejected this derivation and tried to find another instead of it which would harmonize better with my views on the aetiology of the neuroses. . . . What prospect should I have had by any other method of revealing such a [sexual] connection, against her own views and assertions, in this recalcitrant patient who was so prejudiced against me and every form of mundane therapy?" (1895d, S.E., 2:274). Elsewhere he depicts himself in equally frank terms as "leading back the attention of patients with phobias and obsessions to the repressed sexual ideas *in spite of all their protestations*" (1894a, S.E., 3:57; italics added).

As psychoanalytic theory grew more sophisticated, so did Freud's ability and persistence as a clinician. Philip Rieff gives us the following relevant summary of Freud's clinical method in the famous case history of Dora. Freud had surmised that Dora, aged seventeen, was in a repressed state of love with Herr K., a middle-aged friend of the family, whose wife was in turn having an extramarital affair with Dora's father. Rieff's summary begins at the point where Freud was attempting to persuade his rather uncooperative patient that a recent attack of appendicitis was actually a hysterical symptom and represented an unconscious phantasy of defloration by Herr K., and of consequent hysterical pregnancy and childbirth. "Dora expressed disbelief. Freud applauds his own persistence; he speaks of using facts against the patient and reports how he overwhelmed Dora with interpretations, pounding away at her argument, until 'Dora disputed the facts no longer' " (Rieff 1959:82; Freud 1905e, S.E., 7:104). It is no wonder that Dora and others of Freud's patients occasionally responded to this sort of treatment by prematurely terminating their analyses with him.[29]

Whatever one may choose to say about the scientific merits of Freud's clinical technique—for example, he clearly sought confirmations, not falsifications, of his theories, and he also tended to treat recalcitrant clinical exceptions as evidence, in the last resort, of a purely "hereditary" sexual neurosis—this same technique, pursued with dedication and an endless expenditure of personal effort, was what distinguished him as a remarkably successful analyst. Many who sought to duplicate Freud's procedures soon found themselves unequal to the ruthlessness with which "free associations" had to be extracted from their patients in order to produce results. In his article "A Medium in the Bud," G. Stanley Hall later recalled his professional amazement as well as his personal embarrassment at how Freud and Jung, on the occasion of their visit to America in 1909, were able to discover the obvious sexual motive underlying a young girl's claims to spiritualistic powers after only a few brief minutes of questioning:

> In a short interview with her they at once diagnosed the true nature of it all, and to my surprise she frankly confessed that her chief motive from the first had been to win the love of her adored one. . . . The erotic motivation was obvious and the German savants saw little further to interest them in the case, and I was a trifle mortified that now the purpose so long hidden from us was so conscious and so openly confessed. (1918:156)

As time went on, the sheer frequency with which Freud and his followers were able to trace psychoneuroses to childhood sexual com-

---

29. See Origins, p. 215, for a reference to other such desertions. By the time he wrote his six papers on technique, between 1911 and 1914, Freud had become much more relaxed in his clinical methodology. In these later years, he specifically recognized the disadvantages of an overly active approach to his patients and added that "the premature communication of a solution" had formerly brought many of his analyses to an "untimely end" (1913c, S.E., 12:141). The maturation of his technique evidently reflected his own transformation from an investigator in eager search of a theoretical understanding of the neuroses, to a practitioner whose mature theories and greater self-confidence allowed him to bide his time in communicating "solutions" to his patients.

plexes led him, as a strict determinist, to assert one further claim.
Even if he *was* wrong, and sexuality was eventually disproved as the
sole specific cause of psychoneurosis, Freud still insisted that only
the purely sexual cases should be called by the established psychiatric
labels for each standard form of neurosis. "I thoroughly dislike the
notion that my opinions are correct," he protested to a still skeptical
Carl Jung in 1908, "but only in regard to a part of the cases. (Substitute
point of view for opinions.) That is not possible. It must be one
thing or the other. These characteristics are fundamental, they can't
vary from one set of cases to another. Or rather: they are so vital that
an entirely different name should be given to the cases to which they
do not apply. Thus far, you know, no one has seen this other [nonsexual]
hysteria, Dem[entia] pr[aecox], etc. . . . There. Now I have
avowed the full extent of my fanaticism . . ." (*Freud/Jung Letters,*
p. 141).

One final manifestation of Freud's steadfast belief in psychic determinism
is also worth noting. His contemporary critics often said
that his theories found such ready confirmation because he questioned
suggestively and implanted his own preconceptions within the
minds of his patients. Unlike his critics, however, Freud as psychic
determinist drew a sharp and justified procedural line between the
danger of accidentally reading one's thoughts into a patient's mind and
the medically unavoidable necessity of taking an active, theory-laden
attitude whenever psychoanalyzing a patient. Furthermore, whether a
patient's responses were truth or phantasy, they were still psychically
determined, as Freud pointed out before the Vienna Psychoanalytic Society
in 1910; hence they also had to be psychoanalytically meaningful:

> . . . if one wants to come up with anything, one cannot avoid asking some
> leading questions. Besides, the patient can be influenced only in a direction
> that suggests itself to him. One has to take the risk of being at first
> misled by the patient. *For in neurosis, the reality is that of thought, and
> not that of the external world.* (*Minutes,* 2:453; italics added)

Although the tortuous intellectual path that finally led Freud to discover
the importance of phantasy life in the neuroses also involved
him in the professionally embarrassing blunder of the seduction theory,
it is certain that he would never have reached this momentous
insight had not his fundamental faith in psychic determinism guided
him to it—and to his psychoanalytic Promised Land.

OVERVIEW AND AFTERMATH OF THE
BREUER–FREUD COLLABORATION

Depending upon one's perspective, it is possible to see Josef Breuer
either as vindicated by his increasingly cautious—but, nota bene,
hardly puritanical or narrow-minded—stand on psychoanalysis in the

1890s,[30] or as typical of the great majority of Freud's scientific contemporaries who unfortunately failed to recognize true genius in their midst. Breuer himself would certainly have disavowed both of these portrayals, as he essentially did in his 1907 letter to August Forel, written many years after his estrangement from Freud. "I have already said," Breuer told Forel, "that personally I have now parted from Freud entirely, and naturally this was not a wholly painless process. But I still regard Freud's work as magnificent: built up on the most laborious study in his private practice and of the greatest importance—even though no small part of its structure will doubtless crumble away again" (trans. Cranefield 1958:320). And while the issue of sexuality became the symbolic crux of their scientific divergence, Breuer himself refused to accept only Freud's claim that *every* neurosis has a specific sexual cause. Thus, in many respects it is Freud's position, not Breuer's, that requires the greatest retrospective understanding on the part of the historian of psychoanalysis. I shall briefly summarize, then, the logical context within which Freud's own views on this subject first arose.

First and foremost, sexuality emerged in the 1890s as one of the most plausible causes of neurotic complaints on the basis of Breuer and Freud's clinical experience. At first surprised by sexuality's importance, Freud came to see it as "the indispensable 'organic foundation'" for a scientific explanation of mental disease (*Freud/Jung Letters*, pp. 140–41). Reinforcing this reductionist premise in Freud's mind was a sophisticated physicalist model, devised jointly with Josef Breuer, in which the organism's state of mental health could be grasped wholly in terms of various fundamental hypotheses depicting the economics and the dynamics of libido as a simple form of displaceable "quantity."

Freud's biological premises included far-reaching phylogenetic as well as purely physiological considerations during the mid-1890s. Having addressed himself to the formal philosophical problem of what constitutes a causal explanation of disease, he psychoanalytically resolved the issue of "bad heredity" into the one *recurrent* cause of neurosis—repressed and unsatisfied sexuality—which he deemed to be civilization's congenital burden, increasing from generation to generation by Lamarckian inheritance.

Finally, Freud's aggressive, theory-laden application of the free association technique yielded abundant empirical confirmations, as well as other related discoveries about human psychosexual development, that were largely denied to his more diplomatic colleagues.

Within the general philosophical context I have described, the estrangement between Breuer and Freud was, more than anything else,

30. Although Freud himself rejected Breuer's notion of hypnoid states as unnecessary and misleading, it has now been revived in the current understanding of normal and abnormal mental processes (see Cranefield 1970a:448; and Stewart 1967:82). Similarly, on the issue of sexuality, it was Breuer, not Freud, who came nearer to the truth. See also Shakow and Rapaport 1964:201, n. 17; and Stewart 1967:18.

simply a matter of incompatible scientific styles. Where Breuer advocated an eclectic approach to understanding hysterical phenomena, Freud sought rigid and incontrovertible laws that suited his more dogmatic and revolutionary self-image in science. What Breuer saw as Freud's greatest intellectual weakness—his fanatical propensity for exclusive scientific formulations—Freud valued as one of his most courageous and fruitful abilities, while sorely regretting its absence in his friend. All else that came between them was mostly derivative, a symptom but not a cause of the real conflict between their respective approaches to the mysteries of the human mind.

As for the personal estrangement between Breuer and Freud, this too was an outgrowth of their increasingly manifest differences on the proper method of science. Freud, for his own part, was especially unable to get along with anyone who could not take a clear and definite stand on fundamental scientific issues (Jones 1953:255). When Breuer was not able to follow him in all his ideas, Freud's initial impatience gradually turned to resentment and finally to extreme criticism of Breuer's personality, so much so that the editors of the Fliess correspondence felt compelled to omit from publication most of the vitriolic and unattractive side of Freud revealed by his bitter remarks about Breuer.[31] By 1897, Freud was telling Fliess that the very sight of Breuer would make him want to emigrate,[32] and he even took to avoiding Breuer's neighborhood for fear of having to meet him on the street (1901b, S.E., 6:137–38; Roazen 1975:78). Many years later Breuer's daughter recalled just such an accidental meeting between the two men when she and her father, now elderly, were out walking one day. Breuer instinctively threw open his arms, while Freud, head down and doing his best to ignore his old friend, marched briskly by.[33]

The bitter emotional feelings left by the break did not affect Freud's later, public attitude toward Breuer's valuable contributions to psychoanalysis, and he was always unstinting in his recognition of Breuer's integral importance in this respect. On the other hand, Freud's autobiographical rationalizations of the precise causes of their scientific falling-out became considerably clouded with the years. Freud was soon—in April 1900—referring to Breuer's notion of hypnoid states, which he himself had provisionally endorsed in Studies on Hysteria (1895d), as "that unfortunate idea that had been forced on me" and, a year later, as a "superfluous and misleading" idea.[34] Most of all, Breuer's doubts about certain of Freud's more peculiarly psychoanalytic ideas became increasingly reduced in Freud's mind—as did those of his later critics—to the category of reactionary "resis-

31. See Jones (1953:254–55, 288–89), who, in addition to commenting upon this point, has made available some of the less offensive unpublished passages.

32. Unpublished Fliess correspondence, letter of 29 March 1897; cited by Jones 1953:255.

33. Hannah Breuer to Ernest Jones, 21 April 1954, Jones archives; cited by Roazen 1975:80.

34. Unpublished Fliess correspondence, letter of 28 April 1900, cited by Jones 1953:274; and Freud 1905e [1901], S.E., 7:27, n. 1.

tances" to unpleasant psychoanalytic truths—so much so, in fact, that he eventually repressed from memory how far Breuer had actually gone in *Studies on Hysteria* (1895d) in proclaiming the predominantly sexual causes of neurosis. Thus, Josef Breuer, who in many important respects was both the first psychoanalyst and one of the most sympathetic Viennese supporters of Freud's psychoanalytic discoveries in the 1890s, also became, with the passage of time, the first major victim of psychoanalytically reconstructed history.

4

Freud's Three Major Psychoanalytic Problems and the *Project for a Scientific Psychology* (1895)

As I pointed out in the previous chapter, Freud's decision to abandon the use of hypnotism not only pointed up a more dynamic interplay of mental forces within the neurotic mind, but also helped to demonstrate the fundamental roles of resistance and repression in inhibiting the cathartic mode of therapy. At the clinical level, catharsis was accordingly replaced by psychoanalysis, while at the more theoretical level, as Freud later explained it in his *Autobiography*, "The theory of repression became the corner-stone of our understanding of the neuroses." Indeed, as he also intimated, it would be feasible to reconstruct the subsequent history of psychoanalysis around his development of the repression theory. "It is possible to take repression as a centre and to bring all the elements of psycho-analytic theory into relation with it" (1925*d*, *S.E.*, 20:30).

To be more precise, Freud's personal statements on this score must be taken to include a simultaneous endorsement of the considerably more all-embracing construct of "defense" (*Abwehr*) in psychoanalytic theory. He himself made a clear distinction, particularly in the early 1890s, between neuroses that seemed to arise via *Verdrängung* or "repression" and others that could be attributed to independent forms of defense—for example, projection, displacement, and denial. Nor would he have objected in the least to our viewing defense instead of repression as the nuclear concept of his psychoanalytic work; for in 1926, after revising his thinking on the problem of anxiety, Freud formally restored to the term "defense" the all-inclusive status that it had possessed in his earlier psychoanalytic writings (1893–96).

Freud's development of the concept of defense comprises his solutions to three distinct, albeit intimately related, psychological problems: (1) What determines the specific "choice of neurosis"? That is, why does a given neurotic adopt one form of pathological defense (repression, projection, displacement, etc.) rather than another? (2) Why sex? Why is sexuality so invariably found to be the motive for each different form of neurotic defense? Freud's previous and largely physiological-physicalist justifications still left much to be said on this controversial issue. And finally (3) what constitutes the mechanism of repression—particularly in its pathological extremes? It was around these three problems, rather than around that of repression (Verdrängung) proper, that Freud coordinated the theoretical tenets of psychoanalysis during the remainder of his life.

In the balance of Part One and throughout Part Two of this book, I shall accordingly attempt to reconstruct the inner core of psychoanalytic theory in terms of its specific relevance to each of these separate but overlapping preoccupations in Freud's psychoanalytic writings. In the present chapter I shall consider the three years from the publication of Breuer and Freud's "Preliminary Communication" in early 1893 to the beginning of Freud's intensive scientific exchange of ideas with Wilhelm Fliess in early 1896. It was during this period that Freud, working more independently of Josef Breuer, sought to parlay the Breuer-Freud psychophysicalist model of hysteria into a unified theory of all the major forms of neurosis.

PROBLEM ONE: THE CHOICE OF NEUROSIS

Such early views—save perhaps the seduction theory—as Freud developed between 1893 and 1896 on this subject are generally given scant attention in most biographical treatments of him.[1] This is hardly surprising, even if it is to be greatly regretted for historical reasons. To begin with, the choice of neurosis, by far the most clinically complex and theoretically multifaceted of Freud's three problems, involved him in numerous false starts and in endless, highly technical speculations on the whole subject. Not only is it often difficult to follow Freud's early train of thought on this topic; but even more to the point, he himself was eventually forced to repudiate the bulk of

1. Walter Stewart's *Psychoanalysis: The First Ten Years* (1967:42–115) remains a conspicuous exception to this tendency; and in this review of the choice-of-neurosis problem, I am particularly indebted to Stewart's comprehensive analysis of this aspect of Freud's neurological career in the 1890s.

the specific etiological mechanisms that he at one time thought he had discovered during this period.

Nevertheless, there are at least three compelling reasons why Freud's earliest ideas on the choice of neurosis should be given more attention than they have usually received from historians of psychoanalysis. First, to omit them is to neglect the principal focus of Freud's clinical attentions during these three years. Second, in spite of the unfruitful nature of much of this early work, familiarity with this aspect of his psychoanalytic career makes it far easier to understand his later thoughts about the neuroses, especially his espousal of a close etiological relationship between sexuality and the "essential" causes of neurosis. Third and last, scrutiny of a person's conceptual errors, particularly if he has eventually succeeded in overcoming them, often tells far more about how his mind works than do even the most copiously documented episodes of conceptual triumph. This point is particularly applicable to Freud's work on the choice of neurosis.

The choice-of-neurosis problem arose at a purely pragmatic level before patients had even entered into psychotherapeutic treatment with Freud. As he himself stressed at the very beginning of his "Psychotherapy" chapter in *Studies on Hysteria* (1895d), any attempt to apply the cathartic method to hysteria soon encountered a major obstacle (in addition to the impossibility of effecting a deep hypnotic trance in every patient). How could a physician distinguish *in advance* purely hysterical symptoms from the many similar symptoms manifested in certain other nonhysterical forms of neurosis? In short, which patients were truly hysterics, and which were not? That is to say, which were to be selected for the arduous and generally prolonged therapeutic treatment known as catharsis? Often one simply could not be sure.

Thus, Freud frequently used the cathartic method on a patient he thought to be hysterical, only to discover that catharsis yielded few of the results he had originally anticipated. To make matters more complicated, many prospective patients, perhaps the majority, exhibited what appeared to be the combined symptoms of several "textbook" forms of neurosis. What, then, was unique to the etiology of hysteria in such complex cases, and what was not?

Freud soon divined that many neurotic symptoms could be distinguished by a temporal factor from those specific to traumatic hysteria and other manifest psychoneuroses. The psychoneuroses, including hysteria, increasingly proved to have been determined in childhood, while a second group of neuroses displayed a much more contemporary derivation from abnormal sexual practices like coitus interruptus, prolonged continence, and masturbation. Freud therefore named this second group the *actual* neuroses, after the German term *aktuelle*, meaning "current."

It was the actual neuroses rather than the psychoneuroses (those stemming from childhood causes) that first put Freud on the track of a possible sexual universal in neuroses. In February 1893, writing in manuscript Draft B of the Fliess correspondence, Freud announced this point of view: "It may be taken as common knowledge that *neurasthenia* [a form of Freud's actual neuroses] is a frequent result of an abnormal sexual life. The contention which I am putting forward and desire to test by observations is that neurasthenia is always *only* a sexual neurosis" (*Origins*, p. 66).

The development of Freud's ideas on the actual neuroses can be followed in the Fliess correspondence from manuscript Drafts A and B in late 1892 and early 1893, to their far more refined formulations in Drafts E and G (mid-1894 and January 1895), and finally to their various published treatments in the 1890s (1895b, 1895f, 1898a). Freud's general approach to the problem, as stated in his earliest manuscript drafts, was purely "toxicological." In other words, sufferers from the actual neuroses were somehow being neurologically poisoned by their own abnormal deployment of a sexual substance emanating from the reproductive organs.

This idea in turn inspired a formal psychophysiological criterion for distinguishing normal affects from purely neurotic ones. "*In the neurosis*," Freud accordingly announced to his medical colleagues in 1895, "*the nervous system is reacting against a source of excitation which is internal, whereas in the corresponding* [normal] *affect it is reacting against an analogous source of excitation which is external*" (1895b, S.E., 3:112; Freud's italics). Thus anxiety, to give a specific illustration, arises normally through the psyche's perception of a nearby source of external danger; or it can arise neurotically, Freud began to surmise, from the toxicological effects of improperly discharged somatic libido.

More explicitly still, Freud went on to develop his earliest views on the choice of neurosis in close cooperation with the following schematic picture of sexuality (Fig. 4.1). Although this diagram does not appear in the Fliess correspondence until Draft G in early 1895, it was nevertheless Freud's constant conceptual aid, as he tells us in this same draft, in developing much of his earlier thinking on the subject of neurosis (*Origins*, pp. 103–4). Briefly interpreted, his schematic picture of sexuality depicts the organism's initial perception of a sexual object [1] as alerting (via the dotted line) the psychical group [2]. The psychical group becomes, in turn, a source of nervous conductivity leading (via the continuing dotted line) across the somatic-psychical boundary to the genital end organ [3]. There somatic sexual excitation (S.S.) is released. After passing through the spinal chord, somatic sexual excitation (S.S.) contributes to a heightening of erotic tension [4], which, having traversed the somatic-psychical boundary once again, arouses the psychical sexual group (Ps.S.) [5] to its peak potential for sexual receptivity. At this point a totally uninhibited organism would take steps through vigorous motoric activity [6] to place the sexual object in a favorable position. If successful, orgasmic reflex action discharges the accumulated tension in the end organ [7], thus triggering the simultaneous sensation of voluptuous feelings [8] in the psychical sexual group.

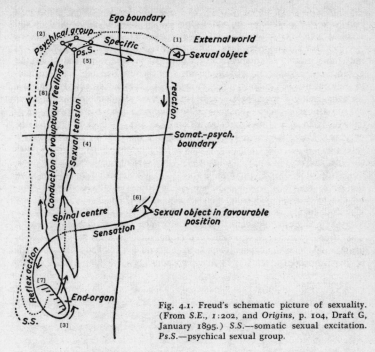

Fig. 4.1. Freud's schematic picture of sexuality. (From *S.E.*, 1:202, and *Origins*, p. 104, Draft G, January 1895.) *S.S.*—somatic sexual excitation. *Ps.S.*—psychical sexual group.

The basic dualist aspect of Freud's model provides for two logical sources of potentially neurotic disturbance within the organism: soma and psyche. By following out the natural combinations and permutations of this psychophysiological model, one may distinguish *four* classes of neurotic etiology. Each of these four classes is in turn uniquely characterized by whether its distinguishing pathological excitation traverses the somatic-psychical boundary or remains instead within its locus of innervational origin.[2]

1. Somatic neurosis. Somatic sexual excitation may poison the soma, Freud thought, without ever entering the psyche. His category of the actual neuroses—particularly anxiety neurosis—fully exemplified this particular principle. He later called such anxiety neuroses "the somatic counterpart of hysteria," an expression that aptly conveys the differential affective origins—soma versus psyche—but similar somatic symptoms manifested in both neuroses (1895b, *S.E.*, 3:115).

2. Soma to psyche. Alternatively, Freud reasoned that somatic sexual excitation may gain successful access to the psyche but, upon failing to find adequate discharge, may encounter psychical defense against prolonged, undischarged sexual tension. The consequence of

2. The four-part analysis offered here is mine, not Freud's, although it is fully implicit in his psychophysicalist logic about the neuroses.

such psychical defense against libido would be the development of purely *psycho*pathological symptoms—for example, obsessions and phobias.

3. *The psyche and internal psychical hemorrhaging.* Looking at the whole matter from the psyche's point of view, the psychical sexual group can become the victim of an insufficient linkage with its terminal organ—as is the fate, for example, of many well-brought-up and sexually anesthetic women—and therefore be forced to replenish its continually low level of psychical sexual excitation by drawing upon closely associated nonsexual neurones (a sort of neuronal "suction" process). Early in 1895, Freud likened this third form of neurosis to "an internal haemorrhage" and clinically equated it in Draft G with chronic melancholia (*S.E.*, *1*:205–6; *Origins*, pp. 107–8). In a word, the symptoms of melancholia—a sort of psychopathological *"mourning over loss of libido"*—were simply an unconscious neurotic counterpart to normal mourning. Freud also related the melancholic state of mind to its neurotic opposite, mania—a psychosis involving an overwhelming of the psychical sexual group by excessive somatic sexual excitation. Mania, as opposed to melancholia, is therefore a Class 2 (soma-to-psyche) neurosis. (See Figs. 4.2 and 4.3 for Freud's schematic representation of these two forms of neurosis.)

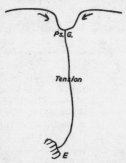

Fig. 4.2. Freud's schematic representation of melancholia. (From *S.E.*, *1*:205, and *Origins,* p. 108, Draft G, January 1895.) *Ps.G.*—psychical sexual group. *E*—end organ.

Fig. 4.3. Freud's schematic representation of mania. (From *S.E.*, *1*:205, and *Origins,* p. 108, Draft G, January 1895.) *Ps.S.*—psychical sexual excitation.

4. *Psyche to soma—the theory of conversion.* Finally, in the neurosis of hysteria, Freud assumed that the accumulation of a traumatic and unabreacted quota of affect within the psyche induced defense (repression) and caused a somatic conversion of emotion—that is, a transformation of this trauma into bodily symptoms following psychically analyzable paths of discharge.

So much for the purely theoretical side of the problem. Clinically speaking, Freud encountered these four classes of neurosis in two more general groups: those of Class 1 (or the actual neuroses) and those of Classes 2, 3, and 4 (or the neuropsychoses of defense).

From work with his patients, Freud became convinced in the 1893–95 period that he had found ample confirmation of his various psycho-physiological formulations in the following life-history particulars.

The Actual Neuroses

Two forms of actual neurosis were to be distinguished from one another in Freud's scheme: neurasthenia (characterized by lassitude, headaches, indigestion, perceptual sensitivities, and a wide variety of other complaints) and anxiety neurosis. Neurasthenia was invariably the result, he contended, of excessive adolescent masturbation (*Origins*, p. 68, Draft B; also Freud 1895b, S.E., 3:109), and it generally appeared with the onset of puberty. The specific symptoms of neurasthenia could be attributed to three consequences of such excessive onanism: (1) to the neurasthenic's reduced ability to tolerate an accumulated level of sexual tension—an impairment caused by "facilitation by repetition" and by the neurasthenic's gradual habituation to an ever-lower threshold of sexual discharge (see Stewart 1967:67); (2) to a weakening of the psychical sexual group (through decreased desire for an external libidinal object) and to a simultaneously diminished production of somatic sexuality: hence the symptoms of exhaustion, ultimately sexual in nature; and (3) to the tendency for the neurasthenic's remaining sexual potency to leak prematurely out of the genital organs and into the nervous system, "as it were, through a hole" (*Origins*, p. 108, Draft G, January 1895).

In contrast to neurasthenia, the clinical picture of anxiety neurosis proved considerably more problematical, at least to begin with. In Draft B of the Fliess correspondence (8 February 1893), Freud was still inclined to attribute neurotic anxiety to purely psychogenic causes. For instance, anxiety after coitus interruptus could be ascribed to fear of an unwanted pregnancy or to either partner's repressed resentment in the wake of insufficient sexual satisfaction (*Origins*, pp. 71, 88–89). All the same, by the time he composed Draft E ("How Anxiety Originates") in mid-1894, Freud had come to see neurotic anxiety, like neurasthenia, in purely *somatic* terms. Two key clinical discoveries changed his mind: that totally anesthetic women, who should not suffer psychically from coitus interruptus, still seemed to contract anxiety neuroses; and that among the victims of anxiety neurosis were some sexual partners with absolutely no fear of pregnancy (*Origins*, pp. 88–89). At the same time, he had noticed that the usual symptoms of anxiety attacks in both sexes—accelerated breathing, palpitations, sweating, and the like—involved the same general paths of innervation that are normally taken by somatic sexual tension in the course of coitus itself (*Origins*, p. 93; Freud 1895b, S.E., 3:111).

Neurotic anxiety, then, began to look as if it were none other than transformed somatic (sexual) excitation. Such a transformation presumably took place whenever somatic sexual excitation was not fully converted into its psychical counterpart and thus into a sexually satisfying copulation (*Origins*, pp. 90–91). Freud blamed such neurotic dysfunctions in the female upon ejaculatio praecox in the male and, for both partners, upon coitus interruptus and prolonged sexual abstinence. In the male, Freud reduced the latter etiological factor to accumulated "pressure on the walls of the seminal vesicles"—a pressure that periodically surpasses a pathological "threshold," he claimed, in those who remain abstinent too long. He also spoke of an analogous, but as yet unknown, chemical process in the female form of this neurotic etiology (1895b, S.E., 3:108).

Freud's new, somatic theory of the actual neuroses called for a special form of treatment. Unlike the symptoms of the psychoneuroses, those of the actual neuroses were "not further reducible by psychological analysis, nor amenable to psychotherapy" (1895b, S.E., 3:97; Freud's italics). Treatment was therefore limited to the physician's direct advice to the patient concerning the specific sources of noxious inadequacy in his or her sexual life. With regard to the prophylaxis of such neuroses at a more collective and societal level, Freud was later to urge in outspoken terms that "it is positively a matter of public interest that men should enter upon sexual relations with full potency" (1898a, S.E., 3:278; Freud's italics).

As late as 1920, Freud was still calling his early 1890s discovery that neurotic anxiety arises out of transformed libido "one of the most important results of psycho-analytic research," and he compared the phenomenon to that of wine turning to vinegar (S.E., 7:224 n., addition to the fourth edition of Freud's Three Essays on the Theory of Sexuality). Nevertheless, despite the wealth of confirming clinical evidence, he eventually did change his mind on this subject after 1926, when he finally gave up the idea that anxiety is physically derived from libido. Whether he was initially misled on this problem because neurotics have, or at least tend to report, more abnormal sexual relationships than do normal individuals, or whether the contemporary dearth of really safe and tolerable methods of contraception should instead be held responsible for Freud's error, I cannot say. Most probably his early formulations on anxiety neurosis were a product of these two influences. More to the point, it was largely his prior physicalist assumptions about the nature of neurosis that influenced him in the first place to entertain such a direct toxicological relationship between neurotic anxiety and inadequate sexual satisfaction.[3]

The Neuropsychoses of Defense

Turning briefly to the neuropsychoses of defense—that is, to the second of Freud's two major clinical categories of neurotic illness—

3. It is worth noting that when Freud finally did change his mind on the problem of anxiety—attributing this affect to the ego rather than to transformed libido—he seems to have done so for reasons more *theoretical* than *clinical*, as he himself admitted at the time. Thereafter, he simply lost interest, as he confessed, in the economic side of the problem. See Freud 1926d, S.E., 20:140; also Stewart 1967: 161–76. Still Freud never gave up the idea that some form of peculiarly primal anxiety had a purely economic and toxicological origin in early life (Freud 1933a, S.E., 22:81). For a further historical review of Freud's thinking on the problem of anxiety, see James Strachey's Editor's Introduction to Freud 1926d, S.E., 20:77–86.

we see that he devoted four of ten articles drafted between January 1894 and February 1896 to the challenging psychological problem of distinguishing the major forms of psychoneurosis from one another (Freud 1894a, 1895c, 1895h, and 1896b). Four psychoneuroses in particular were the focus of his clinical researches at this time: hysteria, obsessional and phobic types, hallucinatory psychoses, and paranoia.

Whereas hysteria seemed to be characterized by defense against an incompatible idea and a concomitant capacity for somatic conversion of affect into symptoms, neuroses involving obsessions and phobias, Freud argued, were somehow unable to make use of the basic conversion mechanism. Instead, an alternative form of defense was involved, one by which the psyche somehow achieved a separation between the incompatible (sexual) idea and its quantitative measure of libidinal affect.[4] As such an isolated affect was thought to be physically conserved, Freud had to account for its subsequent fate. This he did by assuming an unconscious attachment of the "free" affect to another more compatible idea. To cite an example, a young and prudish girl came to Freud with an obsessional fear of urinating whenever she was in a public place. He traced the obsession back to an episode at a theater during which the young girl had indulged in erotic reveries upon seeing an attractive male acquaintance seated near her. After inducing an erectionlike process in herself, the girl's phantasies had terminated in the need to urinate, forcing her to leave the concert hall. Subsequent efforts to fend off such unseemly sexual impulses led to repression of her erotic thoughts and then to her obsessional fear of urinating in public. Freud characterized this pathological process as one of "false connection," a distinguishing attribute of obsessions and phobias that neatly explained their bizarre and often nonsensical nature (1894a, S.E., 3:51–52, 56).

In hallucinatory psychoses, Freud's third clinical form of defense neurosis, the ego has apparently succeeded in an even more energetic form of defense; that is, it has rejected both the incompatible sexual idea and its accompanying quota of libidinal affect." The pathogenic result is what Freud called "a flight into psychosis," since the ego usually proves unable to reject both *idea and affect* without also rejecting a substantial part of reality. Thereafter, such individuals become increasingly prey to the sort of "hallucinatory" defenses that must inevitably characterize a mind lacking a secure hold on reality (1894a, S.E., 3:58–60).

For want of sufficient clinical experience, Freud developed and published his theory of paranoia after the other three etiological interpretations. On 24 January 1895, he first sketched out his theory on this subject in Draft H of the correspondence with Fliess, but it did

4. I should remind the reader that Freud envisioned psychical *affect* to be a quantitative measure of the excitation or "emotion" (e.g., love, hate, anger, fear, anxiety, etc.) that is "attached" to every idea. In terms of their source, he viewed such affects as "the psychical representatives" of somatic impulses or, more simply, as purely somatic (instinctual) impulses that "cathect" ideas in the process of attaining psychical expression. See further, Strachey, Editor's Note to Freud 1915c, S.E., 14:111–16.

not appear in print until almost a year later (Freud 1896*b*). The paranoid individual, Freud maintained in his 1896 publication, is one who differs from other psychoneurotics by fully accepting the existence of the incompatible (sexual) idea. Defense is nevertheless achieved in paranoia and entails *projection* of that incompatible idea onto the external world, whence comes the paranoid's sense of persecution, his delusions, and his extreme distrust of other people. With the added cooperation of repression, the paranoid individual's projected ideas may also become completely divorced from their original sexual content (*Origins*, pp. 113–15; Freud 1896*b*, *S.E.*, 3:184–85).

The Seduction Theory

By early 1896, further clinical investigation had led Freud to one additional refinement in his thinking on the neuropsychoses of defense —namely, the claim that they were all caused by childhood sexual traumas (seductions), perpetrated either by an adult or by a much older child. He dated the seductions of hysterics to the first four years of childhood and assumed the experiences to be passive and generally unpleasurable. He placed the seductions of obsessional neurotics slightly later in childhood (four to eight years of age) and assumed the child's role in the seduction to be more active. Unlike the seductions of hysterics, such later experiences, Freud thought, generated pleasure at the time—hence the endless self-reproaches of obsessional neurotics (*Origins*, pp. 146–55, 163–67). Finally, paranoia was to be correlated with an even later, but also prepubescent, seduction; it was, as he maintained, the neurosis least dependent upon either "infantile determinants" or childhood repressions, and hence a "defensive neurosis *par excellence*" (*Origins*, p. 165).

By mid-1896 this, then, was the state of Freud's thinking on the choice of neurosis. But notwithstanding his impressive discoveries, both clinical and theoretical, during the previous two and one-half years, his real psychoanalytic difficulties had only begun. Freud's second major, and lifelong, psychoanalytic problem will illuminate the precise reasons for this predicament.

PROBLEM TWO: WHY SEX?

As far as the clinical category of actual neurosis (neurasthenia and anxiety neurosis) was concerned, the all-important role of sexuality as a potentially neurotic toxin presented little further difficulty for Freud's theoretical formulations. He considered these various toxicological disorders as mirroring the more general physiological pattern exhibited by other well-known forms of somatic poisoning (*Origins*, p. 85; and Freud 1908*d*, *S.E.*, 9:185).

The psychoneuroses (hysteria, obsessional neurosis, hallucinatory psychosis, and paranoia) harbored, however, a major conceptual stumbling block not encountered in the actual neuroses. Why was it that *only* sexual matters, *and no others*, were able to provoke pathological defense and repression? By the time *Studies on Hysteria* was published in mid-1895, Freud had privately begun to feel uncomfortable about this whole matter. Despite his psychophysiological (economic) rationalization of the issue, he still felt that there must be a more inevitable and all-embracing scientific explanation of such an invariable etiological link. "It is quite impossible," he privately conceded in the early fall of 1895, "to suppose that distressing sexual affects so greatly exceed all other unpleasurable affects in intensity. It must be another characteristic of sexual ideas that can explain how it is that sexual ideas are alone subjected to [pathological] repression" (*S.E.*, 1:352; *Origins*, p. 409). After all, Freud knew full well that the greatest psychical unpleasure could be aroused by emotions like "remorse over bad actions"; but such alternative, nonsexual etiologies were simply never encountered, he adamantly insisted, in hysteria and other psychoneuroses.

The Theory of Deferred Action

With the formulation of the seduction theory, there came an apparent solution to this enigma. Known as the theory of "deferred action," it was first set forth in published form by Freud in two papers he finished almost simultaneously and sent off to different medical journals the same day—5 February 1896 (Freud 1896a and 1896b).[5]

According to Freud's new theory, childhood sexual seductions exerted a uniquely delayed psychophysical effect upon the human nervous system. Unlike other traumatic experiences, he argued, precocious sexual stimulation would normally have no psychopathological repercussions upon the nervous system at the time of its occurrence. He based this conclusion on the absence of a sexual instinct in infancy and early childhood and on the young child's psychical inability to comprehend the act of seduction. The *memory* of the event would nonetheless remain; and, with the arrival of puberty, this mnemic psychical trace, long since forgotten and relegated to the unconscious portion of the mind, would suddenly be reawakened. "Thanks to the [physiological] change due to puberty," Freud reasoned, "the memory will display a power which was completely lacking from the event itself. *The memory will operate as though it were a contemporary event*. What happens is, as it were, *a posthumous action by a sexual trauma*" (1896a, *S.E.*, 3:154; see also 1896b, *S.E.*, 3:166–67, n. 2). It was precisely this delayed physiological aspect of the overall process,

5. Both the seduction theory and the theory of deferred action made their first appearance in Freud's correspondence with Fliess four months earlier in connection with his famous *Project for a Scientific Psychology*. See *Origins*, pp. 413–14; and p. 126, letter of 8 October 1895.

he further insisted, that explained why traumatic seduction memories often become permanently, and pathologically, entrenched within the unconscious.

What is particularly worth underscoring about Freud's theory of deferred action is its outspoken denial of a sexual instinct in childhood. In October 1895, in a letter to his friend Fliess explaining the new theory, Freud plainly defined the term *presexual* as "before puberty, before the production of the sexual substance . . ." (*Origins*, p. 127).

How, then, did Freud account for the more active and aggressive childhood sexual experiences he reconstructed in analyses of his obsessional neurotics? Such cases, he confidently declared, always imply an even earlier experience in childhood of forcible seduction. Compelled by the memory, the victim—usually a male—attempts to repeat the experience with a girl of his own age.[6] "In view of this," Freud concluded, "I am inclined to suppose that children cannot find their way to acts of sexual aggression unless they have been seduced previously. The foundations for a neurosis would accordingly always be laid in childhood by adults . . ." (1896c, S.E., 3:208–9). And thus it was that adults—nursemaids, teachers, relatives, strangers, etc.—and, for female hysterics, mostly the father, came to assume an important role in Freud's theory of the psychoneuroses.

Indeed, so far did he go in his denial of spontaneous infantile sexuality in 1896 that he even thought childhood masturbation—the evidence for which was so frequently encountered in the anamneses of hysterics—to be a consequence of a prior seduction. Masturbation was *not*, he emphasized, an agent of hysteria (1896b, S.E., 3:165).

It was, of course, the inherent contradiction between Freud's assumptions about childhood sexual innocence and the actual facts of human psychosexual development that eventually invalidated his seduction hypothesis. But for the time being, his apparent solution to the inevitability of sex in psychoneurosis had the fruitful effect of turning his immediate attention to explaining pathological defense.

Problem Three: Pathological Defense (Repression)

Of Freud's three great psychoanalytic problems, the riddle of pathological defense (repression) was easily the most refractory and also the most critical to psychoanalytic theory as a whole. The reason for this special importance is not hard to find. Since the concept of repression formed the nucleus of his increasingly psychodynamic approach to the neuroses, a knowledge of the precise mechanisms ex-

6. Freud was specific in limiting the child's capacity for such perverse acts to the *later* years of childhood—after age four in males and after age eight in females (*Origins*, p. 149, Draft K, 1 January 1896; and p. 164, letter of 30 May 1896).

hibited in repression promised both the last and the clearest word on the other two problems. At the purely clinical level, Freud had already gone far toward obtaining a clearer understanding of the various mental processes in pathological repression. What continued to baffle him, as Ernest Jones (1953:280) points out, were its precise physiological mechanisms.

But why did Freud ever consider it necessary to formulate a physiological solution to the problem of repression? Before answering this question, we must first recognize that his search for a physiological solution was, from the very start, motivated by a much more specific enigma than that of repression as a whole. It was necessary, above all, to account for the difference between normal, everyday psychical defense against unpleasant or intolerable ideas and the clinically more elusive phenomenon of repression followed by complete amnesia concerning what has been repressed. Freud was happy to think in purely psychological terms about the former sort of repressions—for example, the intentional fending off and forgetting of unpleasant thoughts; and this is the self-assured, psychological side of Freud that one sees in his discussions of normal psychical defense in works like *The Interpretation of Dreams* and *The Psychopathology of Everyday Life*. But there was clearly something profoundly different about the latter and highly pathological form of repression; and it was *this difference* that Freud sought to account for in detailed physiological terms.

Finally, the fact that Freud had come to see the neuroses as a toxicological consequence of improperly utilized libido, itself obviously somatic and chemical in nature, made it axiomatic that whatever was capable of pathologically inhibiting such a quantity also had to be something quantitative—and hence physiological. Freud's theory of deferred action to childhood trauma had given him what he believed was a first, crude, and partly organic insight into the problem. Now he wanted to know the precise neurological and chemical details of the whole process. It was in his celebrated and controversial *Project for a Scientific Psychology* that he finally sought to achieve a comprehensive physiological explanation of how pathological repression differs from its normal counterpart.

THE *Project for a Scientific Psychology* (1895)

Just a month after completing his final chapter for *Studies on Hysteria*, Freud announced to Fliess that an ambitious new undertaking, which he described as a "Psychology for Neurologists," was bedeviling his scientific imagination. "I am so deep in the 'Psychology for Neurologists,'" he reported in a letter of 27 April 1895, "that it quite consumes me, until I have to break off out of sheer exhaustion. I have never been so intensely preoccupied by anything. And will anything come of it? I hope so, but the going is hard and slow" (*Origins*, p. 118). Throughout the summer of 1895, he continued to relay to Fliess intermittent reports of progress and frustration with his latest fascination. "Freud's intellect is soaring at its highest," Josef Breuer wrote to Fliess in July 1895. "I gaze after him as a hen at a hawk" (quoted in Jones 1953:242). It was not until early September, when Freud visited Berlin to solicit Fliess's advice on a number of unsolved problems in connection with the *Project*, that Freud became sufficiently confident about his latest venture to put pen and ink to paper. Reinforced by his friend's enthusiasm for the *Project*, Freud began writing out the whole business the minute he boarded the train back to Vienna. Within a month he had filled two notebooks totaling one hundred manuscript sheets (eighty-eight printed pages in the original German-language version). The two manuscript notebooks were dispatched to Fliess on 8 October 1895 for the latter's perusal and criticism. A third notebook, dealing with the "Psychopathology of Repression," was held back by Freud, who apparently found this last section considerably more problematical and slow-going than the material treated in the earlier notebooks.

The two surviving notebooks were published only posthumously, after having been discovered among Freud's letters to Fliess, and were given the German editor's title *Entwurf einer Psychologie* (Sketch of a Psychology). The work has since become known to English-speaking students of Freud's writings by the title James Strachey gave it: *Project for a Scientific Psychology*. Strachey has characterized it as an "extraordinarily ingenious working model of the mind as a piece of neurological machinery" (*S.E.*, 4:xvii). In its most immediate historical context, this document may be seen as Freud's own version of the "Theoretical" chapter that Josef Breuer had been assigned to write that same year for *Studies on Hysteria* (Stewart 1967:19). Once absorbed in the matter, Freud became increasingly ambitious. In May 1895, he explained his ultimate goals to Fliess:

> . . . a man like me cannot live without a hobby-horse, a consuming passion—in Schiller's words a tyrant. I have found my tyrant, and in his service I know no limits. My tyrant is psychology; it has always been my distant, beckoning goal and now, since I have hit on the neuroses, it has come so much the nearer. I am plagued with two ambitions: to see how the theory of mental functioning takes shape if quantitative considerations, a sort of economics of nerve-force, are introduced into it; and secondly, to extract from psychopathology what may be of benefit to normal psychology. Actually a satisfactory general theory of neuropsychotic disturbances is impossible if it cannot be brought into association with clear assumptions about normal mental processes. (*Origins*, pp. 119–20)

In both of these two aims—that of reducing the mental apparatus to the laws of psychophysics and that of uniting normal with abnormal psychology—Freud was undoubtedly inspired by the recent publication of a similar model of the mind devised by his former teacher Sigmund

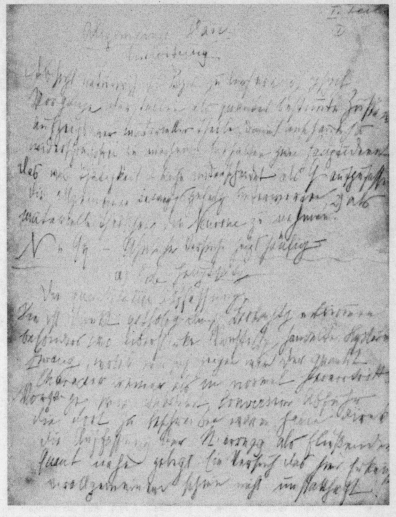

The first manuscript page of Freud's *Project*, written in pencil. The page bears the heading "General Scheme. Introduction."

Exner (1894). Entitled *Entwurf zu einer physiologischen Erklärung der psychischen Erscheinungen* (Sketch of a Physiological Explanation of Psychical Phenomena), Exner's work had attempted, like Freud's *Project*, to deal with the problems of perception, judgment, memory, ideation, and so forth through purely quantitative, physicalist constructs. Exner's model started from the notion of intracerebral excitation. Such excitation, he had argued, undergoes continual "summations" of energy within each neurone, and the energized neurones are discharged only after attaining critical firing "thresholds." At a more general level still, this neuronal model of mind was regulated by the physiological dictates of the pleasure-unpleasure principle. Exner's intracerebral excitation possessed the further capacity for what he called *Ausfahren von Bahnen* (a facilitation of the pattern of energy flow based upon the previous passage of energy through a given neuronal pathway). This last concept, crucial to Exner's whole scheme, was later adopted by Freud in the *Project* under the term *Bahnung* ("facilitation").[7] Freud's concept of "cathexis" (*Besetzung*), the occupying of a neurone by a quantity of energy, was in turn influenced by Exner's general model.

The surviving portion of the *Project* comprises three formal parts: a "General Scheme," setting forth the various introductory premises of the undertaking; a section on "Psychopathology"; and, lastly, an "Attempt to Represent Normal Psychical Processes." The *Project*'s fundamental physicalist orientation to mind is spelled out in the first sentence of the General Scheme: "The intention is to furnish a psychology that shall be a natural science: that is, to represent psychical processes as quantitatively determinate states of specifiable material particles, thus making those processes perspicuous and free from contradiction" (*S.E.*, *1*:295; *Origins*, p. 355).[8] Freud availed himself of two fundamental assumptions at the outset of this general undertaking: that what differentiates activity from rest is to be designated as a quantity (Q) "subject to the general laws of motion"; and that the "specifiable material particles" are none other than the neurones, themselves presumed to be physiologically distinct cellular entities interconnected by numerous *contact-barriers*.

Freud's most fundamental law of neurone activity is introduced in Part I of the *Project* as the principle of *neuronal inertia*, according to

7. As Peter Amacher (1965) has demonstrated, both Exner's *Entwurf* (1894) and Freud's *Project* exhibit close conceptual ties to the ideas of Freud's two former teachers Brücke and Meynert. Like Freud's other previous metapsychological efforts, the energetics of the *Project* owes much to the traditions of Herbart and Fechner (see Chapter 2; and Ellenberger 1970:479).

8. Although I have employed throughout this chapter a double referencing system for all *Project* citations (that is, to both the *Standard Edition* and *The Origins of Psycho-Analysis*), I have taken all quotations from the *Standard Edition* translation of this document. The *Standard Edition* translation is considerably revised and more accurate than that originally provided (also by James Strachey) for publication in the *Origins* some twenty years earlier. Strachey's more recent translation is accompanied by a much-expanded and historically valuable series of editorial commentaries—both on the *Project* itself and on its various conceptual ties with Freud's other published writings.

which it is the natural tendency of all neurones to divest themselves by reflex movement of all Q_η (or psychical quantity); whence also comes in Freud's overall *Project* scheme the biological basis of the sensory-(reception)/motor-(discharge) dichotomy in nervous functioning. This normal, inertial pattern of neuronal discharge, which Freud equates with an *experience of satisfaction*, is further termed the *primary function* of the nervous system. In contrast, the *secondary function* is said to be that which governs the organism's attempts to flee from all forms of excessive (undischargeable) stimulus. Such excessive stimuli represent the source of all pain in Freud's model.

He reasons that in the very simplest organisms the energy required for the secondary function, or flight, would be proportional to the Q of the painful outside stimulus, thus allowing primary and secondary functions to obey the general law of neuronal inertia. But matters are undoubtedly not so simple in organisms of higher complexity, where one has to take into account totally endogenous (somatic) sources of stimulus—principally those triggered by the needs of hunger, respiration, and sexuality. This advanced capacity for generating endogenous sources of stimulus, which presumably has evolved under external biological pressures or "the exigencies of life," thus is a biological compromise between the *ideal* form of the law of neuronal inertia and its expression in higher organic nature. At the same time, such endogenous cravings (hunger, respiration, sexuality) compel the organism to maintain within itself a constant source of reserve Q_η (the biological source for all spontaneous mobility) in order to cope with moments of periodic need. The law of neuronal inertia therefore becomes the law of *constancy of* Q_η in higher organisms.

To account for perception, memory, and consciousness in the *Project*, Freud found it necessary to postulate three separate systems of neurones: the ϕ (phi), the ψ (psi), and the ω (omega) systems. To each system Freud ascribes certain neurophysiological properties, such as permeability and impermeability, that accord with their assigned psychical functions. For example, mnemic (ψ) neurones, being initially impermeable at their contact-barriers, are said to become increasingly permeable with each passage of Q_η. This capacity for contact-barrier modification supplies Freud's psychical model with the physiological foundations of memory and higher cognition. Thus, by matching pleasurable and unpleasurable memories against current perceptions, Freud's $\phi\psi\omega$ model is said to be capable of reality testing and primitive judgment.

The *Project* is sufficiently complex that a summary of its contents cannot do it full justice. But a brief list of the topics treated by Freud will perhaps suffice to convey the ambitious nature of this undertaking. Wishing, hallucinatory states, various ego functions (including judgment, defense, cognition, expecting, remembering, observing, criticizing, and theorizing), the psychopathology of hysteria, and sleep and dreaming are all discussed in terms of his neurophysiological model. In this last context, the *Project* sets forth Freud's wish-fulfillment theory of dreams. Dreaming is energized by extremely small residues of $Q\dot{\eta}$ that are normally left over in the ψ-system during certain portions of the sleeping period. Most dreams fulfill wishes because secondary processes become relaxed during sleep, and $Q\dot{\eta}$, obeying the law of neuronal inertia, readily discharges itself along the highly facilitated pathways that mark previous experiences of satisfaction. Dreams, then, are essentially primary-process hallucinations.

The *Project*'s Place in Psychoanalytic History

No other document in the history of psychoanalysis has provoked such a large body of discussion with such a minimum of agreement as has Freud's *Project*. Nevertheless, in spite of what one chooses to say about it, it still deserves, and has tended to receive, its due in sheer intellectual respect. The *Project* has even prompted some students of Freud's ideas to make elaborate comparisons between it and more recent achievements in the kindred field of cybernetics.[9] Ernest Jones (1953:383–84) remarks that Freud's *Project* was nothing less than "a magnificent *tour de force*," simultaneously expressing in its "conservative" loyalties to neurophysiological reductionism and in its "freely imaginative" constructs what Jones himself sees as the two extreme poles of Freud's remarkable intellect.

At the very peak of his enthrallment with the *Project,* Freud was hardly able to contain himself with delight. "One strenuous night last week," he vaunted to Fliess on 20 October 1895, "when I was in the stage of painful discomfort in which my brain works best, the barriers suddenly lifted, the veils dropped, and it was possible to see from the details of neurosis all the way to the very conditioning of consciousness. Everything fell into place, the cogs meshed, and the thing really seemed to be a machine which in a moment would run of itself" (*Origins*, p. 129). Thereafter, Freud's interest in the whole undertaking alternately waxed and waned until, by the end of November, he was reporting to Fliess in a much more self-critical light, "I no longer understand the state of mind in which I concocted the psychology; I cannot conceive how I came to inflict it on you. . . . it seems to me to have been a kind of aberration" (*Origins*, p. 134).

One last attempt to revise his model of the mind occupies part of a letter to Fliess written on 1 January 1896. With the arrival of the new year, Freud's principal concerns turned once again to the more concrete plane of his clinical work and to his many still-unsolved problems in psychopathology. And he soon altogether abandoned the *Project* itself. As Jones (1953:381) observes, Freud never even requested the

9. Specifically, comparisons have been made to the electronic models of brain functioning developed by Donald Hebb, Karl Lashley, Norbert Wiener, and others; see Jones 1953:393; Pribram 1962, 1965; and Pribram and Gill 1976.

return of the two notebooks that had cost him so much mental effort; and so it was that these notebooks only became known to the world two decades after Fliess's death and a full decade after Freud's own.

Therein would seem to lie the lion's share of the *Project*'s highly controversial nature. For much of this controversy, if we overlook for a moment the undeniable complexities of the *Project* itself, derives from this document's having only become available to students of Freud's theories some fifty-five years after he drafted it and half a century after the publication of his first major psychoanalytic work, *The Interpretation of Dreams* (1900*a*). Thus, in 1950, a long-established view of Freud's intellectual development was suddenly confronted by a largely unanticipated chapter in the history of psychoanalysis. For there, in the neuroanatomical language of the *Project,* as in the later *Interpretation of Dreams,* are the concepts of primary and secondary processes; the principles of pleasure-unpleasure, constancy, and reality testing; the concept of cathexis; the theories of psychical regression and hallucination; the systems of perception, memory, unconscious and preconscious psychic activity; and even Freud's wish-fulfillment theory of dreams.

Not unexpectedly, the more traditional contingent of psychoanalytic historians has tended to see the *Project* as the last remnant of Freud's "need to neurologize" and has placed much weight upon his never having asked for the return of the manuscript that had cost him so much time and mental anguish. Ernest Jones (1953:381) speaks of Freud as having been "relieved of an oppressive burden" when he finally dispatched the surviving portions of the *Project* to Fliess. Similarly, James Strachey, who has referred to the *Project* as essentially "a torso, disavowed by its creator" (*S.E.,* 1:293), has contrasted its overwhelmingly mechanistic and "pre-id" scientific concerns with Freud's later and far more psychodynamic writings: "Internal forces are scarcely more than secondary reactions to external ones [in the *Project*]. The id, in fact, is still to be discovered" (*S.E.,* 1:291–92).[10]

Only recently have scholars taken account of the various conceptual *continuities* that this controversial document indicates about Freud's intellectual development. Kanzer (1973:102) takes this newer approach when he calls the *Project* "a fountain of Freudian thought"— as does Wollheim (1971:59), who speaks confidently of the "powerful and probably incalculable influence" that the *Project* exerted over all Freud's later ideas. Indeed, Wollheim even goes so far as to insist that most of Freud's greatest work was achieved in the *Project*'s conceptual "shadow."

Perhaps the most ardent spokesman for the cause of historical and especially neurophysiological continuity in Freud's life is Robert Holt. As I noted in Chapter 1, Holt (1965*a*:94) has repeatedly insisted that

10. Kris (1954:27, 350–51), Erikson (1955), Suzanne Bernfeld (1955), and Brierley (1967) are all in essential agreement with Jones and Strachey in concluding that Freud did not allow the *Project* to languish without extremely good psychoanalytic cause.

many of the most important and often seemingly arbitrary aspects of psychoanalytic theory have their origins in "hidden biological assumptions" derived from Freud's prepsychoanalytic career. According to Holt, Freud's apparently psychological description of the psychical apparatus in the famous seventh chapter of *The Interpretation of Dreams* (1900a) was no more than a "convenient fiction"—one that "had the paradoxical effect of *preserving* these [biological] assumptions by hiding their original nature, and by transferring the operations of the apparatus into a conceptual realm where they were insulated from correction by progress in neurophysiology and brain anatomy" (1968a:208). Peter Amacher (1965) concurs with this judgment; and it is upon his careful historical documentation of the *Project*'s various intellectual roots that Robert Holt has based his own historical claims.

It would nevertheless be a mistake to conclude that such emphasis upon the historical theme of continuity, which has generally been advanced by younger and seemingly less partisan spokesmen for Freud, has by any means won the day in recent discussion of the *Project*'s place in psychoanalytic history. For example, Paul Cranefield (1970b:54), who, as a seasoned historian of nineteenth-century physiology and as a physiologist by profession, might well be expected to support the revisionist position of Holt et al., nevertheless speaks clearly for the opposite camp when he refers to the *Project*'s "temporary baneful effect" upon those historians who have seen this document as part of the "main line" in Freud's psychoanalytic thought. To confuse matters more, when one carefully rereads the writings of previous Freud scholars on this issue, it becomes almost impossible to find anyone—even those members of the psychoanalytic movement's old guard, like Ernest Jones or Ernst Kris—who would deny the historical judgment of the always perspicacious Strachey when he concedes that "the *Project*, or rather its invisible ghost, haunts the whole series of Freud's theoretical writings to the very end" (*S.E.*, 1:290).

Precisely what, then, has all the fuss been about? The answer is that it makes a considerable difference exactly how one interprets the relevance of this *Project* "ghost" for psychoanalysis *as we now know it.* Did Freud, as Jones (1953:395) and Kris (1954:47) argue, simply retain old-fashioned neurological terms (e.g., "cathexis") while giving them a new and independent psychoanalytic meaning in *The Interpretation of Dreams* (1900a) and subsequent works? Or, are the outmoded nineteenth-century neurological constructs so evident in the *Project* still holding up the creaking scaffolding of present-day psychoanalysis, as Robert Holt insists, and has their cryptic nature insulated psychoanalysis from a much-needed rejuvenation within the fertile field of neurophysiology where it originated?

Two Widespread Misconceptions about the Project

Given the quasi-political cast to this debate over the *Project*—in which the true believers of psychoanalysis, a "soft" science, are apparently divided from the tough-minded champions of a "hard" science approach to mind—it is not so surprising that a number of basic misconceptions about the *Project* have arisen over the years. In pinpointing the following two prevalent misconceptions, I endorse the helpful lead of Kanzer (1973), with whose more specific views on the *Project* itself I am not altogether in agreement.

Both of the erroneous conceptions to which Kanzer has drawn attention underscore the largely typological manner in which the *Project* has so often been viewed in debates over its proper place in psychoanalytic history. According to the first of these two misunderstandings, the *Project* represents Freud's "last desperate effort to cling to the safety of cerebral anatomy" and is therefore a conceptual hangover from his earlier neurological education within the famous Helmholtz school of medicine (Jones 1953:384). Complementing this first misunderstanding is the second, namely, that Freud abandoned the *Project* as an abject failure shortly after having written it. As I have already discussed the specific Helmholtz school aspect of these two claims, stressing its several implicit fallacies (Chapter 2), here I shall address the view that the *Project* was only a "neurological" document.

In fact, much of the *Project*, if not its bulk, was only ostensibly a neurological document. For the various properties of Freud's neuroanatomical model were defined not so much by the findings of current neurological science as by his previous clinical and abstract metapsychological insights. Freud was convinced that psychology must have a physical basis, and he logically hoped that psychological laws might turn out to exhibit many of the same fundamental principles as the neurophysiological events upon which they are causally dependent (Wollheim 1971:34). Thus many of the neuropsychological constructs in the *Project* were already implicit in the earlier, and more abstract, theory of mind developed with Josef Breuer in *Studies on Hysteria* (1895d)—and later appeared in *The Interpretation of Dreams* (1900a). The most notable of these constructs included (1) a necessary difference between the systems of memory and perception, (2) the mechanisms of hallucination and regression, (3) the principles of pleasure and constancy, and (4) the fundamental Freudian contrast between primary and secondary processes. Freud later credited this last insight, although perhaps a bit too generously, to Josef Breuer's distinction in *Studies on Hysteria* (1895d) between cerebral excitation in states of waking and sleeping. (See Freud 1915e, *S.E.*, *14*:188; 1920g, *S.E.*, *18*:26–27; and Holt 1962.)

So, too, many of the fruitful derivatives of Freud's *Project* attempt at neurophysiological reductionism had lasting *psychological* implications. Walter Stewart (1967:29), who joins me in rejecting the "need to neurologize" theme in Freud scholarship, has also emphasized that the *Project*, with its highly concrete neuroanatomical images, must have exerted a powerfully heuristic effect upon Freud's overall psychological thinking. And, indeed, one must not forget that Freud first wrote about such fundamental notions as reality testing and the wish-fulfillment meaning of dreams within the *Project* itself. Even Ernest Jones (1953:354), in commenting upon the second of these psychoanalytic innovations, admits that Freud had come upon the meaning of dreams more from an a priori physicalist than from a purely empirical point of view (see also Amacher 1965:74).

I must therefore wholly endorse the judicious opinion of James Strachey that most of the ideas Freud advanced in the *Project* were "constructed with more than half an eye to psychological events" (*S.E.*, 3:64). On the other hand, I do not go so far as Kanzer's argument that the neurophysiological constructs of the *Project* were nothing but "clinical" and "psychological" generalizations (1973:91). It is clear that the *Project* also made abundant use of contemporary neurological concepts, most notably those of neuronal contact-barriers (for which Sherrington introduced the term "synapse" in 1897), *Bahnung* (or the process of facilitation between neurones), and the complementary principles of energy summation and neuronal firing thresholds. Kanzer's attempt to reduce Freud's *Project* metapsychology to purely clinical inductions is, to me, patently unconvincing and only seems to substitute one unfortunate historical extreme for another.

One last point about the *Project*—a point to which only James Strachey (*S.E.*, 1:305, n. 3) has given much historical notice—should also be emphasized here. This work contains not one but two distinctly different biological models—a neurophysiological or "mechanical" one, as Freud sometimes called it, and an organismic, evolutionary, or "biological" one. Thus, in seeking to legitimate his hypothetical distinction between ϕ (or perceptual) and ψ (or psychical-mnemic) neurones, Freud had momentarily considered what he termed "a Darwinian line of thought" before ultimately settling upon a mechanical solution to that problem (*S.E.*, 1:303; *Origins*, p. 365). In the process, he had briefly recognized the possibility of a more phylogenetic-historical justification for these two neuronal systems—namely, that no higher organism could survive and compete in the struggle for existence without first evolving the permeable/impermeable functional distinction he had proposed.

Similarly, when Freud found himself unable to explain certain other psychological phenomena in purely mechanical terms, he again appealed to more organismic, phylogenetic, or "biological" rules, as he called them. He formally enunciated two such rules, those of *attention* and *primary defense*, when his mechanical paradigm proved insufficient to master the psychological problems of intentionality and foresight. So it transpired that, when necessary, Freud was able to renounce in the *Project* the concepts of a reductionist physiologist in favor of concepts proper to an organismic and evolutionary biologist. The importance of this conceptual step cannot be overestimated. For it was Freud's two biological rules, which he believed to be "biologically justified" and "left over in the course of psychical evolution," that had finally allowed him to envision an impressively self-governing model of the mind. "Taught biologically" by previous, inherited experiences, the hypothetical organism in Freud's *Project* was enabled by these organismic and evolutionary principles to make ever higher "biological acquisitions" in its nervous system (*S.E.*, 1:322, 361, 370; *Origins*, pp. 383–84, 417, 428). In this way, and in this way alone, Freud's *Project* model of mind was made applicable to more than just amoebalike behavior. Thus in the *Project*, his two biological models—the purely mechanical and the organismic-evolutionary—were at times decided rivals for his supposedly "neurological" loyalties.

To conclude, the *Project* is neither a purely neurological document nor a projection of wholly psychological insights onto imagined neuro-anatomical structures; rather, it combines clinical insights and data, Freud's most fundamental psychophysicalist assumptions, certain undeniably mechanical and neuroanatomical constructs, and a number of organismic, evolutionary, and biological ideas—all into one remarkably well-integrated psychobiological system.

I pass now to the second common misconception about Freud's *Project*, namely, that this document was "disavowed by its creator" shortly after being written (Strachey, *S.E.*, 1:293; and Jones 1953:381–83). True, Freud himself termed it "a kind of aberration" in his 29 November 1895 letter to Fliess. Yet from a 1 January 1896 letter to Fliess, we know that he was at work upon major revisions of the *Project*; and he was presumably reworking at least part of the *Project* model still further when, four months later, he reported that he was getting "a higher and higher opinion of the chemical neurone theory" (*Origins*, p. 162).

What, then, if anything, did Freud abandon? Why did he exhibit such ambivalence toward the *Project*? And why did he continue to work upon it even after he had ostensibly disowned it? To answer these questions, it is necessary to emphasize once again that the *Project* consisted of a mosaic of ideas, approaches, and highly ambitious scientific goals, some of which Freud continued to uphold and some of which he did not. Above all, his initial motives for undertaking the *Project* hold the key to each of these questions.

First of all, Freud's reasons for undertaking the *Project* included the two high ambitions announced to Fliess in May 1895: to bridge the existing conceptual gap between normal and pathological mental functioning, and to reduce the general laws of mind to purely mechanical-physiological considerations. Freud also had a third and more modest reason—that is, his desire to come to neurophysiological terms with his most crucial and still-unsolved psychoanalytic problem, the secret of pathological defense (repression). Of these three motives, I submit that the third and last holds the principal solution to the various enigmas that cluster around this controversial document.

Pathological Repression: The "Core of the Riddle"

The evidence for the preceding assertion is so remarkably straight-forward that it is difficult to understand how it could be so consistently overlooked in Freud scholarship. For it was invariably the problem of defense, and particularly that of pathological repression, that formed the focal point for all of Freud's personal evaluations of the whole. In a letter of 6 August 1895, written in the midst of the *Project*'s conceptual germination, he was ecstatic over the thought that he had finally solved this, his most elusive, psychoanalytic problem. But only ten days later he was compelled to announce to Fliess that his previous rejoicing had been premature, and that he had for the time being thrown the whole of the $\phi\psi\omega$ model aside in general despair: "This psychology is really an incubus. . . . *All I was trying to do was to explain defence*, but I found myself explaining something from the very heart of nature. I found myself wrestling with the problems of quality, sleep, memory —in short, the whole of psychology. Now I want to hear no more of it" (*Origins*, p. 123; italics added). His intellectual fortitude revived once more, Freud nevertheless continued in the actual writing of the *Project* to reckon the general problems of defense and repression as the real "core of the riddle" (*S.E.*, *1*:352; *Origins*, p. 410).

Freud's unrelenting difficulties with the problems of defense and pathological repression in the *Project* bring up the important but far too little emphasized fact that he never finished this work. Furthermore, it was its most critical part—"The Psychopathology of Repression" in the third, and now lost, notebook—that he failed to complete to his personal satisfaction and thus withheld from Fliess. Indeed, on 8 October 1895, the day Freud sent off the first two *Project* notebooks to Fliess, he made it clear that this third notebook really contained the key to the entire scheme:

> From that point [completion of the first two notebooks] I had to start from scratch again, and I have been alternately proud and happy and abashed and miserable, until now, after an excess of mental torment, I just apathetically tell myself that it does not hang together yet and perhaps never will. What does not hang together yet is not the [more general psychological] mechanism—I could be patient about that—but the [mechanical] explanation of repression, clinical knowledge of which has incidentally made great strides. . . . But the mechanical explanation is not coming off, and I am inclined to listen to the still, small voice which tells me that my explanation will not do. (*Origins*, p. 126)

Thus, it was not so much that Freud abandoned what he had already written in the *Project* (and what has therefore been preserved among the Fliess papers for us to read) as that he abandoned what he was still struggling to write. And, therefore, this *missing* portion, not the parts we have, holds the real key to assessing the *Project*'s place in psychoanalytic history.[11]

11. While this point, based as it partly is upon Freud's own testimony, may not seem in need of much additional emphasis, it is nevertheless a fact that Freud scholars have generally persisted in treating the *Project* as if it were a completed document. Otherwise, such scholars would wonder far less about the "uncomfortable divorce" that supposedly exists between the clinical and the theoretical aspects of this document—e.g., Jones 1953:384; and Strachey, *S.E.*, *1*:291. For clearly a main

Precisely what, then, were the difficulties that prompted Freud's extreme disgruntlement about his attempts to devise a purely mechanical theory of defense and repression? The principal difficulty that he had encountered in the *Project* itself (others cropped up in the *Project's* immediate wake) was to provide a mechanical explanation for defense against unpleasure without having to assume the existence of an "observing" ego. Freud's *Project* theory of defense had taken its starting point from what he termed his "puzzling but indispensable" hypothesis of *key* neurones. Supposing a in Figure 4.4 to be a hostile memory image and b to be its associated key neurone storing a chemical measure of unpleasure, Freud had envisioned a defensive inhibition (or lateral cathexis) by the ego stemming from a, β, γ, and δ to divert the normal flow of $Q\dot\eta$ away from key neurone b and into other more friendly mnemic images. Hence, b has been repressed.

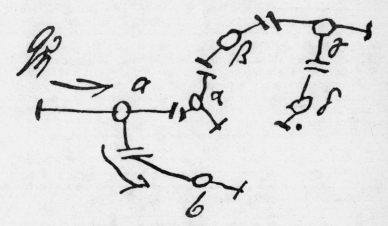

Fig. 4.4. Freud's schematic representation of primary defense (repression). (From *S.E.*, *1*:324, and *Origins*, p. 385.)

Unfortunately such a scheme required that Freud postulate yet another hypothetical mechanism, that of *attention*, which somehow was supposed to forewarn the "mechanical" ego of each imminent fresh cathexis of a hostile memory trace. In addition, *biological experience* (apparently innate) was presumed to assist such primary defenses. Freud termed these two indispensable principles his biological rules of

goal of this missing portion of the *Project* was to bridge this uncomfortable gap, as Freud had earlier sought to do, briefly, in the "Psychopathology" section. So, too, this missing portion holds a major key to the puzzle of why Freud never asked Wilhelm Fliess to return the *Project*. Having failed to complete this work to his own satisfaction, Freud apparently had no further use for the more introductory parts which Fliess continued to hold with Freud's other drafts and letters while waiting for the final, but never completed, installment.

attention and primary defense, and he was unable to reduce them further in the *Project*, except to say that they were a necessary evolutionary acquisition (*S.E.*, *1*:371; *Origins*, p. 429).

As Freud well knew, his rules of attention and primary defense amounted to little more than the ad hoc postulation of precisely those psychical capabilities that he, in the spring of 1895, had originally set out to explain in purely mechanical terms. "How *primary defence*, [that is,] non-cathexis owing to a threat of unpleasure, is to be represented mechanically—this, I confess, I am unable to say," Freud had frankly admitted toward the end of the *Project* (*S.E.*, *1*:370; *Origins*, p. 428). "From this point onwards," he therefore declared in the midst of Part III, "I shall venture to leave unanswered the question of finding a mechanical representation of biological rules such as this; I shall be content if henceforth I am able to remain faithful to a clearly demonstrable course of development" (*S.E.*, *1*:370–71; *Origins*, p. 428).

Again, what did Freud really abandon after completing the first three parts of the *Project*? The best answer is that he abandoned one reductionistic goal in science—a mechanical-physiological one—and, without being fully happy about it, adopted another, and more evolutionary one, in its stead.[12] In brief, he abandoned his previous belief that he could come to terms with both defense and pathological repression in purely mechanical terms. "Perhaps in the end," he glumly acknowledged to Fliess two months after sending off the surviving portions of the *Project*, "I may have to learn to content myself with the clinical explanation of the neuroses" (*Origins*, p. 137).

Freud did not abandon the hope, however, that his psychoanalytic ideas would someday find a firmer basis in neurophysiology (Holt 1965*a*:101). As he himself later insisted in *Beyond the Pleasure Principle*, "The deficiencies in our description [of the mind] would probably vanish if we were already in a position to replace the psychological terms by physiological or chemical ones" (1920*g*, *S.E.*, *18*:60).[13]

Reconstruction of the Missing Part IV:
"The Psychopathology of Repression"

Thus far I have dealt with the problem of defense in the *Project* in its simplest and most abstract form—that of primary defense against unpleasure. Although primary defense was problem enough for Freud, it was the far more baffling one of pathological repression that he, as a clinician, had really hoped to resolve in the *Project*. One would

12. The "Summary and Conclusion" of this chapter, as well as Part Two of this book, will deal further with the importance of such a shift in reductionist strategy for Freud's subsequent psychoanalytic thinking.

13. It is instructive that just four pages after making the oft-quoted statement in the seventh chapter of *The Interpretation of Dreams* that "I shall remain upon psychological ground" (1900*a*, *S.E.*, 5:536), Freud nevertheless went on to mention how extremely helpful it would be to have a neurophysiological grasp of a certain psychological point that was still perplexing him; that point was his hypothetical distinction between the functional properties of the more impermeable memory and permeable perceptual systems.

therefore like to know just what clinical aspects of the repression enigma confronted him at this time.

In spite of the loss of the last and unfinished portion of the *Project,* it is possible to reconstruct these conceptual difficulties from what Freud wrote about them in the six months or so after the work itself formally came to a standstill. Two of these difficulties stand out from all the others: the "reversal of affect" associated with certain premature and originally pleasurable childhood sexual experiences, and the disconcertingly high degree of variability in the aftereffects of such premature sexual experiences.

I shall consider first the reversal of affect. As originally set forth in the *Project,* in his subsequent letters to Fliess, and in three papers published during 1896, Freud's seduction theory had addressed itself to apparent instances of sexual "assault," "shock," and "unpleasure" that each of his psychoneurotic patients had experienced in childhood. He spoke of "all the abuses known to debauched and impotent persons," including perverted abuse of the buccal and rectal cavities, as being among the highly traumatic features of these assaults (*Origins,* pp. 126–27; see also Freud 1896c, S.E., 3:214). In other cases of childhood seduction, Freud believed that no affect—pleasurable or unpleasurable— was experienced in infancy. In such cases it was the chemical changes of puberty, and hence the deferred action of the seduction, that called forth all of the traumatic unpleasure associated with the original sexual assault (Freud 1896a, S.E., 3:154).

This line of reasoning was all well and good for the theory of hysteria. Unfortunately for Freud, his clinical distinction between the passive and generally unpleasurable childhood assaults associated with the etiology of hysteria and the much later, active, and apparently pleasurable experiences in the clinical histories of his obsessional neurotics created a major difficulty for the theory of repression. Any satisfactory theory of pathological repression must explain both the mechanism of repression and its motive. For painful or even non-affect-producing sexual assaults in childhood, the theory of deferred action seemed to encompass both aspects of the problem. But what was the motive for the subsequent repression of the active and originally pleasurable sexual experiences that supposedly underlay obsessional neurosis?

Freud's purely psychological answer to this question was that guilt, arising by deferred action of these pleasurable sexual experiences, is the motive for later repression (*Origins,* p. 127). But he also wondered why it was not equally possible for deferred action to cause a diametrically opposite state of affairs. Why, that is, did deferred action not foster a compulsive need for repeating the originally pleasurable sexual experience, giving rise, with the arrival of puberty, to a hypersexual, immoral, and perhaps even perverse sexual disposition? [14] Freud had realized this inherent contradiction in his theory by 1 January 1896, when he composed Draft K of the Fliess correspon-

14. Childhood seduction was a widely accepted explanation at the time for most forms of sexual perversion; see Chapter 8.

dence; for in it he asked, "How does it come about that analogous conditions sometimes give rise to perversion or simple immorality instead of to neurosis?" (*Origins*, p. 147). Freud, in short, was stumped by this particular riddle. And it made the unsolved problem of the mechanical repression of unpleasure look trivial by comparison, for he at least understood the motive for repression of unpleasurable memories.

Freud's triumphant sense of discovery upon announcing his seduction theory in October 1895 was soon transformed into a cautious and self-critical assessment of the idea. "I have started doubting the pleasure-pain explanation of hysteria and obsessional neurosis which I announced with so much enthusiasm," he wrote to Fliess late in October, only three weeks after that announcement. "Unquestionably those are the essential factors," he added. "But I have not yet put the pieces of the puzzle in the right place" (*Origins*, p. 131).

Undaunted by his theoretical setback, Freud continued to generate interesting speculations about the reversal of affect. One simple way around this dilemma, he proposed in January 1896, was to place more emphasis upon the previous and unpleasurable seduction in each of his obsessional neurotic's clinical histories. Such prior seductions would then be the cause of all the later repressions (*Origins*, p. 149, Draft K). Unfortunately this idea created yet another puzzle. For what was the motive for the obsessional neurotic's active initiation of a later and pleasurable childhood sexual liaison if his only previous sexual associations were purely painful? Freud's tentative answer was to assume that the first sexual experience had probably been *very early*; but he did not find this idea wholly convincing, since he indicates in the same draft that perhaps the whole problem of reversal of affect will have to be accounted for by a more general theory of human sexuality (*Origins*, pp. 148–49). It was, in fact, this last hypothesis that not only solved the reversal-of-affect problem just eleven months later but also led him to recognize the truly dynamic and infantile source of man's unconscious.

The variability in aftereffects of premature sexual experience—Freud's other post-*Project* enigma—was an offshoot of the reversal-of-affect problem. For Freud had begun to learn, in part from his skeptical medical colleagues, that many people who are *not* neurotic can recall traumatic instances of having been sexually abused as children. He forthrightly acknowledged this discrepant finding in a 21 April 1896 lecture ("The Aetiology of Hysteria") he delivered before the Verein für Psychiatrie und Neurologie (Society for Psychiatry and Neurology), where he also presented his counterargument that all those healthy individuals who could recall such traumas were not neurotic precisely because they had *conscious* access to their unpleasant childhood experiences. "But what decides," he further confessed in this lecture, "whether those experiences produce conscious or unconscious memories—whether that is conditioned by the content of the experiences, or by the time at which they occur, or by later influences—that is a fresh problem, which we shall prudently avoid." The general mechanism of deferred action, he frankly conceded in his talk, was in need of further illumination on this and related points (1896c, *S.E.*, 3:211–13).

Just a few days after this lecture, Freud dryly reported to his friend Fliess that "the donkeys gave it an icy reception," and he added that the great psychiatrist Richard von Krafft-Ebing, who had been in the chair, had declared that the seduction theory "sounds like a scientific fairy tale" (unpublished Fliess correspondence, quoted in *S.E.*, 3:189, and Schur 1972:104). It took Freud another year and a half before he, too, finally reached the same conclusion about his theory.

Although Freud declined, as I have said, to speculate in public on the reason for such variability in the aftereffects of childhood seductions, he had not kept silent on this issue in his private correspondence with Wilhelm Fliess. Freud had done his best to overcome this problem in his earlier Draft K of 1 January 1896,[15] in which he entertained the thought that both sexual and social-class differences might possibly underlie variability of outcome:

> We shall be plunged deep into the riddles of psychology if we enquire into the origin of the unpleasure which is released by premature sexual stimulation and without which the occurrence of a repression cannot be explained. The most plausible answer will recall the fact that shame and morality are the repressing forces and that the neighbourhood in which nature has placed the sexual organs must inevitably arouse disgust at the same time as sexual experiences. Where there is no shame (as in male persons) or no morality (as in the lower classes of society), there too, infantile sexual stimulation will not lead to repression nor, consequently, to neurosis. (*Origins*, p. 147)

Yet as Freud also realized, libido was all too accustomed to overriding such minor psychological aversions to the ano-genital region during normal, adult sexual activity. Besides, had it not been among *working-class* men, he recalled in this same context (1896c, *S.E.*, 3:210), that his teacher Charcot had found the bulk of his male hysterics? Freud was therefore inclined to look to as yet undetermined "deeper links" to resolve the mysterious theoretical relationship between sexuality and pathological repression. "So long as we have no correct theory of the sexual process," he concluded in Draft K, "the problem of the origin of the unpleasure operating in repression will remain unsolved" (*Origins*, p. 148).

All these concerns of Freud's led to endless discussion and further speculation in his subsequent correspondence with Fliess. The victim's age at the time of the seduction, the age at which the repression occurs, whether the event has been laid down as a verbal or a visual memory, the maturity of the cognitive and perceptual apparatuses at the time of the sexual experience, the precise nature of the sexual experience, the number of repetitions of such experiences—Freud tossed

15. In the light of Krafft-Ebing's sarcastic remark about Freud's seduction theory the following April, it is amusing that Freud himself gave this January draft, entitled "The Neuroses of Defence," the subtitle "A Christmas Fairy Tale."

around all these possibilities and others until he had exhausted virtually every conceivable alternative. It was to Fliess ultimately that Freud, in candid desperation, increasingly looked for help in attempting to solve the problem of pathological repression in biological terms. "I am in a rather gloomy state," Freud wrote to his friend on 30 June 1896, nine months after drafting the *Project for a Scientific Psychology,* "and all I can say is that I am looking forward to our [next] congress. . . . I have run into some doubts about my repression theory which a suggestion from you . . . may resolve. Anxiety, chemical factors, etc.—perhaps you may supply me with solid ground on which I shall be able to give up explaining things psychologically and start finding a firm basis in physiology!" (*Origins,* p. 169).

SUMMARY AND CONCLUSION

I believe that the *Project,* and particularly Freud's ambivalent attitude toward it, are best understood in relation to the three psychoanalytic problems—the choice of neurosis, the importance of sex, and the mechanism of pathological repression—that dominated his clinical attention at the time he was engaged in drafting this document. And it is the problem of pathological repression that proves most relevant of all to understanding the *Project*'s place in psychoanalytic history.

As for the *Project* itself, it is a multifaceted work reflecting far more than the reductionist manifesto that ostensibly proclaimed its guiding rationale. In particular, it is important to remember:

1. That it is both a psychological and a neurological document and was consequently, like all of Freud's previous theorizing about the mental apparatus, written in a sophisticated dualist spirit. Freud formulated his various physicalist constructs "with more than half an eye to psychological events" (Strachey, *S.E.,* 3:64), while much of the *Project*'s supposedly neurological cast was indeed little more than a projection of previously formulated psychophysicalist constructs onto hypothetical neurophysiological structures. Hence it follows that much of the continuity between the *Project* and Freud's later theory of the mind stems just as naturally and inevitably from these constructs as from anything unique to the ostensible neuroanatomy of the document itself.

2. That it exerted a considerable heuristic effect upon Freud's thinking independently of its neuroanatomical validity and inspired new psychological constructs that were to retain a permanent role in psychoanalytic theory: among them, reality testing, the formal distinction between primary and secondary processes, and the wish-fulfillment theory of dreams.

3. That Freud by no means immediately abandoned the *Project* but continued to grapple with the problems of defense and pathological re-

pression in his never-completed Part IV, "The Psychopathology of Repression."

4. That in the course of writing the *Project*, Freud did abandon his initial dream of devising a neurophysiological, and hence *purely mechanical*, theory of defense (repression). Inasmuch as this ambition was Freud's most immediate and practical concern in the *Project*, his long-range goal of developing a truly mechanical model of the entire psychical apparatus soon began to strike even him as "a kind of aberration" (*Origins*, p. 134). Still, he never abandoned the assumption that psychoanalysis would someday come to terms with the neurophysiological side of mental activity.

5. And finally, that the *Project* endorsed two quite different biological models—a "mechanical" one and a more organismic, evolutionary, and "biological" one. It is often assumed, erroneously, that there is only one form of reductionism in science—to the laws of physics and chemistry. But in certain sciences, particularly the life sciences, there are two major forms of reductionism—physical-chemical and historical-evolutionary; each supplements the other and explains attributes of living organisms that the other cannot (Mayr 1961). As far as Freud's intellectual development is concerned, the full significance of this methodological observation lies in the differential historical fates that each of these biological models had in the *Project*'s wake, as I shall explain in Part Two. It is sufficient to note here that Freud's incipient *Project* goals shared the typical prejudice of "hard" sciences that physical-chemical reductionism is the only "good" form of reductionism. Then, in writing the *Project*, and especially in his attempts to solve the specific problems of defense and repression, he found it necessary to renounce this physicalist-reductionist prejudice in favor of organic and evolutionary explanations. Thus, while not a "main-line" document, as Cranefield (1970b:54) rightly insists, the *Project* nevertheless contains the (at first) reluctant biogenetic seed of Freud's later and far more enthusiastic endorsement of the *developmental* point of view in psychoanalysis.

PART TWO

PSYCHOANALYSIS: THE BIRTH OF A GENETIC PSYCHOBIOLOGY

5

Wilhelm Fliess
and the Mathematics of
Human Sexual Biology

WILHELM FLIESS: THE MAN AND HIS SCIENTIFIC IDEAS

Who was this Wilhelm Fliess, who claimed so much of Freud's intellectual confidence and respect during the years of the latter's most fundamental psychoanalytic discoveries?

At the time of their first encounter in 1887, Wilhelm Fliess (1858–1928) was a Berlin nose-and-throat specialist. In the fall of that year, Fliess came to Vienna to undertake some postgraduate studies, and Josef Breuer, an acquaintance of his, suggested he attend Freud's lectures on neurology. Freud and Fliess soon became fast friends, given their mutual admiration for each other's scientific talents. Indeed, no other friendship in Freud's lifetime was to become so close as this one. A correspondence between the two began shortly after their first meeting, and by 1892 the formal *Sie* ("you") in their letters had given way to the informal *Du*.

According to Ernst Kris, who married Fliess's psychoanalyst niece Marianne Rie and who later wrote the extensive review of Fliess's life and scientific ideas to accompany the publication of Freud's letters to him, everyone who ever knew Wilhelm Fliess found him a man of highly impressive personality and intellect. Besides being well read in virtually the entire field of medicine, he is said to have possessed a comprehensive and imaginative grasp of current biological knowledge. To these qualities may be added his fondness for far-reaching speculation and a dogmatic infatuation with his own scientific ideas (Kris 1954:4).

Sigmund Freud
and Wilhelm Fliess
(*right*) in the
summer of 1890.

Although Freud's formal association with Fliess spanned the fifteen
years from 1887 to 1902, their closest and most intimate contact encompassed only a third of this period, beginning just as Freud's scientific relationship with Breuer was drawing to a close in late 1894 and
ending, at least as far as their mutual exchange of scientific ideas was
concerned, in the summer of 1900. It was then that Fliess, who apparently felt his own scientific work was not being given sufficient attention in their intellectual partnership, decided to withdraw from the
association. During their more intimate period, the two men not only
corresponded frequently (Freud's letters and postcards to Fliess averaged
one every ten days), but they also exchanged numerous and sometimes
lengthy manuscript drafts detailing, among other matters, clinical points of interest from their respective medical practices, preliminary versions of their forthcoming scientific publications, and, of
course, constant news about their latest scientific findings. Freud, for
his own part, would sometimes ask for the return of these prepublica-
tion sketches; but many such drafts, written as informal progress reports on the problems facing him in his psychoanalytic work, were later
found among his letters to Fliess when this correspondence came to be
edited for publication in the late 1940s.

The story of the survival of Freud's letters and drafts to Fliess constitutes a dramatic and curious historical episode in its own right.
Sometime after Fliess's death in 1928, his widow sold Freud's side of the

correspondence to a Berlin bookseller, Reinhold Stahl, under the strict agreement that these letters were not to be offered for resale to Freud himself. Frau Fliess surmised, correctly as it turned out, that Freud would wish to destroy them. After the Nazis came to power in 1933, Stahl successfully smuggled the letters out of Germany into France. There they were sold for 12,000 francs ($480) to Princess Marie Bonaparte, who, as a devoted disciple of Freud's, immediately recognized their scientific and historical value. Freud, who was indignant about the sale of the letters, later tried in vain to acquire them back from the princess. As for Fliess's letters, which unfortunately did not survive, Freud described their fate with the following confession to Marie Bonaparte in 1937: "I don't know till this very day whether I destroyed them, or only hid them ingeniously. . . . Our correspondence was of the most intimate nature, 'as you can surmise" (quoted in Schur 1965:13).

Thus the correspondence gives us only a partial insight into the unusually close intellectual relationship between these two men. Fliess's voice necessarily remains silent, except where it is occasionally possible to reconstruct his comments and advice to Freud from Freud's replies.

Nor were all of Freud's letters to Fliess published in *Aus den Anfängen der Psychoanalyse* (1950a), which was later translated into English as *The Origins of Psycho-Analysis* (1954e). Of 284 letters, post-cards, and drafts, only 168 items were selected for publication by the editors of *Aus den Anfängen*, and many of these were published only in part. Although the editors claimed that the unpublished portions dealt only with unimportant matters (e.g., details about arrangements for meetings, news about family and friends, and certain of Freud's attempts to follow Fliess's biological law of "periods"), those few scholars who have since had access to this correspondence, particularly Ernest Jones and Max Schur, have unearthed a veritable wealth of new biographical material for their own studies of Freud's life.[1]

Unfortunately even the availability of a complete edition of Freud's letters to Fliess would hardly solve many of the most important enigmas that have come to surround the intellectual relationship of these two men. Part of the historian's problem stems from the fact that they exchanged many of their scientific ideas orally. To this end the two

1. It is to be hoped that someday a complete, unexpurgated edition of these letters will be published and thus put an end to the secrecy and the privileged access that have long been associated with them. Freud's manuscript letters and drafts to Fliess were donated to the Library of Congress in 1970 by Freud's daughter Anna, under the restriction that they not be seen again until the year 2000. My own efforts to see this correspondence in 1975 were consequently fruitless. More recently, Anna Freud altered the terms of her 1970 bequest to allow these letters to be seen subject to her personal approval. Nevertheless, my own request to see these letters was denied because, as I was informed by Anna Freud, plans are underway to publish the full text of these letters. I am further informed by the general editor of this projected work, who was previously granted permission by Anna Freud to see these letters for private study, that no activity has yet begun on the transcription or translation of the letters and that publication, which will be simultaneous in German and in English, is as much as seven to ten years in the future.

friends arranged frequent meetings—or scientific "congresses," as Freud liked to call them—either in Vienna, Berlin, or when the opportunity for joint travel arose, in places like Salzburg, Nuremberg, Breslau, or Innsbruck. It was during these congresses, often lasting for several days, that they enthusiastically communicated their latest scientific findings and helped each other with unsolved problems.

Freud's letters to Fliess provide repeated testimony to the high value he placed upon these regular meetings. In June of 1896 he spoke of "looking forward to our congress as to a slaking of hunger and thirst," while in March 1898 he wrote that his ability to work had become "a function of the distance of our congresses" (*Origins*, pp. 169, 248). And on 3 April 1898: "After each of our Congresses I have been newly fortified for weeks, new ideas pressed forward, pleasure in hard work was restored, and the flickering hope of finding one's way through the jungle burned for a while steadily and brilliantly. This time of abstinence teaches me nothing, since I have always known what our meetings meant to me" (unpublished Fliess correspondence; quoted in Jones 1953:302). In the years of Freud's "splendid isolation," preceding world notoriety and the advent of his first followers, Fliess became his "only audience" (*Origins*, p. 337). "Your praise is nectar and ambrosia to me," he commented to Fliess in a letter of 14 July 1894 (unpublished Fliess correspondence; quoted in Jones 1953:298).

From the published correspondence it is also clear that Fliess was expected, above all, to assist Freud in finding the physiological basis of his clinico-psychological findings during the early 1890s (*Origins*, p. 76). Both men were strongly united by their common faith in the strict determinism of all vital phenomena, as well as by their desire to achieve a *complete* scientific (i.e., reductionistic) explanation of those particular vital phenomena that happened to concern their respective medical interests. Fliess's Christmas present to Freud in 1898 was, appropriately, a two-volume set of Helmholtz's lectures (Kris 1954:10). Physics, chemistry, and, for Fliess, particularly mathematics were to be the foundations of the mature sort of scientific explanation that both men sought to achieve in their medical theories. It was Fliess, significantly, who encouraged Freud to continue with the *Project for a Scientific Psychology* when he began to bog down under the manifold frustrations of this ambitious undertaking (*Origins*, p. 124).

The two men were also united by their common interest in sexuality. For this was the principal subject of Fliess's scientific researches during the period of his closest association with Freud. It is therefore to Fliess's scientific work that we must turn if we are to understand the intensity of friendship between these two investigators as well as their scientific collaboration.

Fliess's Principal Scientific Preoccupations

Throughout the 1890s Wilhelm Fliess was occupied in gathering a massive body of scientific evidence, from the overlapping fields of re-

Hermann von Helmholtz
(1821–94), the scientific idol
of Freud and Fliess
during the 1890s.

productive biology and clinical medicine, in an effort to support the
truth of three unusual scientific ideas. He was particularly eager to
make these ideas the "foundations for an exact biology"—a phrase later
used as the subtitle of his magnum opus, *Der Ablauf des Lebens* (The
Course of Life, 1906*b*).

The first idea, which he published at Freud's urging, dealt with a
new and complex clinical entity that Fliess believed to be a "reflex
neurosis" emanating from the nose (Fliess 1893*a*, 1893*b*, 1893*c*). To
this particular pathological condition he ascribed a host of well-diversi-
fied symptoms: pains in the head, shoulders, arms, and stomach, as
well as disturbances in the general functioning of the cardiac, respira-
tory, gastric, and reproductive systems. Fliess further claimed that
such symptoms, whenever of purely nasal origin, could be relieved by
anesthetizing with cocaine a certain responsible region within the interior of the nose. Fliess's cocaine-based remedy thus provided yet
another medical tie between him and Freud.

All such nasal disorders were supposed by Fliess to arise from two
principal sources: organic disturbances within the nose itself (due to
aftereffects of various infectious diseases), and vasomotor (functional) disturbances associated with the human reproductive system.
To explain the latter connection, Fliess assumed a special physiological
link between the nose and the genitalia, an association he localized

within certain "genital spots" (*Genitalstellen*) inside the interior of the nose itself (Fliess 1895, 1897). Painful menstruation (dysmenorrhea) and its analogue, painful childbirth, were jointly referred by Fliess to a pathological condition in these so-called genital spots.

On the basis of this purported nasogenital link, Fliess went on to insist that Freud's category of the actual neuroses was frequently associated, by virtue of its endogenous, sexual origins, with the complicating symptoms of a nasal reflex neurosis. In clinical proof of all this, Fliess cited, among other evidence, the phenomenon of visible swelling by the turbinate bone during menstruation, the occurrence of vicarious nosebleeding during menstruation and pregnancy, and the fact that cocaine applications to the nose were capable of inducing accidental abortions.

The link between the nose and the female menstrual cycle in turn led Fliess to his second preoccupation, namely, the regular vital periodicities manifested by all physiological processes. In a scientific monograph of 1897, *Die Beziehungen zwischen Nase und weiblichen Geschlechtsorganen* (The Relations between the Nose and the Female Sexual Organs), Fliess attempted to show that symptoms of the nasal reflex neuroses, as well as attacks of migraine, nasal bleeding, and various other homologous by-products of the female sexual cycle, followed a regular 28-day sequence like menstruation itself. To account for the many temporal irregularities normally displayed in menstruation and its related medical syndromes, Fliess was soon induced to postulate the independent existence of a second, or 23-day, cycle in human physiology. For reasons that I shall discuss later, he considered this second cycle to be a "male" analogue of the typical female menstrual period. Both periods were present in both sexes, he argued; and it was this last claim that formed the basis for his third crucial scientific insight—the essential *bisexuality* of all human beings.

On the basis of his three scientific "discoveries," Fliess proceeded to erect an even more global conception of human physiology. He summed up this nascent scientific Weltanschauung, which he spent the remainder of his life's work perfecting, in the Preface to his 1897 monograph:

> . . . woman's menstrual bleeding is the expression of a process that appertains to both sexes and the beginning of which is not just connected with puberty.
>
> The facts before us compel us to emphasize an additional factor. They teach us that, besides the menstrual process of the twenty-eight-day type, still another group of periodic processes exists with a twenty-three-day cycle, to which people of every age and both sexes are equally subject.
>
> To these two groups of periodic processes one was able to provide the interpretation that they have a solid inner relation with male and female sexual characteristics. And it is only in accordance with our actual bisexual constitution if both—only with different stress—are present in every man and woman.
>
> Once in the possession of such knowledge, the further insight

emerged that the development and decay of our organism takes place in fits and starts [*schubweise*] during these sexual periods and that the day of our death is just as much determined by them as that of our birth. The disturbances of illnesses are subject to the same temporal laws as are these periodic processes themselves.

The mother transmits the periods to her child, determining its sex by the nature of the period that is transmitted first. The periods then continue in the child and pass with the same rhythm through the generations. They can no more arise anew than energy itself, and their temporal form persists as long as organized beings reproduce themselves sexually. Their existence is accordingly not limited to mankind, but is common to the animal kingdom and probably to the whole organic world. Indeed, the wonderful exactitude with which the period of 23 or 28 whole days is maintained allows one to presume a profound relationship between astronomical conditions and the creation of organisms. (1897: iii–iv)

By 1906, when Fliess published his major work on these various biomedical and cosmological themes, he had taken to confirming his theories by means of an elaborate use of higher multiples, using not only 23 and 28 from the two cycles but also their sum (51) and their difference (5). He considered other related numbers, like 23^2, 28^2, $28 \cdot 23$, $51 \cdot 23$, $5 \cdot 23$, and so forth, as equally significant temporal sums within his full-blown periodicity theory. So, too, additions and subtractions of these higher multiples—for example, $3 \cdot 28 \pm 2 \cdot 23$—often entered into Fliess's calculations of such important vital intervals as the length of life, the time between a woman's childbirths, and the onset and the duration of major episodes of disease. Naturally all these combinations and permutations of 23 and 28 made it easy to confirm his theory.

Posterity's Judgment of Fliess

The standard and, indeed, the virtually unanimous judgment of posterity regarding Fliess's scientific ideas is that they constitute a remarkably well-developed form of pseudoscience. Ernst Kris (1954) has collected a number of scientific opinions on Fliess's work from past and present gynecologists and otolaryngologists; and while these specialists have occasionally acknowledged the genuineness of certain of Fliess's "facts," all are agreed that his theoretical superstructure was quite out of touch with scientific reality. According to Aebly (1928), Fliess was suffering from the overvaluation of an idea. Similarly, Riebold (1942), who calls Fliess "a player with numbers," adds that his work definitely belongs to the realm of the psychopathological. And many others, including Freud's numerous biographers,[2] have reaffirmed

2. Jones (1953:290–91, 313), for example, states that Fliess's scientific thinking clearly had "a pathological basis alien to Freud's," while Eissler (1971: 169) has commented that Fliess was "victimized by a set of paranoid ideas." For other similar judgments by Freud's biographers, see, among others, Erikson 1955:13; Natenberg 1955:117; Bakan 1958:61–63; Lauzon 1963:46; Gardner 1966:108; Robert 1966:92; Costigan 1967:59; Ellenberger 1970:545; and Balogh 1971:43.

Blumenfeld's (1926:51) general conclusion that Fliess's work "verges on the mystical" (see also Kris [1954:5–6, 8–9, 40], whose collection of opinions I am summarizing).

As for Fliess's claim to have turned biology into a natural, mathematical science, Martin Gardner—otherwise known for his monthly *Scientific American* column "Mathematical Games," as well as for his delightful book *Fads and Fallacies in the Name of Science* (1957)—has delivered the last and perhaps the most damaging blow to Fliess's "Teutonic crackpottery." Fliess, Gardner explains (1966), analyzed all his periodicity data in terms of the general formula $x \cdot 23 \pm y \cdot 28$. Unfortunately Fliess's mathematical abilities must have been limited to elementary arithmetic, Gardner asserts, for what Fliess did not seem to realize was that any two positive integers that possess, like 23 and 28, no common divisor, can be used with his general formula $x \cdot 23 \pm y \cdot 28$ to derive *any* positive number whatsoever. Thus, there was no positive integer that Fliess's formula could not produce, given the right juggling of the values of x and y.

From Gardner's mathematical observation it is also possible to see why Fliess might have become so enamored with the numbers 23 and 28. Taking the 28-day menstrual cycle as a physiological "given" and presuming its occasional irregularities to be the product of a *second* periodic cycle, most numbers within a 16-day range centered around the 28th day—that is, from 20 to 36—turn out to share a common divisor. If one eliminates these as well as four other numbers within plus or minus 3 of 28, one is left with only two candidates for Fliess's formula: 23 and 33. It is interesting that modern Fliessians (and to this day Fliess's theories boast a considerable following in Germany, Switzerland, Japan, and the United States) have added a 33-day cycle to Fliess's original two-cycle system. One of Fliess's most ardent disciples, Bruno Saaler, also found such a 33-day period in his own periodicity researches while Fliess was still alive, and asked his mentor about it. Fliess replied that he, too, had found considerable evidence for such a period, but he had finally concluded that it was really to be explained as the difference between $2 \cdot 28$—that is, 56—and 23 (Saaler 1921:360).

History's subsequent and highly disparaging verdict on Fliess's theories stands in marked contrast to Freud's attitude toward him and his work in the 1890s. For, lacking insight into the flaws of Fliess's mathematical reasoning, Freud enthusiastically accepted his friend's "discoveries" as major scientific breakthroughs in the fields of biology and medicine. Freud intended to name one of his two youngest children after Fliess, but, as Jones (1953:291) dryly remarks, "fortunately they were both girls." For a time they even talked of writing a book together in 1894—probably on the subject of anxiety neurosis and its nasal reflex counterpart (see Jones 1953:304; and Schur 1972:69). Freud had only the highest praise for Fliess's findings on this latter topic and expressed his hope in 1893 that the phenomenon of nasal reflex neurosis would be given Fliess's name. He referred to it in his own publications (1895*b* [1894], *S.E.*, 3:90); and he lectured on Fliess's "enthralling [nasal] material" in his course on neurology at the University of Vienna (*Origins*, pp. 74, 188).

Freud even permitted Fliess to operate repeatedly upon his own nose and sinuses—Fliess surgically removed and cauterized part of Freud's turbinate bone—in the hope of dispelling certain neurotic symptoms! To Fliess, Freud likewise referred at least one known psychoanalytic patient for similar surgical treatment in order to correct a case of hysterical gastric pains purportedly complicated by a nasal reflex neurosis affecting the same region. The patient nearly died of a hemorrhage when another physician discovered, and then attempted to remove, a half-meter strip of iodoform gauze that Fliess had inadvertently left inside the patient's nasal cavity.[3]

Freud's medical faith in Fliess was hardly perturbed even by this near fatal episode. Fliess remained, as Freud expressed it in an unpublished letter of 20 April 1895, "the healer, the prototype of the man into whose hands one confidently entrusts one's life and that of one's family" (quoted in Schur 1972:83).

As for Fliess's theory of periodicity, Freud personally provided his friend with considerable data—from himself, his family, and his clinical case histories—in order to help substantiate it. Freud's father, for instance, who died on 23 October 1896, turns out to have succumbed on his periodic day. Not only that. Born the same day as Bismarck, who lived 1087 · 28 days, Freud's father passed away exactly 644 (28 · 23) days earlier (see Fig. 5.1; and Fliess 1906b:154). And this, too, Freud took seriously.[4]

Herr Prof. Sigmund Freud aus Wien hat mich ehemals darauf aufmerksam gemacht, daß sein Vater, der an demselben Tage wie Bismarck geboren wurde, um 28.23 Tage früher gestorben sei.

$$\left.\begin{array}{ll} \text{Herr Freud sen.} & \text{1. April} \quad 1815 \\ & \text{24. Oktober } 1896 \dagger \end{array}\right\} 29792$$

$$= 38 \cdot 28^2 = 3 \cdot 28^3 - 2 \cdot 23 \cdot 28^2 = 28^3 + 2 \cdot 28^2 \Delta$$

$$= (28 + 2\,\Delta)\, 28^2.$$

Fig. 5.1. Fliess's biorhythmic calculations concerning Freud's father Jacob, who was born the same day as Bismarck, and who died exactly 23 · 28 days earlier, on a periodic day (38 · 28 · 28). (From Fliess 1906b: 154.)

There is equally no doubt that Freud for many years believed the major vicissitudes in his own mental and physical states could be ex-

3. See Schur (1972:77–90) for further details on these nasal operations.

4. Freud's conviction that Fliess's periodicity theories held true for the span of life may be dated to early 1896, when Fliess was rapidly developing his ideas on this subject and was communicating them to Freud in a series of manuscript drafts and letters. It is therefore not surprising that Freud should have checked to see whether his father's death took place on a critical day. In his manuscript on the nose and the female sexual organs, which was written in early 1896, Fliess had already documented the case of Goethe, who lived exactly 1077 · 28 days (13 cycles longer than Freud's father). This and other historical examples are annotated in the margin of Freud's personal copy (Fliess 1897:209; Freud library, London). Fliess's monograph was already in press when Freud's father died; hence the confirming example of Jacob Freud was not included in this 1897 publication.

plained in terms of Fliess's laws. In this connection, he apparently kept
a periodicity calendar for Fliess and wrote more than once to his friend
of having just gone through "bad period days" (*Origins*, pp. 170, 192,
235).[5] So great was his admiration for Fliess's pioneering discoveries in
this domain that Freud, in 1898, bestowed upon his friend the title of
"the Kepler of biology" (Jones 1953:304).

Naturally Freud's acceptance of Fliess's "male" and "female" periods
entailed his acceptance of the theory of bisexuality. In a letter to Fliess
written on 4 January 1898, Freud called this idea "the most significant
for my subject since that of defence" (*Origins*, p. 242); and this particular idea was indeed to play an important role in his theory of the
psychoneuroses.

Freud's unqualified support for Fliess's work went so far as to include his resignation from the editorial board of the *Wiener klinische
Rundschau* when the editor-in-chief, Dr. Heinrich Paschkis, refused to
redress the wrong done to Fliess by a devastating reviewer of his 1897
monograph (Ry. 1898). To Fliess, Freud contemptuously described the
review in question as "a sample of that type of insolence which is characteristic of absolute ignorance." [6] Three years later, in his essay *On
Dreams*, Freud offered the following retrospective comment on this
incident: "The unfavorable reception of my [Berlin] friend's work had
made a profound impression on me. It contained, in my opinion, a fundamental biological discovery, which is only now—many years later—
beginning to find favour with the experts" (1901*a*, *S.E.*, 5:663). Freud
also admitted that he had strongly identified himself with his innovative
friend's fate, imagining that his own future scientific reception would
undoubtedly be similar.

Confronted by such incontrovertible evidence of Freud's steadfast
adherence to Fliess's pseudoscientific theories in the 1890s, Freud's
biographers have nevertheless been remarkably successful in salvaging
Freud's rational respectability. To this end, his faith in his friend's
ideas has for the most part been taken as testimony to his fortunately
short-lived gullibility (a tendency to which Freud was clearly not im-
mune) and, more especially, to the peculiar nature of his personal and
scientific ordeal throughout the 1890s. According to Jones (1953:287,
295) and Kris (1954:14), Freud elevated Fliess, who was obviously
"intellectually his inferior," to his own level in the 1890s. In this way he
filled his pressing need for a friendly critic whom he could endow with
"all sorts of imaginary qualities, keen judgment and restraint" during
the most intellectually creative decade of his life (Jones 1953:295).
Fliess therefore became a replacement for Josef Breuer and acted as a
willing and encouraging listener, occasionally as "a censor," but as little
else. "Whatever help . . . Fliess gave to Freud, it must have been essen-

5. To these few published references must be added Freud's many unpublished discussions about Fliess's theory—e.g., *Origins*, pp. 179, n. 1, 181, n. 2;
Jones 1953:288, 300, 302, 304; and Schur 1972:96, 106–7, 111, 116, 133, 143–44,
147.

6. For this and other unpublished extracts from Freud's letters to Fliess dealing with this episode, see Schur 1972:144, letters of 14 and 27 April 1898.

tially that of psychological encouragement; the purely intellectual assistance could only have been minimal" (p. 303). "So the talks were duologues rather than dialogues," Jones also concludes (p. 303).

Within this particular historical context, Freud's acceptance of Fliess's bizzare theories has thus been attributed to their strong personal friendship, which was not without an obvious neurotic side as well. For, among the most important of Freud's neurotic symptoms in the mid-1890s was his conviction, apparently on the basis of a prediction by Fliess, that he would not survive the age of 51—the sum of 23 and 28 (see Jones 1953:310, 348, 357). During a moment of more optimistic medical self-assessment, Freud also became persuaded that his most troublesome symptom, arrhythmia of the heart, might be of purely nasal origin—hence the nasal operations, which even succeeded in bringing about a sudden improvement in Freud's condition (Jones 1953:311).

At another historical level, both Freud's neurosis and his peculiar intellectual and emotional dependence upon Fliess in the 1890s have been rationalized as by-products of his pioneering efforts to explore the often "terrifying" depths of his own unconscious mind during this same period. His relationship to Fliess is therefore to be seen as a prototypic "transference relationship," in which Freud relived, in his attitude toward this convenient father substitute, the early dependence and latent hostility of his unconscious Oedipus complex (Jones 1953:307; see also Eissler 1971:279). "Without someone to play this thankless role," runs one such judgment of the Freud-Fliess relationship, "Freud's self-analysis might well have been impossible" (Costigan 1967:53–54). Shakow and Rapaport (1964:44) have probably best summed up this reasoning when they suggest that Fliess's function as a transference figure in Freud's life "may account in part for the unaccountable in the relationship." Excepting, then, Fliess's generally acknowledged value as a transference figure, occasional literary critic, and faithful listener in Freud's life during the 1890s, little allowance has been made by Freud's biographers for Fliess's having any constructive influence upon Freud. Indeed, a recent biographer has gone so far as to speak of "the extraordinary emotional and intellectual bondage" in which Fliess held Freud for nearly a decade (Robert 1966:99).

Despite such negative evaluations of Fliess's intellectual contributions, this historical consensus has not been unanimous. Two voices, albeit lone ones, have managed to find a few good words to say about Fliess—words that go beyond the standard attribution of menial functions that he supposedly served in Freud's life.

Kurt Eissler, who is well known to Freud scholars as one of the most staunch defenders of Freud's honor and intellectual integrity (e.g., Eissler 1966, 1971), has stressed that we have no way of knowing how often Fliess may have made, either in writing or in person, significant and insightful remarks to Freud dealing specifically with the latter's psychoanalytic work. Nor does Eissler seem to find Fliess's scientific vision of turning biology into an exact, mathematical science as unrealistic as some have found it. "It is my impression . . . ," Eissler writes, "that Fliess's greatness is . . . underestimated in psychoanalytic circles. . . . one day biology may discover, even though it looks quite improbable at present, that the totality of life is indeed regulated by rhythm, and that the sequence of biological phenomena that we can observe are variations of an all-embracing principle. . . . Thus it is not inconceivable that Fliess may, in some far-distant future, come to high honors" (1971:169–70). Finally, speaking of certain puzzling questions that are associated with the eventual estrangement beween Freud and Fliess, Eissler candidly concludes that "an unsolved enigma still surrounds the relationship of these two men" (p. 171).

Precisely what that "unsolved enigma" might be is a subject to which the psychiatrist and historian of medicine Iago Galdston (1956) long ago devoted an outspoken, heterodox, and thought-provoking essay. According to him, the early biographers of Freud, like Ernest Jones and Ernst Kris, cited nothing but the most derogatory opinions concerning Fliess's scientific work. Nor did they make any effort to understand Fliess's theories in their specific historical-biomedical context. That context, Galdston argues, was *Naturphilosophie* and its numerous offshots in Romantic medicine. It was through Fliess, Galdston further insists, that these historical traditions in turn excited "the profoundest effect" upon Freud himself. Virtually all of Fliess's major ideas—periodicity, bisexuality, polarity,[7] and man's dependence upon the world process—were part of a Romantic tradition in medicine, Galdston points out—a tradition in which more "vitalistic" ideas, and particularly the crucial psychoanalytic notions of "intention and purpose," found refuge during the philosophical onslaught of the so-called Helmholtz school of physical-chemical reductionism. It is thus in the writings of adherents to *Naturphilosophie* and Romantic medicine (among other figures, Galdston specifically cites Leibnitz, Kant, Fichte, Schelling, Goethe, Carus, Oken, Novalis, and Bachofen) that one discovers important anticipations of Freud's theories of dream interpretation, the unconscious, repression, the ego, the id, and the superego, as well as the concepts of Eros and Thanatos (life and death instincts). "Tragic," Galdston declares (1956:495), ". . . is the disparagement and calumny heaped upon Fliess's person and memory by the adulating partisans of Freud"!

Galdston's divergent position has had surprisingly little impact upon subsequent Freud scholarship. It is nevertheless interesting to observe the manifest similarities between Galdston's line of thinking and that of the more influential Cranefield (1966a, 1966b, 1970b). Without speaking specifically of Fliess, Cranefield has ascribed an analogous set of vitalistic interests in Freud's thinking to the same generally unrecognized influence of the *Naturphilosophie* tradition. But unlike

7. Fliess's theory of bisexuality later became associated with ideas about bilaterality (particularly left- and right-handedness) in man. Fliess believed the secondary sexual characteristics of the nondominant bisexual disposition to be generally more pronounced in left-handed individuals (Fliess 1906b:537–71).

Galdston, Cranefield argues that many of the basic philosophical-psychological preoccupations of the *Naturphilosophen* survived within the supposedly antithetical corpus of the nineteenth-century biophysics movement in which Freud was partially trained (see Chapter 2).

Whether it was indirectly from the biophysics tradition or directly from Romantic medicine that Freud's purported involvement with *Naturphilosophie* stemmed, let us not forget that, like him, Wilhelm Fliess was an ardent adherent of biophysical ideals. Thus, to establish his argument about Fliess's "profound" influence upon Freud, Galdston need only have shown that Fliess indeed transmitted to Freud certain basic ideas on the meaning of dreams, the nature of the unconscious, the role of intentionality in thought, and so forth. But this Galdston has not done. Nor did Fliess discuss such ideas in his published works, which are instead characterized by purely reductionist, mathematical aims and by a rigid biological fatalism. In my opinion, Galdston has been far too eager to tie Freud to Romantic medicine and, in the process, too quick to cast Fliess in a historical role that he does not readily fill. As Galdston himself concedes, "I doubt that Fliess would have relished being counted among the Romanticists" (1956:499).

Thus like other Freud scholars, I cannot accept Galdston's provocative argument concerning Wilhelm Fliess's instrumental role in Freud's life. Nevertheless, I *do* concur with this scholar on one important point: that Fliess's much-maligned theories are indeed far more understandable and plausible in their historical context than is generally realized today. As we shall see, it is this forgotten context, not Freud's intellectual and emotional "bondage" to Fliess, that really explains Freud's high interest in, and acceptance of, Fliess's scientific work. Finally I must strenuously agree with Galdston that Fliess's scientific views, along with the context of biological logic that served to support them, became of decisive importance for Sigmund Freud's intellectual development. In fact, I have absolutely no hesitation in asserting that, along with Brücke, Charcot, and Breuer, Wilhelm Fliess is the fourth, the last, and perhaps the most important of the quaternary of personal friends and scientific contemporaries who most influenced Freud's psychoanalytic thinking during the crucial years of discovery.

THE BIOMEDICAL CONTEXT OF FLIESS'S THEORIES

Nose and Sex

Surprising as it may seem, Fliess was hardly alone during the early 1890s in suspecting a physiological connection between the nose and the female sexual organs. Even his severest critics acknowledged that the medical observations he claimed in support of his theory had been known to physicians since ancient times (e.g., Senator 1914:37); but such knowledge had remained "an old wives' tale" throughout most of the nineteenth century. The situation changed in the early 1880s when the Baltimore laryngologist and later professor of medicine at Johns Hopkins, John Noland Mackenzie, put this ancient lore upon a new and impressively comprehensive medical foundation (Mackenzie 1884).[8] His medical evidence for nasogenital phenomena was essentially the same as that later presented independently by Fliess, although Mackenzie stressed certain facts that Fliess apparently took for granted in his own publications. Speaking in 1898 at a major medical conference in Montreal, Mackenzie expressed nothing but praise for Fliess's researches. After surveying five pre-Fliessian publications on the question of nasogenital disorders, Mackenzie reported: "Fliess's elaborate monograph [1897], written in apparent ignorance of the work done by me in this special field before him, is a model of painstaking labour, and is valuable as an independent contribution to the study of this important subject" (1898:111).

Mackenzie marshaled his own findings under six major categories: (1) Nasal tissue indeed appears to swell on a regular basis during menstruation. (2) Vicarious, monthly nasal bleeding is found not only during menstruation but in pregnancy and even in males at the time of puberty. (3) In Mackenzie's own words: "To render the relationship to which I wish to call attention more intelligible, it is necessary to recall the anatomical fact that in man, covering . . . the septum [of the nose], is a structure which is essentially the anatomical analogue of the erectile tissue of the penis" (1898:113). (Indeed, the genitalia, the nipples, and the nose are the only parts of the body to possess such erectile tissue.) Also, there generally occurs during sexual arousal a simultaneous erection of all such tissues throughout the body. (4) According to Mackenzie, this last circumstance explains why some individuals suffer from chronic nasal disturbances (nosebleeding, sneezing, and simple occlusion) during moments of intense sexual excitation. (5) Genitourinary irritations are sometimes dependent upon prior affections of the nasal passages. And on a more anatomical-developmental level, cases of arrested physical development of the genital organs are occasionally associated with an absence of both olfactory lobes and nerves. (6) Mackenzie believed that all such afflictions of the nasal mucous membranes were probably "the [phylogenetic] connecting link between the sense of smell and erethism of the reproductive organs

8. A pioneer American laryngologist, John Noland Mackenzie (1853–1925) received his medical degree from the University of Virginia in 1876 and then undertook postgraduate studies with Max Oertel in Munich and with Leopold von Schroetter and Carl Stoerk in Vienna (1879–80). (Stoerk was one of the six men who in 1887 nominated Sigmund Freud for membership in the Vienna Society of Physicians; see Sablik 1968:108.) After his return to America, Mackenzie held clinical professorships at the University of Maryland (1887–97) and Johns Hopkins Medical School (1889–1912) and also became coeditor of the *Maryland Medical Journal* and American editor of the prestigious British *Journal of Laryngology and Rhinology*. "Quickly recognized everywhere as an authority of the first rank, he was elected a fellow of the American Laryngological Association in 1883 and became its vice-president in 1886 and its president in 1889. Widely known and appreciated abroad, he was a corresponding fellow of the leading British, French, and German associations" (Delavan 1933:94).

exhibited in the lower animals" (1898:117–18). It was in this implicit phylogenetic connection that Mackenzie specifically attributed perversions of smell to pathological reversions to "the purely animal type." Summing up the phenomena of nasal pathology in general, and those of the "nasal reflex neuroses" specifically, Mackenzie suggested that such disturbances are probably a direct result of the major reduction in olfactory acuity that has accompanied human evolution and the advent of civilized life (1898:118).

Although Mackenzie claimed no experience with the use of cocaine in attempting to cure such Fliessian problems as painful menstruation, he clearly took most seriously Fliess's notion of "genital zones" in the nose. In this connection Mackenzie testified that masturbators frequently suffer from concurrent nasal disease, olfactory disturbances, and nosebleeding. Like Fliess (1897:182), he noted that changes in the genitals can be reflected by changes in the nasal membrane, and vice versa. "Curiously enough," he further volunteered, "the genital zones of Fliess correspond exactly with the most sensitive portions of the sensitive [nasal] reflex area mapped out by me in 1883" (1898:122). Nor was Mackenzie surprised by Fliess's report of several cases of accidental abortion due to galvanocaustic operations on the nose, for analogous medical observations had been known to Pliny in ancient times.

Even before his 1898 declaration of support for Fliess's researches, Mackenzie's work did much to pave the way for their reception. In German-speaking countries, Mackenzie's early (1884) findings had received a prompt and favorable discussion from Freud's noted colleague at the University of Vienna, Richard von Krafft-Ebing.[9] Like Mackenzie, Krafft-Ebing drew attention to the relevance of the nasogenital relationship to certain enigmatic problems of sexual pathology, and he cited patients plagued by olfactory hallucinations apparently induced through excessive masturbation. Similarly, he argued that a pathological disturbance of the nasogenital relationship entered into certain sexual perversions like foot fetishism and particularly *coprolagnia* (the impulse to perform disgusting acts involving filth and feces). Indeed, so closely linked with sexuality did Krafft-Ebing believe the olfactory sense to be that he envisioned the two functions as controlled by proximal areas within the cerebral cortex. Always in touch with the most recent medical literature, he later added to the tenth (1898) edition of his *Psychopathia Sexualis* a few additional lines of text that warmly referred his readers to Wilhelm Fliess's (1897) recent confirmation and extension of Mackenzie's original findings.

9. See his *Psychopathia Sexualis*, Section II, "Physiological Facts," 1886 and later editions. It does not appear that Fliess himself knew of Mackenzie's prior American work—at least not until 1902 when a medical editor for the Carl Marhold Press added a footnote to a monograph of Fliess's in order to list Mackenzie's previous contributions to this subject (Fliess 1902:2 n.). For a more complete review of the history of this field, see Semon (1900), who credits the Freiburg otolaryngologist Wilhelm Hack (1884) with developing the notion of nasal reflex neuroses independently of the Mackenzie-Fliess theory of nasogenital disorders. Fliess, who was influenced by Hack's doctrine, was treating nasal reflex neuroses with cocaine applications as early as 1886 (Fliess 1893a:8).

By the late 1890s, the area of research pioneered by Mackenzie in 1884 in America and shortly thereafter by Fliess in Germany had come to be a common topic of discussion among rhinologists. To cite one illustration, in the same periodical (the much-respected *Journal of Laryngology, Rhinology, and Otology*) and year in which Mackenzie issued his 1898 review article on this subject, there appeared a paper discussing the frequent association between nasal catarrh and enuresis (bed-wetting) among children. Also in this same journal and volume is an article by a Dutch physician, Willem Meyjes, entitled "On the Etiology of Some Nasal Reflex Neuroses," which reports the cure of such afflictions by no less a remedy than cocaine applications to the nose. Although Meyjes does not mention Fliess, the latter's well-known views undoubtedly inspired this 1898 replication of his cocaine-therapy technique.

Within German-speaking countries the Mackenzie-Fliess naso-genital theory gained prominence in yet another historically unappreciated biological context, by providing important new corroboration for a pet evolutionary hypothesis put forth some twenty years earlier by the illustrious biologist and ardent Darwinian, Ernst Haeckel. Haeckel had theorized in his *Anthropogenie oder Entwickelungsgeschichte des Menschen* (Anthropogeny or Evolutionary History of Man) that "erotic chemotropisms"—that is to say, chemically based sex stimulants affecting taste and smell—were phylogenetically the "primal source" of all sexual attraction in nature (1874a:656–57).[10] It was the subsequent biomedical findings of Mackenzie and Fliess that helped to bring Haeckel's neglected hypothesis to the attention of sexologists around the turn of the century. When sexologist Iwan Bloch published his two-volume *Beiträge zur Aetiologie der Psychopathia sexualis* (1902–3), he duly cited Haeckel's evolutionary hypothesis immediately before discussing both Wilhelm Fliess's researches and their more recent confirmation in forty-seven clinical histories by Arthur Schiff (1901).[11]

Sigmund Freud, for his own part, was fully aware of the general evolutionary context in which Fliess's theories were discussed around the turn of the century; for he underscored Bloch's discussion of Haeckel's *primal-smell* theory of sex in the margin of his personal copy of that work (1902–3, 2:201; Freud library, London). And again, some years later Freud apparently acquired and reread a second copy of Bloch's book, in which he marked the same general discussion of Haeckel's theory that he had before.[12]

10. He was even more explicit in the fourth (1891, *1*:147; 2:886, n. 195) and later editions; see also Haeckel 1913:259.
11. Bloch, Haeckel, and Fliess were all three to become founding members of the Berlin Ärztliche Gesellschaft für Sexualwissenschaft und Eugenik (Medical Society for Sexual Science and Eugenics) in 1913. This organization in turn provided a prominent forum for the discussion and dissemination of Fliess's theories. For a general review of late-nineteenth-century literature on sexuality and olfaction, see Kern 1975: Chapter 5.
12. This second copy of Bloch's *Beiträge zur Aetiologie der Psychopathia sexualis* (1902–3)—now in the possession of the Health Sciences Library, Columbia University, New York—is inscribed by Bloch to Friedrich S. Krauss (dated 16 October 1902). Krauss, a Viennese cultural anthropologist and folklorist, frequently

Thus, the real issue in the debates that surrounded Fliess's theory of nasal reflex neuroses in the late 1890s was much more complex scientifically and historically than Freud's biographers have generally grasped. The distinguished neurologist Moritz Benedikt, even as one of Fliess's most ardent Viennese critics, could still write that he had been "immediately" impressed by many of Fliess's controversial clinical findings, so plausible did they seem in their implicit phylogenetic context. What Benedikt and other critics contested was Fliess's general theory of "nasal reflex neuroses" and, in particular, the clinical frequency that he persisted in claiming for such disorders (Benedikt 1901:361). Yet, many contemporary physicians were hardly troubled by such seemingly fine points. Even the ever-cautious Josef Breuer, after some initial hesitation, appears to have accepted the whole of Fliess's nasal theory by the mid-1890s (Origins, p. 121), while Richard von Krafft-Ebing's enthusiastic endorsement of the Mackenzie-Fliess doctrine stands in considerable contrast to the "benevolent scepticism" with which he tended to view many of Sigmund Freud's psychoanalytic claims about this same time (Origins, p. 184, n. 1).

As late as 1914, almost twenty years after their formulation, Fliess's ideas on nasogenital disorders were still being openly discussed and zealously defended on an evolutionary as well as on a clinico-medical basis. One lively focal point for these later debates was the experimental research by Koblanck and Roeder in 1912, which showed that young rabbits that had had Fliess's "genital spots" surgically removed from their noses uniformly suffered an inhibition of development in their genital organs. Defending both Fliess's theories and Koblanck and Roeder's experimental support for them at the Medical Society for Sexual Science in Berlin, one obviously impatient physician summed up the scientific argument with the words: "All this petty quibbling can change nothing. The relationship between the nose and genitalia is one that is founded deep in the history of evolutionary development" (Siegmund 1914:77; see also Bloch 1914:8–9). How, his supporters apparently wondered, could Fliess's detractors be so blind to the biological validity and importance of his nasal discoveries?

---

attended meetings of the Vienna Psychoanalytic Society after 1910. It seems possible that Freud acquired this second copy through Krauss sometime during the next three or four years, a period when he was particularly concerned with the kinds of anthropological and phylogenetic issues treated in Bloch's book. See Chapters 8 and 10 of this book. Still, one might also legitimately suspect that the markings in this volume are actually those of Friedrich Krauss. Krauss died in May 1938, and his own library may subsequently have gone to the same Viennese bookseller who acquired much of Freud's library in the spring of 1938. I did not, however, encounter other signs of Krauss's personal library in the New York Freud collection. Unfortunately, the New York copy of Bloch's *Beiträge* bears only scattered marginal marks of emphasis, and none of these are in colored pencil, a characteristic feature of Freud's annotations as a whole (and of almost all those from the New York library that I have confidently attributed to Freud). In any event, whether the marginalia in this copy are those of Freud or Krauss, it is evident that Haeckel's primal-smell theory of sex aroused topical interest around the turn of the century.

From 1939 to 1978 the American portion of Freud's personal library was housed at the New York State Psychiatric Institute, which made the original acquisition. For a history of this acquisition and a listing of the contents, see Lewis and Landis (1957).

It is against this background of biological and medical debate over Fliess's theories that the clinical support of his numerous coworkers must also be considered, for a surprising number of them found that his methods of cocaine application and nasal cauterization actually worked! [13] Ries, writing in America, has reported the dramatic reversal of medical opinion that greeted Fliess's initially incredible nasal theories: "The method becoming more generally known made friends out of scoffers, and many a man who began to experiment with it in the hope of discrediting it and exposing its fallacy wound up as a disciple and an apostle. Wherever the method was subjected to impartial tests it has achieved an amazing number of successes, and the experience of the last six years has procured for it many friends who would be loath to part with it if not forced thereto by very weighty reasons" (1903:377). Even the critics acknowledged these successful case histories, attributing them, however, to suggestion—the same charge later used by many of Freud's critics when he and his followers pointed to their own therapeutic successes with the psychoanalytic method. Yet numerous experimenters who took careful steps to preclude suggestion found that this particular factor could not explain why cocaine solutions worked and water did not, why the cocaine solutions uniformly took eight minutes to act—instead of having a more immediate effect, as they should have done if suggestion was involved—or why cauterization of the nose often produced permanent results.

As for the success of Fliess's methods, he himself, at the Medical Society for Sexual Science in 1914 (see note 13), was able to speak of a 75 percent confirmation of his clinical procedures in over three hundred separate medical publications! Nor is the important grain of scientific truth in Fliess's now-defunct nasal theories any less significant today than it was when he and Mackenzie began to publicize the physiological relations between the nose and the genitalia in the 1880s and 1890s. Only Fliess's more ambitious and peculiar theory of the "nasal reflex neuroses," together with his method of therapeutic treatment, eventually proved ephemeral. [14]

Vital Periodicity

If Fliess's nasogenital theory was hardly as bizarre as Freud's biographers have tended to maintain, his scientific interests in vital

13. See Meyjes 1898; also, Schiff's lecture of 1901, and the favorable remarks by Weil, Gomperz, Grossmann, Halban, Chrobak, and Benedikt that followed this lecture at the Society of Physicians in Vienna (*Deutsche Medizinal-Zeitung*, 22:152–53, 177, 202); the review of Fliess's methods by the American physician Emil Ries (1903); and the later comments by Fliess, Bloch, Koblanck, Roeder, Saaler, and Siegmund in *Zeitschrift für Sexualwissenschaft*, 1 (1914):7–8, 76–78.

14. The specific use of cocaine in the treatment of nasal disorders nevertheless remains one of the few success stories in the history of this otherwise problematic drug. According to Henderson and Johns (1977:41), this drug is unrivaled in nasal therapy today for its fast action, its prolonged duration, and its strong vasoconstricting and decongestive effects. "Cocaine finds its most extensive use in *nasal surgery*. In a recent survey of 4000 otolaryngologists, 94% said that they utilize cocaine routinely for anesthesia in nasal surgery" (Henderson and Johns 1977:34).

and sexual periodicity were becoming positively fashionable by the mid-1890s. Indeed, the study of vital periodicity had passed through a long and honorable history before Fliess turned to it in the 1890s.[15] The lengthy list of previous researchers into the biomedical implications of vital periodicity includes, among others, Charles Darwin, who in *The Descent of Man* had addressed himself to "that mysterious law" common to both man and lower animals "which causes certain normal processes, such as gestation, as well as the maturation and duration of various diseases, to follow lunar periods" (1871, *1*:12).

Darwin recognized not only the biological significance of the 28-day lunar cycle in most living creatures, but also the existence of regular weekly cycles, together with their even multiples, in virtually all temporal aspects of growth, reproduction, and disease known to life science. Darwin's explanation for such weekly periodic processes assumed that man and his vertebrate relations must be descended from an even lower, originally tidal-dependent, marine organism similar to the present-day ascidians.

The ascidians, or sea squirts, appear in adult form to be potato-sized sea plants. They are exclusively found, fixed to firm supports, in tidal zones. In the mid-1860s, the remarkable discovery was made by Russia's leading nineteenth-century embryologist, Aleksandr Kovalevsky (1840–1901), that the larval form of the ascidian, which resembles a microscopic tadpole, possesses a rudimentary notochord (Fig. 5.2) and is therefore related to the most primitive of all true vertebrates (Kovalevsky 1866 and 1868; see also Adams 1973). The ascidians were consequently recognized as animals, not plants, and were considered by many to be a "missing link" between invertebrates and the lowest true vertebrates.[16]

In England Charles Darwin (1871) and in Germany Ernst Haeckel (1868, 1874a) quickly seized upon Kovalevsky's discovery as a major corroboration of the theory of evolution. They thought that one branch of primitive ascidianlike creatures had evolved into the vertebrates (fishes, amphibians, reptiles, birds, and mammals), while another, retrogressing, had become the present-day ascidians. "Thus, if we may rely on embryology, ever the safest guide in classification," Darwin concluded in *The Descent of Man,* "it seems that we have at last gained a clue to the source whence the Vertebrata were derived" (1871, *1*:205–6; 1874:160).[17]

Not only did the ascidian hypothesis help to explain much that was otherwise puzzling in higher vertebrate morphology—including why man possesses such aquatic adaptations in early embryonic life

15. See Ellis (1900a:53–121) for a comprehensive survey of Fliess's precursors.

16. The honor of being the lowest true vertebrate had previously fallen to the lancelot or amphioxus, a primitive fish that was once mistakenly classified with the worms. For a more general historical review of the reception and controversies that greeted the famous ascidian hypothesis of vertebrate descent, see Russell 1916: Chapter XV, especially pp. 269–73.

17. This quotation and those that follow are from the 1874 edition of *The Descent of Man.*

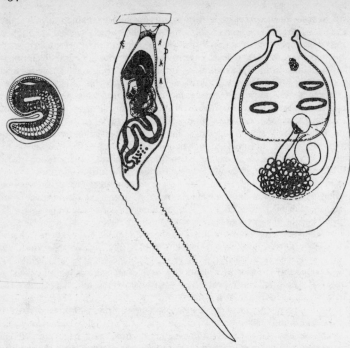

Fig. 5.2. The development of the ascidian (*Ascidia intestinalis*). *Left to right*: embryo, with a well-formed notochord and tail; larval form attached to a support, with the notochord largely reabsorbed; young adult. (From Kovalevsky 1866: Plate 2, Fig. 20; Plate 3, Figs. 29 and 35.)

as rudimentary gill slits—but it also shed light upon the mysterious law of vital periodicity governing the functions of all vertebrate creatures. "The inhabitants of the seashore must be greatly affected by the tides," Darwin reasoned. And he explained further:

> . . . animals living either about the *mean* high-water mark, or about the *mean* low-water mark, pass through a complete cycle of tidal changes in a fortnight. Consequently, their food supply will undergo marked changes week by week. The vital functions of such animals, living under these conditions for many generations, can hardly fail to run their course in regular weekly periods. Now it is a mysterious fact that in the higher and now terrestrial Vertebrata, as well as in other classes, many normal and abnormal processes have one or more whole weeks as their periods; this would be rendered intelligible if the Vertebrata are descended from an animal allied to the existing tidal Ascidians. (1874:164–65 n., expanded from the 1871 edition [1871, 1:212 n.])

Charles Darwin about 1854, five years before the *Origin of Species*.
Photograph by Maull and Fox of London.

As striking illustrations of both the prevalence and the indelible nature of this law, Darwin went on to cite that the eggs of the pigeon hatch
in precisely two weeks, those of the hen in three, those of the duck
in four, those of the goose in five, and those of the ostrich in seven
whole weeks.

But why, asked Darwin, had such weekly periods survived so uniformly in higher organisms? He attributed this rhythmic persistence
to natural selection, which must have favored in gestation and other
periodic biological functions only those temporal alterations that har-

monized with the original, preexisting cycles of the ancestors. Such "preadaptive" transmutations, Darwin reasoned, would have been those occurring "abruptly by a whole week." "This conclusion, if sound," he summed up, "is highly remarkable; for the period of gestation in each mammal, and the hatching of each bird's eggs, and many other vital processes, thus betray to us the primordial birthplace of these animals" (1871, *1*:212 n.; 1874:165 n.).

Darwin's interest in vital periodicity was apparently aroused by the researches of his fellow countryman Thomas Laycock, who had treated the subject in a provocative series of eleven separate studies published in the early 1840s.[18] Among other sources of biological evidence, Laycock claimed to have reviewed the gestation periods of 129 different species of birds and mammals. Of these, he found 67 (52 percent) to have their gravid period in a definite number of weeks or months and another 24 (18 percent) to be within plus or minus one day of having it so (for a total of 70 percent). Of the remaining 39 species (30 percent), most had gestation periods close to the predicted value, although Laycock frankly conceded that in many of these instances the facts were too loosely stated in the available literature to be of critical weight either for or against the theory (1842*a*, 1843*b*).

Like Fliess half a century later, Laycock believed that temporal cycles govern the duration of many stages in the development of organisms. He drew much of his evidence on this score from the life cycles of insects, showing that the sequence of principal stages (ovum, larva and its moults, pupa, imago or "puberty" stage, and adult life-span) often follows multiples of seven whole days.

Diseases, too, Laycock insisted, tend to run their course in three-and-one-half and seven-day multiples. "One might almost venture to assert that the *scientific* observation and treatment of disease are im-

---

18. Darwin must have been familiar as well with his grandfather Erasmus Darwin's stimulating treatment of solar and lunar influences upon biological processes. See Erasmus Darwin's discussion of "The Periods of Disease" in *Zoonomia* (1794–96: Section XXXVI). Laycock's researches encompassed biomedical documentation of recurring periods of twelve hours (the barometric day); twenty-four hours (the solar day); three-and-one-half days (the "lunar week"); seven days (the solar week); twenty-eight days (the lunar month); the solar year; and cycles of seven and eighteen years (the latter being a recurring lunar and eclipse cycle). See Laycock 1840:44–47; 1842*a*, *b*; 1843*a–g*; and 1844.

A neurophysiologist and neurologist like Freud, Thomas Laycock (1812–76) was a prolific scientific writer and published some three hundred articles and half a dozen books in his lifetime. His widely read *Treatise on the Nervous Diseases of Women: Comprising an Inquiry into the Nature, Causes, and Treatment of Spinal and Hysterical Disorders* recognized hysteria in the male, attributed hysteria in the female primarily to sexual causes, and, on more Fliessian lines, argued that menstruation does not cease during pregnancy (1840:8–9, 46–47). More important for the history of psychology, Laycock was one of the earliest to develop a theory of the reflex action of the brain. He later combined this doctrine with a remarkably Freudian view of unconscious mental activity in order to explain dreaming, states of delirium, and various other mental disorders. He was one of the first neurologists to apply the theory of evolution to explaining the comparative structure and function of the nervous system in man and other vertebrates (see Laycock 1860; 1869 edition, *1*:414–15). Through his famous pupil John Hughlings Jackson, Laycock's views on the "evolution and dissolution" of nervous functioning were later to have a major influence on Freud (see Chapter 7).

possible, without a knowledge of the mysterious revolutions continually taking place in the system" (1842a:162). In this last connection, he pointed to the remarkable coincidence between such views and the famous "critical days" of Hippocratic medicine—that is, the 7th, 14th, 21st, and 28th days. Setting forth one last anticipation of Wilhelm Fliess's theories, Laycock (1842b:425–27) suggested that twins, siblings, and perhaps even successive generations might all share identical constitutional periodicities in their vital cycles.

Through Darwin, Laycock's and Darwin's own views on the biological importance of vital periodicity were widely circulated among subsequent students of this captivating subject.[19] Havelock Ellis, one of the great turn-of-the-century pioneers in the scientific study of sexuality, mentioned both men prominently and devoted a large portion of the second volume of his *Studies in the Psychology of Sex* to "the phenomena of sexual periodicity" (1900a:53–121, especially 55, 73, 75). "Throughout the vegetable and animal worlds the sexual functions are periodic," Ellis wrote. "From the usually annual period of flowering in plants, with its play of sperm cell and germ cell, and consequent seed production, through the varying sexual energies of animals, up to the monthly effervescence of the generating organism in woman, . . . from first to last we find unfailing evidence of the periodicity of sex." But such rhythms are not only sexual, Ellis insisted: "It is the character of all biological activity, alike on the physical and the psychic sides" (1900a:53–54). Following the Italian anthropologist Mantegazza rather than Darwin, Ellis attributed the 28-day menstrual cycle in the human species to a phylogenetic residue of the favorable opportunities for courting, long provided by the light of the full moon (1900a:55).

The ideas of Darwin and Laycock were likewise cited by the Swedish chemist and physicist Svante Arrhenius (1859–1927), himself a Nobel Prize laureate in 1903 for his development of "Arrhenius's theory" of electrolytic dissociation. In the late 1890s, Arrhenius had claimed the discovery of two separate periods of air-electrical activity in Stockholm, following intervals of 25.93 and 27.32 days, respectively. On the basis of these meteorological findings, he went on to refer the 26.68-day menstrual cycle average in that city to the mean effect of these two electrical periodicities—themselves averaging 26.62 days, a difference of only .06 days (Arrhenius 1898:403–5).

Also cognizant of Darwin's and Laycock's work on this subject was Friedrich Schatz in Germany. In 1904, picking up on Arrhenius's find-

19. Freud presumably read Darwin's *Descent of Man* soon after it appeared in 1871; see Freud's *Autobiography* (1925d, S.E., 20:8). Freud also purchased a German translation of *The Descent of Man* in 1875, which bears the inscription "Sigismund Freud, *stud. med.*, 1875" (Freud library, London).

In their own right, Laycock's various medical writings were well known to physicians throughout the late nineteenth century. To cite an example that is also relevant to Wilhelm Fliess's later work, Krafft-Ebing mentions Laycock's *Nervous Diseases of Women* (1840:18–20) for its observations on the sexually stimulating effect exerted by musk upon women (*Psychopathia Sexualis*, 1886 and later editions, section on "Physiological Facts"). This reference immediately precedes Krafft-Ebing's discussion of Mackenzie and Fliess.

ings, Schatz suggested that the period of human gestation (270–80 days) might be the physiological expression of ten multiples of Arrhenius's 27.32-day electrical air pattern (Schatz 1904–6:202, 605). The span of mammalian gestations, seen as even multiples of 23 and 28, was also an important aspect of Wilhelm Fliess's contemporary theories on this subject (1897:87, 235–36).

Within the field of psychiatry, the subject of vital 28-day cycles had become particularly well recognized by the turn of the century. Englishman Thomas Clouston (1891:116) capitalized upon such medical observations in his efforts to substantiate the important role played by sexuality in most forms of adolescent insanity. "This periodicity," he concluded, "is an accurate pathological reflection of the moral periodicity of all nervous energizing, and especially of the reproductive capacity and *nisus*. This [periodic] form of insanity has the closest relation to the function of reproduction." Similarly, Richard von Krafft-Ebing, who always had something pertinent to say on Wilhelm Fliess's favorite scientific topics, devoted a whole monograph to the subject of periodic "menstrual psychoses" in 1902, the year of his death. In his *Psychopathia Sexualis*, Krafft-Ebing had previously recognized equivalent phenomena in the male sex—for example, regular monthly homosexual urges and the case of a microcephalic imbecile whose sexual impulses were manifested "periodically and intensively, as in animals" (1899 trans.:447).

Many more examples could be added to this list of turn-of-the-century studies of vital periodicity. Like the relationship between the nose and the genitals, the subject of vital periodicity had become a hot topic for scientific research around this time. Indeed, not a few contemporary researchers believed with Wilhelm Fliess that vital periodicity, together with its manifest links to biochemistry, might soon provide a major scientific breakthrough on the level of Charles Darwin's momentous achievements half a century before. As one enthusiastic worker in this field commented in an 1897 essay provocatively entitled "Periodicity, a Physiological Law in the Male Sex as well as in the Female": "Gravitation and evolution had to run the gauntlet of 'ist' and 'ism,' but are now undeniable laws. The medical man has now, so to speak, to devote himself to the astronomy of microscopic bodies" (Green 1897:726). Backed by the influential precedent of Charles Darwin and scores of others, Wilhelm Fliess could not have expressed his own scientific intentions any better.

Bisexuality in Man

The embryologically remarkable ascidians, proclaimed by Darwin and other zoologists as the probable ancestor of all vertebrate organisms, were the subject of another much-discussed evolutionary problem in the late nineteenth century; and this additional problem now brings us to Wilhelm Fliess's third major scientific interest: bisexuality in man. During the early embryonic stages of vertebrates, including man, the sexual organs of both sexes are plainly visible. In human beings it is only after the third month of embryonic life that one of these two sets of organs begins to atrophy. On the basis of such anatomical facts, Wilhelm Fliess claimed much of the justification for his theory of bisexual periodicities (1897:223). It was from identical facts, moreover, that Charles Darwin had earlier reasoned in *The Descent of Man* that "some extremely remote progenitor of the whole vertebrate kingdom appears to have been hermaphrodite or androgynous" (1871, 1:207). In Darwin's view, one of the most likely candidates for this missing bisexual link was none other than the hermaphroditic ascidians (1871, 1:205).

Thus the persistence of man's ancient bisexual nature, albeit in rudimentary form, was an idea no more incredible from the evolutionary point of view than was the mysterious persistence of weekly and monthly periodic cycles throughout the vertebrate kingdom. As with vital periodicity, the notion of bisexuality had begun to attract considerable discussion in the late nineteenth century among biomedically oriented physicians. To men like Richard von Krafft-Ebing, the idea of constitutional bisexuality provided one of the most promising solutions to the enigmas of homosexuality and other forms of psychosexual hermaphroditism. In *Psychopathia Sexualis*, Krafft-Ebing quoted with definite approbation the following evolutionary explanation of the problem by fellow psychiatrist James G. Kiernan: "The original bisexuality of the ancestors of the race, shown in the rudimentary female organs of the male, could not fail to occasion functional, if not organic reversions, when mental or physical manifestations were interfered with by disease or congenital defect [. . .]. It seems certain that a femininely functionating brain can occupy a male body and *vice versa*" (Kiernan 1888:129–30; *Psychopathia Sexualis*, 1899 trans.:332).

In this same biotheoretical context, Krafft-Ebing presented in *Psychopathia Sexualis* the instructive case history of a woman who underwent a spontaneous sexual transformation at the age of thirty. In June of 1891 this woman suddenly grew a full beard, developed hair on her abdomen and chest, and experienced a drastic voice change from that of a "soprano" to that of a "lieutenant." Temperamentally the patient assumed a psychically aggressive demeanor, and she even showed signs of a progressive "masculinization" of the external genitalia. Krafft-Ebing commented on the case, with Kiernan's theory in mind: "Interesting illustration of the bi-sexual predisposition, and of the possibility of continued existence of a second sexuality in a latent state, under conditions hitherto unknown" (1899 trans.:335). In support of the probably organic and *atavistic*, or reversionary, nature of such pathological phenomena, Krafft-Ebing cited the researches of zoologist Carl Claus, an expert on both hermaphroditism and (sexual) alternation of generations in lower animals. Krafft-Ebing was particularly impressed by Claus's discovery that certain forms of Crustacea live the first part of their lives as males and the second part as females (see Claus 1891:490).

Carl Claus was the same professor with whom young Sigmund Freud had taken an elective course in general biology and Darwinism in 1874, his first year as a medical student at the University of Vienna. It is more than likely that the evolution of sex was a prime topic of discussion in this course, for Claus was just then engaged in his pioneering studies of sex in Crustacea. Impressed by his young student, Claus twice obtained for Freud, in March and September 1876, traveling grants to his newly founded marine laboratory in Trieste. While Freud was at the Trieste laboratory, Claus personally directed his first piece of scientific research—a study of the male sex organs of the eel (Freud 1877b).[20]

There can be little question that Freud was also exposed about this same time to the important biological discoveries, and their wider bearing on the theory of evolution, that figures like Haeckel, Kovalevsky, and Claus were making during the 1870s. Freud's second major piece of scientific research, under the direction of Ernst Brücke, had dealt with the evolutionary relationship of the spinal nerves of *Ammocoetes* (*Petromyzon planeri*) to those of higher vertebrates (Freud 1877a, 1878a). Not only is petromyzon itself bisexual, but, more important, it is virtually the closest zoological relative to the primitive amphioxus and hence, hypothetically, to the remarkable little ascidians that had prompted so much lively biological controversy during Freud's student days. Finally, it was in this wider context of evolutionary debate that Brücke specifically assigned the petromyzon problem to young Freud (Bernfeld 1949:176). Thus, when Wilhelm Fliess brought the theory of bisexuality to Freud's attention in the mid-1890s, he found in the latter a biologically prepared listener who not only had trained with a leader in this field but also had conducted firsthand research himself on a bisexual progenitor of man.

The Evidence for a 23-Day Sexual Cycle in Man

Returning now to the subject of Wilhelm Fliess's various scientific innovations, I should like to emphasize that his only really new idea was the controversial claim to have discovered a 23-day physiological cycle in man. But even here he was forced to share the honors of simultaneous discovery with another of his biological contemporaries, Edinburgh University Professor of Comparative Embryology and Vertebrate Morphology, John Beard.

This convergence of scientific interest upon the biological significance of 23 days in human life is not as surprising as one might think. Twenty-three days is the average interval between the termination of one menstruation and the beginning of the next. Furthermore, in both biochemical and particularly evolutionary biological terms, this 23-day period has considerable scientific fascination. Let us begin by

20. For a more detailed treatment of Freud's scientific relationship with Claus, see Ritvo 1972.

looking at John Beard's theory, where this evolutionary logic is more explicit than it is in Fliess's presentation.

Beard's researches are reported in a closely reasoned monograph, *The Span of Gestation and the Cause of Birth*, which was published in Jena, Germany, in 1897, the same year as Fliess's monograph on the relations between the nose and the female sexual organs. Beard sought to demonstrate that the time required from the last day of menstruation to the completion of the next ovulation in women, approximately 23 days, is of far greater biological significance than the full 28-day cycle. He rested his argument on the following series of evolutionary and comparative embryological facts.

In the embryological development of every species, there comes a point at which the embryo is finally recognizable in all its essential parts. In man, this point, defined by Beard as "the critical period," comes between the 46th and 47th day of embryonic life. Why, he asked, do some organisms come into the world only long after this critical period is reached? In other words, why are not all organisms born, as are most species of marsupials, when the critical period is attained, and when the primitive yolk-sac placenta of these marsupials is no longer able to nourish the young? Beard's answer was that the postmarsupial evolution of an allantoic placenta had allowed gradual prolongation of gestation (with all of its well-known evolutionary benefits). But in marsupials, which lack this innovation, the embryo *must* be born when its parts are roughly complete, and when its source of uterine nourishment is gone.

Meanwhile, as the gestation interval was gradually prolonged in man's early progenitors, the relatively short period of mammalian ovulation had to be biologically suppressed during pregnancy. In the interests of maximum reproduction, the first postpartum ovulation in such evolving organisms would logically have occurred shortly after each birth. Copulation and reimpregnation indeed does follow such an efficient pattern—within "a few hours" as Beard specifically noted—in many small mammals (1897:31).

The relentless evolutionary pressure toward maximizing reproductive efficiency, Beard further reasoned, would have created the following cyclical constraints between ovulation, gestation, and birth. With the progressive lengthening of gestation, the chemical mechanisms coordinating sequential ovulation and birth could only have been preserved by maintaining each new period of gestation as an even and higher multiple of the original periods of gestation and ovulation.[21] Now it just so happens that in the mouse (*Mus musculus*) the average length of gestation ($19\frac{1}{4}$–$19\frac{2}{3}$ days) is just short of twice the ovulation period ($9\frac{5}{6}$–10 days) and exactly twice the length of the critical period ($9\frac{2}{3}$–$9\frac{5}{6}$ days), while in sheep the period of gestation (145–50 days) is ten times the length of the ovulation cycle and five times that of the critical period (Beard 1897:98).

---

21. Cf. Darwin's similar hypothesis in *The Descent of Man* (1871, 1:212 n.).

All this suggested to Beard that whole multiples should invariably prevail between the ovulation cycle, the critical period (itself the original length of gestation), and the current gestation period of each higher species of Mammalia. Something of a masterpiece in hypothetico-deductive reasoning, Beard's monograph was empirically supported by considerable quantitative data from comparative embryology and reproductive biology. His information showed that such whole multiples were indeed to be found in the mouse, rabbit, dog, cat, cavy, pig, sheep, cow, horse, and even man!

These findings bring us to Beard's analysis of the relationship between menstrual and ovulatory cycles in human beings. In the human female, Beard reasoned, menstruation represents the abortion of an unfertilized egg. It also represents the abortion of a missing 23-day-old embryo, one that would have been half the age at which such embryos now reach their critical period and technically become "fetuses." According to Beard's theory, 23 days must have been the original length of gestation in man's ancestors; afterward it doubled to the present critical period and then was augmented, again by whole multiples, until it reached the present gestation span of 276–80 days. The aboriginal period of gestation has nevertheless been preserved, Beard argued, in the present period of ovulation, which is triggered anew by each abortive "birth" (menstruation) of an unfertilized embryo. In Beard's interpretation, then, the period of ovulation is to be seen as extending from the very *end* of one menstruation to the very *beginning* of the next (1897:73). Menstruation itself, in Beard's theory, is merely a *superadded* phenomenon—and peculiarly long in the human female on account of the highly evolved nature of placental reproduction in our species.

One important implication of Beard's theory was that in man the usual length of gestation (276–80 days) could be understood as precisely twelve times the average ovulation cycle (23–23½ days) and six times the critical period (46–47 days) and not, as most physicians then commonly believed, ten times the 28-day menstrual cycle. In corroboration of his theory, Beard presented considerable statistical evidence showing that spontaneous abortions tend to be most frequent at multiples of the 23-day ovulation cycle (1897:81). He also suggested, in a remarkable anticipation of Wilhelm Fliess's own thinking, that much of the apparent irregularity of the menstrual cycle could be minimized by measuring the biologically more constant interval from the end of one menstruation to the beginning of the next—that is, 23 days (1897:75).

Although Wilhelm Fliess reached essentially the same conclusion as John Beard regarding the independent existence of a 23-day sexual cycle in man, he seems to have done so from a more physicalist point of view. Nevertheless, Beard's basic hypothesis about menstrual bleeding being a *superadded* and *eliminatory-destructive* sexual phenomenon was closely tied up with Fliess's thinking on this problem. This connection is underscored by the fact that Fliess's rival discovery emerged in intimate scientific cooperation with his studies of conception, menstruation, and the length of gestation in human beings.[22]

Fliess approached the problem in terms of the physiological investments of energy associated with these cyclical processes. Indeed, his central preoccupation in scientific life was an abiding concern with the organism as a conduit of vital energy. For him, conception, menstruation, gestation, birth, growth, and disease all had to be accounted for in these implicitly Helmholtzian terms.

The key to Fliess's thinking lies in his analysis of the course of gestation. He was well aware that during pregnancy menstruation appears to cease only superficially. That is because the most characteristic feature of the female cycle, the last four or five days of uterine bleeding, is biologically suppressed (Fliess 1897:47). Now, from his physicalist perspective on the problem, this temporarily suppressed source of energy had to be conserved, thus allowing the summation of physiological forces that energized embryonic growth and finally birth itself (1897:47, 113). It was apparently this bioenergetic line of reasoning that first suggested to Fliess that human sexual chemistry in general—as opposed to its more uniquely "female" component, which aborts and destructs unfertilized sexual products—possesses a second or 23-day component, as Beard himself had concluded. In fact, this second rhythm could be seen in Fliess's bioenergetic terms as the really active and procreative component of the human sexual cycle. So, too, when his friend Freud later came to the conclusion that libido, which the latter always conceived as inherently "active," must be predominantly *masculine* and therefore corresponds to Fliess's 23-day substance, he was simply building upon Fliess's logic.[23]

Another compelling influence behind Fliess's discovery of a 23-day cycle in man was his conviction that the statistical irregularities of menstruation and gestation could not be a matter of chance. A parsimonious assumption in this connection was that a second cycle was introducing irregularities into the customary 28-day pattern; and the theory of bisexuality lent suggestive support to the hypothesis that this second cycle was not only characteristic of the male sex but present in *both* sexes. Hence it was that Fliess, for all of the preceding reasons, came to accept the existence of two independent sexual periods in human physiology.

But what really cemented his conviction in the biological reality of his 23-day male cycle was a compelling source of data not consid-

22. It should be noted that much of Fliess's scientific work on this subject originated from observations on himself and his family. Fliess's wife became pregnant with her first child in March 1895 and delivered on 29 December 1895, precisely the interval in which Fliess developed his ideas on the 23-day masculine cycle. What is more, during her pregnancy his wife's periods varied from a lower limit of 23 days to an upper limit of 33 (*Origins*, p. 158; see earlier, p. 142, for the significance of 33 days). Fliess, a rigid determinist like Freud, may have seen a likely universal in this particularly amenable source of data.

23. Freud never gave up the idea that libido is masculine. See *Origins*, pp. 179–80, where he also relates the intellectual superiority of males to Fliess's bioenergetic theory; and *Three Essays*, 1905d, S.E., 7:219.

ered by John Beard. For his own part, Fliess was interested not only in the problems of gestation and conception (including the possible prevention of conception by the rhythm method), but also in the causes of sex determination in the offspring. He believed that these problems were somehow related, an assumption that has since proved to be correct (see, for example, Trivers and Willard 1973). The logic that led Fliess to this particular conviction was the following. Within the context of his general theory about sexual chemistry, he thought that the sex of offspring might be determined by the precise disposition of the mother's chemical cycles at the time of conception. This hypothesis led him to look at the *primary sexual ratio* in human beings (that is, the numerical ratio between males and females *at birth*), a proportion that he sought to relate to the two temporal cycles present in the mother.

The normal ratio between the sexes at birth is roughly 105 or 106 males to every 100 females. On the basis of his theory of bisexual periods, Fliess (1897:224) predicted that this ratio should be 121.7 per 100 (= 28/23). But males are known to show a much higher intrauterine, as well as postnatal, mortality rate than females. Citing data from Carl Düsing's (1884) authoritative monograph on the regulation of the sex ratio in man, animals, and plants, Fliess noted that the human dead-born sexual ratio was 129 males to 100 females (based on a figure of 10 million dead-born fetuses). Numerically, this finding is intriguing for Fliess's theory, because

$$\frac{129 \text{ dead-born males}}{106 \text{ live-born males}} = 1.217 = \frac{28}{23} \text{ (exactly)!}$$

In other words, the higher intrauterine death rate among males appeared to be somehow related to Fliess's two periodic cycles. But this was precisely as it should have been in his theory, for he held that illness, mortality, and hence general life-span in man should be roughly proportional to the frequency of each sex's dominant cycle.

If one now assumes, as Fliess did, that roughly 27 out of 28 females conceived survive pregnancy, but that only 22 out of every 23 males do so, one can easily derive the primary sexual ratio at birth by the following mathematical calculation:

$$\frac{129 \text{ dead-born males}}{100 \text{ dead-born females}} \times \frac{22 \text{ surviving males/dead-born male}}{27 \text{ surviving females/dead-born female}}$$

$$= \frac{105 \text{ surviving males}}{100 \text{ surviving females}}$$

Fliess even produced independent biological statistics from Düsing (1884:55) to show that roughly 2 fetuses die *in utero* for every 51 born alive—precisely the figure required by his theory:

$$\frac{1+1}{28+23} = \frac{2 \text{ dead-born fetuses}}{51 \text{ live-born fetuses}}$$

(See Fliess 1897:223–24; 1906*b*:417–18, 421–22.)

Finally, the higher intrauterine death rate of males implied that Fliess's theoretical prediction of the ratio of *conceived* male and female offspring (121.7/100) might not be far from the actual case. Citing additional data from Düsing (1884:50)—this time based upon a sample of 21,000 live births—Fliess (1897:226) was able to show that monthly variations in the human primary sexual ratio approach, but never exceed, the predicted ratio of 121.7 males per 100 females. (Düsing records 120.5 surviving males/100 females for the month of November—i.e., for those terminal gestations that have been subjected to the mildest seasonal influences.)

The figures 23 and 28 therefore predicted not only the sexual ratio of conceived offspring but also the differential mortality rates of males and females *in utero*, as well as the average primary sexual ratio at birth. All a bit strange in scientific retrospect, but nonetheless quite true! In January 1898, Freud himself called Fliess's primary sex ratio data "highly impressive" (Schur 1971:142; unpublished Fliess correspondence). And indeed they were impressive. Although hardly as convinced by these results as was either Fliess or Freud, the level-headed Havelock Ellis surveyed the theories of both John Beard and Wilhelm Fliess at the turn of the century and was compelled to admit that "these attempts to prove a new physiological cycle [in human beings] deserve careful study and further investigation" (1900a:83).[24]

Two Major Misconceptions Concerning Fliess's Theory of Periodicity

There are two further misunderstandings about Fliess's theories that we are finally in a position to correct; and correct them we must in order to convey the full and rational nature of his influence upon Freud during the 1890s. First, Fliess definitely did not choose the number 23 in his general formula $x \cdot 23 \pm y \cdot 28$ because it allowed him to derive, in conjunction with 28, any and all positive integers, as critics from his own time up to ours (e.g., Gardner 1966) have suggested. Fliess was simply not that stupid, either biologically or mathematically. Indeed, he was fully aware of such mathematical criticism and devoted two whole chapters in *Der Ablauf des Lebens* (1906b:342–437) to refuting it![25]

His theory was valid, Fliess argued, because it fitted the data as observed in day-to-day biological processes; and higher multiples of 23

24. According to Kris (1954:9 n.), Fliess's scientific ideas were never discussed outside of Germany. This claim is patently false. See also Ellis (1928, 1:36, 90, 109, 113, 250; 2:290; 3:180; and especially 4:69), Mackenzie (1898), and Ries (1903) for further English and American citations of Fliess's theories.

25. See, for example, Henning (1910) and Fliess (1907, 1911) for many additional references.

and 28 played no major role in the initial exposition of his theory (Fliess 1897).[26] All in all, it would not be going too far to say that the remarkable mathematical versatility of 23 and 28 in Fliess's basic formula was purely an unforeseen consequence of his prior biological train of thought. Only later did he apparently realize this mathematical versatility, which proved to be a veritable nuisance in his efforts to win converts to his biological conceptions.

In short, Fliess's so-called number mysticism must be understood within the context of his sincere, if erroneous, belief in his various fundamental biological premises. Unfortunately most of Freud's biographers have not even begun to realize what these premises were or to what a sophisticated theory they lent their plausible support. To cite perhaps the most glaring example of this historical disregard, Fliess has long been held responsible for predicting, on the basis of his biorhythm theory, that Freud would die at 51 (the sum of 23 and 28).[27] And yet periods of *years* had absolutely no significance in Fliess's theory.[28] In actuality, Freud himself made this superstitious prediction in a letter he wrote Fliess a full year before his friend had even begun to speak about a 23-day cycle.[29] Freud founded this famous prediction upon his own knowledge of several colleagues who had died suddenly at this critical age (1900a, S.E., 5:438–39). He was also obsessed at various times with the fear that he would die at 41 and 42, 61 and 62, and 81½—ages that were as little significant to Fliess's theory as was 51.[30] Thus, the "death-at-51" story, long a symbol of Fliess's "number mysticism" and "Teutonic crackpottery," is largely a myth—one that tells us something about Sigmund Freud and his subsequent biographers, but nothing about Fliess.

This conclusion brings us to the second and perhaps the more important of the two major historical misunderstandings about Fliess's theory of vital periodicity. This theory is not to be confused with the more rigid "Swiss" system of crisscrossing cycles, with which Martin Gardner (1966) and others have generally equated the original Fliessian version. In the Swiss system (which has an extra 33-day, "intellectual" cycle), three biorhythms are conceived as following a rising and falling pattern, with each cycle reaching its maximum and minimum every

26. When Fliess later turned to the analysis of data in terms of his general formula $x \cdot 23 \pm y \cdot 28$, he fully recognized that x and y could not just be juggled by him *at random* if 23 and 28 days were biologically *real* cycles (1906b:342). Rather, there had to be certain simple and recurring patterns in x and y themselves, starting with the integers 0 and 1—a perfectly logical conclusion that, for extremely large temporal sums, pushed Fliess into much of the "numerology" (i.e., complex mathematics) that characterized his later book of 1906.

27. See, for example, Jones 1953:310, 348; Bakan 1958:308; Lauzon 1963:47; Gardner 1966:109; Costigan 1967:52; Schur 1972:187; and Strachey, S.E., 5:439, n. 6.

28. The only one who has ever noticed this inconsistency is the English-language translator, Patrick Evans, of Lauzon's French biography of Freud (1963: translator's footnote to p. 47).

29. Unpublished Fliess correspondence, letter of 22 June 1894; quoted in Schur 1972:53; see also pp. 100–101.

30. For documentation of this point, see Schur (1972:53, 159, 184–87, 231–32, and 301); but Schur himself still holds to the traditional explanation of the "51" figure.

23, 28, and 33 days, respectively.[31] "Critical days" are accordingly assumed to coincide with each maximum and minimum, as well as with each cycle's return to the zero line, and more especially, with a simultaneous occurrence of critical points in two or all three cycles (see Fig. 5.3).

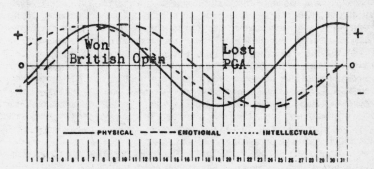

Fig. 5.3. The later, "Swiss" version of Fliess's periodicity theory. The chart depicts points at which Arnold Palmer won and lost major golf tournaments during July 1962. (From Thommen 1964:89.)

Fliess's theory, in contrast to this later version, was considerably more sophisticated and, at the same time, duly appreciative of the complexities to be expected in detecting possible periodicities in living processes. Fliess was fully aware that the 28-day menstrual cycle does not confine itself to producing just 4 or 5 days' symptoms every 23rd through 28th day or, for that matter, at regular 14-day intervals—that is, at the maximum and minimum points in the Swiss interpretation of the matter. Women manifest a wide variety of menstrual-cycle symptoms, including attacks of migraine, cramps, nosebleeding, slight mid-cycle sanguineous discharges, or so-called *Nebenmenstruation*, and so forth, at various times *throughout* their 28-day period. Nor did Fliess expect all the phenomena of life, any more than those pertaining to menstruation, to follow entirely like clockwork at uninterrupted intervals of 23 and 28 days. Such a theory would have proved most easy to refute.

What Fliess *did* expect was that different vital and pathological manifestations would intermittently occur in various bodily organs throughout each cycle and that the presence of recurring patterns would reveal itself by phenomena like migraine, *Nebenmenstruation*, and other organic symptoms following one another at intervals of 23 and 28 days. To document these cyclical patterns, one therefore had

31. Discovery of the 33-day "intellectual" cycle was announced in the 1920s by Alfred Teltscher, a doctor of engineering and teacher at Innsbruck who collected information on the performance of high school and university students. A series of Swiss investigators subsequently combined Fliess's two cycles with the Teltscher cycle to create the present three-cycle system. See Wernli 1959; and Thommen 1964: Chapters 1 and 2.

to group one's medical data into various independent series of periodically, and presumably physiologically, related symptoms. This was just
what Fliess (1897) initially did with his patient's histories, and he
employed up to five or six "male" and "female" series in each of the
clinical histories he published.

To accommodate this more complex conception of vital periodicity, Fliess later came to believe that human sexual chemistry was
governed by 23-day and 28-day *substances*, themselves built up from
subunits possessing life-spans of twenty-four hours (Fliess 1906*b*:41–
42). Further, he reasoned that, in the bisexual organism, chemical
unions of these two periodic sexual substances would produce a chemical entity having a 51-day life-span. The significance of the number 5
in Fleiss's later theory comes from the assumption that two 28-day substances might form a chemical equivalent of a 51-day bisexual substance by combining and freeing themselves in the process of 5 leftover
units. Other temporal combinations were seen by Fliess as biochemically
possible, although increasingly unlikely.

The purely empirical test of Fliess's theory was whether a minimal
number of periodic series could suffice to explain large numbers of
recorded symptom-days over a prolonged span of time. Fliess, on the
basis of tens of thousands of medical observations, claimed this to be
the case. Today, of course, we know that he was mistaken; and thus we
come to the question of his "observations" and where they went wrong.

In the study of vital periodicity, just as in many other areas of
scientific research, it is particularly difficult to keep one's prior expectations from influencing both one's collection and evaluation of relevant
data. As one recent student of biorhythms has confessed in connection
with his work on periodic growth lines in coral formations: "The trouble
is that counting growth lines is not easy, as anyone who has tried can
testify. It is constantly necessary to make subjective decisions about
whether a line is really a line or where an annual or monthly series
begins or ends. As a result it is not surprising that counts often come
out close to the hypothetical values" (J. W. Evans, quoted in Schopf
1976:375). Even Gregor Mendel's revolutionary experiments in plant
genetics are known to have suffered from this same sort of statistical
shortcoming owing to his prior knowledge of the expected results
(Fisher 1936; Wright 1966).

Thus, Wilhelm Fliess was, above all, a victim of his own prior
expectations; and as the latter had a substantial biological foundation,
it was all the easier to find confirmations of his theory.[32] After all,
much of his data was derived from entirely bona fide 28-day, and even
some 23-day, manifestations of his female patients. Then again, when
Fliess encountered clear exceptions to his laws, which of course he did,

32. Fliess's misdirection was undoubtedly compounded by the effects of suggestion upon his patients. According to Ruble (1977), women who are led to believe
that they are about to menstruate report a significantly higher degree of associated
symptoms, which indicates a psychosocial bias in the self-reporting of menstrual-
related changes.

he was able to compare them to the observed exceptions found even in Newton's, Galileo's, and Kepler's physical laws. Finally, Fliess believed that some of the exceptions to his biorhythmic laws could be attributed to the interference of other periodic cycles, such as the annual one (1906*b*:416–17). In all these respects, his ultimate scientific self-deception on the basis of prior biological assumptions was hardly the sort of totally "psychopathological" affair that Freud's biographers have so often proclaimed it. Many scientists have found themselves deluded, like Fliess, by a theory that simply seemed too good to be untrue.

Fliess's Scientific Interests in Retrospect

There was, in short, enough method and consistency to Fliess's madness to convince many—Sigmund Freud included—from a whole generation of scientific contemporaries that he had made a series of profound scientific discoveries. Above all, to those contemporaries who shared Fliess's biological assumptions, his ideas seemed to occupy the visionary forefront, not the lunatic fringe, of "hard" science. Some even interpreted resistance to his discoveries as a sign that he, like the long-unappreciated Gregor Mendel, was simply too far ahead of his times.[33] By 1913, when the Medical Society for Sexual Science was founded in Berlin, partly to help gain recognition for Fliess, there were some individuals, like Albert Eulenburg, the eminent neurologist, ardent Fliessian, and first president of that society, who thought that Freudian psychoanalysis, not Fliessian sexual biology, was the real pseudoscience of the two great medical "systems" of the day.[34]

Were all these Fliessian ideas, to return for a moment to Iago Galdston's (1956) hypothesis, really the unrecognized legacy of nineteenth-century Romantic medicine, or were they perhaps Pythagorean and mystical in inspiration, as Henning (1910) long ago maintained? My response to these two theses is definitely in the negative. To attribute to Fliess so-called Romantic and mystical tendencies is to misunderstand what he was really trying to do. True, his various scientific interests had many ostensible ties both to Romantic medicine and to the doctrines of Pythagoras, Hippocrates, and other ancient Greek medical "mystics." But these same interests were no more Romantic or mystical to Fliess and his supporters than they are today in physiological research being carried out on biological clocks, on male and female sexual hormones and their bisexual presence in each of us, on the importance of olfaction in mammalian sexuality, or on the possible cerebral lo-

33. Saaler (1914:345–46) specifically mentions Mendel.
34. For further reference to Fliess and the new Society for Sexual Science, see Freud's letter of 6 April 1914 to Karl Abraham (*Freud/Abraham Letters*, p. 171). For Eulenburg's contrasting views on Fliess and psychoanalysis, see Bloch's obituary notice of Eulenburg (1917:243).

calization of rational (*left*-hemisphere) and more intuitive (*right*-hemisphere) mental abilities.[35]

Like Sigmund Freud, Fliess was a rigid determinist and hence the bearer of perhaps the most influential of all the legacies to Freud's scientific generation from Helmholtzian-biophysical and *post*-Romantic medicine. "From now on," Fliess urged at one point in his magnum opus of 1906, "we may definitely delete the word 'chance' from the biological sphere of events" (p. 415). His related faith in mathematics as the ultimate basis of exact science was in turn a Galilean or a Newtonian view of science as much as it was a Pythagorean one. As a committed biological reductionist, Fliess looked forward to the creation of a whole new science of mathematical biochemistry, not back to the "mysticism" or number "mumbo-jumbo" of his predecessors.

As for Fliess's influence upon Freud, it was the physiological and particularly evolutionary framework implicit in Fliess's ideas that led Freud to take him so seriously. Man, said Charles Darwin in 1871, was descended from a bisexual, lunar-cycle-dependent, tidal organism whose libido, said Ernst Haeckel in 1874, was originally triggered by chemotropisms (smell in the wider sense). Without always doing so explicitly, Fliess definitely played upon this evolutionary logic and, in the process, offered concrete clinico-physiological findings that finally made such well-known evolutionary speculations seem "mechanically" respectable.

"My first impression," so Freud enviously greeted Fliess's reports of scientific discovery in 1895, "was one of amazement at the existence of someone who was an even greater visionary than I, and that he should be my friend Wilhelm" (*Origins*, p. 130). To be sure, Fliess's scientific vision proved far more ephemeral than Freud's. And yet it exerted a lasting influence upon Freud that was second to none in his life.

---

35. Although I have not treated Fliess's views on bilaterality and the assumed association between bisexual proportionalities and lateral dominance, the grain of truth common to his other scientific work lurks here as well. Citing recent data on bilateral differences that emerge according to sex in gonadal weight, fingerprint patterns, and other traits as early as the fourth month of pregnancy, a contemporary student of the problem concludes: "In the embryo, the relationship of male to female bears a dominance relationship which is essentially similar to that manifested by right and left sides. This relationship holds in man and probably in other mammals . . ." (Mittwoch 1977:76). Freud, although initially skeptical of Fliess's claims on this subject, later seems to have endorsed the general truth contained in them. See *Origins*, pp. 242–44, letter of 4 January 1898; *Leonardo da Vinci*, 1910c, *S.E.*, 11:136; Jones 1955:447; and Schur 1972:141, who cites an unpublished letter of Freud's to Fliess, dated 22 January 1898.

6

Freud's Psychoanalytic
Transformation
of the Fliessian Id

WILHELM FLIESS ON SPONTANEOUS INFANTILE SEXUALITY

Amidst all the provocative and multifarious scientific ideas championed by Wilhelm Fliess in the mid-1890s, there is one additional aspect of his scientific repertoire that was bound to have aroused Sigmund Freud's interests. I am referring to Fliess's systematic and, in many respects, pioneering investigations concerning the existence and the causes of childhood sexuality.

Yet what a truly remarkable fact it is that not a single word has been uttered in the voluminous secondary literature on Freud concerning Fliess's discoveries on this most Freudian of topics.[1] More remarkable still, it is not possible to blame such odd historical neglect upon our fragmentary knowledge of Fliess's scientific association with Freud. On the contrary, Fliess published his ideas on infantile sexuality for all to see in his scientific monograph of 1897.

There can be no mistake. Fliess's whole theory of vital periodicity implied the necessary existence of spontaneous infantile sexuality. According to this theory, both the 23-day male and the 28-day female cycle

---

1. Since making this assertion, I have found an exception to it in a publication by Stephen Kern (1973:122, 125) that deals with the general discovery of childhood sexuality. I have nevertheless allowed my statement to stand inasmuch as Kern, who mentions Fliess's observations on sensual thumb-sucking in childhood, seems not to have appreciated that they were part of a far more comprehensive conception of childhood sexuality and, more important still, that this conception was integral to his overall theory of human development and exerted a considerable influence upon Freud.

were present in each sex throughout the course of life. The mother's two sexual periods were transmitted to the child in earliest embryonic life and were supposed to determine the sex of the offspring and to regulate its further maturation and overall vital activities until the day of its death. Growth to Fliess was therefore just another form by which sexual chemistry expresses itself in a wider, asexual mode of biological reproduction (1897:237; 1906b:513). "Each sex and every age of life," so Fliess claimed in his 1897 monograph, "is subject to them [the male 23-day and female 28-day sexual rhythms]. The development of individual tissues . . . and functions . . . is linked to their temporal exactness" (1897:212).

It was to show that his two periodic rhythms were biochemically *sexual* in nature that Fliess was drawn to the problem of infantile sexuality. To begin with, his claims as to the sexual regulation of major developmental milestones in life—the appearance of teeth or first attempts at walking and speech, etc.—according to cycles of 23 and 28 days were contentions with absolutely no proof. Indeed, his pansexualist unification of biorhythms, sexual chemistry, and a theory of the entire human life cycle seemed to contradict contemporary scientific belief in the absence of sexual phenomena before puberty. And so it was that Fliess seized eagerly upon the little-recognized evidence for spontaneous infantile sexuality, and particularly for the periodicity of its manifestations, as a major corroboration of his overall system of ideas. He boldly asserted his case as follows in the monograph of 1897:

> Among children, in whom development proceeds in the same periodic thrusts [as found in adults], subtle indications from among the cluster of anxiety symptoms [2] betray the fact that these thrusts are essentially of a sexual nature. Such symptoms are singultus [attacks of sobbing] and diarrhea ("teething diarrhea"). An alert examination finds these symptoms exceedingly frequently in periodic sequences. But it finds still more direct symptomology in the periodically intensified impulse toward sucking [*Lutschen oder Ludeln*] . . . and, with little boys, in direct erections of the penis on such days (even as early as the first months of life!). Moreover, the sexual nature of these thrusts reveals itself by extremely small streaks of blood emanating from the nose and in admixtures of blood or blood-colored substance in the saliva and urine. Let it be noted: all this only in periodic (28- or 23-day) sequence. (1897:198)

In other words, Fliess ascribed 23-day male and 28-day female sexual cycles to earliest infancy, as his theory demanded he do. Accordingly, his average infant was not just sexual, it was doubly so—*bi*sexual!

Thus, when Sigmund Freud later wrote in *An Outline of Psycho-Analysis* that one of "the most unexpected" findings of all his psychoanalytic researches had been the discovery that "sexual life does not begin only at puberty, but starts with plain manifestations soon after

---

2. Fliess is alluding here to Freud's theory of anxiety neurosis and to the sexual nature of this disorder. See Fliess (1897:199), where this point is explicitly made.

birth" (1940a, S.E., 23:152–53), he was in fact echoing one of Wilhelm Fliess's equally pioneering insights.

I shall take up at some length in a later section of this chapter the issue of Freud's precise debt to Fliess for this particular discovery; but for the moment it suffices to say that Fliess set forth his provocative views on spontaneous infantile sexuality at a time when Freud, obsessed by his faith in a traumatic (seduction) theory of psychoneuroses, was intent on minimizing just such a possibility (see earlier, Chapter 4, pp. 111–12). Further, when Freud finally did give up his seduction theory, he replaced it with an etiological conception that was considerably more Fliessian in scope. Indeed, Freud's own later theory of human psychosexual development reveals the impact of Fliess's influence at five important points, which alone justify a complete reappraisal of Fliess's scientific relationship with Freud during the origins of psychoanalysis.

I. Fliess's "Organological" Emphasis: The Component Nature of Infantile Sexuality

Wilhelm Fliess perceived sexuality to be a highly variegated phenomenon in childhood, in both its basic chemical nature and its various forms of possible "organological" expression. His fundamental conception of sexuality as having two dominant component impulses, the male and female bisexual drives, is merely the most prominent illustration of his multiform conception of human sexuality. Like Freud, Fliess was concerned with what is commonly known in psychoanalytic parlance as *erotogenic zones*—that is to say, those parts of the body (including the nose) that are capable of contributing to sexual excitement in its wider, nongenital sense. Indeed, Fliess published his views on this aspect of the later Freudian libido theory even before Freud; and it is also interesting to note the peculiarly psychoanalytic mode of argumentation (that is, the use of etymologies) that Fliess himself adopted in making such claims about childhood sexuality:

> I would just like to point out that the sucking movements that small children make with their lips and tongue on periodic days . . . , the so-called *"Ludeln,"* [3] as well as thumb-sucking, must be considered as an equivalent of masturbation. Such activity likewise brings on anxiety, sometimes combined with neurasthenia, just as does true masturbation. It comes on impulsively and is, on this account, so difficult to wean children from. . . . The role which the word "sweet" [*süss*] later plays in the language of love has its initial physiological root here. With lips and tongue the child first tastes lactose [*Milchzucker*] at his mother's breast,

3. English possesses no real equivalent for the German nursery terms *Ludeln* and *Lutschen* ("thumb-sucking") used by Fliess (see also Fliess 1897:198). Both terms were later employed by Freud, along with *wonnesaugen* ("to suck sensually"), to describe sexual manifestations of the so-called oral phase of childhood development. In this connection, see the editor's footnote to Freud's *Three Essays* (1905d, S.E., 7:179 n.). See also Lindner (1879:68), who had previously used all three terms in his study of childhood thumb-sucking.

and they provide him with his earliest experience of satisfaction. "Sweet" [*süss*] is related to the French *sucer* (to suck) and to *Zucker, suggar, sugere*. (1897:185 n.)

Thus, not only did Fliess seem to accept the idea of an "oral" component in childhood sexuality, but he also believed that such activity could induce a childhood neurosis!

As Fliess was quite a student of etymologies, by Freud's own admission (*Origins*, p. 194), it is natural to wonder what influence, if any, this interest may have had upon Freud's well-known psychoanalytic penchant for linguistic evidence. Compare Fliess's etymological analysis of the German word *süss* in 1897 with Freud's similar observations on this subject in his case history of the "Wolf Man" some twenty years later: "Permanent marks have been left by this oral phase of sexuality upon the usages of language. People commonly speak, for instance, of an 'appetizing' love-object, and describe persons they are fond of as 'sweet' [*süss*]" (1918*b*, S.E., *17*:107).

In addition to discussing oral masturbatory activities in childhood, Fliess did not fail to connect the various *excretory* organs with potential expressions of sexuality in young children. Speaking, for instance, of bed-wetting in childhood, Fliess asserted:

> The enuresis of children (and urticaria) [4] also appears only at periodic intervals. Childhood enuresis resembles the urge to urinate by which so many women are tormented and which also in fact occurs at periodic intervals among adults. Its relationship with sexual processes was apparently already known to the ancients (*castus raro mingit* ["the chaste rarely urinate"]). But only if one knows its exact periodic relationship, can one understand why among older people, following the extinction of the sexual function, the bladder becomes less "retentive" and how it might come to be that in some men, directly after castration and in an often mysterious way, that incessant impulse to urinate suddenly disappears, which at times can make life miserable for those with prostate disorders. (1897:175)

Freud, I might add, could not have expressed better what was to become his own psychoanalytic position on the sexual nature of childhood bed-wetting.[5]

Fliess's views did not stop with enuresis. He was equally convinced of a close physiological tie between the *anal* excretory function and the sexual manifestations of children. Witness his careful documentation

---

4. *Urticaria:* a form of skin rash, which, according to Fliess (1897:217), was of a sexual (toxic) nature. Urticaria is largely confined to the mucous membranes and thus can be seen, in such Fliessian terms, as a neurotic disorder par excellence of childhood erotogenic zones.

5. Compare Freud's equation of enuresis with childhood onanism in his *Three Essays* (1905*d*), where he writes that such activities "are mostly displayed on behalf of the still undeveloped sexual apparatus by the *urinary* apparatus, which thus acts, as it were, as the former's trustee. Most of the so-called bladder disorders of this period are sexual disturbances: nocturnal enuresis, unless it represents an epileptic fit, corresponds to a nocturnal emission" (S.E., 7:190). For a comprehensive listing of Freud's discussions on this subject, see the Editor's Note to Freud 1932*a*, S.E., 22:185–86.

of periodic patterns of bowel functioning in childhood (1897:193). So, too, he stood on Freudian ground when he drew a connection in his sexual theory between hemorrhoids in adults and those "reflex-neuroses" associated with the reproductive system (1897:217).[6]

When Freud later laid psychoanalytic claim to the discovery of infantile sexuality, he stressed two aspects of his innovations that are particularly relevant to Fliess's pioneering views on this subject— namely, the *polymorphously perverse* nature of infantile sexuality and its specific association with the doctrine of infantile *erotogenic zones* (Freud 1905d, S.E., 7:191–93; 1940a, S.E., 23:152). That Fliess indeed played a part in these two related insights is underscored by the correspondence between him and Freud. More than once in letters to his friend, Freud alluded to such ideas about sexuality as being part of Fliess's "organological" approach to the human sexual function. Freud accordingly described one of his case histories to Fliess in early 1897 as being of special "organological interest" on account of the patient's use of "oral sexual organs," while just six months later he acknowledged his deference to Fliess in this area of the latter's expertise with the words: "The organological side is waiting for you; I have made no progress with it" (*Origins*, pp. 184, 212).[7]

II. Latency, Sublimation, and Reaction
Formation as Fliessian Concepts

It was Wilhelm Fliess whom Freud credited in the *Three Essays on the Theory of Sexuality* as his source for the term *period of sexual latency* (1905d, S.E., 7:178, n. 1). Freud scholars have been content to let the whole matter go at that: Freud's linguistic debt to Fliess.[8] Fliess's monograph of 1897 shows most clearly that his influence upon Freud was by no means confined to the term alone. Behind Fliess's use of it

6. Cf. Freud's *Three Essays* (1905d), under the heading of "Activity of the Anal Zone": "Like the labial zone, the anal zone is well suited by its position to act as a medium through which sexuality may attach itself to other somatic functions. . . . If we bear in mind the erotogenic significance of the outlet of the intestinal canal, which persists, at all events in a modified form, we shall not be inclined to scoff at the influence of *haemorrhoids*, to which old-fashioned medicine used to attach so much importance in explaining neurotic conditions" (*S.E.*, 7:185–86; italics added).

7. See also *Origins*, p. 183, where Freud likewise refers to "your [Fliess's] organology"; and pp. 185, 327.

8. The term itself (*die sexuelle Latenzperiode*) was hardly original to Fliess. Richard von Krafft-Ebing had used the expression "latent period" to describe the stage of human sexual life that precedes full development of the sex organs (*Psychopathia Sexualis*, 1899 trans.:270). Inasmuch as Krafft-Ebing, though, was not a believer in either the widespread existence or the normalcy of spontaneous infantile sexuality, his conception of the latent period was significantly different from that later espoused by Freud and Fliess (see Krafft-Ebing 1904:86). The notion of a "latency of sexual function" is also found in the writings of Havelock Ellis (1900a: 29 n.), who had in mind the inactive sexual phase that alternates with the periodic expression of the sexual function in most lower animals. The idea of "latency" probably carried similar zoological implications for Fliess as well (e.g., *Origins*, p. 210).

The specific term *period of sexual latency* does not appear in any of Fliess's published writings. Fliess likely communicated it to Freud during one of their many conversations.

was a sophisticated and, above all, dynamic-genetic conception of human sexual development—one that encompassed the basic Freudian notions of *sublimation* and *reaction formation*.

But, first, I must briefly explain how Freud envisioned the latency period in psychoanalytic terms. In the *Three Essays on the Theory of Sexuality,* he placed this developmental process between the fifth year and puberty and described it as follows:

> It is during this period of total or only partial latency that are built up the mental forces which are later to impede the course of the sexual instinct and, like dams, restrict its flow—disgust, feelings of shame [i.e., reaction formations] and the claims of aesthetic and moral ideas [sublimations]. One gets an impression from civilized children that the construction of these dams is a product of education, and no doubt education has much to do with it. But in reality this development is organically determined and fixed by heredity, and it can occasionally occur without any help at all from education. (1905d, *S.E.,* 7:177–78)

One should not be misled by the term itself into thinking that Freud saw the latency period as devoid of sexual activity. Rather, he envisioned a partial muffling of childhood sexual impulses during this interval and did not rule out occasional resurgences of the unruly infantile id. "Thus the activity of those [infantile] impulses," he emphasized in 1905, "does not cease even during this period of latency, though their energy is diverted, wholly or in great part, from their sexual use and directed to other ends" (*S.E.,* 7:178).

Freud held two key processes, sublimation and reaction formation, responsible for diverting libido into other psychical channels during the latency period. It is these two psychical mechanisms, not the seeming cessation of sexual activity, that constitute the essence of "latency" in Freud's later theory. What is more, this highly dynamic conception of sexual latency is fundamental to Freud's mature conception of human psychosexual development.

Although Fliess did not employ the same language as Freud—that is, "sublimation" and "reaction formation"—he nonetheless clearly endorsed the basic concepts behind these terms in his sexual theory of 1897.[9] Fliess, as I have said, was dedicated to discovering the basic *Entwicklungsmechanik* ("developmental mechanics") of life.[10] As

9. Ernest Jones (1953:317), who apparently misread a remark by Freud (*S.E.,* 7:178, n. 1), has erroneously attributed to Fliess the origins of the specific term *sublimation.* Actually, both the term and the concept were already in common circulation in Freud's day, and they may be traced to Novalis, Schopenhauer, and Nietzsche, among others (Ellenberger 1970:505). Although Richard von Krafft-Ebing did not employ this term, he believed, like Nietzsche and the others, that civilization, ethics, and the highest poetic arts were all founded in human sexual feeling (*Psychopathia Sexualis,* 1886 and later editions, Section I, "Fragments of a System of Psychology of Sexual Life"). See Chapter 8 of this book.

10. In characterizing Fliess's approach to human development as a form of *Entwicklungsmechanik,* I do not mean to imply that he belonged to Wilhelm Roux's contemporary embryological school of the same name. But Fliess shared with Roux and most other German embryologists of the 1880s and 1890s the same biophysical ideals that made Roux's term *Entwicklungsmechanik* such an appropriate descrip-

an unflinching reductionist in such matters, he sought to derive the higher achievements of human development, including the psychical ones, from their lower, physiological determinants. In his mind, these physiological determinants were sexual substances, a circumstance that logically entailed his endorsement of the sublimation concept, especially as it applied to the prepubertal period of human development. For the period from conception to puberty in Fliess's scheme of human development was dominated by sublimated sexuality in the service of growth. "During childhood," he wrote of his two sexual-chemical rhythms, "they accumulate the energies [through physiological growth] that the human being is in a position to spend from puberty on and with which he preserves the species." Once this accumulation was finally exhausted through sexual reproduction—that is, at the time of menopause—Fliess held that the organism's biorhythms "alter their prognostication and cause the body to decay in just as wavelike a manner as they have built it up" (1897:212).

Was Freud influenced by Fliess's bioenergetic-developmental thinking about human sexuality? Indeed he was! In his first published reference to the existence of a sexual life in the child, Freud espoused Fliess's bioenergetic conception of the latency period:

> We do wrong to ignore the sexual life of children entirely; in my experience, children are capable of every psychical sexual activity, and many somatic sexual ones as well. . . . Nevertheless it is true that the organization and evolution of the human species strives to avoid any great degree of sexual activity during childhood. It seems that in man the sexual instinctual forces are meant to be stored up so that, on their release at puberty, they may serve great cultural ends. (W. Fliess.) (1898a, S.E., 3:280–81)

Three years later, in the "Dora" case history, Freud referred to this same process by the formal term *sublimation*. There, in almost identical wording, he wrote that the child's sexual impulses, "by being suppressed or by being diverted to higher, asexual aims—by being sublimated— are destined to provide the energy for a great number of our cultural achievements" (1905e [1901], S.E., 7:50). Thus it was in full scientific cooperation with Fliess's ideas that Freud extended the economic (energy-dependent) point of view in psychoanalysis to encompass a developmental perspective on human psychosexuality.

To arrive at a slightly more orthodox psychoanalytic notion of this whole process, it only remained for Freud to specify the various psychodynamic conflicts that promote sublimation. But even in this step

---

tion of this developmental approach. At the same time, Fliess's theory that periods of energy, transmitted from generation to generation, somehow regulate embryological development was paralleled by several similar biophysical conceptions among contemporary German biologists. For example, Breuer's teacher Ewald Hering (1870) and Ernst Haeckel (1876) had already proposed that heredity was merely "memory" stored in the form of molecular vibrations or periods of motions (see Gould 1977: 96–99).

he was not without a hint or two from Fliess as to the precise psychological derivatives, or Freudian reaction formations, of the latency period.

Most instructive in this regard is Fliess's medical interest in the
case history of Fritz L., aged three and three-quarters when he came
under Fliess's care in the fall of 1895 (Fliess 1897:192–94). About the
time of little Fritz's third birthday, an alert nursemaid had noticed that
her precocious charge had developed a "conspicuous interest in the
naked female body," and that his curiosity was accompanied by "pronounced feelings of shame" during his waking hours. At night Fritz was
said to suffer from repeated attacks of anxiety, crying, and *pavor
nocturnus*—symptoms that all betrayed their sexual etiology by "the
stiff penis" and attacks of urticaria that regularly accompanied them.
Fliess, after successfully analyzing the boy's symptoms into their male
and female periodic series, was able to classify the case as a simple
Freudian anxiety neurosis (he specifically mentioned Freud by name in
this connection).

Equally instructive about Fliess's case was the light it shed upon
the psychological origins of shame in childhood. "The early feelings of
shame," he proclaimed, "the aroused libido—which has as its fate a
frustrated excitation—and the anxiety that appears so very promptly,
prove a clear chain of cause and effect. And the singultus [attacks of
sobbing, *pavor nocturnus*, etc.] documents its sexual origins by the
erect penis which accompanies it" (1897:194). So, too, Fliess concluded,
did the Bible endorse the primal-sexual roots of shame when it attributed the origins of this particular emotion, along with fear (*Angst*),
to the moment when Adam discovered his nakedness before God. (Such
a sharp student of etymologies as Fliess could hardly have overlooked
the fact that the German language specifically relates "shame" [*Scham*]
to the genital organs: e.g., *Schamteile* ["genitals"], *Schamgegend*
["pubic region"], *Schamglied* ["penis"], *Schamgang* ["vagina"], and so
forth.)

Did this Fliessian prototype of Freudian reaction formation exert
an influence upon Freud's later conception of this process? The most we
can say from the available evidence is that they grew to be of one mind
on the whole subject of reaction formation in the late 1890s and exchanged views as freely on this developmental question as on all their
other scientific work. Thus Freud, in discussing both the childhood
origins of shame and the early link between that emotion and the perception of nakedness, concludes his account of this question in *The Interpretation of Dreams* with the same biblical story cited by Fliess just
three years earlier (1900a, S.E., 4:245).[11] Similarly, with Fliess's partial
help and inspiration, Freud later reduced one other major agent of or-

---

11. See also 1905d, S.E., 7:177, where Freud specifically includes shame among
the forces of reaction formation.

Of course, one can hardly insist that Freud was indebted to Fliess for the use
of such a celebrated story as that of Adam and Eve and the adoption of fig leaves.
Yet Havelock Ellis, who also refers to the same biblical story when discussing the
sexual roots of modesty and shame, specifically cites Fliess's priority (*Studies in the
Psychology of Sex*, 1900a:27 n.).

ganic repression—the sense of disgust—to a reaction formation peculiar to the organs of taste and smell (*Origins*, pp. 192, 231–34).

Finally, it is possible to see in Freud's mature conception of the latency period, with its automatic developmental processes of repression, sublimation, and reaction formation, one further bond with Fliess's scientific thinking: their joint conception of latency as an innate, physiological process. As Freud himself expressed it in *Three Essays on the Theory of Sexuality*, "this development is organically determined and fixed by heredity . . ." (1905d, *S.E.*, 7:177).

III. Libidinal Development: Its Periodic Ebb and Flow

Without recognizing its possible conceptual tie to Wilhelm Fliess, Richard Wollheim has given us the following synopsis of Freud's theory of libidinal maturation: "The most general feature of infantile sexual development, as recounted by Freud, is that it is *periodic* or *oscillatory*, the oscillations being explained partly in terms of the waning and reinforcement of the sexual impulse, partly in terms of the building up of mental forces opposed to sexuality . . ." (1971:120; italics added).[12] Did Freud's "periodic" and "oscillatory" conception of this developmental process owe anything to his friend Wilhelm Fliess? It most certainly did. Not only did Freud accept the periodic nature of childhood sexual development à la Fliess, but he also endorsed Fliess's medical extension of this conception to include the periodic nature of childhood anxiety neuroses. While discussing the sexual nature of adults' anxiety dreams in *The Interpretation of Dreams*, Freud went on to comment along just such Fliessian lines: "I should have no hesitation in giving the same explanation of the attacks of night terrors accompanied by hallucinations (*pavor nocturnus*) which are so frequent in children. In this case too it can only be a question of sexual impulses which have not been understood and which have been repudiated." To this conclusion there is appended the following indirect but patent reference to the theories of Wilhelm Fliess: "Investigation would probably show a periodicity in the occurrence of the attacks, since an increase in sexual libido can be brought about not only by accidental exciting impressions but also by successive waves [*schubweise*] of spontaneous developmental processes" (1900a, *S.E.*, 5:585).

Freud's use of the German expression *schubweise* in the preceding passage is particularly worthy of commentary. *Schub* ("push," "shove," "thrust," etc.) and *schubweise* ("by thrusts") were developmental terms Fliess used throughout his monograph of 1897 in order to express the periodic ebb and flow that he personally attributed to all developmental processes in human beings. As such, these terms were unique to his writings in this scientific and biophysical context. Freud adopted these terms from Fliess and introduced them into his correspondence with his friend soon after reading the latter's monograph of 1897. In English translation, this linguistic tie between Fliess and

12. See also Freud (1905d, *S.E.*, 7:176) for corroboration of this précis.

Freud has largely been lost. Thus, Eric Mosbacher's English rendition of these terms in Freud's letters to Fliess (e.g., *Entwicklungsschübe* as "progressive steps of development" and *Schübe* as "steps" of development) has unfortunately obliterated both the precise scientific meaning of these terms in German, where *Schub* is specifically used in physics to mean "thrust," and their peculiarly Fliessian, biorhythmic significance.[13]

In short, both Freud and Fliess had in mind a truly *thrust*like conception of infantile sexual development—a conception directly linked to Fliess's two periodic laws. Freud acknowledged this Fliessian tie more explicitly in 1913 when he admitted that the problem of pathological "fixations" of libido lies partly in developmental biology. "Since Wilhelm Fliess's writings have revealed the biological significance of certain periods of time," Freud added to his assertion in a footnote, "it has become conceivable that disturbances of development may be traceable to temporal changes in the successive waves of development [*Entwicklungsschüben*]" (1913*i*, *S.E.*, *12*:318, n. 1).

It was likewise Fliess's *Entwicklungsschubmechanik* that helped Freud to rationalize in biochemical-developmental terms the extreme frequency of childhood (anxiety) neuroses. "Anxiety hysterias are the most common of all psychoneurotic disorders," Freud asserted in 1909. "But, above all, they are those which make their appearance earliest in life; they are *par excellence* the neuroses of childhood" (1909*b*, *S.E.*, *10*:116).[14]

There were, of course, many physicians who immediately denied the sexual nature of such childhood neuroses. But just as quickly, Freud fell back upon the rationale provided by Fliess's own *Entwicklungsschubmechanik*. Responding to Carl Gustav Jung, who like so many others balked at accepting the sexual nature of childhood neuroses, Freud counterclaimed: "Only the sentence about child hysteria struck me as incorrect. The conditions here are the same, probably because every thrust of growth [*jeder Wachstumsschub*] creates the same conditions as the great thrust of puberty (every increase in libido, I mean)" (*Freud/Jung Letters*, p. 140, letter of 19 April 1908). Such, then, was the nature of the Fliessian periodicity that, according to Ernst Kris (1954:43), contributed nothing to the creation of psychoanalysis and supposedly lay at the very "periphery" of Freud's scientific interests.[15]

Above all, one should not see Freud as a passive and gullible convert to Fliess's theory of the *Entwicklungsschubmechanik* of life. The periodic ebb and flow of vital phenomena that concerned these two investigators was one that they had jointly sought to corroborate in the

13. See *Anfänge*, p. 247; and *Origins*, p. 233, letter of 14 November 1897. In the *Standard Edition* of Freud's works, translator James Strachey's choice of the words "successive waves [of development]" as an English equivalent for *Entwicklungsschübe* and "by successive waves" for *schubweise* is considerably more accurate but still not entirely adequate. E.g., *S.E.*, *1*:270, and *S.E.*, *5*:585.

14. Cf. Fliess's (1897:192, 199) similar remarks, including the case of little Fritz.

15. See also Jones (1953:317) for an equally defensive historical appraisal on this subject.

mid-1890s by collecting relevant data from their various patients, relatives, spouses, and even their own children. In fact, Fliess's growing interest in child development, which closely paralleled Freud's, coincided with Frau Fliess's confinement with their first child in the spring of 1895 (Fliess 1906b:6). What Fliess wanted to know at the outset of these studies was whether the child develops during embryonic life according to the periods of the mother. Fliess even got Freud into the act of testing this newest extension of Fliessian theory. Fliess's first child (Robert) and Freud's sixth and last child (Anna—who, for a time, was slated as a possible "Wilhelm," after Fliess) were born the same month (December 1895). Just how far Freud's scientific cooperation with Fliess's researches proceeded may be gathered from the following anonymous, but surely Freudian, observation subsequently attributed to "a friendly colleague" by Fliess, who cited his anonymous friend "word for word":

> My wife (VI para [delivery]) felt the first movements of the child on July 10th [1895]. On the 3rd of December came the beginning of labor and birth. On the 29th day of February her period resumed again. My wife has always been regular since puberty. Her period runs somewhat over 29 days. Now, from the 3rd of December to the 29th of February exactly $88 = 3 \times 29\frac{1}{3}$ days elapsed and from the 10th of July to the 3rd of December $146 = 5 \times 29\frac{1}{5}$ days passed. For a period of somewhat over 29 days the birth therefore ensued right on time and the first movements of the child fall on the 5th menstrual date. (1897:128)

That these observations were made by Sigmund Freud and dealt with his wife and youngest child Anna seems more than likely on the basis of the following five points of indirect evidence. First, Anna was indeed born on 3 December 1895. Second, she was Frau Freud's sixth delivery. Third, the written summary of evidence provided by Fliess's anonymous colleague required familiarity with Fliess's unpublished theoretical expectations. Thus, the information could only have come from someone like Freud who was in close scientific contact with Fliess in the early summer of 1895. Fourth, the particular expression *befreundeter College* ("friendly colleague") employed by Fliess in referring to his anonymous collaborator is one that Freud and Fliess had previously agreed upon for just such discreet acknowledgments of mutual scientific debt (*Anfänge*, p. 84, *Manuskript C*, Spring 1893; *Origins*, p. 75). Fifth, Fliess later used birth information on *all* the Freud children in his larger book *Der Ablauf des Lebens* (1906b:60). (See Figs. 6.1 and 6.2.)

We should not be too surprised, then, that Freud, actively engaged as he was in applying Fliess's theories to himself, his patients, his wife, and even his children, also found Fliess's *Entwicklungsschubmechanik* most useful for the understanding of infantile psychosexual development. True, Freud eventually came to question the extreme rigidity with which Fliess himself was wont to apply his periodic laws,

Zwölftes Beispiel.

Frau Marie Freuds Kinder

$$\left.\begin{array}{lll}\text{Grete} & \text{4. August} & 1887 \\ \text{Lili} & \text{22. November} & 1888 \\ \text{Martha} & \text{17. November} & 1892\end{array}\right\} \begin{array}{l}476 = \text{I} \\ 1456 = \text{II.}\end{array}$$

$$\begin{array}{l}\text{I} = 476 = 17.28 \\ \text{II} = 1456 = 52.28 \\ \hline \text{I} + \text{II} = 1932 = 69.28 = 3.23.28.\end{array}$$

Fig. 6.1. Fliess's biorhythmic calculations concerning the temporal intervals separating the birth dates of the three children of Marie Freud (Freud's sister). The interval between the first and the second child (I) is an even multiple of 28, as is the interval between the second and the third child (II). Finally, the interval between the first and the last child (I + II) is an even multiple of 23 · 28. (From Fliess 1906b:51.)

17. Beispiel.

Professor Sigmund Freuds Kinder:

$$\left.\begin{array}{lll}\text{Mathilde} & \text{16. Oktober} & 1887 \\ \text{Martin} & \text{7. Dezember} & 1889 \\ \text{Oliver} & \text{19. Februar} & 1891 \\ \text{Ernst} & \text{6. April} & 1892 \\ \text{Sophie} & \text{12. April} & 1893 \\ \text{Anna} & \text{3. Dezember} & 1895\end{array}\right\} \begin{array}{l}783 = \text{I} \\ 439 = \text{II} \\ 412 = \text{III} \\ 371 = \text{IV} \\ 965 = \text{V.}\end{array}$$

$$\begin{array}{l}\text{I} = 783 = 14.28 + 17.23 \\ \text{II} = 439 = 5.28 + 13.23 \\ \text{III} = 412 = 18.28 - 4.23 \\ \text{IV} = 371 = 19.28 - 7.23 \\ \text{V} = 965 = 9.28 + 31.23.\end{array}$$

Hier erkennen wir zuerst, daß

$$\text{III} + \text{IV} = \text{I}.$$

Ferner daß

$$\text{V} = \boxed{14.23 + 17.23} + 9.28$$

also in seinem umrandeten Teile biologisch = I und nur um 9.28 vermehrt ist.

Fig. 6.2. Fliess's biorhythmic calculations concerning the temporal intervals separating the birth dates of Freud's six children. The analysis illustrates Fliess's later search for regularities in the values of x and y within his general formula $x \cdot 23 \pm y \cdot 28$. The interval between the third and the fifth child (III + IV) exactly equals the interval between the first and second child (I), or 783 days. The interval between the fifth and the sixth child (V) exhibits the same number of cycles ($31 = 14 + 17$), plus 9, as the interval between the first and the second child (I). (From Fliess 1906b:60.)

but he seems never to have questioned Fleiss's central premise that life, sexual as well as otherwise, is governed by a periodic ebb and flow.[16]

IV. Bisexuality, Neurosis, and the Nature of the Unconscious Mind

It was Wilhelm Fliess who first convinced Freud that all human beings are bisexual, and that this physiological fact is of major relevance for the theory of the neuroses. In contrast to the preceding topics, this fourth aspect of Fliess's influence upon Freud has not been overlooked by Freud scholars, who have generally followed Freud in acknowledging its beneficence (1905d, S.E., 7:166, n. 1, 220 n.).[17] What is not perhaps sufficiently appreciated by most historians of psychoanalysis is just how extensively this notion of bisexuality served to link Freud's psychoanalytic conception of human development to the biological theory championed by Fliess. In his thinking on the bisexual nature of man, Fliess sought to interconnect the following four scientific problems: the etiology of homosexuality, the mechanism of repression, the etiology of psychoneurosis, and the nature of the unconscious mind. I shall briefly review these four ideas in sequence in order to show how they influenced Freud.

A natural corollary to Fliess's views on the embryonic bisexuality of the human fetus was his interpretation of hermaphrodites and homosexuals as victims of a disturbance or inhibition in the normal course of sexual development.[18] Spurred on as he was by his contact with Freud, Fliess approached this whole issue in a protopsychoanalytic fashion and developed, in the process, an ingenious psychobiological solution to the problem of repression. Although Freud eventually rejected certain of Fliess's specific suggestions on this problem, he was nevertheless inspired by them and continued to praise their "attractive" nature and their "bold simplicity."

In Fliess's view, as Freud later explained it, "The dominant sex of the person, that which is the more strongly developed, has repressed the mental representation of the subordinated sex into the unconscious. Therefore the nucleus of the unconscious (that is to say, the repressed) is in each human being that side of him which belongs to the opposite sex" (1919e, S.E., 17:200–201).[19]

Fliess apparently communicated his bisexual theory of repression

16. For further documentation of this last point, see the *Freud/Abraham Letters*, p. 209, letter of 25 January 1915; *Letters*, p. 315, to Josef Popper-Lynkeus, 4 August 1916; and Freud 1920g, S.E., 18:45.

17. See also Jones 1953:317; Kris 1954:42; and Strachey, S.E., 7:127.

18. Although Fliess apparently adopted his conclusions on this subject independently of those medical specialists like Krafft-Ebing who reached similar conclusions in the 1890s, he was certainly aware of such supporting viewpoints in later years: e.g., Fliess 1906a:10; 1906b:472–87. See also Chapters 5 and 8 in this book.

19. It was on the basis of this theory, which also provided for variable degrees of repression in different individuals, that Fliess (1906b:508) later developed an explanation of psychosexual attraction in terms of "bisexual complementarity." According to this notion, a feminine man should tend to attract a masculine woman, and vice versa. See also *Origins*, p. 241, n. 2.

to Freud during their Nuremberg congress in April 1897, and it was certainly known to Freud by October of that year, when he briefly alluded to it in a letter to Fliess (*Origins*, p. 224).[20] Although Freud was more inclined at the time to view the masculine side as the primary target of repression in both sexes (*Origins*, p. 224), he was nevertheless quite intrigued throughout the late 1890s by Fliess's dynamic, psychobiological approach to the whole problem. It was in this same context that Freud came to accept Fliess's clinical assertion that all neurotics exhibit unconscious fixations of the libido upon members of their own sex. This last insight, communicated by Fliess during their Nuremberg congress (April 1897) or possibly during their subsequent Breslau congress (December 1897), was taken over by Freud without further qualification and is specifically credited to Fliess in the *Three Essays on the Theory of Sexuality* (1905*d*, S.E., 7:166, n. 1).

Three further and equally permanent psychoanalytic corollaries may be traced to Fliess's theory of bisexuality in man. First, Fliess's biological framework subsequently allowed Freud to attribute homosexuality—a perversion—to insufficient repression of the embryonic bisexual disposition. Freud did much to improve upon this idea after 1900, but the general point of view provided by bisexuality theory was never outmoded by his later psychoanalytic thoughts on this subject. Second, Fliess's claim about the unconscious homosexual complexes of all neurotics demanded a conceptual link between Freud's theory of psychoneurosis and the problem of perversion. If neurotics are homosexuals but have *repressed* their homosexuality, then such afflictions could be seen broadly as a "negative" state of perversion. This last idea constitutes one of Freud's most fundamental psychoanalytic insights within his later theory of psychosexual development (1905*d*, S.E., 7:165, 170–72). Third and last, Fliess's theory suggested a general paradigm by which sundry forms of psychoneurosis might be conceived, like repressed homosexuality, as inhibitions in the development of specific libidinal component impulses. This particular insight, developed and perfected by Freud, was to become a bulwark of the psychoanalytic theory of neuroses (e.g., Freud 1916–17, S.E., 16:364).

In summing up the various implications of bisexuality theory for the understanding of psychoneurosis, Freud called it "the decisive factor" in 1905, adding that "without taking bisexuality into account I think it would scarcely be possible to arrive at an understanding of the sexual manifestations that are actually to be observed in men and women" (1905*d*, S.E., 7:220).

V. *Childhood Onanism and the Etiology of Neurosis*

The fifth and last point of theoretical agreement between Freud and Fliess constitutes more a conceptual overlap than an instance, like the previous four, of Fliess's direct influence upon Freud. Both their

20. See also Fliess 1906*a*:10; and Jones 1953:318 n.

theories of human psychosexual development were formulated at a time when medical views on the supposed evils of masturbation were undergoing dramatic change. An all but universal medical diagnosis in the 1870s and 1880s, the attribution of neuroses and even insanity to "masturbatory excesses" had virtually vanished by the 1930s and early 1940s. This change was effected largely by the pioneering medical efforts of Havelock Ellis, Albert Moll, and other contemporary sexologists, who, by systematically collecting information on the problem, found healthy and mentally disturbed individuals to differ little in their autoerotic practices.[21]

Freud, for all his progressive views on sexuality, remained a partisan of the old school, as did Fliess. Freud's second son Oliver once came to his father with adolescent worries about masturbation, only to receive a stern warning about the many dangers inherent in this practice. As a result of this painful incident, Freud's son reports that he was never able to enjoy the sort of close relationship with his father that his older brother Jean-Martin had achieved (Roazen 1975:15; 22 April 1966 interview with Oliver Freud).

What is also not appreciated about Freud is how integral his medical views on masturbation were to his overall theory of the neuroses. After his abandonment of the seduction theory in 1897, his theory of the neuroses became, in significant part, a theory about infantile sexual masturbation. It was childhood masturbation that he later blamed for the neurotic phantasies that had misled him in the first place. Such phantasies, Freud wrote, "were intended to cover up the auto-erotic activities of the first years of childhood, to embellish it and raise it to a higher plane" (1914d, S.E., 14:18). Speaking before the members of the Vienna Psychoanalytic Society in 1912, Freud summed up his medical views on the deleterious effects of masturbation: "A priori, one is forced to oppose the assertion that masturbation has to be harmless; on the contrary, there must be cases in which masturbation is harmful. Since the etiology of the neuroses is given by way of the conflict between infantile sexuality and the opposition of the ego (repression), masturbation, which is only an executive of infantile sexuality, cannot a priori be presented as harmless" (Minutes, 4:93; meeting of 24 April 1912).

Freud and Wilhelm Fliess were united in their endorsement of the harmful consequences of such onanistic activities by their toxicological conception of the whole problem. Included in this toxicological analysis was the assumption of permanent organic alterations (by reflex action) in disparate parts of the body. Freud even appealed to Fliess's nasal reflex theory in this physiological context. Of his famous patient Dora and her complaints about gastric pains, Freud had maintained along such Fliessian lines: "It is well known that gastric pains occur especially often in those who masturbate. According to a personal communication made to me by Wilhelm Fliess, it is precisely gastralgias of this

21. See Ellis 1898a:293; Moll 1909, trans. 1912a:182; and Chapter 8 of this book.

character which can be interrupted by an application of cocaine to the 'gastric spot' discovered by him in the nose, and which can be cured by the cauterization of the same spot" (1905e [1901], S.E., 7:78). How fortunate it was for Dora that she did not live any closer to Berlin— and to Fliess!

Finally, during the late 1890s, Freud was able to extract from Fliess's theories a general physicalist rationale as to why sexual activity in childhood, either onanistic or induced, should pose a pathological threat to the developing organism. After citing Fliess's idea in 1898 that "the sexual instinctual forces" are meant to be stored up so that they may serve, after puberty, "great cultural ends," Freud added: "Considerations of this sort may make it possible to understand why the sexual experiences of childhood are bound to have a pathogenic effect" (1898a, S.E., 3:281). In spite of many emendations, Freud's mature theory of the neuroses continued to support this toxicological-bioenergetic conception of sexual pathology that had bound him to Wilhelm Fliess in the 1890s.

Fliess's Mathematical Biology of the Id

To sum up, Fliess's whole theory of human development provided (1) a novel and compelling biological justification for the observed facts about spontaneous infantile sexuality, (2) a dynamic account of how such early sexual manifestations undergo step-by-step (schubweise) development and differentiation, accompanied by repression in the unconscious, and (3) a sophisticated logic for sexuality's intimate medical ties to the neuroses. While Fliess's ideas do not by any means constitute a complete Freudian theory, they certainly rank as a not-too-distant intellectual relative. It is because of such manifold proto-Freudian aspects of Fliess's scientific thinking that I would designate Fliess's theory of psychosexual development as an important anticipation of Freud's own notion of the id.[22] For as we have seen, Wilhelm Fliess, like Sigmund Freud, assumed the unconscious mind to be the repository of those biologically innate and repressed sexual impulses that have proved incompatible with the normal adult psychosexual organization.

22. To be sure, this anticipation is not of the id in its mature, topographical conception—that is to say, as the undifferentiated reservoir of instinctual energy from which the ego is later partitioned by the process of repression. Rather, I am referring instead to the dynamic and developmental aspects of the id concept as they first manifested themselves in Freud's thinking during the late 1890s. Psychoanalysts have themselves provided the historical precedent for this earlier and more general meaning of the term id by dating Freud's discovery of that concept to the 1897–1900 period. Thus Ernest Jones (1953:283) ascribes the beginning of the id concept to a 2 May 1897 letter to Fliess in which the "dynamic" conception of psychosexual development is clearly adumbrated. Ernst Kris agrees with Jones, adding that the 2 May 1897 insight "subsequently led to a complete revision" of psychoanalytic theory (Origins, p. 197, n. 1). See also Stewart 1967:114–15. It was, of course, Freud's acceptance of spontaneous infantile sexuality that made for this watershed in his psychoanalytic thinking (Strachey, S.E., 1:292). The specific term das Es ("the id") was never employed by Fliess in his own scientific writings. Nor was it used by Freud until The Ego and the Id (1923b) and later publications. What I am concerned with, then, is the common presence of the dynamic concept, not the specific term, in both these men's thinking.

And it should not come as much of a surprise, except perhaps to Freud's followers-turned-biographers, that many of the conceptual ties between Freud and Fliess were long ago pointed out by certain of Freud's better-informed medical contemporaries. In a 1910 review of Wilhelm Fliess's scientific work, Hans Henning complained that "Fliess's friend Sigmund Freud" was just as busy as Fliess himself in the single-minded attempt to reduce everything to sexuality (1910:232). Iwan Bloch, in a 1914 article on the problems and goals of sexual science, was even more explicit about the conceptual similarities between these two thinkers. After reviewing the scientific contributions of both, and noting the common impetus that their findings had contributed to the chemical theory of an "inner [sexual] secretion," Bloch mentioned three great problems of sexual pathology that had been illuminated by such recent researches: (1) infantile and childhood onanism (the chemical aspect of which was now clearly established, nota bene, by the *periodicity* of the impulse); (2) the causes of homosexuality (rooted in our constitutional bisexuality); and (3) the intimate relationship between sexuality and nervous disorders, particularly the neuroses and psychoses (1914:8–9). Needless to say, Bloch could hardly have given a better summary of the various scientific interests that had indeed united Freud with Fliess during the period of their most intense scientific collaboration.

Similarly, in 1908 Wilhelm Stekel, one of Freud's earliest followers, made considerable use of Fliess's monograph of 1897, including citations from the case history of little Fritz, in proselytizing the Freudian interpretation of childhood anxiety attacks (1908:82–83, 110). And to give just one last example, Bruno Saaler, a physician who wrote on both Freudian and Fliessian subjects throughout the second decade of the twentieth century, claimed in 1914 to have achieved a simultaneous confirmation of the masculine nature of infantile libido (Freud's theory) and the 23-day nature of the male sexual cycle (Fliess's theory) after he had successfully documented a 23-day period in a neurotic's "anal-erotic" symptoms (1914:338–39; see also Saaler 1912:910).

There is perhaps no better testimony to the convergence of Freud's and Fliess's respective ideas on human psychosexual development than the fact that in 1901 Freud, in a deliberate effort to win back Fliess on the brink of their personal estrangement, was willing to let him be coauthor of his forthcoming book on the sexual theory. This planned work, Freud informed Fliess at the time, was to be called "Bisexuality in Man" (*Origins*, pp. 334–35).[23] It was another four years before that seminal work eventually came out—minus Fliess's cooperation—under the better-known title *Three Essays on the Theory of Sexuality* (1905d). Although Fliess's acknowledged influence upon this later Freudian book is limited to the two specific notions of bisexuality and the undercur-

23. Traditional Freud scholarship has generally made light of this collaboration offer, which Fliess refused. One of Freud's biographers actually finds it "astonishing" that Freud should have made such a proposal as late as 1901 (Costigan 1967:62).

rent of homosexuality in every neurotic, it would not be too much to say
that behind Freud's *Three Essays* there lurks the long-unrecognized
specter of Fliessian sexual biology.

THE PSYCHOANALYTIC TRANSFORMATION OF THE FLIESSIAN ID

Two Preliminary Historical Questions

Before developing Freud's scientific relationship with Wilhelm
Fliess in more detail, I must consider two important questions arising
out of the historical evidence presented thus far. The first and perhaps
the most natural of these is, Who really influenced whom? In other
words, how much of the basic similarity between their respective views
on human development was perhaps due to Freud's prior intellectual
influence *upon Fliess*, as later manifested in the latter's proto-Freudian
monograph of 1897? After all, these two exchanged their scientific ideas
on sexuality and other subjects quite freely, as Freud's comments to
Fliess, just before reading the latter's monograph of 1897 in an early
manuscript draft, certainly evince: "I shall read 'Nose and Sex' immediately, of course. . . . I hope you also mention some of our fundamental
views on sexuality in it . . ." (*Origins*, p. 157, letter of 13 February
1896).

Unfortunately, the loss of Fliess's side of the correspondence de-
prives us of much that would otherwise have been most useful in
answering this question. But more unfortunately still, the lamentable
decision by the editors of Freud's letters to Fliess not to publish certain portions of them in which Freud specifically sought to relate his
work to Fliess's own makes it difficult to benefit fully even from this
invaluable source material.[24]

Nevertheless, to give a preliminary response to this problem of
influence, I can at least make the following claim: that independently
of any final answers in this connection, the suggestion that historians
of psychoanalysis ought to entertain such questions about Freud's scientific relationship to Fliess is, in and of itself, no small step forward
in the historical understanding of Freud's thinking. For, putting aside
for a moment the more technical issue of *who* really influenced *whom*
(and *how*), it is still true that many of the ideas embodied in Fliess's
published discussions of human psychosexual development constitute

---

24. How far had Fliess's ideas developed at various important turning points
in Freud's intellectual development? Ideally a Freud scholar would like to be able
to answer such a question in order to determine what Freud himself may have contributed to Fliess's thinking that might otherwise mistakenly be ascribed to Fliess's
apparent influence. Concerning the editors' flagrant disregard for such historical
issues in the published version of Freud's correspondence with Fliess, I am reminded
of the comment made long ago by Iago Galdston: "In the Fliess letters, ingenuously
labelled *Aus den Anfängen der Psychoanalyse*, (and not Freud's letters to Fliess)
they sought for and found Freud, not Fliess" (1956:491).

an important and much-neglected collaborative phase through which Freud's thinking likewise passed. Furthermore, this was a phase that Freud himself never quite *sur*passed, at least in many key respects, even long after he had parted intellectual and personal company with Wilhelm Fliess. Thus it is unnecessary to assign detailed priorities between these two men in order to demolish the traditional claim that Fliess's scientific views were like "alien bodies" that could only exert "a drag on Freud's painful progress from physiology to psychology" (Kris 1954:45–46; Jones 1953:300).[25]

Indeed, I would be fully justified in saying that it is difficult to conceive Freud's scientific relationship with Fliess except as they themselves did—that is, as a mutual, step-by-step collaboration involving a constant exchange of scientific ideas from initially separate, but increasingly overlapping, scientific domains. Fliess's monograph of 1897 contains at least twelve different references to Freud's published ideas on hysteria, anxiety neurosis, neurasthenia, the noxious effects of masturbation, and so forth (see pp. 12, 99, 110, 142, 182, 192, 197–99, 218). And Freud, who witnessed the gradual evolution of Fliess's scientific discoveries in a succession of letters and manuscript drafts, certainly testified to the growing convergence of interests between himself and Fliess when he wrote to his friend on 1 January 1896: "Your letters, such as the last for instance, contain a wealth of scientific penetration and imagination about which all I can say, unfortunately, is that I am fascinated and overwhelmed. The thought that we should both be busy with *the same work* is the happiest that I could have just now" (*Origins*, p. 141; italics added). And what was this "same work"? It was the study of human sexuality, of the neuroses, and, above all, of the overall course of human life in both its normal and its pathological manifestations.

The fact that much will continue to remain problematical about Fliess's precise influence on Freud, and vice versa, should not be allowed to obscure one further point. Matters of intellectual priority rarely constitute the really important aspect of a collaborative relationship, either in science or in any other field of knowledge. And Fliess's thought-provoking conceptions were not so terribly original that Freud could not have encountered them by another route. Thus Fliess's greatest assistance to Freud was undoubtedly as an intellectual catalyst, who brought to Freud's attention in the mid-1890s fruitful ideas and approaches that he later met with again in fields like sexual physiology, evolutionary theory, and *psychopathia sexualis*—developments that I shall enlarge upon in Chapters 7 and 8.

What *was* unique to Wilhelm Fliess, and therefore deserves special emphasis, was his dynamic, biogenetic synthesis of his ideas, which in turn made them so compelling to Freud and others. Also unique to

---

25. Consider as well the following equally representative comment by Robert: "It can be assumed . . . that when Freud came to think that the links between his psychology and physiology and physics were looser than he had first believed—*for instance, when he discovered infantile sexuality*—Fliess had some difficulty in following him along a path so far removed from his own" (1966:98; italics added).

Fliess were certain clinical observations and, especially, his novel claims of proof in connection with the little-known phenomena of spontaneous infantile sexuality (e.g., the periodicity of their manifestations). Thus as late as 1899, Hermann Rohleder, in a scholarly medical monograph on masturbation subsequently cited by Freud in his *Three Essays* (1905*d*), was able to assert that sixteen months was the earliest age at which an erection had ever been reported in the medical literature (1899:46). In contrast, Fliess was claiming such spontaneous erections as a regular phenomenon in the *first few weeks* of life—probably on the basis of firsthand observations of his son Robert.[26]

Sigmund Freud surely must have been impressed by such medically novel observations as Fliess was making on childhood erections and related topics. To Freud, the anatomical and the psychological always played complementary roles in the understanding of human development. Years later he announced to one of his patients along these lines, "People had no idea of this childhood development of sex until analysis brought it out," and added as a seemingly irrefutable proof that "the young child has erections during the first few months" (Blanton 1971: 52, 26 March 1930 conversation with Freud).

The relative novelty of Fliess's observations on infantile sexuality brings up one more point. Freud, unlike Fliess, had far less opportunity to familiarize himself with such somatically impressive data about infantile sexuality through personal observation of his *own* children. C. G. Jung later recalled how surprised he was in 1907 to discover that Freud's wife knew "absolutely nothing" about her husband's psychoanalytic work (Billinsky 1969:42, 10 May 1957 interview with Jung). Frau Freud is also reported as having once said that "psychoanalysis stops at the door of the children's room" (Ellenberger 1970:458)—an attribution that seems authentic in the light of one particularly humorous passage in the Fliess correspondence. "Why do I not go to the nursery and—experiment?" Freud wrote to his friend in February 1897 in connection with a request for information on early childhood attitudes toward excrement. "Because with twelve-and-a-half hours' work I have no time, and because the womenfolk do not back me in my investigations" (*Origins*, p. 192).

Wilhelm Fliess faced no such maternal obstacles to his sexual researches at home. He kept a daily record book in which he recorded his firstborn son's every maturational milestone, affliction, and trace of sexual activity.[27] And a passage in Fliess's large work *Der Ablauf des Lebens* (1906*b*:487) proudly identifies certain previously anonymous observations on infantile menstrual rhythms (blood in saliva and urine) as having been made on his eldest son during the first week of life (see Fliess 1897:166, 198, observation of January 1896). Following his son's birth on 29 December 1895, Fliess must therefore have been a

---

26. It is now well known, of course, that erections occur regularly in earliest infancy, especially during the stage of *paradoxical* or REM sleep. See Chodoff 1966: 511–12.

27. For a reference to this notebook, see Pfennig 1912:381–82.

constant source of valuable information to Freud concerning his first-born's development, both sexual and otherwise (cf. *Origins*, p. 155, letter of 6 February 1896). Prior to Freud's self-analysis, Fliess had even informed Freud that his son Robert, now in the second year of life, had become sexually aroused by the sight of his mother's naked body—the same and supposedly quite revolutionary, self-analytic revelation that *later* occurred to Freud in October 1897 when he attempted to penetrate the shroud of his infantile amnesia (*Origins*, p. 219). Small wonder, then, that he looked eagerly to Fliess and to the arrival of Fliess's second child in 1898 for corroboration of his self-analytic inferences on the sexual roots of childhood sibling rivalry (*Origins*, p. 265).[28]

Wilhelm Fliess's discoveries on the subject of infantile sexuality bring me to the second question concerning Freud's debt to him. If the spontaneous, Fliessian conception of infantile sexual development proved in the end so fruitful for understanding neurotic phenomena, why did Freud ever develop his own antithetical seduction theory of neurosis? (The seduction theory, which dates from the fall of 1895, was announced contemporaneously with Fliess's treatment of little Fritz and only a few months prior to the birth of Fliess's first son.) And why, to pursue this question further, did these two friends not realize sooner the apparent inconsistency between Fliess's findings on spontaneous infantile sexuality and the traumatic etiology involving "deferred action" that Freud had premised on the child's asexual nature (see pp. 111–12)? In fact, it was not until two years later, in the fall of 1897, that Freud finally gave up his seduction theory; and only then did he replace this erroneous notion with the spontaneous conception of infantile sexual life championed by Fliess.

The solution to this historical puzzle is not as difficult as it might at first seem. For this conceptual inconsistency simply did not exist for either Freud or Fliess prior to the autumn of 1897. The inclination to see Freud's thinking on the psychoneuroses between 1895 and 1897 as somehow antithetical to Fliess's findings during this same period is

28. Elenore Fliess, in a biography of her husband Robert, has briefly described the home life that allowed his father and mother to utilize him and his siblings as objects of psychosexual research. According to Elenore Fliess, Wilhelm Fliess was a man "who however charming to patients and acquaintances was a tyrant at home. His children were second-class citizens, from diet to schooling. The mother, intelligent and quite efficient, would appear to have been more impressed with her husband's off-beat (and quite unsubstantiable) physiologic theories than with her parental responsibilities" (1974:10). It is not without significance that the principal subject of Wilhelm Fliess's pioneering infant studies should have become a psychoanalyst who had little good to say about his own father. Yet prior to the 1930s, Robert Fliess actively supported his father's controversial periodicity theories (Schlieper 1928). His father's death in 1928, and especially Robert's subsequent training as an analyst during his late thirties, seem to have precipitated a considerable reevaluation of his father and his father's theories (R. Fliess 1956:xviii). When George Thommen, an American Neo-Fliessian, contacted Robert Fliess in the early 1960s, Fliess refused to speak to him on the telephone; and Thommen was told by a second party that "the doctor did not wish to be involved" (personal communication from George Thommen, letter of 8 September 1977). Robert Fliess died in 1970 after a distinguished career as a psychoanalyst.

in turn linked to a fundamental misconception of traditional psychoanalytic history—namely, to the presumption that Freud only came to
appreciate the existence of infantile sexuality after recognizing, in the
fall of 1897, the "phantasy" nature of his patients' seduction accusations.

In actuality, Freud was entirely aware prior to the fall of 1897—
through Wilhelm Fliess as well as through other sources (see Chapter
8)—that spontaneous infantile sexual manifestations were not as un-
common in human development as most people then tended to believe.
What Freud was *not* aware of between the time of his formulation of
the seduction theory (October 1895) and his abandonment of it two
years later was the potential relevance of such spontaneous infantile
sexual experiences for his theory of the *psycho*neuroses. Following the
great Charcot, Freud had steadfastly presumed until late 1897 that the
psychoneuroses had to be explained in terms of a repressed, *traumatic*
experience (cf. Freud 1914d, S.E., 14:17). It is in this particular connection that one must understand Freud's attempts to downplay the relationship between spontaneous childhood masturbation and the etiology
of hysteria (1896b, S.E., 3:165). And following Freud's own logic, Fliess
had confined all his remarks on the sexual neuroses of childhood to the
nonpsychoneurotic category of the *actual* neuroses. (The actual neuroses, it will be recalled, were thought to involve purely somatic,
toxicological disturbances in sexual chemistry.) For these disorders,
Fliess considered seductions and periodic sexual *Schübe* in childhood
to be alternative etiological agents; and in this connection he specifically
cited Freud's seduction reports as well as the "loathsome" practice of
some nursemaids who quiet young infants by stroking their genitals
(1897:199).

Furthermore, it seems likely that both Fliess and Freud, united as
they already were in the mid-1890s by their sexual-toxicological point
of view, converged as one mind upon the notion that a sexual (actual)
neurosis could manifest itself even in earliest childhood. In his manuscript draft to Fliess entitled "How Anxiety Originates" (Draft E, June
1894), Freud had already spoken of anxiety in "virginal" (i.e., early
adolescent) subjects as one of seven possible classes of anxiety neurosis
(*Origins*, pp. 89–92). Fliess responded to this draft with a number of
critical comments, as we know from Freud's next letter; and when
Freud finally drew up his ideas for publication in January 1895, he
had significantly extended those on neurotic anxiety toward the views
that Fliess was beginning to endorse in the sphere of child development.[29] Speaking of *pavor nocturnus* in adults, Freud went on to com-

29. Whether Fliess suggested this extension to Freud is impossible to say on
the available evidence. However, an observation by Freud, probably made of one of
his children, also seems to have influenced his thinking. In a footnote in his *Three
Essays* (1905d), he wrote: "For this explanation of the [sexual] origin of infantile
anxiety I have to thank a three-year-old boy whom I once heard calling out of a
dark room: 'Auntie, speak to me! I'm frightened because it's so dark.' His aunt
answered him. 'What good would that do? You can't see me.' 'That doesn't matter,'
replied the child, 'if anyone speaks, it gets light.' Thus what he was afraid of was
not the dark, but the absence of someone he loved; and he could feel sure of being
soothed as soon as he had evidence of that person's presence" (S.E., 7:224 n.).

ment: "I have become convinced, moreover, that the *pavor nocturnus* of children, too, exhibits a form which belongs to [sexual] anxiety neurosis. The streak of hysteria about it, the linking of the anxiety with the reproduction of an appropriate experience or a dream, causes the *pavor nocturnus* of children to appear as something special. But the *pavor* can also emerge in a pure form, without any dream or recurring hallucination" (1895b, S.E., 3:95). Hence the *sexual* periodicity that Wilhelm Fliess soon found to be associated with such symptoms of childhood anxiety neurosis—and that Freud himself later alluded to in *The Interpretation of Dreams* (1900a, S.E., 5:585)—could hardly have come as a surprise to Freud during the interval in which the seduction theory simultaneously took shape in his mind. Rather, he actively sought out such seduction confessions from his psychoneurotic patients in a "deterministic" effort to distinguish their traumatic clinical pictures from the toxicological ones found in the actual neuroses. The only tie that he evidently glimpsed at this time between spontaneous childhood sexuality and the etiology of *psycho*neurosis was the idea that extremely precocious sexual development might suffice to explain the early emergence of hysterical symptoms (prior to the age of eight) in certain rare instances. Even here, though, Freud continued to assume that a prior seduction had been the essential cause of the hysteria (1896c, S.E., 3:212).

At the same time, it should not be forgotten that Freud's seduction theory of neurosis was based upon many *true* instances of traumatic seduction, instances confirmed by independent testimony of the seducer or by some other reliable witness (1896c, S.E., 3:206–8; and *Origins*, p. 183). Thus, when Freud later wrote that "the effects of seduction do not help to reveal the early history of the sexual instinct; they rather confuse our view of it by presenting children prematurely with a sexual object for which the infantile sexual instinct at first shows no need," he was indeed being autobiographically accurate (1905d, S.E., 7:191). But the seduction confessions of his hysterical patients confused this whole issue not so much by masking spontaneous sexuality from Freud's view (via the projection of unconsciously wished-for deeds onto innocent parents) as by making all nontraumatic forms of sexual activity seem irrelevant to a subsequent psychoneurosis. Fliess's influence therefore consisted, in part, of his independent pursuit of a genetic, spontaneous, and biological conception of human sexual development that only became fully relevant to Freud and psychoanalysis when the seduction theory finally collapsed.

In sum, understanding Wilhelm Fliess's influence upon Freud requires us to think about it not so much as a direct transmission of

---

Freud's second son turned three years of age on 19 February 1894. Freud's first published reference to the theory of childhood anxiety comes in January 1895—that is to say, before this son's fourth birthday. Although Aunt Minna Bernays was not yet living with the Freud family, we know that she did occasionally visit on a temporary basis—e.g., for several months in late 1895 and early 1896, when Freud's third son, Ernst, was in his third year (*Origins*, p. 135).

previously unknown facts from Fliess to Freud, but rather as what might more appropriately be termed a "transformation" in scientific ideas (Cohen 1966, 1979). In this respect, then, the history of Freud's changed emphasis upon the importance, the extent, and the precise nature of spontaneous infantile sexuality proves considerably different from the traditional scenario of his sudden and largely "self-analytic" realization in late 1897 that sexuality must develop from birth on. As we shall shortly see, Freud's psychoanalytic transformation of the Fliessian id occurred to a significant extent in Fliess's mind as well, in the course of a constant scientific dialogue between these two men on the subjects of normal and abnormal human psychosexual development.

Finally, this intellectual transformation may be said to involve three major elements: (1) Freud's attempts, actively encouraged by Fliess, to use the theories of periodicity and bisexuality to map out various "critical stages" in the development of human psychosexual organization; (2) Freud's speculations on the relationship between "organic" repression, bisexuality, and the sense of smell; and (3) his gradual insight into the phantasy life of neurotics, especially its dynamic psychoanalytic relationship to the developing id.

"Critical Stages" in the Development of the Psychosexual Organization

Turning now to the late autumn of 1895 and to Freud's post-*Project* correspondence with Fliess, we see a Freud who was becoming increasingly preoccupied by the way in which Fliess's various researches might revitalize his own psychoanalytic work. Indeed, Freud's initial response to Fliess's manuscript on the nose and the female sexual organs was nothing short of ebullient. "I read through your draft in a single breath," Freud replied to his friend on 1 March 1896. And he continued: "I liked tremendously its easy assurance, the natural, almost self-evident way in which each point leads to the next, its unpretentious unfolding of riches and—last but not least—the wealth of glimpses of new riddles and new explanations" (*Origins*, p. 158). Hardly a man of false praise, Freud was clearly impressed by Fliess's findings.

Among these "new riddles and new explanations," Freud singled out three points of special interest. First, he was struck by Fliess's efforts to bridge the gap between the theory of periodicity and his own ideas on the actual neuroses. He responded to this development: "I think I am just beginning to understand the anxiety neurosis now; the menstrual period is its physiological pattern, and it is a toxic state the physiological foundation for which is an organic process" (*Origins*, p. 159). In this same connection, he also acknowledged to Fliess that the theory of periodicity, as Fliess himself had maintained, supplied a useful retort to Löwenfeld (1895), who had recently objected to Freud's conception of anxiety neurosis. Löwenfeld stressed the temporal unpredictability of such attacks, a point that he believed Freud's sexual-toxicological conception could not explain, while Fliess had found such supposedly "irregular" attacks to follow his two sexual cycles (Fliess 1897:197).

Second, Freud spoke to Fliess of being "delighted with the idea of the male menopause," noting that it might be "the final conditioning factor" for anxiety neurosis in aging men.

What interested Freud most of all in his reading of Fliess's manuscript was a third idea that promised a possible solution to two of his three most pressing psychoanalytic problems—that is, pathological repression and the related problem of the choice of neurosis. In reference to Fliess's (1897:212) findings on sexual *Schübe* and infantile dentition, Freud excitedly announced, "It occurs to me that the limits of repression in my theory of the neuroses, *i.e.*, the time after which a sexual experience works not posthumously but directly, coincide with the second dentition" (*Origins*, p. 159). In a paper published three months later, Freud espoused this particular idea in print, fixing the critical "boundary" point at the age of eight (1896c, *S.E.*, 3:212).

Freud's remarks on second dentition have an implicit but little-appreciated biological logic, with which he was apparently familiar from his medical student days. Furthermore, in endorsing this interpretation of dentition, he was in the distinguished biomedical company of Wilhelm Fliess's illustrious precursor Thomas Laycock. In an article entitled "On the Major Periods of Development in Man" (1843f), Laycock had pointed out the several important biological links between sexual development, teething, and disease. "In animals generally," Laycock wrote, "the development of the teeth is closely connected with the evolution of the reproductive organs. The tusks of the stallion, wild boar, and walrus, are sexual, and are simply canine teeth of an unusual size" (p. 256). Premature sexual development is often coincident with either the first dentition (ca. forty months) or the second (ca. seven to eight years), Laycock observed; and like Fliess, he conceived of this whole sex-linked process in terms of a constitutional "thrust" in development around these two critical times. "It is probable, indeed," he argued, "that sexual development takes place in these [premature] cases as well as normally, *per saltum*, an effort being made just at the time when certain teeth are appearing; after the tooth is perfected, and the constitutional effort has ceased, so also will the nisus in the ovaries or testes" (p. 256). As signposts of intensified sexual development, such periods of teething were claimed by Laycock to involve heightened liability to a variety of diseases (p. 257).

Although Freud was apparently unaware of Laycock's views, the intimate biological link between sexuality and dentition was certainly known to him from more contemporary sources. Charles Darwin, in particular, covered much of this same ground when, in *The Descent of Man*, he (1) listed tusks and enlarged canines among the most important mammalian secondary sexual characteristics, (2) commented upon the regularly "inverse relationship" between the development of horns and the length of canine teeth, and (3) emphasized the inhibitory effect that castration generally exerts upon the development of horns and antlers in mammals (1871, 2:241–58; 1874:502–14). Freud was familiar with Darwin's *Descent* from his medical student days, and the sexual nature of horns and canine teeth was probably a topic of discussion during Carl Claus's course "General Biology and Darwinism," which Freud had attended in 1874. Facts such as these, then, justified the peculiar sexual significance that Freud, under Fliess's biological tutelage, began to associate with dentition in his 1890s theory of psychosexual development.

Throughout the spring and summer of 1896, Freud continued to puzzle over the interrelated problems of repression, possible critical stages in psychosexual development, and the choice of neurosis. He also continued to look to Fliess for further scientific assistance in overcoming these problems. On 30 June 1896 he candidly confessed:

> I am in a rather gloomy state, and all I can say is that I am looking forward to our congress as to a slaking of hunger and thirst. I shall bring with me nothing but a pair of open ears, and shall be all agape. Also I expect great things—so self-centered am I—for my own purposes. I have run into some doubts about my repression theory which a suggestion from you, like the one about male and female menstruation in the same individual, may resolve. Anxiety, chemical factors, etc.—perhaps you may supply me with solid ground on which I shall be able to give up explaining things psychologically and start finding a firm basis in physiology! (*Origins*, p. 169)

Freud's appeal to Fliess for further assistance directly presages his 4 December 1896 announcement of a scheme designed to "cement our work together and put my column on your base . . ." (*Origins*, p. 172). Just two days later Freud revealed this consolidating conception to Fliess in a letter that adumbrates a number of Freud's most important insights into human psychosexuality.

Freud had five premises for this conception: (1) the *Project* neurone theory, with its various systems of perception, unconsciousness, preconsciousness, and consciousness; (2) the notion of mind temporally stratified in "psychical layers" according to the various epochs of psychosexual development; (3) the hypothesis that memories maintain their access to consciousness by being successively "transcribed" from one psychical layer to the next; (4) the theory of sexual periodicity; and (5) the theory of bisexuality.

The basic thrust of Freud's approach in this letter was to explain pathological repression, and hence neurosis, as a failure in mnemic transcription at different critical stages in development. From the outset of his analysis, we see a major alteration in his whole understanding of the problem. For the first time he speaks of the potentially pleasurable nature of most childhood sexual experiences, even very early ones. Proceeding from this premise, which he was naturally anxious to harmonize with his traumatic theory of the psychoneuroses, Freud once again acknowledges two separate enigmas associated with pathological repression: Why, he asks himself, does pathological repression occur at all in such instances—that is, when only pleasure has been experienced? And why do similar childhood experiences often have such variable pathogenic outcomes—why, that is, do they lead to psychoneurosis in some individuals and to perversion in others?

To answer the first of these questions, Freud reaffirms the hypothesis of a pathogenic "reversal of affect" in connection with all such premature, pleasurable sexual experiences—a reversal that somehow prevents, he adds, the transcription of associated mnemic traces. Crucial to this working hypothesis is his further decision to equate libido with Fliess's 23-day masculine substance and repression with the 28-day female (anxiety) substance. By associating Fliess's 28-day female substance with repression and the reversal of affect, Freud arrives at the following ingenious solution to the variability-of-outcome problem:

> In order to explain why the outcome is sometimes perversion and sometimes neurosis, I avail myself of the universal bisexuality of human beings. In a purely male being there would be a surplus of masculine release at the two [critical] sexual boundaries [postulated by Freud as occurring around four and eight years of age], consequently pleasure would be generated and at the same time perversion; in a purely female being there would be a surplus of *unpleasurable* substance at these two points of time. During the first phases the releases would run parallel (*i.e.*, there would be a normal surplus of pleasure). This explains the preference of true females for the defensive neuroses. (*Origins*, p. 179)

"Thus hysteria is in fact not repudiated *sexuality* but rather repudiated perversion" (p. 180), Freud concludes, in setting forth one of his most fundamental psychoanalytic propositions.

Freud's first mention of "erotogenic zones" also appears in this same letter and builds upon the theory of bisexual development just enunciated in sketching out a unified ontogenetic conception of sublimation, reaction formation, and moral development. "Behind this [new conception]," Freud remarks about his complementary interpretation of neuroses and perversion, "lies the notion of abandoned *erotogenic zones*. That is to say, during childhood sexual release would seem to be obtainable from very many parts of the body; but at a later time they are only able to release the 28-day anxiety substance and none other. This differentiation and limitation would thus underlie advances in culture and the development of morality, both social and individual" (p. 180). With this one passage, which concludes the scientific message of Freud's 6 December 1896 letter to Fliess, psychoanalysis was pointing toward a whole theory of civilization—a theme that was subsequently elaborated by Freud in much greater detail in *Totem and Taboo* (1912–13) and later works.

Three notable achievements mark Freud's efforts to cement his "column" upon Fliess's theoretical "base." First, in a single sweep, the theory of bisexuality did away with two of Freud's most perplexing post-*Project* difficulties—namely, the reversal of affect associated with many originally pleasurable childhood sexual experiences, and the variability of outcome following upon childhood seductions.

Second, I have already commented (p. 184) that Fliess's ideas on bisexuality were to prove instrumental to Freud's conceptualization of neurosis as the repressed "negative" of perversion. Freud's 6 December letter substantiates this claim.

Third and last, the theories of bisexuality and biorhythmic development fruitfully directed Freud's psychoanalytic attention toward possible critical stages in infantile psychosexual development. He set forth an immediate corollary of this new line of thought in several unpublished manuscript pages of this same letter and sought to relate such critical stages to various higher multiples of Fliess's 28-day female period.[30] It was this last aspect of Freud's 6 December letter that motivated a subsequent and likewise unpublished portion of Freud's next letter to Fliess (17 December 1896), in which he further discussed the theory of periodicity along these same developmental lines.[31] In short, Freud's previously environmental preoccupation with the *type* of seduction (and its purportedly traumatic consequences) was beginning to give way to a more developmental and organic-chemical concern with the child's precise reactions to premature, and apparently often pleasurable, sexual experiences. Both in chronology and reasoning, Freud had advanced more than halfway toward his crucial decision to abandon the seduction theory.

Repression and the Sense of Smell

Freud's 6 December 1896 insight into the importance of various "abandoned [childhood] erotogenic zones" opened the psychoanalytic door to yet another Fliessian-inspired, psychobiological theory. Intended by Freud as a complement to his bisexual analysis of repression, this new approach focused upon the nose. To Wilhelm Fliess, it will be recalled, the nose was a sex-linked organ—an erotogenic zone par excellence. He likewise considered all strong-smelling substances to be the disintegrated products of sexual metabolism, an idea that Freud had come to share by 1 January 1896, in connection with a jointly developed theory of migraine attacks (*Origins*, p. 144). Freud then went one step further and, in a combined ontogenetic-phylogenetic analysis,

30. The existence of this and one other unpublished discussion of Fliess's periodicity theory in such Freudian-developmental terms is briefly alluded to in editorial footnotes to *The Origins of Psycho-Analysis* (1954e:179, n. 1, 181, n. 2). The length of the first of these two discussions is mentioned by Strachey (*S.E.*, 1:238, n. 1). Freud's unpublished calculations are probably concerned with multiples of 28^2. Even multiples of $n \cdot 28 \cdot 28$ days occur at the following ages: 2 years and 2 months, $4\frac{1}{3}$ years, $6\frac{1}{2}$ years, $8\frac{2}{3}$ years, 11 years, 13 years, and 15 years. In his 6 December 1896 letter to Fliess, Freud was preoccupied with psychosexual changes occurring hypothetically at ages $1\frac{1}{2}$, 4, 8, and 14–15. The last three ages coincide closely with $n \cdot 28 \cdot 28$ days for $n = 2$, 4, and 7. One and one-half years is approximately 23^2 days.

31. See also Jones (1953:300), who mentions that Freud discussed 23- and 28-day sexual substances in yet another unpublished passage of the Fliess correspondence, from a letter of 1 March 1897.

seized upon the sense of smell as a major agent in the developmental processes of reaction formation and repression. His first intimation of this idea is expressed in a letter to Fliess of 11 January 1897, just a month after his earliest mention of the erotogenic zones. In this letter Freud declares:

> The perversions regularly lead into zoophilia, and have an animal character. They are not to be explained by the functioning of erotogenic zones which have later been abandoned [in normal individuals], but by the operation of erotogenic *sensations* which have subsequently lost their force [in normal individuals]. In this connection it will be remembered that the principal sense in animals (for sexual purposes as well as others) is that of smell, which has been [phylogenetically] deposed from that position in human beings. So long as the sense of smell (and of taste) is dominant, hair, faeces, and the whole surface of the body—and blood as well—have a sexually exciting effect. The increase in the sense of smell in hysteria [which, according to Freud, is a state of repressed perversion] is no doubt connected with this. (*Origins*, pp. 186–87)

In other words, Freud was saying, the organs of taste and particularly of smell must somehow trigger the reaction formations that in turn serve to delimit normal, adult sexual interests from that far more extensive repertoire shared by children, perverts, and lower animals. One would be curious to know just what Fliess made of all this!

As for Freud, his latest ideas on this Fliessian subject soon pointed the way to evolutionary speculations about upright posture and its psychophysiological repercussions in man. Before turning to Freud's thinking along these lines, I must make a significant historical observation about Freud's basic phylogenetic argument.

Virtually no aspect of Freud's metapsychology has received as little historical appreciation within its late-nineteenth-century biological context as has his notion of abandoned erotogenic zones. Part of this historical lacuna undoubtedly derives from his telegraphic omission in his letters to Fliess of an important biological assumption that was apparently taken for granted by both of them. At any event, what Freud does *not* state, but nevertheless seems to have had in mind in relating abandoned erotogenic zones to repression and the sense of smell, is Ernst Haeckel's *biogenetic law*—better known as the theory that "ontogeny is the short and rapid recapitulation of phylogeny" (Haeckel 1866, 2:300). Returning for a moment to Freud's general hypothesis, if lower animals indeed possess a widened sphere of sexual interests paralleling their heightened sense of smell; and if mankind has lost such "polymorphously perverse" sexual interests in the course of human evolution; then, according to Haeckel's law, the child must necessarily recapitulate both the process by which the zones were gradually extinguished in man and the concomitant acquisition of olfactory "disgust" toward these zones.

Freud's 6 December 1896 allusion to the abandoned erotogenic zones had already endorsed the first, or recapitulation-extinction, aspect of these two biogenetic inferences—that is, when he wrote that "during childhood sexual release would seem to be obtainable from very many parts of the body; but at a later time they are only able to release the 28-day anxiety substance and none other" (*Origins*, p. 180). (Fliess's theory of bisexuality, particularly his bisexual theory of repression and the unconscious, had a similar recapitulatory logic.)

It is hardly surprising, then, that only two months later Freud was actively pumping his friend for information on the second, or disgust-acquisition, aspect of this implicit biogenetic hypothesis. At what age, he asked Fliess, is disgust toward excrement first sensed by infants? "The answer would be interesting theoretically," he declared (*Origins*, p. 192). And, in a letter of 12 June 1897, he alluded to this potential biogenetic key, and to Fliess's own involvement in it, even more directly. "At Aussee," he wrote of their planned meeting in August, "I know a wonderful wood full of ferns and mushrooms, where *you shall reveal to me the secrets of the world of the lower animals and the world of children.* I am agape as never before for what you have to say—and I hope that the world will not hear it before me, and that instead of a short article you will give us within a year a small book which will reveal organic secrets [of development] in periods of 28 and 23" (*Origins*, p. 210; italics added). There can, in short, be little question, as subsequent letters to Fliess make even more evident, that the famed biogenetic law was of major hypothetico-deductive influence upon Freud's thinking throughout the 1896–97 period.

It was not, however, until after his abandonment of the seduction theory in the autumn of 1897 that Freud at last found himself free to pull together all the various organic, biogenetic, and psychological components of his previous year's thinking. Triumphantly calling it his "synthesis" to date (14 November 1897), Freud introduced this latest developmental conception in connection with a phylogenetic scheme for relating olfaction to upright posture in man:

> A few weeks ago I mentioned that I wanted to get behind [the phenomenon of] repression to the essential that lies behind it, and that is what I am writing to you about now.
>
> I have often suspected that something organic played a part in repression; I have told you before that it is a question of the attitude adopted to former sexual zones, and I added that I had been pleased to come across the same idea in Moll.[32] Privately, I would not concede priority in the idea to anyone; in my case the suggestion was linked to the changed part played by the sensations of smell: upright carriage was adopted, the nose was raised from the ground, and at the same time a number of what had formerly been interesting sensations connected with the earth became repellent—by a process of which I am still ignorant. ("He turns up his nose" = "he regards himself as something particularly noble.") Now, the zones which no longer produce a release of sexuality in normal and mature human beings must be the regions of the anus and of the mouth and throat. . . . In animals these sexual zones retain

32. For a discussion of Albert Moll's (1897*b*) similar thoughts on this subject, see Chapter 8.

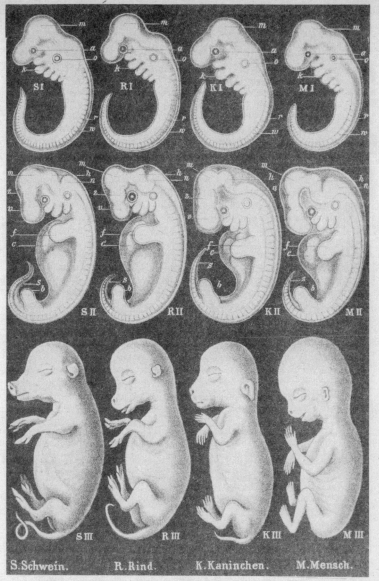

Ernst Haeckel's illustration of the biogenetic law. *Left to right*: embryos of the pig, cow, rabbit, and human as they recapitulate their common ancestry. In accordance with recapitulation theory, the embryos show greatest similarity in the earliest stages of their development. (From Haeckel 1877: Plate 7.)

their power . . . ; where they do so in human beings the result is perversion. We must suppose that in infancy sexual release is not so much localized as it becomes later [note Freud's continuing hypothetico-deductive and biogenetic logic here], so that zones which are later abandoned (and possibly the whole surface of the body) stimulate to some extent the production of something that is analogous to the later release of sexuality. (*Origins*, pp. 231–32)

To derive a theory of repression from this biogenetic vision of human sexual evolution was now but a simple intellectual step. As Freud went on to explain to Fliess, childhood memories associated with *abandoned* erotogenic zones should increasingly evoke disgust—not pleasure—at each successive step in development. "To put it crudely," he wrote, "the current memory stinks just as an actual object may stink; and just as we turn away our sense organ (the head and nose) in disgust, so do the preconscious and our conscious apprehension turn away from the memory. This is *repression*" (p. 232).

Continuing this line of argument, Freud repeated to Fliess their jointly espoused theory that morality, shame, and many other higher intellectual processes must emerge from the "progressive steps" (Fliess's *Entwicklungsschübe* in the original German) by which polymorphously perverse infantile sexuality is extinguished. Freud then remarked that sexual development in the female, as opposed to the male, seems to require an additional step in organic repression at the time of puberty— one that extinguishes the clitoral, or masculine, zone and thereby prepares the way for the subsequent innervation of the vaginal zone.[33]

33. Feminists will be inclined to see in this last, and surprisingly influential, psychoanalytic idea both a typical reflection of Freud's sexism and a clear sign of his ignorance about the female sex. Without wishing to deny either of these retrospective judgments about Freud, I must nevertheless expand a bit here upon the largely unappreciated nineteenth-century context of Freud's views on female sexuality. First, the myth of the "vaginal orgasm" was widely held in Freud's day—i.e., his views were typical, not atypical, of the then current understanding of female sexuality. It may also be assumed that common Victorian, and Western, stereotypes about masculinity (i.e., as the locus of rationality, strength, self-control, etc.) and femininity (as the locus of irrationality, weakness, and self-indulgence) helped to make such views plausible in two additional ways: (1) the "irrational" female seemed to need just such an extra wave of adolescent repression against the unruly id, while the male did not; and (2) many females, taught not to enjoy sexuality, were indeed anesthetic in the male "leading zone" (or clitoris). Finally, for anyone who held, as Freud did, that each sex suppresses its embryonic representation of the opposite sex in the course of human ontogeny, it made perfect biological sense that a female was not a true female until her archaic "male" zone had been extinguished.

Professor Jerome Kagan of Harvard University has pointed out to me that the masculine-feminine, rational-irrational dichotomy mentioned above also corresponds to Freud's further structural dichotomy between (rational) ego and (irrational) id. While this is certainly true in a general sense—and is, moreover, a rather striking and little-noted "externalist" commentary upon Freud's philosophy of mind—it is nevertheless a curious fact that he chose to associate (impulsive) libido with the masculine (i.e., active) side of man rather than with the feminine side, as one might otherwise have expected on this basis. (See, for example, Freud's *Three Essays*, 1905d, *S.E.*, 7:219.) The troublesome id, of course, is not entirely synonymous with libido in Freud's theory; it is synonymous only with the instincts as a whole and, in the adult, includes the repressed. A comment made by Freud in 1910 is relevant in the latter connection: "Neurosis always has a 'feminine' character. . . . Whatever is of the libido has a masculine character, and whatever is repression is of a feminine character" (*Minutes*, 2:432).

The complementary nature of bisexuality theory and Freud's new olfaction hypothesis about "organic repression" is nicely revealed by the next crucial passage in his 14 November 1897 letter to Fliess, where he once again takes up the variability-of-outcome problem:

> And now for the neuroses. Experiences in childhood which merely affect the genitals never produce neuroses in males (or masculine females) but only compulsive masturbation and libido. But since as a rule experiences in childhood also affect the two other sexual zones, the possibility remains open for males also that libido awakened by deferred action may lead to repression and neurosis. In so far as a memory refers to an experience connected with the genitals, what it produces by deferred action will be libido. But in so far as it refers to the anus, mouth, etc., it will produce internal disgust. . . . It ought not to be difficult to take in the psychological side of this; the decisive organic factor is whether the abandonment of the sexual zones takes place according to the masculine or the feminine type of development or whether it does not take place at all. (*Origins,* pp. 233–34)

In a nutshell, the psychoneuroses are now to be seen in terms of the specific erotogenic zone stimulated in childhood, the subsequent onset of the sense of disgust, and the overall bisexual disposition of the individual concerned. To this series of inferences (which broadly prefigures the whole Freudian theory of oral, anal, phallic, and genital psychosexual stages), Freud also appended the far-reaching psychoanalytic comment that "the choice of neurosis . . . probably depends on the nature (that is, the chronological relation) of the step [*des Schubes*] in development which enables repression to occur . . ." (p. 234).

Regarding his latest series of psychoanalytic insights as set forth in this 14 November 1897 letter, Freud concluded: "The main value of my synthesis lies in its linking together the neurotic and normal processes" (p. 234).

There are three historical points of interest about this particularly fascinating and, in general, insufficiently appreciated letter. First, Freud's letter represents the culmination of a year and one-half of ongoing efforts to place his metapsychological "column" upon Fliess's "base." More particularly, between Freud's letter to Fliess of 6 December 1896 and his letter of 14 November 1897 there exists a clear evolution of ideas along psychoanalytically transformed Fliessian lines. Second, Freud's initial psychoanalytic insights into the notions of psychosexual stages, the polymorphously perverse nature of infantile sexuality, and neurosis as the repressed "negative" of perversion were all achieved in close connection with Fliessian sexual biology. Moreover, none of these three fundamental insights was in any way associated either with Freud's self-analysis or with his discovery of his own Oedipus complex —events to which so much of Freud's thinking about infantile sexuality is usually ascribed.[34] Indeed, the most important results of Freud's self-

34. E.g., Fine 1963:218; Amacher 1965:82–84; 1974:222; and see earlier, Chapter 1, pp. 18–19.

analysis, as we shall see, must themselves be viewed as part of his psychoanalytic transformation of the Fliessian id. Third, Freud never abandoned his twofold hypothesis about the crucial roles of smell and of the bisexual disposition in organic repression. In fact, he continued to expand upon these ideas in later works (see Chapter 10.) True, he was later to supplement these constitutional factors with further psychoanalytic insights into the psychological side of the problem—for example, the Oedipus complex, castration anxiety, threats to narcissism, the superego, etc.; but he himself never saw any conflict between his organic theory of repression—with its major controlling role in the biogenetic unfolding of sexual development—and the more psychological theory that increasingly built upon it in order to account for individual differences in this general developmental course. Thus, he who believes with Amacher (1965:83) that Freud's 14 November 1897 ideas about repression are historically "not important" because he later developed them in a more psychological manner surely has failed to comprehend Freud's psychoanalytic transformation of the Fliessian id.

Childhood Sexual Impulses and the Etiology of Hysterical Seduction Phantasies

Speaking of what he termed "a big advance in insight," Freud excitedly announced to Fliess on 2 May 1897 that "the psychical structures which in hysteria are subjected to repression are not properly speaking memories, because no one sets his memory working without good cause, but *impulses* deriving from the primal scenes" (*Origins*, pp. 196–97; italics added). It is this particular insight, Ernst Kris declares in an editorial note to Freud's letter, that "subsequently led to a complete revision of his psychoanalytic hypotheses and turned psychoanalysis into a psychology of the instincts." Freud "has nearly discovered the 'id' (the meaning of instinct)," Kris contends (*Origins*, p. 197, n. 1).

It was this same insight that paved the immediate way for the collapse of Freud's seduction theory. For having once recognized that the proper target of defense is a libidinal impulse and not a memory, Freud was near to seeing that the psychical products of repressed instinctual impulses—that is, neurotic phantasies—could be just as "psychically real" to the neurotic as reality itself.

It would be strange, indeed, in the light of what I have already said in this chapter, to find that Fliess's dynamic, developmental conception of the sexual instinct was not in some way connected with these last psychoanalytic insights. After all, Freud's hypothesis about the etiological consequences of seduction was originally premised upon an explicit minimization of spontaneous infantile sexuality (see earlier, pp. 111–12). At the same time, Wilhelm Fliess's biorhythmic-sexual vision of human development had prompted Freud to accommodate his theory of childhood sexual traumas to include the potentially *pleasurable* nature of many infantile sexual experiences. Having sought on this account to explain a universal "reversal of [sexual] affect" in Fliessian terms, it only remained for Freud to take the next logical step in order to see how such repressed sexual impulses might generate phantasies (including phantasies *of seduction*) among highly neurotic individuals. While I do not wish to downplay, by any means, the magnitude of Freud's personal achievement in reaching this last insight, I am also inclined to count it among the most important of the post-*Project* derivatives of his scientific relationship with Fliess.

Was Freud himself consciously aware of any overlap between Fliess's biochemical, developmental vision of libidinal impulses and his own growing insight into the etiology of neurotic phantasies? Judging from the Fliess correspondence, I believe he was. For example, in Draft M, dated 25 May 1897, Freud went so far as to speak of phantasies in explicitly chemical terms. In hysteria, he commented, they arise "automatically (by a chemical process)"; similarly, he compared their psychical formation to "a process of fusion and distortion analogous to the decomposition of a chemical body which is combined with another one." Not a far distant shade, I submit, of Wilhelm Fliess's two combining bisexual substances! In the very same draft, Freud also speaks of "good grounds for suspecting that the arousing of the repressed material is not left to chance but follows *the laws of development*" (*Origins*, pp. 204–5; italics added). When one also recalls that it was only one month earlier, during their congress at Nuremberg, that Fliess had proposed to Freud that dreams and other psychical undercurrents in a woman might derive from the repressed (23-day) male component of her psyche, it does not seem surprising that Freud may have been thinking of such psychical phenomena at this time in specifically biochemical and Fliessian-developmental terms. As for the Nuremberg congress more generally, in Freud's eyes it was one of the most fruitful of all their many scientific meetings: "I need a new impetus from you . . . ," Freud wrote to his friend on 18 June 1897. "Nuremberg kept me going for 2 months." [35]

On the other hand, not at all implicit in Fliess's biogenetic and psychobiological views was Sigmund Freud's unique psychoanalytic transformation of them. Essential to this most creative of transformations was Freud's relation of repressed libidinal impulses and their sublimation in phantasy life to the complex mechanism of neurotic symptom formation.

Thus, in early May 1897, Freud had already begun to grasp the power of such phantasy-laden "sublimations" (his first use of this term) in provoking "highly improbable charges" against other people (*Origins*, p. 198). Then, less than a month later, he drew near to recognizing the Oedipus complex. Writing in Draft N under the subheading "Impulses," he asserted: "Hostile impulses against parents (a wish that they should die) are also an integral part of neuroses." In neurotic sons, he added, the death wish is directed against the father while in daughters it is against the mother (*Origins*, p. 207). Finally, by early July, Freud was viewing the psychoneuroses in terms of a vicious and dynamic circle of perverse libidinal impulses undergoing continual repression and resurgence. "The result," he announced to Fliess, "is all these distortions of memory and phantasies, either about the past or the future. I am learning the rules which govern the formation of these structures, *and the reasons why they are stronger than real memories*, and have thus learned new things about the characteristics of processes in the unconscious. Side by side with these structures perverse impulses arise, and the repression of these phantasies and impulses . . . gives rise . . . to new motives for clinging to the illness" (*Origins*, p. 212; italics added). To sum up, by July 1897, Freud no longer conceived the etiology of psychoneurosis as being so simple as he once had —that is, in terms of childhood sexual traumas operating by "deferred action" at puberty. With his greater insight into the dynamics of psychosexual development—in significant part assisted by Wilhelm Fliess— matters had become much more complex indeed.

Abandonment of the Seduction Theory

In the light of his growing insight into libidinal impulses and phantasies in the neuroses, it is not too surprising that Freud began, during the spring and summer of 1897, to have serious misgivings about his seduction etiology (*Origins*, pp. 192, 194, 206). In mid-August he spoke to Fliess of being "tortured with grave doubts" about his whole seduction-theory approach (*Origins*, p. 213). Then, in a fateful letter of 21 September, following his return to Vienna from his summer holidays,[36] he at last revealed to his Berlin friend "the great secret which has been slowly dawning on me in recent months"—namely, that the seduction confessions were, in most instances at least, simply not true (*Origins*, p. 215).

Freud cited four main reasons as having prompted him to take this difficult intellectual step: (1) lack of complete therapeutic success with his patients; (2) the astonishingly frequent degree of parental perversion implied by the theory (even Freud's own father was implicated by virtue of his brother and sisters' hysterical tendencies);[37] (3) the difficulty of separating truth from "emotionally-charged fiction" in the unconscious; and (4) the apparent impossibility of ever completely overcoming conscious resistance in patients and therefore gaining reliable access to "the secret of [repressed] infantile experiences" (*Origins*,

36. In late August, Freud departed for Italy and Venice for nearly a month of travel and sightseeing. He was accompanied by his wife, his younger brother Alexander, and a Berlin colleague and pupil, Dr. Felix Gattel (Jones 1953:334). Did Felix Gattel's systematic attempt to corroborate Freud's sexual theories at Krafft-Ebing's Psychiatric Clinic in the summer and fall of 1897 play any part in Freud's decision to give up the seduction theory at this time? I treat this issue separately as an open question in Appendix C.

37. Freud's comment about his father is omitted in *Anfänge* and *Origins* but is included by James Strachey in the subsequent version of this letter published in *S.E.*, 1:259. See also Jones 1953:322.

pp. 215–16). It is of interest that Freud had convincingly dismissed in print the second and the third reasons as long as a year and a half before (1896c, S.E., 3:204, 207–8).[38]

Of more interest, as Jones (1953:267) has specifically noted, is Freud's immediate reaction to his setback: he was considerably more cheerful and optimistic than his later reference to "helpless bewilderment" suggests ("History of the Psycho-Analytic Movement," 1914d, S.E., 14:17). Actually, what he described to Fliess at the time as a feeling of "triumph" was perhaps not so surprising when one appreciates the remarkable progress he had made in the last year and one-half toward understanding the long and dynamic course of human psychosexual development. True, Freud was hardly overjoyed by the many new uncertainties that he now faced in his theory of psychoneurosis. And yet his optimism foreshadowed his progress over the next few weeks. Within a month, he had not only formulated the notion of the Oedipus complex—now seen as a universal phenomenon—but he was also talking with renewed confidence about "big, general framework factors . . . which [constitutionally] determine [psychosexual] development, and other minor factors which fill in the picture and vary according to individual experiences" (Origins, p. 226).

Finally, by the middle of November, Freud had effectively plugged the seduction-theory gap in his thinking with the major psychobiological synthesis (of upright posture, abandoned erotogenic zones, organic repression, and bisexuality theory) that I have already described. Free at last of the seduction theory, he was able to give psychoanalytic primacy to the polymorphously perverse nature of the infantile sexual disposition, together with its biogenetically predetermined course of extinction in healthy individuals. In short, by the end of 1897 psychoanalysis had become a psychology of the id.

Self-Analysis

Freud's famous self-analysis, whose beginning dates from midsummer of 1897, may now be seen in a more historically realistic light than has generally been the case in the secondary accounts of his life. According to the traditional view, Freud's self-analysis led directly to his abandonment of the seduction theory and, more important, to his discoveries of infantile sexuality, the Oedipus complex, the theory of dreams, the free association technique, the concepts of transference and resistance, and even the unconscious (e.g., Fine 1973:29). "Psychoanalysis proper," concludes another spokesman for this traditional position, "is essentially a product of Freud's self-analysis" (Wells 1960:189).[39]

38. See also 1896a, S.E., 3:153. For a discussion of the changing import of the second objection, see Appendix C.

39. See Chapter 1, pp. 18–19, for a more complete list of historical judgments about the "epic" proportions and "unprecedented results" that were supposedly entailed in Freud's self-analytic journey into the forbidding depths of his own unconscious mind.

I certainly do not wish to minimize either the difficulties or the important psychological achievements that are customarily attributed to Freud's self-analysis. He himself described this analysis as "harder than any other" (*Origins*, p. 214) and also considered it an invaluable step in his intellectual development; but with the passage of time, it has tended to become an overburdened catchall for many developments in his thinking that have hitherto possessed no better historical explanation. As such, the inordinate number of discoveries referred to his self-analysis has done much to reinforce the widespread myth that he was intellectually "isolated" in the 1890s.[40] Postponing until Chapter 13 a detailed analysis of the considerable political function served by such myths in psychoanalytic history, I shall consider here the myth of self-analysis in its specific historical context.

To begin with, it seems highly unlikely that Freud's self-analysis played anything like the "decisive" role that has so often been attributed to it in connection with his abandonment of the seduction theory.[41] The decision to abandon the seduction theory was the culmination of a long conceptual transformation, influenced much more by Fliess and by the inherent flaws of the seduction theory itself than by self-analysis. What is more, major temporal inconsistencies have always plagued this historical hypothesis, which has depended upon the dubious claim that the self-analysis definitely *preceded* Freud's abandonment of the seduction theory. Although it is true that he first speaks of his intention to undertake a systematic self-analysis on 14 August 1897—that is to say, a full month before abandoning his seduction etiology—he also seems to have made little real progress, if any, in this direction before departing some ten days later for nearly a month of travel in Italy. As Freud himself wrote to Fliess on 14 November 1897, not long after his return to Vienna: "Before the holidays I mentioned that my most important patient was myself, and after my holiday trip my self-analysis, *of which there had previously been no trace*, began" (*Origins*, p. 231; italics added).

Jones (1953:236), among others, dismisses this contradictory passage as evidence of a curious "lapse in memory" on Freud's part.[42] It

40. The traditional claim that Freud and Fliess conducted "duologues rather than dialogues" throughout their intimate relationship forms a significant part of this myth (Jones 1953:303).

41. E.g., Jones 1953:265, 325; Kris 1950*a*:113. For further references, see Chapter 13, p. 492, Myth 15.

42. Schur (1972:109–12) goes even further to save the traditional historical view and argues that Freud's self-analysis must have been *unconsciously* under way many months before his first formal (14 August 1897) intimations about it to Fliess. Schur's argument seems patently unconvincing and also involves a major contradiction in terms, to wit: in Freudian theory the unconscious does not yield its repressed secrets without a *conscious* and concerted conflict with the analysand's own ego. Nevertheless, some such argument is clearly necessary for those like Schur, Kris, and Jones who would attribute to Freud's self-analysis his May 1897 discoveries of (1) the true locus of psychical defense (sexual impulses as opposed to memories) and (2) the powerful "psychical reality" that is embodied in the neurotic's phantasy life.

Others (e.g., Ellenberger 1970:445–46; Buxbaum 1951; and Anzieu 1959) would assign the beginning of Freud's self-analysis to his discovery of the meaning of seems equally plausible, however, that Freud simply found it impossible simultaneously to begin a detailed self-analysis and to sightsee actively in his beloved Italy. Also, Freud was dependent upon his dreams for his self-analysis; and while traveling in a foreign country, they may well have been of limited self-analytic value. It was only in early October (and therefore several weeks *after* his decision to abandon the seduction theory) that he began to report to Fliess real signs of self-analytic progress (*Origins*, pp. 218–28).

Nor did Freud's self-analysis serve, as Freud scholars commonly claim, as the "heroic" vehicle for his discovery of the hidden world of spontaneous infantile sexuality. It is clear that he was already looking for evidence of sexual activity in his own childhood (spontaneous or otherwise) when he finally undertook this self-analysis.

What, then, was the real scientific value of Freud's self-analysis? Self-analysis finally allowed him to confirm from his own experience just how remarkably widespread the opportunities were in every *normal* childhood for both traumatic and spontaneous sexual activity. At the same time, self-analysis enabled Freud to extend significantly his understanding of the various psychological correlates of such early sexual experiences. He was able to recall feelings of jealousy and hatred at the birth of a younger male sibling, one year his junior (and who died after only eight months of life). He also recognized love for the mother and jealousy of the father in the early years of his childhood and therefore concluded that such feelings must be a universal concomitant of this period of life (if not so pronounced or so early as in the clinical histories of psychoneurotics). He even recalled that "libido towards *matrem* was aroused" when, at the age of two, he had seen his mother in the nude. It is in this connection that he acknowledged Fliess's previous and identical conclusion about his own son (*Origins*, p. 219).

And finally, Freud discovered that his "primary originator" in neurosis had been a childhood nurse—his demanding "instructress in sexual matters" as he called her, apparently in reference to his difficult toilet training (*Origins*, pp. 218–25). When Freud, with the help of his mother, was subsequently able to confirm many of his recollections of his nurse, he was emboldened to reaffirm his wavering belief in the ability of psychoanalysis to recover *reliable* evidence about early childhood sexual experiences. It was primarily for this reason that he also seems, temporarily at least, to have revived his belief in many of the "horrible perverse details" that his hysterical patients had previously told him (*Origins*, p. 221).[43]

---

dreams—i.e., as early as July 1895, when he interpreted the famous dream of "Irma's injection" along "wish-fulfillment" lines. I, on the other hand, make a sharp distinction between Freud's self-directed attempts at *dream* analysis, which indeed date from mid-1895 and even earlier, and his subsequent decision to undertake a systematic self-analysis in August 1897. It was only with the latter decision that he finally began to use his dreams as a means of overcoming his personal amnesia of early childhood sexual memories.

43. See also Strachey's comments to this effect in *S.E.*, 1:260–61, n. 4.

One last point. Self-analysis helped to confirm the importance of something Freud had already begun to surmise from his previous clinical work: that dreams, which contain "the whole psychology of the neuroses in a nutshell" (*Origins*, p. 212), can provide invaluable assistance in overcoming therapeutic resistances and hence childhood amnesia.

Further Developments in the Libido Theory (1897–1905)

It has frequently been said that it took Freud some time (until after the turn of the century) to become "entirely reconciled" to his momentous discoveries about infantile sexuality.[44] While there is indeed an important grain of truth to this historical claim, there is also considerable inaccuracy in it as well. Once again it is necessary to reiterate that Freud's personal enlightenment on the subject of infantile sexuality constituted not so much a sudden "discovery" (in the usual sense of the word) as it did a prolonged series of transformations in his previous appreciation of the exact relevance of spontaneous infantile sexual manifestations for explaining psychoneurosis.

In his paper "Sexuality in the Aetiology of the Neuroses," for instance, Freud commented unambiguously about the existence of infantile sexuality: "We do wrong to ignore the sexual life of children entirely; in my experience, *children are capable of every psychical sexual activity, and many somatic ones as well.* Just as the whole human sexual apparatus is not comprised in the external genitals and the two reproductive glands, so human sexual life does not begin only with puberty, as on a rough inspection it may appear to do" (1898a, S.E., 3:280; italics added). True, he then went on to proclaim that "the organization and evolution of the human species strives to avoid any great degree of sexual activity during childhood," adding that in man these "sexual instinctual forces are meant to be stored up so that, on their release at puberty, they may serve great cultural ends. (W. Fliess)" (pp. 280–81). Nevertheless, what has seemed to Jones, Strachey, and others like an ambivalent retraction of the first of Freud's assertions—that children display unmistakable sexual impulses—by the second—that our species seeks to avoid such infantile activities—represented no such inconsistency to either Freud or Fliess. For, as I have already said, a dynamic opposition between waves of spontaneous infantile sexual release and the agents of sexual "latency" was entirely necessary to both of them in the late 1890s in order to explain the potentially pathological nature of sexuality in childhood as well as the underlying psychophysiological mechanism controlling the delayed (i.e., postpubertal) outbreak of psychoneurosis.

Freud's equally unequivocal endorsement of spontaneous infantile sexuality during this same period can likewise be seen from his pub-

44. E.g., Strachey, Editor's Note to Freud 1905d, S.E., 7:128–29; and Jones 1953:322–23.

lished letters to Fliess of 27 September 1898 and 3 January 1899 (*Origins*, pp. 267 and 271). In particular, Freud's development of a new theory of paranoia in December 1899 leaves no doubt about his general views on this subject, set forth in a discussion of his perennial problem, the choice of neurosis:

> The lowest of the sexual strata is auto-erotism, which renounces any psychosexual aim and seeks only local gratification. This is superseded by allo-erotism (homo- and hetero-), but undoubtedly survives as an independent tendency. Hysteria (and its variant, obsessional neurosis) is allo-erotic; the main highway it follows is identification with the loved person. Paranoia dissolves the identification again, re-establishes all the loved persons of childhood . . . and dissolves the ego itself into extraneous persons. So I have come to regard paranoia as a surge forward of the auto-erotic tendency, a regression to a former state. (*Origins*, pp. 303-4, letter of 9 December 1899)

In other words, by late 1899 psychoanalysis was venturing to assert a direct relationship between the infantile stage of libidinal fixation and the specific type, and severity, of neurosis. Freud's insight in this regard involved a significant revision in his previous psychoanalytic thinking; for he had formerly considered paranoia as the neurosis least dependent upon childhood determinants (see, for example, *Origins*, p. 165).

What Freud did *not* fully decide about infantile sexuality until at least 1901 was how much emphasis to give to the deferred action of infantile sexual experiences and how much to give, on the other hand, to the more dynamic psychoanalytic notion of libidinal fixations during childhood. Thus, as Freud came more to realize how virtually no one (even the perfectly healthy) manages to escape sexual experiences in childhood, his theoretical emphasis underwent a corresponding shift from the importance of premature sexuality per se to the more peculiarly psychoanalytic question of whether a pathological fixation of the libido has ensued from such early sexual experiences.

The mechanism of fixation was in turn seen by Freud as creating an inhibition in further libidinal development, and as inducing later *regressions* to the weak fixation points of libidinal organization. Within this more mature Freudian perspective on neurosis, the principle of deferred action became significantly less important in psychoanalytic theory—a still necessary but no longer sufficient explanation of later psychoneurosis (Freud 1918*b*, *S.E.*, 17:45 n.).

By the time Freud wrote up his case history of Dora in early 1901, he had apparently reached this later etiological point of view, although a trace of the older scheme is still to be seen in his discussion of the time of fixation. Speaking of the Oedipus complex, he wrote that such rudimentary feelings of sexual love may become fixated either in childhood itself or as late as puberty. "The decisive factor in this connection," he concluded, "is no doubt the early appearance of true genital sensations, either spontaneously or as a result of seduction or masturbation"

(1905e [1901], S.E., 7:57, n. 1). According to Freud's revised etiological scheme, then, the more neurotic the individual, the greater the likelihood that the fixations occurred during childhood itself.

Freud's mature theory of psychoneurosis involved a second big shift in his thinking about infantile sexuality, a shift closely linked to the general notion of psychopathological fixations that I have just surveyed. He recognized libidinal fixations as having three possible consequences—neurosis, normality, or perversion—with the particular outcome being attributed largely to *heredity*—that is, to whether there is an organic disposition toward repressing the fixation. As Freud later summarized this theoretical change in views, "accidental influences have been replaced by constitutional factors and 'defence' in the purely psychological sense has been replaced by organic 'sexual repression'" (1906a, S.E., 7:278).[45] With his revised position on the role of heredity in the psychoneuroses, and with his increasingly dynamic emphasis upon childhood libidinal fixations, Freud's later theory of human sexual development was essentially complete in its fundamental outlines.

Although he informed Fliess in late 1899 that a book on sexuality would probably be "the immediate successor" to his *Interpretation of Dreams* (*Origins*, p. 300), it was almost six more years before he finally published his major work on this subject. (No doubt Freud's personal estrangement from Fliess, which dates from the summer of 1900 and which I shall take up shortly, had something to do with this delay.) Published in 1905 under the title *Drei Abhandlungen zur Sexualtheorie*, Freud's treatise was a remarkably compact eighty-seven pages in the original edition. In spite of its brevity, few would argue with James Strachey's assertion: "Freud's *Three Essays on the Theory of Sexuality* stand, there can be no doubt, beside his *Interpretation of Dreams* as his most momentous and original contributions to human knowledge" (Editor's Note to Freud 1905d, S.E., 7:126).

Freud frankly acknowledges the first essay, "The Sexual Aberrations," to be a general compendium of current information from the writings of Krafft-Ebing, Havelock Ellis, Albert Moll, and other sexologists. By way of introduction, he proposes that sexual perversions be classified in binary terms—either as deviations with respect to *object* (for instance, homosexuality) or deviations with respect to *aim* (sadism, masochism, and so forth). The etiological roots of homosexuality, discussed at considerable length, are attributed to man's innate bisexual disposition as well as to various disturbances that can affect the sexual instinct during its long development. In the 1905 edition, Freud did not choose to specify what these various disturbing influences might be; in 1910 and 1915, he expanded his discussion on this topic and ascribed homosexuality, in part, to "narcissistic object-choice and a retention of the erotic significance of the anal zone" (1905d, S.E., 7:146 n.).

In the same essay, the psychoneuroses are defined as the (repressed) "negative" of perversion. Both neurosis and perversion may be jointly construed in terms of various "component [sexual] instincts" and

45. See also the "Dora" case history, S.E., 7:87–88.

the associated erotogenic zones of childhood. "A formula begins to take shape," this first essay concludes, "which lays it down that the sexuality of neurotics has remained in, or been brought back to, an infantile state" (1905d, S.E., 7:172).

Freud's second essay, entitled "Infantile Sexuality," begins by comparing the remarkable amnesia that conceals from us our early childhood experiences with the equally peculiar phenomenon of *hysterical* amnesia. It then details the course of sexual development along the following lines. The newborn child comes into the world with germs of the sexual instinct already present. These germs continue to develop by periodic advances—advances that are countered by suppressions, reaction formations, and sublimations (the psychical agents of the latency period). The phenomenon of sexual latency is ascribed to organic as well as to cultural factors and is further related, through the specific notion of sublimation, both to individual educability and to the achievements of higher civilization.

Freud's third and last essay, "The Transformations of Puberty," delineates the adolescent consolidation of the component instincts under the primacy of the genitals. In the male this process is straightforward. In the female, however, a fresh wave of repression is necessary in order to extinguish the infantile, masculine sexual zone in women—the region of the clitoris—and to allow the subsequent awakening of a new leading zone, the vagina.

Adolescence also presents each individual with the critical task of finding an appropriate sexual object. At first such sexual objects are taken in phantasy life only—a process that inevitably revives the incestuous libidinal ties of childhood. These phantasies must be overcome, says Freud, if a normal sexual life is to ensue. Most individuals accomplish this feat by gradually detaching themselves from the parental authority that they accepted so unquestioningly in childhood. Psychoneurosis becomes the individual's unhappy fate if there instead occurs a repudiation of the demands of normal sexuality, followed by an unconscious return to the incestuous object choice of childhood.

The Summary of Freud's *Three Essays* reemphasizes the intimate cooperation between hereditary predisposition and acquired influences in the etiology of psychoneurosis. Together these dual influences orchestrate the outcome of sexual development. "Every step on this long path of development can become a point of fixation . . . ," Freud concludes. Above all, it is the psychobiological influences of sublimations, reaction formations, and waves of repression (*Verdrängungsschübe*) that determine the specific adult sexual disposition (1905d, S.E., 7:235, 237–39).

As set forth in the *Three Essays on the Theory of Sexuality*, Freud's libido theory was complete in its most essential features. Although he would make many subsequent modifications in it, his fundamental biogenetic unification of heredity with environment, biology with psychology, and neurosis with normality and perversion represents the essence of his conception and is the culmination as well of his psychoanalytic transformation of Fliessian sexual biology.

THE ESTRANGEMENT

Having so often wondered what Sigmund Freud saw in Wilhelm Fliess in the first place, Freud's biographers have generally viewed their estrangement after 1900 as inevitable as well as long overdue. These biographers have usually cited three different circumstances as precipitating the final break. To those who have dwelt upon Fliess's role as a "transference" figure, both Freud's unusual dependence upon Fliess in the 1890s and subsequent break with his friend after the turn of the century are clear reflections of his Oedipus complex.[46] To wit, Freud's temporary overestimation of Fliess's intellectual capabilities mirrored his childhood overestimation of his father's wisdom and authority, while his latent skepticism and hostility toward Fliess (the "father figure") was bound to emerge once his self-analysis revealed this complex (Jones 1953:307).

Closely related to this historical explanation of the estrangement is another, namely, that the break became necessary when Freud finally refused to follow Fliess in his "ever more fanciful hypotheses."[47] Fliess became indignant (so goes this account), attacked Freud's work, and subsequently implicated him in a needless and highly "paranoid" priority dispute.

Still others have seen the break as stemming from a fundamental incompatibility between their respective scientific approaches to the psyche. Along such lines, Ernst Kris claims that the estrangement was a necessary step in Freud's establishment of psychoanalysis as an "independent" and purely psychological science (1954:35, 45–46). "After the beginning of Freud's self-analysis in 1897," Kris asserts, "Fliess's influence could only hinder this development" (p. 45). And similarly, "When Fliess attempted to link the unconscious to the problem of bisexuality by stating that the impulses of the opposite sex are regularly repressed, Freud revolted against the attempt to 'biologize psychodynamics,' and the relationship between the two came to an end" (Kris 1950a:115).[48]

In spite of the considerable credence given to these various explanations of the estrangement, I must question them all. To begin with, they all rest upon the common but incorrect assumption that Freud, having outgrown his need for Fliess's friendship and scientific advice, was the one who terminated the relationship (e.g., Schur 1972:209). That this was not the case is amply borne out by Freud's correspondence with Fliess, as I shall shortly show.[49]

---

46. E.g., Jones 1953:307; Kris 1954:43; Erikson 1955:4; Robert 1966:150; and Costigan 1967:60–61.

47. See, for example, Schur 1972:96, whose words I quote; Kazin 1962:358; and Kris 1954:40–41.

48. See also Erikson 1955:13; and Jones 1953:300, 313–14.

49. Those Freud scholars who have been forced to acknowledge this historical fact have still been able to argue that Freud's "unconscious" hostility toward Fliess, which the latter eventually detected and came to resent, really precipitated the

What, then, came between these two men? I see the estrangement as bound up with three interrelated aspects of their relationship: Freud's enthusiastic acceptance and subsequent transformation of Fliess's scientific ideas into several key psychoanalytic constructs; the growing scientific rivalry that this transformation introduced into their previous intellectual relationship; and Freud's increasingly neurotic personal relationship with Fliess. I shall begin by taking up the last of these aspects.

Freud's Neurosis

From about 1894 to about 1900, Freud suffered the symptoms of a psychosomatic illness. His complaints included highly depressed moods, disquieting self-doubts, an obsessive preoccupation with his own death, and various gastrointestinal and cardiac disturbances.

That Wilhelm Fliess played an important role in Freud's neurosis is evident from Freud's letters to his friend during this period. Writing on 7 July 1897, for example, Freud confessed: "I still do not know what has been happening to me. Something from the deepest depths of my own neurosis has ranged itself against my taking a further step in understanding of the neuroses, *and you have somehow been involved*. My inability to write seems to be aimed at hindering our intercourse. I have no proofs of this, but merely feelings of a very obscure nature" (*Origins*, p. 212; italics added). More than one interpretation of this most interesting passage is possible,[50] but this is mine.

That Freud should have implicated his friend in both his neurotic symptoms and his scientific problems during the summer of 1897 is hardly surprising. On the brink of abandoning his seduction theory of neurosis, an already unnerved Freud was beginning to see Fliess's views on sexual development as a definite forewarning of his blunder. "When this point [the existence of spontaneous infantile sexuality] had been clarified," Freud later reflected on his mistake, "the 'traumatic' element in the sexual experiences of childhood lost its importance and what was left was the realization that infantile sexual activity (whether spontaneous or provoked) prescribes the direction that will be taken by later sexual life after maturity" (1906a, S.E., 7:274).

---

estrangement. Moreover, inasmuch as the Freudian psyche is often assumed to exhibit an excessively friendly emotion for its unconsciously intended opposite, Freud's repeated testimony to his supreme admiration for Fliess has naturally provided ready evidence for such a convoluted psychoanalytic point of view. See, for example, Jones 1953:312–14; Erikson 1955:4, 13; and Kris 1954:43.

50. Jones (1953:306), Kris (1954:43, 212 n.), and Erikson (1955:9), among others, have interpreted this passage as an important sign of Freud's beginning self-analysis and hence his growing insight into his transference relationship with Fliess. Two points seem especially relevant in questioning this interpretation—at least as the only possible one. First, Freud's formal self-analysis, as already explained, seems to have begun in mid-August, not early July, of 1897 and even then it was slow to yield much in the way of results. Second, in this passage, Freud clearly associates his relationship with Fliess both with his neurosis and, more explicitly, with his current difficulties in understanding "*the neuroses*." The latter problem, as I have already maintained, was a derivative not just of their emotional (and peculiarly oedipal) relationship but of their *scientific* relationship as well.

Nor is it coincidental that Freud's neurotic symptoms became greatly intensified at this time. The collapse of his seduction theory (his would-be discovery of "the source of the Nile") effectively smashed his hopes for quick fame and recognition as a neurologist. Moreover, his scientific mistake, already published in several scientific papers, was professionally embarrassing. Indeed, it was fully *seven* years before Freud finally admitted his error in print to the highly skeptical medical community that had never really believed him in the first place! No wonder, then, that he developed a fairly severe case of neurosis about this time, and that he also considered his friend Fliess to be involved in his scientific difficulties.

In making this point, I am not saying the Freud's neurosis lacked other provocations; to be sure, it had multiple determinants. His neurosis has also had many differing interpretations. Jones (1953: 305–11), among others, sees it as an expression of the unconscious material that was attempting to emerge from Freud's psyche during the late 1890s, a process that ultimately ended in his discovery of his own Oedipus complex.

On the other hand, Henri Ellenberger (1970:444–50) considers Freud's neurosis, his self-analysis, the relationship with Fliess, and the elaboration of psychoanalysis as all part of "a creative illness." The characteristics of a creative illness are polymorphous, according to Ellenberger. They include depression; symptoms of a severe neurosis or even psychosis; excessive preoccupation with obscure intellectual problems; a sense of utter isolation, of ordeal, and of searching for "an elusive truth"; continual doubts about one's ability to reach that great and secret principle; and a euphoric return to health once the discovery, or series of discoveries, has finally been made. Such illnesses, Ellenberger maintains, are to be seen among shamans, mystics, creative writers, and many philosophers. Mesmer, Fechner, Nietzsche, Freud, and Jung all suffered from a creative illness at some time in their lives. In Freud's case, Ellenberger believes, Wilhelm Fliess took on the role of "the shaman master before the shaman apprentice" and thus facilitated Freud's passage through his creative illness. This is a variant of the traditional "transference" hypothesis about Fliess.

Whereas Ellenberger, Jones, and most other Freud scholars tend to stress the creative derivatives of Freud's neurotic illness, I prefer to concentrate upon its *causes*. Freud was not only an ambitious and creative thinker but also a man obsessed with *being* creative—a self-styled "conquistador" in the world of science.[51] In the mid-1890s his obsession and his self-doubts about being able to satisfy it reached a peak.[52] His equally obsessive fear of premature death throughout this

---

51. Unpublished Fliess correspondence, quoted in Schur 1972:201.

52. Eissler (1971:258–59), speaking of the medical-student period in Freud's life (1882–86), has reached a similar conclusion in relating Freud's "wild and probably pathological ambition," together with his fear of accepting "a subordinate position in the history of ideas," to the many psychical conflicts he experienced during this earlier period. Eissler believes that Freud had learned to master such conflicts by the time he visited Charcot in Paris. I, on the other hand, prefer to think more in terms of a "return of the repressed" during the late 1890s.

period (including his specific phobia about railway travel) is particularly suggestive of his conflict-ridden preoccupation with creative (immortal) achievement.[53] I believe that this obsessional need for intellectual immortality was the principal cause both of his neurosis and, indirectly, of his subsequent estrangement from Fliess.

With the abandonment of the seduction theory, Freud's motives for psychoneurosis could hardly have been more justified. The whole reliability of the psychoanalytic method, not to mention the various theoretical and therapeutic claims that Freud had erected in its name, was temporarily cast into grave doubt by his error. Additionally, his long-range goal of using his psychopathological findings to illuminate the whole of psychology was given an equally serious setback. "One thing I have learned . . . which makes an old man of me," he gloomily admitted to Fliess in a letter of 23 October 1898. "If the ascertaining of the few points required for the explanation of the neuroses involves so much work, time and error, how can I ever hope to gain an insight into the whole of mental activity, which was once something I proudly looked forward to?" (*Origins*, p. 269).

To sum up, Freud's personal and scientific relationship with Fliess furnished only a partial catalyst for his mid-1890s outbreak of neurosis. But Fliess's scientific work indeed helped to bring on Freud's crisis of intellectual confidence at that time and thus facilitated his latent predisposition to neurotic symptomology. In the process the Freud-Fliess relationship sowed the seeds of its own destruction.

Rivalry and Reductionism

Freud's abandonment of the seduction theory created a wholly new and potentially divisive dimension to his scientific relationship with Fliess. Prior to the fall of 1897, Freud had happily envisioned the two of them, in spite of their many overlapping interests in the fields of physiology and toxicological medicine, as reigning in separate but equal scientific domains: "We share like the two beggars, one of whom allotted himself the province of Posen; you take the biological, I the psychological" (*Origins*, p. 211). Then, with the abandonment of the seduction theory in September 1897, all this suddenly changed as Freud also abandoned his extreme environmentalism and in its stead began to speak of "big, general framework factors" in human development and of "other minor factors which fill in the picture and vary according to individual experiences" (*Origins*, p. 226).

At the heart of the altered relationship between the two scientists was the issue of how much biological reductionism was necessary and appropriate in Freud's increasingly genetic conception of human thought and behavior. Fliess obviously thought there should be as much as possible, and Freud—in principle at least—was in basic accord. Turning his attention to dreams, for example, Freud still looked to the

53. This point is also set forth by Ernest Becker in his provocative study *The Denial of Death* (1973:97–105).

biological side of the problem in early 1898 in deriving one of his most daring theoretical propositions about them:

> It seems to me as if the wish-fulfillment theory gives only the psychological and not the biological, or rather metapsychological explanation [of dreaming]. (Incidentally I am going to ask you seriously whether I should use the term "metapsychology" for my psychology which leads behind consciousness.) Biologically dream-life seems to me to proceed directly from the residue of the prehistoric stage of life (one to three years), which is the source of the unconscious and alone contains the aetiology of all the psychoneuroses; the stage which is normally obscured by an amnesia similar to hysteria. . . . The repetition of experiences of the prehistoric period is a wish-fulfillment in itself and for its own sake; a recent wish leads to a dream only if it can be associated with material from that period, if the recent wish is a derivative of a prehistoric wish or can get itself adopted by such a wish. I do not know yet to what extent I shall be able to stick to this extreme theory, or let it loose in the dream book." (*Origins*, pp. 246–47, letter of 10 March 1898)

Thus, the biological-developmental point of view continued to be of important theoretical inspiration to Freud, even in his work on dreams.[54]

At times, however, Freud's concern with the biological side of the psyche must have seemed insufficient to Fliess, for the latter evidently questioned him on this point—and received the following response on 22 September 1898: "But I am not in the least in disagreement with you, and have no desire at all to leave the psychology hanging in the air with no organic basis. But, beyond a feeling of conviction [that there must be such a basis], I have nothing, either theoretical or therapeutic, to work on, and so I must behave as if I were confronted by psychological factors only. I have no idea yet why I cannot yet fit it together [the psychological and the organic]" (*Origins*, p. 264).

In these general terms, the problem of reductionism was still harmless enough. But Fliess meanwhile had been busy extending his own theories—both along with, and independently of, Freud—into the overlapping provinces of psychology, human psychosexual development, and neuropathology. (The absence of Fliess's replies to Freud's letters should not fool one into thinking of him as just a passive or disinterested observer of Freud's psychoanalytic transformation of his ideas.) At the same time, Fliess, who was reading and criticizing *The Interpretation of Dreams* in both manuscript and proof, continued to be an enthusiastic supporter of Freud's most recent psychological innovations; and he even sought to stir up reviewers in Berlin for this book (*Origins*, p. 313). He therefore felt increasingly entitled to comment upon Freud's psychoanalytic work and, more important, to integrate their respective views on the course of life. After all, was not the organic skeleton in Freud's developmental approach partly explained by Fliess's own domain of sexual biology—for example, the notions of bisexuality; the erotogenic zones; possible critical periods in the development of libido and psyche; and organic, sexual repression? But

54. See also *The Interpretation of Dreams*, 1900a, *S.E.*, 5:605–7.

Fliess's zealous attitude raised the further issue of just *whose* scientific domain—Freud's or Fliess's—was really the more important in Freud's work.

It seems likely that Freud had already sensed this potential conflict even before his abandonment of the seduction theory finally brought this issue to a head. As early as April 1897, for example, a dream had apparently revealed to him an accumulation of unconscious "irritation" at Fliess, who, as he frankly told his friend, seemed to be "always claiming something special" for himself (*Origins,* p. 194). A committed reductionist, Fliess was indeed claiming something special for himself in their intimate scientific association. Moreover, Freud's acceptance and extensive psychoanalytic application of Fliess's biological ideas did not make it any easier to argue with his friend when the latter finally began to press the point. As Freud tried to explain in September 1901, apparently in response to a comment by Fliess on bisexuality and the unconscious: "One cannot simply say 'the conscious is the dominant, the unconscious the underlying, [bi]sexual factor' without grossly oversimplifying the very complicated nature of the case, though it is, of course, the basic fact" (*Origins,* p. 337).

In short, Freud wanted to use Fliess's ideas and suggestions—in his own psychoanalytically transformed terms. His previous dependence upon Fliess gradually turned to rivalry, and he began to see their scientific work as potentially competing. Writing to Karl Abraham on 6 April 1914, in connection wih the newly founded Berlin Society for Sexual Science, Freud conceded as much about his attitude toward Fliess's work: "The Society is designed to achieve recognition for Fliess. Rightly so, because he is the only mind among them and the possessor of a bit of unrecognized truth. But the subjection of our psycho-analysis to a Fliessian sexual biology would be no less a disaster than its subjection to any system of ethics, metaphysics, or anything of the sort. . . . We must at all costs remain independent and maintain our equal rights. Ultimately we shall be able to come together with all the parallel sciences" (*Freud/Abraham Letters,* p. 171). It is in this same vein that I interpret Freud's purported statement in 1913, made before the Vienna Psychoanalytic Society, that he had been forced by Fliess's domineering manner to take the idea of bisexuality "as his own discovery":

> Evening of reports. Rosenstein on Fliess's [theory of] periodicity. Freud replied at great length about his scientific relations with Fliess and how after Fliess had brought the matter of bisexuality to his attention he later on had to hold on to this as his own discovery. On the occasion of his break with Fliess: the difference in their methods, psychological instead of organismic. (Lou Andreas-Salomé, *The Freud Journal,* 1964:87)[55]

Prior to the summer of 1900, when their estrangement reached a point of open crisis, Freud's ambivalence toward Fliess and his methods was still largely latent. Nevertheless, one can detect increasing

55. This discussion is largely omitted from *Minutes,* 4:154–56; meeting of 29 January 1913.

signs of mutual rivalry, as from Freud's report to his friend of the following wish-fulfillment dream in late 1899: "Absurdity in dreams! It is astonishing how often you appear in them. In the *non vixit* dream I find I am delighted to have survived you . . ." (*Origins*, p. 299).[56]

Contrary to his unconscious wish "to survive Fliess," Freud received no indication from the publication of *The Interpretation of Dreams* (1900*a*) that his ambition was to be realized in a purely intellectual sense. In his depression over the indifferent reaction to his theory of dreaming, Freud temporarily found his need for scientific companionship at a low ebb.[57] He therefore declined to meet with Fliess, who was eager for a congress at Easter in 1900. "In point of fact it is more probable that I shall avoid you . . . ," Freud responded to Fliess's proposal on 23 March. "Inwardly I am deeply impoverished. I have had to demolish all my castles in the air, and I have just plucked up enough courage to start rebuilding them. . . . In your company . . . your fine and positive biological discoveries would rouse my innermost (impersonal) envy. The upshot would be that I should unburden my woes to you for the whole five days and come back agitated and dissatisfied for the summer. . . . No one can help me in what oppresses me, it is my cross, which I must bear . . ." (*Origins*, p. 314).

Was it actually possible, Freud seems to have anxiously wondered, that Fliess, and not he, might turn out to be the scientific "survivor" of the two? In a letter of 7 May 1900, Freud echoes such an apprehension while comparing himself with his friend in the following forlorn terms:

> When your book [Fliess 1906*b*] is published none of us will be able to pass the judgment on it which, as in the case of all great new achievements, is reserved for posterity; but the beauty of the conception, the originality of the ideas, the simple coherence of the whole and the conviction with which it is written will create an impression which will provide the first compensation for the arduous wrestling with the demon. With me it is different. No critic . . . can see more clearly than I the disproportion there is between the problems and my answers to them, and it will be a fitting punishment for me that none of the unexplored regions of the mind in which I have been the first mortal to set foot will ever bear my name or submit to my laws. (*Origins*, p. 318)

All of these uneasy undercurrents in their relationship—Freud's scientific rivalry with Fliess, his partly neurotic state of depression, and his latent concern lest psychoanalysis be engulfed by Fliessian sexual biology—finally came to a head in the summer of 1900 when Freud and Fliess met for a congress at Achensee. Fliess later described at some length this meeting and the incident that led to their formal estrangement:

56. See also Freud 1900*a*, *S.E.*, 5:421–25, 480–87.
57. Actually, as has been shown by Bry and Rifkin (1962), Freud's *Interpretation of Dreams* not only was widely reviewed by his contemporaries but also was given high praise by many reviewers. However, I must postpone a further discussion of the reception of this book until Chapter 9.

I often used to have meetings with Freud for scientific discussions. In Berlin, Vienna, Salzburg, Dresden, Nuremberg, Breslau, Innsbruck, for instance. The last meeting was at Achensee in the summer of 1900. On that occasion Freud showed a violence towards me which was at first unintelligible to me. The reason was that in a discussion of Freud's observations of his patients I claimed that periodic processes were unquestionably at work in the psyche, as elsewhere; and maintained in particular that they had an effect on those psychopathic phenomena on the analysis of which Freud was engaged for therapeutic purposes. Hence neither sudden deteriorations nor sudden improvements were to be attributed to the analysis and its influence alone. I supported my view with my own observations. During the rest of the discussion I thought I detected a personal animosity against me on Freud's part which sprang from envy. Freud had earlier said to me in Vienna: "It's just as well that we're friends. Otherwise I should burst with envy if I heard that anyone was making such discoveries in Berlin!" In my astonishment I told my wife about this exclamation at the time, as well as our friend, Frau Hofkapellmeister Schalk, *née* Hopfen, who was then in Vienna and will gladly confirm it.

The result of the situation at Achensee in the summer of 1900 was that I quietly withdrew from Freud and dropped our regular correspondence. Since that time Freud has heard no more from me about my scientific findings. . . . (Fliess 1906a:16–17; *Origins*, p. 324 n.)

From their subsequent, but dwindling, correspondence we can see that there was considerably more to the Achensee argument and its immediate aftermath than what Fliess himself related in 1906. Freud responded to Fliess's suggestions about periodic processes in the psyche with the words, "But you're undermining the whole value of my work"; whereupon Fliess, angered and hurt by what he considered to be Freud's ambivalent attitude toward his own scientific discoveries, accused Freud of reading his psychoanalytic thoughts into the minds of his patients (*Origins*, pp. 336–37).

It would be a flagrant misreading of this particular dispute, however, to say with traditional Freud scholarship that Freud had simply begun to recognize the "pseudoscientific" nature of Fliess's theories. Ironically, it was Fliess who made this particular accusation about Freud's work (and not without good reason—viz., his firsthand acquaintance with Freud's seduction-theory fiasco), while Freud, on the contrary, continued to believe in Fliess's theory of biological periodicity long after they had parted intellectual company (see earlier, p. 183). True, Freud came to see Fliess's periodic cycles as subject to considerably greater environmental interference than Fliess was inclined to believe (*Origins*, p. 272). But the Achensee dispute hinged upon an even more general issue, namely, whether Fliess's periodicity theory should be given any place at all in a psychological conception of mental events. "The mathematical conception and the psychological one prove to be incompatible," Freud categorically insisted many years later in a 1913 discussion of Fliess's periodic laws at the Vienna Psychoanalytic Society (*Minutes*, 4:155). If Wilhelm Fliess failed in the

summer of 1900 to see this inherent incompatibility, so also did psychoanalysts Paul Federn, Hanns Sachs, Eduard Hitschmann, and Gaston
Rosenstein—all of whom argued against Freud thirteen years later at
this same meeting of the society:

> FEDERN does not see the contradiction that has just been men-
> tioned [by Freud]. Tabular comparisons he made from this [Fliessian]
> point of view reveal that in some cases the periodic influence comes
> clearly to the fore as soon as during the course of treatment the psycho-
> genic repetition of symptoms subsides. . . .
>
> HITSCHMANN, too, is of the opinion that the influence exerted by
> psychic factors is no evidence against periodicity. This view finds sup-
> port in the female "period," which can indeed also be influenced by
> psychic factors. (*Minutes*, 4:155)

Freud's disciples must surely have sensed more than a rational scientific
objection in his aversion to combining Fliessian periodicity theory with
the psychoanalytic point of view.

The notion of psychical periodicities was only part of the problem
underlying Freud's growing ambivalence toward Fliess's scientific work
around the turn of the century. The theory of bisexuality offered an
equal, if not greater, threat to Freud's quest for an independent psychoanalytic science of mind. Moreover, it was regarding this notion of
bisexuality that Freud's behavior must have seemed most perplexing
of all to Fliess. From letter to letter and congress to congress, Freud's
attitude on the subject switched from hot to cold and back again. In
January 1898, Freud was lauding the concept of bisexuality as "the
most significant for my subject since that of defence"—no small praise
(*Origins*, p. 242). Two months later he does not "in the least underestimate bisexuality" but nevertheless feels "remote from it at the moment" (*Origins*, pp. 247–48). With *The Interpretation of Dreams* almost
complete, Freud was once more enthusiastic about Fliess's brainchild.
"Now for bisexuality!" he writes in a letter of 1 August 1899. "I am sure
you are right about it. And I am accustoming myself to the idea of regarding every sexual act as a process in which four persons are involved. We shall have a lot to discuss about that" (*Origins*, p. 289).

Then, during their fateful meeting at Achensee in the summer of
1900, the notion of bisexuality became the subject of an odd priority
dispute between the two. Freud later reported this incident in his
Psychopathology of Everyday Life under the heading "The Forgetting
of Impressions and Knowledge":

> One day in the summer of 1901 [actually 1900] I remarked to a friend
> with whom I used at that time to have a lively exchange of scientific
> ideas: "These problems of the neuroses are only to be solved if we base
> ourselves wholly and completely on the assumption of the original bi-
> sexuality of the individual." To which he replied: "That's what I told
> you two and a half years ago at Br. [Breslau, December 1897] when we

went for that evening walk. But you wouldn't hear of it then." It is painful to be requested in this way to surrender one's originality. I could not recall any such conversation or this pronouncement of my friend's. One of
us must have been mistaken and on the *"cui prodest?"* ["Who benefits?"]
principle it must have been myself. Indeed, in the course of the next
week I remembered the whole incident, which was just as my friend
had tried to recall it to me; I even recollected the answer I had given
him at the time: "I've not accepted that yet; I'm not inclined to go into
the question." (1901*b*, *S.E.*, 6:143–44)

As Ernest Jones (1953:315) frankly remarks in connection with this
episode, Freud's was indeed "a very severe case of amnesia."

In sum, it was as a result of Freud's amnesia about Fliess's priority
in applying bisexuality theory to the psyche, together with Freud's reluctance to endorse periodicity theory in this same sphere, that Fliess
began to judge his friend an envious ingrate and decided to withdraw
from their scientific relationship. As candid as Freud was in later acknowledging his unconscious attempt to plagiarize Fliess's originality,
Fliess had had enough, and he remained intractable in his decision.

At first Freud could not believe that Fliess would allow such a
valuable friendship to come to an end. When he finally realized that
Fliess was serious, he still thought he could placate his friend by
recognizing bisexuality theory "once and for all" in connection with his
famous "Dora" case history (*Origins*, p. 327, letter of 30 January 1901;
and *S.E.*, 7:60, 114, where Fliess, however, is *not* credited for this
notion). Then, in an effort of dubious tact, Freud sought to win back
Fliess's friendship in late 1901 with the announcement that his next
book would be called "Bisexuality in Man," for which he would need
Fliess's considerable help! The purpose of this new book, he stated,
was to establish the idea that "repression and the neuroses, and thus
the independence of the unconscious, presuppose bisexuality" (*Origins*,
p. 337)—in other words, just what Fliess had been telling him all
along. Freud even offered Fliess coauthorship for his help on the
anatomical and biological sides of the question. Fliess apparently interpreted this proposal as an attempt to rob him further of his discoveries, and he flatly refused it. He also turned down Freud's subsequent plea for a reunion in January 1902 (Jones 1953:134).[58] By the end
of 1902 their regular correspondence had ceased, and their friendship
of fifteen years had come to an end.

The Weininger-Swoboda Affair

Two years after the termination of their regular correspondence,
Freud received a concerned letter from Wilhelm Fliess asking what
he knew about a recently published book, *Geschlecht und Charakter*
(Sex and Character, 1903), written by a brilliant young Viennese philosopher named Otto Weininger (1880–1903). Weininger's work, which

---

58. Based upon unpublished portions of the Fliess correspondence.

Otto Weininger about 1900. At twenty-three, he stunned the world with his book *Sex and Character* (1903) and then committed suicide the same year.

was creating a literary sensation at the time,[59] presented a highly speculative and far-ranging metaphysical disquisition on the general theme of bisexuality in man. Bisexuality, claimed Weininger, characterizes the vital activities of every organ and every cell. From this idea of the "permanent bisexual condition," which he claimed as his own discovery (1903:10), Weininger had developed an elaborate theory of human character types, including the key notion that "male" and "female" substances vary proportionately in different individuals. Weininger explained the phenomenon of sexual attraction by his associated "law of bisexual complementarity"—with a ¾ masculine and ¼ feminine man, for instance, attracting a ¾ feminine and ¼ masculine woman (and vice versa).

Astonished to see both his theory of bisexuality and his notion of complementary bisexual attraction expounded by Weininger, Wilhelm

59. The success of Weininger's book may be judged by its having reached a 26th edition in 1925. A Danish translation appeared in 1905, an English translation in 1906, and a Polish translation in 1921. See also Ellenberger 1970:293, 545, 788–89. Abrahamsen's *The Mind and Death of a Genius* (1946) presents the best account of Weininger's life and work and also contains two letters to the author from Freud discussing his relations with Weininger.

Fliess surmised that his ideas had been communicated to Weininger through Freud's pupil (and Weininger's close friend), one Hermann Swoboda (1873–1963). Fliess therefore wrote to Freud on 20 July 1904 in order to ask if his suspicions were justified. "I have no doubt," Fliess charged, "that Weininger obtained knowledge of my ideas through you and that there was an abuse of other people's property on his part. What do you know about it? I beg you to give me a candid answer . . ." (Fliess 1906a:19; trans. Brome 1967:7).[60]

Freud answered on 23 July: "I too believe that the late Weininger broke into private property with a key he picked up by chance. That is all I know about it." Swoboda, he continued, had been his onetime patient, not his pupil. And all he had ever mentioned to Swoboda was the general notion of bisexuality in the psyche and its specific relevance to the "streak of homosexuality in every neurotic." Such topics of discussion, Freud added, were a normal part of every therapeutic treatment. Swoboda must have mentioned these ideas to Weininger, whereupon Weininger apparently "clapped his hand to his forehead and rushed home to write this book." But whether this reconstruction was really the source of Weininger's knowledge on the subject, Freud emphasized he was in no position to judge; after all, the idea of bisexuality was part of the current literature in sexual pathology; and he mentioned Krafft-Ebing's *Psychopathia Sexualis* in this connection.

For his own part, Freud informed Fliess that in his forthcoming book on the sexual theory he planned to "avoid the theme of bisexuality as much as possible." In two places, however, he would have to discuss this idea (when dealing with the problem of homosexuality and with the homosexual undercurrent in every neurosis). He promised to put a note in these discussions to the effect that he had first learned of the importance of bisexuality from Fliess. As for Weininger, Freud maintained: "I have had no part in his 'discovery' which does seem to infringe your ideas. I did *not* read his book before publication" (Fliess 1906a:19–20; trans. Brome 1967:7–8; italics added). "It was perhaps the only occasion in Freud's life," Jones remarks (1953:315), "when he was for a moment not completely straightforward."

Fliess, who was clearly not satisfied by Freud's explanation, replied on 26 July with his trump card: "Obviously what Oskar Rie [Fliess's brother-in-law and Freud's old collaborator on the subject of childhood cerebral paralyses] told me, in all innocence, when I mentioned Weininger, was incorrect. He said that Weininger had been to you with his manuscript and you, after examining it, had advised him against publication, because the contents were rubbish. In that case, I would have thought that you would have warned both him and myself of the theft." Nor had Weininger got the idea of persistent and inevitable bisexuality elsewhere, Fliess maintained, since he claimed this particular discovery as his own. Finally, had not Freud himself

60. None of the following interchange of letters, which includes the only surviving specimens from Fliess's side of the correspondence, was included in *The Origins of Psycho-Analysis* (1954e).

once complained to him about Swoboda *as a pupil?* (Fliess 1906*a*: 21–22; trans. Brome 1967:8–9).

Responding to Fliess's second letter on 27 July 1904, Freud decided to make a clean breast of the whole matter. "I see that you have more right on your side than I originally thought," he replied; Swoboda had indeed been his pupil, as well as his patient. In addition, Freud had read Weininger's book before its publication, although the manuscript "certainly read quite differently from the published book." Also, Freud had recognized the theme of bisexuality at that time and had surmised that Fliess was indeed Weininger's unacknowledged source for this idea. He was now sorry that he had "handed over" Fliess's discoveries through Swoboda, and under the embarrassing circumstances he felt compelled to psychoanalyze his own curious behavior: "Together with my own attempt to steal this idea from you [in 1900] I can understand my behavior towards W. [Weininger] and my subsequent loss of memory."

In any event, as Freud went on to argue, the idea of bisexuality was more current than Fliess seemed to realize: "In my eyes you have always been the originator of the theory of bisexuality (1901),[61] but I'm afraid that if you look through the literature, you will find that many have run you very close." Still, he confessed: "I have often secretly reproached myself, as I now do openly, with my generosity or carelessness in making free with your property." [62] But all the same, Freud said, Fliess would just have to learn that "ideas cannot be patented." Then, in a passage that certainly did nothing to appease Fliess, he concluded, "It is, however, not my fault if you only find the time and inclination to write to me on such a trivial matter" (Fliess 1906*a*:22–23; trans. Brome 1967:9–10). On this inauspicious note, their correspondence came to an end.

Meanwhile the whole episode had taken on a new complexion. When the psychotic Weininger had committed suicide in 1903, he left his library and all his papers to his friend Swoboda (Brome 1967:11), who in 1904 published a book on the periods of the human organism in their psychological and biological significance. Therein he discussed the existence of periods of 23 and 28 *days* as well as *hours*, briefly recognizing Wilhelm Fliess's previous findings on this subject (to which he had been specifically alerted by Freud). Unfortunately Swoboda also tried to claim that he had made these discoveries *independently* of Fliess, and that he had been, moreover, the first to document such periodic processes in the psyche.

61. Freud, of course, had first learned of Fliess's theory of bisexuality five years earlier than the date he cited in this letter—that is, when Fliess, in the spring of 1896, sent him the manuscript of his 1897 monograph. Not surprisingly, Fliess was further angered by Freud's postdating of his discovery in this letter, which he later made public along with the rest of their 1904 correspondence (1906*a*:22).

62. Jones (1955:409–10), speaking from personal experience, was later to point up Freud's annoying inability to keep confidential matters to himself: "Freud was not a man who found it easy to keep someone else's secrets. He had indeed the reputation of being distinctly indiscreet. It may be remembered that the final break with his friend Fliess came about over a matter of this sort."

Fliess was not fooled by Swoboda's claims. Had not Freud written him the following words out of the blue in April 1904 even before the whole Weininger episode had come to his attention?: "You will have received a book from Dr. Swoboda, the *intellectual originator of which I am in many respects,* although I wouldn't like to be the author" (Fliess 1906a:18; trans. Brome 1967:12; italics added).[63] Convinced of duplicity on all sides, Fliess decided to publish his most recent correspondence with Freud in an attempt to establish his claim of plagiarism (1906a). At the same time, Fliess's friend and admirer, the Berlin librarian, mathematician, and historian Richard Pfennig, published a pamphlet attacking Weininger, Swoboda, and Freud and defending Fliess's scientific priorities in great detail (Pfennig 1906). Wrote Pfennig of Freud's involvement: "It is not our task here to criticize the way that Professor Freud used his friendship for Fliess. Suffice it to say that after his original denial that Swoboda was his pupil and his careful silence on the main point at issue—namely, his knowledge of Weininger's work before its publication—he deigns to make a confession [of these facts], the candor of which can only be called cynical" (1906:31).

Freud was indignant and acted quickly to protect himself from public scandal by sending letters to two major journals. To Karl Kraus, editor of *Die Fackel* (The Torch), he angrily protested on 12 January 1906:

> Dr. Fliess of Berlin has induced R. Pfenning [*sic*] to publish a pamphlet attacking O. Weininger and H. Swoboda in which both young authors are accused of the most flagrant plagiarism and abused in the cruelest fashion. The cogency of this fabrication may be judged by the fact that I myself, a friend of Fliess for many years, am accused of being the one who imparted to Weininger and Swoboda the information (gained from my contact with Fliess) which has served as a basis for their unauthorized publications.
>
> I trust it is not necessary for me to defend myself in detail against such absurd slander. . . .
>
> . . . What concerns us here is the defense against the presumptuousness of a brutal personality and the banning of a petty personal ambition from the temple of science. (*Letters,* pp. 250–51)

Nevertheless, Freud was careful in his letter to Kraus to warn Weininger's friends and relatives that they should avoid any legal action in this matter, inasmuch as the unauthorized publication of Freud's private letters indeed proved that Weininger had stolen Fliess's scientific property!

Freud's second letter was directed to Magnus Hirschfeld, editor of the Berlin *Jahrbuch für sexuelle Zwischenstufen* (Yearbook for Sexually

63. Freud had written this letter in an unsuccessful attempt to get Fliess to cooperate upon a new journal, and in this same letter had also identified Swoboda as his pupil. Freud's influence upon Swoboda's book of 1904 was indeed considerable, as can be seen from his discussions of periodicity in dreaming, in neurasthenia, and in hysteria (1904:49–68, 112–22).

Freud in 1906 (age 50).

Intermediate Stages). "May I direct your attention," Freud wrote, "to a pamphlet entitled *Wilhelm Fliess und seine Nachentdecker* [Wilhelm Fliess and his Subsequent Discoverers]. . . . It is a disgusting scribble, which amongst other things casts absurd aspersions on me. . . . Actually we have to do with the fantasy of an ambitious man who in his loneliness has lost the capacity to judge what is right and what is permissible. . . . It is not pleasant for me to utter harsh words in public about someone with whom I have for twelve years been associated in the most intimate friendship and thereby provoke him to further insults" (quoted in Jones 1953:316). Evidently what really perturbed Freud was Fliess's decision to reveal the whole nasty matter to the public.

Swoboda responded with an acrimonious publication of his own (1906) and also sued Fliess for libel and for the unauthorized publication of Freud's private letters. According to Siegfried Bernfeld, Swoboda lost the case because his Viennese lawyer was sadly ignorant of German libel laws (Bernfeld to Ernest Jones, 26 May 1952; Roazen 1975:93).

Freud's subsequent references to Fliess and the troublesome notion of bisexuality reveal a lingering animosity over the whole priority dispute. In his *Three Essays on the Theory of Sexuality*, Freud assiduously cited eight different authors who had previously written on the universality of a bisexual disposition in man.[64] To the second edition (1910) he added a reference to Weininger's and Fliess's more recent claims in this regard. Unfortunately, since Freud mentions only the date of Fliess's big book (1906), and not that of his earlier monograph (1897), Fliess's predecessors appear to be nine in number instead of just five—the original eight plus Weininger!

As for his *personal* indebtedness to Fliess, Freud credited him for having first pointed out the undercurrent of homosexuality in every psychoneurotic as well as for having brought to his attention the "decisive" importance of bisexuality in psychosexual development. The latter reference, however, was deleted from the second and later editions of the *Three Essays*, undoubtedly in response to the Pfennig-Fliess publications of 1906. All this, according to Ernst Kris (1954:42), is supposed to constitute "scrupulous" documentation of Freud's intellectual debts to Fliess—documentation that omitted, I might add, any reference to Fliess's pioneering views on infantile sexuality—the theme of the second of Freud's *Three Essays*.

Priority and Plagiarism as Transformational Constructs

Let us step back for a moment from the Weininger-Swoboda affair and ask what it tells us about Freud and his relationship to Wilhelm Fliess. The affair has received sharply contrasting interpre-

64. That list comprises Gley (1884), Kiernan (1888), Lydston (1889), Chevalier (1893), Krafft-Ebing (1895), Hirschfeld (1899), Arduin (1900), and Herman (1903); see 1905*d*, *S.E.*, 7:141–43. I omit discussion of these sources here since they will be treated in Chapter 8.

tations from Freud scholars. Is it, for instance, as Roazen claims, yet
another illustration of "the theme of plagiarism [that] can be found
almost everywhere one turns in Freud's career" (1969:88)? Or should
we instead take the diametrically opposed view of Eissler (1971:171):
"In my opinion, the correct biographical approach would be to cite
Fliess as the prototype of the scientist whose efforts are hampered by
his paranoid tendencies, and who wastes time and effort in a useless
and destructive fight about priorities—a fight that, if anything, actually
makes him appear a fool in the eyes of posterity"? As Eissler correctly
emphasizes at another point, the real issue is whether Fliess had already published his theory of universal bisexuality in 1897, thus making it impossible for Freud to "betray" his secret to Weininger. Eissler
(1971:163–64) concludes that Fliess had indeed done so. In contrast
to Eissler, I must disagree and argue instead that this whole episode
must be interpreted in terms of the intellectual transformation of
which it was a part.

From Fliess's point of view, the notion of universal bisexuality
in man had undergone a significant development in his own thinking
since the appearance of his monograph of 1897, in which he had announced his discovery of two universal bisexual rhythms.[65] Then, over
the next two years, Fliess had continued to develop this general notion, extending it in novel developmental and psychological directions
to encompass three distinct innovations.

The first of these was a dynamic theory of the unconscious psyche
in man—a theory that attributed this unconscious portion of the mind
to a repression of the latent sex within the bisexual constitution.
Fliess's second innovation posited differential levels of repression in the
adult population—differences that would necessarily express themselves in the average bisexual composition of every organ and cell. Here
he also had in mind the specific notions of bilaterality and handedness,
with which he was able to implement his theory in the empirical
realm. This second insight paved the way for Fliess's third innovation,
namely, his theory of "complementary" bisexual attraction—an idea
that Weininger had also made central to his own book.

Although Weininger or anyone else might conceivably have anticipated all three of Fliess's ideas independently, Fliess surmised
correctly that Weininger himself had not done so—at least in regard to
the key notion of a persistent bisexuality in normal adults.[66] In this

---

65. Weininger (1903:499–500), in an Appendix, did in fact briefly credit Fliess
(1897) with having discovered "the most interesting and stimulating things" about
periodicity, and he even predicted that Fliess's book might become famous one day
with further progress in this promising branch of the biological sciences. Obviously,
to Weininger and Fliess alike the theory of bisexual periodicities was distinct from
the more global one of bisexuality that each later claimed to have discovered.

66. Weininger probably derived the associated law of sexual complementarity
on his own. See Eissler (1971:164–68), with whom I agree on this point. Both Pfennig and Fliess attempted to argue that Weininger's knowledge of biology was so
poor that he could not possibly have reached such an insight by himself. But Weininger's 133-page Appendix ("Zusätze und Nachweise") contradicts this claim and
shows that he was widely read in the works of Darwin, Weismann, Haeckel, Naegeli,

form, the idea *was* new, and Weininger, who was familiar with his and Fliess's biomedical predecessors in connection with the bisexual disposition of inverts, premised his own priority on just this transformed point (Weininger 1903:10, 469).[67] Sincerely convinced, like Weininger, that he was the originator of new and profound insights about an admittedly old idea, Fliess did what he thought necessary to protect his priorities. Such a response can hardly be considered "paranoid," as Eissler (1971:171) and others have labeled it.[68]

As for Freud's behavior in this whole affair, I see it as the culmination of the growing ambivalence and intellectual rivalry that developed out of his psychoanalytic transformation of the Fliessian id. Freud was fully aware of Fliess's instrumental role in this transformation, yet he never quite reconciled himself to giving credit where credit was due. When he later discovered from the literature on sexual pathology just how current the general notion of bisexuality had become for explaining homosexuality, he allowed this knowledge to serve as the dubious rationale for failing to protect Fliess's priorities. Did not Fliess, after nearly fifteen years of intimate friendship and scientific collaboration, deserve better from Freud? Fliess obviously thought he did; and given the unusual nature of their collaboration, in which so many unpublished ideas were freely communicated, it is difficult not to agree with him. As he remarked, with some pathos, in *Der Ablauf des Lebens*, "With Freud I was in friendly communication for many years. To him I confided without reserve all my scientific thoughts and germinal ideas" (1906b:583).[69]

In the final analysis, Freud's disregard for his old friend's priorities reflected an unmistakable desire for revenge in the wake of Fliess's distressing desertion of both him and his psychoanalytic cause. Psychoanalysis itself became a source of comfort to Freud in helping to rationalize the whole affair. Years later he took consolatory refuge in his own theories in order to explain the violence with which Fliess had reacted to the betrayal of his ideas. Writing to Sándor Ferenczi about Fliess in January 1910, Freud declared: "The conviction that his father, who died of erysipelas after suffering for many years from nasal suppuration, could have been saved was what made him into a doctor,

---

Claus, the Hertwig brothers, de Vries, and many other contemporary biologists. According to Abrahamsen (1946:58), the original title of Weininger's doctoral dissertation (which became his later book) was "Sex and Character: A Psychobiological Study." In his Appendix to this work (which is not included in the English translation), Weininger noted that the idea of bisexual complementarity in sexual attraction had previously been suggested by two men—Arthur Schopenhauer (1844, 2:623–28) and Albert Moll (1897b:193). Nevertheless, Weininger claimed to have reached his similar insight independently of these two sources.

67. The bisexual theory of homosexuality (which holds that sexual inversion is due to a pathological inhibition in early sexual development or, alternatively, to a reversion to the hermaphroditic ancestral state) is indeed a different proposition from the more Fliessian notion that the latent sex survives in a dynamic, biochemical, and unconscious form in every normal adult human being.

68. See also Jones 1953:316. On the motivational importance of priorities in science, see Merton 1976.

69. See also Galdston 1956:496, n. 14.

and indeed into a rhinologist. The sudden death of his only sister two years later, . . . led—as a consolation—to the fatalistic theory of pre-destined lethal dates. This piece of analysis, very unwelcome to him, was the real reason for the break between us which he engineered in such a pathological (paranoic) fashion" (quoted in Jones 1955: 446–47).

Aftermath of the Estrangement

The estrangement, as Jones (1953:318) has observed, left a con-siderable scar upon Freud's emotional life. As late as 1910, he was disturbed by a dream repeated over a series of nights—a dream that had as its basic content a possible reconciliation with his old friend. At last Freud succeeded in divining the hidden "hypocritical" meaning of this dream, which he traced to an unconscious wish that he might abandon the remnants of his former regard for Fliess and "free myself from him completely" (*The Interpretation of Dreams, S.E.,* 4:145 n.; footnote added to the 1911 edition).

Another dramatic sequel to their break was later reported by Ernest Jones. Freud had asked five of his followers to meet him in Munich on 24 November 1912 to discuss editorial matters about their new journal, the *Zentralblatt für Psychoanalyse.* As they were finishing their luncheon together in the Park Hotel, Freud suddenly began to admonish the two Swiss, Jung and Riklin, for publishing papers on psy-choanalysis without mentioning his name. Jung responded by saying that they had thought this quite unnecessary, Freud's name being so well known in this connection. "He [Freud] persisted," Jones recounts, "and I remember thinking he was taking the matter rather personally. Suddenly, to our consternation, he fell on the floor in a dead faint. The sturdy Jung swiftly carried him to a couch in the lounge, where he soon revived. His first words as he was coming to were strange: 'How sweet it must be to die' . . ." (Jones 1953:317; cf. Jung 1963:153). Freud later confessed to Jones that he had previously had two similar attacks in the same room of the Park Hotel, in 1906 and 1908, and that the explanation for the attacks was tied up with his relationship with Fliess. "I saw Munich first," Freud related to Jones, "when I visited Fliess during his illness and this town seems to have acquired a strong connection with my relation to that man. There is some piece of unruly homosexual feeling at the root of the matter" (Jones 1953:317). Jones subsequently learned from Freud that it was not just the town but the very dining room in which he had fainted at the Park Hotel that Freud so strongly associated with his memories of Fliess. It seems that their final argument during the Achensee congress in 1900 took place in this same dining room.

As for Fliess, throughout the first three decades of the twentieth century he and his small but loyal band of followers continued to pub-lish books and articles on the various psychobiological topics that he had championed during the 1890s.[70] To this day, his theories of periodicity have a following, particularly in Germany, Switzerland, America, and Japan. Certain physicians in Swiss hospitals continue to choose the most propitious dates for surgery in accordance with a modified version of Fliess's original system (Gardner 1966:111).

To the end of his life, which came in 1928, Fliess preserved a considerable interest in psychoanalysis, reading the latest publications by Freud and referring suitable patients to Freud's Berlin followers for psychoanalytic treatment (Schur 1972:70, 387). In 1911 he entered into an intimate and permanent friendship with psychoanalyst Karl Abraham, who described Fliess to Freud at that time as "perhaps the most valuable [acquaintance] I could make among colleagues in Berlin" (*Freud/Abraham Letters*, p. 102). Abraham, who was largely responsible for reviving Fliess's interest in psychoanalysis, in turn became a disciple of his periodicity theories. In 1925, when Abraham underwent a gall bladder operation, he insisted upon the date's being scheduled according to Fliess's calculations (Jones 1957:115–16). Fliess's eldest son Robert—the guinea pig in his earliest studies of infantile sexuality and *Entwicklungsschubmechanik*—later became a prominent psychoanalyst, as did his niece, Marianne Kris.

In spite of such continuing psychoanalytic ties, Freud and Fliess never communicated with one another again after the brief exchange of letters that accompanied the Weininger-Swoboda affair. In a way, Freud always felt he had been unjustly deserted by Fliess, and he apparently never forgave him for that. Although he was later to speak of the "magnificent conception" (*grossartige Konzeption*—1920g, *S.E.*, 18:45) of Fliess's scientific work, he consistently sought to discourage his followers from pursuing Fliessian points of view. In 1925, to Abraham's report that Fliess had expressed concern over Freud's deteriorating state of health, the latter responded with signs of lingering bitterness: "This expression of sympathy after twenty years leaves me rather cold" (Jones 1957:116).

70. Besides *Der Ablauf des Lebens* (1906b; 2nd ed., 1923), Fliess published three other books on periodicity: *Vom Leben und Tod* (Of Life and Death, 1909; 5th ed., 1925), *Das Jahr im Lebendigen* (The Year in Living Things, 1918c; 2nd ed., 1924), and *Zur Periodenlehre* (On the Periodicity Theory, 1925). Shorter articles on bilaterality, bisexuality, and periodicity theory include Fliess 1907, 1908, 1911, 1914, 1918a, and 1918b. Fliess's 1902 work on the nasal reflex neuroses and their therapeutic treatment reached a second edition in 1910 and a third in 1926.

Among Fliess's followers, Pfennig (1912, 1918), Saaler (1914, 1921), and Schlieper (1909) were perhaps the most prominent. Hermann Swoboda, who remained independent of Fliess's following, nevertheless continued to publish on Fliessian themes. See Swoboda 1905, 1909, 1917. In the 1930s, Fliess's theories were taken up by a number of German and Swiss investigators. Recently, and in spite of their repeated refutation, these theories have attracted a following in Japan, where, according to Neo-Fliessian George Thommen (1973: Chap. 5), they have been adopted by over five thousand companies in an effort to improve safety and production. In America, the three-cycle system has been promoted into a $1000-a-week business by George Thommen and has also been applied to sports forecasting (see Gittelson 1977). Needless to say, Fliessian biorhythms work best when the application is retrospective, or when a knowledge of the theory alters the subjects' behavioral patterns.

Wilhelm Fliess
in his
later years.

Freud's Theory of Paranoia

Freud owed one last intellectual debt to Fliess: the theory of
paranoia, which Freud derived in significant part by psychoanalyzing
Fliess's behavior in the course of their estrangement. "Do not forget that
it was through him [Fliess]," he wrote to Karl Abraham in a letter of
3 March 1911, "that both of us came to understand the secret of
paranoia ('The Psycho-sexual Differences')" (*Freud/Abraham Letters*,
p. 103). What Freud had in mind was the inference that paranoia is
rooted in an unsuccessful defense against homosexual impulses—a
process often brought on by a regression of the libido after a major
falling-out with a member of the same sex (1911c, *S.E.*, 12:62). Fliess
was apparently unable, Freud concluded from their estrangement, to
redirect the homosexual cathexis upon which all such close relationships are partly based. Commenting about Fliess to Ferenczi in 1910,
Freud proclaimed: "You not only noticed, but also understood, that I
no longer have any need to uncover my personality completely, and
you correctly traced this back to the traumatic reason for it. Since

Fliess's case, with the overcoming of which you recently saw me occupied, that need has been extinguished. A part of the homosexual
cathexis has been withdrawn and made use of to enlarge my own ego.
I have succeeded where the paranoiac fails" (quoted in Jones 1955:83).
Thus, even in estrangement Fliess remained a source of influence upon
Freud—a theme I shall take up once again when I examine the various
reasons for Freud's increasingly crypto-biological identity as a man of
mental science (Chapter 12).

THE FLIESS PERIOD IN RETROSPECT

Contrary to the consensus of most Freud scholars, it is irrelevant to
the assessment of Wilhelm Fliess's influence upon Freud that Fliess's
scientific ideas eventually proved to be "pathological" (incorrect) science
in hindsight. What matters historically is that Freud (as well as many
of his scientific contemporaries) not only defended the truth and the
importance of Fliess's discoveries but also was directly inspired by his
ideas to think in new and fruitful ways about sexuality and its role in
human development. In particular, Fliess's unsuccessful attempt to
present his ideas in mathematical terms should not be allowed to obscure his considerable nonmathematic importance for the history of
psychoanalysis. As Freud wrote to his friend in a last and plaintive
effort to salvage their former scientific relationship: "I do not believe
that anything qualitative, any point of view which arose out of the
calculations, was wasted on me" (*Origins*, p. 336).

In short, Fliess was far more than just a proofreader for Freud's
Interpretation of Dreams and other early psychoanalytic works (Jones
1953:298). He was, in fact, a largely unrecognized source of inspiration for much of Sigmund Freud's whole psychosexual perspective on
human development.

From Physicalism to Geneticism

In spite of their contrasting scientific methodologies in later years
(mathematical organicism vs. the psychoanalytic method), the early
careers of Freud and Fliess exemplify a historically binding similarity.
When they first met in the late 1880s, both men were already deeply
imbued with the mid-nineteenth-century Helmholtzian and biophysical
legacies to their contemporary world of scientific ideas. More important, their collaboration reached its height at a time when they were
jointly moving from a static and mechanical application of such physicalist points of view toward a distinctly genetic conception of life.
Together they in turn used this developmental perspective in their ambitious and global attempts to understand the nature of the unconscious

psyche in man. Finally, both men took sexuality for granted as the psychobiological focal point of their respective explanatory schemes.

In Fliess's case, the increasingly genetic scope that he sought in his *Entwicklungsschubmechanik* led him logically to give full and universal recognition to many neglected manifestations of spontaneous infantile sexual life. Moreover, he took this important step in his research fully a year and a half before Sigmund Freud, still under the sway of his misguided seduction theory, finally realized that his theory of the neuroses was incompatible with the more spontaneous conception of infantile sexuality endorsed by Fliess. Thus, when Freud's understanding of the somatic and biological sides to the problem of human sexual development changed (in intimate conjunction with his knowledge of Fliess's scientific ideas), so too did his psychological views. It is to Fliess that we must therefore ascribe a major historical role in the development of Freud's far-reaching conception of the id.

Freud did not just borrow from Fliess. Rather, he *transformed* Fliess's ideas in a way quite revealing of his own creative genius. The nature of this creative transformation may be best understood by briefly reviewing how Fliess's scientific ideas helped to resolve Freud's three great psychoanalytic problems: (1) Why sex? (2) the mechanism of pathological repression, and (3) the choice of neurosis.[71]

As for "Why sex?" Freud replaced the notion of a deferred reaction to sexual trauma by the more dynamic and Fliessian mechanisms of sexual latency, sublimation, reaction formation, and the pathological fixation of infantile, polymorphously perverse, sexual impulses.

With regard to pathological repression, purely psychical defense against traumas gave way in Freud's theory to a largely organic conception of the repression of infantile sexual impulses. Under Fliess's scientific tutelage, Freud related this new theory of repression to (1) the sense of smell and man's phylogenetic assumption of an upright posture, (2) the theory of bisexuality, and (3) the biogenetic law (that ontogeny recapitulates phylogeny).

With the abandonment of the seduction theory, Freud reassessed the choice-of-neurosis problem in two basic ways. First, he sought that lack of an organic repression of childhood sexual impulses accounted for sexual *perversion*, and repression for *neurosis*, with the precise outcome being determined by individual (congenital) differences, by male-female differences (themselves related to Fliess's conception of bisexual proportionalities), and, finally, by social-class differences. Second, Freud came to see the *specific* choice of neurosis in terms of the precise stage (with its dominant erotogenic zones and characteristic libidinal aims and objects) in which a fixation of the infantile sexual impulse had taken place.

71. These three problems, as described in Chapter 4, had led Freud to his ill-fated seduction theory in the first place and had also caused him to abandon his ambitious attempt in the *Project for a Scientific Psychology* (1895) to explain all of mental functioning in purely mechanical-physiological terms. For even in the *Project*, Freud had begun to realize the unavoidable need in psychoanalytic theory for a more genetic point of view.

In all three of these productive psychoanalytic transformations, Fliess's variegated conception of the sexual instinct (bisexuality, the erotogenic zones, etc.) proved instrumental in prompting Freud's renunciation of the extreme environmentalism that had temporarily led him astray in the mid-1890s.

The Freud–Fliess Relationship in Its Wider Darwinian and Evolutionary Contexts

Perhaps Fliess's most commendable historical achievement, as Hirsch (1928:424) long ago pointed out, was his attempt to establish a far-ranging unification of medicine and biology at a time when his medical colleagues were largely concerned with specialized inquiries. Similarly, Freud himself summed up this aspect of Fliess's synthetic temperament as a man of science when he once marveled at having encountered "an even greater visionary than I" (*Origins*, p. 130).

Above all, a belief in Fliess's scientific vision required rationalization of his various theories in terms of their largely unspoken, but nonetheless manifestly *evolutionary*, perspective on human sexuality. Nose and sex, vital periodicity, bisexuality, and the existence of a childhood sexual instinct—all these subjects had their logical roots deep in late-nineteenth-century evolutionary doctrine. In other words, Fliess played his Helmholtzian and bioenergetic tunes to a largely Darwinian score.

In this sense, the long-misunderstood role of Fliess in Freud's intellectual life reflects, in microcosm, the crypto-biological nature of Freud's entire psychoanalytic legacy to the twentieth century. For it was precisely this new evolutionary vision that, after the *Project for a Scientific Psychology* (1895), exerted the greatest single, and most far-reaching, theoretical influence upon Freud's conception of human psychosexual development. As for the series of myths that have continued to surround Freud's famous self-analysis, it was Fliessian sexual biology, evolutionary theory, and the biogenetic law—not just Freud's clinical work or his self-analysis per se—that served to inspire his far-reaching discoveries during the Fliess period.

Finally, just as Wilhelm Fliess's scientific views were part of a common (and surprisingly rational) scientific context, so too were Freud's efforts at transforming the Fliessian id for his own psychoanalytic purposes. This last assertion leads directly to the next two chapters, where I shall consider the pervasive and highly fruitful influence that evolutionary theory (Darwinism) had upon child psychology, the emerging science of sexual pathology, and the general biomedical background from which Freud's most fundamental psychoanalytic ideas emerged. Although I have placed these chapters after the Fliess period, the influence on Freud of the various intellectual traditions explored in them was fully contemporaneous with that of Wilhelm Fliess.

7

The Darwinian Revolution's Legacy to Psychology and Psychoanalysis

When Charles Darwin, in his celebrated book *On the Origin of Species* (1859), announced to a disbelieving world that the supposed Organic Creation was no "creation" at all but rather the result of a natural, evolutionary process; when, in the guise of his theory of natural selection, he presented the world with a convincing new rationale for such heterodox views; and when, in *The Descent of Man* (1871), he finally included man himself in this evolutionary vision—in short, when he accomplished all these feats, he probably did more than any other individual to pave the way for Sigmund Freud and the psychoanalytic revolution. And it is certainly no coincidence that Freud's early follower Ernest Jones (1913:xii), as a proud Englishman, championed in Freud a new "Darwin of the Mind" almost as soon as he had become familiar with Freud's theories.[1]

Yet like all men who occasionally take note of their ties to the past, neither Freud nor Jones, nor any of Freud's other followers for that matter, ever realized just how pervasive this particular intellectual influence really was. Nor should any of them have been expected to do so, for Darwin's legacy to the generations that followed him was so extensive as to create, at times, its own invisibility. Educated men and women read about Darwinian ideas firsthand, secondhand, thirdhand, and nth-hand—where, of course, they were often no longer

1. Jones later developed this theme in his biography of Freud (1957:304, 309–14). Others who have commented upon Darwin's influence on Freud include, most notably, Wyss 1958:278–80; Brosin 1960:376–78; Rapaport 1960a:11–12, 22–23; Shakow and Rapaport 1964:14–32, 37–41; Ritvo 1965, 1972, 1974; Burnham 1967:54–56; Ellenberger 1970:236–37; and Gruber 1974:239–41.

identified as being specifically Darwinian. True, even after the initial furor over Darwin's ideas had given way to reasoned discussion, many still chose to reject his views on evolution (the theories of natural selection, sexual selection, pangenesis, and so forth); but in the broader sense one was Darwinian all the same, just as twentieth-century man is Freudian *malgré lui*.

It is in this "broader sense" that I shall often refer in this chapter to Darwin's influence upon Freud and his generation. More specifically, this overall Darwinian influence encompasses (1) Darwin's evolutionary publications; (2) certain aspects of his unpublished researches that nevertheless came into circulation after his death; (3) the ideas of other pre-Darwinian evolutionists, especially those of Jean-Baptiste Lamarck, whose work finally gained acceptance through Darwin's own achievements; (4) those who were influenced by Darwin, Wallace, and other early Darwinians, and who subsequently extended their theories into the many disparate subfields of the life sciences; and (5) those, like Herbert Spencer in England and Ernst Haeckel in Germany, who played an important role in popularizing Darwin's theories—and the doctrine of evolution in general.

Darwin's high degree of "invisible" influence was especially true for the sciences of man, which were soon suffused with Darwinian and rival lines of evolutionary thinking. This influence reached Sigmund Freud by three distinct but overlapping routes—namely, comparative psychology in general and child psychology in particular; medical psychology; and Darwin's direct contributions to the incipient science of mind that Freud himself chose to call psychoanalysis.

DARWIN AS PSYCHOLOGIST

As much as the title "Darwin of the Mind" is appropriate for Sigmund Freud, the first Darwin of the mind was unquestionably Charles Darwin himself. Yet the full extent of Darwin's contributions to psychology has not generally been appreciated. To begin with, the dispersed nature of his writings on psychological themes has prevented his being identified with a single, great exposition of his ideas as an evolutionary psychologist. At the same time, much, if not the bulk, of his psychological researches remained unpublished in his own lifetime. Still, that Darwin's personal interest in psychology was "fundamental to his system" has been convincingly maintained by Ghiselin (1973:964). And Darwin's overall influence upon psychology was indeed enormous. Edwin Boring (1950:743) goes so far as to list him, along with Freud, Helmholtz, and James, as one of the four great influences upon twentieth-century psychology. And of these four, Boring ranks Darwin and Freud as the most important of all.

Born in 1809, Darwin prepared for a career in the ministry by

240 THE BIRTH OF A GENETIC PSYCHOBIOLOGY

graduating from Cambridge University in 1830. An unusual opportunity intervened, however, when he was offered the position of unpaid naturalist aboard H.M.S. *Beagle*. After enlisting his famous uncle Josiah Wedgwood's support in the venture, Darwin successfully convinced his hesitant father that an oceanic voyage as a ship's naturalist would not be demeaning to his intended profession as a clergyman. For five years (December 1831 to October 1836) Darwin circumnavigated the globe, spending most of this time in the vicinity of the South American continent, where he conducted detailed studies of the geology and the natural history of this great land mass and its neighboring islands.

During the voyage, four great classes of biological phenomena came to Darwin's attention: (1) the intimate anatomical relationship between the past (fossil) and present land mammals of the South American continent; (2) the manner in which closely related species replace one another geographically as one moves from one major district to another; (3) the remarkable organisms of the Galapagos Archipelago, which, although belonging to a distinct "center of creation," were allied to those of the nearby continent; and (4) the curious circumstance that each island within the Galapagos group often possessed its own distinct species of giant land tortoise, bird life, and many other native animals and plants. Such facts suggested to Darwin that species might not be permanent "creations" after all but rather the product of slow evolutionary change. Within six months of his return to England (that is, by March of 1837), the twenty-eight-year-old Darwin was convinced of the truth of the evolutionary theory. In July of that same year, Darwin opened the first of a series of four notebooks entitled "Transmutation of Species."

In addition to systematically pursuing in these "Transmutation" notebooks evidence that related to evolution and its possible mechanisms, Darwin began to generate ideas on a much more heterodox question, namely, the evolution of man, mind, and the whole of human behavior. Soon his speculations on the evolution of man had become so numerous that in July of 1838 he decided to begin a separate series of notebooks, labeled *M* and *N*.[2] Written during the year and one-half

2. The letter *M* probably stands for "Metaphysics," the term by which Darwin consistently designated his studies on human psychology. (In Darwin's day, psychology was still a formal part of philosophy.) The letter *N*, used for the second notebook, is merely an alphabetical continuation of this metaphysical notebook series, in the style of Darwin's companion notebooks on geology (*A*) and species transmutation (*B, C, D,* and *E*). Darwin's *M* and *N* notebooks have been transcribed and published with a valuable commentary by Howard Gruber and Paul Barrett in *Darwin on Man* (1974). This work also contains a lengthy and stimulating essay, entitled "A Psychological Study of Scientific Creativity," in which Gruber traces the early development of Darwin's theory of evolution by natural selection and discusses the impact of this theory upon Darwin's conception of mind and man. Gruber's chapter "Darwin as Psychologist" (pp. 218–42) has been of particular assistance in my own treatment of this theme. See also Ghiselin (1969:187–213; 1973) for further discussions of Darwin's contributions (according to Ghiselin, still largely unassimilated) to psychology.

Darwin's notebooks on the transmutation of species have been published by Sir Gavin de Beer (1960–61) and by de Beer et al. (1967). De Beer (1964) also has written one of the best biographical introductions to Darwin's life and thought. For a useful review of recent Darwin scholarship, see Greene 1975.

from mid-1838 to the end of 1839, Darwin's *M* and *N* notebooks contain, some thirty-odd years before *The Descent of Man* (1871), a revolutionary new framework for the understanding of man. "Origin of man now proved," Darwin triumphantly proclaimed in the midst of notebook *M*. "—Metaphysics must flourish.—He who understands baboon would do more toward metaphysics than Locke" (*M*, p. 84).

The range of topics covered by Darwin in these notebooks is indeed breathtaking. His faith in the necessary continuity between man and lower animals led him to examine, among other questions, the evolution of intelligence, the nature and the origins of instincts, and the expression of emotions in man and other animals. His interest in the last of these subjects was particularly inspired. Confronted with the immense difficulty of proving man's intellectual and behavioral continuity with lower animals, Darwin soon perceived how this continuity betrays itself in numerous bodily gestures and sundry forms of nonverbal communication. For instance, the basic human facial expressions—aggression, surprise, fear, laughing, and so forth—depend in both man and his closest zoological relatives upon the same sets of highly specialized muscular movements. By correlating mind with body in such a physiognomic fashion, Darwin generated considerable evidence for his views on the descent of man, while also pioneering an important subdiscipline of the present-day science of ethology (see Ekman 1973). Darwin's researches on facial expression and other manifestations of the emotions were later published as *The Expression of the Emotions in Man and Animals* (1872). Although he had originally intended to use this material as part of *The Descent of Man* (1871), he found the subject so extensive that it required a book of its own.

It was equally as an evolutionary biologist turned psychologist that Darwin began in the *M* and *N* notebooks to examine the phenomena of memory, association, habit, imagination, language, motivation, will, and even creative scientific thinking. Grappling with the writings of the foremost philosophers and psychologists available to him, Darwin clearly foresaw a whole new biological psychology in place of the sterile arguments of traditional metaphysicians. "To study Metaphysics, as they have always been studied," he argued in notebook *N*, "appears to me to be like puzzling at astronomy without mechanics.—Experience shows the problem of the mind cannot be solved by attacking the citadel itself. —the mind is function of body.—we must bring some *stabile* foundation to argue from" (*N*, p. 5). Evolution, he clearly surmised, with its genetic approach to psychological phenomena, was to be an important new mainstay of such a "stabile foundation."

Finally, it was as an increasingly committed evolutionary materialist that Darwin undertook to explore a whole medley of later Freudian themes centering upon the relation between mind and body and, particularly, upon the many nonrational aspects of human thought and behavior. Darwin's notebooks touch repeatedly upon unconscious mental processes and conflicts; upon psychopathology (including double consciousness, mania, delirium, senility, intoxication, and a variety of other psychosomatic phenomena); upon the psychopathology of every-day life (for example, forgetting and involuntary recall); upon dream-ing (Darwin records three of his own dreams and subjects them to partial psychological analysis); upon the psychology of love and the phenomena of sexual excitation ("—We need not feel so much surprise at male animals smelling vagina of females.—when it is recollected that smell of one's own pud[enda is] not disagree[able]"[*M*, p. 85]); and, finally, upon the evolution of the aesthetic sense, of morality, and of religious belief.

While much in these notebooks sounds remarkably like Freud him-self, I must stress that Darwin and Freud were preoccupied by differ-ing scientific problems. The important historical parallels should there-fore be confined to the general manner in which both scientists took the nonrational and instinctual forces in man for granted (Gruber 1974:239). One can certainly hear the Freud of *Civilization and Its Discontents* (1930*a*) speaking, for example, when Darwin exclaims in notebook *M* that "the mind of man is no more perfect than instincts of animals. . . . —Our descent, then, is the origin of our evil passions!!—The Devil under form of Baboon is our grandfather!—" (*M*, p. 123).

It was toward the end of September 1838, just as he was finishing notebook *M*, that Darwin happened to read Thomas Malthus's *Essay on the Principle of Population* (1798; 6th ed., 1826) as part of his am-bitious program of "metaphysical" studies, and was thereby led to formulate his celebrated theory of natural selection. Malthus had shown that human population, which tends to grow at a geometric rate, is always held in constant check by the means of subsistence, which gen-erally grow at an arithmetic rate. Famine, disease, wars, and sexual restraint were the "checks" that Malthus held responsible for limiting both population growth and human happiness. Darwin deduced that in a state of nature, where the food supply is on the average constant, this struggle for existence must be even more intense than what Malthus had described for human populations. And he reasoned that in the long run the strongest and most adapted must tend to survive, and that evolution must result from this relentless process of "natural se-lection." "Here, then," he wrote in his *Autobiography*, "I had at last got a theory by which to work . . ." (1958 [1876]:120).

For almost twenty years, Darwin patiently continued to amass evi-dence in favor of his evolutionary convictions until he was finally prompted in 1858, by Alfred Russel Wallace's independent formulation of the theory of natural selection, to rush into print an early "ab-stract" of his own evolutionary views. Yet in 1859, Darwin contented himself in the *Origin of Species* with but one terse reference to the question of man: "Psychology will be based on a new foundation, that of the necessary acquirement of each mental power and capacity by graduation. Light will be thrown on the origin of man and his history" (1859:488).

Although Darwin's obvious caution about the question of man has long appeared to historians as a sign of his "conservative" temperament, one must also respect the fact that, in the *Origin*, he wanted to *convince* people far more than he feared any persecution stemming from his views on evolution and man (Simpson 1974:134). Indeed, a decade later, both *The Descent of Man* (1871) and Darwin's closely related book *The Expression of the Emotions in Man and Animals* (1872) exerted such considerable influence owing to the thoroughness and the maturity of argument that were made possible by his prudent schedule of publication. It was in these two later works, *Descent* and *Expression*, that Darwin made greatest use of the psychological views that he had long been developing in connection with his theory of human evolution.

Sigmund Freud owned, read, and always praised Darwin's major works on evolutionary themes; he also made substantial use of them, particularly *Descent* and *Expression*, in his published writings—most notably, in *Studies on Hysteria* (1895d) and in *Totem and Taboo* (1912–13).[3] Darwin's observations concerning the role of emotional expression in discharging excess nervous energy probably contributed to Breuer and Freud's similar ideas about hysterical conversion. Speaking in *Studies on Hysteria* of Frau Emmy von N.'s highly active motoric symptoms during hysterical states, Freud noted that such behavior "reminds one forcibly of one of the principles laid down by Darwin to explain the expression of the emotions—the principle of the overflow of excitation [Darwin 1872: Chapter 3], which accounts, for instance, for dogs wagging their tails" (1895d, S.E., 2:91). In his *Psychopathology of Everyday Life* (1901b), Freud cited a particularly perceptive, self-analytic observation by Darwin that was first brought to Freud's attention by Ernest Jones (1911:480): Darwin, upon discovering that he had a habit of forgetting facts that were contrary to his theories, had followed "a golden rule" of making an immediate written record of such unpleasant items.[4]

Darwin and Child Psychology

Freud's overall debt to Darwin as a psychologist is perhaps nowhere more apparent than in Darwin's influence upon the nascent field of child psychology, where he was an important pioneer. His evolutionary concern with documenting the mental continuity between man and lower animals led him as early as 1838 to propose the "Natural History of Babies" as a fruitful topic for future inquiries (*M* notebook, p. 157). To begin with, he had conducted such observations upon the children of friends and relatives. But after his marriage in January 1839 and the birth of his first child, William, in December of that year, Darwin at last had a more convenient object for his psychological studies. He kept a detailed and, to begin with, day-by-day record of his firstborn's mental and behavioral development for at least the first three years of

3. See Ritvo (1972) for further details on Freud's personal collection of Darwin's published works.
4. See Freud 1901b, S.E., 6:148 (addition to the 4th [1912] edition); see also Darwin 1958:123.

Daguerreotype of
Charles Darwin in 1842,
with his eldest child
William (the subject
of his baby biography).

life. When the family grew (eventually to ten children, eight of whom
survived infancy), Darwin studied the comparative rates of development exhibited by his various children's mental faculties.

It was fully in keeping both with the growing interest in child development in the latter part of the nineteenth century and with this
field's intimate relevance to evolutionary theory that Darwin later decided to publish these observations in the first formal journal of psychology—*Mind*—founded in 1876. One of the earliest known attempts
of its kind, Darwin's "A Biographical Sketch of an Infant" (1877) traces
the early development of motor phenomena, the emotions (notably
anger, fear, pleasure, and affection), reasoning capabilities, the moral
sense, and the ability to communicate.

The immediate inspiration for Darwin's publication of his findings
was a similar undertaking by the French psychologist Hippolyte Taine
that had appeared in translation in the preceding issue of *Mind* (Taine
1877; originally 1876). Taine's study of his daughter's linguistic development in the first year and one-half of life had touched upon the views
of Darwin's well-known critic, Max Müller. Strenuously opposed to
man's equation with animal, Müller, a linguist, believed that both lan-

guage and thought ("language without speaking") were the sole prerogatives of mankind. Taine, like Darwin, had chosen to emphasize both the natural origins of language and the spontaneous acquisition of such linguistic abilities as a result of the child's own experiences. Along these lines, Taine believed that children would eventually create a language of their own if not otherwise supplied one by adults. He saw only a matter of degree in the communicative differences between creatures of differing levels of intelligence (including children, idiots, savages, and higher animal forms). "Speaking generally, the child presents in a passing state the mental characteristics that are found in a fixed state in primitive civilizations, very much as the human embryo presents in a passing state the physical characteristics that are found in a fixed state in the classes of inferior animals" (1877:259).[5]

If Taine's study was suggestive, Darwin's was even more so. In his own child biography, Darwin stressed the observation that preverbal infants, like many animals, seem to understand spoken words even though they cannot articulate such words themselves. He also pointed to the early appearance of meaningful intonations in children's babblings, to the highly inventive quality of the child's first words, and to the wealth of preverbal information that is both conveyed and understood by the infant through facial expressions and simple gestures alone.

More directly relevant to Darwin's impact upon Sigmund Freud are the great naturalist's remarks on the emergence of childhood emotions. When Darwin had taken his two-year-old son to the London Zoological Gardens, he had been surprised to observe the child's fear of the larger and more exotic animals. "May we not suspect," Darwin conjectured, "that the vague but very real fears of childhood, which are quite independent of experience, are the inherited effects of real dangers and abject superstitions during ancient savage times? It is quite conformable with what we know of the transmission of formerly well-developed characters, that they should appear [in the descendants] at an early period of life, and afterwards disappear" (1877:288). Darwin's position on inherited childhood fears was later reiterated by American psychologist and ardent Darwinian G. Stanley Hall in his 1914 publication "A Synthetic Genetic Study of Fear." Freud, in turn, enlisted the support of both Hall and Darwin in likewise arguing that many childhood fears—especially neurotic phobias—are phylogenetically endowed (1916–17, S.E., 16:399).[6]

5. Taine (1876:22), apparently misunderstanding Müller's position, considered his own evolutionary views as basically compatible with those of the English linguist. On Müller's opposition to Darwin and the *gradualist* conception of language and thought, see Müller (1902, 1:477–78, 523–24), which includes a 3 July 1873 letter to Müller from Darwin and a 13 October 1875 response from Müller, briefly discussing their differences.

6. Freud's Darwin reference is to *The Expression of the Emotions* (1872:38), where Darwin relates how he once induced a poisonous snake to strike at him from behind a protective glass partition, and how, against his own will, he had instinctively recoiled at the moment of the snake's attack. If from no other source, Freud was familiar with Darwin's *Expression* from having attended as a medical student Theodor Meynert's lectures on psychiatry. See Meynert 1884:251–62; Amacher 1965: 36–37; and Ritvo 1974:180.

Darwin on the expression of childhood emotions (weeping): "Infants whilst young do not shed tears or weep, as is well known to nurses and medical men. . . . It would appear as if the lacrymal glands require some practice in the individual before they are easily excited into action, in somewhat the same manner as various inherited consensual movements and tastes require some exercise before they are fixed and perfected. This is all the more likely with a habit like weeping, which must have been acquired since the period when man branched off from the common progenitor of the genus Homo and of the non-weeping anthropomorphous apes" (1872:152–53).

It was this same line of reasoning that allowed Freud to claim that the child enters the world with a store of *"instinctive* knowledge"— knowledge that shapes much that is fundamental in the overall pattern of Freudian psychosexual development. Speaking of the Oedipus complex and other such childhood conflicts, Freud declared: "Whenever experiences fail to fit in with the hereditary schema, they become remodelled in the imagination—a process which might very profitably be followed out in detail. It is precisely such cases that are calculated to convince us of the independent existence of the schema. We are often able to see the schema triumphing over the experience of the individual . . ." (1918b [1914], *S.E.*, 17:119).

Darwin's work in comparative and child psychology was linked to psychoanalysis by manifold ties, most of them indirect. One of the more important indirect ties was established by the work of Darwin's younger friend and colleague George John Romanes (1848–94). Romanes first met Darwin after the latter had noticed a letter he had written to *Nature*, dealing with the vexing Darwinian problem of the evolution of the flat fish (Romanes 1873). The young biologist was soon invited to visit Darwin, and the two scientists developed a close friendship lasting until the latter's death. It was partly personal contact with Darwin that encouraged Romanes to apply the theory of evolution to the still young fields of comparative and child psychology. Later, he became interested in the problem of heredity. His three-volume work *Darwin and After Darwin* (1892–97) tackled the major theoretical problems in evolutionary biology prior to the rediscovery of Mendel's laws in 1900.

In the early 1880s, while Freud was still a student of medicine, an aging Darwin had put the bulk of his unpublished researches in psychology at the disposal of Romanes. After Darwin's death in 1882, Romanes published much of this unknown manuscript material, including an essay by Darwin on the subject of instinct, as part of his *Mental Evolution in Animals* (1883). Five years later, Romanes followed this work with a companion study on child development entitled *Mental Evolution in Man* (1888), which was read and carefully annotated by Freud—probably during the early 1890s.[7]

7. Romanes's *Mental Evolution in Man*, which deals heavily with language and its evolutionary relationship to thought, is, in fact, the most annotated work of those that comprise the 1,200-item Freud acquisition of the Health Sciences Library, Columbia University. Freud's copy bears, in his characteristic hand, marginal markings and brief comments on 117 of the total 439 pages of text. See also Shakow and Rapaport 1964:43 n.

Anna Freud, from a perusal of photocopies of the more extensively annotated passages of the Romanes volume and taking into account where her father's interests lay in the years following its publication, has suggested that he probably made these marginal markings in 1895 while he was working on the *Project for a Scientific Psychology* (Bowlby 1969:12–14). The relationship between language and thought was indeed a major concern of Part III of the *Project* and was a topic much discussed by Freud in a number of his letters to Fliess around this same period (*Origins*, pp. 64–67, 174–75). This relationship was touched upon in a specifically Darwinian light in *Studies on Hysteria* (1895d). Nevertheless, after carefully examining Freud's copy of the Romanes volume, I have been unable to find justification for such a precise dating of Freud's marginalia. Freud's comments make no reference to either the *Project* itself or its peculiar terminology. Moreover, most of the annotations are limited to marks of emphasis, question marks, and brief exclamatory expressions—as is generally characteristic of Freud's marginalia. My own guess (and it is only a guess) is that Freud read Romanes's *Mental Evolu-*

Romanes's main objective in these two works, particularly in *Mental Evolution in Man*, was to demonstrate to psychologists just how air-tight the case had become for man's naturalistic descent from apelike progenitors. Romanes was a wholehearted supporter of Ernst Haeckel's famous biogenetic law, and he included, to this end, a large fold-out diagram opposite the title page of each of these two books. In this diagram (Fig. 7.1), Romanes set forth the many parallel stages that he believed united the ontogeny of man with the phylogenetic series beneath him. From a letter he wrote to Darwin dated 6 February 1880, we know that Romanes originally constructed this diagram by comparing the details of Darwin's baby biography with others from *The Descent of Man* (E. Romanes 1896:96). Furthermore, both Darwin and his botanist son Francis actively followed the progress of Romanes's researches in comparative and human psychology. In a letter to Romanes of 2 September 1878, Darwin enthusiastically relayed his son Francis's suggestion that Romanes ought to keep "an idiot, a deaf mute, a monkey, and a baby" in his house (E. Romanes 1896:78).

Like Darwin before him, Romanes was particularly attuned to the evolutionary continuity displayed by the emotional characteristics of man. In *Mental Evolution in Man*, he proclaimed that "the emotional life of animals is so strikingly similar to the emotional life of man—and especially of young children—that I think the similarity ought fairly to be taken as direct evidence of a genetic continuity between them" (1888:7). Of more direct relevance to psychoanalysis is the precise *order* in which Romanes asserted that the emotions first emerge in childhood. In his large fold-out diagram, Romanes placed the first manifestations of the sexual emotions at seven weeks (!)—sandwiching them between surprise and fear (at about three weeks) and the first sentiments of shame and morality (at about fifteen months). Nor should such a proto-Freudian conception of early childhood (in which sexuality emerges before morality) surprise us in the work of Romanes. As predominantly human traits in Romanes's phylogenetic scheme, shame and morality formed a major biogenetic watershed between man and his lower zoological relatives. But as sexually reproducing organisms, these lower relatives demanded through Romanes's recapitulatory logic that sexual drives be imputed to the early stages of human infancy. Although Romanes did not elaborate further on the precise nature of these infantile sexual emotions,[8] what he probably had in mind was

---

tion in Man (1888) within a decade or so of its publication, but most probably in the earlier half of that decade. It is strange that Freud does not refer to this work in any of his published writings—for example, in the list of books on child psychology that he said were known to him in his *Three Essays on the Theory of Sexuality* (1905d, S.E., 7:173–74, n. 2).

8. Romanes had planned to follow up his *Mental Evolution in Man*, which was mostly concerned with the development of language and thought, with a series of companion studies on the development of intellect, emotions, volition, morality, and religious belief. Unfortunately his early death in 1894, of an undiagnosed disease, prevented him from realizing this more extensive project. Presumably the subject of sexuality would have received further discussion in the volume on emotional development (see Romanes 1888:vi).

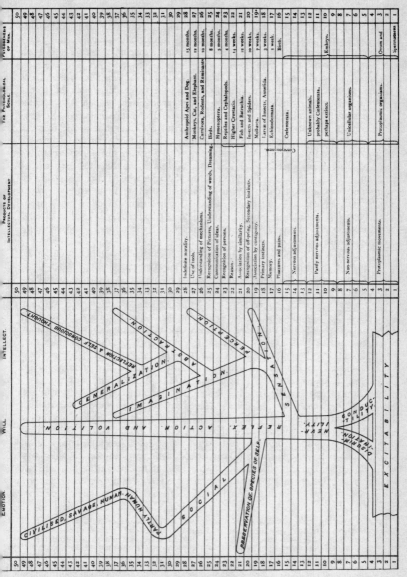

Fig. 7.1. George John Romanes's comparative depiction of the leading features of animal psychogenesis. *Left to right*: an evolutionary tree of the emotions, will, and intellect; specific stages of animal intelligence; the phylogenetic scale; and the ontogenetic scale. (From Romanes 1888: Frontispiece.)

an alert observation from Darwin's baby biography. For it was at precisely seven weeks of age that his infant son's contented smiles and "swimming eyes" while sucking at the breast had convinced Darwin that children are indeed capable of sensual experiences at such an early age (Darwin 1877:288).[9]

In addition to Darwin's immediate influence upon the work of Romanes, his pervasive influence on child psychology may be traced through numerous other routes. Even among less biologically oriented students of childhood, it became increasingly common under Darwin's general influence for authors to speak of the emergence of congenital "instincts" in childhood and to compare such instincts with those of lower animals (Burnham 1974:198). The German physiologist-psychologist William Preyer took just this approach in the first major book on child development (1882), as did the English psychologist and personal acquaintance of Darwin's, James Sully (1892, 2:193; 1896:5). (The significance of this trend is perhaps more evident in German-speaking countries, where, prior to Darwin, the words *Instinkt* and *Trieb* ["drive"] were carefully reserved for animals and man, respectively.)

It was in this new vein, and guided by an explicitly evolutionary line of thought, that the German philosopher-psychologist Karl Groos devoted two widely read books to the subject of play in animals (1896) and in man (1899). Groos interpreted youthful play behavior as a necessary process of "preactivity," or "practice," for instincts that are later to be called upon in the struggle for existence. In man, Groos held, play is itself a generalized instinct. By facilitating a high degree of learning in childhood, the instinct for play has helped to pave the evolutionary way for man's unique freedom from more specialized instincts. Groos did not hesitate to include sexuality among such regularly "preactive" childhood instincts (1899:326; see Chapter 8 in this book).

In America, Groos's *Die Spiele der Thiere* (The Play of Animals) and *Die Spiele der Menschen* (The Play of Man) were translated by Elizabeth L. Baldwin, the wife of American psychologist and evolutionary theorist James Mark Baldwin (Groos 1898, 1901). In addition to contributing laudatory prefaces to these American editions, James Baldwin had already made an independent contribution to child psychology under the title *Mental Development in the Child and the Race* (1895). Rampantly biogenetic, like so many child psychology works of this period,[10] Baldwin's book anticipated the general approach to

9. Darwin's inference was anticipated by his grandfather Erasmus Darwin, who was also an evolutionist and had already argued in *Zoonomia* (1801, 1:200-201) that the infant's pleasurable sensations while breast-feeding later find mature expression in man's highest aesthetic undertakings (see Ellenberger 1970:504).

10. The theme of recapitulation was given prominent emphasis by British psychologists James Sully (1884:62; 1896:5, 8, 234) and Alexander Chamberlain (1900:446-47), and by the American psychologist G. Stanley Hall (1904, 2:648-748). Hall, who devoted considerable discussion to Karl Groos's theory of play, added a biogenetic twist to this theory with the claim that play represents "the motor habits and the spirit of the past of the race, persisting in the present, as rudimentary functions. . . ." Hall also believed that recapitulation was a prerequisite for the child's successful journey toward fully civilized behavior (1904, 1:202-3).

social psychology that Sigmund Freud was to take after 1910. To Baldwin the infant was "an embryo person . . . ; and he is, in these early stages, plainly recapitulating the items in the social history of the race." Baldwin concluded, "The embryology of society is open to study in the nursery" (1895:156). Freud was familiar with the works of Baldwin (1895), Groos (1899), Sully (1896), and Preyer (1882) and later referred briefly to all four in his *Three Essays on the Theory of Sexuality* (1905d).

To sum up, by the 1890s the post-Darwinian rush to child psychology had reached the point at which even Freud was wondering in private how much room for originality remained. Commenting on Baldwin's *Mental Development in the Child and the Race* (1895) in a November 1897 letter to Fliess, Freud wistfully exclaimed: "It is interesting that writers are now turning so much to child psychology. Today I received another book on the subject, by James Mark Baldwin. So one still remains a child of one's age, even with something one had thought was one's very own" (*Origins*, p. 228).

DARWINISM AND MEDICAL PSYCHOLOGY

The history of psychology in the nineteenth century may be viewed as essentially a development away from philosophy and toward biology (Young 1970:vii). Medical psychology, particularly psychiatry, is no exception to this trend (Ellenberger 1970:284). At the vanguard of this general shift in emphasis were two main influences: the brain anatomists, represented most notably by Theodor Meynert (1833–92) and Carl Wernicke (1848–1905); and Darwin and post-Darwinian evolutionary theory. I have already discussed the extensive influence that Meynert and the wider physicalist-neuroanatomical tradition exerted upon Freud, culminating in the *Project for a Scientific Psychology* (1895), and shall deal here with Darwin's general influence upon medical psychology.

Briefly, Darwin provided the late-nineteenth-century medical community with a simple, persuasive conception of the essential instinctual forces that underlie vital activity. Where Meynert and other anatomist-psychiatrists had sought for the causes of mental illness in localized brain lesions, a new breed of Darwinian psychotherapists turned their medical attentions to a dynamic and nonlocalized model of *instincts and their vicissitudes*. This Darwinian paradigm had as its supreme virtue a dependence upon just two basic and all-encompassing instinctual drives—the will to survive and the urge to reproduce.

For a comprehensive review of theories comparing childhood to phylogenetically lower forms, see Chamberlain (1900), especially the chapters "The Child as Revealer of the Past" (pp. 213–85), "The Child and the Savage" (pp. 287–353), and "The Child and the Criminal" (pp. 355–95). A discerning treatment of the biogenetic law (fact and fallacy), together with its influential history, is offered by Stephen Gould's *Ontogeny and Phylogeny* (1977: especially 115–166).

Darwin on Sex

It is not generally recognized that Darwin's *The Descent of Man, and Selection in Relation to Sex* (1871) was really two books in one, with roughly two thirds of it being devoted to the subject matter announced in the latter half of the title. In fact, the major message of Darwin's *Descent of Man* was the claim that a phenomenon called sexual selection can and does act independently of the Darwinian principle of natural selection. But Darwin was saying even more than this— namely, that the ultimate test of biological success lies in *reproduction*, not in "the survival of the fittest." For if the fittest do not reproduce, Darwin well knew, they are generally of no evolutionary import to the species.

In order to convince his readers of both the independent existence and the immense power of sexual selection, Darwin patiently catalogued hundreds of examples of sexual dimorphism among animals, pointing out how adaptively such characteristics subserve either courtship (and female "choice" over the courting males) or battle among the males for possession of the females. How could such incredibly cumbersome ornaments as the giant tail fan of the peacock or the splendid secondary wing feathers of the male Argus pheasant justify their biological evolution, Darwin shrewdly asked, unless these dramatic structures had returned in reproductive advantage what they clearly sacrified in anatomical fitness? In sum, Darwin's basic intent in explicating the doctrine of sexual selection was to establish how closely sexual attraction, love, jealousy, and various other sexual emotions are all tied to the evolution and the operation of the nervous system itself:

> He who admits the principle of sexual selection will be led to the remarkable conclusion that the nervous system not only regulates most of the existing functions of the body, but has indirectly influenced the progressive development of various bodily structures and of certain mental qualities. Courage, pugnacity, perseverance; strength and size of body, weapons of all kinds, musical organs, both vocal and instrumental, bright colours and ornamental appendages, have all been indirectly gained by the one sex or the other, through the exertion of choice, the influence of love and jealousy, and the appreciation of the beautiful in sound, colour or form; and these powers of the mind manifestly depend on the development of the brain. (1871, 2:402; 1874:617)

Thus it was that Charles Darwin, who, perhaps more than anyone else in the nineteenth century, singled out the biological importance of the instincts for survival and for reproduction, laid before the medical community a dynamic and dualist paradigm of instinct that seemed to encompass the whole of organic behavior.

The notion that "love and hunger" rule the world is, of course, ancient and not original to Darwin. But it was Darwin who first provided a theoretical superstructure for recognizing these two instincts *and no others* as the primary basis of all animal behavior. As Havelock Ellis later observed in this connection, "The immense importance of sex is indeed implicit in the biological conception of life as it began to take shape in the middle of the last century and the ancient dictum that hunger and love are the pillars of life became developed in all the human sciences" (1939a:316).

Darwin's influence provided an important scientific sanction for many previously speculative and philosophical trends in nineteenth-century thought, and this sanction was doubtless conducive to the belated popularity achieved by Arthur Schopenhauer's (1788–1860) philosophy. Schopenhauer's famous work *Die Welt als Wille und Vorstellung* (The World as Will and Idea, 1819; 2nd ed., 1844) emphasized the unconscious and irrational aspects of the will. Behind the operation of the will were two instincts, the conservative and the sexual; and Schopenhauer considered the sexual instinct to be by far the more important of the two. "Man is incarnate sexual instinct," he wrote, "since he owes his origin to copulation and the wish of his wishes is to copulate. . . . The sexual act is the unceasing thought of the unchaste and the involuntary, the ever recurring daydream of the chaste, the key of all intimations, an ever ready matter for fun, an inexhaustible source of jokes" (1844, 2:588; trans. Ellenberger 1970:209). In emphasizing the opposition between the instincts and the intellect, Schopenhauer attributed insanity to the process of repression.

It has long been pointed out, by Freud among others, how closely Schopenhauer anticipated many of the central tenets of psychoanalysis. Thomas Mann once wrote that Freud's theories were Schopenhauer's doctrines "translated from metaphysics into psychology" (quoted in Ellenberger 1970:542). Freud later claimed that he read Schopenhauer very late in life and that any coincidence between their views was "not to be traced to my acquaintance with his teaching" (*Autobiography*, 1925d, S.E., 20:59). Freud did, however, consult Eduard von Hartmann's famous *Philosophie des Unbewussten* (Philosophy of the Unconscious, 1869) when writing *The Interpretation of Dreams*, and Hartmann was a zealous disciple both of Schopenhauer and of Darwin.[11]

Darwinian Instinct Theory: The Immediate Medical Impact

Darwin's message, reinforced as it was by the German philosophical tradition, did not go unheeded among students of psychopathology.

11. In the 1870s, Hartmann wrote three separate works on Darwinian theory, one of which was entitled *Das Unbewusste vom Standpunkt der Physiologie und Descendenztheorie* (The Unconscious from the Standpoint of Physiology and Evolutionary Theory, 1872). These three Darwinian works were later incorporated into the third volume of the *Philosophie des Unbewussten* (10th ed., 1890), and it was this edition that Freud consulted when writing *The Interpretation of Dreams* (1900a, S.E., 4:134). Of additional relevance in this connection is that Schopenhauer's own emphasis upon sexuality and the "will to live" in human motivation was intimately tied to his pre-Darwinian support of evolutionary theory (Lovejoy 1959). The influence of Schopenhauer upon Freud is difficult to trace in any detail because of Freud's own reluctance to associate his psychoanalytic insights with prior philosophical assumptions. This problem will be touched upon again in Chapter 13. On the influence of Schopenhauer and other nineteenth-century philosophers of the unconscious (especially Hartmann and Nietzsche), see Ellenberger (1970:208–10, 275–78, 542–43) and the additional sources cited therein.

Within eight years of *The Descent of Man*, the great German psychiatrist Richard von Krafft-Ebing had endorsed self-preservation and sexual gratification as the only two instinctual aims known to physiology. In his celebrated *Lehrbuch der Psychiatrie* (Textbook of Psychiatry, 1879–80, 1:65), and later in his *Psychopathia Sexualis* (1886), Krafft-Ebing traced the most basic features of human psychopathology in terms of the vicissitudes and the perversions of just these two fundamental drives of life. The same doctrine was later espoused in Berlin by psychotherapist and sexologist Albert Moll (1891:205–6, n. 3) and in Leipzig by neurologist Hermann Rohleder (1901:5), both of whom refer back in this connection to Krafft-Ebing; by professor of legal medicine at Lyon, Alexander Lacassagne (see Preface to Chevalier 1893:v); by English psychiatrist Thomas Clouston (1891:9); by gynecologist A. F. A. King (1891:517) and by child psychologist G. Stanley Hall (1904, 2:9, 60–62, 69–70) in America; and by scores of others. Sigmund Freud was later to acknowledge this general Darwinian influence, although he characteristically expressed it in a more literary manner: "In what was at first my utter perplexity, I took as my starting-point a saying of the poet-philosopher, Schiller, that 'hunger and love are what moves the world' " (1930*a*, *S.E.*, 21:117).[12]

Of these two primal instincts—the self-preservative and the reproductive—it was the reproductive that offered by far the greater theoretical attraction for late-nineteenth-century students of mental pathology. Darwin had claimed, for his own part, that no aspect of animal physiology is as liable to variation as is the reproductive system— especially among animals that have been removed from a state of nature (1868, 2: Chapter 18; and 1874:189). In Germany, Albert Moll later extended such Darwinian observations in the course of *Untersuchungen über die Libido sexualis* (Investigations into the Libido Sexualis), arguing that cultural development had greatly contributed to sexual perversion within the human species (1897*b*:386–87). Sigmund Freud, who read Moll's *Libido Sexualis* with considerable interest in the late 1890s, carefully marked this and similar passages in the margins of his personal copy of that work (Freud library, London). At the same time, the increasing practice of family limitation—or "the problem of Malthusianism," as Freud termed it—struck him as yet another incontestable raison d'être for the widespread existence of psychosexual maladies (*Origins*, p. 72, Draft B, 8 February 1893; Freud 1898*a*, *S.E.*, 3:276–77). Thus it was that Darwin, together with his *spiritus rectus*, Thomas Malthus, provided important new justifications for reinstating a sexual etiology in medical psychology at a time when this traditional pathogen had largely fallen into disrepute.

Accordingly, from about 1880 to 1900 there occurred a major revival in interest among neurologists and psychopathologists in documenting the many pernicious and often disguised manifestations of the sexual impulse in neurotic complaints (Ellenberger 1970:291, 300–

---

12. Cf. 1914*c*, *S.E.*, 14:79; and 1933*a*, *S.E.*, 22:95–96, where Freud speaks in a more explicitly biological vein. See also Burnham 1974:205.

301). In 1890, the Zurich physician Alexander Peyer could cite a dozen supporters when he implicated coitus interruptus as a frequent cause of neurasthenia. Similarly, Freud's Viennese colleague Moritz Benedikt had achieved dramatic success in the cure of hysteria by extracting from his patients their reluctant confessions of a pathogenic, and usually sexual, secret (Benedikt 1894).

Of more ingeniously Darwinian nature was the theory of hysteria proposed about this time by the American gynecologist A. F. A. King (1841–1914). Recognizing two departments of neurophysiological government, the self-preservative and the reproductive, King hypothesized that an occasional disharmony between them underlay the mysterious phenomenon of double consciousness, or double personality, so often encountered in hysteria. In hysterical attacks, King claimed, "the reproductive ego" temporarily gains ascendancy over "the self-preservative ego," causing the patient to suffer paroxysms and loss of consciousness. Such helpless states, he said, must be understood in their proper phylogenetic context—one in which the hysterical individual, almost always a woman, would soon have been cured of her troubles by "a youthful Apollo of the woods" (1891:521). Thus the function of the hysterical attack was to facilitate insemination by this uninhibited and lust-seeking Apollo of primeval times. It was only with the advent of civilization and sexual constraint, King maintained, that hysteria had become such a chronic disease owing to social proscription of the most natural form of treatment.

King believed that his argument was borne out by the most common characteristics of hysteria: (1) its predominant appearance in women between the times of puberty and menopause; (2) its tendency to occur in *single* women (together with its well-known cure by marriage); (3) the temporal association of hysterical attacks with the spring and summer months; (4) the fact that such attacks rarely occur when the patient is alone; (5) the failure of the attacks to impair the patient's physical beauty; and (6) the greater frequency of hysteria among the idle (or those who have been freed from the struggle for existence). In connection with this last observation, King noted that hysterical fits and other chronic hysterical symptoms had previously been reported as cured by a sudden threat to the patient's life. One long-paralyzed hysteric suddenly walked, he related, when she faced the imminent prospect of burning to death.

English neurologist Thomas Clouston (1840–1915) was another physician who fully sympathized in the pre-Freudian era both with the sexual theory of hysteria and with the post-Darwinian model of instinct from which this theory was gaining so much encouragement (Clouston 1883 [1892 ed.:16]); and he specifically cited Herbert Spencer and G. J. Romanes in this connection. Havelock Ellis, who later prided himself on his early (1898b) acceptance of the Breuer-Freud theory of hysteria, nevertheless recalled in the year of his death that Thomas Clouston had endorsed a sexual interpretation of this disease ahead of all of them (1939a:311). Clouston did not limit his interest in sexual etiol-

ogy to hysteria. In *The Neuroses of Development* (1891), he predicted
that the closest associations would soon be found between the development of the sexual function and innumerable disturbances in the
nervous system:

> I believe, if our knowledge of heredity and physiology were sufficiently
> advanced, we should be able to fit into such a [sexual-developmental]
> scheme, and to show the true [etiological] relationship of the acephalous
> foetus, the hare-lipped, the cleft-palated, and the open-spined child, the
> congenital imbecile, the deaf and dumb, the cases of infantile delirium
> and *pavor nocturnus*, the convulsions of teething, those of chorea and
> epilepsy occurring before twenty-five, the speech defect of stammering,
> infantile paralysis, megrim, Friedreich's disease, hysteria in girls, pos-
> sibly phthisis, and acute rheumatism, the insanities of puberty and ado-
> lescence, as well as many moral perversions, volitional paralyses, and in-
> tellectual peculiarities which are met with in both sexes during the
> developmental period of life. (1891:4)

Even Freud's friend Wilhelm Fliess (1906b) was unable to enlarge significantly upon Clouston's own far-reaching, pansexualist vision.

Although Freud never cited Thomas Clouston in any of his own
writings, he would certainly have known of Clouston from the contemporary neurological literature. In America, Clouston's conception of
"the neuroses of development" was picked up by James Mark Baldwin in
his *Mental Development in the Child and the Race* (1895), which Freud
did read. In a manner reminiscent of Freud's *Totem and Taboo* (1912–
13), Baldwin suggested that all such developmental neuroses were probably linked by ontogenetic recapitulation to major "crises" that had
once taken place in the phylogeny of the race (1895:27–28 n.). It remained for Freud to attempt a more elaborate formulation of this idea
(see Chapter 10).

So great was the medical ascendancy of the sexual factor between
1880 and 1910 that it began to appear to many physicians as if Darwinism had finally been disowned by one of its principal intellectual
stepchildren. Wilhelm Fliess's critic Henning commented about both
Fliess and Freud in this light when he complained of their joint efforts
to displace the Darwinian "principle of selection" in favor of a rampant
pansexualist philosophy (1910:232). One of Fliess's disciples later expanded on this theme when he insisted that Fliess's theory of complementary bisexual "object choice," not Charles Darwin's "victory of the
stronger," was what really explained the manifold mysteries of human
sexual attraction (Saaler 1914:346). Within the psychoanalytic movement, a major split developed about this same time (ca. 1910) between
the loyal Freudian libido theorists and Alfred Adler and his followers,
including G. Stanley Hall in America, who reacted against this sexual
trend and chose to reinstate the primacy of the "self-preservative"
instincts.

In sum, Freud's medical generation witnessed, under the general
influence of Darwin and evolutionary theory, a major revival of interest

in sexual etiology. The opposition Freud encountered for his own part in this trend was largely because he pursued such a Darwinian logic further than most of his medical contemporaries ventured to do.

DARWINISM AND PSYCHOANALYSIS: AN OVERVIEW

Struggle and Conflict as Mental Paradigm

As much as Freud believed in the importance of sexuality, he could still rightfully protest against the charge of being a pansexualist. Indeed, his theory of mind remained faithfully dualist from beginning to end. Although his etiological emphasis eventually shifted after 1920 from an original opposition between ego and libido to one between "life" and "death" instincts, his preoccupation with twofold psychical conflict never faltered. As such, his dynamic emphasis upon "the struggle for existence" within the psyche was psychologically Darwinian to the core (Ritvo 1974:187). "Opposition between ideas," he once commented, "is only an expression of struggles between the various instincts" (1910i, S.E., 11:213–14). At the same time, Freud never relinquished his belief that the ultimate causes of neurosis lie in the conflict between instincts as a whole and the demands and restrictions that human civilization has placed upon them.

Freud was not unaware of the conceptual parallel between his dynamic paradigm of mind and the Darwinian concept of struggle. The year before his death, he jotted down the following brief memorandum: "The individual perishes from his internal conflicts, the species in its struggle with the external world to which it is no longer adapted.—This deserves to be included in Moses [and Monotheism]" (1941f, S.E., 23:299). Similar views of an internal, Darwinian struggle for existence had long been advocated in the physiological and embryological fields by Herbert Spencer (1864–67) in England and by Wilhelm Roux (1881) in Germany. As we shall see later in this chapter, Freud not only knew of Wilhelm Roux's work but repeatedly cited his findings in connection with his own theories of human development.

Historical Truth: The Past as Key to the Present

Both Darwin and Freud shared a facility for bringing unforeseen meaning to the seemingly trivial. In doing so, both sought in the past a key to the present. To biologists before Darwin, the many useless rudimentary organs in nature—like wisdom teeth and the appendix in adult man, and the gill slits and tail in the early stages of human embryological development—often seemed like arbitrary quirks of Creative Fiat. Darwin demonstrated the historical meaning of such organs, and he likewise explained their state of atrophy by the same mode of reasoning.

Freud adopted a similar historical approach when he sought to introduce psychoanalytic meaning into such disparate phenomena as symptom formation, dreams, slips of the tongue and pen, bungled actions, and so forth. Although the nature of Freud's clinical material originally led him back into the prehistory of each neurotic's childhood, it was Charles Darwin whom he cited in *Studies on Hysteria* (1895d) when he first endeavored to justify the hidden symbolisms inherent in many bizarre hysterical symptoms. Speaking of Frau Cäcilie M., perhaps his most gifted hysteric, Freud argued that a host of neuralgias (for instance, a stabbing sensation near the patient's heart) had been determined by abreactions following the everyday patterns of speech (for example, "the 'stab in the heart,'" which is linguistically associated with a severe insult). "All these [neurotic] sensations and innervations," Freud wrote, "belong to the field of 'The Expression of the Emotions,' which, as Darwin [1872] has taught us, consist of actions which *originally had a meaning and served a purpose*" (*S.E.*, 2:181; italics added). Both linguistic usage and hysterical affects could be seen, according to Freud's Darwinian interpretation, as arising from a common phylogenetic root. His later interest in the evolution of language, together with its bearing upon the "archaic" laws of the unconscious, was a natural continuation of this earlier line of thought (e.g., Freud 1910e).

Also stemming directly from this Darwinian-historical point of view were Freud's efforts to place human morality, social laws, and religious institutions in an elaborate phylogenetic perspective—as he did, for example, in *Totem and Taboo* (1912–13), *The Future of an Illusion* (1927c), and *Moses and Monotheism* (1939a) (see Chapter 10). It was in this same Darwinian-historical spirit that Freud later distinguished the purely *material* truth embodied in such social institutions from the *historical* truth that originally inspired their evolution (*Moses and Monotheism*, 1939a, *S.E.*, 23:127–32).

Psychosexual Stages and the Biogenetic Law

Why are oral and anal zones such basic sources of infantile sexual excitation in Freudian theory? Granted that feeding at the mother's breast constitutes a highly pleasurable experience for the hungry infant, how could Freud conceive of this activity as a form of sexual experience? Many non-Freudians have long been amazed by his nonchalant assurance about the answer to this debatable question.[13] Moreover,

13. "Any fruitful discussion of various psychoanalytic theses," Erich Fromm intimated as early as 1932, "would have to begin with a critique of the central role given to the [infantile] erogenous zones" (1932:166, n. 5). More specific as well as more critical of Freud on this point is Stanislav Andreski: "Had he said that the infant's thought and behavior were guided by the quest for sensual gratifications instead of calling them sexual; had he refrained from calling the infant a 'polymorphous pervert,' and found a more sober label for its propensity to find pleasure in sucking its mother's breast or its thumb, or in relieving the tension in its bladder or bowels, Freud would have formulated a more tenable theory, but one which would be less apt for the role of a surrogate religion" (1972:162). Similarly,

upon Freud's equation of "sensual" with "sexual" in infantile emotions rests much that automatically follows in psychoanalytic theory—a circumstance that he himself once acknowledged: "Psycho-analysis stands or falls with the recognition of the sexual component instincts, of the erotogenic zones and of the extension thus made possible of the concept of a 'sexual function' in contrast to the narrower 'genital function'" (1913i, S.E., 12:323).

It was over precisely this issue of the "extended" conception of sexuality in human infancy that Freud and Carl Gustav Jung later parted scientific company. Jung's position was that infantile sexual manifestations in the clinical record of adult neurotics have generally been *retroactively* introduced by the patient into his or her childhood recollections. In other words, both neurosis and infantile polymorphous perversity originate with the onset of puberty (Jung 1913:104–7, 125, 168). Freud managed to circumvent this theoretical objection—one that he himself had acknowledged in his letters to Fliess as early as 1897 (*Origins*, p. 216)—by his implicit endorsement of a biogenetic conception of human sexual development.

According to the "fundamental biogenetic law," as advanced by Ernst Haeckel (1866, 1868, 1874a) and other late-nineteenth-century evolutionary thinkers, "ontogeny recapitulates phylogeny": that is to say, in man, the development from fetus to adulthood (ontogeny) provides a brief recapitulation of the entire history of the race (phylogeny). Freud's implicit endorsement of this law constitutes perhaps the least appreciated source of a priori biological influence in all of psychoanalytic theory.[14] For if the developing child recapitulates the history of the race, it must likewise recapitulate the *sexual* history of the race. In other words, the prepubertal human being must have the innate potential to experience all of the archaic forms of sexual pleasure that once characterized the mature life stages of our remote ancestors. Not only did this biogenetic logic underlie Freud's earliest (mid-1890s) insights into the "extended" and "polymorphously perverse" nature of infantile sexual activity, but it also gave him, in later years, his most

---

Rudolf Allers has offered the following protest in connection with Freud's claim, in *Three Essays* (1905d, S.E., 7:182), that the sexual nature of sucking in childhood is self-evident from the infant's facial expressions when nursing: "Such a statement cannot but amaze the unprejudiced reader. . . . Freud simply assumes identity of expression means identity of experience" (1940:116–17). See also, on this general issue of Freud's "enlarged" conception of infantile libido, Paul Näcke 1906:166; Albert Moll 1909, 1912a trans.:173; Hinrichsen 1914:142; Leopold Löwenfeld 1914:9; Albert Eulenburg 1914:34; Karen Horney 1939:51–52; Havelock Ellis 1939a:313; and Magnus Hirschfeld 1948:46. For a more recent critique of Freud's theory of infantile sexuality, including a comprehensive review of the empirical, experimental, and psychoanalytic evidence on this subject, see Chodoff 1966.

14. See earlier, Chapter 6, pp. 199–204. Yazmajian (1967) has partially anticipated my own argument regarding biogenetic assumptions in psychoanalytic theory, but he attributes the introduction of these assumptions to Abraham (1924), who was only expanding upon themes that Freud himself had already endorsed as early as 1896 (*Origins*, p. 180). I have treated separately in Chapter 12 the various historical reasons that have interfered with the proper recognition of Freud's biogenetic propensities.

Ernst Haeckel in 1870 (age 36).

irrefutable justification for these views. Here is what he had to say on this key point in his *Introductory Lectures on Psycho-Analysis*:

> In forming our judgement of the two courses of [instinctual] development—both of the ego and of the libido—we must lay emphasis on a consideration which has not often hitherto been taken into account. For both of them are at bottom heritages, abbreviated recapitulations, of the development which all mankind has passed through from its primaeval days over long periods of time. In the case of the development of the libido, this *phylogenetic* origin is, I venture to think, immediately obvious. Consider how in one class of animals the genital apparatus is brought into the closest relation to the mouth, while in another it cannot be distinguished from the excretory apparatus, and in yet others it is linked to the motor organs—all of which you will find attractively set out in W. Bölsche's valuable book [1911–13]. Among animals one can find, so to speak in petrified form, every species of perversion of the [human] sexual organization. (1916–17, *S.E.*, *16*:354)

Freud elaborated on this recapitulatory logic when he maintained in other writings that each major substage in the child's "pregenital" phase of sexual development has preserved a specific legacy of this phylogenetic influence.[15]

In the previous passage from his *Introductory Lectures*, Freud appealed to Wilhelm Bölsche's *Das Liebesleben in der Natur* (Love-Life in Nature)—a best-selling work that reflects perhaps better than any other the tremendous joint influence of Darwin and his German exponent Ernst Haeckel (1834–1919) in preparing the way for Freud's theory of psychosexual stages. Wilhelm Bölsche (1861–1939), a popular science writer as well as novelist, was also known in lay intellectual circles for his biographies of Darwin and Haeckel. Like Freud, Bölsche was part of the late-nineteenth-century materialist effort to use evolutionary theory in placing man's moral faculties and cultural institutions in a wholly naturalistic-historical light. His rambling and highly lyrical *Das Liebesleben* was an unabashed part of this attempt, extolling the many marvels of sex while cataloging in prosaic detail the remarkable diversity in nature's modes of sexual union.[16]

In his theory of sexual evolution, Bölsche started with Ernst Haeckel's famous notion of the primeval gastraea. Haeckel, in the early 1870s, had noticed that multicellular animal organisms follow a common pattern in their earliest stages of embryological development. Specifically he maintained that the fertilized zygote invaginates to create a primitive stomach, a mouth, and, later, an anal orifice (Fig. 7.2). Haeckel concluded that this gastraea (from the Greek *gaster*, meaning "stomach") was both a crucial turning point in the evolution of higher animal life (with many simple marine organisms remaining fixated at this general stage) and a basic form from which all higher organisms were ultimately descended (1874b, 1875).[17]

Seizing upon this suggestive gastraea theory, Bölsche portrayed the evolution of sexual sensitivity as a phenomenon that had become grad-

15. Freud made this assertion in his section "The Phases of Development of the Sexual Organization," added to the *Three Essays on the Theory of Sexuality* in 1915: "We shall give the name of 'pregenital' to organizations of sexual life in which the genital zones have not yet taken over their predominant part. We have hitherto identified two such organizations [the oral and the anal stages], which almost seem as though they were harking back to early animal forms of life" (1905d, S.E., 7:198). It was at about this same time that Freud wrote in the "Wolf Man" case history that "the pregenital organizations in man should be regarded as vestiges of conditions which have been permanently retained in several classes of animals" (1918b [1914], S.E., 17:108). For Freud's general support of the biogenetic law, and his further comments upon its high relevance for psychoanalytic theory, see his Preface to the third (1915) edition of *Three Essays* (1905d, S.E., 7:131), his essay on Leonardo da Vinci (1910c, S.E., 11:97), and the Schreber case history (1911c, S.E., 12:82).

16. Originally published between 1898 and 1903 in three volumes, Bölsche's *Das Liebesleben in der Natur* had sold nearly 80,000 copies by 1927. In 1931 an English translation appeared. We do not know when Freud read Bölsche, but his London library includes first-edition copies of the second (1900) and third (1903) volumes, and a third-edition (1909) copy of the first volume of this work. The 1909 copy bears the inscription "Freud 22.XI.09." The other volumes are not dated by Freud.

In addition to his biographies of Darwin (1898) and Haeckel (1900; English trans. 1906), Bölsche was author of *Die Abstammung des Menschen* (1904; English trans. as *The Evolution of Man*, 1905). For a brief biographical account of Bölsche's life, see Bolle 1955.

17. See Russell (1916:288–301) for further historical comments on Haeckel's theory and its reception by fellow biologists.

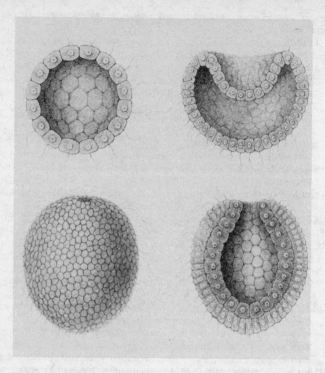

Fig. 7.2. Gastrulation in *Gastrophysema*, a sponge. (From Haeckel 1875: Plate 8.)

ually dispersed from the original "skin" of the preinvaginated gastraea to the later-evolved, and increasingly specialized, gastraeal organs of sexuality.[18] Bölsche included in this basic phylogenetic sequence (1) the gastraeal mouth, followed by (2) the primitive cloaca, (3) the anus, and finally (4) the genitalia.

In Bölsche's lyrical account, with the advent of the simplest form of reproduction (fission), eating became "the earliest prerequisite of love." "With the firstlings of life there was no opposition between eating and love; eating was a purely logical condition of love" (1898–1903; 1931 trans.:293). True sexual reproduction—originally "a sort of higher

18. Haeckel himself had previously broached the whole topic of the gastraea's acquisition of specialized sexual capabilities and called this issue "one of the most difficult problems of ontogeny and phylogeny" (1874b:45). Freud's old teacher Carl Claus wrote a critical review of Haeckel's gastraea theory the year that Freud enrolled in Claus's "General Biology and Darwinism" (Claus 1874). It seems more than likely that Haeckel's theory, which aroused much attention at the time, was a subject of lively discussion in that course.

eating" in Bölsche's characterization—began with the fusion of two whole organisms. Eventually the fusion of multicellular organisms became impractical, and sexual reproduction was soon achieved through the coalescence of specialized sexual cells. This new form of sexual union was increasingly effected by physical copulation. At first each primitive gastraea turned its mouth-intestine "gateway" toward its partner's analogous orifice. Sexual evolution subsequently paralleled the increasing specialization of the gastraea's central gut. "Anal love" evolved and then "disappeared in both sexes at a certain height of evolution" (1931 trans.:672–73). Penis and vagina appeared with the crocodiles as a means of introducing greater efficiency into the awkward process of "anus pressed against anus" (1931 trans.:633–34).

From this grand evolutionary point of view, human sexuality was to be seen as a comparatively stunted and localized process. Still, residues of ancestral sexuality were not without their occasional influence in human beings:

> . . . you must not picture this localization confined in too extreme a fashion to one spot; light excitations of sensual pleasure are possible on the entire skin of the body, and they are able to sound along faintly now and again, now here and now there; now as before. The erotically excited kiss as well as the inward feeling of physical well-being, which is so difficult to describe, of a mother nursing her child at her breast, feeds on fare that is both coarse and indefinitely fine and becoming finer; but all this in the sense of the primæval evolutionary fact, that in the beginning the whole skin was the seat of sensual pleasure. (1931 trans.:673)

Although Bölsche did not extend such biogenetic views to the sphere of human infancy, he, like Sigmund Freud, believed that many peculiar characteristics of this early period of life were only fully comprehensible in the light of biogenetic theory. He referred in this connection to the child's transient ability to grasp objects with the toe: "You think of the fundamental biogenetic law which points more strongly in infancy to ancestral characteristics! It is irrefutable . . ." (1931 trans.:441). It remained for Freud to supply the sexual complement to this Bölschean portrait of child development.

Yet even in this controversial step Freud was not alone. Of those who recognized the existence of infantile sexuality around the turn of the century, a sizable proportion sought, like Freud himself, to legitimize such heterodox claims by appealing to the biogenetic law. Included among this group are Freud's early follower Wilhelm Stekel (1895:247), writing even before the two had met; Freud's American supporter G. Stanley Hall (1904:2:101–2); the Swiss zoologist and psychotherapist August Forel (1905; 1911 trans.:10, 40, 192–207); the neurologist Hermann Rohleder (1907:1:56, 173, 544); the sociologist Franz Müller-Lyer (1912:33; 1913, 1917 ed.:32–33); and the Fliessian psychoanalyst Bruno Saaler (1912:904).[19]

19. To this list of names I might add Wilhelm Fliess (1897), Albert Moll (1897b:44–46), Havelock Ellis (1898a, 1900b), Karl Groos (1899:326), Sanford

It is likewise no accident that Karl Abraham, the disciple who contributed the most to the psychoanalytic theory of libidinal stages, was himself a former embryologist (Brown 1961:21). Quick to endorse Freud's general biogenetic statements, Abraham referred to the ontogenetic half of this doctrine when he emphasized that the human anus is developed from the primitive blastopore mouth (Abraham 1924). His astute propaganda for the theory of infantile sexuality did not go unnoticed by Freud.[20]

To conclude, what many critics of psychoanalytic theory have considered an arbitrary equation of sensual with sexual in early childhood experience was not so at all to Freud. Biogenetically, Freud, as well as certain of his contemporaries, perceived no other choice in the matter.

Freud's Fundamental Mechanisms of Pathological Development

After 1900, besides the two cardinal tenets of repression and the sexual content of the repressed (see Chapters 3, 4, and 6), Freud developed the three key developmental hypotheses of fixation, regression, and the special pertinacity of early impressions. Unlike the theory of repression, which Freud derived from clinical material and only later associated with biological hypotheses, these three psychoanalytic notions were rooted in biology from the moment of his first endorsement of them. They are also among the earliest tools of his explanatory medical repertoire, dating from his prepsychoanalytic work in neuroanatomy, childhood cerebral paralyses, and aphasia. But even though conceived early, these notions came into play in psychoanalysis proper only after the genetic viewpoint finally became the nuclear consideration of Freud's metapsychology.

Fixation. A fixation may relate either to an anatomical structure or to a behavioral attribute—in Freudian theory, to an instinct, its source, its aims, and its objects. Furthermore, these two differing senses of the concept of fixations spring from different intellectual sources.[21]

By the mid-nineteenth century, the notion of anatomical fixations (or "arrests in development") was well established in the fields of embryology, teratology (the study of monstrous births), and medical pathology. Such "arrests," or "inhibitions," in development were understood

---

Bell (1902), and Robert Müller (1907:14–18), who all treated infantile sexuality in a broadly Darwinian, if less explicitly biogenetic, spirit. I include here the less biologically oriented Sanford Bell owing to the influence that his Clark University teacher, G. Stanley Hall, had upon his decision to undertake his questionnaire study on childhood sexuality. See Ross 1972:383–84.

20. See *Three Essays,* 1905d, S.E., 7:199 n., note added to the 1924 edition; and 1933a, S.E., 22:100.

21. I do not discuss here a number of other meanings that the term *fixation* (*Fixierung*) had in Freud's early writings—namely, (1) a concentrated hypnotic stare, (2) a symptom that has become "permanently established," and (3) an idea that has become "fixated" to a memory. See, in this connection, James Strachey's editorial note to Freud 1892–93, S.E., 1:125 n.

to arise from a congenital anomaly or, alternatively, from an injury to the immature organism. Sigmund Freud received firsthand experience in the diagnosis of such phenomena from his work as a specialist on childhood cerebral paralyses (1888a, 1891a, 1891c, 1897a). Writing in the last and most comprehensive of this series of studies, he distinguished three forms of cerebral lesion in his postmortem materials: (1) *traumatic* (caused by physical accidents); (2) *vascular* (due to disturbances in circulation); and (3) *inflammatory* (the result of infections). The outcome of all three forms, he reported, is invariably "inhibitions in development" of the surrounding brain tissue (1897a: Chap. 4, § 2–4; Chap. 5, §B [a]).

Turning to the subject of instinctual fixations—the dynamic and Freudian version of this medical concept—there is a direct line of influence between Darwin, late-nineteenth-century students of animal behavior, and Sigmund Freud. Darwin, proceeding on the Lamarckian basis of the inheritance of acquired characteristics, had paid close attention, in *Variation of Animals and Plants under Domestication* (1868) and *The Descent of Man* (1871), to the way in which instincts, inhibited or otherwise altered by new habits, might help to account for evolutionary change. Writing in *Variation of Animals and Plants,* he reported along these lines: "An animal when once accustomed to an unnatural diet, which can generally be effected only during youth, dislikes its proper food, as Spallanzani found to be the case with a pigeon which had been long fed on meat. . . . The caterpillars of the *Bombyx hesperus* feed in a state of nature on the leaves of the *Café diable,* but, after having been reared on the Ailanthus, they would not touch the *Café diable,* and actually died of hunger" (1868, 2:304).

Darwin's suggestive observations on this score soon yielded to a more comprehensive theory of instinctual fixations, a theory that encompassed an early experimental insight into the celebrated ethological phenomenon of "imprinting." It was as an ardent spokesman for both Darwinian and Spencerian theories of instinct that Douglas Spalding (1873) conducted the following series of pioneering investigations upon newly hatched chicks. Having hooded some twenty of these little creatures just as they exited from the shell, Spalding allowed his experimental subjects to remain blinded for one to three days. Upon removing the blindfolds, Spalding observed his chicks with the closest attention. He discovered that a chick blinded for up to three days could, with sight restored, peck at an approaching fly on the first attempt with nearly "infallible accuracy." Similarly, chicks made deaf upon hatching (Spalding sealed their ears with gum and then carefully tested them for hearing) were immediately attracted to their mother's call once the gum was removed at the end of the third day. Even blindfolded chicks, he found, relentlessly pursued a cackling sound. Spalding also ascertained that chicks will faithfully follow the first moving object that they see—be it a mother hen or any other creature, including a human being—and he therefore counted an instinct "to follow" among the innate behavioral patterns he had experimentally documented. Finally he determined that the instincts of the chick emerge at critical times, and that they are occasionally lost if they are not practiced at these times. Chicks unhooded after four days, for example, refused to follow Spalding about and instead showed only intense fear at his approach. In a like manner, chicks kept deaf for as long as ten days were no longer able to recognize their mother's call. Spalding compared these transitory learning abilities to the sucking instinct in human infants, an instinct that, although almost perfect at birth, is soon lost if the child is spoon-fed for several days.

Picking up on Spalding's experiments, George Romanes later reported in his *Mental Evolution in Animals* (1883:212–18) that hens without previous maternal experience will raise a brood of young belonging to another species (for example, ducklings, peachicks, and, in one of Romanes's experiments, three orphaned ferrets). One zealous hen in Romanes's studies raised three successive broods of ducklings and then showed the greatest consternation when a fourth brood (this time of chicks) refused to take to the water like the last three!

William James (1842–1910), in his monumental *Principles of Psychology*, subsequently synthesized the experimental work of Romanes and Spalding into two general laws of instinctual perversion: the law of "the *inhibition of instincts by habits*" (covering the exclusive attachment of an instinct to its first-eliciting object); and the law of "the *transitoriness of instincts*" (1890, 2:394).

It was through the field of sexual pathology that William James's two laws, together with relevant clinical details about human beings, came to the attention of Sigmund Freud in the 1890s. James's laws were applied by Albert Moll to developmental disorders of the "libido sexualis" in a work that Freud carefully read in 1897 (Moll 1897b:466–67, 500; see Chapter 8 in this book). Similarly, in *Sexual Inversion*, Havelock Ellis endorsed the idea that strong homosexual impressions at an early age could bring about inverted object choice and an "arrest" in subsequent psychosexual development (1897:138–39). (Ellis had bisexuality theory in mind, among other points, when he drew this conclusion.) Joining Ellis in support of the theory of instinctual fixations was a female physician from America, whose views he presented in an anonymous appendix to *Sexual Inversion*. In her treatment of this subject, Dr. K. cited the distinguished authority of none other than Charles Darwin, referring to his observations, already cited here, on the plasticity of youthful eating habits among animals.[22]

22. See Ellis 1897, Appendix E, p. 198. Freud owned, and from the evidence of his annotations, read with care the 1896 German translation of Ellis's *Sexual Inversion* (Freud library, New York). It is not known precisely when Freud read this work, although it was probably around the turn of the century, when he first spoke to Fliess about "collecting material for the sexual theory" (*Origins*, p. 309, letter of 26 January 1900), and certainly by 1905, when Freud's *Three Essays* appeared in print. Ellis's book, incidentally, was published in German translation a year before the English-language version became available.

Another student of sexual pathology whose works were known to Freud, and who cited similar zoological findings in explaining the problem of sexual perversion, was Albert von Schrenck-Notzing (1898–99:24).

Behind the developmental theory of arrests and fixations there lies a further important biological assumption, one fully recognized by Darwin and other evolutionarily minded thinkers—namely, that such pathological states invariably resemble the permanent forms of lower organisms. In *The Descent of Man*, under the specific heading "Arrest in Development," Darwin took as his paradigmatic example the microcephalous idiot. Such idiots resemble the lower types of mankind, Darwin related, in most of their general cranial features, in the protruding jaw, and in the remarkable hairiness of their bodies. Judged in more behavioral terms, such idiots betrayed their arrested capabilities in their love of imitation, grimacing, climbing furniture and trees, crawling on all fours, and in their occasionally smelling each mouthful of food before consuming it (1871, 1:121–22; 1874:35–36). It was under this same general rubric that Richard von Krafft-Ebing, in his *Lehrbuch der Psychiatrie*, classified several well-known forms of mental disease—for example, idiocy and so-called moral insanity (1879–80, 2:200–214). In his *Psychopathia Sexualis*, he later reported the particularly instructive case of an imbecile whose sexual impulses were "manifested periodically and intensively, as in animals" (1899 trans.:447).

Freud was fully conversant from his student days with the evolutionary implications of such developmental arrests. Ernst Brücke had assigned Freud as his first major research topic at the Physiological Institute the problem of ascertaining the nature of large and peculiar "Reissner cells" found scattered throughout the spinal chord of *Ammocoetes (Petromyzon)*, a primitive genus of fish. When Freud undertook this research project, the spinal chord of lower vertebrates was known to be characterized by an arrangement of *bipolar* ganglion cells. Higher vertebrates were believed to possess exclusively *unipolar* ganglia. Freud was able to show that the spinal chord of petromyzon possesses both types of cells—itself an important anatomical contribution to evolutionary theory (see Fig. 7.3). As for the Reissner cells (located in the posterior nerve root), Freud discovered that they, too, were a form of spinal ganglion cell but had remained within the spinal chord. Finally, he observed certain Reissner-like cellular elements on the surface of the spinal chord, between the posterior nerve root and the peripheral ganglia (see Fig. 7.4). Deducing that these cells were the evolutionary link between the central and the peripheral ganglia, he proclaimed that "it is not surprising if, in an animal that in many respects represents a permanent embryo, there are cells that have remained behind and that indicate the path the spinal ganglion cells once traveled" (1878a:139). To use Freud's later psychoanalytic terminology, such laggard cells were "fixated" in the midst of their evolutionary course.

Years later Freud found this evolutionary-anatomical parallel to his psychoanalytic findings of important didactic use in his *Introductory Lectures on Psycho-Analysis*. After describing his youthful discoveries about petromyzon, with its laggard ganglion cells, Freud went on to say:

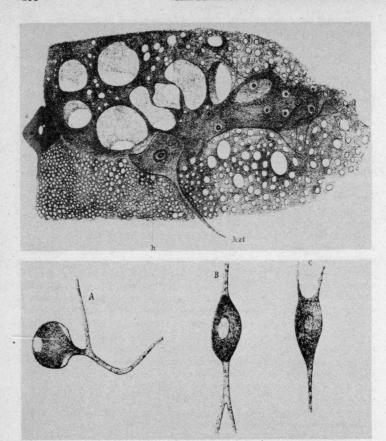

Fig. 7.3. Unipolar, bipolar, and tripolar ganglia from the spinal chord of *Ammocoetes* (*Petromyzon planeri*). *Above*: a unipolar ganglion or Reissner cell (*h*) located near the central canal (*c*) of the spinal chord. *Below*: ganglia in the periphery showing all stages of transition between (*A*) unipolar, (*B*) bipolar, and (*C*) tripolar forms. (From Freud 1877*a*: Fig. 1; and 1878*a*: Plate 1, Fig. 4.)

I will therefore declare without more ado that I regard it as possible in the case of every particular sexual trend that some portions of it have stayed behind at earlier stages of its development, even though other portions may have reached their final goal. . . . Let me further make it clear that we propose to describe the lagging behind of a part trend at an earlier stage as a *fixation*—a fixation, that is, of the instinct. (1916–17, S.E., 16:340)

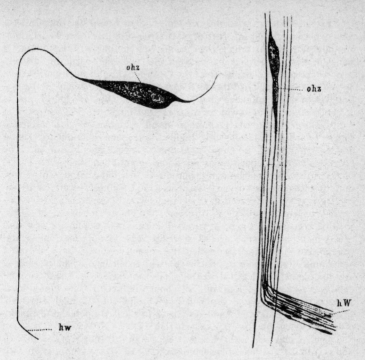

Fig. 7.4. A transitional cellular element (*ohz*) between the central canal and the posterior nerve root (*hW*) in *Ammocoetes* (*Petromyzon planeri*). *Left*: the cell in isolation. *Right*: the cell *in situ*, overlying the nerve fibers of other cells. The transitional cell possesses features intermediate between the unipolar Reissner cells (Fig. 7.3, [*h*]) and the peripheral (bipolar) ganglia (Fig. 7.3, [*B*]). (From Freud 1978a: Plate 3, Figs. 3 and 4.)

Regression. The concepts of fixation and regression possess complementary roles in Freudian theory. Freud held that the neurotic falls ill either from a developmental inhibition in the libido or from a subsequent libidinal regression to a point of partial fixation (1912–13, *S.E.*, 13:17); and that there is every possible degree of cooperation between these two etiological extremes (1916–17, *S.E.*, 16:364). Frustration in adult sexual life generally triggers the regressive side of this neurotic process (1912c, *S.E.*, 12:231–32).[23]

23. I am speaking here primarily of *temporal* regression. Freud distinguished three forms of regression: *temporal, topographical,* and *formal,* although ultimately he held them all to be fundamentally the same—i.e., as tending toward the "primitive" (1900a, *S.E.*, 5:548; paragraph added in 1914). Historically the notion of temporal regression came first in Freud's thinking. See S. W. Jackson 1969.

Freud scholars have long pointed out that Freud was indebted for this general concept of regression to the English neurologist John Hughlings Jackson (1835–1911) and his notion of "dissolution." [24] Jackson, in turn, derived his ideas on the "evolution" and the "dissolution" of the nervous system from the evolutionary philosophy of Herbert Spencer (1855, 1862). Although Jackson's doctrine of psychical dissolution was of great influence upon Freud, it is only one of several aspects of his theory of mind to which Freud was indebted.

Jackson conceived the human mind in terms of a hierarchical series of functional levels, with "higher," voluntary functions overlaying and "keeping down" the more involuntary, "lower" ones (1884:58). The lower functional capacities of mind, he maintained, had been superseded in the course of human evolution by the higher ones, which now serve to integrate and oversee the whole; and a similar evolutionary sequence was to be observed in individual mental development. In senescence, various neurological diseases, and most forms of insanity, Jackson recognized a general reversal of this evolutionary process and called such phenomena, after Herbert Spencer, "dissolutions" in mental functioning.[25] He also taught that the lower functional levels of mind —dynamically and subconsciously present in all healthy individuals— are temporarily unleashed during states of sleeping and dreaming (1894:412, 415 n.). "Find out all about dreams," Freud later quoted Jackson as saying, "and you will have found out all about insanity" (1900a, S.E., 5:569; note added in 1914 and based upon the testimony of Ernest Jones, who heard Jackson's remark).

One of Jackson's most detailed applications of the theory of dissolution was to the problem of speech disorders (1879). In conjunction with his dissolution theory, he appealed to an ingenious model of cognitive

24. See, for example, Jelliffe 1937; Stengel 1953, 1963; and particularly S. W. Jackson 1969.

25. Jackson (1879:309) explicitly credited Spencer for this term. Spencer, who had discussed the idea of dissolution in the context of healthy senescence, had not himself realized its potential application to nervous diseases. (Later he privately acknowledged Jackson's innovation in this regard. See Duncan 1908, 2:335; Spencer to E. L. Youmans, 9 January 1883.) In addition to Spencer's role in bringing this doctrine to Jackson's attention, there is good reason to believe that Jackson was influenced by one of his principal teachers, Thomas Laycock, whose treatise *Mind and Brain* (1860; 2nd ed., 1869, *1*:ii, 414–15) had endorsed a similar theory. Laycock, who also preceded Jackson in espousing a hierarchical-developmental model of nervous functioning, set forth his doctrine of "retrocession" or "disvolution" in disease in the 1869 edition of *Mind and Brain*. Laycock's theory may have been in partial response to the publication of Darwin's evolutionary views, but Laycock also reported that he had "long taught" the doctrine of retrocession to his medical students (1869, *1*:ii). Inasmuch as such doctrines were recognized by certain nonevolutionary physicians before Darwin and Spencer, this claim seems plausible. Jackson later acknowledged Laycock's independent influence on him when he wrote about Laycock's "reflex theory" of the brain in 1875: "I have used as synonymous with dissolution, the expression 'Reduction to a more Automatic Condition.' The phenomena of dissolution, as seen in cases of 'Diseases of the Mind,' seem to me to illustrate in a very striking way Laycock's doctrines of the Reflex Function of the Brain and Herbert Spencer's doctrines on Evolution of the Nervous System. Insanity is dissolution . . ." (1875:38, n. 1). On this historical issue, see S. W. Jackson 1969:763–65; Magoun 1960:189–90; and Greenblatt 1965. Pagel (1954) has traced the notion of pathological regressions to a number of early nineteenth-century medical thinkers.

malfunctioning in which the recurrent fixed utterances of aphasiatics were attributed to a Darwinian "survival of the fittest" among states of conflicting mental discharge. In aphasia, Jackson believed, such fixed utterances, usually words or phrases learned early in life, represent the permanent victors in the aphasiatic's struggle to speak.

It was through this last area of Jackson's medical researches that the theory of dissolution came to Freud's attention. In *On Aphasia* (1891*b*), Freud had nothing but praise for Jackson's views on the subject and made them part of his theoretical critique of the then popular Wernicke-Lichtheim theory of aphasic disorders. This theory ascribed the extraordinary variety of aphasic phenomena to hypothetical lesions within one or more of the three main localized centers of the speech apparatus —the motoric, the acoustic, and the visual. Freud pointed up the many inadequacies inherent in the Wernicke-Lichtheim localization model and proposed instead a dynamic and developmental approach to the problem. It is these last two features that justify Bernfeld's (1944:357) characterization of *On Aphasia* as the first "Freudian" book.

Freud was particularly emphatic about the difficulty of knowing whether a lesion is *in* a certain speech center or is merely disturbing the paths of association *between* centers; and because of this difficulty, a rigid appeal to localized lesions seemed both premature and grossly oversimplified. What is really important, he insisted, is an appreciation of how a hypothetical lesion might affect the whole system, dynamically understood; and he set forth such a scheme in his monograph. Freud's model even took into account individual differences in verbal learning. For example, given two individuals with an identical lesion within the acoustic center, one who has learned much of his verbal capabilities through reading should suffer milder speech disturbances than one who is illiterate.

At the heart of his attack upon localization theory, Freud placed his endorsement of Jackson's doctrine of mental dissolutions:

> In assessing the functions of the speech apparatus under pathological conditions we are adopting as a guiding principle Hughlings Jackson's doctrine that all these modes of reaction represent instances of functional retrogression (dis-involution) of a highly organized apparatus, and therefore correspond to earlier states of its functional development. This means that under all circumstances an arrangement of associations which, having been acquired later, belongs to a higher level of functioning, will be lost, while an earlier and simpler one will be preserved. From this point of view, a great number of aphasic phenomena can be explained. (1891*b*; 1953*a* trans.:87)

Elsewhere in his monograph, Freud made it clear that Jackson's doctrine of dissolution had other wide-ranging applications for neuropathology: such retrogressive phenomena were necessarily "inherent in the general properties of an apparatus equipped for association . . ." (1953*a* trans.:89).

Freud's theory of aphasia had a direct influence upon his subsequent conception of the neuroses. Speaking of libidinal regressions some sixteen years later, in 1907, he commented that such regressive phenomena are to be expected "wherever developmental processes are involved" (*Minutes, 1*: 101). Nor had he forgotten by this late date the intellectual debt that he owed to Hughlings Jackson in this regard, for he wrote to Karl Abraham that same year:

> I have always assumed that the individuals generally described as idiopathic who later become obviously paranoid have only inadequately completed the necessary development from auto-erotism to object-love. With a proportion of cases of dementia this factor would supply the predisposition that we have been seeking for the later illness, and that would fit in admirably with the general pathological view that illness always implies a regression in development. (The *evolution* and *involution* of British authors.) (*Freud/Abraham Letters*, p. 5, letter of 26 July 1907)

Finally, the Jackson-Freud theory of psychical regression united Freud's conceptions of dreaming and the neuroses, in which *temporal* regressions are so pronounced, within a common biogenetic context. Through the study of dreams and neuroses, Freud wrote in 1919, one ultimately perceives "a phylogenetic childhood—a picture of the development of the human race, of which the individual's development is in fact an abbreviated recapitulation influenced by the chance circumstances of life." It was for this reason, he further concluded, that psychoanalysis could "claim a high place among the sciences which are concerned with the reconstruction of the earliest and most obscure periods of the beginnings of the human race" (1900a, *S.E.*, 5: 548–49; discussion added in 1919).

According to Stengel (1963: 348), it was through Freud that Jackson's ideas entered psychiatry. Although this assertion is perhaps true from the point of view of the enormous influence that Freud's ideas subsequently exerted in psychiatry as well as in psychology, it nevertheless obscures the fact that Jackson's dynamic approach to mind, including the general concept of regression, had already achieved widespread circulation independently of Freud before the turn of the century. In England, for example, both Sully (1884: 683) and Clouston (1883; 1892 ed.: 16, 508; 1891: 5, 113) applied Jackson's dynamic-developmental doctrines to mental diseases; [26] while in America Adolf Meyer, the Swiss psychiatrist who had studied with Jackson in 1891 before immigrating to the United States, also endorsed his doctrines.[27] In France similar notions of *dissolution, involution,* and *regression,*

26. Sully (1893: 362) also described a regressive trend in dreaming: "Now our dreams are a means of conserving these successive [earlier] personalities. When asleep we go back to the old ways of looking at things and of feeling about them, to impulses and activities which long ago dominated us. . . ." Freud subsequently cited this passage in the 1914 and later editions of his *Interpretation of Dreams* (1900a, *S.E.*, 4: 60; 5: 591).

27. On Meyer, see Ellenberger (1970: 291), who also cites British neurologist Henry Head and German neuropsychiatrist Kurt Goldstein as important exponents of Jackson's doctrines.

found in the writings of numerous contemporary neurologists and psychologists, were probably derived from the combined influence of Spencer, Jackson, and French psychiatrist J. Moreau (1845). Charles Féré, in a book owned by Freud—*L'Instinct sexuel: Évolution et dissolution* (1899 [London library])—gave a particularly good synopsis of the doctrine of regression:

> When the circumstances of life become abnormal, when nutrition abates as in old age, the hierarchy of instincts becomes disturbed, the instincts relative to the social group and to the species tend to subordinate themselves to the more egoistic instincts; there occurs an involution which has been interpreted as a tendency to regression, to the return to an ancestral or infantile state. (1899:5)[28]

Clearly Freud was in good medical company when he, too, applied the concept of regression to mental pathology.

The pertinacity of early impressions. In his Summary of the *Three Essays on the Theory of Sexuality,* Freud appealed to a third prerequisite of psychoneurosis besides the mechanisms of fixation and regression. Calling it "a provisional psychological concept" and a psychical factor "of unknown origin," he proclaimed the "pertinacity of early impressions" to be an essential component in his theory of the childhood origins of psychoneurosis (1905d, S.E., 7:242). In *Introductory Lectures on Psycho-Analysis* (1916–17) and again in *An Outline of Psycho-Analysis* (1940a [1938]), Freud offered a biological "analogy" in justification of this important principle. The embryological experiments of Wilhelm Roux (1850–1924), he said, had convincingly shown that the prick of a needle into an embryonic cell mass induces far more damage during the early stages of growth than it does at a later stage (S.E., 16:361; S.E., 23:185).[29] As it turns out, Freud was personally familiar with this general embryological principle from his earliest work on childhood cerebral paralyses. There, too, the sooner the lesion occurs, the more extensive is the resulting inhibition in brain development. In his last major monograph on the subject of cerebral paralysis, Freud (1897a:229) compared this basic principle to the same embryological experiments he later cited in a more psychological context in 1916 and 1938.

28. For further appeals to the doctrine of regression, see Ribot (1881:90–105; 1897:226–27, 423, 436), Janet (1889:305–14, 366–443; 1898, 1:469), Dallemagne (1894:601, 609), and Sollier (1900:163–165). Freud's copy (London library) of Sollier's *Le Problème de la mémoire* (1900) bears Freud's personal underscorings of Sollier's terms *la régression* (p. 163) and *involution* (p. 165) in speaking of the loss of recent memories (and the corresponding return of memories from early childhood) as a result of senescence. Sollier ascribed this general law of memory regression to Ribot (1881:48, 51), who drew upon Spencer and Hughlings Jackson. Dallemagne (1894:601) mentioned Spencer. Janet credited his concept of regression (*désagrégation psychologique*) to Moreau as the latter's "fundamental law of mental illness" (1898, 1:469). See once again Ellenberger (1970:290, 360, 403) on the independent influence of Moreau.

29. See also Freud's 31 October 1934 discussion of this subject with Joseph Wortis (1954:53).

Freud as Psycho-Lamarckian

One last general influence of evolutionary thinking upon Freud stems not from Darwinism per se but rather from the widespread influence of Jean-Baptiste Lamarck (1744–1829) and his theory of the inheritance of acquired characteristics. Freud, as a zealous psycho-Lamarckian, occupied an extreme wing of the Neo-Lamarckian phalanx in post-Darwinian theory.[30] He fully subscribed to the psycho-Lamarckian efforts of individuals like August Pauly (1850–1914), the German biologist who so greatly influenced the celebrated embryologist Hans Spemann (Jones 1957:312).[31] The position of thinkers like Pauly was that internal physiological needs and the organism's efforts to satisfy such needs—not the principle of natural selection—are the primary agents of evolutionary change. Since such adaptive reactions to internal needs are inherited, evolution could proceed far more straightforwardly, and rapidly, than along purely Darwinian lines. Freud became so enamored of this position that during the First World War he considered making a major psychoanalytic contribution to this psycho-Lamarckian cause, in collaboration with Sándor Ferenczi. He described this plan to Karl Abraham in a letter of 11 November 1917:

30. Ritvo (1965) has sought to attribute Freud's Lamarckian position on heredity to the influence of Charles Darwin, inasmuch as Darwin had openly endorsed this Lamarckian principle of evolutionary change as an important supplemental factor to natural selection. Such heavy emphasis upon Darwin, however, is inappropriate in this context. In Freud's scientific generation (i.e., those born before 1860) virtually all biologists, including his university professors in this field, were Lamarckians to an extent—in addition to whatever other theories of evolutionary change they may have espoused. In any event, Freud's endorsement of Lamarck's ideas on the importance of internal "needs" as an agent of evolutionary change was utterly non-Darwinian. Darwin called this aspect of his French predecessor's theory the "Lamarck nonsense of a 'tendency to progression,' 'adaptations from the slow willing of animals,' &c.!" (1887, 2:23; Darwin to Joseph Hooker, 11 January 1844). I might add that Ritvo's publication of 1965 suggests a much too immediate line of influence between Darwin and Freud. In more recent publications, Ritvo (1972; especially 1974:181) has acknowledged more indirect sources for Darwin's influence upon Freud. In particular, Ritvo has emphasized Freud's 1870s contact with his Vienna University teacher Carl Claus, who was both a Lamarckian and a Haeckelian biogeneticist. Regarding Haeckel, Ernst Cassirer (1950:163) points out that he was one of the major late-nineteenth-century psycho-Lamarckians within German-speaking countries (particularly in his later writings).

Freud's psycho-Lamarckian propensities may owe something to the influence of Ewald Hering (1834–1918), Josef Breuer's principal scientific mentor. Hering's views on this subject were expressed in a famous lecture delivered at the Viennese Imperial Academy of Sciences in 1870. Entitled "Über das Gedächtniss als eine allgemeine Function der organisirten Materie" ("On Memory as a General Function of Organized Matter"), Hering's lecture had emphasized the close connection between heredity and memory, thus giving the inheritance of acquired characteristics a partly psychological foundation. Like Freud, Hering was a dualist in his approach to mental phenomena. According to Jones (1953:222), Hering invited Freud to join him as his assistant in Prague while Freud was still attached to Brücke's Physiological Institute. For further details on Hering's theory of heredity, see Russell (1930:112–13, 123–26) and Gould (1977:99–100), and, for an English translation of Hering's famous lecture, Butler's *Unconscious Memory* (1880).

31. For Pauly's work (especially 1905) and its influence, see Baltzer 1967: 8–10, 36, 48, 130–31, 141–42; Spemann 1948:145–50, 157–64; and Hamburger 1969:1125.

The idea is to put Lamarck entirely on our ground and to show that the "necessity" that according to him creates and transforms organisms is nothing but the power of unconscious ideas over one's own body, of which we see the remnants in hysteria, in short the "omnipotence of thoughts." This would actually supply a psycho-analytic explanation of [biological] adaptation; it would put the coping stone on psycho-analysis. There would be two linked principles of progressive change, adaptation of one's body and subsequent transformation of the external world (autoplasticity and heteroplasticity), etc. (*Freud/Abraham Letters*, pp. 261–62)

Such a scheme, he related to Ferenczi, would leave a desirable psychoanalytic "visiting card" for biologists (Jones 1957:312).

Although Freud subsequently dropped the project (for reasons that are unclear), he steadfastly maintained his psycho-Lamarckian position to the end of his life, confidently dismissing the mounting attacks upon the Lamarckian viewpoint with hardly an afterthought. "Lamarck's theory of evolution," he once proclaimed, "coincides with the final outcome of psychoanalytic thinking" (*Letters*, p. 317, to Georg Groddeck, 5 June 1917).[32]

SUMMARY AND CONCLUSION:

DARWIN'S INFLUENCE IN RETROSPECT

It is certainly fitting that the influence of Charles Darwin, the man whose evolutionary writings did so much to encourage young Freud in the study of biology and medicine (Chapter 1), should have been so instrumental in turning psychoanalysis into a dynamic, and especially a genetic, psychobiology of mind. Indeed, perhaps nowhere was the impact of Darwin, direct and indirect, more exemplary or fruitful outside of biology proper than within Freudian psychoanalysis. Yet it was not until Freud had freed himself from the quest for a neurophysiological theory of mind (Chapter 4) that he finally began to reap the full benefits of this Darwinian legacy within psychoanalytic theory. By then— the late 1890s—Darwin's influence upon Freud's scientific generation had become so extensive that Freud himself probably never knew just how much he really owed to this one intellectual source. Darwinian assumptions (1) pervaded the whole nascent discipline of child psychology from which Freud drew, and to which he in turn contributed, so much; (2) reinforced the immense importance of sexuality in the contemporary understanding of psychopathology; (3) alerted Freud and others to the manifold potentials of historical reductionism (the use of the

32. See Chapter 10 for the use Freud made of this Lamarckian position when he extended psychoanalytic theory into the wider realms of anthropology, sociology, and the history of religion.

past as a key to the present); (4) underlay Freud's fundamental conceptions of infantile erotogenic zones, of human psychosexual stages, and of the archaic nature of the unconscious; and (5) contributed a number of major psychical concepts—like those of fixation and regression—to Freud's overall theory of psychopathology. Finally, the simultaneous influence of Lamarckian notions served to convince Freud that psychoanalysis, with its insight into conscious and unconscious psychical adaptation, was itself a culminatory achievement in evolutionary theory. It was doubtless for reasons such as these that Freud, toward the end of his life, recommended that the study of evolution be included in every prospective psychoanalyst's program of training (1927a, S.E., 20:252).

At the same time, the revolutionary doctrines of Darwin and Freud brought about a kindred metaphysical shift in Western intellectual thought. As Freud himself once proclaimed, the universal narcissism of mankind has suffered three great blows at the hands of post-Renaissance science. The first or *cosmological* blow came when Copernicus insisted that the earth was not the center of the universe. The second or *biological* blow was rendered by Darwin and his supporters when they showed that man was not separate from lower animals in the organic scheme of things. The third great blow—the *psychological* one—was delivered by psychoanalysis, Freud claimed, when it showed that "*the ego is not master in its own house*" (1917a, S.E., 17:139–43).

Nevertheless, if Freud and his followers were the ones who indeed delivered this third blow to man's narcissistic pride, their achievement was a direct extension of the second, or Darwinian, blow. For it was Darwin who handed Freud that most powerful instrument—namely, evolutionary theory's stress upon the dynamic, the instinctual, and, above all, the *nonrational* in human behavior.

Finally, more than any other scientific influence, the post-Darwinian Zeitgeist provided a powerful common denominator, linking Freud to his intimate friend and scientific colleague Wilhelm Fliess, on the one hand, and to the rise of the sexology movement, on the other. For in order to rationalize and embrace Wilhelm Fliess's "visionary" discoveries in the 1890s, Freud found it necessary to draw from the evolutionary and psychobiological wellsprings that inspired the parallel rise of the sexology movement. And within the nascent sexology movement—itself largely inspired by Darwinism—virtually every important aspect of Freud's own theory of psychosexual development can be found. Therefore I now turn to this movement and to the small group of Freudian "alter egos" who pioneered its earliest years.

8

Freud and the Sexologists

It was in December 1896 that Freud first took the fundamental step of equating neurosis with a pathologically repressed, or *"negative,"* state of sexual perversion (*Origins,* pp. 180, 189). And with this one key insight, psychoanalysis became an integral part of the nascent science of sexology. From December 1896 on, Freud accordingly found it imperative to explain the problem of sexual perversion simultaneously with that of the psychoneuroses. This is precisely what he proceeded to do; and he eventually went so far as to sanction therapeutic treatment of the "positive" forms of sexual perversion as a regular part of his psychoanalytic enterprise (1905*d, S.E.,* 7:232, n. 1 [added in 1915]).

In the historical alliance of psychoanalysis with sexology, it is a reflection of Freud's subsequent greatness that his name has become associated with many important ideas about human sexuality that he did not originate. Terms and constructs like *libido, component instincts, erotogenic zones, autoerotism,* and *narcissism*—all generally associated in twentieth-century consciousness with Freud's name alone—were actually brought into scientific circulation between 1880 and 1900 by other contemporary students of sexology.[1] Similarly, the problematical

---

1. For the pre-Freudian use of the term *libido,* see Benedikt (1868:448–54), where the word occurs nine times in seven pages, Meynert (1890:195), Krafft-Ebing (1889:1–6), Moll (1891:123–39), and, for additional examples, Ellenberger (1970:303, 328). The notion that libido consists of "component [*komponenten*] drives" may be found, among other sources, in the writings of Moll (1897*b*:29) and Bloch (1902–3, 2:189, 192). Freud (1905*d*) later spoke of the libido's *Partialtriebe* (translated "component instincts") as well as of libidinal *Komponenten.* The notion of erotogenic zones comes from the French. Ernest Chambard (1881:65) seems to have been the first to speak of erogenic centers (*centres-érogènes*) in the Freudian sense, and he provided a comprehensive description of such zones. Féré (1883:131) subsequently emphasized the similarity between such *zones érogènes* and Charcot's well-known *zones hystérogènes,* an analogy that Chambard himself had apparently overlooked. See also Binet and Féré's *Le Magnétisme animal* (1887:112) and Krafft-Ebing's *Psychopathia Sexualis* (1886 and later editions: Section II, "Physiological Facts"). For a comprehensive historical review of this last derivation in terms, see Kern (1975:130–31) and Havelock Ellis (1928, 7:111–20). It was Ellis who introduced the terms *autoerotism* and *Narcissus-like* in describing cer-

The sexual nature of thumb-sucking as illustrated by the Hungarian pediatrician Lindner (1879:74). His paper on this subject was later cited by Freud in the *Three Essays on the Theory of Sexuality* (1905*d*), a citation that perhaps owes something to Fliess (1897:185 n.), who also seems to have drawn on Lindner.

subject of infantile sexuality had been repeatedly discussed by pediatricians, educators, and sexologists before Freud himself broached this issue in his *Three Essays on the Theory of Sexuality* (1905*d*). Stephen Kern (1973, 1975), who has presented by far the most detailed historical survey to date on the subject of childhood sexuality, lists over a dozen publications between 1867 and 1905 in which Freud's views were clearly presaged; and other anticipations could be added to this list. Not only did many of these writers, like Henry Maudsley (1867:284), S. Lindner (1879), Bernard Pérez (1886:272), Friedrich Scholz (1891: 151), Paul Sollier (1891:84), Jules Dallemagne (1894:525), Wilhelm Stekel (1895:247), Karl Groos (1899:326), Hermann Rohleder (1901: 14–16), Iwan Bloch (1902–3, 2:253–58), and Lewis Terman (1905: 174), recognize the relative normalcy of sexual manifestations in childhood; but a few others, like Max Dessoir (1894), Albert Moll (1897*b*), Havelock Ellis (1898*a*, 1900*b*, 1901), and Sanford Bell (1902), went even further in arguing that the normal human libido develops in sequential, prepubertal stages—attaching itself to different "love" objects in the process. Still others before Freud had noted possible characterological consequences of excessive infantile sucking, while toilet training had been specifically connected by several pre-Freudians with the personal traits of orderliness, cleanliness, punctu-

---

tain aspects of normal sexual activity (Ellis 1898*a*). Näcke (1899*b*:375) subsequently translated Ellis's concept of narcissism into German as *Narcismus,* referring it, as Ellis had not, to certain forms of sexual perversion. Freud adopted this term around 1910 (e.g., *Three Essays,* 1905*d,* S.E., 7:145 n.; note added to the second edition). Unknown to Ellis, Näcke, and Freud, Alfred Binet (1887:264 n.) preceded them all by comparing certain fetishists who take themselves as their preferred sexual object to the famous fable of Narcissus.

ality, and pedantry.[2] As Kern concludes, "almost every element of Freud's theory of child sexuality was exactly anticipated, or in some way implied or suggested, before him" (1973:137).

Yet no one has sufficiently shown in connection with this sizable body of pre-Freudian literature what sort of theoretical rationale, if any, tied together these observations and claims. The importance of the known "facts" about infantile sexual development underwent continual alteration between 1880 and 1910 as differing theories, including Freud's own, were developed to encompass them. Similarly, what has also not been established is how this body of contemporary knowledge about human sexuality interacted in the late 1890s and early 1900s with the psychoanalytic paradigm that Freud himself was attempting to develop. From whom did Freud draw in this related field of study? And what did he add to the previous understanding of human psychosexual development? It is to these specific historical problems that I now turn.

THE EMERGENT SCIENCE OF SEXUAL PATHOLOGY

The formal, scientific study of sexual pathology began to emerge as a recognized field of inquiry in the 1870s and early 1880s. Who were the early pioneers in this nascent science? At the head of the first page of his *Three Essays on the Theory of Sexuality* (1905*d*), Freud credited much of his own knowledge in this field to the writings of Richard Krafft-Ebing, Albert Moll, P. J. Möbius, Havelock Ellis, Albert Schrenck-Notzing, Leopold Löwenfeld, Albert Eulenburg, Iwan Bloch, and Magnus Hirschfeld.

Of these nine pioneers, it was Richard von Krafft-Ebing (1840–1902), professor of psychiatry and Freud's distinguished colleague at the University of Vienna, who did more than anyone else to put sexual pathology "on the map" as a respected branch of medical science. Iwan Bloch (1902–3, 2:xv) spoke for most of his contemporaries when he proclaimed Krafft-Ebing "the true founder of modern sexual pathology." Similarly, Havelock Ellis (1933:222) later honored Krafft-Ebing as "the first great clinician of sexual inversion." Although not the first person to consider the general problem seriously, it was nevertheless Krafft-Ebing who successfully transformed the approach to it from one of stringent legal containment and great social taboo to one of legitimate and sympathetic medical concern.[3] He spoke of perverts as "step-

2. See particularly Scholz (1891:112) and, for additional references, Kern (1973, 1975).
3. Of Krafft-Ebing's precursors, the most important are Carl Heinrich Ulrichs and Carl Westphal, about whom more will be said. Other notable pioneers in the study of sexual perversion include Casper 1863, 1881; Lombroso 1876, 1881, 1893 (with Ferrero), 1894; Charcot and Magnan 1882; and Tarnowsky 1886. A comprehensive bibliography of pre-1900 literature on sexual perversion (particularly homosexuality) may be found in the *Jahrbuch für sexuelle Zwischenstufen, 1* (1899):215–38. For a general history of the study and treatment of sexual pathology, see Heine 1936; and Wettley and Leibbrand 1959.

children of nature" and repeatedly appealed for greater judicial le-
niency whenever such victims of sexual compulsion were brought before the courts. Both as a physician and as a respected forensic witness,
Krafft-Ebing diagnosed perverts as mentally afflicted and, hence, only
partially responsible individuals:

> In former years I considered *conträre Sexualempfindung* ["contrary sex-
> ual feeling"] as a result of neuro-psychical degeneration, and I believe
> that this view is warranted by more recent investigations. As we study
> into the abnormal and diseased conditions from which this malady re-
> sults, the ideas of horror and criminality connected with it disappear,
> and there arises in our minds the sense of duty to investigate what at
> first sight seems so repulsive, and to distinguish, if may be, between a
> perversion of natural instincts which is the result of disease, and the
> criminal offences of a perverted mind against the laws of morality and
> social decency. By doing so the investigations of science will become the
> means of rescuing the honor and re-establishing the social position of
> many an unfortunate whom unthinking prejudice and ignorance would
> class among depraved criminals. It would not be the first time that
> science has rendered a service to justice and to society by teaching that
> what seem to be immoral conditions and actions are but the results of
> disease. (Quoted in Lydston 1889:254)

Krafft-Ebing was also cognizant of the pervert's frequent burden of mental suffering, fears of exposure, blackmail, and so forth, and he threw
the great weight of his medical reputation in favor of selected legal
reforms in the existing German and Austrian statutes, particularly
those dealing with homosexuality.

His sympathy with the plight of sexual deviates was an attitude
shaped by family tradition. His progressive maternal grandfather, the
eminent Heidelberg criminal lawyer Karl Josef Mittermaier (1787–1867),
had previously earned himself popular designation as "the last hope of
the damned" for his spirited defense of such deviates in mid-nineteenth-
century courts (Peterson 1904). Having come under his grandfather's
tutelage as a young Heidelberg University medical student, Krafft-Ebing
absorbed much of this liberal family outlook. It was upon hearing the
famous psychiatrist Wilhelm Griesinger lecture in Zurich, where
Krafft-Ebing had briefly gone as a medical student to recover from a
severe attack of typhoid, that he finally settled upon his medical specialty of mental diseases.

After taking his medical degree in 1863, Krafft-Ebing promptly began building his reputation as one of the foremost psychiatrists on the
Continent. He was quickly rewarded for his diligence by a professorship
in psychiatry at Strasbourg in 1872 and one at Graz the following year.
His *Lehrbuch der gerichtlichen Psychopathologie* (1875) and his *Lehrbuch der Psychiatrie auf klinischer Grundlage* (1879–80) established
his reputation worldwide.

As early as 1866, at the age of twenty-six, Krafft-Ebing had become
interested in the problem of homosexuality through encountering the

Richard von Krafft-Ebing
about 1900.

pioneering works on this subject by Carl Heinrich Ulrichs. Krafft-Ebing later attributed his ambition of erecting a whole science of sexual pathology to Ulrichs's influence. Ulrichs (1826–95), a Hanoverian legal official, was also a self-confessed homosexual. In a series of works published from 1864 onward, at first under the pseudonym of Numa Numantius, Ulrichs had openly discussed the problem of sexual inversion and had sought for a revision of the German legal codes in this domain.[4] It was Ulrichs who coined the term *urning* in reference to homosexuals (an allusion to Uranos in Plato's *Symposium*). He believed that uranism was a hereditary abnormality producing, in men, "a female soul in a male body" ("*Memnon*," 1898 [1868], 7:87). In his numerous publications, he championed a biological theory of homosexual love, citing in this connection the evidence of man's embryonic bisexuality up to the twelfth fetal week, as well as observations by Charles Darwin and Robert Chambers on hermaphroditism in lower animals and plants (1898 [1868], 7:26–33, 133–36).

Ulrichs's writings exerted little direct influence upon the medical world when they were first issued in the 1860s and 1870s, but they did stimulate both Krafft-Ebing and Carl Westphal, editor of the *Archiv für Psychiatrie und Nervenkrankheiten*, to pursue the problem in a

4. Ulrichs's works have been collected into twelve short volumes. See Ulrichs 1898; and for Ulrichs's influence upon Krafft-Ebing, Hirschfeld's Foreword to the first volume, pp. 7–8, where there is also published a grateful 29 January 1879 letter from Krafft-Ebing to Ulrichs.

more systematic, clinical light. Westphal (1870) soon lent his support to the congenital view of homosexuality, coining the expression *conträre Sexualempfindung* ("contrary sexual feeling") for such sexually inverted individuals. He also threw open his journal to clinical studies by others, among them Krafft-Ebing, whose first publication on the subject of sexual pathology appeared there in 1877.

Thereafter, Krafft-Ebing gradually widened his sphere of expertise to include the clinical study of virtually all known classes of perverts—among them lust murderers, necrophiliacs, sadists, masochists, transvestites, nymphomaniacs, exhibitionists, fetishists of all imaginable kinds, lovers of urine and excrement (coprophiliacs), voyeurs, renifleurs, and an endless succession of patients whose only concern for the other sex was a desire for something other than the normal form of coitus. In 1886 the first edition of Krafft-Ebing's famous *Psychopathia sexualis, mit besonderer Berücksichtigung der conträren Sexualempfindung* (Psychopathia Sexualis, with Especial Reference to Antipathic Sexual Instinct) appeared in print; it offered a clinical analysis and formal classification of most major perversions. From that date, Krafft-Ebing's notoriety as a physician of sexual anomalies grew rapidly. Sexually abnormal people from all over the world began sending him their autobiographical histories and requesting his medical advice on how to overcome their afflictions. Some even suggested detailed theoretical explanations of their sexual problems—explanations that Krafft-Ebing often communicated to fellow physicians in successive editions of his book. In a remarkably Freudian-sounding analysis, one such individual insisted that the higher proportion of nervous afflictions among homosexual patients was a purely incidental by-product of the homosexual's constant attempts to "repress" his abnormal libido (1899 trans.:542–46).

Although the *Psychopathia Sexualis* enjoyed immense success, finding its way into seven languages and going through twelve editions in its author's lifetime, Krafft-Ebing himself was far from being a seeker after notoriety. As Victor Robinson (1953:iv–v) has commented about him: "Krafft-Ebing was a physician who wrote for physicians. He did not want the public to read his book, so he gave it a scientific title, employed technical terms, and inscribed the most exciting parts in Latin. . . . It was annoying not to understand the cryptic phrase in the lady's letter: 'While you whine like a dog under the lashes of my servants, you shall witness another *favoritus sudorem pedum mihi lambit.*' " Still, the public was hardly to be foiled by such subterfuges, for most of the book was written in the vernacular. It was this feature of the *Psychopathia Sexualis* that prompted the *British Medical Journal* to lament in 1893 not only the book's recent translation into English (by an initially anonymous translator), but also the fact that Krafft-Ebing had not written his *entire* book in Latin and thus veiled it "in the decent obscurity of a dead language" (p. 1325).

Nonetheless, by the mid-1890s it had become clear to most physicians, particularly those in German-speaking countries, that Krafft-Ebing—already an acknowledged pioneer in the study of hypnotism, hysteria, criminal psychopathology, epilepsy, menstrual psychoses, and many other subjects—had established sexual pathology as an important new branch of medical psychology. With its sober, systematic, and Baconian approach to the whole problem of perversions, the *Psychopathia Sexualis* quickly inspired an almost exponential growth in the scientific literature on sexual deviations. The *Psychopathia Sexualis* itself grew from 45 case histories and 110 pages in 1886 to 238 case histories and 437 pages by the twelfth edition of 1903. In 1899, Magnus Hirschfeld founded the *Jahrbuch für sexuelle Zwischenstufen*, a formal journal for the study of homosexuality and related perversions; and between 1898 and 1908 there appeared over a thousand publications on the subject of homosexuality alone (Hirschfeld 1948:190).

Krafft-Ebing's Theory of "Psychopathia Sexualis"

Although primarily a book about sexual pathology, *Psychopathia Sexualis* (1886) devoted a Preface and three introductory chapters to a broad treatment of the psychology and the physiology of sex. With Friedrich Schiller before him, Krafft-Ebing proclaimed in his Preface that love and hunger govern all world affairs; and he approvingly cited Henry Maudsley's (1872) view that sexual feeling is the primary basis of all social life. Altruism, ethics, aestheticism, and even religious sentiment, he argued, have their deepest roots in sexual feeling. "If man were deprived of sexual distinction and the nobler enjoyments arising therefrom, all poetry and probably all moral tendency would be eliminated from his life" (1899 trans.:1). Particularly in religious devotion, he asserted, the closest parallels are manifested with different forms of sexual perversion—for example, rituals of self-punishment, castigation, and whipping, which are obvious forms of sadomasochism. Finally, Krafft-Ebing saw culture and civilization as having emerged owing to refinements and suppressions of the sexual instinct in man. "Life is a never-ceasing duel between the animal instinct and morality" (1899 trans.:5).

Krafft-Ebing's theory of sexual pathology was straightforward and based upon his general dictum as a psychiatrist that mental illness creates no new instincts but only augments, diminishes, or perverts those that already exist (1879–80, *1*:65). In this connection he set forth a descriptive, four-part system of classification involving *anesthesias* (absence of sexual feeling), *hyperesthesias* (abnormally increased sexual desire), *paradoxias* (manifestations of sexuality in childhood and old age), and *paresthesias* (the sexual perversions proper). In the last of these four categories, Krafft-Ebing distinguished sadism, masochism, fetishism, and homosexuality as the principal subforms. And it was he who coined the terms *sadism, masochism, sexual bondage,* and *psychical hermaphroditism.*

Looking at the sexual perversions from a causal-etiological point of view, Krafft-Ebing held that modern civilization, with its great demands upon the nervous system, was the primary agent of such instinctual malfunctions. Commenting upon the sexual debauchery of Greece, of the Roman Empire, and of seventeenth- and eighteenth-century France, he insisted that "the most monstrous excesses of sexual life . . . can always be traced to psycho-pathological or neuro-pathological conditions of the nations involved" (1899 trans.:6–7). Widely known as the theory of "neuro-psychopathic degeneration," this general doctrine had been borrowed by Krafft-Ebing from the French psychiatrist Bénédict Morel (1857), whose influence pervaded psychiatric theory during the latter half of the nineteenth century. According to Morel's view, a predisposition to either insanity, perversion, or a host of other neurological disorders could be congenitally inherited from a "tainted" relative, himself (or herself) the victim of severe alcoholism, syphilis, debauchery, epilepsy, mental illness, or a variety of other pathogenic agents of neuro-psychopathic heredity. Prior to Krafft-Ebing, the more popular view, particularly that of educators, had been that homosexuality and most other perversions were acquired through seduction, bad example, vice, and similar environmental agents of corrupt habit formation. Although Krafft-Ebing (1877) had at first stressed the need for open-mindedness on this question, he soon ruled out the possibility of truly acquired perversion, except under the most unusual circumstances. It was in this context that he strongly emphasized the distinction between congenital *perversion* and acquired *perversity*—with the latter phenomenon being ascribed to premeditated choice (for instance, homosexual activity faute de mieux, as in prisons).

In considering Krafft-Ebing's views on sexual perversion, it is important to keep in mind that, in spite of his desire to bring greater compassion to the treatment of sexual perversions, he himself was by no means free from the prejudices of his times. Owing to the difficulty of obtaining clinical histories, he had premised his initial theory on a comparatively small number of generally severe cases, often derived from criminal proceedings. His first discussion of homosexuality (1877) described only thirteen such cases, and by 1882 he had collected only four more. Of these seventeen cases, thirteen displayed hereditary taint in the form of insanity in the patient's close ancestry, while the other four were complicated by neuroses. Ten years later, in the seventh edition of the *Psychopathia Sexualis*, Krafft-Ebing had successfully documented hereditary taint in all but four of his forty-seven reported case histories involving homosexuality. He admitted these few cases as acquired and blamed them on excessive masturbation in early youth. Adolescent onanism, he believed, destroys the masturbator's sexual ideals and eventually undermines a normal desire for the opposite sex. (He also laid auxiliary blame upon debauched habits, upon seductions and mutual masturbation in boarding schools, and upon the limitations to normal sexual activity in prisons, ships, garrisons, and the like.)

The atypical nature of Krafft-Ebing's earliest case materials is only part of the reason behind his endorsement of degeneration theory. It is also true that his clinical zeal in adding to these pioneering case histories left a certain psychological clarity to be desired. As Havelock Ellis later observed:

> Krafft-Ebing's methods were open to some objection. His mind was not
> of a severely critical order. He poured out the new and ever-enlarged
> editions of his book with extraordinary rapidity. . . . Krafft-Ebing's great
> service lay in the clinical enthusiasm with which he approached the
> study of sexual perversions. With the firm conviction that he was con-
> quering a great neglected field of morbid psychology which rightly be-
> longs to the physician, he accumulated without any false shame a vast
> mass of detailed histories. . . . (1928, 2:69–70)

And Ellis concluded, "It is as a clinician, rather than as a psychologist,
that we must regard Krafft-Ebing."

Still, it is to Krafft-Ebing's considerable credit that he began, toward
the very end of his life, to reassess his views on the problem of sexual
perversion—and he did so in the light of the newer findings by those
fellow sexologists whose entrance into the field he had inspired.

The Challenge from Association Psychology

No sooner had Krafft-Ebing's *Psychopathia Sexualis* (1886) appeared
than its general theory of sexual perversion was challenged by the
French psychologist Alfred Binet (1857–1911). Differentiating himself
from alienists [5] like Krafft-Ebing, who were preoccupied with the medical and forensic aspects of perversion, Binet (1887) explicitly set out
to study the *acquirement* of sexual perversions and, particularly, to elucidate the psychological laws governing this process. For Binet, these
laws were to be found in association psychology.

Taking *fetishism* (a term he coined) as his main point of focus,
Binet argued that the customary medical appeal to the hereditary nature of such perversions did not solve the more fundamental problem
of how such aberrations had been acquired by a given patient's ancestors. Nor could hereditary taint in any way explain the specific form
taken by each case of fetishism—why, that is, one fetishist falls ob-
sessionally in love with a particular color of eyes; or why another
becomes attached to a certain physical form, bodily odor, or object of
attire. Thus, in Binet's opinion, to emphasize the hereditary nature
of such afflictions was only to displace the problem back to another
unknown.

Binet's solution lay in the power of early childhood experiences.
Drawing upon the published case histories of Westphal and Krafft-Ebing,
as well as those of fellow countrymen Charcot and Magnan (1882),
Binet noted that virtually every case of sexual perversion reveals a
childhood incident that has left an indelible influence upon the patient's
sexual life. One of Charcot and Magnan's famous cases involved a man

---

5. "Alienist" (from the French *aliéné* = "insane"): one who treats diseases of
the mind, especially diseases involving the legal problems of insanity. The term
enjoyed widespread usage around the turn of the century (as in the title *The
Alienist and Neurologist*, an American journal of mental disorders).

who had slept with his parents as a young child, and who had first experienced erections at the age of five while seeing his mother dressed in her night bonnet. From then on, the mere sight of a night bonnet had served to arouse violent sexual excitement in this patient. Cases like this were typical, Binet testified; and whenever such childhood incidents were not specifically mentioned by a patient, Binet believed them to have been forgotten, or else insufficiently sought after, by the interviewing physician.

What was new and controversial about Binet's position was not, however, his seeming rejection of congenital degeneration as a cause of sexual pathology. Indeed, he himself partly supported that theory when he admitted that most people have been exposed to the same pathogenic experiences reported by fetishists and yet have not become perverted. Both the precocity and the peculiar "omnipotence" of the fetishist's childhood sexual associations, Binet therefore concluded, pointed to a congenital "morbid state" in such pathological instances (1887:167).

The real innovation in Binet's theory of perversion was his claim that the major forms of sexual pathology—homosexuality, sadism, masochism, fetishism, and so forth—could be unified under his associationist theory with the simple assumption that each was always specifically determined by *chance* events. In other words, a fetishist could just as well have become a sadist or a homosexual, given exposure to a different determining event in early childhood. Binet's theory also had the novel virtue of uniting the psychology of sexual pathology with that of normal love. All people are fetishists to some extent, he maintained. Everyone has a slight preference for one particular color of hair or one type of sexual partner over another—often determined by one's first love. Only an exaggeration of this normal tendency is necessary for a perversion to result, while love itself, Binet provocatively suggested, is merely a complicated fetishism—a harmonious symphony of fixed obsessions about the loved person.

Binet's associationist point of view, together with his environmentalist approach to sexual perversion, soon received the influential support in Vienna of two of Freud's teachers, Theodor Meynert (1890:185) and Sigmund Exner (1894:345). More influential still was the medical backing of Albert von Schrenck-Notzing of Munich, a man whose diligence both as clinician and psychotherapist led to the unexpected discovery that perverts could be cured by hypnotism and suggestion therapy.[6] Schrenck-Notzing's first cure was announced in August 1889 at the First International Congress of Hypnotism, held in Paris. Among the many notable figures in attendance at this congress were Bernheim, Binet, Forel, William James, Liébeault, Lombroso, Magnan,

---

6. Schrenck-Notzing was preceded by several alienists in this form of attempted cure, particularly by Charcot and Magnan (1882) and by Krafft-Ebing, who was treating homosexuals with hypnotic suggestion therapy as early as 1888 (see Krafft-Ebing 1899 trans.:440). However, no one persisted more than Schrenck-Notzing in this respect—or drew quite the same conclusions from such findings as he did.

Myers, and thirty-three-year-old Sigmund Freud. Schrenck-Notzing reported that his patient, a homosexual from a "tainted" family, had required forty-five hypnotic sessions over four months in order to reverse his inverted tendencies (1889:319). Three years later, in his widely read monograph on suggestion therapy and the sexual sense, Schrenck-Notzing was able to report seventy similar cases in which homosexual and other perverse inclinations had either been completely cured or significantly reduced through hypnotic therapy. (Besides hypnotic suggestions, Schrenck-Notzing's treatment included trips to local brothels in order to reinforce these therapeutic suggestions!) If homosexuality could be cured by such external influences, then it also stood to reason —at least in his opinion—that homosexuality and other perversions might be *totally* acquired through influences of an analogous sort. Schrenck-Notzing concluded from such findings, in open disagreement with Krafft-Ebing and other contemporary congenitalists: "The more the number of cases accumulates in which lasting therapeutic results have been achieved, the more insignificant appears the proportion for which, according to our views, the hereditary disposition can be claimed in the origin of these anomalies" (1892:149).

The theory of Binet and Schrenck-Notzing was subsequently carried one step closer to the views of Sigmund Freud when Jules Dallemagne (1894:525–27) and, following him, Théodule Ribot (1896:254–55) insisted that precocious childhood sexual experiences, even though forgotten, may persist in the unconscious and thereby form the psychological foundation of adult sexual experience. "The existence of an unconscious subpersonality—director of the conscious personality—reveals itself in this [sexual-pathological] sphere, more than any other, with an undeniable clarity" (Dallemagne 1894:527; also quoted by Ribot 1896: 255). Thus, by the mid-1890s, a relatively Freudian theory of psychosexual pathology had already gained limited currency independently of Freud.

Krafft-Ebing's Response

Krafft-Ebing replied to Binet, Schrenck-Notzing, and other proponents of the acquired conception of perversion that their environmentalist theory was premised on the faulty assumption that homosexuality and fetishism are paradigmatic of sexual deviation. Rather, it was sadism and masochism, the active and passive representatives of the impulse to subjugation, that Krafft-Ebing considered the most "fundamental forms" of psychosexual aberration (*Psychopathia Sexualis*, 1899 trans.:206). And the reason was, as Krafft-Ebing pointed out, that with these two disorders sexual hyperesthesia reaches its most bizarre extreme. Thus, while the associationist theory had some plausibility for explaining milder perversions like homosexuality and fetishism (and Krafft-Ebing was willing to endorse this theory for the specific choice of fetish), it was totally unable to explain how an accidental childhood sexual association, even in the most precocious individual, could by it-

self lead to sadistic or masochistic inclinations. Whenever there is precocity, Krafft-Ebing objected, the number of sexual associations in
childhood must be large as well as heterogeneous. Yet the circumstance
that a whipping, for example, or even the mere sight of a whipping, or
the witnessing of a chicken being strangled, could somehow induce a
lasting pathological association with sexuality suggested to Krafft-Ebing
that the general choice of perversion was already latent in the individuals concerned (1899 trans.:205 n.). In short, he continued to see truly
acquired sexual anomalies as both rare and, whenever documented,
predominantly "perversities," not "perversions."

By the mid-1890s, there were plenty of supporters for both positions in the general debate between Krafft-Ebing and his critics—with
sides about equally drawn.[7] In part, the whole argument may be seen
as a reflection of the timeless nature-nurture controversy within the life
sciences. And as always in such timeless debates, there was no short-
age of medical evidence supporting both points of view.

At the same time, this 1890s polemic over the causes of sexual
perversion was closely linked in German-speaking countries to an opposition between a Darwinian, or strictly hereditary, explanation of the
problem, on the one hand, and an environmentalist-psychopathological
explanation on the other. In these terms, the controversy was one over
preformation versus *epigenesis*,[8] with Darwinism smacking of prefor-
mationism to orthodox physicalists like Theodor Meynert and Sigmund

---

7. In fact, there were really four different positions extending across a single
spectrum: (1) those individuals accepting hereditary neuro-psychopathic taint
(*Belastung*) as the principal cause of perversions—a group that included Krafft-
Ebing (1882, 1886), Charcot and Magnan (1882), Gley (1884), Chevalier (1893),
and Féré (1896); (2) those who emphasized the congenital element, but who admitted that hereditary perversion may appear without any other signs of neuro-
psychopathic degeneration—a group including a wavering Westphal (1870, 1876),
Kiernan (1888, 1891), Lydston (1889), Eulenburg (1895), Moll (1891, 1897b), and
Ellis (1896a, 1896b, 1897); (3) those accepting the congenital element in some
cases, but admitting the possible acquirement of perversion in nonpredisposed individuals—a group including Tarnowsky (1886); perhaps Binet (1887), who nevertheless also stressed hereditary predisposition; and definitely Schrenck-Notzing
(1892, 1895); and (4) those who argued for the existence and the plurality of
purely acquired perversion—a group including Hoche (1896), Cramer (1897),
Kautzner (1899), and Iwan Bloch (1902–3). For a comprehensive survey of views
on this subject, see Moll 1897b:646–60, 667–70.

Matters become more confused when one discovers that some alienists, like
Tarnowsky (1886) and Lydston (1889), emphasized the acquirement of perversion
through organic factors such as brain diseases, while others, like Schrenck-Notzing
(1898–99:23), stressed that a predisposition to perversion could be acquired during
intrauterine life—a noninherited, but still congenital, cause of perversion.

8. *Preformation* and *epigenesis* are two opposing theories of embryological
development in the history of that discipline. The theory of preformation holds that
the organism is entirely "preformed" within the developing embryo and needs only
to increase in size, and to take on opaque coloration, in order to become visible to
the embryologist. In an extreme, eighteenth-century version of this theory called
emboîtement, it was maintained that every organism contains all its descendants in
successively encapsulated form. By contrast, the theory of epigenesis posits that
each embryo is created gradually, and de novo, out of smaller physiological subunits. The theory of preformation was dominant in the latter part of the eighteenth
century but was eclipsed in the early nineteenth century by the theory of epigenesis.
Thus, the Darwinian theory of inherited perversions, which seemed preformationist
to some, later met with opposition for this reason. For further details on the
preformation-epigenesis debate, see Roger 1963.

Exner. As Albert Moll (1891:185) commented about this time, Krafft-Ebing's theory of hereditary perversion was really just an elaboration of Charles Darwin's views in *The Descent of Man* (1874) concerning the hereditary transmission of marked moral qualities within the same family. Darwin had written: "I have heard of authentic cases in which a desire to steal and a tendency to lie appeared to run in families of the upper ranks; and as stealing is a rare crime in the wealthy classes, we can hardly account by accidental coincidence for the tendency occurring in two or three members of the same family." Insanity, Darwin believed, is "notoriously often inherited" (1874:123–24). To Theodor Meynert (1884:256) and Schrenck-Notzing (1892:155), both proponents of the acquired theory of sexual perversion, such logic was an untenable appeal to the direct inheritance of specific "ideas" independently of experience.

Finally, one last feature of this debate over the nature and nurture of sexual perversions is particularly worth emphasizing. Both sides had based their opposing theories upon the same fundamental premise, namely, that the emergence of spontaneous sexual impulses in early childhood is a typical sign of neuropathic degeneration. To the congenitalists, like Krafft-Ebing, precocious sexuality implied that the individual was tainted and hence his perversion innate. To the environmentalists, like Binet and Schrenck-Notzing, precocious sexual activity had provided the morbid mechanism by which a wide variety of perversions were supposedly acquirable at an impressionable age. Thus the same premise had led to conflicting interpretations of the clinical facts.

This paradoxical situation did not last long. At its root, of course, lay the key issue of just how unusual, precocious, and abnormal is childhood sexuality. And when this series of questions was finally resolved around the turn of the century, the resulting clarification forced a major reassessment by nativists and environmentalists alike on the whole problem of sexual perversion.

The Passing of Degeneration Theory and the Emergence of "Libido Sexualis" as a Biogenetic Concept

The solution to the 1890s paradox in sexology—and, with it, to the problem of infantile sexuality—came primarily through three new sources of information: (1) the introduction of a biological-developmental paradigm of sex inspired by the theory of evolution;[9] (2) the work of a new and younger generation of sexologists who, cognizant of this more naturalistic explanation of sexual anomalies, began to look at the

9. See also Chapter 7, where this influence is briefly treated on a more general historical level.

neglected problem of *normal* sexual development; and (3) the anthropological study of sexual practices in other cultures and other times.

The Phylogeny of Sex

A phylogenetic perspective on human sexual development was pioneered primarily in America, although it was not exclusively confined to that country. But it was a series of American investigators who first placed the problem of sexual perversion in a more naturalistic, biological, and particularly Darwinian light, which reflected, moreover, a peculiar American emphasis upon developmental and functionalist interpretations of psychological phenomena. In part a reaction against the pseudoexactitude of German psychophysics, the functionalist program (led by William James, John Dewey, J. R. Angell, and G. Stanley Hall) sought to make psychology the study of the organism's adaptations to its environment. William James's attitude toward the great Fechner's brand of "exact" psychological science succinctly captures the American discontent with German methods:

> The Fechnerian *Maasformel* and the conception of it as an ultimate 'psychophysic law' will remain an 'idol of the den,' if ever there was one. . . . [I]t would be terrible if even such a dear old man as this could saddle our Science forever with his patient whimsies, and, in a world so full of more nutritious objects of attention, compel all future students to plough through . . . his own works. . . . Those who desire this dreadful literature can find it; . . . but I will not even enumerate it in a footnote. (1890, *1*:549)

Clearly something new was needed in psychology, according to James; and in America, Darwin's theories, together with a more naturalistic approach to human behavior, were a significant part of the functionalist response during the general period from 1880 to 1910.

James himself developed this trend in remarkably Freudian directions as far as the problem of sex was concerned (Shakow and Rapaport 1964:38–39). Touching upon love and sexuality in the chapter on instinct written for his *Principles of Psychology* (1890), James maintained that a normal human instinct of "personal isolation," once overcome by habit, may yield to the most varied forms of vice in the sphere of sexual activity:

> The fondness of the ancients and of modern Orientals for forms of unnatural vice, of which the notion affects us with horror, is probably a mere case of the way in which this instinct [of personal isolation] may be inhibited by habit. We can hardly suppose that the ancients had by gift of Nature a propensity of which we are devoid, and were all victims of what is now a pathological aberration limited to individuals. It is more probable that with them the instinct of physical aversion toward a certain class of objects was inhibited early in life by *habits*, formed under

the influence of *example;* and that then a kind of sexual appetite, of which very likely most men possess the germinal possibility, developed itself in an unrestricted way. (1890, 2:438–39)

One finds, significantly, no appeal to the doctrines of degeneration or neuro-psychopathic heredity in the developmental theory of perversion held by William James.

The precise basis of James's "germs" of perversion is a problem that was being independently studied during the 1880s by a series of American alienists. The first in this series was an Illinois psychiatrist, Shobal Vail Clevenger (1843–1920), who earned himself the posthumous epithet "Don Quixote of Psychiatry" for his vain crusade against fiscal corruption within state institutions for the insane (Robinson 1919). Besides his classic treatise *Spinal Concussion* (1889) and his psychiatric work as head of the Illinois Eastern Hospital for the Insane, Clevenger was widely known for his researches as a biologist. In addition to his other distinguished accomplishments in this field, he clarified the problematic evolutionary consequences associated with man's adaptation to upright posture (Clevenger 1884). He also published two books in the field of biological psychology—*Comparative Physiology and Psychology* (1885) and *The Evolution of Man and His Mind* (1903)—and claimed Charles Darwin and Herbert Spencer as guiding lights in these endeavors (1885:iv).

Another important aspect of Clevenger's evolutionary thinking encompassed the nature and origins of sexual reproduction, whose ultimate phylogenetic roots he traced to the phenomenon of "protoplasmic hunger." In an article entitled "Hunger the Primitive Desire," he pointed out that cannibalism in amoebas and other single-celled organisms is often followed soon after by a reproductive fission. He elaborated on this suggestive observation:

> Among the numerous speculations upon the origin of the sexual appetite, such as Maudsley's altruistic conclusion, which always seemed to me to be far-fetched, I have encountered none that referred its derivation to hunger. At first glance such a suggestion seems ludicrous enough, but. . . .
> . . . Crabs have been seen to confuse the two desires by actually eating portions of each other while copulating, and in a recent number of the *Scientific American,* a Texan details the *Mantis religiosa* female eating off the head of the male Mantis during conjugation. Some of the female Arachnidæ find it necessary to finish the marital repast by devouring the male, who tries to scamper away from his fate. The bitings and even the embrace of the higher animals appears to have reference to this derivation. (1881:14)

As for hunger itself, Clevenger reduced this primal impulse to "the atomic affinities of inanimate nature," a view that he thought "monistic enough to please Haeckel and Tyndall."

Replying to Clevenger's brief article, Edward Charles Spitzka

(1881),[10] another prominent American psychiatrist (and a personal acquaintance of Clevenger's), emphasized the striking parallel between Clevenger's theory and a number of cases of lust murder that had recently been reported by Richard von Krafft-Ebing (1877). "It is well known," Spitzka amplified upon Clevenger's argument, "that under pathological circumstances, relations obliterated in higher development and absent in health, return and simulate conditions found in lower and even in primitive forms." And he continued:

> There are forms of mental perversion, properly classed under the head of the degenerative mental states, with which a close relation between the hunger appetite and sexual appetite becomes manifest.
> Under the heading "Wollust.—Mordlust-Anthropophagie" Krafft-Ebing describes a form of sexual perversion, where the suffered fails to find gratification unless he or she can bite, eat, murder or mutilate the mate. . . . He gives an instance, where after the act, the ravisher butchered his victim, and would have eaten a piece of the viscera, another where the criminal drank the blood and ate the heart, still another where certain parts of the body were cooked and eaten. (1881:302)

It was probably Spitzka who, as editor of the *American Journal of Neurology and Psychiatry* (1881–84), provided a detailed synopsis in that periodical of Krafft-Ebing's next major publication (1882) on sexual pathology (*1* [1882]:323–25 [anonymous review]).

The evolutionary views of Clevenger and Spitzka quickly inspired the interest of other American alienists. In a series of publications on the problem of perversion, James G. Kiernan (1852–1923), Clevenger's direct superior as Medical Superintendent of the Chicago County Asylum for the Insane, extended Clevenger's own phylogenetic point of view to encompass the problem of homosexuality (Kiernan 1884, 1888, 1891). Along these lines Kiernan wrote: "The original bisexuality of the ancestors of the race, shown in the rudimentary female organs of the male, could not fail to occasion functional, if not organic, reversions when mental or physical manifestations were interfered with by disease or congenital defect." And he concluded that "it seems certain that a femininely functionating brain can occupy a male body, and vice versa. Males may be born with female external genitals and vice versa. The lowest animals are bisexual and the various types of hermaphrodism are more or less complete reversions to the ancestral type" (1888: 129–30).

10. Edward Charles Spitzka (1852–1914) was born of German parents who had immigrated to the United States as a result of the Revolution of 1848—a cause that Spitzka's father had supported (Phalen 1935). Spitzka's background made it natural that he should consider postgraduate studies abroad, which he undertook in Leipzig and Vienna from 1873 to 1876. It was in Vienna that he studied with Freud's teacher Theodor Meynert as well as with the distinguished professor of human and comparative embryology, Samuel Leopold Schenk. Spitzka later made several important contributions of his own to human and comparative neuroanatomy. Spitzka's German ancestry and his postgraduate training made him irrevocably scornful of American work and also explain his early cognizance of the sexological researches of Richard von Krafft-Ebing.

Besides his phylogenetic theory of sexual inversion, Kiernan endorsed Clevenger's "hunger" theory of primal sexual passion, as well as this theory's extension by E. C. Spitzka to the sphere of lust murder. Kiernan observed that, with removal of the normal inhibitions man has acquired in the timeless course of evolution, "the animal in man springs to the surface" (1888:129). It was Kiernan who first insisted that the nine gruesome (and never solved) murders attributed to "Jack the Ripper" between 1887 and 1889 were the work of a sexual deviate. Kiernan viewed all such perverse manifestations of the sexual instinct in terms of a model involving stratified "egos," much like that later set forth in Freudian theory, and wrote in this vein: "Between the cannibalistic sexual intercourse, the expression of protoplasmic hunger in the amoeba, and the picture drawn by Finch and Maudsley, looms a seemingly impassable gap, yet evolution has, as demonstrated by these perversionary atavisms, bridged this gap, and from . . . what would, *a priori*, seem the utmost expression of egotism [i.e., cannibalism], has developed a secondary 'ego,' which inhibits explosive manifestations of egotism, and hence is an efficient moral factor" (1891:217).

It was yet another American physician, G. Frank Lydston (1857–1923), who generalized the theories of Clevenger, Spitzka, and Kiernan into a more strictly developmental (as opposed to atavistic) model of sexual perversion. In Lydston's conception of the matter, perversions were to be blamed either upon "mal-development" or upon "arrested development," with the most severe sexual aberrations approximating "the type of fetal development which exists prior to the commencement of sexual differentiation . . ." (1889:255).

It was through the publications of Kiernan and Lydston in America and, slightly later, through Julien Chevalier's (1893) similar writings in France,[11] that these biogenetic theories of sadism and sexual inversion came to the attention of Richard von Krafft-Ebing, who was particularly enthusiastic about the notion of bisexuality, with its apparent solution to the problem of homosexuality. After disdainfully dismissing the well-known theory of sexual inversion promoted by Schopenhauer (that homosexuality is purposeful in nature and seeks to prevent men over fifty from fathering inferior offspring), Binet's assoc-

---

11. Chevalier (1893:408–19), who spoke only of the problem of sexual inversion, in turn referred back to the remarks of an earlier French colleague, E. Gley (1884:88–92). Gley's discussion had been primarily embryological, while Chevalier's was both embryological and evolutionary in scope. Chevalier was also the first student of homosexuality after Ulrichs, whose own biological arguments had largely been ignored, to cite Charles Darwin in this connection. The nature of Chevalier's evolutionary approach to the problem of inversion is conveyed by the following passage from his treatment of the subject: "I believe, on the strength of the facts—that is to say, by the evidence of anatomy, physiology, embryology, and teratology—that the prime characteristic of man, the least contestable although perhaps the most contested, is his animal nature. It is not repugnant to me in the least to consider ourselves as the most elevated in rank among the animals and to regard ourselves further as the inheritors of the qualities and faults that they [the animals] have bequeathed to the first indistinct races which served as the transition between them and us. All the more so as . . . I consider that it is from the study of sexual evolution in the animal series that one must demand the key to the problem [of homosexuality]" (1893:408–9).

iation theory, and Gley and Magnan's theory that homosexuals have a female brain in a male body—Krafft-Ebing inserted in *Psychopathia Sexualis* a detailed and highly favorable review of the theories of Kiernan, Lydston, and Chevalier (1892:154 n., 229; see also Krafft-Ebing 1895).[12] Krafft-Ebing accepted two further points that Chevalier (1893:410–11, 418–19) in particular had stressed—namely, that proceeding from the original bisexuality of the embryo, an ontogenetic struggle goes on during human development, with one sex conquering the other under normal monosexual (adult) circumstances; and that inverted sexuality is a developmental disturbance in the present state of monosexual evolution, not an atavism in the sense of Cesare Lombroso's well-known theories.[13] Such disturbances, Krafft-Ebing reasoned, could occur either in the anatomical development of the organism (resulting in physical hermaphroditism) or independently in the corresponding psychical centers (resulting in homosexuality or psychical hermaphroditism).

The theory of bisexuality in turn linked Krafft-Ebing's etiological views to the phylogenetic conception of sadism previously advocated by Kiernan and his American colleagues.[14] Krafft-Ebing, as I have said, took sadism and its masochistic opposite to be "the fundamental forms" of psychosexual perversion. Not only were they the most extreme forms of sexual hyperesthesia in his view; but such disorders were also frequently combined, he reported, with other major forms of sexual perversion. Moreover, both sadistic and masochistic tendencies were commonly found together in the same individual. It was this last circumstance that particularly intrigued Krafft-Ebing. If either of these two

12. In this connection, Kiernan is specifically quoted by Krafft-Ebing; see earlier, Chapter 5, p. 159, and this chapter, p. 292.

13. Here I would like to ask a particularly relevant historical question concerning Cesare Lombroso (1836–1909) and his school. Lombroso, the eminent Italian criminal anthropologist whose famous *L'Uomo delinquente* (Criminal Man) was published in 1876, had developed his own evolutionary and biogenetic approach both to criminality and to sexual deviation in the early 1870s. He believed that the "criminal type"—characterized by numerous signs of physical and mental degeneration—was *born*, not made. He further believed the criminal to be "an atavistic being who reproduces in his person the ferocious instincts of primitive humanity and the inferior animals" (1911:xv; see further Gould 1977:120–25). Lombroso's works were well known to Krafft-Ebing, who cited many of the Italian criminologist's case histories. Yet—and this is the interesting question—Krafft-Ebing does not seem to have been inspired theoretically by Lombroso, but drew his evolutionary conceptions instead, at a later date, from the Americans and the French. In part, this choice may reflect Krafft-Ebing's lack of enthusiasm for atavistic theories of sexual inversion (see Krafft-Ebing [1895:111–12], where he objects that the doctrine of atavism fails to explain the true homosexual's simultaneous abhorrence of the opposite sex). At the same time, I get the distinct impression that the ever-cautious Krafft-Ebing was not ready for an evolutionary theory of sexual pathology until the early 1890s, a time when the views of Clevenger, Kiernan, Lydston, and Chevalier were just coming to his attention. Such a "ripeness-of-time" interpretation of this historical question is further corroborated by Krafft-Ebing's neglect of the even earlier biological views of Carl Ulrichs (1898 [1868], 7:26–33, 133–36).

14. Krafft-Ebing erroneously credits this theory to Kiernan, although of course it was actually formulated by Clevenger and Spitzka. Clevenger continued to develop his thinking on the biological bases of sexual perversions; see, for example, his contribution to the discussion that followed Kiernan's (1891:218) published talk before the Chicago Academy of Medicine. See also Clevenger's *The Evolution of Man and His Mind* (1903:344–45), where he treats sodomy and sadism in atavistic terms.

perversions was to be understood theoretically, *both* had to be explained by one and the same etiological hypothesis. Kiernan's theory of sadism, Krafft-Ebing believed, had met this requirement. If reproduction by cannibalism was indeed the primal form of the sexual impulse, then an "instinctive desire to be the victim" would also be explained under the same rubric (*Psychopathia Sexualis*, 1899 trans.:207 n.). Thus the male, as the more active and aggressive representative of the two sexes, had presumably evolved along sadistic lines, whereas the female had fallen heir to the masochistic element in animal reproduction. Masochism, in short, was none other than "an inheritance of the 'bondage' of feminine ancestry"—an interpretation agreeing very nicely, Krafft-Ebing thought, with the medical predilection of males and females for sadism and masochism, respectively (1899 trans.: 199–200 n.). Finally, to account for the presence of masochistic tendencies in the male, Krafft-Ebing assumed such a condition to be a rudimentary form of sexual inversion—"a [bisexual] transference to the male of a perversion really belonging to the female" (1899 trans.:199–200 n.).

It was Krafft-Ebing's endorsement of these various biogenetic points of view that undoubtedly promoted their widespread adoption by other students of sexual pathology during the 1890s. By 1905, the bisexual theory of homosexuality had been advocated by most of the leading sexologists of Europe, including—besides Krafft-Ebing himself—Ellis (1896a:59–60; 1897:132–33), Kurella (1896), Moll (1897b:326–46), Féré (1899:234), Hirschfeld (1899:8–9), Weininger (1903), Herman (1903), and Sigmund Freud (1905d, S.E., 7:141–44). Of these, Krafft-Ebing, Havelock Ellis, and Ellis's German translator Hans Kurella had all further endorsed Julien Chevalier's notion of an internal "struggle" during development between the bisexual *Anlagen*; and Kurella (1896:237) specifically appealed to Wilhelm Roux's embryological doctrines in this context. About this same time, Schaefer (1891), Penta (1893:307), Stekel (1895), Bölsche (1898–1903), Eulenburg (1902), Bloch (1902–3, 2:31–32, 64), Hall (1904, 2:101–2), and many others threw their weight either to atavistic or to biogenetic theories of sexual perversion—particularly in connection with sadomasochism.[15]

Of these two theories of sexual perversion—the *atavistic* and the *biogenetic* (with its greater emphasis upon embryonic "component instincts")—it was the latter that eventually won the day among sexual pathologists. This biogenetic tradition in sexology also went a long way toward effecting the demise of the degeneration theory, with which the doctrine of atavistic depravity had been so closely associated. As long as sexuality had been looked upon as a homogeneous impulse, a congenital conception of sexual pathology had remained synonymous with hereditary degeneration to an atavistic condition. But when the theories

15. Freud's copy of Iwan Bloch's work bears Freud's marginal emphasis next to the sentence, "[Herbert] Spencer, in particular, advocates the evolutionary explanation of cruelty" (2:31 [Freud library, London]). Bloch's reference is to Spencer's *Principles of Psychology* (1870–72, 2:§510–12). Freud also marked Bloch's summary of Schaefer's (1891) evolutionary theory of sadism (2:47 n.), which Krafft-Ebing (1899 trans.:80 n.) had likewise endorsed.

of Clevenger, Kiernan, Chevalier, and others began to separate the
healthy sexual instinct into bisexual and other evolutionary components, it finally became possible to recognize sexual perversion as arising from *developmental* disturbances in these normal, component
impulses.

Richard von Krafft-Ebing took this step at the age of sixty-one, the
year preceding his death. In a review article on homosexuality published in 1901, he declared of the older degeneration theory:

> In view of the realization that contrary sexuality is a congenital
> anomaly, that it represents a disturbance in the evolution of the sexual
> life towards monosexuality and of normal psychical and somatic develop-
> ment in relationship to the kind of reproductive glands [possessed by the
> individual], it is no longer possible to maintain the idea of [degenerate]
> "disease" in this connection. . . .
>
> Not infrequently one runs across neuropathic and psychopathic pre-
> dispositions among homosexuals, for example, constitutional neurasthe-
> nia and hysteria, . . . which may lead to the most severe aberrations of
> the sexual impulse. And yet one can prove that, relatively speaking, het-
> erosexuals are apt to be much more depraved [*Cyniker*] than homo-
> sexuals. (1901b:5)

Through years of patient research, Krafft-Ebing had come to recognize
the noble qualities of many homosexuals, who were frequently, he emphasized, the pride of their nations as authors, poets, artists, statesmen,
and the like (1901b:6–7). As Victor Robinson has remarked, Krafft-
Ebing was "a pioneer who remained a pioneer" (1953:ix).

Krafft-Ebing and Freud

Because of Krafft-Ebing's premier importance in the early sexology
movement, it is all the more noteworthy that Freud knew him personally.
The great psychiatrist had come to the University of Vienna in 1889, at
the height of his medical career. Although skeptical at times of Freud's
scientific ideas (such as his seduction theory of the psychoneuroses),
Krafft-Ebing was one of two professors, along with Hermann Nothnagel, who actively supported Freud's promotion to Extraordinary (Associate) Professor at the University of Vienna—an honor Freud finally
obtained in 1902, the year of Krafft-Ebing's death (*Origins*, pp. 191,
343). That the two men were on good professional terms is further
borne out by the fact that Freud regularly received autographed copies
of Krafft-Ebing's major works—including the *Psychopathia Sexualis* in
its fifth (1890), seventh (1892), ninth (1894), and eleventh (1901) editions. Freud's copy of the ninth edition bears the inscription *"Herrn
College[n] Dr. Freud freundschaftlich v[om] Verf[asser]"* ("To Herr Colleague Dr. Freud with friendly regards from the author").[16]

16. Freud also owned Krafft-Ebing's *Lehrbuch der Psychiatrie* (1879–80) in
the third (1888) and fifth (1893) editions and his *Lehrbuch der gerichtlichen
Psychopathologie* (1875) in the third (1892) edition. All of these works may be
found in Freud's London library.

It was to the *Psychopathia Sexualis,* that monumental conduit of information and theory on sexual pathology, that Sigmund Freud turned in early 1897 when he first formulated the notion that psychoneurosis is a "repressed" state of perversion. "New valuable evidence of the soundness of my material," Freud announced to his friend Fliess on 3 January, "is provided by its agreement with the perversions described by Krafft" (*Origins,* pp. 183–84). (In early 1897, Freud would have been reading the ninth [1894] edition of the *Psychopathia Sexualis,* and details of the case histories are heavily marked in his copy with marginal emphases.) Just three weeks later, Freud excitedly amplified upon this new line of thought, "Perverted sexual actions are always alike, always have a meaning, and are based on a pattern which can be understood" (*Origins,* p. 189). Such, of course, was the basic message of the *Psychopathia Sexualis,* although Freud doubtless had novel psychoanalytic points of view to add to it.

It was from Krafft-Ebing's *Psychopathia Sexualis* that Freud apparently learned that the notion of bisexuality had come to play a major role, independently of Wilhelm Fliess, in the contemporary literature on sexual perversion. (In 1904, when Fliess asked Freud where he had come across the ideas of Krafft-Ebing, Kiernan, and Chevalier on this subject, Freud cited the *Psychopathia Sexualis* (see Fliess 1906a:21–23). That this work was also probably a stimulus during the late 1890s to Freud's nascent views on the "biogeny" of sex can be seen not only from his contemporaneous letters to Fliess but also from his later psychoanalytic writings. Freud subsequently endorsed the "cannibalistic" theory of sadism and referred as well to a "cannibalistic" or "oral" stage in childhood sexual development. Like Krafft-Ebing before him, Freud emphasized the intimate link between sadomasochism, masculinity-femininity, and man's bisexual disposition (*Three Essays,* 1905*d*, *S.E.,* 7:159–60, 198). But most important of all, Freud always conceived of sexual perversions (and neuroses) in terms of developmental "arrests" approximating the fixed adult stages of our animal ancestors (see once again Chapter 7, pp. 258–64).

The Science of Normal Sexual Development

While the biogenetic conception of sexual perversion ultimately banished hereditary degeneration from its central position in the theory of sexual pathology,[17] it did not succeed in altering a closely related belief—namely, that *precocious* sexual activity is a major indication of a congenital predisposition to perversion. On this issue, Krafft-Ebing

17. After 1900, the theory of degeneration was retained by many theorists as a subsidiary concept. In giving qualified support to the degeneration doctrine in his *Three Essays,* Freud insisted upon the "remarkable fact" that more than half of his severe cases of psychoneurosis involved patients whose fathers had suffered from syphilis (1905*d*, *S.E.,* 7:236). Freud still held to this view thirty years later (Wortis 1954:133; discussion of 4 January 1935).

and his environmentalist opponents had all been in general agreement. Within European countries, three men—Max Dessoir, Albert Moll, and Havelock Ellis—successfully undermined this common assumption by making known the unexpected finding that the early anamneses of perverted individuals do not differ essentially in their reports of precocious sexual activity from those of predominantly normal individuals.[18]

Max Dessoir (1867–1947) was the first of these investigators to report his discoveries in this connection. A German psychologist and philosopher, Dessoir (1888, 1890) had already established a considerable reputation for himself as a student of hypnotism, of the unconscious mind, and of the problem of split personality when, in the early 1890s, he turned his attention to the psychology of sex. In a study published in 1894, Dessoir described the evolution of the sexual instinct and specified two major stages in it. The first of these he called an "undifferentiated" stage, which appeared in girls, he claimed, between the ages of twelve and fourteen, and in boys between the ages of thirteen and fifteen. During this first stage, the sexual instinct may express itself in either a heterosexual or a homosexual manner. Undifferentiated libidinal impulses may even attach themselves to animals at this time. All this is normal, Dessoir insisted, and is followed by a stage of "differentiation," in which heterosexual relationships become the exclusive goal of the libido. Some individuals, nonetheless, remain in an "embryonic" state, continuing to express homosexual, bisexual, or other perverse inclinations as adults.

Dessoir's two-stage scheme was at first used by association psychologists to bolster their theory of acquired perversion. When "precocious," such an undifferentiated sexual impulse seemed all the more reason to environmentalists for emphasizing the critical role of accidental factors in pathological associations—for example, Schrenck-Notzing (1892:154, 288–89), who already knew of Dessoir's theory two years before its formal publication. Similarly, Havelock Ellis (1897:37–39), in spite of siding with the hereditary interpretation of homosexuality, at first judged Dessoir's analysis as providing considerable support to the environmentalist conception of perversion. Ellis soon had reason to retract this conclusion, however, when Dessoir's German colleague Albert Moll extended Dessoir's theory back into early childhood and, buttressing this extension with new clinical evidence, established a persuasive rival interpretation of the whole matter.

18. Although Sanford Bell (1902) and G. Stanley Hall (1904) in America must not be forgotten in this regard, their work was largely independent of, and subsequent to, that body of research that was most important for Freud's own thinking. Bell's study, which Hall inspired and later summarized in 1904, described five stages in the emergence of love, beginning as early as the age of two and one-half. From an analysis of 2,500 questionnaires, Bell concluded that the emotion of love most often emerges in the third year of life. Nevertheless, he did not consider genital sensations to be normal in early childhood, and he wrote that childhood love "has about as little of physical sexuality in it as an apple-blossom has of the apple that develops from it" (1902:333). Freud later cited Bell's study in the first edition of his *Three Essays* (1905d, S.E., 7:174 n.). Hall's work came to Freud's attention at a later date.

Albert Moll's Contributions to Sexual Science

Compared with Havelock Ellis or Sigmund Freud, Albert Moll is an obscure figure today—a standing that is in marked contrast to his pre-eminence as a neurologist and sexologist around the turn of the century. After Krafft-Ebing's death in 1902, Moll was possibly the best-known authority on sexual pathology in all of Europe. His major publications were designated "classics" at this time by fellow sexologist Hermann Rohleder (1907, 2:23). The ever discriminating Paul Näcke (1899a: 170) bestowed his "unrestricted praise" on Moll's theories. And Havelock Ellis honored Moll in his seven-volume *Studies in the Psychology of Sex* by citing Moll's authority on the problems of sex more than any other individual.[19] In later years (the second and third decades of the twentieth century), Moll's fame as a sexologist and psychotherapist was gradually eclipsed by none other than Sigmund Freud (cf. Eissler 1971: 175). After 1933, Moll's reputation suffered a further setback in Germany as his books were systematically destroyed by the Nazis; and in a curious twist of fate, he died in 1939, in relative anonymity, the same day as his world-celebrated rival Sigmund Freud (Ellenberger 1970: 859–60).

Moll's intellectual relationship to Freud has long been obscured by his harsh criticisms of psychoanalysis after the turn of the century, as well as by the intense animosity that Freud developed toward him as a result. Six years younger than Freud, Moll (1862–1939) had much in common with his Viennese medical counterpart. Like Freud, Moll was the son of a Jewish merchant. He took his medical degree at the University of Berlin in 1885 and spent the next two years doing post-graduate studies, first in Vienna, where he came to know Nothnagel, Meynert, Benedikt, and probably Freud; then in London, where he worked with David Ferrier and Hughlings Jackson, among other medical figures; and afterward in Paris, where he studied with the great Charcot (Moll 1936). In Paris, Moll attended Charcot's lectures and clinic and was also invited, like Freud, to Charcot's famous parties. Through Charcot, he met Binet, Féré, Gilles de la Tourette, and many other members of Charcot's entourage. After studying with Charcot, Moll visited Nancy, where he learned the technique of hypnotic suggestion therapy from Liébeault and Bernheim. Thereafter he attached himself to the Nancy school of hypnotic therapy; and upon his return to Berlin, he became one of the earliest German neurologists to campaign for the new methods of psychotherapy (Dessoir 1947:129). He later spoke, like Freud, of having been "isolated" from his older and more conservative colleagues during these pioneering years (1936:33).

Moll's first book, *Der Hypnotismus* (1889), established his reputa-

19. The rank order of Ellis's (1928) citations may be looked upon as a convenient "Who's Who" of eminent sexologists around the turn of the century. Moll, leading the field with 120 citations, is followed by Iwan Bloch (96), Richard von Krafft-Ebing (77), Charles Féré (76), Sigmund Freud (75), Magnus Hirschfeld (71), and Paul Näcke (57).

tion worldwide. William James (1890, 2:615) rated it "the best com-
pendious work on the subject . . . extraordinarily complete and judicious." Havelock Ellis, who arranged for Moll's book to be translated
into English as part of his Contemporary Science Series, later reported
that it had become the best seller of the entire fifty-volume series
(1939b:213).

Before long, the use of hypnotic suggestion therapy involved Moll
in the psychotherapeutic treatment of sexual perversions. His work in
this field led to the publication in 1891 of *Die conträre Sexualempfindung* (Contrary Sexual Feeling), which carried a laudatory Preface
by Richard von Krafft-Ebing. Writing on the same subject six years
later, Havelock Ellis (1897:31) called Moll's work "the most important
discussion of sexual inversion which has yet appeared"; and Ellis subsequently reported that it had "speedily superseded all previous books
as a complete statement and judicious discussion" of the whole problem (1928, 2:71). Contrasting Krafft-Ebing, the tireless compiler of case
histories, with his younger German colleague, Ellis commended Moll
for attacking the causes of perversion and for doing so "as a psychologist even more than as a physician." It was Albert Moll, Ellis declared,
who successfully "cleared away various ancient prejudices and superstitions which even Krafft-Ebing sometimes incautiously repeated"
(1928, 2:71).

During the 1890s, Moll corresponded with Krafft-Ebing on a regular
basis and received increasingly high praise from the master for his dili-
gent contributions to the field of sexual science. Many of Moll's case
histories were subsequently used by Krafft-Ebing in successive editions
of the *Psychopathia Sexualis*. Furthermore, Krafft-Ebing's decision
around the turn of the century to separate the doctrine of degeneration
from the theory of homosexuality was in response to the thinking of
his younger and more critical colleague Moll.

Even in the first edition of *Die conträre Sexualempfindung* (1891:
162), Moll had insisted that degeneration could not be diagnosed in
every case of inversion. Indeed, when inversion itself was the sole visible sign of degeneration, it was purely circular reasoning, Moll contended, to blame the inversion on this cause; at most, degeneration
was purely a secondary cause of perversion. Moll's own theory of sexual
aberrations was unpretentious. Since all biological organs and functions
are susceptible to variations and anomalies, why should the sexual instinct be any different (1891:189–90)? Although Moll's conception of
sexual perversion became considerably more sophisticated with the
years, he never wavered from this basic biological position.

Moll was also highly critical of another belief shared by most sexual pathologists during the 1890s—namely, that early sexual activity
is an important correlate of later perversion. Already in his book on
homosexuality, he had reported that mutual masturbation is often practiced in childhood by individuals who later show no signs of inversion.
In fact, he had learned of a veritable "epidemic" of this sort that had
broken out in a Berlin boarding school many years before. And yet not

Albert Moll (1862–1939).

one of the many youths involved was known to have become a homo-sexual (1891:167, n. 1).

It was to correct the common misapprehension of moralists, de-generacy theorists, and association psychologists alike regarding child-hood sexuality that Moll subsequently undertook an ambitious theo-retical work, *Untersuchungen über die Libido sexualis* (Investigations into the Libido Sexualis, 1897b), in which both normal and abnormal sexual development were to be treated side by side. It was, as he stated in his Preface to this book, the regrettable failure of previous sexolo-gists to study *normal* sexuality that was largely responsible for existing disagreements about *abnormal* sexuality.

The *Libido Sexualis*, some 850 pages in length, appeared in two parts in the spring and summer of 1897. Part One treated normal sex-uality and its typical developmental course. Part Two examined sexual pathology in its various clinical, theoretical, and forensic aspects. Both parts of the *Libido Sexualis* were read shortly after their publication by Sigmund Freud, whose personal copy of that work is heavily anno-tated in his hand (Freud library, London; see also Appendix D).

Moll's guiding theoretical orientation in the *Libido Sexualis* was evolutionary and Neo-Darwinian; Krafft-Ebing, Charles Darwin, and August Weismann—the ardent German Neo-Darwinian—are the three most cited authors, in that order.[20] The starting point of Moll's theoretical disquisition on sex was his analysis of the sexual impulse into two major component instincts, which he termed the *Detumescenztrieb* and the *Contrectationtrieb*. By the first or "detumescence" drive, Moll had in mind "an impulse to bring about a transformation in the genitals"—a definition that he believed to be equally applicable to men, women, and children. His second term, derived from the Latin root *contrecto* ("to touch" or "to feel") specified the impulse to touch, fondle, or kiss the sexual object (1897*b*:10). Moll thought the evidence for the existence of these two instincts was to be observed most clearly in man's evolutionary history. Man's most primitive ancestors undoubtedly reproduced asexually, by budding or fission (the primordial modes of tumescence/detumescence). The instinct of contrection, on the other hand, emerged later in the evolutionary series—with the advent of the first bisexual organisms (both the ascidians and the amphioxus are mentioned in this regard). Hermaphroditism was followed by the evolution of monosexuality, achieved by a regular suppression in ontogeny of one of the two embryonic sets of sexual organs.

Turning to the ontogeny of the sexual impulse in human beings, Moll emphasized two important points based upon his numerous clinical inquiries on this subject: that either impulse (detumescence or contrectation) may emerge first, at least at a level that is perceived by consciousness; and that both impulses often emerge well before puberty in sexually normal individuals. In support of the latter claim, Moll declared:

> . . . we are familiar in literary history with numerous cases of prominent poets who in their early childhood fell in love with women, that is at a time when we could not as yet speak of physical puberty. Let me mention Dante, who fell in love with Beatrice at the age of nine; Canova [who fell in love] at the age of five; Alfieri, at the age of ten; and Byron, who at the age of eight, is said to have fallen in love with Mary Duff. Sollier [1891:91–94] makes mention of the fact that in idiots we may sometimes observe the impulse towards the other sex long before physical puberty. He rightfully adds that this is also the case with normal individuals. At any rate, I may state, on the basis of many questions which I have addressed to numerous persons, that the inclination towards the other sex, with all its signs of sexual passion, may be observed long before the onset of puberty. I have known cases in which at the age of five or six there were indubitable inclinations originating from the sex instinct. (1897*b*:43–44; 1933 trans.:67 [with slight retranslation, here and below])[21]

20. Darwin's theories, and their much-debated status in contemporary science, were of special interest to Moll, who said in the *Libido Sexualis* (1897*b*; 1933 trans.:270) that he was planning to write a separate work on this subject—although he never did so. It is curious that Moll did not mention this projected work in the German edition (1897*b*); see the corresponding page (217).

21. This passage on childhood sexuality and the precocious loves of famous poets is scored in the margin of Freud's personal copy. Freud later mentioned Dante and Byron before the Vienna Psychoanalytic Society as instructive instances of "those who are precocious mentally and sexually [and] fall sexually in love before their time . . ." (*Minutes*, 4:4; meeting of 3 January 1912).

To Moll, particular confirmation of the normalcy of such child-hood sexual experiences came from the realm of natural history. Just as in human beings, he reported, flirtations and love play are commonly observed in higher animals long before physical puberty. Citing Karl Groos's *The Play of Animals* (1896:230 ff., 253 ff.) in support of this claim, Moll contended that sex play in human beings likewise constitutes an adaptive "preactivity" of the animal instinct. (On this last point, he anticipated Groos's own logic about childhood sexuality in *The Play of Man* [1899:326].) Moll concluded of such biological findings:

> These observations on animals, in my opinion, are exceedingly important in order to destroy the common belief that physical puberty is a necessary preliminary condition for the sexual inclination of male and female. *On the contrary, as has already been mentioned several times, the psychic element, in a number of cases, may develop much earlier than physical puberty.* (1897b:44; 1933 trans.:67-68; italics added to indicate text scored in the margin of Freud's copy)

Jealousy, shame, and even the child's preferential expressions of love toward the opposite-sex parent (for example, kissing) are all colored by the sexual element during childhood (1897b:55).

Further, Moll claimed that such early sexual activities in man were not confined to contrectation, or love attachments, alone. Children may have erections and begin masturbating as early as the first or second year of life, he reported. Moreover, both detumescence and contrectation impulses may emerge precociously in one and the same individual. As an example, he cited the case of a seven-year-old girl who had seduced her three-year-old brother into mutually pleasurable genital manipulations (1897b:46-47).[22]

It was in this context of prevalent childhood sexual activity that Moll threw his support to Max Dessoir's (1894) dual-stage theory of human sexual development. But unlike Dessoir, who had confined his two stages to the period surrounding puberty, Moll explicitly extended Dessoir's first (undifferentiated) stage back into early childhood. Even the early emergence of homosexual or other perverse inclinations, Moll argued from this point of view, was hardly a proof of degeneracy or an irrefutable explanation of later perversion. Such anomalous impulses often emerge in childhood, he attested, only to become normal, heterosexual ones at the time of puberty (1897b:421, 425; scored in the margin of Freud's copy). Once again, Moll stressed his discovery that

22. Moll presented 78 case histories in the *Libido Sexualis*. Of these, he was able to supply information on the first emergence of the sexual impulse (contrectation or detumescence) in 49 instances. Most of these case histories involved sexual perverts of one sort or another and are therefore somewhat independent of Moll's observations about normal sexual development. Nevertheless, inasmuch as Moll held there to be little difference in the first emergence of sexual impulses in those who are normal and in those who are subsequently perverted, it is worth noting that he was able to document sexual activity during or before the *eighth year of life* in more than 60 percent (31) of these case histories: 2 in the first year of life (as reported by the parents); 1 in the second year of life; 1 in the third; 4 in the fourth; 2 in the fifth; 5 in the sixth; 5 in the seventh; 4 in the eighth; and 7 more in "early childhood."

homosexual seductions and mutual masturbation prior to puberty occur frequently among children who are subsequently normal (1897*b*:462–63). Even sadistic or masochistic tendencies can emerge in early childhood, only to fade away with the onset of normal heterosexual tendencies (1897*b*:325 n.; scored in the margin of Freud's copy). So, too, early homosexual fetishes may subsequently become heterosexually directed when puberty is finally reached (1897*b*:320; scored by Freud).

The essential causes of perversion, Moll accordingly insisted, are those that determine why a perverse inclination in childhood fails to transform itself into normal heterosexuality at the time of puberty (pp. 425, 514). Neither the association psychologists nor the degeneration theorists, he believed, had solved this problem with their appeal to precocious sexual experiences. "Were a single sexual experience, and, indeed, the first sexual experience, to induce a lasting association between the sex drive and the object of the first sexual experience, then we would have to find sexual perversion everywhere. Where are there to be found people who initially satisfied their sexual impulse in a normal manner?" (pp. 469–70).

It was to rectify the theoretical shortcomings of the association psychologists, on the one hand, and those of degeneration theorists, on the other, that Moll proposed his latest theory of sexual pathology. Basing himself squarely upon Darwinian principles, he interpreted perversion in terms of a congenital weakness in one or more of a large complex of elements that together constitute the normal, heterosexual "reaction capacity" in man (p. 474; scored in the margin of Freud's copy). Among normal individuals, Moll submitted, the potential for being heterosexually aroused emerges (or intensifies) at the time of puberty, in conjunction with the secondary sexual characteristics; but in some individuals there exists a congenital weakness in this heterosexual reaction complex, just as there exist variations in all biological traits.

At a more cultural-historical level, Moll related such instinctual defects to man's adoption of clothing as well as to man's reduced sense of smell compared with animals. Clothing, for example, obscures the visual stimuli upon which heterosexual attraction normally depends in the biological sphere, while the sexual role of smell has always been paramount for the Mammalia. Thus, the influence of culture has made the inheritance of sexual drives far less certain in civilized man, Moll believed (p. 399; scored in the margin by Freud). As Moll was fully cognizant of August Weismann's (1892) critique of the inheritance of acquired characteristics, he was careful to show how these evolutionary conclusions could be supported from either a Lamarckian or a purely Neo-Darwinian (selectionist) point of view.

Two additional considerations, besides a prerequisite weakness in the normal heterosexual impulse, complete Moll's theory of sexual perversion. First, he assumed there to be congenital predispositions to differing kinds of perversion. He attributed homosexuality to a disturbance in normal monosexual development and cited Krafft-Ebing and bisexuality theory in this regard (pp. 326–28). Second, Moll endorsed the possible "inhibition of instincts by habits," referring to William James's well-known law in this context (see earlier, Chapter 7). In clinical support of this principle, he cited the example of two brothers, both of whom became sadists; yet each sought to humiliate his wife in a separate fashion that was clearly determined by individual experience (p. 500). Moll believed that such ontogenetic experiences could determine, within limits, the precise association of congenitally perverse impulses.

A conservative document in the light of the environmentalist, psychoanalytic ideas that were to supersede it, Moll's *Libido Sexualis* (1897*b*) nevertheless presented a number of important innovations at the time of its publication. Not the least of these was its exhaustive treatment of normal sexual development side by side with that of sexual pathology. More impressive still was its synthesis of clinical data with biological theory in arguing for the normalcy of childhood sexuality.

Havelock Ellis: Studies in the Psychology of Sex

Havelock Ellis (1859–1939) spent the early years of his adolescence puzzling in darkness over the problem of sex. (As he candidly admits in his autobiography, he was particularly troubled at this time by seminal emissions during sleep.) So greatly struck was young Ellis by the lack of scientific literature on this vital topic, and so contemptuous was he of the obscurantist writings on sex that came into his hands, that he resolved at the age of sixteen to devote his life's work to the scientific study of sexuality (1939*b*:126–27). "I determined," he later reflected on his decision, "that I would . . . spare the youth of future generations the trouble and perplexity which this ignorance had caused me" (1936, 1:ix).

In pursuit of this goal, Ellis undertook a formal medical education, even though he never intended to practice that profession. Then, at the age of thirty, he launched himself into a prolific literary and scientific career. Besides his own writings, Ellis occupied himself for many years by editing two major book series: the twenty-six-volume Mermaid Series, through which he republished the best plays of Shakespeare's contemporaries; and the fifty-volume Contemporary Science Series, the first volume of which was Geddes and Thomson's widely read *The Evolution of Sex* (1889).[23] After writing two books of his own in the Contemporary Science Series—*The Criminal* (1890) and *Man and Woman* (1894)—Ellis turned his attention in the mid-1890s to his chief life's work, the *Studies in the Psychology of Sex*.

Published over a thirteen-year period (1897–1910), Ellis's *Studies* originally encompassed six volumes. The first dealt with sexual inversion (1897) and was written with John Addington Symonds, who had

---

23. Freud owned and annotated *Sex* (1914), a related volume by Geddes and Thomson, which briefly discussed his psychoanalytic theories (Freud library, London; see pp. 118, 138, 144, 150–53).

first suggested the work but died in 1893 during the early stages of the collaboration. *Sexual Inversion* was followed by *The Evolution of Modesty* (1900a [1899]), which also included Ellis's studies on sexual periodicity and on autoerotism; *Analysis of the Sexual Impulse* (1903); *Sexual Selection in Man* (1905); *Erotic Symbolism* (1906); and *Sex in Relation to Society* (1910a). Ellis says in his autobiography that when he finally finished the sixth volume, he could identify himself with Gibbon completing his monumental *History*; and in his personal diary Ellis wrote at the time, "The work that I was born to do is done" (1939b:432). A supplementary seventh volume (*Eonism and other Supplementary Studies*) was added to the series in 1928.

The scope of Ellis's documentation in the *Studies* is truly breathtaking. He was uncommonly at home with the medical literature of his day and cited more than two thousand authors in the *Studies* from at least half a dozen different languages. Each volume is an encyclopedic compendium of contemporary information on the various topics he treated. At once informative, judicious, and readable, the series enjoyed an immense success that included its translation into numerous foreign languages.

Publication of his first volume in the series, *Sexual Inversion,* soon became the occasion for the famous prosecution of *Queen* v. *Bedborough* in 1898. Bedborough, a bookseller of radical reputation, was arrested in 1898 for selling a copy of Ellis's book to a London police detective.[24] He was thereupon charged by a grand jury with seeking "to vitiate and corrupt the morals of the liege subjects of our Lady the Queen, to debauch and poison the minds of divers of the liege subjects of our said Lady the Queen, and to raise and create in them lustful desires, and to bring the liege subjects into a state of wickedness, lewdness, and debauchery" (Ellis 1936, *1*:xvii). In spite of the formidable defense organized by Ellis and other sympathizers, Bedborough pleaded guilty to the charges against him, with the understanding that he would receive a suspended sentence. Thereafter, Ellis, who was himself still liable to prosecution in Great Britain, arranged to have the *Studies* published in the United States by the F. A. Davis Company. But even in America, the sale of Ellis's *Studies* was restricted to doctors and lawyers until the early 1930s. Only then did a series of court cases finally sanction public availability of sex information in the United States.[25]

Ellis's *Sexual Inversion* (1897) was primarily a compilation of other authoritative views on this subject, although Ellis did make known many new case histories collected by his colleague Symonds. Like Albert Moll, to whose opinions he frequently referred, Ellis believed homosexuality should be separated from a condition of neuropathic degeneration by virtue of its common expression as the only

24. Peterson (1928:237–62) provides a detailed account of this episode in his biography of Ellis, which includes a verbatim account of the trial. Ellis published a pamphlet defending his own involvement in this prosecution; see his *Note on the Bedborough Trial* (1898c).
25. Several of these legal cases are briefly reviewed by Morris L. Ernst in his Foreword to Ellis's *Studies* (1936 ed., *1*:vi–vii).

Havelock Ellis in 1898,
the year he made
contact with Freud.

stigma of that presumed etiology. (Moll, in fact, is specifically mentioned on this point, which is scored in the margin of Freud's German-
language copy of this work.) [26] Also like Moll, Ellis adopted a largely
congenitalist approach to the problem, endorsing (1) the theory of bisexuality, (2) the principle of arrested development, and (3) Max
Dessoir's two stages of sexual differentiation. Although Ellis believed
that congenitally inverted propensities tend to emerge spontaneously in
many individuals, he also stressed that such inclinations may remain
wholly latent in those who have remained free of homosexual influences
throughout their lives. He therefore acknowledged the importance of
examples set at school, of seductions, and of disappointments in normal love in eliciting such latent tendencies (1897:138–40; 1896b:
244–45, 247; text underlined and scored on the last two points in Freud's
German-language copy).

Publication of *Sexual Inversion* as the first work in the *Studies*

26. See Ellis 1897:32, 137; and 1896b:243–44 (Freud library, New York).

series had diverted Ellis from his original intention to begin his researches with normal sexuality. (When the *Studies* were later republished in America, he moved the volume on sexual inversion to the
second position in the series.) Having completed the first volume, Ellis
resumed his initial plan, issuing in 1898 his famous study of "autoerotism" in *The Alienist and Neurologist.* Under this heading, Ellis
discussed the many self-gratifying forms through which sexual impulses are expressed among human beings. He took this opportunity to
incorporate within his concept of autoerotism the recent discoveries by
Breuer and Freud on the subject of hysteria. As sexual derivatives, Ellis
proclaimed, the symptoms of hysteria documented so thoroughly by
Breuer and Freud were to be included among autoerotic phenomena.
Ellis (1898*b*) developed this theme in a subsequent article and dispatched a reprint copy to a much-pleased Freud (*Origins,* p. 271). A
regular exchange of letters and publications between the two investigators dates from about this time.

In addition to the problem of hysteria, Ellis's ideas on autoerotism
encompassed the issue of childhood sexuality. On this delicate question he flatly maintained, "There appears to be no limit to the age at
which spontaneous masturbation may begin to appear" (1898*a*:283). He
recorded the case of an eight-month-old female infant who was able to
induce complete orgasm by closing her eyes, clenching her fists, and
tightly crossing her thighs (1898*a*:270; passage scored in the margin
of Freud's reprint copy [Freud library, New York]).

Ellis followed up his 1898 study of autoerotism, which he later incorporated into the second volume of the *Studies* (1900*a*), with the publication of "The Analysis of the Sexual Impulse" (1900*b*), which he
later used as the lead essay for the third volume of the *Studies* (1903).
This article surveyed recent theories of the sexual instinct, including
those of Féré, Clevenger, Spitzka, Kiernan, and Moll. Of these, Moll's
theory received by far the most favorable appraisal. Designating the
Libido Sexualis (1897*b*) as "the most thorough attempt yet undertaken
to investigate the fundamental problems of the sexual impulse," Ellis
acknowledged of Moll's two fundamental drives of contrectation and
detumescence: "It seems to me undoubtedly true that these two instincts do correspond to the essential phenomena" (1900*b*:252).

Ellis's survey article offered several provocative views of his own
on the oral and anal nature of childhood sexuality, a subject on which
he anticipated much of the Freudian doctrine. He referred to the pleasurable anal, urethral, and bladder sensations reported by a number of
his personal informants who, as children, had regularly practiced the
voluntary retention of urine and excreta for this purpose. "It is true,"
Ellis (1900*b*:247–48) declared, "that, especially in early life, the emotions caused by forced repression of the excretions are frequently massive
or acute in the highest degree, and the joy of relief correspondingly great. (I recall the remark by a lady that in childhood the long-
delayed opportunity of emptying the bladder was often 'like Heaven.')"
Speaking of the tender bond in the mother-child relationship, Ellis

felt no hesitation in comparing the process of breast-feeding to that of the adult sexual act:

> The analogy is indeed very close, though I do not know, or cannot recall, that it has been pointed out: the erectile nipple corresponds to the erectile penis, the eager watery mouth of the infant to the moist and throbbing vagina, the vitally albuminous milk to the vitally albuminous semen: The complete mutual satisfaction, physical and psychic, of mother and child, in the transfer from one to the other of a precious organized fluid, is the one true physiological analogy to the relationship of a man and a woman at the climax of the sexual act. (1900b:250)

Sigmund Freud later referred approvingly to this description of the erotic relationship between mother and child in his *Three Essays on the Theory of Sexuality* (1905d, S.E., 7:223 n.).[27] Also like Ellis, Freud maintained that such early forms of sexual pleasure are regularly given up (both naturally and as a result of toilet training) in the course of normal psychosexual development.

It was in connection with his researches on autoerotism that Ellis began systematically collecting autobiographical narratives relating to the sexual development of normal individuals. These he published, first in article form in 1901, and subsequently as appendices to the later volumes of his *Studies in the Psychology of Sex* (see especially Ellis 1903: Appendix B). Ellis's narrative collection proved most influential in demonstrating the wide variety of perverse forms that sexuality may normally assume in its early developmental stages (the Moll-Dessoir theory). Publication of these case histories was later lauded by Freud (1905d), who was particularly indebted both to Havelock Ellis and to Albert Moll for having clarified the whole issue of childhood sexual development.

The Influence of Moll and Ellis

In assessing the influence of Albert Moll and Havelock Ellis around the turn of the century, I should emphasize one general point at the outset. Neither Moll nor Ellis, for all of the innovative efforts of each to advance the science of sexology, was particularly revolutionary in what he published. Rather, each man gave similar expression at about the same time to clinical findings and ideas that were emerging, as it were, almost inevitably from within the whole sexology movement of which they, Sigmund Freud, and many other investigators were all a part. Nevertheless, inasmuch as Moll and Ellis were more progressive, more biologically sophisticated, and more clinically informed than the

27. Freud's personal reprint of this article by Ellis (1900b) is listed among the 1,200 items of Freud's library that were offered for sale in 1939 by Heinrich Hinterberger of Vienna (see Lewis and Landis 1957: item no. 657). Approximately 200 of these items, including this Ellis reprint, never arrived at the New York State Psychiatric Library. The missing items were probably sold separately by Hinterberger before the New York State Psychiatric Library's bid for the whole lot had been tendered.

bulk of their contemporaries, it was primarily through their writings that a new perspective on human sexual development first began to crystallize into a systematic, compelling, and historically consequential form. And in this achievement, both Moll and Ellis deserve to be duly applauded—as indeed they generally were by their contemporaries. Their influence was expressed through three major conceptual changes in the domain of sexology.

The existence and "perverse" nature of childhood sexuality. Along with Max Dessoir and Karl Groos, Moll and Ellis established a developmental conception of the sexual instinct—a conception extending back into early childhood and acknowledging the apparently perverse nature of spontaneous infantile sexual phenomena. Within this developmental conception, sexuality in childhood became comprehensible as a biologically normal and prerequisite part of human maturation. Moreover, this new and largely Darwinian conception of sex, supplemented as it was by detailed autobiographical narratives of healthy individuals, placed the isolated observations on childhood sexuality by Lindner (1879), Pérez (1886), Sollier (1891), Dallemagne (1894), and others within an assimilable context of theory. Prior to this conceptual transformation, such reports had received systematic attention only in the contrasting, pathological context of degeneration doctrine—for example, from Krafft-Ebing, Charcot, Magnan, Binet, Schrenck-Notzing, and others. The discovery of infantile sexuality was therefore a discovery in *theory* as much as it was a discovery of *facts*. For the facts, long known but eschewed, required the proper theory to bring them to recognition as a normal aspect of human development.

Contrary to the Freudian legend, this new conception of sexual development was established in the sphere of sexual studies by Havelock Ellis and Albert Moll several years before Freud's similar views became well known. When Robert Müller published his *Sexualbiologie* (1907), a general survey on this subject, it was from Moll's *Libido Sexualis* (1897*b*), not from Freud's more recently published *Three Essays on the Theory of Sexuality* (1905*d*), that he drew the bulk of his own information on childhood sexuality. (Karl Groos was also cited by Müller.) Similarly, in response to his friend Joseph Wortis's training analysis with Freud in the 1930s—during which the sex theory naturally came up—Havelock Ellis informed Wortis, "The existence of early homosexual traits, or of an undifferentiated sexual attitude, dates from long before Freud . . ." (Wortis 1954:118, letter of 21 December 1934). True, the "undifferentiated" concept of childhood sexuality was hardly the same notion in Max Dessoir's publication of 1894, or even in Moll's *Libido Sexualis* (1897*b*), as it later became in the guise of Freud's own theory of infantile "polymorphous perversity." What we have here is another instance of the *transformation* of scientific ideas (Cohen 1966, 1979). Freud, however, was one of the later conceptual engineers of this particular transformation; he was not the first.

Above all, it was Albert Moll (1897*b*) who added the dynamic element to this undifferentiated-stage concept, by widening it to encompass both perverse "component impulses" and the normalcy of the undifferentiated stage as a passing aspect of overall psychosexual development. Freud himself tacitly acknowledged this aspect of Moll's achievement when he wrote in 1922: "Libido is a term used in the theory of the instincts for describing the dynamic manifestations of sexuality. It was already used in this sense by Moll (1898 [1897b]) and was introduced into psychoanalysis by the present writer" (1923a [1922], S.E., 18:255).

The demise of degeneration theory and ascendancy of the concept of "component predispositions." In effecting the recognition of childhood sexuality, Moll and Ellis also established the variational-congenital nature of sexual perversion over the prevailing views of degeneration theorists and of their rivals, the association psychologists. To be sure, their accomplishment was relative, in that shades of these two vanquished theories remained as subordinate explanations even in their own writings on sex. But the overall balance of power definitely shifted, most notably in 1901 when Krafft-Ebing finally dissociated the most common perversion of all—homosexuality—from a state of psychoneuropathic degeneration.

As for the association psychologists, with their theory of chance occurrences fostering acquired perversions, they too underwent a significant shift in thinking around the turn of the century. Paul Näcke (1899a:172) announced his conversion from the association theory of Schrenck-Notzing to Albert Moll's own views in the course of a highly laudatory review of Moll's *Libido Sexualis* (1897b). Just a few years later, environmentalist Iwan Bloch admitted that the congenitalist views of Krafft-Ebing, Moll, and Ellis were definitely in "ascendancy," and that the theory of acquired perversion had undergone a corresponding "eclipse" (1902–3, 1:8; 1933 trans.:15). Similarly, as late as 1928 Havelock Ellis was able to speak of the lasting victory achieved by himself and Albert Moll some thirty years before:

> It may now be said to be recognized by all authorities, even by Freud . . . , that a congenital predisposition as well as an acquired tendency is necessary to constitute true inversion, apparent exceptions being too few to carry much weight. Krafft-Ebing, Näcke, [and] Iwan Bloch, who at one time believed in the possibility of acquired inversion, all finally abandoned that view, and even Schrenck-Notzing, a vigorous champion of the doctrine of acquired inversion twenty years ago, admits the necessity of a favoring predisposition. . . . (1928, 2:83)

Sigmund Freud became an integral part of this conceptual transformation in the theory of sexuality when he too later confessed, "Accidental influences derived from experience having . . . receded into the background [of my theory], the factors of constitution and heredity necessarily gained the upper hand once more . . ." (1906a, S.E., 7:275).

Refutation of the seduction theorists. Implicit in the preceding two reevaluations by contemporary sexologists was one concerning the etiological significance of childhood seductions. After all, if sexuality is already spontaneously present in a polymorphously perverse spectrum during early childhood, then seductions could hardly be the predominant cause of later perversion (cf. Freud 1905d, S.E., 7:190–91). Both Albert Moll and Havelock Ellis were widely recognized by their contemporaries for their part in bringing about this conceptual retreat by the seduction theorists. Richard von Krafft-Ebing praised his younger colleague Albert Moll in the later editions of the *Psychopathia Sexualis* for having shown "very clearly and convincingly" that homosexual seductions in youth are not the prime cause of sexual inversion (1899 trans.:276 n.), and he specifically cited Moll's findings about mutual masturbation in a Berlin boarding school. Krafft-Ebing's famous remark about Freud's (1896c) seduction theory—namely, that "it sounds like a scientific fairy-tale" (*Origins*, p. 167 n.)—should also be understood in this light. Krafft-Ebing was hardly unacquainted either with the sexual aspects of hysteria or with the fact that children are sometimes sexually molested by their parents, as he had documented many such instances in the *Psychopathia Sexualis*. If Freud's seduction theory nevertheless seemed suspect to him, it was because it purported to establish a purely environmental theory of psychosexual pathology at a time when that theoretical viewpoint seemed to be refuted by the recent work of Albert Moll.

Along analogous lines, Freud later wrote in his *Three Essays on the Theory of Sexuality* that the discovery of homosexual experiences (seductions and mutual masturbation) in the early lives of *normal* individuals had clearly established that other, predisposing influences are necessary for a perversion to develop from them (1905d, S.E., 7:140). Although Freud did not mention his clinical source of information in this connection, at least one reviewer, in praising Freud's logic on this point, was compelled to add that his argument was only a reaffirmation of "Moll's uncited theory" of sexual pathology (Praetorius 1906:731).

If Freud was perhaps a bit taciturn about his intellectual relationship to Albert Moll, he was considerably more outspoken about his debt to Havelock Ellis. In 1934 Freud admitted to Joseph Wortis: "Ellis [1898b] years ago said that we put too much emphasis on early sexual trauma, and he was right; now we are more cautious. . . . School-boys in England, for example, have, most of them, homosexual experiences, but they usually get over them—there must be other [predisposing] factors involved" (Wortis 1954:92). Similarly, in his *Three Essays*, Freud commented even more explicitly about the corrective influence of normal case histories, like those published by his friend Havelock Ellis (1903). After pointing out that such autobiographical narratives should be supplemented by the psychoanalytic technique, he added, "In more than one respect, nevertheless, the statements are valuable, and similar narratives were what led me to make the modification in my aetiological hypotheses which I have mentioned in the text [i.e., his abandonment of the seduction theory]" (1905d, S.E., 7:190–91 n.). Precisely where Freud learned of these "similar narratives," he did not choose to divulge in this discussion of 1905.

Were these "similar narratives" in fact those published by the "un-cited" Albert Moll in 1897, the year that Freud gave up the seduction theory? Although Freud himself never said as much, I believe that reading Moll's *Libido Sexualis* indeed played an important part in Freud's abandonment of the seduction theory during the fall of 1897.[28]

To elucidate Moll's precise influence, I must first explain that Freud already knew of such clinical exceptions to his seduction theory as long as a year and a half before he finally discarded that theory. In an 1896 paper, for example, he had dismissed seduction reports in the lives of normal individuals by saying that the episodes had obviously not been pathologically repressed (1896c, *S.E.*, 3:207, 209–11; here Freud cited Stekel [1895], who had also reported such instances). Why these seductions had not been repressed, Freud did not know at this time; but their existence seemed no immediate threat to his theory. Hence, he was swayed in the fall of 1897 not so much by the discov-ery of such exceptions as by the wider theoretical context in which he, partly under Moll's influence, was forced to reconsider them.

I base this inference upon the following points of historical evi-dence. First, Freud indeed read Albert Moll's *Libido Sexualis* sometime after its appearance, in two separate parts, in the spring and early summer of 1897 and apparently just before he finally gave up his se-duction theory in late September of that year (for evidence substan-tiating this conclusion, see Appendix D).

Second, the conceptual impact of Moll's *Libido Sexualis* upon Freud at this time must be juxtaposed against Freud's continuing preoccupa-tion with his one great, still unsolved psychoanalytic problem. As previ-ously reviewed in Chapter 4, this problem involved the enigma of pathological repression, together with its two subproblems: What is re-pression's organic mechanism? and, Why does pathological repression manifest itself so unpredictably after childhood seductions? Moll's *Libido Sexualis* inspired provisional solutions to each of these subprob-lems, by making it possible for Freud to conceive of differing forms of childhood sexuality as being related to different consequences in adult sexual life.

Years later Freud spoke in precisely these terms when he re-counted that his discovery of infantile sexuality had been coincident upon his realizing that a certain degree of "normal" childhood sexuality must be essential to "the later events of normal [adult] sexuality" (Andreas-Salomé 1964 [1912–13]:90; record of a comment by Freud at the Vienna Psychoanalytic Society, meeting of 5 February 1913). What Freud meant by this remark is elucidated in his *Three Essays on*

---

28. Freud's published references to Moll—whom, as I have already mentioned, he greatly despised—are eight in number: of these, two are favorable (one of these was later deleted), two are neutral (and briefly mention Moll's notions of detumes-cence and contrectation), and the remaining four are disparaging. Freud listed Moll in 1910 (*Three Essays*, 2nd ed.) among those backward physicians who were still denying the existence of infantile sexuality! See Freud 1905d, *S.E.*, 7:174 n. (I shall treat Freud's curious accusation more fully in Chapter 13.) In any event, Freud's published citations of Moll's writings are not a reliable guide to the latter's influence upon Freud in the late 1890s.

the Theory of Sexuality, where he asserted that a certain degree of genital masturbation in childhood seems preordained by Nature as a means of establishing the primacy of this zone over the other erotogenic zones of childhood (1905*d*, *S.E.*, 7:188, n. 1). This important insight may be compared to two key, and closely related, ideas advanced by Albert Moll in the *Libido Sexualis*: that most aspects of childhood sex play should be seen, with Karl Groos (1896), as an adaptive "preactivity" of the adult sexual instinct (a point made in a paragraph partially scored in the margin of Freud's copy [Moll 1897*b*:44, 437]); and that a weak heterosexual impulse is a prerequisite for later perversion (p. 474; also scored by Freud).

Freud first alluded to this crucial distinction between genital and nongenital childhood sexuality in a 14 November 1897 letter to Fliess in which he also mentioned Albert Moll. The reference to Moll appears in Freud's discussion of abandoned erotogenic zones and their assumed link to the notion of organic repression. The same insight, Freud confessed to Fliess, had been independently reached by Albert Moll:

> I have often suspected that something organic played a part in repression; I have told you before that it is a question of the attitude adopted to former sexual zones, and I added that I had been pleased to come across the same idea in Moll [1897*b*]. Privately, I would not concede priority in the idea to anyone; in my case the suggestion was linked to the changed part played by sensations of smell. . . . (*Origins*, p. 231)

In other words, Moll's views on the cultural-historical reduction of sexual stimuli (through the adoption of clothing, perfumes, standards of cleanliness, etc.) complemented Freud's dawning insight into the hereditary-phylogenetic nature of pathological repression. Some infantile sexual experiences prove pathological, Freud now surmised, because they relate to biogenetically abandoned erotogenic zones and to an associated tendency to organic repression. Other sexual experiences are not harmful as long as they relate to later heterosexuality, an outcome they actually help to promote. What was important, then, Freud had begun to see, was not the influence of seductions per se but rather the nature of sexual experiences, which may be beneficial as well as harmful and spontaneous as well as induced.

Finally, Moll's *Libido Sexualis* was notable for one other important insight that was not lost upon Freud at this time. As a clinician, Moll faced a problem similar to that confronting Freud in the mid-1890s: How does one know whether autobiographical confessions of childhood sexual activity are really true? Indeed, they are often not so, Moll contended, citing a variety of psychological reasons: distortions of memory, the patient's desire to rationalize a perversion as innate, subsequent repression of normal heterosexual memories, and so forth. Not only did Moll discuss this point in some detail in the *Libido Sexualis* (1897*b*: 315–16), but he also compared it with the problem of weighing the often outrageous complaints and accusations of hysterical patients, and he cautioned moderation in believing hysterics and perverts alike. To be sure, there was nothing terribly new in Moll's recommendation; but this timely reminder, in a passage scored by Freud in the margin of his personal copy of Moll's book, could hardly have come at a more appropriate time in Freud's wavering support for the seduction theory. In *The Sexual Life of the Child* (1909), Moll later warned against the danger of accepting too readily the accusations of sexual misconduct that little girls often lodge against men, and called it *"one of the gravest scandals of our present penal system"* that such charges were so frequently believed by judges. The problem was particularly marked, he also emphasized, with *child hysterics* (1912a trans.:204, 228; Moll's italics). Similarly, Iwan Bloch (1902–3, *1*:174–77) supported Moll's call for caution when he noted that in spite of the "enormously important" role of childhood seductions as documented by Krafft-Ebing, Moll, and Ellis, Moll's (1897b:46) report of a seven-year-old girl seducing her own brother was a clear caveat for suspecting that little girls may sometimes make false sexual accusations against adults.

That Freud was more than just passingly impressed by Moll's warning in the *Libido Sexualis* (1897b) is reinforced by the following (and later deleted) reference to the whole problem in the first edition of Freud's *Three Essays*: "Many writers, *especially Moll* [*insbesondere von Moll*], have insisted with justice that the dates assigned by inverts themselves for the appearance of their tendency to inversion are untrustworthy, since they may have repressed the evidence of their heterosexual feelings from their memory" (1905d, *S.E.*, 7:137, n. 2; italics added to indicate Freud's subsequent deletion, which is not among those that have been systematically restored, in editorial footnotes, to the *Standard Edition* of Freud's works). Now if Moll was right, and if the positive perversions do not depend so exclusively upon childhood sexual activity as had previously been thought, then neither must the "negative" perversions of psychoneurotics. It was Freud's immediate conclusion upon abandoning the seduction theory that both hereditary predisposition and the distorting phantasies of puberty should be given far more weight in his problematic theory of hysteria (*Origins,* p. 216). Seen in the context of Albert Moll's similar recommendations, Freud's decision to abandon the seduction theory is an important indication of his debt to Moll and to the sexology movement that Moll, among others, helped to found.

SEX FROM THE ANTHROPOLOGICAL POINT OF VIEW

Simultaneously with the influence of biogenetic propositions about sex, on the one hand, and the study of normal sexual development, on the other, Freud's sex theories developed in close association with a third major perspective on human sexuality, which was derived from sociological and anthropological studies of the sexual customs prevailing among other peoples and in other times.

Among the early pioneers of sexology, this anthropological interest was initially focused upon the example of the ancient Greeks, with their widespread cultivation of homosexual practices—particularly male love for young boys. As mentioned before, the prevalence of such homosexual activities among the Greeks had sufficiently impressed American psychologist William James (1890, 2:438–39) for him to proclaim that homosexual inclinations must be innate in all of us, although normally kept in check by an instinct for interpersonal "isolation." Speaking of the "embarrassing" historical neglect of William James's anticipations of Freud, Shakow, and Rapaport (1964:38–39) have supposed that Freud himself never knew how close James had come to his own later views on perversions. Actually James's ideas on this score were brought to the attention of European students of sexual inversion, including Freud, by Havelock Ellis (1896b:129) and, somewhat more fully, by Albert Moll (1897b:135, 677–78). Freud's copy of Ellis's *Sexual Inversion* (1896b) bears his marginal mark next to the relevant claim that sexual inversion is "a kind of sexual appetite, of which very likely most men possess the germinal possibility . . ." (quoted from James 1890, 2:439). Freud also scored the passage in Moll (1897b:135) that discusses James's instinct for interpersonal isolation, but he did not score the longer discussion of James's views on homosexuality (pp. 677–78).

Perhaps the fullest expression of the anthropological approach to sex around the turn of the century was that attained in Iwan Bloch's *Beiträge zur Aetiologie der Psychopathia sexualis* (Contributions to the Etiology of Psychopathia Sexualis), published in two volumes in 1902 and 1903. Drawing upon German anthropologist Hermann Heinrich Ploss's *Das Weib in der Natur- und Völkerkunde* (The Woman in Natural Science and Ethnology, 1885); upon Viennese ethnologist Friedrich S. Krauss's studies of the southern Slavs; upon Captain J. G. Bourke's (1891) detailed survey of excrement's multifarious liturgical roles in primitive societies; and upon a wide variety of other ethnological sources—Bloch showed that perversions were to be found universally in every culture and in every historical period. The history of religions, particularly primitive religions, he further maintained, was a special branch of the history of perverse sexual institutions, among which he mentioned prostitution, fetishism, phallic cults, exhibitionism, sadism, masochism, sodomy, and homosexuality. Given appropriate cultural influences, Bloch went so far as to insist, every sensory organ could function as an erotogenic zone and thereby form the basis for a perverse sexual impulse; and in this connection he cited Wilhelm Fliess's views on the nose. (See Bloch 1902–3, 2:192–206. Freud's personal copy [London library] bears his marginal markings throughout this section on erotogenic zones.)

An ardent critic of Krafft-Ebing's notion of congenital *psychopathia sexualis*, Bloch believed sexual aberrations to be far more often acquired than not. He attributed them to two principal causes: the need for varied sexual stimuli that is found among sexually hyperesthetic individuals—a psychophysiological theory previously suggested by Hoche (1896); and the influence exerted upon the sexual instinct by accidental, external conditions. Bloch thought that the former principle governed perversions arising in the later years of adulthood, and that the latter explained those arising through chance associations in childhood (1902–3, 2:363–65).

Iwan Bloch's *Beiträge* also touched upon the subject of childhood sexuality from an anthropological point of view. He noted the great frequency of copulatory attempts and other forms of sex play among the children of primitive peoples, and that these children's elders did not generally look down upon such childhood activities as abnormal or indecent (2:253–58).

From the evidence of his numerous annotations of Bloch's *Beiträge,* Freud read it with considerable interest. He later spoke highly of Bloch's efforts to divorce the subject of *psychopathia sexualis* from the doctrine of degeneration. Sometime prior to its publication, Freud added the following footnote to the manuscript of his "Dora" case history (1905*e* [originally drafted in 1901]), in which he had briefly adumbrated Bloch's anthropological approach to sexual perversions: "These remarks upon the sexual perversions had been written some years before the appearance of Bloch's excellent book [1902–3] . . ." (*S.E.,* 7:51, n. 1). Similarly, in the *Three Essays* Freud credited Bloch with having replaced the "pathological" approach to the study of sexual inversion with an "anthropological" one (1905*d*, *S.E.,* 7:139, n. 2).

In later years Freud found welcome psychoanalytic allies in a number of the anthropological sources that had originally inspired Bloch's *Beiträge.* Bloch's valuable Viennese source on the sexual customs of the southern Slavs, Friedrich S. Krauss, developed a serious interest in Freud's theories, and after 1910 he was frequently a guest at the Vienna Psychoanalytic Society. (It may have been at this time that Freud acquired Krauss's personal copy, autographed by Iwan Bloch, of Bloch's *Beiträge* [Freud library, New York].) As early as 1904, Krauss had founded *Anthropophyteia,* a journal devoted to researches on the history and the ethnology of sexual morality. Appearing from time to time in this journal were collections of obscene jokes from different cultures. At Krauss's invitation, Freud (1910*f*) contributed a letter to *Anthropophyteia* in which he explained from a psychoanalytic point of view the considerable scientific value of these anthropological collections. Such jokes, Freud believed, betrayed the unconscious sexual component impulses (particularly the coprophilic ones) of mankind.

Two years later, when Freud was engaged in writing *Totem and Taboo* (1912–13), Ernest Jones sent him a copy of J. G. Bourke's *Scatalogic Rites of All Nations* (1891)—another of Iwan Bloch's sources. It was in collaboration with Krauss and his journal that Freud arranged to have Bourke's work translated into German—a translation to which Freud contributed an enthusiastic Preface (1913*k*), where he discussed the coprophilic components of the infantile sexual instinct from psychoanalytic, as well as biogenetic, points of view.

In sum, the collective efforts of historians, ethnologists, and anthropologists to escape the narrow confines of the late-nineteenth-century, Victorian conception of sexuality played an important role in the sexual revolution that is now associated with Sigmund Freud's name. Not only was Freud himself in close touch with this anthropological movement; but he was also, at least in the later years of his life, an influential participant in it.

SUMMARY AND CONCLUSIONS

Freud's achievements in the sphere of sexology can be looked upon from two complementary points of view. On the one hand, they are an extensive synthesis of existing ideas and positions of investigators who, by 1900, had become well informed, independently of Freud, on the whole problem of human psychosexual development. At the same time, Freud contributed distinct psychoanalytic innovations and conceptual transformations.

Infantile sexuality. With Max Dessoir (1894), Albert Moll (1897*b*), Havelock Ellis (1898*a*), Karl Groos (1899), and others, Freud accepted the normalcy of spontaneous "polymorphously perverse" infantile sexuality; he endorsed a developmental conception of libido (including sequential stages); and, above all, he rationalized such phenomena within a biological, and Darwinian, conception of sex. In all of this, Freud's views were paralleled by those of his friend Wilhelm Fliess. Thus, the ideas of Freud, Fliess, and the sexologists were all part of a major conceptual offshoot of the Darwinian revolution. It was Havelock Ellis—always conscious of the wider historical trends in the scientific study of sex—who later expressed this conclusion most clearly:

> It was during the second half of the nineteenth century, when a new biological conception, under the inspiration of Darwin, was slowly permeating medicine, that the idea of infantile and youthful "perversion" began to be undermined; on the one hand the new scientific study of sex, started by the pioneering work of Krafft-Ebing at the end of the third quarter of the century, showed how common are such so-called "perversions" in early life while, on the other hand, the conception of evolution began to make it clear that we must not apply developed adult standards to undeveloped creatures, what is natural at one stage not necessarily being natural at the previous stage. (1933:105)

Recapitulation and regression. With Stekel (1895), Bölsche (1898–1903), G. Stanley Hall (1904), and many others, Freud applied Ernst Haeckel's fundamental biogenetic law ("ontogeny recapitulates phylogeny") to the problem of sexual development. In disease, Freud recognized the reverse of this biogenetic process. Along with Spitzka (1881), Kiernan (1888), and particularly Féré (1899), Freud accordingly envisioned pathological regressions, or dissolutions, in the sexual sphere (see also Chapter 7). Finally, turning the tables on contemporary psychiatric theory, Freud used the bedrock of sexual pathology to explain psychopathology.

Bisexuality, the component instincts, and their psychoneurotic sequelae. With Kiernan (1888), Lydston (1889), Chevalier (1893), Krafft-Ebing (1895), Fliess (1897), and others, Freud endorsed the "decisive" importance of bisexuality in human psychosexual development. At the same time, he was among those scientists who soon extended a more general phylogenetic paradigm of sex to encompass numerous other "component impulses" of the human sexual instinct (sadism, masochism, coprophilia, etc.). It was doubtless on account of these psychobiological features of his medical thinking that Freud was described by his environmentalist contemporary Iwan Bloch as having "gone further than any other writer in biologico-physiological derivation of sexual perversions" (1907; 1910 trans.:756).

The role of environment. But Freud also went further than anyone else in accounting for sexual perversions within a sophisticated environmentalist, cultural, and psychological conception. Along with William James (1890), Albert Moll (1897*b*), Havelock Ellis (1897), and particularly Iwan Bloch (1902–3), Freud accepted the anthropological ubiquity of perverse sexual drives, enthusiastically welcoming this new approach to the scientific study of sex. More important still, with Binet (1887), Schrenck-Notzing (1892), Dallemagne (1894), and Ribot (1896), Freud gave theoretical primacy to unconscious libidinal fixations, to childhood traumas, and to the psychogenic nature of most neurotic symptoms. In doing so, he showed how rich are the psychological, and particularly the intrafamilial, forces that play upon "the germs of perversion" in all of us. Freud also discovered how pathogenic phantasies develop out of these germs of infantile sexual activity, as well as how such phantasies can intervene between the real events of childhood and the subsequent symptoms of neurosis. Through his notions of the Oedipus complex, the castration complex, and so forth, Freud enriched this etiological conception with far-reaching clinical insight.

The nature and nurture of psychosexual pathology. Finally, Freud's theory of sexual pathology synthesized the contrasting positions of the nativists and the environmentalists within his own notion of "a 'complemental series'" (1905*d*, *S.E.*, 7:170–71, 239–40). In this etiological notion, Freud recognized every possible combination of hereditary predisposition with environmental determinism. His flexibility on the degree of "innateness" or "acquiredness" in sexual pathology was a novel and fruitful position in an old and tired debate. His approach allowed him, above all, to adopt and exploit the best theoretical ideas advanced by the two opposing camps in contemporary sexology. More of a psychologist than Krafft-Ebing, Moll, or Ellis, Freud was also far more of a biologist than Binet, Schrenck-Notzing, or Bloch. It is this dual construction to his theorizing as a sexologist that has made so enduring Freud's thinking as a psychoanalyst.

9

Dreams and
the Psychopathology of
Everyday Life

A dream is "a (disguised) fulfillment of a (suppressed or repressed) wish" (*S.E.*, 4:160). With this discovery, which Freud first announced to the world in his book *Die Traumdeutung* (The Interpretation of Dreams, 1900a), the psychoanalytic art of analyzing dreams became what he proclaimed as "the royal road to a knowledge of the unconscious activities of the mind" (*S.E.*, 5:608). *The Interpretation of Dreams* has generally been considered Freud's single most important work, nothing short of magnificent in its psychological achievement. In keeping with the book's epochal status, although it appeared in early November 1899, it was postdated by the publisher into the new century. "Insight such as this falls to one's lot but once in a lifetime," Freud wrote in 1932 in his Preface to the third English edition (*S.E.*, 4:xxxii). And as James Strachey notes in his Editor's Introduction to this work, *The Interpretation of Dreams* was one of the two books—the other being the *Three Essays on the Theory of Sexuality* (1905d)—that Freud kept systematically up to date in successive editions.

If *The Interpretation of Dreams* is Freud's greatest book, it is today also one of his least understood, as Henri Ellenberger (1970:450) has insisted. The reasons for such a current lack of understanding are several, and I believe that they exemplify most of the basic misunderstandings about Freud's psychoanalytic achievements as a whole.[1]

---

1. Ellenberger (1970:450–51) would ascribe the inaccessible nature of Freud's book to (1) the many revisions, additions, and deletions that *The Interpretation of Dreams* underwent in Freud's lifetime; (2) the frequently difficult-to-translate nuances in Freud's original German-language dream discussions; and (3) the implicit, but largely unappreciated, context of fin-de-siècle Viennese life that the book as a whole reflects. See pp. 346–50 for my discussion of the misunderstandings about this work.

Specifically, the problem of properly appreciating this book may be conveniently subdivided into the three separate issues of (1) its historical origins, (2) its precise claims to originality, and (3) its relationship to the rest of Freud's psychoanalytic thought.

THE PREHISTORY OF FREUD'S DREAM THEORY

More than once Freud has said that he first discovered the meaning and importance of dreams when patients, complying with the technique of free association, began spontaneously reporting their dreams to him. Thereupon, Freud determined to treat his patients' dreams as extensions of their symptoms and to assume that dreams, too, have a meaning (1900a, S.E., 4:100–101; 1914d, S.E., 14:19; 1916–17, S.E., 15:83; 1925d, S.E., 20:43). As Jones (1953:350) comments about this discovery, it was "a perfect example of serendipity."

Although it may have been serendipitous that some of Freud's patients began reporting their dreams to him, it was hardly accidental that he then sought for a hidden meaning in them. Freud, as Jones himself documents, had a keen interest in the interpretation of dreams long before he realized that they might possess a more special, psychoanalytic application. A good dreamer, Freud had kept notebooks of his own dreams during his medical-school days (and perhaps even earlier).[2] In these notebooks he had systematically analyzed dreams as possible portents of the future. To his fiancée, Martha, he reported on 19 July 1883 a blissful dream of a landscape, "which according to the private notebook on dreams which I have composed from my experience indicates traveling" (unpublished letter, quoted in Jones 1953:351). Freud related several other dreams to his future wife in their 1880s correspondence, and on at least one occasion he anticipated a basic feature of his later theory of dream formation with the comment: "I never dream about matters that have occupied me during the day, only of such themes as were touched on once in the course of the day and then broken off" (unpublished letter of 30 June 1882, quoted in Jones 1953:351).[3]

Freud's first published reference to dreams was in the "Preliminary Communication" on hysteria, published jointly with Josef Breuer in January 1893. There we find two observations on this topic: that hysterical patients are momentarily insane during hypnoid states, "as we all are in dreams"; and that hysterical symptoms may involve "symbolic" associations "such as healthy people form in dreams" (1893a, S.E., 2:5, 13). The latter claim about symbolic associations points directly to Freud's subsequent ideas on dream symbolism.

Freud's next published observation on dreams occurs in a footnote

2. Freud's early notebooks on dreams have not survived.
3. See also *The Interpretation of Dreams*, 1900a, S.E., 4:18, 79, 177; and for Freud's other early comments on dreams, *Letters*, p. 101.

that he drafted between 1894 and the spring of 1895 and appended to the case history of Frau Emmy von N. in *Studies on Hysteria*. There Freud narrated how for several weeks he had slept on a harder bed than usual and had recalled his dreams upon awakening with much greater vividness. He took the trouble to write these dreams down in order that he might "try to solve them." Two Freudian generalizations about dreams emerged at this time: the tendency for dreams to work out ideas and impressions that have been dwelt upon only cursorily during the day (cf. Freud's similar insight of 1882), and the dream's compulsion to link together any ideas, however unrelated, that happen to be present in the same state of consciousness (1895d, *S.E.*, 2:69 n.). Like the former "working out" idea, the latter notion of "compulsive association" found a subsidiary place in Freud's mature theory of dream formation (1900a, *S.E.* 4:179).

An anticipation of the later wish-fulfillment theory of dreams was related by Freud in a 4 March 1895 letter to Wilhelm Fliess, where he described a "convenience" dream of Josef Breuer's nephew, a young doctor who was a reluctant riser in the mornings. Having heard himself being called by his landlady one morning, Breuer's nephew promptly hallucinated his name on a hospital bed chart-board and concluded that there was no need for him to rise, since he must already be at work (*Origins*, p. 115; *Interpretation*, *S.E.*, 4:125). In his letter to Fliess, Freud compared this dream with a wishful "dream psychosis" experienced by one of his patients.

From all of the above, it is apparent that Freud, before he actually discovered the specific *wish-fulfillment* meaning of dreams in July 1895 (during his analysis of the famous dream about "Irma's injection"), had been diligently attempting "to solve" dreams for more than a decade. One might say that he eventually gave scientific expression to an earlier, personal predilection for interpreting dreams, and that it merely remained for him to translate a symbolic "portent of the future" (his original, superstitious theory of dreams) into a "disguised wish" of the present and childhood past. Thus, when Freud once wrote that he had entertained no interest in the subject of dreams prior to his discovery of their psychoanalytic importance in the 1890s, he was evidently allowing his Baconian self-image as a scientist to obscure the truth of the matter (1914d, *S.E.*, 14:19).

Freud was considerably more accurate and outspoken when it came to acknowledging his major predecessors in dream theory. Prior to Freud, the literature on dreams was already quite voluminous, as he discovered to his chagrin when he decided to write a historical survey chapter for his book. Furthermore, like the psychoanalytic theory of psychosexual development, Freud's theory of dreams had been anticipated piecemeal in almost every major constituent by prior students of the problem. For example, the claim that dreams have a hidden meaning, that they are wish-fulfillments, that they represent disguised expressions of unacceptable thoughts, that they elicit the archaic features of man's psyche, that they involve a regression to the dreamer's childhood experiences and successive personalities, that they fulfill the wish to sleep, and that they come about by the condensation and displacement of ideas—all these Freudian insights and more were made by other students of dreaming prior to Freud.[4] Some of these anticipations Freud had previously been exposed to as a medical student; some he learned about when reading the literature on dreams in the late 1890s; and some he encountered only after he had developed and published his own theory on the subject. Freud's theoretical conception was characterized by its unusually exhaustive and synthetic approach and by its peculiar emphasis upon a number of key ideas like wish-fulfillment, dream-censorship, and the wider primary/secondary process model of the mind in which these notions were conjointly cast.

Freud's most important precursors in the theory of dreaming, at least for him personally, are probably the least discussed in psychoanalytic history, because they were largely anonymous. I am speaking of the age-old proponents of the popular, lay conception of dreaming, as set forth in the Bible—for example, Joseph's interpretations of the Pharaoh's prophetic dreams—and in countless cheap dream books that were widely available in Freud's day. Two methods of dream interpretation are generally used in these popular sources. In most biblical instances, dreams are transposed as a symbolic whole in order to uncover their hidden, prophetic meaning. Joseph, for example, interprets the Pharaoh's famous dream of seven fat cows that are followed and then eaten by seven thin cows as foretelling seven years of Egyptian plenty that are to be followed by seven years of famine. Contrasting with this method, the popular dream books of Freud's day generally treated the dream piecemeal as a series of brief messages to be deciphered according to a fixed cryptographic key (for example, the reception of a "letter" stands for impending "trouble"). Although Freud did not specifically mention ever having studied such dream books, the private dream notebooks he kept in the early 1880s were clearly patterned after them. He later discussed both biblical and popular methods of dream "decoding" as part of his historical survey in *The Interpretation of Dreams* (*S.E.*, 4:96–99), and he also made explicit his sentimental support for these more popular conceptions of dreaming when he chose the provocative title of his book (Ellenberger 1970:452). *Traumdeutung*, unlike, say, *Deutung des Traums*, reminded his German readers of the fortune-teller's slogan as well as of the related word *Sterndeutung* ("astrology").

With regard to the scientific literature on dreaming, the ideas of

4. For a comprehensive survey of pre-Freudian theories of dreaming, see Ellenberger's *Discovery of the Unconscious* (1970:303–11, 493), on which I have drawn liberally for what immediately follows. Freud's own historical survey of his predecessors in the first edition of *Die Traumdeutung* runs to sixty-five pages and is broken down into eight subsections: (1) dreams and their relation to waking mental life; (2) the material and (3) sources of dreams; (4) forgetting of dreams; (5) distinctive psychological features of dreams; (6) morality in dreams; (7) various comprehensive theories of dreaming and dream function; and (8) the relation between dreams and mental pathology. The Bibliography of Freud's book includes references to 79 different works on dreams, most of which are mentioned in the text. In later editions, Freud added a second bibliographical list of over 200 works—most of them psychoanalytic—written since 1900 and increased the first (pre-1900) list to 260 items.

psychiatrist Wilhelm Griesinger overlapped closely with Freud's thinking. Griesinger (1861:106) had maintained that dreams share with psychoses the common feature of being "the imaginary fulfillment of
wishes [*die imaginäre Erfüllung von . . . Wünschen*]." Freud's teacher
in psychiatry, Theodor Meynert, who himself followed Griesinger on
many points, had further analyzed this "wish-fulfillment" syndrome in
connection with states of acute hallucinatory psychosis, the so-called
Meynert's amentia (Jones 1953:353). Freud discussed cases of this sort
in his first paper on the neuropsychoses of defense (1894*a*, *S.E.*, 3:
58–59), so he was not unacquainted with the syndrome that Meynert
(1889–90:40) had compared to both dream and infantile (primary-
ego) mental states. Like Meynert and Griesinger, Freud eventually, in
early 1899, linked this psychiatric condition with his own theory of
dreams (*Origins*, p. 277), and he repeatedly cited Griesinger's authority
on this point in *The Interpretation of Dreams* (*S.E.*, 4:91, 134, 230
n.).[5]

In a more diagnostic vein, certain sexual pathologists had previously recognized the wishful nature of dreams and had applied this
insight in assessing perverse sexual desires in their patients. Albert
Moll (1891:193) emphasized this point in *Die conträre Sexualempfindung*, claiming that dreams are one of the most reliable indicators of
perverse sexual inclinations. He reported that many perverts who have
been therapeutically cured of their sexual aberrations in a waking state
of consciousness may still continue to dream of perverse experiences at
night. Paul Näcke later set forth similar diagnostic views in an article
in which he proclaimed, "Clearer and clearer comes to light the colossal
influence of the genital sphere upon the formation of ego-complexes
and upon the character of mankind" (1899*b*:356, 380).

The issues of whether a dreamer is responsible for the moral character of his dreams, and what that moral character reveals about his
"inner self," were also discussed by students of dreaming in the late
nineteenth century. Freud reviewed a spectrum of opinions on this
subject in *The Interpretation of Dreams*, citing, with approval, the following words of Hildebrandt: "It is impossible to think of any action
in a dream for which the original motive has not in some way or other
—whether as a wish, or desire or impulse—passed through the waking mind" (Hildebrandt 1875:51; Freud, *S.E.*, 4:69). Some years after
publishing his famous work on dreams, Freud ran across the related
ideas of a Viennese engineer, Josef Popper, who had independently set
forth what Freud acknowledged as "the core" of his own dream-distortion theory. Popper's views were first stated in *Phantasien eines*

5. Presumably Freud culled Griesinger's specific comments on dreams from
his reading of the dream literature in 1898 or 1899—that is, some three years after
he had independently developed his own wish-fulfillment theory of dreaming with
his July 1895 interpretation of the dream about "Irma's injection" (*Origins*, p. 322).
Nevertheless, the psychiatric ideas of Griesinger and Meynert must have provided
a conducive background to the whole "wish-fulfillment" theory of dreaming. For
Meynert's concept of amentia and its ties to Freud's own thinking, see Amacher
1965:37–41.

Realisten (Phantasies of a Realist, 1899), published almost simultaneously with Freud's *Interpretation*. Writing under the pseudonym of Lynkeus, Popper had explained in a chapter entitled "Dreaming like Waking" that the dreams of the unchaste, in contrast to those of the virtuous, are commonly senseless and fragmented owing to an intervening distortion and censorship of the original dream-thoughts (2:149–63). Freud added to the second (1909) edition of *The Interpretation of Dreams* a footnote in which he quoted from Popper's book at some length (see *S.E.*, 4:308–9; and also Freud 1923f and 1932c).

Freud's other major precursors in the theory of dreams include three great pioneers of the subject, Karl Albert Scherner, Alfred Maury, and Hervey de Saint-Denys. Influenced by the Romantic tradition, Scherner's *Das Leben des Traums* (The Life of the Dream) appeared in 1861 and set forth a symbolic theory of dream interpretation. Scherner attempted to correlate dream symbols with various bodily sensations experienced during sleep, and he related the human body as a whole to the symbol of a house. Scherner was particularly thorough in his enumeration of sexual symbols. As symbolic equivalents of the male sexual organs, he listed pointed objects of all sorts, and, for the female sex, he mentioned narrow passageways through courtyards and other similarly confined spaces. Scherner believed pubic hair to be symbolized by fur. Freud later praised Scherner as "the true discoverer of symbolism in dreams," adding that Scherner's views on this subject had merely been resurrected and given proper recognition by his own psychoanalytic theory of dream symbolism (*S.E.*, 5:359 n.; note added in 1911).

Alfred Maury (1861) and Hervey de Saint-Denys (1867) introduced the experimental method of dream investigation. While he was sleeping, Maury had an assistant stimulate him with noises, odors, and other sensory cues. On being awakened several minutes later, Maury systematically recorded the dreams that had ensued. The smell of perfume, for instance, induced a dream of being in a Cairo perfume merchant's shop. He also related dream images to past experiences in his life—experiences that often had long since been forgotten. Freud knew of Maury's (1861) work and cited him repeatedly in *The Interpretation of Dreams*.

It remained for Hervey de Saint-Denys, however, to carry the self-analytic technique of dream interpretation to its most herculean extreme in the late nineteenth century. In his anonymously published *Les Rêves et les moyens de les diriger* (Dreams and the Means of Directing Them, 1867), Hervey described the three stages through which his self-analytic technique evolved. First he learned how to recognize when he was dreaming. Then he taught himself to wake up after each dream so that he might record his dreams in special notebooks. Finally, he sought to alter the course of his dreams as he pleased, a technique that was successful but that met with certain limitations. For instance, when Hervey once attempted to kill himself in the course of a dream by jumping off a tall tower, he instantly found himself transposed into the crowd below, where he witnessed another man falling off the same tower. Over a twenty-year period, Hervey recorded more than two thousand dreams, many of them "self-directed" by his remarkable experimental method. His general theory of dreaming was based upon a conception of memory revival. He also achieved a clear insight into the psychoanalytic notions of condensation and displacement in connection with dreams—that is, the superimposition and fragmentation of real-life entities and experiences. Hervey's (1867) book had become a rare item by the 1890s, and Freud reported that he was unable, in spite of all his efforts, to procure a copy of it (S.E., 4:61). Many of Hervey's findings were indirectly known to Freud, however, from other works on dreaming—for example, Maury's (1861) book in its second (1878) edition.

Three final students of dreaming, although not of the stature of Scherner, Maury, or Hervey de Saint-Denys, also deserve mention on account of the high value that Freud placed upon their theoretical insights into the problem. The first, Yves Delage (1891), was a French biologist whose model of dreaming, with its emphasis upon day-to-day sensory impressions as "accumulators of energy" tending to inhibit and conflict with one another, approximates the economic and dynamic postulates of Freud's theory. Delage attributed the motive force of dreams to a previous "suppression" of psychic material during the day —a view that Freud cited approvingly (S.E., 4:82; 5:591). Freud gave considerable credit as well to the views of English psychologist James Sully (1893), who had discussed not only the cryptographic nature of dreams but also the phenomenon of personality regression during dreaming (S.E., 4:60, 135, n. 2). "Now our dreams," Sully (1893:362) reported of such regressions, "are a means of conserving these [earlier] successive personalities. When asleep we go back to the old ways of looking at things and of feeling about them, to impulses and activities which long ago dominated us . . ." (quoted twice by Freud, S.E., 4:60; 5:591). Finally, Freud believed with Havelock Ellis (1899:721) that dreams call forth "an archaic world of vast emotions and imperfect thoughts," the detailed investigation of which promised to clarify the primeval stages of human mental evolution (S.E., 4:60; 5:591).

Several of the writers whose views I have reviewed here (especially Scherner and Sully) concurred with Freud that dreams serve a useful psychical function, and that they often possess, additionally, a *hidden* meaning. Nevertheless, the dominant pre-Freudian theory of dreaming in late-nineteenth-century scientific and medical circles was based on a much more physiological tradition and stood, as Freud later emphasized, in basic opposition to his own views. According to the prevailing physiological explanation, the dream was simply an incidental reaction to the various sensory and somatic stimuli normally impinging upon the mind during a state of sleep; it was a predominantly corporeal process, "a kind of twitching of a mind that is otherwise asleep" (1925*d*, S.E., 20:43). In other words, neither meaning nor a beneficial psychical function was accorded to dreams by the reigning somatic theories of the period.[6] Thus, if Freud's contention that dreams have hidden meaning was not entirely novel among students of dreams, his views certainly expressed a minority position within *scientific* circles—a position that had not been defended in such exhaustive fashion since the work of Scherner (1861).

Freud's Early Theory of Dreams

Another little-appreciated aspect of Freud's thinking about dreams is that he held two distinct theories between 1895 and 1900. Or I might say that his theory of dreams passed through two major *stages*, with the later reformulation encompassing the earlier.[7]

Freud reached his early theory of dreams deductively in the process of thinking about the *Project for a Scientific Psychology* (see Amacher 1965:73–74). Having envisioned primary-process mental phenomena as movements of psychic energy following previous experiences of satisfaction (or the neuronal pathways of least "resistance"), Freud found it logical to view dreams as similar primary-process activities. Dreams, according to this conception, are simply hallucinations motivated by the small residues of energy that are ordinarily left over in an otherwise sleeping (or energyless) mind. It was the quantitative diminution of all secondary processes during sleep, Freud had argued in the *Project*, that allowed most normal dreams to follow a natural —and completely wishful—pattern of hallucinatory discharge. Freud's famous 24 July 1895 interpretation of the dream about "Irma's injection" fixed this theory in his mind at the more empirical level when he first realized that the motivating "dream-wish" might have to be inferred from certain ideational *missing links* that were somehow absent from the conscious manifestations of the dream (*Project*, *S.E.*, 1: 341–43). By restoring these missing links through the technique of free association, Freud recognized that his otherwise nonsensical dream

6. Freud cited Strümpell (1877), Binz (1878), Maury (1861; 2nd ed., 1878), and, to a lesser extent, Robert (1886) as the major proponents of this somatic conception. See Freud 1900a, *S.E.*, 4:76–82.

7. Freud himself confounded his two different dream theories in his "History of the Psycho-Analytic Movement," where he wrote, "*The Interpretation of Dreams* . . . was finished in all essentials at the beginning of 1896 but was not written out until the summer of 1899" (1914d, *S.E.*, 14:22; see also Freud 1925j, *S.E.*, 19:248). James Strachey seems to agree with Freud's statement, while adding "some qualifications" to it (Editor's Introduction to *The Interpretation of Dreams*, *S.E.*, 4:xviii–xix). On the other hand, Jones (1953:351–54), Kris (*Origins*, p. 400, n. 1), Schur (1972:153), and others have questioned Freud's claim. Jones, for instance, compares the *Project* (1895) discussion of dreams to the theory published in 1900 "as a cottage to a mansion" (1953:354). Of principal concern to Jones, Kris, and Schur is to portray Freud's self-analysis in the fall of 1897 as the revolutionary catalyst in his understanding of the dreaming process; and thus, their views tend to attribute to his self-analysis many theoretical insights that he actually derived from the Fliess relationship, from sexual theory, and from biological and particularly *biogenetic* considerations (see my discussion of Freud's self-analysis in Chapter 6).

concerning his patient Irma had actually sought to exculpate him from an embarrassing inability to cure Irma's hysterical symptoms.

The immediate circumstances associated with this famous dream were as follows.[8] Irma, a young woman who was on very friendly terms with Freud and his family, had been receiving psychoanalytic treatment from Freud in the summer of 1895. After several months of therapy, the patient was only partially cured, and Freud had become unsure whether he should keep her on. He had therefore proposed a solution to her, but she was not inclined to accept it. The day before the dream, Freud was visited by his friend "Otto" (Oskar Rie), who had been staying with the patient's family at a summer resort. Otto reproved Freud for his failure to cure Irma of all her symptoms. That evening Freud wrote out Irma's case history so that he might present it to "Dr. M." (Josef Breuer) in order to justify his treatment of the case. Later that night Freud dreamt that he met Irma at a large party and said to her, "If you still get pains, it's really only your fault." Irma looked "pale and puffy," and Freud wondered if she might not have an organic disease after all. He therefore examined his patient and detected white patches and scabs in her mouth. Otto and Dr. M., who were also present in the dream, then examined the patient for themselves; and it was agreed by all that Irma had contracted "an infection." The three physicians further determined that the infection had originated from an injection previously given to the patient by Otto, who had apparently used a dirty syringe.

Upon interpretation the next morning, Freud's dream revealed the fulfillment of at least two unconscious wishes. First, the dream had excused him of responsibility for Irma's pains by blaming them on Otto (Oskar Rie). Simultaneously the dream had exercised revenge upon Otto for his annoying remarks about Freud's unsuccessful therapy (*Origins*, p. 403; *Interpretation*, 1900a, S.E., 4:106–21).

There is no mention of either repression or censorship in Freud's brief *Project* discussion of the Irma dream. The *Project*, as James Strachey has commented, contains a "pre-id" model of the mind (*S.E.*, 1:292). Freud had yet to appreciate the elaborate distortions that are intentionally introduced into dreams by the "dream-work" in order to cover up the egoistic, hostile, and lustful nature of most dream-wishes. Instead, Freud's *Project* theory of dream distortion still possesses remnants of the dominant physiological theory of dreaming—namely, that a dream is psychically imperfect and hence garbled in its true, wish-fulfillment meaning.

In contrast, Freud's later (1900) conception of dream distortion was based upon a dynamic-genetic model of human psychosexual development. With the discovery of the id, the primary reason for

8. Schur (1972:79–89) has pointed out certain parallels between the content of the Irma dream and the case history of Emma, upon whom Wilhelm Fliess had previously conducted a nasal operation with such near-fatal consequences (see Chapter 5). According to Schur's variant interpretation of this dream, its main wish was to exculpate *Fliess*, not Freud, from the charge of incompetent medical treatment.

dreaming became genetic rather than economic: that is, we dream because the infantile id clamors for nightly self-expression, rather than because impinging energy residues or unresolved daytime conflicts happen to discharge themselves in the sleeping mind. Additionally, it was Freud's genetic, id-based model of dreaming that (1) allowed him to ascribe *universal* validity to his wish-fulfillment formula [9] and (2) united the theories of psychoneurosis, human psychosexual development, and dream distortion into a single structure.

As I have already shown in Chapters 6 to 8, Freud's discovery of the id stemmed not only from his clinical and self-analytic study of dreams in 1895–97, but also from his scientific relationship with Wilhelm Fliess, from the influence of contemporary sexologists, and, most of all, from his own increasingly biogenetic conception of human psychosexual development between 1896 and 1899. In short, the discovery of the id, and the impact of that discovery upon the theories of neurosis and psychosexual development, largely made possible Freud's mature theory of dreaming, not vice versa, as is so often erroneously maintained.[10]

FREUD'S MATURE (GENETIC) THEORY OF DREAMS

Freud's mature, genetic theory of dreams is formally distinguished from his earlier theory by two major claims and by a number of sub-corollaries. These claims are (1) that every dream is an attempt to fulfill a wish, even nightmares and anxiety dreams, and (2) that every dream represents a wish-fulfillment dating from early childhood, as well as a wish-fulfillment from current mental life. Let us consider the first claim.

Freud, as I have mentioned, was well aware that the wishful

9. It is important to understand, in connection with what follows, that Freud's early (pre-id) theory of dreams did not encompass every dream but was limited to explaining *normal* dreams. Freud made this point clear in the *Project*: "The aim and sense of dreams (of normal ones, at all events) can be established with certainty. They [dreams] are *wish-fulfillments*—that is, primary processes following upon experiences of satisfaction . . ." (*S.E.*, 1:340; *Origins*, p. 402). What Freud evidently declined to theorize about in 1895 were nightmares, anxiety dreams, and other forms of blatantly unpleasant dreams. (Although the term *id* did not become part of the psychoanalytic lexicon until 1923, I have used it here in its generally accepted conceptual sense as applied to the earlier period [see footnote 22, p. 186].)

10. In contrast to my own historical views on this subject, it is commonly claimed that the theory of dreaming, as developed during Freud's self-analysis, was the single major source of inspiration for the theory of infantile sexuality. Robert (1966:178) writes, for example, that "all the works he [Freud] published in the following years [after 1900] sprang from his theory of dreams. . . . Even the *Three Essays on the Theory of Sexuality*, which exist in their own right, owe their first and decisive inspiration to *The Interpretation of Dreams*." Similarly, Reuben Fine considers both the theory of dreams and the libido theory as jointly stemming from Freud's analysis of his own dreams (Fine 1963:68, 218; 1973:29). See also Mannoni 1974:91.

character of dreams had been pointed out before him. In *The Interpretation of Dreams* he cited six other authorities on dreaming, in addition to Griesinger (1861:106), who had anticipated him on this important notion. What was unique to his own theory, Freud declared, was that *every* dream could be proved a wish-fulfillment (*S.E.*, 4:134). He arrived at this remarkable conclusion by the following route. At the clinical and self-analytic levels, his efforts to convince both himself and his often skeptical friends and patients that most dreams are wish-fulfillments required him to pay greater attention to the role of dream distortion and censorship in disguising most people's nightly dreams.[11] Since many of these dreams dealt with repression-laden sexual matters and were likewise related to Freud's own, and to his patients', neurotic problems, Freud increasingly came to see that censorship, not "psychical inefficiency," was the major agent behind dream distortion.

Approaching the matter from a more theoretical point of view, Freud sought to explain the supposed exceptions to his dream theory in terms of analogous patterns of symptom formation he had already worked out in the field of sexual neurosis. A neurotic symptom, like an "exceptional" dream, is generally unpleasant to the person it afflicts. Yet the ultimate origin of all such symptoms, Freud had come to believe by the mid-1890s, was sexual in nature. And sexuality could always be associated in neurotics with a repressed or suppressed *wish*. Here, then, was a psychological paradigm for the enigma of unpleasant dreams. With Freud's increasing appreciation of the spontaneous element in infantile sexuality, he came to apply the same logic to the exceptional dreams of children.

Although Freud's theory of the meaning of dreams allowed for only one general pattern, he nevertheless recognized three major types of dreams as experienced by the dreamer. The first type—pure wish-fulfillment—required little or no interpretation for the motive to be understood. Freud placed "convenience" dreams in this first category, as when one is thirsty and dreams of drinking a refreshing liquid, or when one's bladder is full and one dreams of relieving oneself. Only dreams of Freud's second and third categories—that is, dreams of seemingly indifferent or unpleasant content, respectively—stood in need of further psychoanalytic interpretation in order to show their true, wish-fulfillment nature.

It is at this point in his *Interpretation* argument that Freud introduced his fundamental contrast between *manifest* and *latent* dream-thoughts. What we remember of a dream—namely, the manifest dream-thoughts—may well be indifferent or unpleasant; but what matters to Freud's theory are the latent thoughts that subsequently emerge upon interpreting such dreams, for it is these thoughts that actually instigate dreams and thus contain the dream's true (wish-fulfillment) meaning.

11. See, for example, Freud's 28 April 1897 reference to Fliess's "defence-dream" (*Origins*, p. 194; and *S.E.*, 4:134–62).

Apparent Exceptions to Freud's Early Theory
(as Solved by the Later Theory)

Inasmuch as dreams with a purely indifferent content lie on an explanatory continuum in Freud's theory between totally undisguised wish-fulfillments and dreams of manifestly unpleasurable nature, I shall concentrate my analysis of exceptional dreams upon the latter end of this spectrum. There are four distinct subgroups of unpleasurable dreams in Freud's *Interpretation* conception: (1) elaborately distorted dreams; (2) counter-wish dreams; (3) anxiety dreams; and (4) punishment dreams.[12]

Elaborately distorted dreams. Dreams, like neurotic symptoms, are a compromise formation, whose structure is the product of two separate psychical systems, the unconscious and the preconscious ego (S.E., 5:580–81).[13] A fulfilled wish in one system, however, does not always coincide with a fulfilled wish in the other (S.E., 4:146). For instance, a young female patient dreamt that she was standing before the coffin of her sister's only surviving son. (An elder son had died some time before.) In the course of analyzing this dream, Freud learned that his patient was still in love with a man who had previously broken with her. After a long hiatus, this man had appeared once again at the dreamer's home in order to attend the funeral of the sister's elder child. The death of the sister's other child would have brought about a similar reunion. Thus, beneath the manifest content of this patient's dream, there actually lay an unconscious libidinal wish against which the patient was still struggling in real life (S.E., 4:152–54).

It is the nature of many unconscious wishes, Freud commented about such elaborately distorted dreams, that even the dreamer finds the wish, once it has been laid bare, repugnant to his or her better judgment. Such wishes continually emerge in dreams, however, and it is *these* wishes that justify Freud's formula that "*a dream is a (disguised) fulfillment of a (suppressed or repressed) wish*" (S.E., 4:160; Freud's italics).

Counter-wish dreams. Under the heading of "counter-wish" dreams Freud placed two frequent but distinctly different classes of dreams. In the first, he included those dreams that are motivated by the wish that his theories might be wrong. Dreams of this sort typically appear, he claimed, just after a patient has first learned of the wish-

---

12. I omit a fifth group, the unpleasurable dreams in traumatic neurosis, since Freud was interested in them much later. I will consider this group, however, in Chapter 11 when I discuss Freud's theory of the death instinct. See *Beyond the Pleasure Principle*, 1920g, S.E., 18:32, where Freud discusses this problem.

13. The major division in Freud's topographical model of the mind is between the system Unconscious (which contains the repressed) and the system Preconscious; it is not between preconscious and conscious mental states. Preconscious ideas are *descriptively* unconscious, but they are capable of becoming conscious at any time. Repressed wishes, which form the core of the system Unconscious, are both descriptively unconscious and dynamically so; that is, they never attain direct access to a conscious mental state.

fulfillment theory. By having an unpleasant dream, and thus denying Freud's theory on the subject, a patient is attempting to controvert what Freud has already revealed about the repressed motives of the illness (*S.E.*, 4:151, 157–58). The patient's resistance to treatment is therefore the principal cause of such exceptional dreams. Freud added another class of counter-wish dreams to the second (1909) edition of *Interpretation* when he ascribed certain frustrated wishes, as well as the occurrence of wholly unwished-for events in dreams, to the masochistic inclinations of the dreamer (*S.E.*, 4:159). (Here we see an important tie between Freud's mature theory of dreaming and the psychosexual substratum that increasingly came to support it after 1895.)

Anxiety dreams. Anxiety dreams offer perhaps the greatest apparent obstacle to Freud's theory. As Freud himself admitted in 1900, the idea of considering these dreams as wishful "will meet with very little sympathy from the unenlightened" (*S.E.*, 4:161). Nonetheless, anxiety dreams, too, can be considered as wishful, for upon interpretation, they invariably prove to be dreams of a sexual nature, whose libido has been transformed into neurotic anxiety (*S.E.*, 4:161–62). Thus, the theory of anxiety dreams "forms part of the psychology of the neuroses" (*S.E.*, 5:582).

A specific example will help to elucidate this class of dreams. In the spring of 1897, one of Freud's patients, "an intelligent jurist," challenged Freud's wish-fulfillment theory with the following dream. The jurist (Herr E.) dreamt that just as he was bringing a lady home, he was arrested by a policeman and ordered into a carriage. "I suppose you'll say," declared Herr E. to Freud, "that *this* is a wishful dream." Freud reported his subsequent interrogation of Herr E., together with an interpretation of the dream, in his correspondence with Fliess:

> [Herr E.:] "I had the dream in the morning after I had spent the night with this lady." . . . —[Freud:] Do you know what you were accused of?—"Yes. Of having killed a child."—Was this connected with anything real?—"I was once responsible for the abortion of a child as a result of a *liaison*. I don't like to think about it."—Well now, did nothing happen during the morning before you had the dream?—"Yes. I woke up and had intercourse."—But you took precautions?—"Yes. By withdrawing."— Then you were afraid you might have begotten a child; and the dream showed the fulfillment of your wish that nothing had gone wrong and that you had nipped the child in the bud. You then made use of the [neurotic] anxiety that arises after this kind of [incomplete] intercourse as material for your dream. (*Origins*, pp. 199–200, Draft L, 2 May 1897; see also *Interpretation, S.E.*, 4:155–57)

In Herr E.'s case, the anxiety associated with his dream was already present before his dream took form. The dream simply seized upon this anxiety in order to express a disguised wish. In contrast to this pattern, Freud thought anxiety dreams could arise whenever a repressed (erotic) wish is openly fulfilled in a dream without *sufficient* disguise. A certain portion of libido in the dream is thereupon transformed into anxiety. The dream is usually broken off at this point, and the dreamer awakens in a state of anxious fright.[14]

It was this second formula that proved so useful to Freud in explaining the exceptional dreams of childhood. Since the repressions associated with Freud's theory of psychosexual development are supposed to occur in the later years of childhood, he made a special point of insisting that dreams in early childhood should be models of undisguised wish-fulfillment. Indeed, the openly wishful nature that he attributed to children's dreams was an *experimentum crucis* for the theory, and he reported seven such corroborating dreams in *Interpretation* (S.E., 4:127–31). At least one of these delightful dreams deserves to be mentioned here. Freud's youngest child Anna (aged nineteen months) had an attack of vomiting one day after eating too many wild strawberries. As a consequence, she was made to go without food for the rest of the day. That night she excitedly called out a whole menu in her sleep: "'Anna Freud, stwawbewwies, wild stwawbewwies, omblet, pudden!'" (S.E., 4:130; see also *Origins,* p. 227, letter of 31 October 1897).

Yet, it was precisely children, Freud admitted, who proved to be the commonest victims of anxiety dreams (*pavor nocturnus*). To resolve this contradiction, he espoused the view, previously developed in conjunction with Wilhelm Fliess, that these attacks of night terrors are "a question of sexual impulses which have not been understood and which have been repudiated." A tacit reference to Fliess's *Entwicklungsschubmechanik* follows with the words: "Investigation would probably show a periodicity in the occurrence of the attacks, since an increase in sexual libido can be brought about not only by accidental exciting impressions but also by successive waves of spontaneous developmental processes" (S.E., 5:585; see also Chapter 6, and Fliess 1897:192).

Freud's decision in 1926 to revise his theory of anxiety, and to attribute anxiety's origins to a reaction of the ego rather than to a transformation of the libido, did not really alter his theory of anxiety dreams; and he still maintained their wishful (and libidinal) character. All that changed was the hypothesized derivation of anxiety, not its intimate association with insufficiently disguised dream-wishes.[15]

Punishment dreams. The notion of punishment dreams was incorporated into Freud's theory in 1919. Calling this category "a new addition to the theory of dreams," Freud included in it those dreams prompted by the dreamer's latent wish to be punished for entertaining

14. Freud actually allowed for three separate derivations for anxiety dreams, only two of which I discuss in the text. In the third class of anxiety dreams, a nonlibidinal somatic disturbance (for instance, difficulty in breathing due to disease of the heart or lungs) generates anxietylike symptoms during sleep. Thereupon, a suppressed (and usually sexual) wish employs these preexisting somatic symptoms in order to produce an appropriate anxiety dream (S.E., 4:236). This somatic formula for anxiety dreams reflects Freud's unaltered support, even after 1900, for the dualism of mind and body. Freud's whole theory of anxiety dreams has its roots, of course, in his toxicological theory of anxiety neurosis (see Chapter 4).

15. See further on this point the useful work of Nagera et al. (1969b:107–8), and Freud (1926d; also *Interpretation*, S.E., 5:557; passage added in 1919).

an associated, forbidden wish (*S.E.*, 5:557; passage added to the fifth [1919] edition of *Interpretation*). In such instances, Freud explained, the dreamer's ego has reacted to the forbidden dream-wish at the preconscious level, has successfully repudiated this wish, and has responded with a self-punitive wish that is then taken over by the unconscious and fashioned into a "rejoinder" dream. In 1930 Freud specifically attributed such punishment dreams to the fulfillment of wishes originating in the superego (*S.E.*, 5:476, n. 2, 558, n. 1).

Although "a new addition" to the theory of dreams in 1919, the notion of self-punishment wishes was actually an old standby in the 1890s theory of psychoneurosis, a circumstance that once again reveals how close the two subjects were in Freud's mind. He had recognized as early as May 1897 that neurotic symptoms involve a compromise between two conflicting wishes—a forbidden libidinal impulse and a simultaneous desire for self-punishment (*Origins*, p. 209). By February 1899, he was suggesting to Fliess that this dual-wish aspect of symptom formation might be the major distinction between dreams and symptoms. A dream-wish, by being "kept apart from [waking] reality," seemed to enjoy a certain impunity, whereas the neurotic's libidinal impulses did not (*Origins*, pp. 277–78; *Interpretation*, *S.E.*, 5:569). Gradually, however, Freud encountered more exceptions to this assertion, and in 1919 he admitted that even dreams were not free from self-punitive repercussions. Prior to 1919, Freud had interpreted dreams of this punitive class either as masochistic dreams, as simple anxiety dreams, or as elaborately disguised—"hypocritical"—dreams.[16]

In conclusion, I must emphasize again how important Freud's prior thinking about the neuroses was for his successful treatment of these apparent exceptions to the wish-fulfillment formula. It was this intimate connection that allowed Freud to proclaim that dreams "contain the whole psychology of the neuroses in a nutshell" (*Origins*, p. 212, letter of 7 July 1897).

Basic Mechanisms of Dreaming:
Sleep, Regression, Censorship, and the Dream-Work

Freud's mature theory of dreaming is virtually unparalleled, even today, for the remarkable insight that it brought to bear upon the psychological mechanisms of dreaming. For this achievement alone, *The Interpretation of Dreams* remains an indispensable introduction to this baffling and still insufficiently studied subject. Freud's analysis of the psychology of dreaming has four main features: (1) the state of sleep, (2) regression, (3) censorship, and (4) the dream-work. Some of these notions we have encountered before (in the *Project* and other writings), while some were first introduced only in *The Interpretation of Dreams*.

16. See, for instance, Freud's discussion of the journeyman tailor's recurring dream, and his own dreams about the Chemical Institute (*S.E.*, 5:473–76).

THE STATE OF SLEEP

The psychophysiological state of sleep is characterized by the ego's withdrawal of its cathexes from all the interests of waking life. The ego concentrates these free cathexes upon the wish to sleep. Sleep, in turn, makes dreams possible by relaxing the ego's censoring control over the unconscious. Freud designated this second feature of the sleeping state as "the principal *sine qua non*" of dream formation (*S.E.*, 5:526).

CENSORSHIP AND REGRESSION

Nevertheless, the power of censorship is not totally abolished during sleep. It still remains the task of the censor to ensure that the state of sleep is not disturbed. Wishes emerging from the unconscious at night frequently threaten to disturb sleep by generating intolerable ideas and affects. Censorship acts upon such troublesome wishes in two ways. First, the preconscious greets the wish with an initial round of censorship and flatly prohibits its entry into consciousness. Thereupon, the unconscious wish is forced to proceed in a regressive (backward) direction and obtains visual representation by cathecting the perceptual system. This regressive process is the reverse of the normal, daytime flow of energy from the perceptual system to consciousness and then to motor discharge (see *S.E.*, 5:542–44). Associated memories that have been aroused by the dream-wish become visually cathected in this regressive process, and the dream-wish itself is subjected to considerable distortion by the *dream-work*. These disguised dream-thoughts now make their second attempt to enter consciousness, at which time another, but less severe, round of censorship may occasion gaps within the final, manifest content of the dream (*S.E.*, 4:142–44; 5:529–31; 1916–17, *S.E.*, 15:139).

THE DREAM-WORK

Censorship works in tandem with the dream-work, and it is the latter process that introduces the greater distortion within the dream. The dream-work is carried out by the unconscious. The final result of the dream-work is "a compromise" that aims at satisfying both the unconscious wish and the preconscious censor. Five psychical mechanisms implement the dream-work in Freud's theory: condensation, displacement, pictorial representation (or dramatization), symbolization, and secondary revision.

Condensation. The first great achievement of the dream-work is condensation (1916–17, *S.E.*, 15:171). Freud considered this process to be most clearly demonstrated by the evidence of composite figures and structures in dreams, as when a dream constructs a person who bears the separate features of several acquaintances. Freud compared this process with Francis Galton's famous method of making family portraits by overlaying a different negative image for each member of the family and then making a single print (*S.E.*, 4:293). By allowing the summation of cathectic energies from different ideas and images, condensation is said to facilitate the dream's regressive path toward perceptual representation (*S.E.*, 5:596). Because of condensation, the manifest content of a dream is always much smaller than its latent content (the principle of overdetermination).

Displacement. After condensation, displacement is the second of the two great governing agents of the dream-work. It often operates in unison with condensation, as when the cathexes of two separate ideas are displaced to a common intermediate (*S.E.*, 4:308; 5:339). Displacement may also result in a latent dream-thought being replaced by some other idea that is distantly located along the pathways of psychical association. Displacement, like condensation, serves the purpose of dream distortion by modifying the affective content (degree of interest and intensity) given to the latent dream-thoughts in the manifest dream-façade.

An example of this displacement process is provided by the following specimen dream of a female patient in analysis with Freud:

> She dreamt that she was going to the market with her cook, who was carrying the basket. After she had asked for something, the butcher said to her: "That's not obtainable any longer," and offered her something else, adding "This is good too." She rejected it and went on to the woman who sells vegetables, who tried to get her to buy a peculiar vegetable that was tied up in bundles but was of a black colour. She said: "I don't recognize that; I won't take it." (*S.E.*, 4:183)

Here is Freud's interpretation of the dream. The expression *"That's not obtainable any longer"* was spoken to the patient by Freud several days earlier when he had explained to her that childhood impressions are *"not obtainable any longer* as such," but could nevertheless be recovered in dreams. So Freud was evidently the butcher in the dream. The words *"I don't recognize that"* had been spoken by the patient to her cook during a dispute the previous day and had been followed by the reprimand *"Behave yourself properly!"* It was the second expression (not present in the dream) that was important to the motivating dream-thoughts and had been innocently displaced by the first. The dream concealed the patient's phantasy wish that Freud would make improper sexual advances toward her (*"Behave yourself properly!"*). This interpretation coincides with another distorted allusion in the dream, which Freud recognized in the expression *"Die Fleischbank war schon geschlossen"* ("the meat-shop was closed"). The opposite of this utterance (*"Du hast deine Fleischbank offen"*) is Viennese slang for "your fly is undone." Similarly, the vegetable mentioned in the patient's dream proved to be asparagus. "No knowledgeable person of either sex," Freud commented, "will ask for an interpretation of asparagus" (*S.E.*, 4:184). Evidently the dreamer wished for more than just a psychoanalysis from Freud.

Representation. The third important element in the dream-work is the process of representation. Through this mechanism, unconscious thoughts become modified so that they may be expressed in a predominantly visual—and, to a lesser extent, a verbal or conceptual—form. We have already seen that unconscious instinctual impulses must be content to express themselves indirectly in dreams owing to (1) censorship and (2) the substitute forms that such censored wishes subsequently assume during regression to the perceptual system. A similar indirect expression takes place where abstract thoughts must find an outlet in visual images (*S.E.*, 5:339–40). A few examples will suffice to illustrate this point. A man dreams that he is "*an officer sitting at a table opposite the Emperor.*" According to Freud's interpretation, the latent dream-thoughts are: the man wishes to place himself in opposition to his father. Another man dreams that "*his uncle gave him a kiss in an automobile.*" Interpretation of the dream reveals the disguised theme of autoerotism. Similarly, a patient, during an analysis conducted in French, has a dream in which Freud is represented as an elephant. The latent dream-thoughts are "*Vous me trompez*" ("you [Freud] are deceiving me"; *trompe* = "trunk"). (For the examples cited, see *S.E.*, 5:408–13).

Symbolization. Representation greatly facilitates dream distortion by making use of dream symbols—for example, the Emperor as "father." As a specialized and highly important mode of representation, symbolization deserves separate notice. Although Freud had recognized its role in dreams as early as 1893 (1893*a*, *S.E.*, 2:5), his understanding of the frequency and the importance of symbols was a later addition to the theory. (With its predominant emphasis upon displaced associations, Freud's early [1900] theory of dreams actually constituted a reaction against symbolic theories of dream interpretation.) It was Wilhelm Stekel (1911) whom Freud personally credited with having brought the full importance of dream symbols to his attention (*Interpretation*, *S.E.*, 5:350; passage added in 1925).

A symbol is something that depicts, and stands for, something else, similar to—but distinct from—an allusion, a metaphor, a simile, or a highly indirect representation. Unlike representations, however, symbols are not created during the dream-work, since they already exist in the unconscious and are merely seized upon during dream formation (*S.E.*, 5:349). The dreamer, moreover, knows nothing of symbolic meanings, which therefore escape censorship while subserving representation. Freud considered symbolization as being, along with censorship and the dream-work, an independent means of distortion in dreams. Even without these other two agents of distortion, he argued, the meaning of dreams would still be unclear owing to the presence of symbolic ideas (1916–17, *S.E.*, 15:168). Together with the more laborious procedure of analyzing free associations, symbolic "translations" were one of the two basic methods by which dreams could be interpreted in Freud's mature theory (*S.E.*, 4:241 n.; 5:360).

The index volume to Freud's *Complete Psychological Works* lists 257 symbols mentioned in his writings (*S.E.*, 24:173–76). In dreams, these symbols usually stand for the human body (and its separate organs, particularly the genitals), for parents, sisters, brothers, birth, death, coitus, children, and for numerous other aspects of sexual life. Some of the more well-known symbols in Freudian theory are King and Queen (father and mother); boxes, cases, chests, cupboards, etc. (the womb); walking up or down steps, ladders, or staircases (coitus); baldness, decapitation, hair-cutting (castration); small animals and vermin (children); and long, stiff objects (the penis) (S.E., 5:353–60). The psychoanalytic understanding of dream symbols is corroborated, Freud maintained, by the study of neurotic symptoms, myths, fairy tales, folklore, and jokes (1916–17, S.E., 15:165–68).

Freud traced the dreamer's rich repertoire of symbols to an unconscious biogenetic knowledge, similar to having an inborn understanding of Sanskrit (S.E., 15:165). A major clue to this phylogenetic origin of symbols, he insisted, is the observation that dream symbols are almost always sexual in nature. In this connection, he agreed with philologist Hans Sperber (1912), who maintained that words and language were originally derived from sexual needs—for example, to summon the sexual partner. Gradually, sexual words were applied to the working activities of primal man and so took on double meanings. Work itself became acceptable because of its linguistic equation with the sexual act. As work became more complex, sexual words were applied to each new work form and work tool. Hence it is today that weapons and tools generally stand in dreams for the male genitalia, while materials (things worked upon) stand for the female genitalia (S.E., 15:167).

Freud's phylogenetic ideas on dream symbolism were closely tied up with the archaic regressions that he ascribed to the dreaming process. "The [archaic] prehistory into which the dream-work leads us back," Freud wrote in his *Introductory Lectures*, "is of two kinds—on the one hand, into the individual's prehistory, his childhood, and on the other, in so far as each individual somehow recapitulates in an abbreviated form the entire development of the human race, into phylogenetic prehistory too. . . . It seems to me, for instance, that symbolic connections, which the individual has never acquired by learning, may justly claim to be regarded as a phylogenetic heritage" (S.E., 15:199; cf. S.E., 5:548–49).

Secondary revision. The fifth and last component of the dream-work, secondary revision, supplies the manifest content of the dream with a logical façade based upon "considerations of intelligibility" (*On Dreams*, 1901a, S.E., 5:666). Such secondary revisions inevitably add to dream distortion. Freud considered secondary revision to be closely associated with the rational (secondary) processes of waking thought. It is normal thinking, not the unconscious or the dream-work, that demands of dreams some degree of intelligibility. In 1923 and after, Freud chose to exclude secondary revision from the dream-work on the grounds that it was not actually part of the unconscious (primary-process) mechanisms of dream formation (1923a, S.E., 18:241). Nevertheless, secondary revision continued to have an important role in Freud's overall theory of dream formation.

In conclusion, Freud believed that all the basic processes I have just reviewed (censorship, regression, condensation, displacement, representation, symbolization, and secondary revision) are operational for many hours before a dream finally emerges at night. The dream-work is set in motion during the previous day by experiences that elicit unconscious wishes. When sleep finally sets in, the pace of the dream-work is merely accelerated. A dream, Freud explained, "is like a firework, which takes hours to prepare but goes off in a moment" (*S.E.*, 5:576).

Sources and Motives of Dreaming

The basic mechanisms of dream formation tell us very little about the sources and motives of dreaming, and it is to these aspects of the problem that I now turn. I have already touched upon the motive forces of dreaming in describing how unconscious wishes press their way into consciousness at night via the dual routes of regression to perception and the dream-work. The various sources and motives of dreaming may be further explained in terms of their economic, dynamic, and topographical aspects, on the one hand, and their developmental determinants, on the other.

Economic, dynamic, and topographical causes of dreaming. Every dream, Freud maintained, exhibits some link to thought "residues" of the previous day (*S.E.*, 5:562). These day's residues may be unsolved problems, worries, reflections, intentions, warnings, fears, suppressed thoughts and wishes, or purely indifferent and trivial material (*S.E.*, 5:554–64; 1913*a*, *S.E.*, 12:273–74). The day's residues belong topographically to the preconscious. Such impressions, which have ready access to consciousness, provide the raw material of dreams. But to produce a dream, such residues must get hold of a wish, which brings us to the question of where dream-wishes originate.

Freud delineated four separate categories of dream-wishes: (1) wishes aroused during the day but left unsatisfied (like the day's residues, such wishes are localized in the preconscious); (2) wishes aroused and repudiated during the day (that is, wishes originating in the preconscious and then repressed into the unconscious); (3) unconscious wishes that become active at night; and (4) preconscious, somatic impulses arising at night (hunger, thirst, pain, sexual urges, and the effects of various external stimuli). Although any one of these wishful impulses may contribute to the formation of a dream, Freud held that only an unconscious wish (3) is *indispensable* to the dream, and is the primary instigator of *all* dreams. Thus a preconscious wish that has been aroused during the day must link up with a similar, unconscious wish if it is to contribute to the formation of a dream (*S.E.*, 5:551–54). Freud compared this state of affairs with the relationship between the capitalist and the entrepreneur in business:

> A daytime thought may very well play the part of *entrepreneur* for a dream; but the *entrepreneur*, who, as people say, has the idea and the initiative to carry it out, can do nothing without capital; he needs a *capitalist* who can afford the outlay, and the capitalist who provides the psychical outlay for the dream is invariably and indisputably, whatever may be the thoughts of the previous day, *a wish from the unconscious.* (*S.E.*, 5:561)

Topographically, then, the prime motive for dreaming is an *unconscious* wish.

Looking at the motive of dreams from the economic and the dynamic points of view, Freud appealed to another analogy. As we have already seen, censorship of dream-wishes is necessary to prevent anxiety and unpleasure, the two great disturbers of sleep. Dreaming therefore acts, Freud argued, as "a safety valve" in regulating the nighttime interplay of mental forces, discharging unconscious excitations at the expense of only a small amount of waking activity—the conscious attention that is briefly devoted to the dream (*S.E.*, 5:579, 591).

Developmental motives of dreaming. Freud's insistence that every dream is ultimately motivated by an unconscious wish was linked to a second and equally emphatic claim—that every dream is motivated by an infantile wish (*S.E.*, 5:553, 567, 589). Both of these claims were closely related in Freud's mind, and both derived a priori theoretical support from his developmental conception of the mental apparatus.

In Chapter 7 of *The Interpretation of Dreams*, Freud gave two developmental reasons for why the infantile and the unconscious should play such important roles in dream formation. The first of these reasons points to the ontogenetic relationship between primary and secondary mental processes in human beings. In the course of human development, secondary (inhibitory) processes come to overlay, and belatedly to control, primary (impulsive) ones. Primary processes therefore contain "the core of our being" (that which becomes the unconscious); and this core, Freud insisted, can neither be destroyed nor suppressed, but only redirected, by later secondary processes (*S.E.*, 5:603). The critical question for understanding the motive of dreaming is accordingly: How does this primary-process "core" become dynamically repressed, thereby severing the unconscious—and the source of dreams—from the preconscious in Freud's topographical model of the mind? This key issue brings us to Freud's second developmental reason for dreaming.

There are some infantile wishes, he explained, whose fulfillment would no longer generate pleasure at the level of secondary-process thinking. In the course of development, there has been a *"transformation of affect"* associated with such infantile wishes, one *"which constitutes the essence of what we term 'repression'."* (*S.E.*, 5:604). It is this developmental "reversal of affect" that Freud held responsible for the creation, and sealing off, of the dynamic Unconscious (i.e., the repressed) from the systems Preconscious and Conscious.

So important for his theory of dreaming were the assumptions of (libidinal) repressions and an accompanying reversal of affect that

Freud later went so far as to assert that without these developmental changes we would not dream at all (1916–17, S.E., 16:456–57).[17]

In *The Interpretation of Dreams* (1900a), Freud did not claim to understand these developmental processes—except to associate them with the normal acquisition of disgust in childhood, which, he claimed, is not present to begin with. Privately, however, he considered such a transformation to be a biological process of "organic" repression, a process firmly tied to the laws of infantile psychosexual development. He had already expressed this biological conception of dream life in a letter of 10 March 1898 to Wilhelm Fliess:

> It seems to me as if the wish-fulfillment theory gives only the psychological and not the biological, or rather metapsychological [developmental] explanation. . . . Biologically dream-life seems to me to proceed directly from the residue of the prehistoric stage of life (one to three years), which is the source of the unconscious and alone contains the aetiology of all the psychoneuroses; the stage which is normally obscured by an amnesia similar to hysteria. . . . a recent wish leads to a dream only if it can be associated with material from that period, if the recent wish is a derivative of a prehistoric wish or can get itself adopted by such a wish. I do not know yet to what extent I shall be able to stick to this extreme theory, or let it loose in the dream book. (*Origins*, pp. 246–47)

As we have seen, Freud indeed did stick to this "extreme theory" in *The Interpretation of Dreams*. It was also his extreme emphasis upon the infantile causes of dreaming that made the interpretation of dreams so central to Freudian psychotherapy; for dreams, as disguised *infantile* wishes, became a unique clinical tool for penetrating the amnesic shroud around early childhood events. "The fact that dreams are hypermnesic and have access to material from childhood," Freud proclaimed in 1900, "has become one of the corner-stones of our teaching. Our theory of dreams regards wishes originating in infancy as the *indispensable motive force for the formation of dreams*" (S.E., 5:589; italics added). Thus, dreams, if properly interpreted via the techniques of free association and symbolism, could supply invaluable clues about each patient's psychosexual development (1916–17, S.E., 16:456).

I shall summarize Freud's overall conception of (1) the dream-work and (2) the sources and motives of dreams by stressing the *two-tier* nature of his theory (see Fig. 9.1). The upper tier of Freud's theory focuses upon current causes and includes (1) the preconscious day's residues and (2) the latent dream-thoughts, as well as their final, nighttime product, the manifest content of the dream (9). In contrast

17. Strictly speaking, Freud's assertion that, without libidinal repressions, we would not dream, is imprecise, since primary-process wishes of a nonrepressed type— for example, in connection with hunger or thirst—would still occasionally emerge in dream form as brief hallucinatory wish-fulfillments. Inasmuch, however, as the major Freudian characteristics of dreams (i.e., censorship and the dream-work) would not exist without libidinal repression, Freud's claim may be more correctly restated to indicate that, without such repression, the wish-fulfillment meaning of dreams would be transparent, and dream interpretation entirely unnecessary.

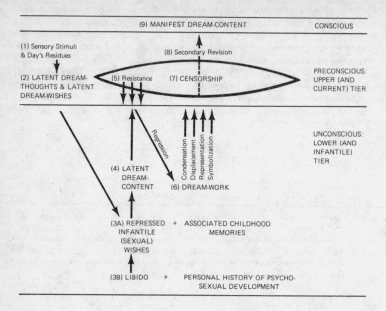

Fig. 9.1. Freud's two-tier conception of dream formation. (Adapted from Ellenberger 1970:491.)

to this, the lower tier is organized around the dreamer's repressed childhood libidinal impulses and associated childhood memories (3A, 3B). The lower tier contains the ultimate motivation and meaning of the dream. The dream-work (6), although executed in the present like the upper-tier functions, makes use of the superseded primary-process mechanisms that once dominated mental life in its earliest stages. Similarly, the latent content (4) of the dream has one foot in the present and one foot in the past (*S.E.*, 5:553). There is, accordingly, both an upper-level meaning to dreams and a deeper, more hidden, lower-level meaning. It is the task of dream interpretation to reveal these two major levels of significance.

THE PROBLEM OF INTERPRETATION: DREAMS, SEXUALITY, AND NEUROSIS

The process of dream interpretation requires that one concentrate upon the first element of a dream, recording all the "involuntary associations" that come to mind in connection with it, and then repeat the same method with every other element. When this procedure is finally completed, the latent dream-content will generally have made itself apparent by its central location within the associative chain of ideas (*S.E.*, 5:527).

Nevertheless, can a dream be interpreted uniquely and objectively by Freud's theory and method? In particular, how does one recognize the "right" interpretation of a dream when faced with the profusion of interrelated thoughts that Freud's free association technique brings to light? Numerous individuals, psychoanalysts and their critics alike, have pondered this question. Nor is the response to it made any easier by Freud's claims that a dream may have several meanings and fulfill several different wishes (the principle of overdetermination), that every element of the dream can stand for its opposite, or that a dream must often be retold backward to yield its true meaning (*S.E.*, 4:219, 328; 5:341, 471). How, then, does one distinguish the true meaning of a dream from, in Philip Rieff's apt words, "the alternative always lurking at the edge of every psychoanalytic interpretation" (1959:112)?

The two-tier nature of Freud's dream theory has a special relevance to this problem of interpretation—a relevance that is not always recognized by readers of *The Interpretation of Dreams*. Thus, whereas the upper-level meaning of dreams frequently seems ambiguous to the uninitiated, Freud saw it as inextricably linked to, and confirmed by, the fixed biological substratum of child development. Put another way, the ultimate (lower-level) meaning of a dream always leads to a Freudian glimpse of early psychosexual development and to a potential or manifest cause of psychoneurosis. As Freud explained to an American audience in 1909: "In dream-life the child that is in man pursues its existence. . . . [From dream analysis] there will be brought home to you with irresistible force the many developments, repressions, sublimations and reaction-formations, by means of which a child with a quite other [than civilized] innate endowment grows into what we call a normal man, the bearer, and in part the [potentially neurotic] victim, of the civilization that has been so painfully acquired" (1910a [1909], *S.E.*, 11:36). It was for these biological and developmental reasons that the study of psychopathology was so crucial to understanding the unconscious material of dreams (1901a, *S.E.*, 5:686). More specifically, Freud believed that the subject matter of neurotics' dreams is always tied to their symptoms and hence to their case histories, which therefore provide constant confirmation of the hidden (infantile) meaning of dreams (*S.E.*, 4:104; 5:673). Dream interpretation is therefore inseparable from formal clinical analysis, at least when properly conducted (1925i, *S.E.*, 19:128). Furthermore, since the correct lower-level interpretation is what *cures* the patient, psychotherapy provides an independent clinical confirmation of Freud's successful understanding of dreams. Finally, the formal clinical study of symptoms, like that of dreams, corroborates the ubiquity of unconscious psychical distortions, as well as the reliability of the free association method in "undoing" these distortions (*S.E.*, 5:528, 531–32, 673).

Nowadays Freud's readers are far more aware of these developmental and clinical connections with the problem of dream interpretation, although the biological substratum of Freud's thinking is less widely appreciated. Nevertheless, his specific dream interpretations seem more acceptable to us than they once did to his colleagues. Similarly, many of the most common categories among Freud's psychoanalytic dream interpretations have become plausible to us in terms of the now-familiar model of human development that directly underlies them. Among these common categories are so-called typical dreams: for example, discovering that one is naked in public (a dream derived from childhood exhibitionist tendencies); dreams involving the death or departure of siblings and parents (related to the Oedipus complex); losing hair or teeth (reflecting castration anxiety); examination dreams (representing sexual "tests" and sexual self-reproaches); flying, falling, and swimming dreams (all related to childhood sexual excitations from movement or bed wetting [= swimming dreams], etc.).[18] But in 1900 Freud's readers were still unaware, for the most part, of this superstructure, and were being asked to believe that the secret meaning of dreams—always a disguised wish-fulfillment—could be reached solely by analyzing "free associations" to one's manifest dream-thoughts. Freud foresaw this dilemma of credibility as he was writing *The Interpretation of Dreams* (1900a); but, despite his concerted efforts to overcome the problem, he was unable to do so to his own satisfaction. His book remained incomplete in three significant ways that conjointly touch upon this problem of interpretation.

Dreams of neurotics. I have already mentioned the considerable importance of Freud's clinical case histories in confirming his theory of dream interpretation. This special importance may be summed up by the following logical formula: If the "ultimate" meaning of dreams is derived from repressed infantile sexual experiences, and if the neurotic's illness is also derived from such repressed experiences, then the dreams of neurotics should generally offer the most dramatic illustrations of Freud's dream-distortion theory. In *The Interpretation of Dreams,* however, Freud could bring himself to exploit such clinical material only sparingly. Explaining the dreams and associated case histories of his patients, he reckoned, would have been a drawn-out process inevitably detracting from the principal focus of his book. At the same time, Freud wanted to base his theory of dreaming on the dreams of *normal* individuals in order to show that psychoanalysis was no longer just a theory of psychopathology (*S.E.,* 4:xxiii, 104). He occasionally did use specimen dreams derived from his neurotic patients, but more often he simply chose to allude to this clinical material as confirming his basic assertions (*S.E.,* 4:150–51, 183–85, 203, 244, 273; 5:349).

Freud's own dreams. Freud could not base his scientific arguments upon the many dreams he collected from healthy acquaintances or from the existing literature on dreams, since it was generally necessary

18. See Freud 1900a, *S.E.,* 4:242–46, 248–67, 271–76; 5:357, 387.

to carry out a lengthy psychoanalysis in order to reveal the hidden meaning of dreams. He therefore found it expedient to rely heavily upon his own dreams—a decision that was not without its own dilemma, for he could not interpret his own dreams fully without revealing considerably more of himself to the public than he reasonably cared to do.[19] Furthermore, the nearer he drew to the ultimate (lower-level) meaning of a dream, the more such potential indiscretions became blatant and demanded that he cut off the published version of the interpretation. Freud had originally intended to include at least one full interpretation from among his own dreams, but this particular specimen (referred to as his "big dream" in letters to Fliess) was discarded prior to publication owing to personal considerations (Origins, pp. 269, 288, letters of 23 October 1898 and 1 August 1899; see also S.E., 4:310). The upshot was that Freud used parts of his dream interpretations to reveal different aspects of his theory but nowhere elected to reveal, as he himself confessed, the complete or ultimate meaning of any of his own dreams (S.E., 4:105, n. 2, 191, 310; 5:559). Even as it stands, The Interpretation of Dreams still required remarkable courage on the part of its author to sustain the degree of self-confession that it required.

"Dreams and the Neuroses." Freud apparently believed he could overcome these various omissions from his argument by writing a concluding chapter to The Interpretation of Dreams entitled "Dreams and the Neuroses" (Origins, p. 248, letter of 15 March 1898). This chapter would have allowed Freud to give a full and ruthless analysis of several patients' dreams while setting forth the various connecting links between dream interpretation, neurotic symptoms, his patients' case histories, the infantile (sexual) determinants of dreaming, and the theory of psychoneurosis more generally. Inasmuch as every major component of the theory of dreams has an antecedent in the theory of psychoneurosis (see Fig. 9.2), Freud's discussion of these points would have greatly assisted the understanding of his theory by those readers who were not already familiar with his other publications (cf. Flournoy 1903:73; and Freud, S.E., 5:588).

Freud's proposed chapter on dreams and neurosis was never written and was replaced instead by a more abstract chapter on dreaming and the mental apparatus (Chapter 7, "The Psychology of the Dream-Processes"). The most likely reason for this substitution is that Freud thought the subject of psychopathology too unwieldy to be introduced at such a late point in his overall argument. Nevertheless, the largely unspoken rationale of the omitted material remained, as he himself confessed to Fliess on 20 June 1898, while working on an early draft of the famous seventh chapter: "All its themes come from the work on

19. Approximately one-fifth (47) of the 226 dreams reported by Freud in The Interpretation of Dreams (8th and last revised edition, 1930) are his own. However, Freud's dreams received far more extensive discussion and analysis than most others he discussed and therefore constitute the bulk of his didactic material, particularly in the less expansive first edition of 1900, in which they formed the nucleus of the argument.

Dream Formation	Symptom Formation
The Dream-Work	
Condensation	Overdetermination
Displacement	Displacement
Representation	Regressive, Hallucinatory Cathexes
Symbolism	Symbolism
(Secondary Revision)	—
Other Principles	
Wish-fulfillment Nature of Dreams	Wish-fulfillment Nature of Hallucinatory Psychoses (and of symptoms more generally)
Censorship	Censorship, Repression
Two-Tier Theory (infantile wish = ultimate cause of dreaming)	Two-Tier Theory (childhood sexual experience = ultimate cause of neurosis)
Latent vs. Manifest Content	Libido vs. Its Disguised Displacement in Symptoms
Dreams as Compromise Formations	Symptoms as Compromise Formations
Self-Punishment Dreams	Self-Punishment Symptoms
Anxiety Dreams = Sexual Dreams	Anxiety Symptoms = Transformed Libido

Fig. 9.2. Comparison between concepts of dream formation and symptom formation.

neurosis, not from that on dreams" (*Origins*, p. 257). The reader who was unacquainted with this omitted material had already taken a great deal on faith in Freud's highly unconventional book. As Jones (1953: 363) frankly comments about the final, abstract form taken by Chapter 7, "It was not an ideal arrangement. . . ."

At all events, the theoretical gap created by this important omission in Freud's argument was later filled by two separate publications: the "Dora" case history (originally entitled "Dreams and Hysteria") and the *Three Essays on the Theory of Sexuality*, both issued in 1905. Through the "Dora" case history, the theory of dreams blends inextricably into the theory of sexuality and hence into the biological substratum of Freud's thinking.

Major Misconceptions Stemming from Freud's (1900) Omissions

I mentioned at the outset of this chapter that *The Interpretation of Dreams* (1900a) has become one of Freud's most misunderstood works. The preceding omissions in it have fostered many of posterity's principal misconceptions about the book. Also of critical relevance to these misunderstandings is the fact that great classics in science, unlike those in literature, cease to be read and so become easy victims of mythology. Only those who have read *The Interpretation of Dreams*, and particularly only those who originally read it in the first edition of

1900, can appreciate what a difficult, albeit fascinating, book it can be to the uninitiated.

Foremost among the historical misunderstandings about *The Interpretation of Dreams* is its curious fate. Psychoanalytic tradition has long emphasized how Freud's masterwork on dreams met with an icy silence and, when discussed at all, was overwhelmed with "annihilating" criticism. After two years, only 351 copies had been sold, and it took another six years to sell the entire first printing of 600 copies (Jones 1953:360–61). Not until 1909 was a second edition finally called for (to be followed by six more editions in Freud's lifetime).

What is generally not understood in this connection is that the initial reception and "meager" sales were not the result either of the book's failure to be reviewed or of the supposedly harsh criticisms that it received from certain of its reviewers. Actually, the book was widely and favorably reviewed in popular and scientific periodicals, and it was recognized by a good number of its reviewers as "epoch-making" and "profound." [20] Collectively, *The Interpretation of Dreams* (1900a) and Freud's shorter essay *On Dreams* (1901a) received at least thirty reviews, totaling some 17,000 words (an average of 570 words per review). Freud's theory was fairly and systematically summarized in these notices and, by the end of 1902, had been brought to the attention of psychologists, psychiatrists, and neurologists, as well as educated lay readers, all over the world. Nevertheless, virtually no reviewer, even the most friendly and respectful, failed to point out the questionable and unprovable nature of many of Freud's dream analyses together with the methodological difficulties entailed in the objective application of his technique. As Freud himself commented to Fliess in a sober moment of self-assessment shortly after his book appeared in print: "Your news of the dozen Berlin readers pleases me greatly. I have readers here too; [but] the time is not yet ripe for followers. There is too much that is new and incredible, *and too little strict proof*" (*Origins*, p. 304; italics added).

Freud's appraisal was indeed prophetic, for some of his most devoted disciples were unimpressed by their first reading of *Interpretation*. Sándor Ferenczi, for one, read and dismissed the book "with a shrug of his shoulders" shortly after it was published, and in 1907 he had to be persuaded to read it again—this time with a better result—by a Hungarian colleague who fortunately happened to be acquainted with both Freud and Carl Gustav Jung (Jones 1955:34). Similarly, Jung read *The Interpretation of Dreams* in 1900 but, as he tells us in his autobiography, "laid the book aside, at the time, because I did not yet grasp it." Only in 1903 did Jung again pick up Freud's book and discover how much it agreed with certain ideas he had independently developed in the meantime as a result of his various word-association tests (1963:147). Elsewhere, Jung writes of this first contact with

20. E.g., Metzentin 1899:389; Näcke 1901a:168; Flournoy 1903:72; see also Bry and Rifkin 1962; Ellenberger 1970:782–74; Decker 1975, 1977; and for a number of representative extracts from these early reviews, see Chapter 13 in this book.

Freud's ideas, "I can assure you that in the beginning I naturally entertained all the objections that are customarily made against Freud in
the literature" (1907, C.W., 3:3).

Even as late as 1911, Jung and his Swiss group were still very
conscious of the didactic inadequacies in Freud's treatment of dreams.
When Freud asked Jung that year if he had any suggested revisions for
the third edition of *Interpretation*, Jung responded with the collective
criticism put forward by his teaching seminar on psychoanalysis at
the Burghölzli—that it was "sorely" difficult to understand Freud's
theory and methods from his book owing to the incomplete nature of
the specimen dreams and the consequent lack of "deeper layer" interpretations. Jung recommended that Freud insert more dreams of neurotics and interpret them fully, so that "the ultimate real motives" of
dreams could be *"ruthlessly* disclosed." Freud answered Jung's criticisms by saying that the time had now come to discontinue publication
of *The Interpretation of Dreams* with the forthcoming edition (!) and
to replace it with a "new and impersonal" work in which the theories
of dreaming and neurosis could be interrelated more adequately. Freud
added that he would announce this decision in his Preface to the third
edition of *Interpretation* and would explain there the various reasons
for it, pretty much in Jung's own words. Nothing ever came of this plan,
as—among other reasons—Freud's astute publisher, Franz Deuticke,
thought it would make a bad impression and so vetoed it (*Freud/Jung
Letters*, pp. 392–96, 422). Thus, *The Interpretation of Dreams*, with all
its omissions and deficiencies, has remained the standard, if problematic, introduction to Freud's science of the mind.

In short, Freud's masterwork on dreams was neither ignored nor
ridiculed by the world in 1900. It was simply not always understood,
partly owing to the novelty and complexity of Freud's ideas, and partly
(as Jung later testified) on account of Freud's incomplete presentation
of his 1900 argument.

As for the supposedly poor sales of Freud's book, *The Interpretation of Dreams* sold, at an annual rate of seventy-five copies per year
over an eight-year period, nearly twice as well as *Studies on Hysteria*
(1895d) and about half as well as Freud's *Jokes and Their Relation to
the Unconscious* (1905c) and *Leonardo da Vinci* (1910c).[21] No doubt
Freud and his publisher were disappointed by the relative sales of
Interpretation, but one should also appreciate that, as works of science
and medicine, none of Freud's early publications were written, published, or distributed with the expectation of today's levels of mass
consumption. Only with Freud's rise to worldwide fame and with his

21. *Studies on Hysteria* (1895d) initially sold 626 copies over a thirteen-year
period, or 48 copies per year. *Jokes* sold 1,050 copies in its first seven years, or 150
copies a year. *Leonardo da Vinci* sold 1,500 copies in nine years, or 167 copies an-
nually. By these standards, Freud's *Three Essays* (1905d) was something of a best
seller, with 1,000 copies being sold in the first five years, or 200 copies per year.
Sales figures are not available for *The Psychopathology of Everyday Life* (1901b),
which was first issued as a book in 1904 and became Freud's most successful pre-
First-World-War publication. The sales figures mentioned above are derived from
Jones 1953:253; 1955:286, 335, 347.

attempts to reach a wider, nonmedical audience did the sales of his books undergo a corresponding increase.[22]

Another insufficiently appreciated circumstance in connection with the "disappointing" sales of Freud's *Interpretation of Dreams* should be mentioned here. Freud published his more condensed essay *On Dreams* (1901a) in the medical series *Grenzfragen des Nerven- und Seelenlebens* (Frontier Problems of Nervous and Mental Life—edited by Leopold Löwenfeld and Hans Kurella), doing so without the prior approval of Franz Deuticke, the publisher of *Interpretation*. Deuticke was greatly perturbed by this decision, claiming that it would interfere with the sales of Freud's bigger book (Freud 1901b, S.E., 6:160). Although the specific sales figures for the shorter essay are not available, there is good reason to believe that Deuticke's prediction was fulfilled. *On Dreams* provided a highly lucid thirty-eight-page introduction to Freud's theory and was in many ways much more successful than the bulky and relatively hard-to-assimilate *Interpretation of Dreams* (with its sixty-five-page historical introduction and its exhaustive treatment of the whole dream problem). Upon initial publication, *On Dreams* received almost twice as many reviews (nineteen vs. eleven) as *Interpretation*. Furthermore, it was eventually translated into ten foreign languages in Freud's lifetime, two more than *Interpretation*. More strikingly, of the twelve foreign languages into which one or the other of these two works was translated, *On Dreams* was the first or only translation in eight instances. From such facts it is not unreasonable to assume that *On Dreams* and *The Interpretation of Dreams* sold collectively at least as many copies as Freud's more popular books on wit and Leonardo da Vinci.

The early reactions to *Interpretation*, including those of subsequently zealous psychoanalysts, show just how important personal contact with Freud was in nurturing the small but dedicated following that slowly began to absorb his doctrines after 1900. Wilhelm Stekel, for instance, had been through a therapeutic analysis with Freud (owing to a personal problem relating to his sex life) before writing a favorable review of *The Interpretation of Dreams* in 1902.[23] It was

22. Thus, the *Five Lectures on Psycho-Analysis* (1910a [1909]), published at the height of controversy over Freud's theories, sold 1,500 copies over an initial two-year period, or 750 copies per year, and eventually over 30,000 copies by the mid-1950s. See Jones 1955:211.

23. Legend, however, has given rise to an entirely different story. In his *Autobiography* (1950:105), Stekel later claimed that he had read a long and adverse review of *The Interpretation of Dreams* in a Viennese weekly (evidently Max Burckhardt's review of 6 and 13 January 1900 in *Die Zeit*), and that he had promptly drafted a rejoinder, which he sent to the *Neues Wiener Tagblatt*. Actually Stekel's review was published in the 29 and 30 January 1902 issues of that periodical—that is, two years later and *after* he had already been through an analysis with Freud. A similar myth surrounds Alfred Adler's conversion to psychoanalysis. According to Phyllis Bottome (1939:56–57), Adler read a hostile review of *The Interpretation of Dreams* in the *Neue Freie Presse* and thereupon wrote a letter of protest to that newspaper. Adler's letter supposedly attracted Freud's attention, causing Freud to send a postcard to Adler thanking him for his support and inviting Adler to pay him a visit. In reality, neither a hostile review nor a response from Adler ever appeared in the *Neue Freie Presse*—or in any other Viennese newspaper, as far as is known. See Ellenberger 1970:583; Brome 1967:17; and Jones 1955:7.

Stekel who later proposed to Freud in the autumn of 1902 that Alfred
Adler, Max Kahane, Rudolf Reitler, and Stekel himself all meet regularly at Freud's home on Wednesday evenings for discussion of Freud's
theories. (This little group, which continued to grow, became the Vienna
Psychoanalytic Society in 1908.) Such personal contact with Freud as
was afforded by the Wednesday evening meetings ensured that these
first followers learned much about Freud's doctrines that was not otherwise available at this time. Despite Freud's later publication of clinically
instructive works like the "Dora" case history, in which dreams were
carefully related to the patient's symptoms, a didactic analysis, either
with Freud or with one of his disciples, eventually became an institutionalized requirement in psychoanalytic training.

Later Developments in the Theory of Dream Interpretation

Freud's later modifications and extensions of his dream theory
should be appreciated within the context of the various problems of
dream interpretation I have just reviewed. As the gaps in Freud's initial
1900 presentation were gradually filled in by his later publications on
the neuroses and on psychosexual development, dream interpretation
became increasingly axiomatic. In particular, the notion of symbolism, which Freud confined predominantly to sexual themes, greatly
circumscribed the problems of dream interpretation by supplementing
the original method of free association with an independent criterion
of dream meaning. Additionally, by providing a direct bridge between
upper- and lower-level dream interpretations, symbolism supplied many
of the ultimate, infantile-sexual meanings of dreams that had merely
been alluded to in 1900. Freud acknowledged the collective impact of
these later theoretical developments when he remarked at the Vienna
Psychoanalytic Society in 1909:

> Proud as he [Freud] was not to have found much to add when the second
> edition of *The Interpretation of Dreams* was being prepared, the book is
> nevertheless incomplete in one definite respect: the role of sexuality de-
> serves to be enlarged in the statement of the dream problem. The better
> one understands dreams, the more one is forced to assign to the sexual
> material a decisive role.
>
> The formulation should be extended to the effect that the dream
> represents the fulfillment of disguised *sexual* wishes.
>
> A second extension is necessary because of the fact that far too little
> importance has been ascribed to the fixed symbolism of dreams. . . .
> [W]hen nothing else can be uncovered, we have to assume [the sym-
> bolic presence of] something sexual. (*Minutes*, 2:218–19; meeting of 28
> April 1909)

Freud's analysis of a student's dream in the 1930s illustrates this more
direct form of interpretation using symbolic translation. Here is the
dream, in the student's own words: "*I dreamed that I was in the gallery
of a theatre and watched a man in military costume doing tricks with a*

sword. I looked down into the orchestra, thought of the danger of a fall, grew frightened and called to my wife for help." Freud's interpretation of the dream is as follows: "Sitting in a theatre always meant watching coitus; children often see something of the sort and associate it, perhaps rightly, with something frightening or with an act of aggression: hence the military aspect. The drawing of a sword from its sheath was a symbol for the sex act, even though the sword was being withdrawn, since dreams often showed the opposite of what they mean. Falling is a constant symbol for femininity, for giving birth or being born. . . . The dream meant I [the trainee] was watching coitus, was identifying myself with the female part and was disturbed by the feminine elements in myself" (Wortis 1954:85, analytic session of 27 November 1934; italics added).

It is equally true, of course, that Freud never claimed that *all* dreams are sexual, as his opponents commonly charged. Imperative-needs dreams (those prompted by hunger, thirst, or the need to excrete) supplied Freud with numerous counterexamples to the allegations of such obtuse critics (*Autobiography*, 1925d, S.E., 20:46). But virtually all dreams that required *interpretation*, Freud confidently insisted in later years, were sexual dreams (1901a, S.E., 5:682; discussion added in 1911).

THE PSYCHOPATHOLOGY OF EVERYDAY LIFE

It was while he was still engaged in writing *The Interpretation of Dreams* (1900a) that Freud first grasped the psychological significance of certain everyday, and often seemingly trivial, mistakes that people make. His earliest mention of this subject occurs in a 26 August 1898 letter to Fliess and describes an instance of name-forgetting accompanied by erroneous substitution of another name in its place. Freud's letter reports the following analytic results in connection with this memory lapse, which involved his forgetting the last name of the poet Julius Mosen: "I was able to prove (i) that I had repressed the name Mosen because of certain associations; (ii) that material from my infancy played a part in the repression; and (iii) that the substitute names that occurred to me arose, just like a symptom, from both [recent and infantile] groups of material. The analysis resolved the thing completely; unfortunately, I cannot make it public any more than my big dream . . ." (*Origins*, pp. 261–62). Characteristically Freud began collecting additional examples of such phenomena, which he gradually recognized as being psychologically related to many other forms of unconscious mistakes. Published in article form in 1898 and 1901, and later collected together and reissued as a book in 1904, Freud's studies on the psychopathology of everyday life affirmed that such diverse dysfunctions as slips of the tongue and of the pen, the losing or mis-

An accidental inkblot, with Freud's circled reference to its possible "secret" meaning and "interpretation" twenty years before the *Psychopathology of Everyday Life*: "Here the pen fell out of my hand and inscribed these secret signs. I beg your forgiveness and ask that you not trouble yourself with an interpretation" (9 August 1882 letter to Martha Bernays). Like the theory of dreams, the notion of "Freudian slips" had a long prehistory in Freud's thinking and was nurtured by the popular psychology of the times.

laying of objects, bungled actions, so-called symptomatic actions, the forgetting of names, and certain forms of errors, all followed the psychical laws he had already worked out for neurotic symptoms and dreams. These *parapraxes* [24] have a hidden meaning, Freud claimed, and arise whenever a conscious intention is sufficiently inhibited by an unconscious one. In other words, such parapraxes are motivated by suppressed (or repressed) impulses or intentions that seize upon opportune moments to betray their presence within the unconscious portion of the psyche.

Because such phenomena are common to all normal individuals, Freud considered them to be one of the best introductions to the existence and the pervasiveness of unconscious mental processes. He often gave parapraxes didactic priority over dreams when explaining the

24. The English term *parapraxis* was invented by the translator of Freud's works to stand for the German word *Fehlleistung* (literally "faulty function" or "faulty act"). See James Strachey's note to Freud 1901*b*, *S.E.*, 6:xii, n. 1.

principles of psychoanalysis to the nonspecialist—as, for example, in Part One of the *Introductory Lectures* (1916–17) and in his contributions to *Scientia* (1913*j*) and Marcuse's encyclopedia (1923*a*). A. A. Brill reports how, as an initial skeptic about Freud's theories, he became a convinced Freudian only after an experience of name-forgetting finally revealed to him the power of the unconscious in such matters. Once converted to Freud's point of view, a whole new world of psychological understanding opened up to practicing psychopathologists, as Brill himself later described in his English translation of *The Psychopathology of Everyday Life*:

> Those were the pioneer days of Freud [and his theories] among psychiatrists, and we observed and studied and noted whatever was done or said about us with unfailing patience and untiring interest and zeal. We made no scruples, for instance, of asking a man at table why he did not use his spoon in the proper way, or why he did such and such a thing in such and such a manner. It was impossible for one to show any degree of hesitation or make some abrupt pause in speaking without being at once called to account. We had to keep ourselves well in hand, ever ready and alert, for there was no telling when and where there would be a new attack. We had to explain why we whistled or hummed some particular tune or why we made some slip in talking or some mistake in writing. But we were glad to do this if for no other reason than to learn to face the truth. (Passage interpolated into Freud's text. See Freud 1938:57)

Nevertheless, Brill's later zeal should not obscure the necessary perseverance by which he and others came to appreciate the psychological significance of parapraxes. Brill's own first analysis of name-forgetting in 1907 was a model of Freudian labor. He spent virtually a whole day producing free associations to no avail, and when this herculean effort failed, he continued his labors into the early hours of the next morning until he finally met with success and psychoanalytic insight. Only a resident, like Brill, at the then-Freudian stronghold of the Burghölzli Clinic in Zurich (where Bleuler, Jung, Abraham, Riklin, Eitingon, and other Freudians were currently working) would have accorded Freud's theory such a patient test. "I have no doubt now," Brill later confessed of his conversion experience, "that had I not been able to find it [the solution to his forgetfulness], I probably would never have continued to take the slightest interest in Freud" (Freud 1938:59).

In spite of such difficulties, many readers must have undergone similar conversion experiences, for *The Psychopathology of Everyday Life* became one of Freud's most popular books. It was second only to his *Introductory Lectures* (1916–17) in number of editions, as well as foreign-language translations, in Freud's lifetime. With successive editions, the work was enlarged to incorporate the best new examples of parapraxes collected by Freud and his disciples. Freud is said to have first suspected that he might be a famous person when, on his way to America to deliver his Clark University lectures in 1909, he found

his cabin steward reading *The Psychopathology of Everyday Life* (Jones
1955:55). A few examples from the book will convey the nature of
Freud's argument and suggest the fascination that it continues to
exert over his readers today.

The forgetting of names and words. A friend who was familiar
with Freud's theories invited him to explain the following instance of
forgetting. The friend, also a Jew, had been lamenting in Freud's presence the persecuted status of the Jewish race. He ended his speech by
appealing to the well-known words from Vergil's *Aeneid* (IV:625) in
which Dido threatens vengeance upon Aeneas: *"Exoriar(e) aliquis nos-
tris ex ossibus ultor"* ("Let someone arise from my bones as an aven-
ger!"). Unfortunately Freud's friend found himself unable to recall the
second word of Dido's proclamation, *aliquis* ("someone"), a word that
Freud, however, was able to supply. By the method of free association,
Freud's friend produced the following series of thoughts about the forgotten word *aliquis*: the notion of dividing the word into *a* and *liquis*;
relics; liquefying, fluidity, fluid; saints' relics; Saint Simon, Saint Bene-
dict, Saint Augustine, and Saint Januarius (the last two being calendar
saints); Saint Januarius's miracle of blood (a phial of this saint's blood,
kept in a church at Naples, is said to liquefy once a year on a particular
holy day); and, finally, a thought that Freud's friend felt to be too intimate to pass on, although he did tell Freud that it concerned an expected message from a certain lady. At this point Freud guessed that his
friend was fearful of hearing that his lady friend's periods had stopped
—an assumption that turned out to be correct. The allusions to *calendar*
saints, *blood* that flows on a particular day, *liquid*, and so forth had all
been unconsciously associated by Freud's friend, through the forgotten
word *aliquis*, to the anxious expectations deriving from an amorous affair. Hence the wish expressed by the friend in their previous conversation—that he might have descendants to avenge the fate of his race—
had met with unconscious interference from the equally fervent hope
that he would not have any immediate descendants issuing from his recent sexual liaison (1901*b*, *S.E.*, 6:8–14).

Another example, which likewise illustrates the motive of "unpleasure" (Freudian *Unlust*) in unconscious forgetting, was later reported to
Freud by Jung and used by Freud in a later edition of *The Psychopathology of Everyday Life*. A certain Herr Y. fell in love with a woman, but
the woman failed to return his love and instead married Herr X. Herr X.
was well known personally to Herr Y. from prior business dealings.
For a long time after the marriage, however, Herr Y. found himself repeatedly unable to recall the name of Herr X. whenever he had to correspond with him (*S.E.*, 6:25).

When the unconscious forgetting of names is accompanied by
paramnesia (recollection of another name that one swears to be correct or similar), the substitute name represents a psychical displacement, just as occurs in the formation of dreams.[25]

25. See Freud's autobiographical explanation of his forgetting the name "Sig-
norelli," and substitute recollection of the names "Botticelli" and "Boltraffio" (*S.E.*,
6:2–7).

Screen memories. Freud's theory of unconscious forgetting and substitute recollections can be extended to explain the general amnesia and isolated recollections associated with the period of early childhood. Why are indifferent and unimportant events often preserved in our memories of childhood, whereas the significant impressions from this period are usually forgotten? Freud's answer is that these indifferent recollections are "screen memories" that have arisen from (1) the repression of really momentous impressions and (2) their mnemic replacement by inconsequential substitutes (1899a; 1901b, S.E., 6:43–52). A screen memory is therefore like the manifest content of a dream. It is simply a disguise, a compromise formation, for a latent memory whose recollection would only evoke unpleasure. The displaced impression may be either an early childhood one or, less commonly, a post-pubertal one (so-called retrogressive displacements). Insight into the problem of screen memories had great importance for Freud's therapeutic technique, since these mnemic screens are generally linked to early repressions.

Slips of the tongue. Prior to Freud, slips of the tongue, slips of the pen, and misreadings had been systematically analyzed from linguistic and physiological points of view only (e.g., Meringer and Mayer 1895). According to this conception, linguistic or acoustic similarities, together with such physiological influences as inattention, lassitude, or psychical degeneration, were considered to be the primary mechanisms of verbal and written parapraxes. Freud's achievement lay in showing how frequently linguistic slips are motivated by more everyday, psychological considerations.[26] A favorite example of Freud's was a slip of the tongue committed by the President of the Lower House of the Austrian Parliament during opening formalities. The President, who apparently had reason to expect a stormy and unfruitful session, greeted the assembly with the words, "Gentlemen: I take notice that a full quorum of members is present and herewith declare the sitting *closed!*" (*S.E.*, 6:59). Another of Freud's favorite examples concerns a professor of anatomy who, in a lecture on the female sexual organs, was heard to declare, "In the case of the female genitals, in spite of many temptations [*Versuchungen*]—I beg your pardon, experiments [*Versuche*] . . ." (*S.E.*, 6:78–79). This same professor, after lecturing on the nasal cavities, once asked his students whether they had understood his explanation of this complicated subject. When he received a positive response, the professor, who was well known for his self-admiration, proclaimed with surprise: "I can hardly believe that, since, even in Vienna with its millions of inhabitants, those who understand the nasal cavities can be counted on one finger, I mean on the fingers of one hand" (*S.E.*, 6:78).

26. Among novelists and playwrights, Freud's psychological conception of linguistic slips had long been understood and used to good advantage as part of dramatic technique. Freud cited several such examples, including one from Shakespeare's *Merchant of Venice*, in *The Psychopathology of Everyday Life* (*S.E.*, 6:96–100, 132–33, 176–77). It was in more than this respect that Freud made a science out of "the kind of psychology used by poets" (the phrase is from Berger's [1896] review of Breuer and Freud's *Studies on Hysteria* [1895d]).

Bungled and symptomatic actions. In these two categories Freud counted such mishaps as husbands and wives who mislay their wedding rings; brides and grooms who "accidentally" fail to show up for the marriage ceremony; attempts to open a door with the wrong key (which indicates where one would rather be); and patients who leave objects behind in the analyst's office, thus signifying their desire to return (*S.E.*, 6:164, 203–6, 214).

Freud concluded his treatment of parapraxes in *The Psychopathology of Everyday Life* with a discussion of psychical determinism and the significance of numbers. Even those numbers that are picked "randomly" out of one's head, Freud insisted, are always determined by unconscious thoughts that may be traced by the method of free association; and he illustrated this claim with several examples (*S.E.*, 6:242–50). Such random-number analyses, which may also be performed on "favorite" numbers, provide an interesting self-test of how far one is prepared to go with Freud on this issue of unconscious psychical determinism.

In summing up his argument in *The Psychopathology of Everyday Life*, Freud compared parapraxes to neurotic symptoms "located in the least important psychical functions." The motives of such parapraxes are always suppressed or repressed feelings of an egoistic, hostile, jealous, or sexual nature. Freud emphasized "personal" and "professional" complexes as foremost among the sources of unconscious interference in parapraxes, and also spoke of "the positively predatory activities of the 'family complex'" in such matters (*S.E.*, 6:23, 40, 276–79).

JOKES AND THEIR RELATION TO THE UNCONSCIOUS

Jokes and Their Relation to the Unconscious (1905c) originated, according to Freud, as "a side-issue directly derived from *The Interpretation of Dreams*" (*Autobiography*, 1925d, *S.E.*, 20:65). The immediate source of inspiration for the book was Wilhelm Fliess, who, while reading the proofs for *The Interpretation of Dreams*, had remarked that Freud's dream analyses were surprisingly full of jokes (*Origins*, p. 297).[27] "In order to throw some light on this impression," Freud later recounted, "I began to investigate jokes and found that their essence lay in the technical methods employed in them, and that these were the same as the means used in the 'dream-work'—that is to say, con-

---

27. Freud had independently begun collecting Jewish jokes and anecdotes as early as 1897 (*Origins*, p. 211). He also credited Theodor Lipps's *Komik und Humor* (1898) with giving him both "the courage" and "the possibility" of undertaking his own studies on this subject (*S.E.*, 8:9 n.). Lipps, a professor of psychology in Munich, was an outspoken advocate of the notion of unconscious mental processes. Freud had approvingly cited Lipps's (1883, 1897) ideas on the unconscious in *The Interpretation of Dreams*.

densation, displacement, the representation of a thing by its opposite or by something very small, and so on" (*Autobiography*, 1925d, *S.E.*, 20:65–66). The intimate overlap in Freud's thinking about dreams and jokes is succinctly conveyed by his use of the term *joke-work* to describe the processes by which a preconscious thought is given over to unconscious revision in the formation of a joke. But unlike a dream, a joke does not attempt to disguise its displaced "allusions" so strenuously, for such elaborate disguises would only stifle the joke's humor. Thus, a typical dream, when properly interpreted, seems like a *bad* joke (*S.E.*, 8:173, 179).

Freud separated jokes into word play, puns, jests, and innocent jokes, on the one hand, and tendentious jokes, on the other (that is, jokes involving a more definite purpose, usually of an obscene or hostile nature). He concluded that innocent jokes, puns, and jests derive their humor from the economy of psychical expenditure achieved by the joke technique. It was as a jest deriving its humor from such an economy of expression that the great medical figure Carl Rokitansky once explained the professions of his four sons: "'Two heal [*heilen*] and two howl [*heulen*]'" (two were doctors and two were singers [*S.E.*, 8:129–30]). Tendentious jokes, Freud submitted, use the same economic technique as a means of lifting psychical repressions. By cleverly bribing the mind's censor with a bit of "fore-pleasure," jokes of this coarser form trigger the release of suppressed affect, which expresses itself as laughter. At the same time, the pleasure of obscene or hostile jokes is partly derived from the momentary savings of psychical energy that is normally employed in maintaining our repressions. It is for these reasons, Freud claimed, that the best jokes are always sexual jokes (*S.E.*, 8:133–37).

Freud's employment of sexual terms and concepts, such as "fore-pleasure," in his economic analysis of humor was not accidental. He wrote his book on jokes simultaneously with the *Three Essays on the Theory of Sexuality* (1905d) and kept the two manuscripts on adjoining tables so that he might work alternately on each one as the mood struck him (Jones 1955:12). More important, the two themes of jokes and sexuality encouraged such a concurrent analysis owing to the basic identity of their underlying psychoanalytic mechanisms. In Freud's conception, innocent jokes may be seen as small, orgasmic outbursts of primary-process activity, while obscene jokes correspond to an orgasm of the repressed. Similarly, Freud viewed the original form of most obscene jokes (smut) as an attempt at seduction of the female by the male (*S.E.*, 8:97, 133).

Jokes and Their Relation to the Unconscious (1905c) is one of Freud's least-read books today, although it was well received upon publication and also sold relatively well. Much of it is difficult to translate, at least without ruining the jokes, and many of the jokes are no longer as humorous as they were in Vienna at the turn of the century. This book nevertheless illustrates Freud's unsurpassed ability to grasp subjects removed from his normal sphere of medical expertise, together with his talent for applying new and far-reaching insights to such material as part of his nascent psychoanalytic enterprise.

Conclusion

Between 1899 and 1905, Freud set forth his basic psychoanalytic corpus of ideas in five major publications: *The Interpretation of Dreams* (1900a [1899]), *The Psychopathology of Everyday Life* (1901b), *Jokes and Their Relation to the Unconscious* (1905c), the "Dora" case history (1905e [1901]), and *Three Essays on the Theory of Sexuality* (1905d). Had Freud written nothing more in his lifetime, psychoanalytic theory would still have been available to the world in virtually all the essential aspects that we recognize today. These five works constitute a magnificent achievement, which certainly places Freud among the most creative scientific minds of all time and has given to the world what is possibly, in the words of Philip Rieff (1959:x), "the most important body of thought committed to paper in the twentieth century."

For Freud himself these publications satisfied a more immediate and pragmatic ambition: they provided him with a compelling theoretical *paradigm* (in the Kuhnian [1962] sense),[28] by which Freud successfully transformed psychoanalysis from a theory of the neuroses into a new and far-reaching psychology of the normal mind. He later offered essentially the same judgment in his *Autobiography* (1925d) when he reflected back upon his remarkable scientific accomplishments at the turn of the century:

> Previously psycho-analysis had only been concerned with solving pathological phenomena and in order to explain them it had often been driven into making assumptions whose comprehensiveness was out of all proportion to the importance of the actual material under consideration. But when it came to dreams, it was no longer dealing with a pathological symptom, but with a phenomenon of normal mental life which might occur in any healthy person. If dreams turned out to be constructed like symptoms, if their explanation required the same assumptions—the repression of impulses, substitutive formation, compromise-formation, the dividing of the conscious and the unconscious into various psychical systems—then psycho-analysis was no longer an auxiliary science in the field of psychopathology, it was rather the starting-point of a new and deeper science of the mind which would be equally indispensable for the understanding of the normal. (*S.E.*, 20:47)

28. According to Kuhn's (1970a:182–87; 1974:463) more recent reformulation of this concept, paradigms are to be seen as jointly composed of (1) a "disciplinary matrix," encompassing a scientific community together with shared symbolic generalizations (like the formula $f = ma$), models (like atomism), and values (like the goal of prediction); and (2) "exemplars" (instances of solved problems, set forth in basic texts). In both of these two general senses, Freud brought a significant new paradigm to psychology.

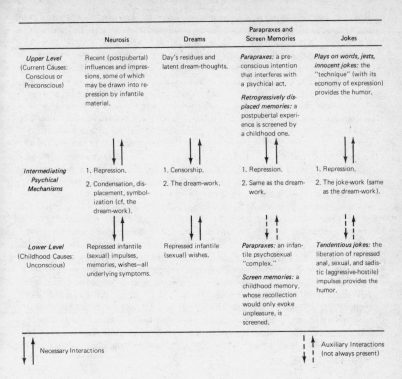

	Neurosis	Dreams	Parapraxes and Screen Memories	Jokes
Upper Level (Current Causes: Conscious or Preconscious)	Recent (postpubertal) influences and impressions, some of which may be drawn into repression by infantile material.	Day's residues and latent dream-thoughts.	*Parapraxes:* a preconscious intention that interferes with a psychical act. *Retrogressively displaced memories:* a postpubertal experience is screened by a childhood one.	*Plays on words, jests, innocent jokes:* the "technique" (with its economy of expression) provides the humor.
Intermediating Psychical Mechanisms	1. Repression. 2. Condensation, displacement, symbolization (cf. the dream-work).	1. Censorship. 2. The dream-work.	1. Repression. 2. Same as the dream-work.	1. Repression. 2. The joke-work (same as the dream-work).
Lower Level (Childhood Causes: Unconscious)	Repressed infantile (sexual) impulses, memories, wishes—all underlying symptoms.	Repressed infantile (sexual) wishes.	*Parapraxes:* an infantile psychosexual "complex." *Screen memories:* a childhood memory, whose recollection would only evoke unpleasure, is screened.	*Tendentious jokes:* the liberation of repressed anal, sexual, and sadistic (aggressive-hostile) impulses provides the humor.

Necessary Interactions

Auxiliary Interactions (not always present)

Fig. 9.3. Freud's two-tier paradigm of human behavior.

In terms of its most general features, Freud's new psychological paradigm combined two major causal tiers (one for *current* causes and one for *childhood* determinants), together with a series of universal psychical mechanisms (like condensation, displacement, censorship, and repression), in achieving his comprehensive model of human behavior. At the same time, Freud's lower-tier assumptions about mental functioning ensured that his own thinking as a psychoanalyst remained thoroughly rooted in biology, even within the newer and more overtly psychological domains that his theories now encompassed. (See Fig. 9.3 for a schematic summary of Freud's overall paradigm of human behavior.)

Viewed from another historical perspective, dreams and parapraxes did for the future psychoanalytic movement what the more limited study of psychoneuroses could not do. Freud's discoveries about dreaming, everyday episodes of forgetting, slips of the tongue, and so forth opened up his theories to the nonspecialist—to psychologists, anthropologists, and educators; to students of music, art, and literature; to intelligent laymen; and even to former patients—issuing them a didactic invitation to begin learning psychoanalysis "self-analytically."

Nor was the scientific gain represented by Freud's new psychoanalytic paradigm limited solely to normal psychology. His discoveries offered contemporary psychopathologists a valuable methodological window into the minds of their patients. Together with the technique of free association, his various doctrines became united into a powerful method of psychotherapy, eventually leading to many further refinements in the understanding of mental pathology. To those physicians who were willing to try this new and daring approach, like the youthful psychiatrist-in-training Carl Gustav Jung, Freud's therapeutic methods seemed a vast improvement upon contemporary procedures, which were mostly confined to providing a classification, not a cure, of the illness (see Jung 1939, C.W., 15:44–45).

With the achievement of his far-reaching paradigm of human behavior—normal and abnormal—Freud soon began to attract adherents. From its small beginning in the autumn of 1902 as the Psychological Wednesday Evenings circle, Freud's following grew steadily with each successive year of the new century. The initial Wednesday discussion group, which met in Freud's waiting room and included—besides Freud—Stekel, Adler, Reitler, and Kahane, was joined in 1903 by several others, including Paul Federn. Eduard Hitschmann was introduced to the group in 1905, and Otto Rank and Isidor Sadger began attending meetings the following year (by which date the organization, which now claimed seventeen members and an average weekly attendance of eleven, had become known as the Psychological Wednesday Society and was keeping formal minutes of its discussions). Two years later, in 1908, Ernest Jones, Sándor Ferenczi, and A. A. Brill made their first contact with Freud. As early as 1904 the eminent Zurich psychiatrist Eugen Bleuler had written to Freud about the interest taken in Freud's theories at the Burghölzli Clinic, where Jung, Riklin, Abraham, and Eitingon, among others, were actively applying Freud's therapeutic procedures. Then, in 1906, Carl Jung began a regular correspondence with Freud that was to continue until their break in 1913–14. By 1908, when the Psychological Wednesday Society was formally renamed the Vienna Psychoanalytic Society, Freud and his movement—surrounded as it was by growing controversy—stood on the brink of worldwide recognition.

10

Evolutionary Biology Resolves Freud's Three Psychoanalytic Problems (1905-39)

A common criticism of Freud's theory of mind is that, notwithstanding his personal genius, his doctrines were severely limited by the peculiar Victorian period in which he lived, by the predominantly upper-class clientele that he treated, as well as by certain personal failings that caused him to overemphasize the importance of sex to the exclusion of all else.[1] Even some of Freud's earliest followers quickly reached such a sober judgment as to the one-sided nature of his teachings. Carl Jung was one of these, and in his autobiography, *Memories, Dreams, Reflections*, he later reminisced about this aspect of Freud's doctrines. Recalling two separate episodes, in 1907 and 1910, Jung reports how struck he was by Freud's dogmatic attitude toward the psyche (especially on the subject of sex), and how he soon began to see Freud, however brilliant, as "a tragic figure . . . , a man in the grip of his daimon" (1963:153). Concerning their first face-to-face encounter, in 1907, Jung recounts:

> Above all, Freud's attitude toward the spirit seemed to me highly questionable. Wherever, in a person or in a work of art, an expression

1. See Wassermann 1958; Rieff 1959:338–39; Ansbacher 1959; Shakow and Rapaport 1964:201, n. 17; Fromm 1970a:45–46; Andreski 1972:138; Becker 1973: 94–96; Lifton 1976:26, 83–84; and Heller 1977.

of spirituality (in the intellectual, not the supernatural sense) came to light, he suspected it, and insinuated that it was repressed sexuality. Anything that could not be directly interpreted as sexuality he referred to as "psychosexuality." I protested that this hypothesis, carried to its logical conclusion, would lead to an annihilating judgment upon culture. Culture would then appear as a mere farce, the morbid consequence of repressed sexuality. "Yes," he assented, "so it is, and that is just a curse of fate against which we are powerless to contend."

. . . There was no mistaking the fact that Freud was emotionally involved in his sexual theory to an extraordinary degree. (1963:149–50)

Three years later, Jung had these impressions dramatically confirmed during another meeting with Freud that foreshadowed their subsequent estrangement:

I can still recall vividly how Freud said to me, "My dear Jung, promise me never to abandon the sexual theory. That is the most essential thing of all. You see, we must make a dogma of it, an unshakable bulwark." He said that to me with great emotion, in the tone of a father saying, "And promise me this one thing, my dear son: that you will go to church every Sunday." In some astonishment I asked him, "A bulwark—against what?" To which he replied, "Against the black tide of mud"—and here he hesitated for a moment, then added—"of occultism."

. . . What Freud seemed to mean by "occultism" was virtually everything that philosophy and religion, including the rising contemporary science of parapsychology, had learned about the psyche. (1963:150–51)

To Jung and other contemporaries, Freud's all-encompassing conception of "psychosexuality" seemed just as "occult"—at best a useful hypothesis for the present but not "an unshakable bulwark" against future enlightenment.

In a similar vein, Izydor Wassermann (1958) has emphasized that Freud's patients belonged predominantly to the upper classes. Proceeding from this observation, Wassermann has drawn an intriguing contrast between Freud and Alfred Adler. After carefully searching Freud's and Adler's clinical writings for indications about the wealth and the social status of their clientele, Wassermann found consistent differences between the two physicians' patients. Specifically, three-quarters (74 percent) of Freud's patients were affluent, and almost none (3 percent) were poor. By Viennese standards, Freud's fees were also high (Jones 1955:389). In contrast to this, three-quarters (75 percent) of Adler's patrons were either middle class (40 percent) or poor (35 percent). Wassermann attributes certain basic theoretical differences between Freud and Adler to this marked contrast in their medical practices. Among Freud's upper-class clientele, "with the instinct of self-preservation completely satisfied, the second most powerful instinct [sex] moves to the frontline" (1958:624). Adler's less affluent patients, on the other hand, found "the problems of material existence . . . much more anxiety-inspiring" (p. 625).

Drawing upon these statistical findings, Heinz Ansbacher (1959) has gone beyond Wassermann's argument in maintaining that Freud's and Adler's *initial choice* of patients derived from major personality differences between the two investigators, which hold the real key to their respective theories. Ansbacher's thesis may be summarized as follows. Freud, his mother's undisputed favorite and a typical firstborn, was conscious of his social status, openly disdainful of *"das Volk,"* valued authority and power over his fellow man, and once wrote that "the unworthiness of human beings, even of analysts, has always made a deep impression on me . . ." (Jones 1955:182).[2] Consistent with such attitudes, Freud assumed man to possess an innate evil component that must constantly be controlled by a higher authority (for instance, by the laws of society, the superego of the individual, the preconscious censor, and so forth). Adler, a laterborn, discounted Freud's "firstborn" notion of the Oedipus complex (with its undue emphasis upon parent-child relations); pioneered in discovering the psychological implications of birth order (i.e., sibling-sibling interactions); and saw his patients as victims of their struggle for greater power (cf. the fate of the younger sibling). He further believed that man is basically good, and that neurosis is potentially eliminable through the promotion of egalitarian attitudes, together with greater social interest.

Also consistent with Adler and Freud's theoretical differences, Ansbacher points out, are their differing modes of therapy. Freud's therapy displays an above/below attitude: the patient, who does not see the analyst, reclines (below) on a couch. Adlerian therapy, by contrast, is more egalitarian: the patient faces his analyst across a table and is considered by the analyst as the *real* expert on the case in question. Thus, each psychologist's theories, Ansbacher concludes, reflect the dominant values of his own psyche, while their closely related choice of patients merely served to reinforce such extrascientific prejudices.

The criticisms of Wassermann, Ansbacher, and Jung, as well as of numerous others who have pointed to overly dogmatic biases in Freud's theories, may strike us now as well taken. Seizing upon selected and historically transient evidence, Freud appears to have generalized his findings into universal laws. Yet it is not sufficiently recognized how fully aware Freud was of the ephemeral cultural-historical influences

2. If Freud displayed many of the qualities of a firstborn, as Ansbacher enumerates (on the basis of Adler's own theories), Freud also possessed many important laterborn traits, such as his high degree of intellectual nonconformity. Freud was his mother's firstborn child but his father's third son; and until he was almost four years old, his two elder brothers lived nearby, as did his nephew and childhood playmate John. The latter, who was one year Freud's senior, was Freud's eldest brother's son. When the Freud family moved to Vienna from Freiberg in 1859, the two elder brothers, along with nephew John, immigrated to Manchester, England. (For further details on Freud's unusual family constellation, see Jones 1953:8–14.) In my view, to be elaborated more fully in a future publication on birth order and revolutionary temperament in science, Freud was a birth-order "hybrid," simultaneously displaying qualities of both firstborn and laterborn temperaments. For Alfred Adler's views on birth order, see Adler 1931; 1956:376–82. For more recent experimental studies of birth order corroborating the typologies mentioned above, see Sampson (1962) and Bragg and Allen (1970), and, for a more general review of the literature, Sutton-Smith and Rosenberg (1970).

that underlay the sexual neuroses of his generation and especially the afflictions of his upper-class clientele. Indeed, he was perfectly willing to concede that primitive societies, or the lower classes of his own society, were far less prone to hysteria and other psychoneuroses on account of the greater permissiveness toward sexual behavior prevailing in those quarters. "In consequence of the inverse relation holding between civilization and the free development of sexuality . . . ," Freud proclaimed in his *Three Essays on the Theory of Sexuality,* "the course taken by the sexual life of a child is just as unimportant for later life where the culture or social level is relatively low as it is important where that level is relatively high" (1905d, S.E., 7:242). As we have also seen, Freud's fourfold causal analysis of mental pathology allowed for a wide variety of nonsexual pathogens in every neurosis (Chapter 3). Accordingly, his etiological theories by no means demanded, a priori, a totally rigid or exclusively sexual formula of neurosis for every patient, historical period, or culture. All that he ever claimed was that, given the circumstances prevailing in all civilized societies known to him, *his* etiological laws would not be violated, and that repressed sexuality would always be found as the "specific" (childhood) determinant of every neurosis.

As we shall see in this chapter, it was actually (and ironically) *because of* Freud's sweeping cultural and historical relativism that he was ultimately able to proclaim the universal views on sex and neurosis that he did, and not, as Carl Jung and others have suggested, because Freud was tragically caught up by his own "daimon" and was thus incapable of placing his clinical findings in a proper sociohistorical framework. This assertion is not to deny that Freud's personality, together with the historical period in which he lived, was of considerable influence upon his theories. But I wish to make clear in this chapter how complex, how sophisticated, and, above all, how rational was the interaction between Freud's scientific and personal Weltanschauungen, as well as how insufficiently his critics have understood this scientific vision.

It is commonly said that Freud's intellectual excursions into human prehistory and, through it, into anthropology, sociology, and evolutionary theory, were "late" and "peripheral" adjuncts to his psychoanalytic thinking.[3] Not so. Works like *Totem and Taboo* (1912–13), *Group Psychology and the Analysis of the Ego* (1921c), *The Future of an Illusion* (1927c), and *Civilization and Its Discontents* (1930a) grew naturally out of his 1890s appraisal of the human animal in relation to the burdens of civilization. Indeed, many of the most important cultural-historical and phylogenetic ideas that Freud publicly announced in the second and third decades of the twentieth century were originally adopted

3. See Wittels 1924b:168; Glover 1950:43; Jones 1957:324; and Ritvo 1974: 187–89. The last of these authors speaks for the others when she writes: "Freud's speculations with these now antiquated biological ideas [recapitulation and Lamarckian inheritance] did no harm to his theory. They may have led those who have read only his later speculative writings on applied psychoanalysis to underestimate his scientific contributions" (p. 189).

by him in the mid-1890s, as the Fliess correspondence amply corroborates. Inasmuch as these same ideas (for example, the biogenetic law and Freud's phylogenetic views on sexual perversion, the component instincts, organic repression, abandoned erotogenic zones, etc.) were fundamental to his initial discovery and subsequent elaboration of the id concept in psychoanalytic theory, the key reformulations of this early period actually proceeded hand in hand with his growing evolutionary conception of man (Chapters 6–8).

Thus, Freud's later works on primitive man and on the origins of religion, law, and civilization are simply a continuation of the basic shift in reductionistic explanation that occurred in his psychoanalytic thinking between 1895 and 1905. That was a shift from *proximate*-causal theory to *ultimate*-causal theory within Freud's abiding lifetime ambition of attaining a synthetic, psychobiological solution to the problems of mind. As Ernst Mayr (1961) has distinguished these two causal approaches in the life sciences, the proximate-causal theorist is someone who studies organic phenomena as they manifest themselves in the lifetime of the individual. This first branch of biological theory asks, How come? Such are the questions of the functional biologist, the physiologist, the endocrinologist, and so forth. To cite another relevant example, Freud's famous *Project for a Scientific Psychology* was written within a zealously neurophysiological and hence *proximate*-causal framework.

The ultimate-causal theorist, in comparison, asks, Why?—and his science, Mayr points out, is evolutionary biology. Although How come? is also implicit in the question of Why?, the functional and the evolutionary biologist tackle very different aspects of biological causality in their day-to-day researches. For instance, why do some birds migrate at certain times of the year? Whereas the functional biologist would explain such migrations in terms of environmental cues (for example, changes in temperature and photoperiodicity) acting upon hormonal and biochemical mechanisms, the evolutionary biologist has learned that migrations constitute a historical acquisition in certain species' genetic programs. The advent of a glacial epoch, for instance, conferred a selective advantage upon certain species of birds that—given their previous ecological habits—headed toward warmer climates in the autumn and then returned to their customary mating sites in the spring. It is this evolutionary account that explains why geese migrate (because their food supply is dependent upon a temperate climate) and why owls do not.

As a pre-1900 psychologist and neuropathologist, Freud may be described as primarily a proximate-causal theorist. For a time, he even hoped that a proximate-causal approach to brain functioning might allow him to grasp the entire working principles of the mental apparatus. As we have seen (Chapter 4), Freud eventually recognized the prematurity of this line of research when his abortive *Project for a Scientific Psychology* (1895) convinced him just how immense this task was and how speculative and inadequate were his own attempts to surmount it.

Freud's study and desk, as photographed by Edmund Engelmann (Vienna, 1938). Freud's fascination with the past is exemplified by his collection of Egyptian, Etruscan, Greek, Roman, and other antiquities, some dating back more than two millennia. Freud began this collection, of which the statuettes shown here constitute only a small part, in the mid-1890s. Also on the desk is a manuscript now believed to be *Moses and Monotheism*.

But he did not by any means lose faith on this account in the critical importance of the biological approach to mind. Rather, his abandonment of neurophysiological reductionism was increasingly counterbalanced by his adoption of a phylogenetic-historical form of reductionism as he continued to wrestle with his most essential, unanswered problems. Indeed, in advocating a genetic psychology after 1900, Freud established perhaps the most comprehensive evolutionary explanation of the origins of human behavior that has yet been formulated in science. Even if he was mistaken in certain of his phylogenetic and anthropological theories, his appeal to these ultimate-causal solutions marks him as a shrewd thinker who fully understood the task of constructing a universal theory of human behavior.[4]

The fundamental continuity of Freud's thought is reinforced by another observation: it was the findings and the unsolved problems of psychopathology that continually motivated him to ask the ultimate-causal questions that he did. The theory of psychoneurosis, even after 1900, remained for him "the motherland where we have first to fortify our dominion against everything and everybody" (quoted in Jones 1955: 140, Freud to Ferenczi, 29 December 1910). When other analysts, like Jung, occasionally strayed too far afield from this motherland, Freud sternly warned them to return in good time to what he designated as "psycho-analysis itself"—the theory of neuroses (1916–17, S.E., 16:379). It should not surprise us, then, that when Freud himself ventured into the neighboring intellectual "colonies" of psychoanalysis (anthropology, religion, sociology, etc.), he did so largely in order to clarify his most basic unsolved problems in the theory of the psychoneuroses.

In the present chapter and the one that follows, I shall elaborate the key role played by ultimate-causal (evolutionary) explanations in resolving Freud's three most fundamental psychoanalytic problems. These three problems (the nature of pathological repression, Why sex?, and the choice of neurosis) were precisely the ones that had proved so recalcitrant in Freud's *Project* attempt to construct a working, neurophysiological model of the mind (Chapter 4). As psychoanalysis matured, new difficulties had naturally arisen, but none ever became quite as central to Freud's overall theoretical vision as his three problems from the 1890s. It was, above all, in order to master these problems that Freud subsequently developed such a remarkable anthropological-phylogenetic scenario about man. Man's evolutionary past, he came to believe, had originally decreed the psychoanalytic laws of human behavior and, more important, had endowed these laws with a universal, transcultural validity.

4. The differential relevancy of proximate- and ultimate-causal considerations to the psychoanalytic vision of man has been specifically recognized by psychiatrist Robert Lifton (1976:18, 62–63), who draws upon Edward O. Wilson's analysis of this causal dichotomy within biological theory. See Wilson's *Sociobiology: The New Synthesis* (1975:23), which, despite its differing theoretical premises, is fully in keeping with the general spirit of Freud's own views on social behavior.

PROBLEM ONE: THE NATURE OF REPRESSION AND MORALITY

Of Freud's three major psychoanalytic problems, the nature of repression (and of civilized morality) was decidedly the most fundamental. As long as the concept of repression remained "the corner-stone" in Freud's theory of psychoneurosis, its resolution claimed highest priority in his work (*Autobiography*, 1925*d*, *S.E.*, 20:30). Not surprisingly, his eventual solution of this problem dictated much that automatically followed in his thinking about his other two psychoanalytic problems. I therefore begin with Freud's assault upon the repression-morality problem.

Four phases may be distinguished in Freud's maturing thoughts about the problem of repression, in the course of which he developed complementary psychological and organic-phylogenetic theories of repression. He unified these two approaches in the fourth and last phase under the concept of the *superego*.

Phase One, 1893–97:
Freud's Early Theory of Repression (Defense)

In this first period, Freud conceptualized repression (or defense) in terms of the ego suppressing certain "incompatible" and generally traumatic ideas (1894*a*, 1896*b*). He believed that pathological defense severed the incompatible idea from its affect, and that the displaced affect, under continued repression, then induced a pathogenic "splitting of the mind" while simultaneously becoming the unconscious energy source for neurotic symptoms. The psychophysiological nature of this early conception is epitomized by the Breuer-Freud theory of *abreaction* as it sought to explain the cathartic cure.

Freud's abandonment of the seduction theory called this whole psychophysiological scheme into question when the "incompatible ideas" turned out to be fictitious. He now realized that normal and neurotic individuals share similar childhood sexual experiences, and that the real key to the problem lies in whether a person has reacted to these experiences with "organic 'sexual repression'" (1906*a*, *S.E.*, 7:276–78).

Phase Two, 1896/97–1913:
Organic Repression and the Sense of Smell

Even before he abandoned the seduction theory in the autumn of 1897, Freud had begun to supplement his psychological theory of repression with an appeal to an organic "reversal of affect" associated with certain forms of childhood sexual experiences (*Origins*, pp. 179–80, 186, letters of 6 December 1896 and 11 January 1897). Under this organic rubric, he later, in *Three Essays on the Theory of Sexuality* (1905*d*), included the acquisition of disgust, shame, aesthetic ideals, and morality. The layman might ascribe such psychical acquisitions to the effects of moral education. "But in reality," Freud asserted, "this development is organically determined and fixed by heredity, and it can occasionally occur without any help at all from education" (S.E., 7:177–78).

During this second phase of his thinking about repression, Freud considered the acquisition of disgust to be the major catalyst of all higher moral sensibilities. He therefore focused his analysis upon disgust as the key to the repression problem. In the "Dora" case history, he wrote: "Such feelings [of disgust] seem originally to be a reaction to the smell (and afterwards also to the sight) of excrement" (1905e [1901], S.E., 7:31). Privately, Freud had long attributed this reaction against excrement to the phylogenetic consequences of man's upright posture. This was the idea about which he had told Fliess in 1897 that he "would not concede priority . . . to anyone," and which he first described to his friend in connection with his biogenetically based notion of "abandoned erotogenic zones" (Origins, pp. 231–34). Freud's next major statement on this subject appears in 1909, during a discussion at the Vienna Psychoanalytic Society:

> We assume that there is no repression that does not have an organic core; this organic repression consists of the substitution of unpleasurable sensations for pleasurable ones. Probably man's detachment from the soil is one of the basic conditions for [the formation of] a neurosis; the olfactory sense is prone, as a consequence of this detachment, toward repression, since it has become useless. The repression of coprophilic tendencies begins in the same way: the bigger the child gets to be, the further it rises away from the ground. In this organic repression psychic factors as yet play no role; it is the repression of pleasurable sensations [and their transformation] into unpleasurable ones that we characterize as a portion of civilization. . . . The entire theory of the neuroses is incomplete as long as no light has been shed on the organic core of repression. (Minutes, 2:323; meeting of 17 November 1909)

The distinction between organic, childhood repressions and the more psychological repressions of adulthood corresponds to Freud's later dichotomy between *primal* and *secondary* repressions (1915d). As we shall see, his ideas on primal repression and the sense of smell were to become paradigmatic for all of his subsequent attempts to resolve the problem of repression in phylogenetic terms. That paradigm, which Freud articulated more fully in the third and next phase of his thinking, conceives of primal repression as an inherited reaction to the loss of archaic pleasures.

Phase Three, 1912/13–1923:
The Phylogenetic Origins of Civilization and Morality

Describing his plan for a four-part study of primitive, totemic religions, Freud briefly previewed to Ernest Jones in 1912 the bearing that he believed his anthropological researches would have upon the problem of repression:

> The true historical source of repression I hope to touch on in the last of the four papers, but I may as well give you the answer now. Any internal—(damn my English)[5]—Every *internal* barrier of repression is the historical result of an *external* obstruction. Thus: the opposition is incorporated within; the history of mankind is deposited in the present-day inborn tendencies to repression. (Jones 1955:455, letter of 1 August 1912; trans. Jones, and his italics)

Although Freud (1907b, 1908d) had previously been intrigued by the interrelations of culture, religion, and neurotic behavior, the immediate stimulus for his venture into these fields was the recent work undertaken by Carl Jung on comparative religion. As Jones (1955:351) notes, Jung's researches for his *Wandlungen und Symbole der Libido* (Transformations and Symbols of the Libido, 1911–12), the first part of which Freud had read in manuscript in 1910, had quickly made the latter uneasy about his Swiss disciple. In countermeasure, Freud had immersed himself in the same subject matter, hoping to reinforce the basic psychoanalytic conclusions from which Jung himself was rapidly departing. Writing to Ferenczi on 8 May 1913, Freud referred to the growing tension between himself and Jung and prophesied that *Totem and Taboo* would not be well received by his Swiss colleague: "I am working on the last section of the Totem, which comes at the right moment to deepen the gap [between us] by fathoms. . . . I have not written anything with so much conviction since *The Interpretation of Dreams*, so I can predict the fate of the essay" (quoted in Jones 1955: 353).

Freud's studies were focused upon the Australian aborigines and their peculiar totemic religions. The aborigines believe that a different totem, generally an animal, is the primordial ancestor of each clan; and they worship these totems as gods. After examining these totemic beliefs closely, Freud seized upon the totem gods and their associated taboos as relics of a major phylogenetic drama that long ago had produced primitive culture. He arrived at this remarkable and much-contested conclusion in the following manner. All totemic worship, he observed, is accompanied by a curious admixture of extreme fear toward, and extreme reverence for, the totem animal. Additionally, the rituals and taboos associated with the totem animal display many striking parallels to the obsessive rituals invented by neurotic patients. In particular, Freud thought he detected close similarities between the ambivalence exhibited toward the totem animal and the ambivalence universally observed in neurotics toward the same-sex parent. Having previously shown that childhood animal phobias reflect a neurotic fear of the father (1909b), Freud took the *animal* nature of most aboriginal totems as corroboration of his psychoanalytic thesis. But why is the totem, Freud asked, a symbolic father figure?

To answer this last question, Freud turned his attention to exogamy and its customary practice in totemic societies. Exogamy is a cultural

---

5. At this point Freud, who had been writing to Jones in English, switched to German: "*Jede innere Verdrängungsschranke ist der historische Erfolg eines äusseren Hindernisses. Also. Verinnerlichung der Widerstände, die Geschichte der Menschheit niedergelegt in ihren heute angeborenen Verdrängungsneigungen.*"

Freud, on the veranda of Berggasse 19, about the time of *Totem and Taboo* (1912–13). Photograph by his eldest son.

institution prohibiting marriage between individuals from the same clan. In his four-volume *Totemism and Exogamy* (1910), James Frazer had recently explained exogamy as a cultural means by which primitive societies protect themselves against the ever-present temptations of incest. Freud accepted Frazer's thesis and used it to complete the psychoanalytic parallel between totemism and neurosis. What Freud inferred was this: that totemic religion (with its characteristic ambivalence toward the totemic father figure) and the universal custom of exogamy (which prevents love for the mother from becoming incestuous) were none other than "the two halves of the familiar Oedipus complex" (Jones 1955:359). In other words, totemic religion was simply an institutionalized oedipal relationship!

Freud's final and most daring step in *Totem and Taboo* (1912–13) was to account for the historical origins of exogamy and totemism. The exogamy problem had been much discussed by contemporary anthropologists, and little agreement had yet been reached on it. After dismissing a number of theories on this subject, Freud proposed his own. His starting point was Charles Darwin's hypothesis in *The Descent of Man* (1871, 2:361–63) that man's early ancestors must have lived together in small hordes. Darwin had reasoned that in such a primitive social state, one old and powerful male would have controlled sexual access to all the females, thereby preventing promiscuity among his younger and subordinate male rivals. Darwin also surmised that the younger males must frequently have been expelled from the horde as soon as they reached sexual maturity. Eventually many of these ejected males, having been successful in winning or stealing sexual partners, would have founded their own hordes and thus have ensured the healthy consequences of outbreeding.

Extrapolating from Darwin's hypothetical state of affairs, Freud suggested that the younger male rivals—essentially a brother clan—must repeatedly have been compelled by their oedipal urges to slay, and to eat, their own father. The consequence of their rebellion was not, however, what the sons had at first envisioned; for, faced with the inevitability of their own quarrels over their father's harem, the sons became extremely ambivalent about their act of murder. They developed a sense of remorse, and they eventually sought to atone for their heinous act by deifying the slain father as the totemic ancestor of the clan. It was now forbidden by law to kill the totem, the symbolic father substitute. Finally, the sons instituted a delayed obedience to their father's will by prohibiting all incestuous relationships, thereby forcing marriage outside the clan. "They thus created out of their filial sense of guilt," Freud declared, "the two fundamental taboos of totemism [the prohibitions against incest and parricide], which for that very reason inevitably correspond to the two repressed wishes of the Oedipus complex" (1912–13, *S.E.*, *13*:143). Freud concluded the fourth and last essay of *Totem and Taboo* with his celebrated assertion that "the beginnings of religion, morals, society and art converge in the Oedipus complex" (*S.E.*, *13*:156).

Freud's argument, ingenious as it stands, was not particularly original. The major themes of *Totem and Taboo* (1912–13) had largely been anticipated by James J. Atkinson's *Primal Law* in 1903, and Freud acknowledged Atkinson's priority in his own publication (*S.E.*, *13*:142 n.). Proceeding, like Freud, from Darwin's notion of the primal horde, Atkinson had inferred both the practical consequences of exogamy for the young males and the repeated acts of parricide, followed by fraternal strife. In Atkinson's view, "Primal Law" arose when maternal love triumphed over paternal jealousy, and the youngest son was finally allowed to remain within "the Cyclopean family." The formal prohibition against incest arose as a result of this compromise. Gradually other sons were allowed to remain, causing kinship laws to become still more complex (Atkinson 1903:209–63). In the light of Atkinson's elaborate argument, Freud's originality lies largely in his having linked the facts about the neuroses with those about totemic religion, including Robertson Smith's (1894) observations on how the totem is occasionally killed and eaten during special religious rituals.

Of particular concern here is the way in which Freud related his theory of primitive religion to the problem of repression. As a convinced Lamarckian, Freud assumed that the phylogenetic events of *Totem and Taboo* were, with countless repetitions over the millennia, organically impressed upon the unconscious recesses of the mind. Speaking the year of his death about the Lamarckian hypothesis of mnemic inheritance, Freud proclaimed, "I have no hesitation in declaring that men have always known (in this special [Lamarckian] way) that they once possessed a primal father and killed him" (1939a, *S.E.*, *23*:101). Given Freud's equal confidence in the biogenetic law, the logic of *Totem and Taboo* greatly expanded the organic theory of repression that he had originally set forth in connection with olfaction and disgust. The ontogenetic acquisition of remorse, guilt, and moral sense now became conceivable to Freud as a phylogenetic precipitate from the primal father complex of early man (1923b, *S.E.*, *19*:37). In addition, Freud was able to include the repression of incestuous impulses among the organic predispositions of human beings. To the 1915 edition of *Three Essays on the Theory of Sexuality*, he accordingly added the following statement: "The barrier against incest is probably among the historical acquisitions of mankind, and, like other moral taboos, has no doubt already become established in many persons by organic inheritance. (Cf. my *Totem and Taboo*, 1912–13.)" (*S.E.*, *7*:225, n. 3). Similarly, four years later Freud insisted that children "are compelled to recapitulate from the history of mankind the repression of an incestuous object-choice, just as at an earlier stage they were obliged to effect an object-choice of that very sort" (1919e, *S.E.*, *17*:188).[6]

6. Like so many of Freud's later, ultimate-causal thoughts on repression, the inverse relationship between incest and civilization was first formulated in the Fliess correspondence (Draft N, 31 May 1897), where he had written: "The horror of incest (as something impious) is based on the fact that, as a result of common sexual life (even in childhood), the members of a family hold together permanently and become incapable of contact with strangers. Thus incest is anti-social and civilization consists in a progressive renunciation of it. Contrariwise the 'superman' [whose sexual behavior during primeval times knew no restraints]" (*Origins*, pp. 209–10; cf. *Group Psychology*, 1921c, *S.E.*, *18*:123).

I shall sum up the third stage in Freud's thinking about repression with the following formula: repression is the phylogenetic price for the evolution of law, religious belief, morality, and higher civilization. In essence, repression amounts to the suppression and dissolution of the Oedipus complex.

Phase Four, 1923–39: The Superego

I now return to the proximate-causal side of Freud's repression theory. Freud's early concept of defense had equated the ego with the agent of repression, and the unconscious with "the repressed." In 1914 he amended this point of view, asserting that repression is effected by "a special psychical agency" associated with the ego's *ideal* ("On Narcissism," 1914c, S.E., 14:95). To this ego ideal, Freud ascribed, besides the chief cause of secondary repression, responsibility for moral conscience, censorship in dreams, and paranoid delusions of "being watched." Nine years later, in 1923, Freud renamed this ego ideal the *superego* and introduced his tripart division of mind into ego, id, and superego. Freud envisaged the ego and the superego as jointly developing out of the *id*—or that part of the mind that contains the core of the unconscious, the source of all the passions, and the biologically innate in man (*The Ego and the Id*, 1923b, S.E., 19:24–25, 34–38). The *ego* was now characterized as "that part of the id which has been modified by the direct influence of the external world . . . ," a process brought about, Freud contended, by the influence of the perceptual system (p. 25). Within the id, and separated from the ego by a barrier of "resistance," Freud located the repressed.

As for the superego, Freud attributed two complementary origins to it: one in childhood and one in the history of the race. In childhood, the superego arises from identification with parental authority, principally with that of the opposite-sex parent, and thus with the major source of prohibition against incestuous impulses. In this developmental way, the Oedipus complex is successfully resolved. The superego is, to use Freud's famous phrase, "the heir to the Oedipus complex" (*S.E.*, 19:48). Normally the ego obeys the moral demands of the superego. But occasionally the ego may react to an overly harsh superego by repressing a part of the superego instead. Thus arises, according to Freud, the unconscious sense of guilt so typical of neurotics (*S.E.*, 19:51–52). Freud's model of superego development was initially conceived in terms of the male sex; and he subsequently admitted that matters were far more complicated in the female sex owing to the little girl's preoedipal attachment to her mother, her lack of castration fears, and the paramount role of *penis envy* in her Oedipus complex. (See Freud 1925j; 1931b; and 1933a: Lecture XXXIII.)

Turning to his second, or historical, derivation for the superego, Freud asserted that conscience and other moral values "were acquired phylogenetically out of the father-complex" he had previously documented in *Totem and Taboo* (1912–13). Originally assimilated by the male sex, these moral values were organically transmitted to women "by cross-inheritance" (*S.E.*, *19*:37). But was it the id or the ego, Freud asked rhetorically, that first acquired the moral trait of conscience in man's prehistory? He replied with the following Lamarckian analysis:

> The super-ego, according to our hypothesis, actually originated from the experiences that led to totemism. The question whether it was the ego or the id that experienced and acquired these things soon comes to nothing. Reflection at once shows us that no external vicissitudes can be experienced or undergone by the id, except by way of the ego, which is the representative of the external world to the id. . . . The experiences of the ego seem at first to be lost for inheritance; but, when they have been repeated often enough and with sufficient strength in many individuals in successive generations, they transform themselves, so to say, into experiences of the id, the impressions of which are preserved by heredity. Thus in the id, which is capable of being inherited, are harboured residues of the existences of countless egos; and, when the ego forms its super-ego out of the id, it may perhaps only be reviving shapes of former egos and be bringing them to resurrection. (*S.E.*, *19*:38)

Seen in these Lamarckian and biogenetic terms, Freud's notion of the superego constitutes an important conceptual watershed between his two formal categories of primal and secondary repression. The superego arises as the last of the great primal repressions and, like them, is reducible to an organic process founded in the ancestral experience of the race. With the appearance of the superego, however, secondary repression becomes possible, and it is this psychological capacity that continues the work of repression in the adult.

In spite of the great importance that Freud ascribed to the superego and to secondary repressions, he continued to view primal repressions, with their organic kernel, as the key to psychopathology. As he asserted in 1926, secondary repressions always "presuppose the operation of earlier, *primal repressions*. . . . There is a danger of overestimating the part played in repression by the super-ego" (1926*d*, *S.E.*, 20:94). Why was the concept of primal-organic repression so important to Freud? The answer to this question is ultimately to be found in his lifelong efforts to understand why neurosis and sexual maladjustment should be so inseparable in man.

PROBLEM TWO: WHY SEX?

For over forty years Freud steadfastly proclaimed to his readers, who were both shocked and fascinated by what he had to say, that sexuality is the one and only *specific* cause of neurosis. "None of the theses of psycho-analysis," Freud frankly confessed in 1923, "has met with such tenacious scepticism or such embittered resistance as this assertion of

the preponderating aetiological significance of sexual life in the neuroses" (1923a, S.E., 18:243). Freud made this etiological claim so frequently in the course of his psychoanalytic career that it is almost
superfluous to cite published examples. As Madison (1961:122) has emphasized about Freud, "He never once veered from his insistence that
sexual motivation is basic to neurosis (and hence to repression)." A
passage from the posthumously published *Outline of Psycho-Analysis*
will serve to demonstrate that Freud never altered his opinion on this
subject: "Theoretically there is no objection to supposing that any sort
of instinctual demand might occasion the same [pathological] repressions and their consequences; but our observation shows us invariably,
so far as we can judge, that the excitations that play this pathogenic
part arise from the component instincts of sexual life. The symptoms of
neuroses are, it might be said, without exception either a substitutive
satisfaction of some sexual urge or measures to prevent such a satisfaction . . ." (1940a, S.E., 23:186).[7]

Given the intimate ties between the problem of pathological repression and Freud's sexual interpretation of neurosis, it is not surprising
to encounter an analogous developmental pattern in his work upon
these two themes. As with the problem of repression, four major
phases may be distinguished in Freud's thinking about sexual etiology.
Freud approached sexuality in the first phase in proximate-causal
terms, whereas he approached it in the next three in a distinctly ultimate-causal manner.

Phase One, 1893–97:
Sexuality as "an Indispensable Premiss"

In this first phase, Freud declared sexuality to be "an indispensable
premiss" in his theory of psychoneurosis owing to its conformity with
his psychophysiological conception of symptom formation (1896c, S.E.,
3:200). With the development of the seduction theory, Freud concluded
that the unusually *late* emergence of the sexual instinct in man (!)
must somehow be responsible for the pathogenic effects that arise from
childhood sexual assaults (1896b, S.E., 3:166–67). Unfortunately, when
the child proved to be far less sexually "innocent" than Freud had at
first assumed, and when most of the seductions claimed by his patients
turned out to be imagined, his theory about the deferred action of
sexual traumas became unsatisfactory. Once again he was confronted
with the problem of why sex, and sex alone, undergoes pathological
repression.

7. For other discussions of this point, see Freud's "Sexuality in the Aetiology
of the Neuroses" (1898a, S.E., 3:268, and passim); "Psycho-Analytic Notes on an
Autobiographical Account of a Case of Paranoia (Dementia Paranoides)" (1911c,
S.E., 12:79); "History of the Psycho-Analytic Movement" (1914d, S.E., 14:29); "Repression" (1915d, S.E., 14:147); *Introductory Lectures* (1916–17, S.E., 16:362–
63); "A Difficulty in the Path of Psycho-Analysis" (1917a, S.E., 17:138); "Introduction to *Psycho-Analysis and the War Neuroses*" (1919d, S.E., 17:208–10); *Autobiography* (1925d, S.E., 20:23–24); and Jones (1955:320).

Phase Two, 1896/97–1913:
Sex, Organic Repression, and Neurosis

Freud responded to the collapse of his seduction theory by rejecting the extreme environmentalism that had previously characterized
his general etiological approach. He replaced the notion of defense
against traumatic seductions with an organic-olfactory theory of repression, attributing man's propensity to sexual neurosis to an excessive repression of pleasurable affects associated with certain infantile erotogenic zones, namely, the mouth, nose, throat, and anus (*Origins*, pp. 232–34, letter of 14 November 1897). Freud expanded upon
this idea in the famous "Rat Man" case history (1909d). The "Rat Man"
(so-named for his obsessional fear of rats) had been a renifleur, or
osphresiolagniac, in his childhood, recognizing everyone he knew by
their distinctive smell. "I have met with the same characteristic," Freud
remarked, "in other neurotics, both in hysterical and in obsessional patients, and I have come to recognize that a tendency to taking pleasure
in smell, which has become extinct since childhood, may play a part
in the genesis of neurosis" (1909d, S.E., 10:247). To this assertion
Freud added the following general statement, which represents his first
published reference to the subject of upright posture in man:

> And here I should like to raise the general question of whether the
> atrophy of the sense of smell (which was an inevitable result of man's
> assumption of an erect posture) and the consequent organic repression
> of his pleasure in smell may not have had a considerable share in the
> origin of his susceptibility to nervous disease. This would afford us some
> explanation of why, with the advance of civilization, it is precisely the
> sexual life that must fall a victim to repression. For we have long known
> the intimate connection in the animal organization between the sexual
> instinct and the function of the olfactory organ. (*S.E.*, 10:247–48)

In publications appearing in 1912 and 1913, Freud reiterated this hypothetical evolutionary connection between sexuality, neurosis, and upright posture in man,[8] and he developed it most completely in *Civilization and Its Discontents* (1930a), as we shall see.

Phase Three, 1913–30:
The "Diphasic Onset" of Sexuality

About the time he published *Totem and Taboo* (1912–13), Freud hit
upon the idea of relating neurosis to the unique "diphasic onset" that

8. See "On the Universal Tendency to Debasement in the Sphere of Love"
(1912d, S.E., 11:189) and "Preface to Bourke's *Scatalogic Rites of All Nations*"
(1913k), where Freud asserts of the excretory functions that "the chief finding from
psycho-analytic research has been the fact that the human infant is obliged to recapitulate during the early part of his development the changes in the attitude of
the human race towards excremental matters which probably had their start when
homo sapiens first raised himself off Mother Earth" (*S.E.*, 12:336).

characterizes human sexual life (1912d, S.E., 11:189). Unlike other animals, man's sexual life, including man's choice of sexual object, Freud asserted, emerges in two waves. An early epoch of sexual efflorescence reaches its peak at the age of five and is interrupted by a period of latency, which is then followed by a new wave of sexual development at the time of puberty (1905d [1915], S.E., 7:200). So literally did Freud subscribe to the biogenetic implications of this claim that, in 1939 and again in his posthumously published *Outline of Psycho-Analysis* (1940a), he suggested that man must be descended from an animal originally reaching sexual maturity at the age of five. The latency period, he argued, was incorporated into man's psychosexual development as a result of certain "momentous" historical circumstances that interrupted the once straight-line course of sexual development (1939a, S.E., 23:75; 1940a, S.E., 23:153 n.; 1926d, S.E., 20:154–55). As a result of these disruptive historical events, mankind is now forced to repress its first (incestuous) choice of sexual object. Neurosis, Freud insisted, is the fate of those who fail to surmount this diphasic pattern. The diphasic onset of sexuality accordingly became "the determining [biological] factor for the origin of neuroses," although Freud subsequently compared the importance of this biological consideration to a second, namely, to the human infant's prolonged dependency upon its parents, which he associated with heightened oedipal problems and with more severe superego development (see 1923a, S.E., 18:246; and 1926d, S.E., 20:154–55).[9]

To what "momentous" historical events did Freud ascribe this unique, diphasic feature of man's sexual life? As we shall see in the next and last step of Freud's thinking about sexual etiology, he ultimately proposed an eclectic resolution of the whole problem. Nevertheless, in the third phase of his thinking, he briefly entertained a much more specific hypothesis, which was suggested to him by Sándor Ferenczi.

According to Ferenczi, who enthusiastically shared Freud's own fervor for biogenetic-Lamarckian generalizations, the phenomenon of

---

9. For further references to the diphasic onset of sexuality, see Freud's addition to the Summary of his *Three Essays on the Theory of Sexuality*, 1905d [1920], S.E., 7:234; *The Ego and the Id*, 1923b, S.E., 19:35; "A Short Account of Psychoanalysis," 1924f, S.E., 19:208; *Autobiography*, 1925d, S.E., 20:37; *The Question of Lay Analysis*, 1926e, S.E., 20:211; and *Moses and Monotheism*, 1939a, S.E., 23:153. Freud's biogenetic explanation of this subject evidently extended to the problem of menopause; in his copy of Geddes and Thomson's *Sex*, he marked the sentence, "It is more likely that the waning of reproductivity about the fiftieth year indicates the end of an older span [of life, i.e., when life used to end]" (1914:141 [Freud library, London]).

James J. Atkinson (1903:230–31), whose ideas on the primal horde coincided so closely with those of Freud, had previously discussed the consequences of man's prolonged infancy and had attributed to this prolongation the creation of "a psychological factor of strangely magnified force as compared with what it is in the mere brute—namely, human maternal love." Prior to Atkinson, philosopher John Fiske had made man's prolonged infancy the subject of an influential evolutionary analysis (1874, 2:344–45, 360–63; 1884:306–19). To the prolongation of infancy, Fiske ascribed higher intelligence, plasticity in learning, the permanent organization of the human family, primitive clan structures, and the foundations of morality.

sexual latency had been induced by the harsh conditions of the great
Ice Age, when man was forced to inhibit his sexuality in order to conserve energy for survival. The Ice Age was but the last of a series of
global catastrophes that Ferenczi saw as having shaped the course of
human sexual evolution. He first put forth this general thesis in 1913:

> Such catastrophes may have been the sites of repression in the history of
> racial development, and the temporal localisation and intensity of such
> catastrophes may have decided the character and the neuroses of the
> race. According to a remark of Professor Freud's, racial character is the
> precipitate of racial history. Having ventured so far beyond the know-
> able, we have no reason to shrink before the last analogy and from
> bringing the last great step in individual repression, the latency period,
> into connection with the last and greatest catastrophe that smote our
> primitive ancestors . . . , i.e. with the misery of the glacial period, which
> we still faithfully recapitulate in our individual life. (1913:237)[10]

Freud mentioned Ferenczi's hypothesis in 1912, at the Vienna Psychoanalytic Society, where he appears to have endorsed it with the words:
"Ontogenetically, the individual repeats this destiny; in the present [sex-
ual] constitution and in the tendency toward repression, that destiny
of the libido has been preserved" (*Minutes*, 4:86). A somewhat less
enthusiastic reference to this hypothesis may be found in *The Ego and
the Id* a decade later (1923b, S.E., 19:35).[11]

With continued encouragement from Freud, Ferenczi developed
his catastrophe theory of psychosexual evolution to an ingenious point
of culmination in his *Versuch einer Genitaltheorie* (Toward a Theory of
Genitality, 1924), about which Freud later said, "It is probable that
some time in the future there will really be a 'bio-analysis,' as Ferenczi
has prophesied, and it will have to cast back to the *Versuch einer*

---

10. That the Ice Age (of which there have actually been several) may have
supplied a major inhibition to human sexual life was not an original hypothesis
with Ferenczi. Fritz Wittels (1924b:171 n.) later complained that he had anticipated
Ferenczi on this point in his *Alles um Liebe* (All about Love, 1912), and that Ferenczi had failed to credit him properly. Ferenczi's originality lay exclusively in pointing to the last glacial epoch as the historical cause of the "latency period" that now
appears in ontogeny. Wittels's own views on this subject were expressed before the
members of the Vienna Psychoanalytic Society as early as 1908 (*Minutes*, 1:347–50;
meeting of 11 March 1908). See also *Minutes*, 4:86, 88; meeting of 27 March 1912.
About the time of Ferenczi's writings on this subject, the Dutch anatomist Louis
Bolk (1926) sought to explain human evolution in terms of a progressive "fetalization," or physiological retardation, of developmental functions. At least two psychoanalysts, Heinz Hartmann (1939:82) and Hans Lampl (1953), tried to reconcile
Freud's notion of sexual latency with Bolk's fetalization theory. Bolk's ideas, founded
upon a Lamarckian-vitalist theory of evolution, have long since been rejected by
biologists (see Gould 1977:356–62). Yazmajian sums up this Neo-Freudian foray
into biology by saying that "[it] epitomizes the erroneous biological thinking, glib
theorizing, and philosophizing that has regularly punctuated psychoanalytic literature . . . in this area over the years" (1967:222).

11. James Strachey, in an editorial footnote to this 1923 passage, asserts that
Freud endorsed Ferenczi's Ice Age hypothesis "more definitely" in *Inhibitions, Symptoms and Anxiety* (1926d, S.E., 20:155). Examination of the relevant text does not
bear out Strachey's claim. Rather, Freud says only that "*something momentous* must
have occurred in the vicissitudes of the human species" to have left the latency
period behind as its historical precipitate (italics added).

	Phylogenesis	Onto- and Perigenesis
I. Catastrophe	Origin of organic life	Maturation of the sex cells
II. Catastrophe	Origin of individual unicellular organisms	"Birth" of mature germ cells from the gonads
III. Catastrophe	Beginning of sexual propagation	Fertilization
	Development of marine life	Development of the embryo in the uterus
IV. Catastrophe	Recession of the ocean; adaptation to terrestrial existence	Birth
	Development of animal species with organs of copulation	Development of the primacy of the genital zone
V. Catastrophe	Ice Ages The Coming of Man	Latency period

Fig. 10.1. Sándor Ferenczi's five catastrophes in the evolution of sexual life. (From Ferenczi 1924; 1968 trans.:69.)

Genitaltheorie" (1933c, S.E., 22:228–29). In this highly fanciful treatise, Ferenczi set forth five great catastrophic events that he believed to be faithfully recapitulated in present human sexual life (see Fig. 10.1). He saw these recapitulations not only in ontogeny but also in what he termed *perigenesis*, or all those biological developments pertaining to the protection and nurture of the embryo. The great biogenetic theorist Ernst Haeckel had believed such specialized placental innovations to be independent of recapitulation and to interfere, moreover, with the embryological corroboration of that law. Ferenczi, "out-Haeckeling" Haeckel, claimed these acquisitions as attempted re-creations, for the sake of the germ cells, of life's earliest, preterrestrial environment.

As the sexual cells first develop, they recapitulate, according to Ferenczi's grand scheme, the origin of life on earth (Catastrophe I). With the expulsion of the sex cells from the gonads, the evolution of the first unicellular organisms is repeated (Catastrophe II). Fertilization coincides with the primeval beginnings of sexual propagation between one-celled creatures; and the subsequent growth of the fertilized embryo inside the mother's watery uterus represents the evolution of complex marine life (Catastrophe III, with its two substages). In the act of birth (i.e., adaptation to terrestrial life) and in the gradual postnatal emergence of the *phallic* stage (i.e., attainment of specialized copulatory organs), Ferenczi's fourth great stage is surmounted. Finally, latency (the ontogenetic precipitate of the Ice Ages) completes this "bioanalytic" scenario. In keeping with this visionary scheme, Ferenczi proclaimed sexual intercourse to be a "regressive" attempt by the penis to return to the moist warmth of the maternal womb and, beyond that, to the original aquatic environment of primeval times (1924; 1968 trans.:54).

Although greatly intrigued by Ferenczi's speculations, Freud (who at one time planned to write a book with him on such Lamarckian-biogenetic themes) nevertheless chose, after 1930, to reaffirm his own alternative explanation for the diphasic onset of human sexual life.[12]

Phase Four, 1930–39: The Final Synthesis

In the course of writing *Civilization and Its Discontents* (1930*a*), Freud summed up more than three decades of thinking about the problem of sexual etiology by suggesting that civilized man's susceptibility to neurosis should be attributed to the following prehistoric sequence of events. Primal man was a creature who moved around on all fours and whose sexual appetite was aroused primarily by olfactory stimuli. Such olfactory stimuli would have been closely linked to the periodicity of menstruation—that is, to the time of estrus. During this primeval epoch, the odor-impelled male would have sought the company of the female only during this estrual phase.

The relationship between the sexes must have changed dramatically, Freud reasoned, following man's adoption of an upright posture. With this particular evolutionary achievement, visual stimuli would have increasingly replaced the intermittent olfactory ones that had previously dominated man's sexual life. With sexual excitation having gradually become continuous through vision, the male acquired a powerful motive for keeping the female near him at all times. And so the primal horde, or family, was founded, and the first great "threshold of human civilization" was passed (1930*a*, S.E., 21:100 n.). Along with this momentous step in hominization, there now emerged the capacities for shame (because the genitals were readily visible and embarrassingly in need of protection), as well as for disgust (owing to the organic repression that greeted excremental and genital odors). Olfactory repression paved the way for civilization's trend toward cleanliness. In a similar manner, the first sublimations and displacements arose from man's organic repudiation of strong odors. Hence one may infer, Freud argued, that "the deepest root of the sexual repression which advances along with civilization is the organic defence of the new form of life achieved with man's erect gait against his earlier animal existence" (S.E., 21:106 n.).

But primal man did not attain a full state of civilization until after the primal family was able to limit the tyrannical ways of the all-powerful father who stood at its head. Freud's scenario returned to the hypothesis of parricide advanced in *Totem and Taboo* (1912–13), as he reviewed the primal taboos and cultural institutions that followed upon this momentous deed (S.E., 21:101).

Although Freud fully admitted the conjectural nature of this phylogenetic scenario, he continued to discuss the remarkable diphasic onset of human sexuality with this scenario in mind (1939*a*, S.E., 23:75; and 1940*a*, S.E., 23:153, 186). More important, he never altered his basic

12. For further details on Freud's planned collaboration with Ferenczi, which the two investigators actively discussed in 1916/17, see Jones 1957:312–13.

conviction that some such momentous drama had once taken place, and that it explained the intimate association between sexuality, culture, and neurosis. "Theory must rest satisfied with a few hints that betray a deeper connection . . . ," Freud commented upon this problem the year of his death. "It is not in psychology but in biology that there is a gap here" (1940a [1939], S.E., 23:186).

PROBLEM THREE: THE CHOICE OF NEUROSIS

Like his other two psychoanalytic problems, the choice of neurosis pre-occupied Freud to the end of his scientific career; its solution was, after all, the final and most practical test of psychoanalysis as a clinical theory of mind. Only by correlating specific developmental influences with specific forms of neurosis could Freud possibly lay claim to a general understanding of mental disease. His thinking on this last problem passed through three distinct phases and involved a general shift in focus from ontogeny to phylogeny.

Phase One, 1893–97:
Actual Neurosis, Psychoneurosis, and the Seduction Theory

In the first phase, Freud sought to explain five basic forms of neurosis in terms of two major classes of proximate causes: those operating currently, as in the actual neuroses, and those dating from childhood, as in the psychoneuroses (see Chapter 4). He never relinquished the distinction between actual neurosis and psychoneurosis, and as late as 1925 he reaffirmed his belief that the actual neuroses are toxic disorders of purely current etiology (Autobiography, 1925d, S.E., 20:25–26). In contrast to this, the seduction theory of psychoneurosis collapsed in the autumn of 1897 and so paved the way for the second phase of Freud's thinking about the choice of neurosis.

Phase Two, 1897–1913:
Developmental (Proximate-Causal) Solutions

By late 1899, Freud had formulated three basic postulates about the choice of neurosis, none of which he was ever to renounce: that the etiology of neurosis is always sexual and represents a repressed perversion; that the evolution/involution paradigm of disease explains the various forms of neurosis as a genetic series; and that neurotic regressions of the libido mimic the archaic sexual organizations of our remote ancestors. Freud clearly set forth the first two assumptions in a 9 November 1899 letter to Fliess (Origins, pp. 303–4). The third assumption, that early libidinal stages approximate ancestral types, was already implicit in Freud's 1896/97 conception of the "polymorphously perverse" nature of infantile sexual life (*Origins*, pp. 180, 186, 231–34); and like the other two assumptions, it became increasingly explicit as he elaborated his theory of psychosexual stages (*Three Essays*, 1905*d* [1915], *S.E.*, 7:198).

After 1900, Freud's real unsolved problem concerning the choice of neurosis became twofold: What specific point of regression characterizes each major form of psychoneurosis? And what determinants favor one point of instinctual fixation, and a later regression to that point, over another? Publicly, Freud remained reserved on this whole topic for more than a decade. As he admitted to Jung in 1907, "I was entirely mistaken in my first attempt at explanation; since then I have been cautious" (*Freud/Jung Letters*, p. 19). But the embarrassing fate of his earlier seduction theory was not the only reason for Freud's reticence. His continuing uncertainty was reinforced by the conviction that unexplored biological considerations would play an important part in the final solution. "We are not in a position," he emphasized in the *Three Essays on the Theory of Sexuality* in 1905, "to give so much as a hint as to the causes of these temporal disturbances of the process of [libidinal] development. A prospect opens before us at this point upon a whole phalanx of biological and perhaps, too, of historical problems of which we have not even come within striking distance" (*S.E.*, 7:241). It was, in fact, the psychological rather than the biological side of the problem that Freud elucidated during the second phase of his thinking.

Not until 1911 did Freud finally make public the general theory of libidinal fixation points that he had intuited as early as 1899. His views were set forth in the famous case history of Daniel Paul Schreber, a German judge who had developed paranoid delusions in the 1890s, and who had subsequently published an autobiographical account of his illness (Schreber 1903; 1955 trans.). Freud's (1911*c* [1910]) analysis of Schreber's mental disorder is unusual insofar as he never met his subject but derived his psychoanalytic conclusions entirely from the judge's written record of his neurosis.

Schreber believed that it was his mission to redeem the world and to return it to its former state of happiness. To achieve this end, he was convinced that he would have to be transformed by God from a man into a woman, in which new form he would then repeople the earth through impregnation by "divine rays." Freud was able to show that Schreber's paranoid delusions initially arose as part of a defense against passive homosexual phantasies (described by Schreber in his *Memoirs* [1903]), and that these phantasies in turn derived from Schreber's relationship with his father and older brother.[13]

At the theoretical level, Freud ascribed Schreber's paranoia to a fixation of the libido during the *narcissistic* stage of development—a stage occurring midway in the libido's maturational journey from auto-

13. More recent studies of Schreber's autocratic father by Niederland (1959*a*, 1959*b*, 1963) and Schatzman (1973) have modified this clinical reconstruction and have revealed Freud's surprising neglect of Schreber's childhood experiences as independently reflected in his father's rigid pedagogical theories. See also Kern 1975: 117–19.

erotism to heterosexual object love. What is initially chosen as a sexual object during this narcissistic stage, Freud argued, is the subject's own ego (whence comes the megalomania of paranoia). Development then proceeds to homosexual object choice (that is, to the choice of an external object with the same kind of genitals) and is followed by heterosexual object choice. Extending this etiological conception, Freud suggested that a far less treatable mental disorder, dementia praecox, was probably the result of an even earlier libidinal fixation, namely, to the stage of autoerotism (1911c, S.E., 12:59–79, especially 60–61, 72, and 77). A psychoneurosis results when sexual frustration in adult life induces libidinal regressions to an earlier point of fixation. After regression there occurs a "*return of the* [primal] *repressed*," and in response to this return, a new round of secondary repressions (1911c, S.E., 12:67–68). The specific choice of neurosis is determined by two considerations: the point of pathological regression, and the corresponding mode of secondary defense (repression, projection, etc.).

Several years later, in 1913, Freud broached the problem of what determines a hysteria instead of an obsessional neurosis (1913i). The symptoms of obsessional neurosis, he contended, represent a regression to the anal-erotic and sadistic stage of the pregenital organization—that is, to a stage normally manifested prior to the age of five. These anal-sadistic components of the libido supply the hostility and compulsiveness underlying the obsessional neurotic's symptoms. In contrast to obsessional neurosis, hysteria involves no major regression in libidinal aim, in spite of the hysteric's repudiation of adult sexual responsibilities. Freud did, however, associate with female hysteria a relatively minor regression from vaginal to clitoral eroticism; and he therefore attributed this neurosis to a previous fixation at the phallic stage, which is not the final stage of development in the normal female.

To sum up, by 1913 he had correlated four major stages of libidinal development (autoerotic, narcissistic-homosexual, anal-sadistic, and phallic) with four major forms of psychoneurosis (dementia praecox, paranoia, obsessional neurosis, and hysteria, respectively). With this genetic solution to the choice-of-neurosis problem, Freud's proximate-causal thinking on the subject was essentially complete, although he was later to make various minor refinements in these conceptions. During the third and last phase of his deliberations, Freud returned to the biological themes that had long been developing in his mind.

Phase Three, 1913–39:
Ultimate Biological Solutions

What was the "whole phalanx of biological and . . . historical problems" that Freud hinted at in 1905 (S.E., 7:241) as being essential to a final solution of the choice-of-neurosis issue? In 1913 he proclaimed as a "general proposition" that the factors determining the specific choice of neurosis (as opposed to whether or not one falls ill) "are in the nature of [hereditary] dispositions and are independent of experiences which operate pathogenically" (1913i, S.E., 12:317). In spite of the strongly

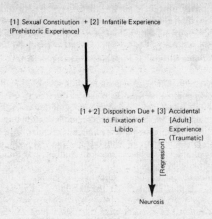

[1] Sexual Constitution + [2] Infantile Experience
(Prehistoric Experience)

[1 + 2] Disposition Due + [3] Accidental
    to Fixation of   [Adult]
       Libido   Experience
                         (Traumatic)

[Regression]

Neurosis

Fig. 10.2. Freud's etiological notion of "a complemental series." (From Freud 1916–17, *S.E.*, *16*:362; slightly redrawn.)

organic slant of this passage, Freud had in mind a cooperative relationship between hereditary predisposition and environmental eliciting causes. "The constitutional factor," he wrote in the third edition of his *Three Essays on the Theory of Sexuality*, "must await experiences before it can make itself felt; the accidental factor must have a constitutional basis in order to come into operation" (1905*d* [1915], *S.E.*, 7:239). In his *Introductory Lectures on Psycho-Analysis* (1916–17), he elaborated upon this conception, arguing that the interplay of pathogenic influences follows what he termed a *complemental series,* in which both hereditary and environmental extremes may be observed at each end. Freud's schematic presentation of his argument (Fig. 10.2) provides for three basic causes of neurosis, numbered here in order of their priority in time: (1) hereditary (and prehistoric) dispositions, (2) infantile impressions, and (3) adult experiences. It is the ancestral and infantile influences that induce the libidinal fixations underlying the psychoneuroses, and that thereby determine the distinguishing symptoms of each neurotic type.

The hereditary side of Freud's complemental series comprises the various biological and historical considerations that Freud introduced, beginning about 1913, into the choice-of-neurosis issue. He set forth these biological and historical considerations in two principal contexts: with regard to the specific *content* of neurosis, which has its roots, he claimed, in prehistoric experience; and in terms of the pathogenic mechanisms of repression, fixation, and regression.

The prehistoric content of neurosis. During the late 1890s, Freud had taken the momentous step of according to his patients' phantasies an independent etiological significance alongside of external reality itself. Now, during the third and final phase of his thinking about the choice of neurosis, he sought to reduce these phantasies to a prehistoric reality. In particular, it was the difficulty of rationalizing the universality and the traumatic efficacy of these phantasies that induced him to reconsider them as "a phylogenetic endowment." Freud broached this issue at some length in his *Introductory Lectures* (1916–17), where he responded to these difficulties in the following manner:

> I am prepared with an answer which I know will seem daring to you. I believe these *primal phantasies*, as I should like to call them, and no doubt a few others as well, are a phylogenetic endowment. In them the individual reaches beyond his own experience into primaeval experience at points where his own experience has been too rudimentary. It seems to me quite possible that all the things that are told to us to-day in analysis as phantasy—the seduction of children, the inflaming of sexual excitement by observing parental intercourse, the threat of castration (or rather castration itself)—were once real occurrences in the primaeval times of the human family, and that children in their phantasies are simply filling in the gap in individual truth with prehistoric truth. I have repeatedly been led to suspect that the psychology of the neuroses has stored up in it more of the antiquities of human development than any other source. (*S.E.*, *16*:370–71)

Freud returned to this theme soon afterward in his famous "Wolf Man" case history, where he remarked more definitely that "a child catches hold of this phylogenetic experience where his own experience fails him. He fills in the gaps in individual truth with prehistoric truth; he replaces occurrences in his own life by occurrences in the life of his ancestors" (1918b, *S.E.*, *17*:97). Freud concluded his discussion of the "Wolf Man" case history by comparing such pervasive remodeling processes to "the far-reaching *instinctive* knowledge of animals" (p. 120). Similarly, in his posthumously published *Outline of Psycho-Analysis* (1940a), Freud dismissed the assumption that a child must be breast-fed in order to pass through an "oral stage" of psychosexual development: "In all this the phylogenetic foundation has so much the upper hand over personal accidental experience that it makes no difference whether a child has really sucked at the breast or has been brought up on the bottle and never enjoyed the tenderness of a mother's care. In both cases the child's development takes the same path . . ." (*S.E.*, *23*:188–89).

It was equally with this biogenetic-Lamarckian theory in mind that Freud later found himself so prepared to dismiss those of his critics who defiantly declared that childhood events like seduction, threats of castration, the witnessing of parental intercourse, and so forth were far too infrequent to warrant Freud's universal claims about their etiological influence. Among such critics, Fritz Wittels (1924a:145) had sarcastically addressed himself to this point in his biography of Freud, written a decade after his resignation from the Vienna Psychoanalytic Society. Duly inscribed by Freud in the margin of his personal copy of this book is his confident handwritten retort *"und die Phylogenese?"* ("and what of phylogeny?" [Freud library, London]).

Also from the vantage point of his biogenetic-Lamarckian presuppositions, Freud was able to attribute to "pure phantasy" a degree of *traumatic* force that was otherwise missing from his general etiological framework. Writing in *Civilization and Its Discontents*, Freud later insisted that the potentially pathological overreactions of children to their oedipal situation were hardly surprising when properly understood as a brief repetition of the more severe experiences with the terrible father of phylogeny (1930a, S.E., 21:131). Similarly, he rationalized the traumatic nature of castration threats by appealing to "a phylogenetic memory-trace" of the actual deed, which long ago was performed by the jealous father of the primal horde whenever his sons became overly troublesome as sexual rivals (1940a, S.E., 23:190 n., 200, 207).

Freud's extreme eagerness to provide a historical and phylogenetic explanation for the principal forms of mental illness is nowhere better exemplified than by a hypothesis he set forth on this subject in a 1915 letter to Sándor Ferenczi:

> In preparing next session's lectures on the transference neuroses I am troubled by phantasies which are hardly suitable for public expression. So listen:
>
> There is a series of chronological starting points in patients which runs thus:
>
> Anxiety hysteria—conversion hysteria—obsessional neurosis—dementia praecox—paranoia—melancholia—mania.
>
> Their libidinal predispositions run in general in the opposite direction: that is to say, the fixation lies with the former set in very late stages of development, with the latter in very early ones. That statement, however, is not faultless.
>
> On the other hand this series seems to repeat phylogenetically an historical origin. What are now neuroses were once phases in human conditions.
>
> With the appearance of privations in the glacial period men became apprehensive: they had every reason for transforming libido into anxiety.
>
> Having learned that propagation was now the enemy of self-preservation and must be restricted, they became—still in the time before speech—hysterical.
>
> After they developed speech and intelligence in the hard school of the glacial period, they formed primal hordes under the two prohibitions of the primal father, their love life having to remain egoistic and aggressive. Compulsion, as in the obsessional neurosis, struggled against any return to the former state. The neuroses that followed belong to the new epoch and were acquired by the sons.
>
> To begin with they were forced to relinquish all sexual objects, or else they were robbed of all libido by being castrated: dementia praecox.
>
> They then learned to organize themselves on a homosexual basis, being driven out by the father. The struggle against that signifies paranoia. Finally they overpowered the father so as to effect an identification with him, triumphed over him and mourned him: mania—melancholia.
>
> Your priority in all this is evident [an allusion to Ferenczi's (1913)

Ice Age theory, mentioned by Freud above]. (Quoted in Jones 1957:330, letter of 12 July 1915)

Although Freud "wisely dropped the whole train of thought," as Jones (1957:330) cynically remarks, he never abandoned the basic assumption that some such phylogenetic scenario held the biological key to the choice of neurosis. That same year, Freud added a similar phylogenetic statement about psychosexual development to the third edition of the *Three Essays on the Theory of Sexuality*, where he now insisted: "The order in which the various instinctual impulses comes into activity seems to be phylogenetically determined; so, too, does the length of time during which they are able to manifest themselves before they succumb to the effects of some freshly emerging instinctual impulse or to some typical repression" (1905*d* [1915], *S.E.*, 7:241). In short, phylogeny was Freud's final answer to many of the difficulties that threatened to undermine his most basic psychoanalytic claims. From the problem of attributing neurosis to phantasies instead of to real events, to the issue of just how universal were the psychosexual stages and neurotic complexes that Freud espoused, phylogenetic suppositions played a paramount role in legitimating his science of the mind.

The biological bases of fixation and regression. Looking at the choice-of-neurosis problem in more ontogenetic terms, Freud sought to supply a biological explanation for two key neurotic mechanisms: fixation and regression. I have already reviewed the general biological and evolutionary foundations that Freud, even in the early 1890s, associated with these two psychoanalytic notions (Chapter 7). Here I shall relate only how he expanded upon these biological underpinnings during this last stage of his thinking.

Freud always believed, as we saw in Chapter 6, that infantile psychosexual development follows a periodic ebb and flow. In one of his most detailed discussions of the choice of neurosis, Freud (1913*i*) united this Fliessian theme of sexual periodicity with his own theory of instinctual fixations and insisted that the whole problem was one for future "biological research." He immediately amplified this statement with the following footnote reference to his old friend: "Since Wilhelm Fliess's writings have revealed the biological significance of certain periods of time it has become conceivable that disturbances of development may be traceable to temporal changes in the successive waves of development [*Entwicklungsschüben*]" (1913*i*, *S.E.*, 12:318, n. 1). Two years later, Freud added a similar version of this hypothesis to the *Three Essays on the Theory of Sexuality* (1905*d* [1915], *S.E.*, 7:241). Like Fliess, Freud now distinguished between minor waves in short-term growth and the major waves associated with critical phases in psychosexual development. Freud's crucial notion of the diphasic onset of human sexuality, which he also added to *Three Essays* in 1915 (*S.E.*, 7: 200), betrays its partial alliance with Fliessian sexual biology in Freud's choice of the words *in zwei Schüben* ("in two waves") to describe this biological process.

Freud's support for the relevance of Fliess's periodic laws to the theory of instinctual fixations must be understood in terms of his long-standing endorsement of two other fundamental psychobiological hypotheses: the primacy of early experience and the biogenetic law. Belief in the primacy of early experience—in which connection he often cited Wilhelm Roux's embryological experiments (see Chapter 7)—allowed Freud to attribute the neuroses of adults to relatively small disturbances in childhood libidinal development. The biogenetic law in turn suggested the biorhythmic implications of this first principle through the following chain of logical inference. If the continuous nature of human libido is one of the major features of present-day human sexuality, and if that feature originally evolved, as Freud believed, not long before the primeval Oedipus complex, then biogenetic considerations just as assuredly implied a strongly periodic pattern for *preoedipal* sexual development. According to this interpretation, chance environmental events would influence the young child differently depending upon the exact configuration of the Fliessian cycles. In Fliess's periodic laws would thus lie a solution to Freud's variability-of-outcome problem. It was precisely this last implication (but without the earlier [1913i] reference to Fliess's laws) that Freud incorporated into the *Three Essays* in 1915 (1905d, S.E., 7:241). If he did not pursue this biological point in more Fliessian detail, one should not forget that he told Karl Abraham in 1911 that further investigation of "the grain of truth that is surely contained in his [Fliess's] theory of periodicity, [is] a possibility that is denied to me for personal reasons" (*Freud/Abraham Letters*, p. 100, letter of 13 February 1911). Finally, Freud's unflinching support for the biogenetic law explains the curious circumstance that he could continue to endorse Fliess's periodicity theories in the context of childhood psychosexual development even though he had vehemently rejected their application, more than a decade earlier, to the mental life of adults (*Origins*, p. 324 n.).

Freud tackled the problem of regression about this same time in an equally biological manner. By 1913, his thinking on the choice of neurosis had evolved an important new distinction between regression to a prior libidinal *object* (for example, to the incestuous object choice so common among hysterics) and the more striking regression to a prior *aim* (for example, to anal-sadistic tendencies, as in obsessional neurosis, or to the narcissistic and autoerotic satisfactions of paranoia and dementia praecox, respectively). In contrast to object-related regressions, Freud viewed the second and more striking form—regressions-in-aim—as an organic process, in accordance with the evolution/involution paradigm of disease. Such regressions-in-aim were true reversals of prior biological development. If one became severely neurotic, the degree of *aim*-regression was now said to be controlled by "the hereditary constitutional factor" (1916–17, S.E., 16:362). But what could be the final, biological cause of such innate predispositions to regress? Freud's answer was twofold: Regressions are triggered by (1) prior instinctual fixations, themselves predetermined in part by ancestral experiences; and by (2) the nature of instinct itself. What Freud meant by this second resolution of the problem was that *"an instinct is an urge inherent in organic life to restore an earlier state of things . . ."* (*S.E.*, *18*:36). I shall explore Freud's insight into the regressive nature of instinct, first announced in *Beyond the Pleasure Principle* (1920*g*), in the following chapter; but for the moment, I offer the following psychoanalytic formula for libidinal regressions: In the neurotic, unconscious points of instinctual fixation exert an attraction upon libido, which when confronted by the frustrations of adulthood, may ultimately express an inherent biological tendency toward regression.

Summary and Conclusion

During more than forty years of thinking about his three great psychoanalytic problems, Freud developed what he considered to be a unified, ultimate-causal solution to all three. That tripart solution involved different facets of a single phylogenetic scenario for early man.

Freud's reconstruction of hominid evolution. Once a creature who walked on all fours like other animals, man came to adopt an upright posture. With this fundamental achievement, Freud stressed, olfaction was deposed as man's dominant sensory capacity. Certain formerly pleasurable smells now became unpleasant, gradually inducing the atrophy and abandonment of various erotogenic zones (nose, mouth, throat, and anus). Sexual excitation in general, increasingly freed from the odor of the menstrual fluids, ceased to be periodic. In order to satisfy his constant sexual cravings, man was now compelled to form primal hordes, or families. Formation of the primal horde was succeeded by father-son conflict over sexual resources, by repeated acts of parricide on the part of the jealous sons, and by the guilt-laden renunciation of the parricidal deeds on the part of the surviving brother clan. Finally, out of the brothers' guilt and their wish for atonement grew the germs of morality, religion, and primal law—in short, the foundations of higher civilization.

Inspired by Freud's phylogenetic scenario, the solution to the problem of pathological repression was readily forthcoming. Repression was to be understood as an organic recapitulation of the various instinctual renunciations that attended man's lengthy psychosexual evolution. Thus, what originally began as psychical defense against stages of development that had been superseded, became, over the millennia, an "organic repression." "Man's archaic heritage," Freud explained in 1919, "forms the nucleus of the unconscious mind; and whatever part of that heritage has to be left behind in the advance to later phases of development, because it is unserviceable or incompatible with what is new and harmful to it, falls a victim to the process of [organic] repression" (1919*e*, *S.E.*, *17*:203–4). Man's susceptibility to neurosis, Freud concluded, is the price of this advancement.

Freud's phylogenetic answer to the problem of pathological repression provided the key to the problem of why neurosis and sex are so inseparably linked. Along with such eminent colleagues as Richard von Krafft-Ebing (1886), Freud saw the evolution of civilization as being primarily at the expense of free sexual expression. Here, then, was the historical precondition explaining the central role of sexuality in modern nervous illnesses. It is therefore no accident that Freud, in his mature years (1905–39), wrote four separate books and the major part of a fifth on the intimate and antagonistic relationship that he perceived between civilization and sexual life.[14] Moreover, it was from his phylogenetic-historical conception of sexuality that Freud drew the conviction that *his* system of psychology must be basic to all human societies, or at least to all societies insofar as they approach a civilized state. As Philip Rieff has aptly remarked in this connection, "There are good reasons why sexuality is for Freud the one really profound subject matter, the demands of the instincts the most fundamental demands. A science that recognizes the instincts is a basic science, examining not this social system or that but the system of civilization as a formed thing in itself" (1959:339).

Freud resolved the problem of the choice of neurosis in the following manner. Ontogenetically, a particular illness was linked to a particular stage of libidinal fixation, to which the libido has later regressed. Freud assumed that both the initial fixation point and the later process of regression were favored by organic predispositions— neuroses once experienced by the race. Such inborn predispositions served, he concluded, as the basic "schema" for ontogenetic development, remodeling many childhood experiences in phantasy according to the universal guidelines of phylogeny.

Of greatest historical concern to us, in the last analysis, are not so much the specific details of Freud's three solutions, as are the underlying premises of these particular solutions. As a committed psychobiologist in his overall approach to the human mind, Freud knew that proximate (that is, psychological and physiological) as well as ultimate (evolutionary) explanations were necessary for a complete theoretical understanding of the subject. Despite the speculative nature of his excursions into phylogenetic theory, Freud fully believed that some such prehistoric drama had to have occurred if his various psychoanalytic claims about repression, sexuality, and neurosis were to possess universal truth.

In sum, Freud's psychoanalytic theories became *more* biological, not less so, after the crucial years of discovery (1895–1900), just as they became increasingly sophisticated in their psychological content. Nor is it odd that the man who initially placed so much theoretical importance upon infantile prehistory and the primacy of early experi-

14. *Totem and Taboo* (1912–13), *Group Psychology and the Analysis of the Ego* (1921c), *The Future of an Illusion* (1927c), *Civilization and Its Discontents* (1930a), and *Moses and Monotheism* (1939a, S.E., 23:especially 97–102, 111–21, 132–34). See also Freud's " 'Civilized' Sexual Morality and Modern Nervous Illness" (1908d), "On the Universal Tendency to Debasement in the Sphere of Love" (1912d), and *Why War?* (1933b).

ence, should have become equally convinced that human prehistory holds the final key to understanding human behavior. But these were not two distinct Sigmund Freuds—the young and empirical as against the old, speculative, and far-ranging—as some commentators would have us believe. The Freud who wrote *Totem and Taboo* (1912–13) and other cultural-historical works was much the same Freud, conceptually speaking, who, between 1895 and 1900, erected his basic psychobiological theory of mind. In particular, the same biogenetic-Lamarckian paradigm of human development inspired both the early and the later achievements, providing the underlying model of human psychosexual evolution for Freud's interpretation of human behavior. From Freud's biogenetic insight into "abandoned erotogenic zones" (1896/97) to his repeated assertion in the 1930s that castration threats and oedipal anxieties derive their terrifying force from phylogenetic residues of actual deeds, psychoanalytic theory continually unfolded one of the most sophisticated psychobiological conceptions of man yet proposed.

11

Life (Eros) and Death Instincts: Culmination of a Biogenetic Romance

One last development in Freud's psychoanalytic thinking remains to be considered, namely, his controversial theory of life and death instincts. Set forth in *Beyond the Pleasure Principle* as a frankly "far-fetched speculation" (1920g, S.E., 18:24), Freud's twofold distinction gradually evolved from a working hypothesis into an essential and permanent part of his theoretical psychology. "To begin with," he confessed during a discussion of his instinct theory a decade later in *Civilization and Its Discontents*, "it was only tentatively that I put forward the views I have developed here, but in the course of time they have gained such a hold upon me that I can no longer think in any other way. To my mind, they are far more serviceable from a theoretical standpoint than any other possible ones; they provide that simplification, without either ignoring or doing violence to the facts, for which we strive in scientific work" (1930a, S.E., 21:119).

In particular, Freud's idea of a *death* instinct has the remarkable distinction among his theories of being the only one that achieved little acceptance even among his own followers. Ernest Jones (1957:266) reports that of the fifty or so psychoanalytic papers devoted to this topic by the 1950s, only half supported Freud's theory in the first decade, only a third during the next decade, and none at all in the decade after that. English psychologist William McDougall, who was sympathetic to many of Freud's psychoanalytic ideas, once colorfully dubbed his death instinct "the most bizarre monster of all his gallery of monsters" (1936:96). According to Jones (1957:277), who in turn draws upon neurologist Rudolf Brun (1953), Freud's theory of the death instinct "contradicts all biological principles" and can claim no support from that direction. Similarly, Robert Holt writes of the death instinct that "Freud's shaky logic in developing his case, the questionable and speculative nature of the facts he adduced, and the general lack of evidential support for this theory are well-known" (1965a:112). Ernest Becker sums up the present-day consensus on this subject when he declares that "Freud's tortuous formulations on the death instinct can now securely be relegated to the dust bin of history" (1973:99). (See also Kline 1972:352.)

The biographical tradition in Freud scholarship has, not surprisingly, sought to relate Freud's death-instinct supposition to his *personal* preoccupation with death. As Jones candidly expresses this biographical rationale, "If so little objective support is to be found for Freud's culminating theory of a death instinct, one is bound to consider the possibility of subjective contributions to its inception, doubtless in connection with the theme of death itself" (1957:278). In support of this rationale, several contemporary events in Freud's personal life have frequently been pressed into service, such as the sudden death from influenza of his daughter Sophie in January 1920, the death of a favorite grandson, and his own incurable affliction with cancer of the jaw (e.g., Wittels 1924b:251; Puner 1947:297–99; and Ekstein 1949). Unfortunately, the precise chronology of these suggestive influences is not entirely consistent with the interpretation that has so often been placed upon them. As Jones has pointed out, *Beyond the Pleasure Principle* was actually written some months before the first of these misfortunes and four years before the other two (1957:280).

Freud himself was shrewd enough to anticipate such attempts to undermine his controversial theory, and he went so far as to ask Max Eitingon, who had read *Beyond the Pleasure Principle* in manuscript during the autumn of 1919, "to certify" that the theory had been in existence while Sophie was still in perfect health (see Jones 1957:40; and Schur 1972:329). When Fritz Wittels (1924a), only four years later, made just such a connecting inference between the death of Freud's daughter and Freud's own revised theory of instincts, Freud responded with the following critical remarks:

> Beyond question, if I had myself been analysing another person in such circumstances, I should have presumed the existence of a connection between my daughter's death and the train of thought presented in *Beyond the Pleasure Principle*. But the inference that such a sequence exists would have been false. The book was written in 1919, when my daughter was still in excellent health. . . . In September, 1919, I had sent the manuscript of the little book to be read by some friends [Eitingon and Abraham] in Berlin. It was finished, except for the discussion concerning the mortality or immortality of the protozoa. What seems true is not always the truth. (*S.E.*, *19*:287 n., letter of 18 December 1923; see also Wittels 1924b:251–52)

Even so, Jones (1957:42, 278) and most other biographers have continued to support a subjective interpretation of Freud's "bizarre" notion, and they have generally considered it sufficient in this connection to cite the terrible events of the First World War (in which three of his sons risked their lives), together with his lifelong preoccupation with death.[1]

As I shall argue in the course of this chapter, Freud's notion of a death instinct, by virtue of its consistently misunderstood status in psychoanalytic theory, exemplifies just how fully his intellectual union of psychology with biology has gone unappreciated in psychoanalysis. For his theory of the death instinct has a perfectly rational logic in his own psychobiological terms. One must not forget how extremely logical Freud was in his thinking. "If any of his theories are unacceptable," Ramzy (1956:120) has rightly emphasized, "this is not due to the way he argued it, but to the premises he started with. . . ." These premises, together with the rigorously logical manner in which Freud followed them out, supply the real key to his death-instinct theory.

Logical considerations were also the immediate stimulus to Freud's whole reformulation of 1920, which sought to restore to his theories the intellectual unity that had been undermined by certain conceptual inconsistencies that emerged in the previous decade or so. Freud scholars have long recognized the existence of these inconsistencies and have generally granted them an important place as catalytic agents in Freud's theoretical reformulations; but I suggest that they were considerably more than mere "catalysts" for an otherwise subjectively determined theory. Instead, that theory must be understood as part of the progressive biologizing of certain key concepts in psychoanalysis from about 1910 to 1920. Additionally, both Freud's need for, and his later articulation of, the death-instinct theory were dependent upon his biogenetic-Lamarckian resolution of his three basic psychoanalytic problems (Chapter 10). Acceptance of these premises, as well as of the death instinct itself, separates Freud as a staunch psychobiologist from the more purely psychological Freud championed by his orthodox followers.

THREE INCONSISTENCIES IN
PSYCHOANALYTIC THEORY (1910–20)

Introduction of the narcissism concept (1911–14). While analyzing the Schreber case, Freud introduced into psychoanalysis the developmental stage of *narcissism*—a "half-way phase" between autoerotism and object love—during which the individual takes himself and his own body as his love object (1911c, S.E., 12:60–61). Three years later, in his paper "On Narcissism," Freud elaborated this new conception by draw-

---

1. See Robert (1966:329), Costigan (1967:229–30), Schur (1972:328–33), Andreski (1972:138), and Fine (1973:178) for additional endorsements of this general historical interpretation.

ing a distinction between ego libido and object libido. In the primary stage of narcissism, he insisted, all libido is ego libido, and only later is it directed out toward objects. The more object libido is deployed, the more ego libido becomes depleted, much as "the body of an amoeba is related to the pseudopodia which it puts out" (1914c, S.E., 14:75).

The question now arose, Freud confessed, as to whether the ego could have any other form of psychical energy at its disposal than that originally derived from primary ego libido. In other words, are the self-preservative ego instincts that Freud (1910i) had previously distinguished on biological grounds from the sexual instincts really distinct after all, or was libido itself perhaps the only form of psychical energy? Such a monistic view of instinct would have controverted Freud's long and adamant dualism in explaining mental activity. Looking back on the problem in his *Autobiography,* he frankly acknowledged, "This was clearly not the last word on the subject; biological considerations seemed to make it impossible to remain content with assuming the existence of only a single class of instincts" (1925d, S.E., 20:57). The issue was a pressing one as well, for it supplied considerable intellectual ammunition for the adversaries of Freudian psychoanalysis. If all psychical energy is really purely libidinous, Freud conceded in *Beyond the Pleasure Principle,* "we shall after all be driven to agree with the critics who suspected from the first that psychoanalysis explains *everything* by sexuality, or with innovators like Jung who, making a hasty judgement, have used the word 'libido' to mean instinctual force in general. Must not this be so?" (1920g, S.E., 18:52).

In 1915, in partial clarification of this problem, Freud acknowledged a formal polarity between love and hate. With regard to the affect of hate, he gave independent recognition to an *aggressive* inclination, which was not, he insisted, of purely libidinal-sadistic nature as he had always previously maintained. Freud associated such aggressive impulses with the self-preservative, or ego, instincts (1915c, S.E., 14:137–39). About this same time, he also reaffirmed his view that attached to the self-preservative instincts are certain other nonlibidinal drives, which he called *ego-interest* (1916–17, S.E., 16:414). Still, the whole distinction between ego (or self-preservative) instincts and libido instincts remained confused prior to his reformulations of 1920. It was only in *Beyond the Pleasure Principle* (1920g) that he finally granted to the impulses of aggression a fully independent status as a primal (death) instinct and divorced it from both libidinal and self-preservative (ego) instincts. With this key step, Freud's binary conception of instinct was finally restored.

Fixation to traumas and the "compulsion to repeat." The second basic inconsistency to be rectified by Freud's death-instinct theory entails a clinical phenomenon known as the *compulsion to repeat.* By 1920 Freud had come to recognize certain classes of neurotic symptoms as involving fixations to, and compulsive repetitions of, traumatic events. The foremost representatives of this clinical syndrome were the traumatic neuroses of wartime. Certain soldiers with no apparent organic injuries nevertheless developed a wide variety of sensory/motor disturbances (tremors, pains, paralyses, etc.), generally after having suffered a traumatic brush with death. Often these soldiers relived in nightly dreams the various traumatic experiences that had first precipitated their symptoms. This last circumstance seemed to contradict Freud's wish-fulfillment theory of dreams, or at least it forced him to consider such traumatic dreams as either masochistic or self-punishing in nature.

Paralleling his observations on the war neuroses, Freud had become aware that a similar tendency to compulsive repetition exists in the transference neuroses. There the patient often reexperiences in relation to the analyst the many painful derivatives of the childhood Oedipus complex. But what could be the motive force, Freud asked himself, for such compulsive regressions to, and repetitions of, totally unpleasurable experiences? Unlike the neurotic's pleasure-seeking libidinal fixations (which undergo a reversal of affect in subsequent development and cause unpleasure only to the secondary system), fixations to trauma draw upon no apparent source of pleasure from any psychical system. Could it be, Freud began to wonder, that there exists a special principle in mental activity that operates independently of the pleasure principle, and that even overrides that principle in certain neurotic disorders? It was this reflection that subsequently inspired the title of *Beyond the Pleasure Principle* (1920g).

The problem of regression (a paradox). A third theoretical inconsistency brings us to an issue that has not been given sufficient attention in Freud studies. After about 1910, Freud had placed greatly increased reliance upon the concept of temporal regression in attempting to explain the choice of neurosis. It was not, however, until "The Disposition to Obsessional Neurosis" (1913i) that he first surmised that such libidinal regressions could take two different forms in the psychoneuroses: one to an earlier *object*, and the other to an earlier *aim* (see Chapter 10). Regression to a prior libidinal object (as in hysteria) involves little more than a change in the libido's specific attachments. A regression-in-aim, by contrast, customarily entails both a change in object and a further change in mode of sexual functioning, a change that reestablishes a lower, nongenital form of psychosexual satisfaction that has long since been superseded in normal development. This more striking form of regression may be compared with those equally constitutional expressions of "involution" witnessed in aphasia and other organic diseases of the nervous system. According to Freud's conception of neurosis, frustration in adult sexual life precipitates both forms of regression. But it was one thing for Freud to believe that frustrated libido may attach itself to a substitute object (either in phantasy or in reality), in conformity with the economic point of view. The mechanism for regressions-in-aim remained much more puzzling.

During the period prior to 1920, Freud's tentative explanation for this second form of regression was to assume that previous fixations of the libido somehow exert "an attraction" upon libido and "lure" that libido into the path of regression. He also spoke of "the adhesiveness" of libidinal fixations and began to refer to a certain "psychical inertia" inherent in libido itself; he called this last characteristic "the funda-mental precondition of neurosis." Finally, he acknowledged that, al-though an aim-regression is intimately linked to mental life, "the most prominent factor in it is the organic one." (See 1915f, S.E., 14:272; and 1916–17, S.E., 16:343–44, 348–49, 359, 364.) But Freud was still unable to say what caused the organically predetermined "inertial" and "regressive" propensities of libido. Not until 1920, in the guise of his death-instinct conception, did he finally offer a convincing answer to this vexing problem in psychoanalytic theory.

Freud's theory of regression developed a second major difficulty prior to 1920. Why do the combined effects of primal repression and reaction formation not preclude all possibility of neurotic regression in adult individuals? After all, primal repression and reaction forma-tion are the essential causes of *forward* development in Freud's theory. It is assumed that these mechanisms catalyze successive renunciations of each major pregenital phase as well as hinder subsequent libidinal regressions back to these abandoned stages. Freud stressed this last point in *Beyond the Pleasure Principle*, where he wrote of the de-veloping libido: "The backward path that leads to complete satisfaction [of the libido] is as a rule obstructed by the resistances which main-tain the [primal] repressions. So there is no alternative but to advance in the direction in which growth is still free . . ." (1920g, S.E., 18:42). Thus, only when no previous organic repressions have occurred during development will the path to regression normally be open in a sexually mature individual. But regression without prior repressions would pro-duce perversion, never neurosis. Once again, to explain the possibility of regressions-in-aim that are capable of inducing a psychoneurosis, Freud had to assume that some unknown force is active in overcoming the counterinfluence of primal repressions.

The increasingly problematic nature of Freud's whole evolution/ involution model of libido was reinforced by yet another circumstance that began to pose difficulties for the regression theory between 1910 and 1920. As we saw in the previous chapter, Freud's three lifelong psychoanalytic problems had induced him to give far more explicit endorsement to his fundamental biogenetic-Lamarckian presupposi-tions. The essence of the biogenetic law is that it mechanically causes the developing organism to pass through all the previous adult stages of its ancestors. In doing so, the organism must not only repeat all these former stages, but it must also *give them up* as the biogenetic process exerts its "forward pull" to each successive stage. Freud endorsed pre-cisely this position in "A Child is Being Beaten," when he wrote that childhood Oedipus complexes "pass away because their time is over, because the children have entered upon a new phase of development in which they are compelled to recapitulate from the history of man-kind the repression of an incestuous object-choice, just as at an earlier stage they were obliged to effect an object-choice of that very sort" (1919e, S.E., 17:188). Similarly, Freud declared in "The Dissolution of the Oedipus Complex" that the Oedipus complex generally resolves itself "according to programme," and that it is therefore "of no great importance what the occasions are which allow this to happen, or, indeed, whether any such occasions can be discovered at all" (1924*d*, *S.E.*, *19*:174). Thus, the automatic consequences of the biogenetic law, upon which Freud had come to rely so heavily in his theoretical work, were in direct conflict with his alternative "frustration-regression" model as proposed for the psychoneuroses. In short, by 1920 Freud desperately needed to inject a formal, *regressive* force into psychoanalytic theory unless he wished his biogenetic machine to undermine his whole evolution/involution paradigm of neurosis.

As we have seen, it was not only the enigma of regression that called for such an urgent addition to psychoanalytic theory. The compulsion to repeat and the problem of fixation to traumas likewise suggested the existence of some such independent, regressive force. It is hardly surprising, then, that Freud came more and more to suspect that the "conservative" nature of instinct itself might hold the key to all his current theoretical dilemmas. But only in 1920 did he finally spell out this much-needed theoretical corrective with the claim that *"an instinct is an urge inherent in organic life to restore an earlier state of things"* (*S.E.*, *18*:36).

FERENCZI'S BIOGENETIC RESOLUTION OF THE EVOLUTION/INVOLUTION PARADOX

In 1913 Freud's colleague Sándor Ferenczi had independently dealt with the general evolution/involution paradox and successfully resolved it in a way that was to prove instrumental to Freud's own thinking. In "Stages in the Development of the Sense of Reality," Ferenczi had sought to reconcile the teleological illusion of spontaneous "strivings toward development" with a materialist and causal-historical view of life. Living organisms, under Ferenczi's materialist conception of the matter, exhibit no progressive tendencies whatsoever. Thus the human fetus displays absolutely no spontaneous efforts to leave the protective envelope of the mother's womb. Only in spite of its wishes and intentions does the fetus find itself "cruelly turned out into the world," choosing, as a result, "to forget (repress) the kinds of satisfaction it had got fond of, and adjust itself to new ones." All of ontogeny follows such a passive pattern of reaction formation and repression, Ferenczi proclaimed, and "the same cruel game is repeated with every new stage of development" (1913:236–37).

From a phylogenetic standpoint, the fundamental passivity of organic life became even more self-evident to Ferenczi. Ontogenetic "progress" in life, he submitted, is merely a passive recapitulation of all former, ancestral reactions to unpleasurable experiences, reactions that must now be compulsively repeated in embryogenesis with each

Freud and Sándor Ferenczi in 1918.

new generation. Even the playful "practising" of young animals is "not the preliminary stages of a future racial function [Karl Groos's (1896) famous theory], but repetitions of phylogenetically acquired capacities" (1913:238, n. 27). Thus the organism seeks only to preserve previous (ontogenetic and phylogenetic) states of existence and, alternatively, to repress those that have proved incompatible with current levels of adaptation. Drawing this idea to its logical conclusion, Ferenczi declared that "one must make oneself familiar with the idea of a tendency of preservation, or *regression-tendency*, also dominating organic life, the tendency to further development, adaptation, etc., depending only on external stimuli" (p. 237, n. 26; italics added). In short, from Ferenczi's biogenetic-Lamarckian vantage point, there was no paradox at all in the evolution/involution dichotomy. The only internal forces within the organism turn out to be regressive and defensive; the illusion of ontogenetic "progress" (spontaneous development) derives solely from the joint operation of these two forces within creatures that are biogenetically destined to repeat the lengthy history of their race.

Beyond the Pleasure Principle

In *Beyond the Pleasure Principle*, Freud took up Sándor Ferenczi's biogenetic mode of reasoning and specifically acknowledged his ingenious solution of 1913 to the progression/regression paradox (1920*g*, *S.E.*, *18*:41–42). External influences upon the organism, Freud agreed, are stored up for future developmental "repetition" and thus create the deceptive appearance of there being "[internal] forces tending towards change and progress, whilst in fact they are merely seeking to reach an ancient goal by paths alike old and new" (*S.E.*, *18*:38). Freud, for his own part, now elevated the regression side of the progression/regression dichotomy into a formal definition of instinct. "*It seems, then, that an instinct is an urge inherent in organic life to restore an earlier state of things* which the living entity has been obliged to abandon under the pressure of external disturbing forces; that is, it is a kind of organic elasticity, or, to put it another way, the expression of the inertia inherent in organic life" (*S.E.*, *18*:36). This formal regressive property of instinct constitutes the "beyond the pleasure principle" in mental functioning, for it impels the organism to reestablish all previous psychical states, whether pleasurable or not.

By accepting this regressive attribute of instinct, Freud believed one could resolve a whole group of previously enigmatic phenomena, including: the compulsion to repeat; the mechanism of fixation to traumas, including the traumatic dreams of war neurotics; the painful psychotherapeutic manifestations of transference; and certain repetitive aspects of children's play. In further biological support of his regressive definition of instinct, Freud cited a series of striking examples from animal behavior. Certain species of fish undertake lengthy migrations at spawning time, returning to the waters where they apparently once resided but have exchanged in the course of time for other habitats. So, too, the remarkable migrations of birds are explained by a similar instinctive compulsion to repeat. And he added his most compelling biological argument:

> . . . but we are quickly relieved of the necessity for seeking for further examples by the reflection that the most impressive proofs of there being an organic compulsion to repeat lie in the phenomena of heredity and the facts of embryology. We see how the germ of a living animal is obliged in the course of its development to recapitulate (even if only in a transient and abbreviated fashion) the structures of all the forms from which it has sprung, instead of proceeding quickly by the shortest path to its final shape. (*S.E.*, *18*:37; see also 1933*a*, *S.E.*, 22:106)

"In the last resort," Freud expounded in a cosmic manner reminiscent of Wilhelm Fliess, "what has left its mark on the development of organisms must be the history of the earth we live in and of its relation to the sun. Every modification which is thus imposed upon the course of the organism's life is accepted by the conservative organic instincts and stored up for further repetition" (*S.E.*, *18*:38).[2]

Freud did not stop here, however. He pursued the conservative nature of instinct to its most logical culmination, suggesting that life must be seeking to restore an ancient state of existence that preceded even life itself—in other words that "*the aim of all life is death*" (*S.E.*, *18*:38). Life must have first arisen, he elaborated, when inanimate matter became cathected by some external force, and an instinct simultaneously came into being which sought to cancel out the tension that had just been acquired. Freud referred this primeval instinct to the dominant economic principle of mental life: the impulse to discharge completely, or to keep at a constant level, the sum of internal psychical tension. Freud also identified this tendency toward a state of tranquility—the so-called Nirvana principle, after Barbara Low—with Gustav Fechner's (1873:94) psychophysical law of stability, as well as with the general trend of the pleasure principle (*S.E.*, *18*:8–9, 55–56).

Life in those primeval times must have been quickly followed by death, Freud continued with his theoretical romance. Occasionally, however, the influence of the external world would have posed various obstacles to an immediate death, and life must thereafter have found itself bound by its conservative instinctual nature to respect all such detours in its strivings for death. And so it was that life-span became

---

2. Freud actually cited Fliess's "magnificent [*grossartige*] conception" of the solar-dependent periodicity of all life just seven pages later, to which reference he added the following critical comment: "When we see, however, how easily and how extensively the influence of external forces is able to modify the date of the appearance of vital phenomena (especially in the plant world)—to precipitate them or hold them back—doubts must be cast upon the rigidity of Fliess's formulas or at least upon whether the laws laid down by him are the sole determining factors" (*S.E.*, *18*:45). Strachey translates Freud's expression "*grossartige Konzeption*" as "large conception," which, as Eissler (1971:170, n. 32) points out, "does not do justice to the praise that Freud actually bestowed on Fliess on that occasion."

lengthened, and that life itself became more than just a fleeting accident of nature.

Yet are there no other instincts in living organisms, Freud asked, than the paradoxical strivings of a death instinct? To this question his response was definite: he argued that the sexual instincts, which ensure the continuation of life by reproduction, constitute a second, and independent, driving force in organic nature. Like the death instinct, the sexual instincts are "conservative," returning life to its simplest form as male and female gametes, which then unite with one another and resume the processes of organic development all over again. It is the sexual instincts that have given rise as well to the immortality of the germ plasm; and in this connection Freud cited August Weismann's (1892) well-known biological dichotomy between mortal soma and immortal germ plasm. The sexual instincts conserve life in one other fashion, Freud asserted, by warding off the trend of the death instinct until a comparatively late point in life. It is to this end that life coalesces great numbers of cells into multicellular organisms, which are thereby better able to withstand the destructive forces of the outside world. In the widest sense, then, the sexual instincts subserve the self-preservational or life instincts that Freud had previously associated with the ego.

And what is the historical source of these sexual-life instincts? Freud ventured the daring hypothesis that living matter was once torn apart into little pieces during primeval times, an event that somehow gave rise to an instinct to reunite these severed parts and hence "to restore an earlier state of things" (*S.E.*, *18*:58, 62).

In bringing *Beyond the Pleasure Principle* to a close, Freud called his dualistic conception of life and death instincts "a provisional one" and carefully emphasized that he himself did not yet know to what extent he really believed in his speculations. The theory was nevertheless justified, he insisted, insofar as it introduced conceptual order into an otherwise bewildering subject matter. To Freud personally, this was just what his theory in fact supplied. All three of his theoretical difficulties between 1910 and 1920 (the issue of narcissism and its challenge to instinctual dualism, the interrelated problems of fixation to trauma and the compulsion to repeat, and the paradox of regression) had been dispelled by the new life/death instinct dichotomy. Thus, the major dualistic opposition that had long been assumed in Freud's theory of mind became one between life instincts (or Eros) — represented by both object libido and ego libido — and the death instinct.[3] Freud further identified the death instinct with the destructive

3. As Robert Lifton (1976:36) has pointed out, the concepts of life and death impose no necessary dualism upon Freud's theory, since life's termination in death can just as readily be encompassed within a unitary scheme of things. The motive for Freud's dichotomy ran deeper still and rested, as I have argued here, upon his equation of the evolution (construction)/involution (dissolution) paradigm of disease with the "forces" of life and death, respectively. Thus the evolution/involution contrast was the true and necessary dualism in Freud's theory and, when also linked to life and death instincts, transferred that necessary dualism onto these instincts.

and aggressive impulses of living beings, impulses that are normally turned outward in the adaptive service of the life instincts. "The deficiencies in our description [of mind]," he wistfully remarked in conclusion, "would probably vanish if we were already in a position to replace the psychological terms by physiological or chemical ones. . . . Biology is truly a land of unlimited possibilities. We may expect it to give us the most surprising information and we cannot guess what answers it will return in a few dozen years to the questions we have put to it" (S.E., 18:60).

Two Common Misconceptions about
Freud's Death Instinct

Before examining two common misconceptions that have tended to obscure the basic logic of Freud's controversial death-instinct theory, I shall look more closely at a rather odd feature of Freud's argument, to which much of the subsequent confusion about this theory may be traced.

As we have seen, Freud took as one of the principal starting points for his death-instinct theory the clinical phenomenon of repetition compulsion. In Beyond the Pleasure Principle, he ascribed this particular syndrome to the instinctual impulse to restore a previous state of affairs (ultimately a state of nonlife); and he identified it, at the economic level, with Gustav Fechner's principle of stability—that is, with the tendency for the psychical apparatus to reduce internal tension to the lowest possible level, or at least to maintain a constant level of that tension. But as Lichtenstein (1935) has rightly pointed out, the compulsion to repeat and the impulse to restore a previous state of affairs are two quite separate phenomena. The repetition compulsion restores an earlier state in its first phase but then, in its second, progresses away from that state. The same two-phase sequence is then repeated over and over again, without any real change occurring in the long run. Regression, on the other hand, lacks the progressive phase that the repetition principle involves. Regression therefore achieves unidirectional change through time, not a denial of change, as does the repetition compulsion. Thus, the two principles are logical opposites, an apparently curious oversight on Freud's part, but an inconsistency that he nevertheless resolved.

Similarly, when Freud equated the repetition compulsion and its motive, the death instinct, with Fechner's principle of stability, he was actually merging several aspects of Fechner's original doctrine. In fact, Fechner (1873:25–41) had distinguished three different forms of the principle of stability:

Gustav Theodor Fechner (1801–87), a founder of nineteenth-century psychophysics. "I was always open to the ideas of G. T. Fechner and have followed that thinker upon many important points" (Freud, *Autobiography*, 1925d, S.E., 20:59).

1. *Absolute stability*, in which there exists no energy or movement in a given system (Freud's state of Nirvana).
2. *Full stability*, in which the parts of the whole are animated by completely regular movements. The solar system is, according to Fechner, an instance of nearly full stability and departs from that state only insofar as the planets exert slight gravitational disturbances among themselves.
3. *Approximate stability*, in which the parts of the whole return to roughly the same position at rhythmical intervals. In this third conceptual class Fechner included periodic physiological processes such as the movements of the heart and blood, and the phenomenon of embryological (biogenetic) repetition.

But unlike Freud's notion of the repetition compulsion, Fechner believed that his third, approximate form of stability provided life with a means of *overcoming* death, in basic opposition to which all living

stable systems stood in Fechner's own scheme. That Freud should have
fused Fechner's animate and inanimate conceptions in his own discussion of the stability problem tells us something very interesting about
his underlying biological assumptions, a point to which I shall return.
For the moment I may say that Freud's theory and Fechner's three
principles (one animate and two inanimate) are by no means identical, even though Fechner may well have been an important influence
upon Freud in this overall context.[4]

Several psychoanalytic writers have not been troubled by this distinction between animate and inanimate forms of the stability principle and have sought to equate Freud's death instinct, through Fechner's inanimate principle of absolute stability, with the second law of
thermodynamics (e.g., Alexander 1921; Bernfeld and Feitelberg 1930;
Lichtenstein 1935; and Saul 1958). The second law of thermodynamics, otherwise known as the law of entropy, specifies that all forms of
energy—for instance, heat—tend to dissipate within a closed system.
Entropy, the measure of unavailable energy within a system, is therefore a directional and irreversible quantity reflecting the tendency of
things to "run themselves down." Seen in terms of this entropy principle, Freud's death instinct has become considerably more palatable
to certain psychoanalysts by virtue of a respectable alliance with the
physical sciences.

Unfortunately a major difficulty is that, in terms of the second
law of thermodynamics, Freud's death instinct ceases to describe a
vital process, as he himself had clearly envisioned it; rather, this conception reduces the death instinct to a purely physical tendency with
no formal biological basis. Lichtenstein (1935:273-74) has seen this
point explicitly, although he believes that the second law of thermodynamics is the only means of salvaging Freud's otherwise shaky notion. But so much of Freud's original conception is lost in the entropy
analogy, and such a dubious understanding of the second law of
thermodynamics is generally exhibited by the proponents of this view,
that one must also wonder whether Freud's theory is really worth salvaging in this manner.[5]

What sharply distinguishes Freud's death-instinct notion from its
beefed-up version as the second law of thermodynamics is its intimate
association with three key psychoanalytic ideas: the compulsion to
repeat, the proclivity of life to restore previous states on a supposedly
instinctual basis, and the overall "vitalistic historicism" that inspired
Freud's thinking on this whole subject. These ideas, particularly the
last two, also differentiate Freud's post-1920 theory of instinct from
his pre-1920 theories on the same subject. As Edward Bibring long ago
commented in this vein, "[Freud's] theory of the primal instincts (the
life and death instincts) was founded upon an essentially changed concept of instinct" (1941:128). That change, as Bibring understood, was

4. On Freud's intellectual relationship to Fechner, see Chapter 2 in this book;
and Ellenberger 1956: especially 210-12.
5. See, for instance, the scathing critiques of the entropy/death-instinct equiv-
alence by Penrose (1931) and Kapp (1931), who speak for the physical sciences on
this point.

from a predominantly mechanistic interpretation, in which instinct was conceived as a form of energy production (and its satisfaction as a pleasurable abreaction of that energy), to the directional-historical view that allowed Freud to proceed beyond the (mechanistic) pleasure principle.[6]

It is highly indicative of Freud's changed conception of instinct that he soon found it necessary to revise his earlier, mechanistic theory of pleasure as simple tension reduction in order to distinguish the separate trends of the Nirvana and the pleasure principles. In "The Economic Problem of Masochism," Freud wrote that "we shall henceforward avoid regarding the two principles as one." There he acknowledged that pleasure often involves an *increase* in tension (one obvious instance being the state of sexual excitation). Pleasure and unpleasure, he concluded, must depend primarily upon "qualitative" not "quantitative" considerations (1924c, S.E., *19*: 160). Similarly, although the trend of the death instinct remained synonymous with that of the earlier (mechanistic) version of the pleasure principle, Freud also used this instinct to explain the compulsive reproduction of traumatic unpleasure. Thus, after 1920 there no longer existed a simple and purely mechanistic equation between instinct, energy level, and pleasure-unpleasure in Freud's overall system of mind, even though the kernel of the older, economic-mechanistic theory remained.

How was it, then, that Freud came to endorse a new element of historicism in psychoanalysis after 1920? This question brings us to the second common misconception about his theory of life and death instincts.

It is often said that Freud's death-instinct theory is totally unsupported by biology (Brun 1953; Jones 1957:277; Holt 1965a:112; Andreski 1972:138); but this assertion must be qualified by asking what sort of biology such commentators have in mind. True, Freud's death instinct seems manifestly un-Darwinian. Any organism possessing an innate urge to die would presumably be at a great "selective" disadvantage in the struggle for existence compared with those organisms possessing only the instincts for life.[7] Freud himself was hardly anti-

6. Holt (1965a:112–13), in tracing Freud's death-instinct theory back to his 1890s passive-reflex model of the mind, is among those who have definitely missed the new "historicism" of Freud's renovations. On the other hand, Karen Horney (1939: 45, 122–23, 133) certainly appreciated Freud's historical reasoning when she spoke of his combined "evolutionistic-mechanistic" thinking in this regard. Perhaps the closest anticipation of my own analysis of this problem may be found in Pratt (1958:20–21), who has clearly perceived Freud's reliance upon the biogenetic law in this context.

7. Nevertheless, orthodox Darwinian theory is quite compatible with a "genetic" theory of death: we die because lethal genes contributing to death often first express themselves after the normal age of reproduction; such lethal genes therefore tend to accumulate in the gene pool in spite of their deleterious effects. See Medawar (1957) and Dawkins (1976:42–45) on this biological point. Freud's use of the term *death instinct* is unfortunate in this biological context, since it generally suggests a conscious striving *forward* to death (an obviously maladaptive trait) rather than a regressive compulsion to restore a primal state of rest (a biologically more neutral trait). This distinction is important, and a failure to appreciate it has caused considerable misunderstanding in connection with Freud's theory, as Glover (1950:56, n. 1) long ago pointed out.

Darwinian, but for all practical purposes he tended to think phylogeneti-cally as a psycho-Lamarckian. Indeed, those who actively endorsed the fundamental biogenetic law, as Freud did, were almost always zealous Lamarckians. For it is the framework of Lamarckian inheritance that explains (1) the biogenetic incorporation of acquired characteristics as well as (2) how, through countless developmental repetitions of such acquisitions, the whole recapitulation process becomes "speeded up" (Gould 1977:96–100).

Now, a psycho-Lamarckian sees as the major agent of evolutionary change the organism's reactions to its physiological needs. Freud, who was already convinced by the facts of embryology, as well as by the clinical problems of the neuroses, that an instinctual tendency to retrograde development must exist, had sought to rationalize that tend-ency in terms of a primal phylogenetic need (the earlier, psychophysi-cal theory of tension reduction). Freud's earlier, mechanistic theory of instinct therefore became a special case of his later historical-direc-tional theory. Above all, however—and here is where Freud made a particularly creative transformation of ideas—he used the biogenetic law as a key conceptual bridge between two otherwise distinct forms of the Fechnerian principle of stability: absolute, inanimate stability (a principle consistent with a historical-directional interpretation); and the animate, repetitive, and ahistorical notion of approximate stability. The biogenetic law epitomizes the compulsion to repeat (an animate and nondirectional process, as Lichtenstein has argued); but this same law, following the earlier lead of Sándor Ferenczi (1913), could be reduced to a historical-directional tendency toward regression, and hence to Fechner's principle of absolute stability. "We may suppose," Freud later said in reiterating this key connection in his *New Introductory Lectures*, "that from the moment at which a state of things that has once been attained is upset, an instinct arises to create it afresh and brings about [regressive] phenomena which can be described as a 'compulsion to repeat.' Thus the whole of embryology is an example of the compulsion to repeat" (1933a, S.E., 22:106).[8] In brief, embryological recapitula-tion always remained for Freud the most impressive demonstration of the biological-instinctual nature of the repetition compulsion and hence of the insufficiency of the mechanistic pleasure principle in ac-counting for human behavior. All in all, his conception of the death in-

8. One sees something of an intermediate link between the logic of Fechner and Freud in the views of the leading American Neo-Lamarckian and biogenetic advocate Edward Drinker Cope (1840–97). Some twenty years after Fechner's (1873) publication of his three principles of stability, and some twenty years before Freud's *Beyond the Pleasure Principle* (1920g), Cope (1896) proposed a fundamental bio-logical dichotomy between *Anagenetic* (life) and *Catagenetic* (death-dissolution) forces. As an ardent psycho-Lamarckian, like Freud, Cope derived Catagenetic forces, which he believed to be physical and chemical, from prior Anagenetic and psy-chically "conscious" ones. He further equated recapitulation with a form of memory and attributed "retrograde evolution" in the animal series to his class of Catagenetic forces. In connection with this theme of retrograde development, Cope (1896:211–14) cited the famous example of the ascidians as well as the researches on the copepoda by Freud's former teacher Carl Claus. See also Cope 1887:422–36. Freud himself later associated the physiological processes of *anabolism* and *catabolism* with his own two classes of life and death instincts (1923b, S.E., 19:41).

stinct was a logical tour de force that has rarely been understood in its proper intellectual perspective, namely, as the culmination of Freud's biogenetic romance about the history of life.

Aftermath of the Eros/Death Instinct Dichotomy

The notion of a death instinct, together with Freud's associated logic concerning the regressive nature of all instincts, was an important catalyst for numerous reformulations in psychoanalytic theory. These various reformulations included (1) Freud's renewed emphasis upon traumatic etiology, (2) his revised theory of anxiety, (3) an important modification in the theory of dreams, (4) the new notion of instinctual *fusions* and *defusions*, (5) certain key aspects of the later, structural theory of mind, (6) much of the general argument embodied in *Civilization and Its Discontents*, and (7) Freud's revised opinion on the therapeutic efficacy of psychoanalysis. Together these seven reformulations encompass most of the important theoretical developments in psychoanalysis during the last two decades of Freud's life.

Renewed emphasis on traumatic etiology. As Ernest Jones (1940a:20) pointed out in his obituary tribute to Freud, Freud's theory of the neuroses passed through three distinct stages. To begin with, Freud placed special etiological emphasis upon the role of childhood sexual traumas. Then, with the abandonment of the seduction theory (1897), he spent the next twenty years elaborating his libido theory, with its contrasting emphasis upon phantasy and wish-fulfillment as the major sources of neurotic symptoms. Under this alternative theory, neurosis was interpreted as the repressed "negative" of a state of perversion. Besides the key concept of repression, theoretical emphasis during this second stage of Freud's thinking was primarily upon the causes of childhood libidinal fixations, which he attributed to unusually precocious or intense sexual emotions during childhood.

Freud's etiological theory entered its third stage with the publication of *Beyond the Pleasure Principle* (1920g). Henceforth traumas, operating independently of repressed perversions, were given increasing recognition as major sources of neurotic symptoms. It was the notion of the death instinct that consolidated this twofold etiology in Freud's thinking.[9] Fundamental to this third-stage view of neurosis, then, was Freud's theoretical insight into the dual pleasure/pain motivation be-

---

9. Freud had by no means excluded the role of trauma during the previous (second) stage of his thinking; for instance, he had continued to acknowledge the great importance of traumas in adulthood as precipitating causes of neurosis (1905d [1915], *S.E.*, 7:240; 1916–17, *S.E.*, 16:362–64). He also recognized the role of infantile traumas in this second stage but generally considered it to be an auxiliary agent of repression (for example, the castration complex with its effect upon the dissolution of the Oedipus complex). During this middle period, Freud candidly acknowledged the existence of a conceptual gap between his past (traumatic) and his current (libidinal or wish-fulfillment) theories of neurosis (1916–17, *S.E.*, 16:274).

hind instinctual fixations. He subsequently extended the role of childhood traumas to include a regular series of developmental disturbances,
or "threats," to libido: birth, loss of the mother as nurturing object, loss
of penis, loss of the mother's love, and loss of the superego's love (1926d
[1925], S.E., 20:82, 130, 136–47).

The following statistic is an indication of the renewed importance
of infantile traumas in psychoanalytic theory after 1920. In the first
three volumes of the Standard Edition of Freud's works (1886e–1899a),
there is an average of thirty-eight references per volume to the subject
of traumatic etiology. With Volumes 4 to 17 (1900a–1919k), this average drops to three references per volume, many of which are autobiographical allusions back to the earlier theory. After 1920 (Volumes 18
to 23), the number of references to traumatic etiology rises sharply to
fourteen per volume.

Revision of the theory of anxiety. With the traumatic etiology given
renewed emphasis in his mature theory of neurosis, Freud also revived
the theory of signal anxiety that he had first adumbrated in his Project for a Scientific Psychology ([1895], S.E., 1:326, n. 1; see also
Freud 1895b, S.E., 3:112). In his mature theory of mind, the ego,
faced with the repeated threat of approaching danger situations, requires a continuous means of vigilance and defense against such
sources of unpleasure. Freud therefore ascribed to anxiety the function
of a "signal" warning the ego to suppress certain instinctual processes
or to avoid certain danger situations. Along with the theory of signal
anxiety, Freud also resuscitated the long-dormant distinction between
repression and other modes of psychical defense (1926d, S.E.,
20:163–64).

Revision of the theory of dreams. Already in Beyond the Pleasure
Principle, Freud had admitted that certain dreams encountered in the
traumatic neuroses of soldiers, as well as certain recurring dreams of
neurotic patients, are in apparent violation of the wish-fulfillment
theory. He therefore attributed these exceptional dreams to the compulsion to repeat and, hence, to the death instinct. In 1933 Freud qualified
this earlier reassessment by saying that such anomalous dreams might
actually represent attempts, albeit unsuccessful, at wish-fulfillment—
that is to say, thwarted desires of transforming the memory of a
trauma into a desirable event. Freud accordingly recast his original
theory of dreaming to accommodate the new conclusion that a dream
is only "an attempt at the fulfillment of a wish" (1933a, S.E., 22:29).

Instinctual fusions and defusions. In his 1923 encyclopedia article
on the libido theory, Freud described the death instinct as working "essentially in silence" and as manifesting itself observably only after being fused with Eros and directed outward as destructive or aggressive
impulses (1923a, S.E., 18:258). Freud now saw sadism as "a classical
example" of such an instinctual fusion, and masochism as the primary
form of the death instinct before being fused with Eros and redirected
toward the outside world. Carrying this notion one step further, Freud
was able to conceptualize development and regression in terms of fusions and defusions, respectively, of the two primal instincts. He be-

lieved these dual processes to correspond, at another level, to the two fundamental physiological activities of *construction* and *dissolution* within the organism (1923*a*, *S.E.*, *18*:258–59; 1923*b*, *S.E.*, *19*:41–42).

Freud lost no time in applying this new perspective to the choice-of-neurosis problem. "Making a swift generalization," he commented about obsessional neurosis in *The Ego and the Id*, "we might conjecture that the essence of a regression of libido (e.g., from the genital to the sadistic-anal phase) lies in a defusion of instincts, just as, conversely, the advance from the earlier phase to the definitive genital one would be conditioned by an accession of erotic components." He gave a similar explanation for melancholia (1923*b*, *S.E.*, *19*:42, 53–55).

The concept of regression thus took on three overlapping definitions in Freud's mature theory of the neuroses: as the trend of the otherwise "silent" death instinct, as a "defusion of instinct," and as a return of the libido (and its component instincts) to earlier stages in their development (1920*g*, *S.E.*, *18*:62; 1926*d*, *S.E.*, *20*:114). Consonant with this dual-instinct conception, Freud believed that libido and the death instinct partake simultaneously in most instances of regression.

The structural theory of mind. As proposed in *The Ego and the Id* (1923*b*), Freud's tripartite structural theory of the mind greatly clarified the dual-instinct theory, particularly in its developmental application. The id, or seat of the unconscious, is said to be the original repository of life (Eros) and death instincts in this tripartite scheme. Within the id, the death instinct aims at tension reduction and thus at an eventual state of Nirvana. Eros, by contrast, continually introduces new tensions into the id, tensions that take the form of those instinctual needs required for the preservation of life and for the continuance of the species. By binding the death instinct with itself, Eros redirects this unruly instinct outward as adaptive aggression. In the course of development, however, sublimations of the libido trigger defusions of this instinctual union and thereby liberate portions of the death instinct. Such defused components of the death instinct become utilized in superego formation, creating the last of the great traumatic threats—loss of an overly harsh superego's love—encountered during child development.

The ego, which, like the superego, is formed from a modified portion of the id, finds itself defensively encased during adulthood between its two harsh taskmasters, the id and the superego. The ego's difficult plight aptly reflects the renewed importance of trauma and defense in Freud's mature psychoanalytic system.

Freud's views on civilization. In 1930 Freud frankly confessed, "I can no longer understand how we can have overlooked the ubiquity of non-erotic aggressivity and destructiveness and can have failed to give it its due place in our interpretation of life" (1930*a*, *S.E.*, *21*:120). In *Civilization and Its Discontents*, where Freud conceded this point, he applied his revised psychoanalytic perspective on aggression to the themes of civilization, human suffering, and war. Eros, he submitted, seeks to bind human beings into ever larger groups (reproductive pairs, families, peoples, nations, and the unity of mankind); but these achievements of civilized life impose inevitable sacrifices upon man's innate sexual and aggressive impulses. In the end, the "primary mutual hostility of human beings" continually threatens civilized society "with disintegration" (p. 112). The evolution of civilization accordingly represents "the struggle between Eros and Death, between the instinct of life and the instinct of destruction, as it works itself out in the human species" (p. 122). The unhappiness of mankind is the collective price for this conflict-ridden achievement.

Freud's revised views on the prospect for therapeutic success. During later years, Freud used the death instinct as an important rationale for explaining the therapeutic limits to psychoanalytic treatment. Although he was never what he once termed "a therapeutic enthusiast," his theory of the death instinct made him considerably more explicit in his conservatism on this theme. "If we take into consideration," he reflected in "Analysis Terminable and Interminable" just two years before his death, "the total picture made up of the phenomena of masochism immanent in so many people, the negative therapeutic reaction and the sense of guilt found in so many neurotics, we shall no longer be able to adhere to the belief that mental events are exclusively governed by the desire for pleasure. . . . Only by the concurrent or mutually opposing action of the two primal instincts—Eros and the death-instinct—, never by one or the other alone, can we explain the rich multiplicity of the phenomena of life" (1937c, S.E., 23:243). Looking back upon a lifetime of intellectual achievement, Freud firmly believed that it was as a science of man and his unconscious mind, not as a mode of psychotherapy, that psychoanalysis must hope for its greatest conceptual recognition from the future (1926f, S.E., 20:265; 1933a, S.E., 22:156–57).

Summary and Conclusion

Robert Fliess, Wilhelm Fliess's psychoanalyst son, recalls Freud's once uttering the following confession about the theory of life and death instincts. "He [Freud] said: 'When, originally, I had this idea I thought to myself: this is either something altogether erroneous [*etwas ganz Abwegiges*], or something very important. . . . Well,' he went on with a smile, 'lately I have found myself more inclined toward the second alternative' " (R. Fliess 1956:3). By the 1930s, Freud's conceptual polarity had become so well integrated into the rest of his psychoanalytic corpus that he could "no longer think in any other way" about the nature of mental life (S.E., 21:119). In sharp contrast to Freud's verdict, subsequent students of his ideas have found themselves both baffled and disturbed by what they have variously described as "shaky logic," "tortuous formulations," and blatant "lack of evidential support" for his death-instinct theory (Holt 1965a:112; Becker 1973:99). For these reasons, the psychoanalytic tradition has constantly sought to rationalize Freud's bizarre doctrine in subjectivist-biographical terms, appealing to his own preoccupation with death in this connection. In this way, Freud is made to appear human after all, while the doctrine of the death instinct is safely and effectively severed from the main body of Freudian thought. But was Freud really blinded by a fatalistic preoccupation with his own death? Or does not his death-instinct theory tell us something that is insufficiently appreciated about Freud's biological orientation toward mind? After all, as a Jew, Freud hardly needed such oft-cited influences as the First World War to remind him of man's frequent brutality to man, and he was far less preoccupied with the subject of his own death when he began *Beyond the Pleasure Principle* at the age of sixty-three than he had been a quarter of a century earlier when his dreams of intellectual fame and immortality still lay unfulfilled.

As I have argued in the course of this chapter, Freud's theory of life and death instincts was actually the natural and inevitable outgrowth of three problems that emerged in psychoanalytic theory between 1910 and 1920. The new dichotomy between Eros and death (1) restored the twofold division of instinct that had been undermined by his earlier theory of narcissism, (2) clarified the otherwise enigmatic clinical phenomena of fixation to trauma and the compulsion to repeat, and (3) provided Freud with a much-needed equilibration between the developmental forces of evolution (progression) and involution (regression). Above all, it is the third and last of these issues—the opposition between evolution and involution—that proves to be the logical key to the whole of Freud's controversial reformulations about instinct. For in order to insist, as he had repeatedly done prior to 1920, that childhood unfolds biogenetically "according to programme," and that phylogenetic experience fills in where ontogenetic experience is lacking, he also needed to posit a *second* force in organic life—one capable of reversing such biogenetic achievements through regressions to previously abandoned stages. The plausibility of Freud's whole evolution/involution paradigm of mental disease depended upon the existence of such an alternative force. In 1920, instinct itself became that second, opposing force in psychoanalytic theory, thereby explaining not only the mechanism of regression but also the mechanisms of fixation to trauma and the compulsion to repeat.

If instinct was really "an urge inherent in organic life to restore an earlier state of things," then a primal stage of nonlife appeared to be the ultimate historical aim of all life. Against the regressive strivings of this hypothetical death instinct, Freud simultaneously juxtaposed the constructive manifestations of Eros (the life and libidinal instincts), to which alternative instinctual agency he attributed life's capacity to combine itself into ever larger unities. Through reproduction, the life instincts were seen to triumph over the death instincts, while in the life instincts' cyclical return to the same pattern of sexual union, Freud saw a sign of their own "conservative" nature. Finally, from the hypothetical fusion of Eros and the death instinct, Freud derived the innate aggressive and destructive drives that are normally directed outward in the service of Eros.

As much as posterity has overwhelmingly rejected his conceptual polarity, one cannot deny from Freud's point of view either the logical elegance of his arguments or the simple and compelling manner in which his theory simultaneously solved so many of his current theoretical problems. Nor is Freud's binary position as unbiological as has so often been claimed, for biology clearly constitutes the very heart of his misunderstood logic. That logic is the ultimate expression of his life-long adherence to various biogenetic and psycho-Lamarckian assumptions that, like the death instinct itself, have found little subsequent favor with Freud's psychoanalytic followers. Significantly, of those few loyal analysts who accepted Freud's controversial theory of the death instinct in the 1920s and 1930s, it was the younger group (Alexander, Bernfeld, Feitelberg, Nunberg, and others) who consistently sought to rationalize this theory in terms of the second law of thermodynamics, while the older group, which was principally confined to Sándor Ferenczi and to Freud himself, understood this concept in its alternative, biogenetic-Lamarckian guise.[10]

Freud's twofold division of instinct also exerted far more influence upon his later psychoanalytic thinking than his followers have generally acknowledged. It is only the defensive propaganda of an embarrassed movement that allows such a perceptive individual as David Rapaport to label Freud's death instinct as "a speculative excursion which does not seem to be an integral part of the [Freudian] theory" (1960a:50). Couched for more than twenty years in terms of libido and wish-fulfillment, Freud's psychoanalytic explanation of the neuroses returned once more, under the guise of the death instinct, to the traumatic etiology that he had originally emphasized in his earliest ideas on this subject. Henceforth, fixation to perverse pleasures (the work of the libido) and fixation to traumas (the work of the death instinct) stood as dual sources of neurosis in Freud's etiological system. The new role accorded to anxiety as an adaptive signal of possible danger situations became a natural psychoanalytic complement to this revised conception of neurosis. So, too, did Freud's subsequent creation of the id/ego/superego trichotomy, in which the ego gained new prominence as "the actual seat of anxiety" (S.E., 19:57). Indeed, the ego and the superego came into their own in psychoanalytic theory only after the death instinct, firmly implanted within the id, paved the way for a more defense-oriented theory of mind. In short, for Freud, ego psychology was the heir to the death instinct. It is in this sense that

10. Those mentioned in the younger group were all under the age of forty when Freud published *Beyond the Pleasure Principle* in 1920. Thus, their formative scientific years date from the new century. Ferenczi was forty-seven, and Freud himself was sixty-four in 1920. Their own formative scientific education was therefore acquired during the late nineteenth century. Although neither the biogenetic law nor Lamarckian theory was thoroughly discredited until after 1930, increasing criticism of these two doctrines dates from the turn of the century. For Ferenczi's views on the death instinct, see Ferenczi 1924; 1968 trans.:66, 94; for Nunberg's views, see Nunberg 1932; 1955 trans.:57–58, 102–3. It is a testimony to the scapegoat role commonly assigned to Ferenczi in orthodox psychoanalytic circles that Flugel (1955:130–31) could recognize the connection between Freud's death instinct and the biogenetic law and yet could credit this connection to the speculative influence of Sándor Ferenczi (1924).

the rejection of the death instinct by most of Freud's followers separates Freud—the psychologist of the id—from the movement's present-day ego psychologists, who have always claimed Freud as their first exponent (cf. Erich Fromm 1970b:33).

Biology as the "Land of Unlimited Possibilities"

Of all of Freud's works, *Beyond the Pleasure Principle* offers perhaps the closest conceptual ties to the unpublished *Project for a Scientific Psychology*, drafted a quarter of a century earlier. One is struck by the bold and frankly speculative vein of both works as well as by their common guiding principle—Freud's attempt to unite psychology with biology in resolving his most fundamental questions about human behavior. Biology, as he reaffirmed in the later work, was indeed "a land of unlimited possibilities" (1920g, *S.E., 18*:60). But there is also a major conceptual gulf between these two theoretical treatises, and that gulf provides a convenient measure of Freud's dramatic shift from *proximate*-causal reductionism (the blend of psychophysics and neurophysiology that dominated his thinking until late 1895) to a more *ultimate*-causal reductionism (one drawing upon historical and evolutionary considerations). In many ways *Beyond the Pleasure Principle* is the culmination of Freud's remarkable biogenetic romance about human psychosexuality, a romance first cultivated some twenty-five years earlier in the wake of his problematic *Project for a Scientific Psychology*. It is historicism, not mechanism or psychophysics, that pervades the innovative logic of *Beyond the Pleasure Principle*. It is also historicism, not mechanism, that enabled Freud to extend his biogenetic romance from the very origins of life itself, through the evolutionary odyssey of primal man, and finally to the conflict-ridden problems of present-day psychological man.

And yet if biology continued to be such a land of fundamental inspirations and "unlimited possibilities" to Freud, how is it that he and his theories have been so consistently misunderstood on this level, and that he himself has remained a veritable "crypto-biologist" to so many of his readers? There can be no doubt, as we shall see in the next chapter, that Freud actively sought to foster this myth about his scientific identity, and that his image as a "pure psychologist" has derived its principal and widespread support from the internal politics surrounding the birth of the psychoanalytic movement. It is to this general theme—distortion in history and the manifold purposes that such distortion has served in the psychoanalytic cause—that we now turn; for one cannot fully understand either Freud or his theories until the two themes of "Freud as crypto-biologist" and "the myth of the hero in psychoanalytic history" are traced to the various political considerations that still shroud the true meaning of his ideas. Part Three of this book therefore aims to be a capsule natural history of the psychoanalytic revolution.

PART THREE

IDEOLOGY, MYTH,
AND HISTORY IN
THE ORIGINS OF
PSYCHOANALYSIS

12

Freud as Crypto-Biologist: The Politics of Scientific Independence

In the preceding chapters of this book, we have followed the differing historical fates of two separate biological paradigms in the growth of psychoanalytic theory. The first paradigm has its roots in the traditions of nineteenth-century neurophysiology and biophysics. Although Freud, in the mid-1890s, relinquished his ambitious goal of establishing psychology as a branch of neurophysiology, he nevertheless retained many of the abstract psychophysical concomitants of this reductionistic quest (see Chapters 4, 9, and 11). After about 1895, however, he systematically adopted a second, and evolutionary, form of biological reductionism in order to secure the solid organic underpinnings that neurophysiology was not then ready to supply. Freud's later theories of infantile sexuality, psychosexual development, the instincts, pathological fixations, repression, the neuroses, and man in relation to culture—in short, the whole of the dynamic-genetic core of psychoanalytic theory—were all suffused with this evolutionary conception of life (see Chapters 6–8, 10, and 11). Above all, it was Freud's continued appeal to biological assumptions that justified his personal conviction that he had finally created a universally valid theory of human thought and behavior.

If biological inspirations were really so important in the development of Freud's psychoanalytic doctrines, we are faced with a series of paradoxical questions: Why, for instance, have Freud and his followers not underscored these key biological sources of their thinking? More especially, why did Freud allow himself to become a *crypto-biologist,* with all the confusion and misunderstanding this dissimulation has created for his theories? And why did he actually seek to encourage

this misapprehension by telling his readers, to cite a characteristic remark: "We have found it necessary to hold aloof from biological considerations during our psycho-analytic work and to refrain from using
them for heuristic purposes . . ."? (See Freud 1913j, S.E., 13:181; and
1914c, S.E., 14:78–79.)

As we shall presently see, Freud had a number of reasons for making such disclaimers. His followers, who absorbed most of these same
persuasions from Freud, in turn possessed motives of their own for
promoting psychoanalysis as a "pure psychology." All these reasons together offer a direct insight into the innermost politics that guided the
psychoanalytic movement in its difficult struggle to gain acceptance
from the scientific establishment. In the course of this chapter, I shall
demonstrate just how consequential these politics have been for psychoanalysis today.

The Quest for an Independent Science

Personal Considerations and the Opposition from Without

Myths in the service of scientific empiricism. Myths about famous
scientific discoveries often share their origins in the venerable philosophical commitment to "empirical" science. Galileo's translators, to
cite a classic example, could not resist reaffirming the empiricist image
of "the Father of Experimental Science": they added the words "by experiment" and deleted the embarrassing "without experiment" when
rendering Galileo's original Italian into English.[1] Writers of scientific
textbooks are even more notorious for their empiricist reconstruc-
tions of scientific discovery. As Cohen remarks of such historical falsifications, they seek "to personify a particular conception of the scientist: proceeding happily by the exercise of 'method' (the 'soul of science')
from experiment to theory" (1974:340–41).

Freud is no exception to this general historical tendency by which
the scientific founding fathers assume a respectable veneer of arch-
empiricism. Freud would have had us believe that virtually the whole
of psychoanalytic theory was kept free of hypotheses—especially biological ones—in order that he should not be misled from his impartial and purely empirical assessment of the facts. "I must . . . emphasize," he proclaimed in his *Three Essays on the Theory of Sexuality,*

1. The work in question was Galileo's *Dialogues Concerning Two New Sciences,*
trans. Henry Crew and Alfonso de Salvio (New York: Macmillan, 1914, and later
reprints); see page 153. For this and additional examples of empiricist distortions
of scientific history, see Koyré (1937, 1943) and Cohen (1974:338–41) on Galileo,
Holton (1969) on Einstein, Fisher (1936) on Mendel, and Thackray (1972:40–41,
62–63) on Dalton. Stephen Brush (1974) provides a useful survey of these and other
historical instances and suggests that the *real* history of science, which so often reveals the nonempirical character of scientific research, should be "X-rated" for science students.

"that the present work is characterized not only by being completely based upon psycho-analytic research, but also by being deliberately independent of the findings of biology. I have carefully avoided introducing any preconceptions, whether derived from general sexual biology or from that of particular animal species, into this study—a study which is concerned with the sexual functions of human beings and which is made possible through the technique of psycho-analysis" (1905d [Preface to the 1915 edition], *S.E.*, 7:131).

In spite of such categorical disclaimers, no student of his works can fail to appreciate that Freud, like most successful scientists, employed a highly hypothetico-deductive methodology in his researches. Nonetheless, what has so often shielded this methodology, and accompanying biological premises, from public recognition is the traditional form of argumentation in which scientific research is cast. The historian, in particular, must constantly be aware that the structure of Freud's published arguments is often the exact reverse of the actual genesis of his ideas. To cite a prime example, Freud later gave didactic priority to dreams and parapraxes in explicating his psychoanalytic theories, even though his understanding of these phenomena was largely dependent upon his previous conceptions of neurotic symptom formation. Like the reader of *The Origin of Species* (1859), whom Darwin first instructed in the extraordinary accomplishments of pigeon breeders before broaching the dangerous doctrines of evolution, the reader of Freud's *Introductory Lectures* (1916–17) is masterfully guided through dreams and slips of the tongue until the controversial psychoanalytic laws of the neuroses seem to beg for spontaneous recognition. (I am indebted to Jacques Roger for this comparison.) Similarly, Wollheim (1971:99–100) has emphasized that Freud deliberately began his book on jokes (1905c) with a lengthy review of individual jokes in order to avoid the obvious imputation that "the new categories [for example, the joke-work] had been selected with an eye to the old and had been forcibly imposed on the [newer] material."

More especially, Freud's denial of hypotheses and presuppositions in psychoanalysis may be seen as a defensive reaction to a common accusation by his opponents, namely, that psychoanalysis was based upon excessive and unfounded speculation. Freud was particularly sensitive to this criticism, apparently owing, as Jones (1955:123) remarks. to a deep fear of "the imaginative, and even speculative, side of his nature which he had striven so hard to suppress or at least to control." "If only one could get the better people to realise," Freud complained to Oskar Pfister in 1909, "that all our theories are based on experience (there is no reason, so far as I am concerned, why they should not try to interpret it differently) and not just fabricated out of thin air or thought up over the writing desk. But the latter is what they all really assume . . ." (*Freud/Pfister Letters*, p. 27).[2] Hence it was that the indispensable "psychoanalytic method" became such an important sym-

2. See also Freud's *Autobiography*, 1925d, *S.E.*, 20:50; and the section "Psycho-Analysis an Empirical Science" in "Psycho-Analysis," 1923a, *S.E.*, 18:253–54.

bol in the psychoanalytic movement, epitomizing the triumph of empirical inquiry over the hostile prejudices of Freud's opponents. Finally, to Freud himself, who was indeed privately disposed toward far-reaching speculation along biological and other lines, it must have been greatly reassuring to think that psychoanalysis really *was* the product of his empirical half.

In later years, followers like Ernest Jones merely echoed Freud's own empiricist tactics when discussing the conceptual relationship between biology and psychoanalysis. "Although I have designated psychoanalysis," Jones wrote in 1930, "as the study of the mind from a biological point of view, it should at once be said that this does not mean any deductive application of biological principles to such a study. On the contrary, Freud's investigations were of an unusually empirical nature . . . , and it was only gradually that the general bearing of them, and particularly their biological import, became manifest" (1930:604). In short, both Freud and his followers quickly learned the political virtues of portraying psychoanalysis as an independent and purely empirical science of mind.

Freud's scientific identity transformed. Between 1890 and 1905, Freud underwent a profound change in his personal identity as a practitioner of science (Holt 1963): in 1890 he still considered himself a neurologist and neuroanatomist; by 1905 he saw himself instead as a revolutionist in psychology. A major consequence was that Freud later opposed having his "prepsychoanalytic" publications on neuroanatomy, aphasia, and other biomedical subjects included in his *Collected Psychological Works*. Freud's decision has exerted the desired effect, for few indeed are the practicing psychoanalysts who have ever read these earlier publications or pondered their implications for the rest of Freud's thought. With the majority of analysts now dependent upon English, French, Spanish, Italian, and other translations of Freud's works, the conceptual gulf between Freud the untranslated biologist and Freud the psychologist has become even more formidable with the years. Historians and political ideologists may haggle over the young Marx as against the mature Marx, but at least these classical disputants have both sets of writings readily available to fuel their debates.[3]

For Freud personally, his growing psychological self-image was closely tied up with his defiant vision of himself as pitted against the established medical theories that he was seeking to overthrow. Existing medical theory was predominantly somatic and physiological; and in contrast to it, Freud erected a sophisticated psychobiology of mind, which seemed to him like a pure psychology that had finally revealed the misguided fallacies of the organicist paradigm of mind. In *The Interpretation of Dreams* (1900a), for instance, Freud had challenged the prevailing somatic theories on that subject. Soon afterward he

3. As a representative of this polemical literary genre, see Althusser's *For Marx* (1969). The difficulties that have long beset students of Freud will be greatly alleviated by the forthcoming publication, in three volumes, of *The Pre-Analytic Works of Sigmund Freud*.

analyzed slips of the tongue and other parapraxes in *The Psycho-pathology of Everyday Life* (1901*b*), not as physiological phenomena (the current theory) but as dynamic, unconsciously motivated distur-bances (Chapter 9). Similarly, in his controversial theory of the psycho-neuroses, Freud reacted against the established doctrine of hereditary degeneration in choosing to emphasize the primacy of early experience. Even after Freud was forced to abandon the extreme environmentalism of his short-lived seduction theory, he never relinquished the revolu-tionary and psychological self-image that he had so fervently cultivated during this Sturm-und-Drang period of his life.

Underlying Freud's transformed self-image, his Jewish identity may also be discerned. Freud himself later pointed up this connection in his *Autobiography*:

> When, in 1873, I first joined the University, I experienced some appre-ciable disappointments. Above all, I found myself inferior and an alien because I was a Jew. . . . These first impressions at the University, how-ever, had one consequence which was afterwards to prove important; for at an early age I was made familiar with the fate of being in the Op-position and of being put under the ban of the "compact majority." The foundations were thus laid for a certain degree of independence of judge-ment. (1925*d*, S.E., 20:9)

Doubtless the general intellectual iconoclasm entailed in his challenge to somatic theory was partly reinforced by his identification with mi-nority causes. Furthermore, his much more vehement opposition to de-generation theory was very likely connected with the anti-Semitic im-plications that were being drawn from that theory even while young Freud was in Paris studying with the great Charcot. In his best-selling work *La France juive* (1886, 1:106), Édouard Drumont had based his anti-Semitic claims about Jewish mental instability upon Charcot's own purported statements concerning Russian Jews "in his course at the Salpêtrière" (see further L. Stewart 1977:222, 228). Freud's later oppo-sition to Charcot's doctrine of neuropathic heredity may well have been fueled by such anti-Semitic implications. Thus, Freud's later self-image as a "pure psychologist" reflected both a reaction against explicitly ra-cial doctrines during a period of growing racial prejudice, and the gen-eral intellectual iconoclasm that characterized his relationship to his teachers. That his psychoanalytic theories remained deeply imbued with biological assumptions was not in conflict with Freud's psychological self-image, for his own "biology" was vastly different from the somatic and hereditarian doctrines that had preceded him in mental science.

"Invisible" biological influences. I have mentioned before that evo-lutionary and Darwinian conceptions of man had become so extensive by the 1890s as to become almost invisible influences to those of Freud's scientific generation (Chapter 7). Such invisibility naturally made it more difficult for investigators like Freud to recognize how far prior biological and biogenetic assumptions were silently guiding their think-ing as clinicians.

G. Stanley Hall, in America, provides an interesting parallel to Freud's own historical insensibility in this respect. No one used evolutionary theory and the biogenetic law more extensively in psychology than either Freud or G. Stanley Hall (see especially Hall's Preface to *Adolescence*, 1904). Like Freud, Hall considered primitive peoples as developmentally arrested racial forms offering instructive parallels to the childhood stages of higher races (1904, 2:648–748). He equated mental pathology with the persistence of primitive forms of behavior, and he viewed childhood play as a necessary "catharsis" (his own term) of these archaic vestiges (1904, 1:x–xi, 163–65). Also like Freud, Hall related early fixations of archaic traits to the later occurrence of sexual perversion (1904, 2:101–2); and he developed his own biogenetic conceptions of repression ("inhibition") and sublimation ("irradiation") to explain human psychosexual development (1904, 1:107–11, 162, 455–57). Yet when one of Hall's disciples, George E. Partridge, later drew together Hall's ideas in such a way as to stress the central role of recapitulation theory, Hall's reaction was one of surprise. He responded to Partridge by saying that "it makes me begin to query whether after all, down below consciousness, I may have some kind of system that, if I live a decade or two more, might be put into a sort of scheme of things called perhaps geneticism" (cited by Ross 1972:376, n. 10, unpublished letter of 1 March 1911, Clark University Papers).

Of course, the striking similarity between the psychologies of Hall and Freud is not really so remarkable when one recognizes the communality of their most basic biological premises. This communality also lies behind Hall's early and enthusiastic interest in Freud's ideas (1904, 1:233, 279, 285; 2:121–22), an interest that subsequently led him to invite his Viennese counterpart to Clark University, where Freud gave his famous lectures and was awarded his first (and only) honorary degree in 1909. Given their similar psychobiological perspectives on man, Hall had become something of a convinced "Freudian" before he had even heard of Sigmund Freud (Ross 1972:394). Both careers, then, were carried along by the same contemporary tide of genetic and Darwinian thinking that had brought the whole field of child psychology to such prominence by the 1890s. One is reminded of Freud's surprise when he, too, suddenly caught a glimpse of this common conceptual flow during that decade. "It is interesting," he confessed in an 1897 letter to Fliess, "that writers are now turning so much to child psychology. . . . So one still remains a child of one's age, even with something one had thought was one's very own" (*Origins*, p. 228).

Biology versus history. Such biological influences as Freud's doctrines embodied were able to achieve their psychoanalytic invisibility in yet another manner. I have several times mentioned that his biological allegiances were divided between two distinct forms of reductionistic reasoning (Chapters 1, 4, 10, and 11). When Freud spoke of his efforts to keep psychoanalysis free from biological points of view, he generally had in mind proximate-causal (physiological) reductionism, not evolutionary biology (e.g., 1916–17, *S.E.*, *16*:393). But as a psycho-Lamarckian, Freud was able to see phylogenetic reductionism as a form of *historical*, rather than strictly biological, explanation. He apparently considered this distinction important enough to alter the published text of one major work. In *The Ego and the Id*, he had initially referred to the origins of the superego as the outcome of "two highly important biological factors: namely, the lengthy duration in man of his childhood helplessness and dependence, and the fact of his Oedipus complex, which we have traced back [phylogenetically] . . . to the diphasic origin of man's sexual life" (1923*b*, *S.E.*, *19*:35). In the 1927 English translation, Freud personally ordered that the first part of this sentence be changed to read that the superego has its origins in "two highly important factors, one of a biological and the other of a historical nature"; and he went on to name them as before. Thus phylogenetic explanations, as historical explanations, were environmental and psychological, not biological, to an ardent psycho-Lamarckian like Freud. It is probably for this same reason that he never formally recognized a genetic (or biogenetic) component in his metapsychology—that is, as a fourth complement to the economic, dynamic, and topographical points of view (cf. Rapaport and Gill 1959:154). Once reduced by the Lamarckian theory to multifarious historical acquisitions, the biogenetic aspect of psychoanalysis apparently seemed less of an abstract universal to Freud than his other three metapsychological dimensions.

Summing up this chapter thus far, Freud's arch-empiricist self-image, his staunch identification with minority causes, his increasingly revolutionary identity as a "pure psychologist," and his failure to appreciate his extensive debt to evolutionary biology all combined forces between 1890 and 1905 and effectively turned psychoanalytic theory into a crypto-biological doctrine. It was during the ensuing decade, however, that Freud acquired the most important motive of all for denying his debt to biology: the opposition toward his theories that emerged from his own psychoanalytic following.

Opposition from Within

Biological theory turned out to be a double-edged sword for Freud and his movement. Various followers began to emphasize different biological assumptions and soon developed rival theories that proved incompatible with Freud's own. What Freud witnessed was a classic encounter between "discipline" and "antidiscipline." According to E. O. Wilson's (1977) characterization of such factionalisms, every field of science stands in epistemological relation to another, usually older and more advanced field, which may be called the *antidiscipline* of the younger field. Biology is the antidiscipline of psychology, just as psychology is itself the antidiscipline of sociology and certain other social sciences. Within this hierarchical progression of scientific domains, there exist large areas of explanatory overlap as well as unique levels of fact and analysis that sharply differentiate each discipline. Nevertheless, it is generally the attitude of the antidiscipline that the discipline closely related to it should be explained exclusively in terms of the antidiscipline's own causal principles. The physicist consequently seeks to reduce chemistry to the laws of physics, while the chemist hopes to reduce biology to chemistry, and so forth along the antidiscipline/discipline progression. Freud, as a onetime biologist, fully recognized both the high promise for psychology of the reductionist quest and its many potential dangers. As a psychoanalyst, he eagerly sought to reduce sociology to psychological points of view (notably in *Group Psychology and the Analysis of the Ego,* 1921c). In turn, he referred his most fundamental psychoanalytic principles to his adjacent antidiscipline, biology. Yet Freud strenuously resented any attempt from the direction of biology to rob psychoanalysis of its independent disciplinary status. He feared the oversimplification of psychological phenomena, as well as potential defections from psychoanalytic theory, at the hands of biologically inclined analysts.

Freud's relationship with Wilhelm Fliess represents the prototype of many such antidiscipline/discipline dissensions within psychoanalysis. During the 1890s Freud had looked to Fliess to provide the biological foundations of his new theory of mind, an expectation that Fliess more than fulfilled (Chapter 6). As late as 1901, Freud planned to write a book entitled "Bisexuality in Man" with Fliess as coauthor (*Origins,* pp. 334–35). The book was to have bridged the remaining psychoanalytic gaps between the theories of perversion, neurosis, and repression. But the planned collaboration, as well as Freud's friendship with Fliess, came to an abrupt end when the issue of whose field was scientifically more essential finally came between the two men.

Estrangement from Fliess had a direct and decisive impact upon Freud's conception of the proper relationship between biology and psychoanalysis. In 1904, with their break virtually complete, Freud told his old friend that he now planned to "avoid the theme of bisexuality as much as possible" (Fliess 1906a:20). Although Freud still called the notion of bisexuality "the decisive factor" in psychosexual development in his *Three Essays on the Theory of Sexuality* (1905d), he remained increasingly aloof from bisexuality theory as a biological concept. Fritz Wittels (1924b:124–25), who later described Freud's general uneasiness about bisexuality during the 1905–10 period, has himself traced this ambivalence back to the Fliess relationship: "Even to-day, I fancy, his mind is not free from a secret antagonism towards the notion. . . . At this [earlier] period he would still, at times, make fun of bisexuality, and warn us against accepting it with too much enthusiasm."

What Freud evidently feared, especially during his movement's formative years, was the possible subordination of psychoanalysis to Fliess's own sexual biology. As late as 1910 in *Leonardo da Vinci,* Freud still hinted at a possible bisexual theory of repression before finally dismissing this line of thought with the firm declaration, "We will not, however, leave the ground of purely psychological research" (1910c, *S.E.,* 11:136). To Ernest Jones, Freud privately mentioned this same issue as he was writing the *Leonardo* essay, and he cited in this connection Leonardo's "bimanual" capability (an allusion to Fliess's interrelated theories of bisexual/bilateral predispositions). "I have not inquired further into his [Leonardo's] handwriting because I avoided by purpose all biological views, restraining myself to the discussion of the psychological ones" (quoted in Jones 1955:347, letter of 15 April 1910). Freud was even more explicit about the Fliessian source of his biological worries in a 1914 letter to Karl Abraham, where in reference to the newly founded Berlin Society for Sexual Science he remarked:

> The society is designed to achieve recognition for Fliess. Rightly so, because he is the only mind among them and the possessor of a bit of unrecognized truth. But the subjection of our psycho-analysis to a Fliessian sexual biology would be no less a disaster than its subjection to any system of ethics, metaphysics, or anything of the sort. You know him, his psychological incapacity and his logical consistency in the physical field. Left hand = woman = the subconscious = anxiety. We must at all costs remain independent and maintain our equal rights. Ultimately we shall be able to come together with all the parallel sciences. (*Freud/ Abraham Letters*, p. 171, letter of 6 April 1914)

After 1910, Freud's continued efforts to claim an independent disciplinary status for psychoanalysis, reinforced as they were by growing opposition from within, steadfastly reflected the lingering specter of Fliess. Freud himself spoke openly of the similar emotional impact that these later disagreements and defections had upon him. "I had quite got over the Fliess affair," he wrote to Ferenczi in 1910. "Adler is a little Fliess come to life again. And his appendage Stekel is at least called Wilhelm" (quoted in Jones 1955:130). Similarly, Freud's dramatic fainting spell in Munich in 1912, which followed upon an argument with Jung and Riklin, was a direct symptom of the neurotic pattern established by the Fliess affair. To Ludwig Binswanger, Freud confessed shortly thereafter, "Repressed feelings, this time directed against Jung, as previously against a predecessor of his [Fliess], naturally play the main part" (Binswanger 1957:49, letter of 1 January 1913).

Although the enduring effect of the Fliess affair on Freud has never been disputed, the specific role of biology (Fliessian and otherwise) in the later dissensions has not been sufficiently recognized by Freud scholars. Indeed, traditional psychoanalytic interpretations of these dissensions have become so reified within Freud historiography as to largely obscure the rational, biological sources of the movement's schisms. Psychoanalysts, trained to think psychoanalytically, consistently saw signs of their mutual disagreements in terms of the classic oedipal formula: Freud—the father—was being challenged by his jealous and unruly sons—Jung, Adler, Stekel, Sadger, and others. To the loyal analysts who remained with Freud, the problem naturally lay in the pathology of the children. To the defectors, these painful incidents provided equally clear-cut testimony to the pathology of the father. Such oedipal rivalries no doubt existed on both sides; but as the dissensions became more pronounced, underlying sources of biological disagreement manifested themselves. Freud's most creative disciples, like Freud himself, had been drawing liberally upon biological assumptions in their work; and Freud, fully aware of the dangerous consequences, let them know what an unpardonable taboo it was to mix psychology with biology. If traditional psychoanalytic historiography has failed to acknowledge these intellectual, and specifically biological, aspects of the debates, it is because the movement has long remained defensively fixated upon its own psychoanalytic rationalizations. Freud and his dissident followers, however, knew much better at the time.

Nor was the analogy with the Fliess case lost upon Freud's rebellious followers. In spite of Freud's estrangement from Fliess, Fliessian and related biological ideas had continued to inspire both innovation and dissension within psychoanalytic circles. Sadger (1907), Adler (1910), and Stekel (1911:71) all sought to make bisexuality into a universal principle of symptom formation, phantasies, and dreaming. On this bisexual basis, they saw psychical phenomena as having two independent sources—one homosexual and one hetereosexual—within the unconscious mind and consequently claimed for bisexuality an essential role in analysis and therapy. Freud, although inclined to support a limited application of this idea for dreams and hysterical symptoms, strenuously rejected the more universal declarations of Sadger, Adler, and Stekel (1908a, S.E., 9:165 n.; 1900a [1911], S.E., 5:396–97).

Fliessian periodicity theory held a similar attraction for Freud's psychoanalytic adherents. Stekel (1908) made repeated use of Fliess's theory of biorhythms in a book on anxiety neuroses, while Freud's one-time student Hermann Swoboda (1904) introduced a modified version of Fliess's theory into dream interpretation. Freud disapproved of both these efforts, although he went so far as to test Swoboda's hypothesis on his own dreams.[4]

It was above all through the work of Adler and Jung and, in America, of G. Stanley Hall that biology proved a particularly instrumental source of the defections that soon beset the psychoanalytic movement. Adler was the first of these three investigators to make known his heterodox views.

ALFRED ADLER (1870–1937)

Along with Stekel, Kahane, Reitler, and Freud, Adler was one of the five physicians who in 1902 founded the Psychological Wednesday Evenings circle at Freud's home. Adler's first major psychoanalytic work was a short booklet entitled *Studie über Minderwertigkeit von Organen* (Study of Organ Inferiority, 1907; trans. 1917a), in which he argued that individuals generally compensate for underdeveloped or abnormal organs and occasionally achieve a higher-than-average capability through overcompensation. Such instances are frequently hereditary, Adler claimed, and often characterize whole families. He pointed in this

4. See *The Freud/Jung Letters*, p. 169, letter of 13 August 1908; and Freud 1900a, S.E., 4:166–69 (additions made in 1909 and 1911).

Alfred Adler in his forties,
about the time of his break with Freud.

connection to musicians coming from families afflicted by hearing
difficulties, as well as to famous artists whose families were plagued by
chronic eye disorders.

Although Adler's work on organ inferiority was somewhat independent of the mainstream of psychoanalytic theory, it offered two
direct points of contact, as Ellenberger (1970:605) has noted. First, if
the defective organ happened to be an erotogenic zone, overcompensation might lead either to neurosis or to perversion, in accordance
with Freud's psychosexual theory. Second, inasmuch as organ systems
contribute to the ultimate success of the sexual being, there could be
no "organ inferiority" without some degree of "sexual inferiority." This
is especially true, Adler thought, whenever groups of organs belonging to
the same defective embryonic segment prove abnormal in the sexually
mature individual.

Whereas the theory of organ inferiority was well received by

Freud's circle, the same cannot be said of its logical successor. The principal source of conflict was bisexuality theory, boldly advanced as part of a frontal assault upon the Oedipus complex and upon Freud's sexual conception of neurosis. Published under the title "Der psychische Hermaphroditismus im Leben und in der Neurose" (Psychical Hermaphroditism in Life and in Neurosis), Adler's new theory was presented before the Vienna Psychoanalytic Society on 23 February 1910 and elicited lively debate in the weeks that followed. Surveying the previously published discussions on bisexuality by Freud, Halban, Krafft-Ebing, Fliess, Weininger, Swoboda, and others, Adler observed that secondary sexual characteristics of the opposite sex appear to be much more frequent among neurotics than among normal individuals. It is this organic predisposition, Adler maintained, that induces the future neurotic to develop a subjective feeling of personal inferiority. Neurotics further associate such feelings of inferiority with all that is weak, passive, bad, and above all feminine, while they see the traits of masculinity and aggression as superior qualities that they lack. Males fall ill, so Adler's argument runs, because of their feminine tendencies. By contrast, females fall ill when an unusually pronounced masculine organization leads to a protest against, and attempted compensation for, their inferior, feminine side.

Within this combined sociobiological framework, Adler sought to explain the phenomena of neurosis, exhibitionism, fetishism, and the oedipal desire to surpass the father and possess the mother. These tendencies are all aggressively rooted, Adler believed, in the drive toward "masculine protest"—or, more broadly, in "the will to power." As he explained to the Vienna Psychoanalytic Society in February 1910, "Those phenomena of neuroses that we call compromise-formations in the true sense of the word—such as doubt, sadomasochistic traits, all forms of the inhibited or perverted aggressive instinct, the phenomena of compulsion and anxiety—these are derived and obtain their power from the battle between the feminine foundation and the masculine protest" (*Minutes*, 2:427). Lest the biological substratum be forgotten, Adler reminded his listeners that sexual periodicity had to be included in these formulations, since the feminine component of bisexuality presupposes a tie with the menstrual cycle.

Freud's immediate objections to Adler's theory of masculine protest are preserved in the recorded minutes of the discussion that followed Adler's oral presentation. Adler's innovations were misguided, Freud unhesitatingly replied, and represented a wholly premature subordination of psychoanalysis to sexual biology:

> . . . one faces his [Adler's] expositions with a certain feeling of alienation, because Adler subjects the psychological material too soon to biological points of view, thus arriving at conclusions that are not yet warranted by the psychological material.
> . . . The example of Fliess, who offers a biological characterization [of the neuroses], has misled many. Fliess saw in the unconscious the elements of the opposite sex. This is wrong. It is true that in the woman one does find in neurosis repressed masculinity, but in the man one finds

only the repression of "masculine" impulses and not of "feminine" ones. Neurosis always has a "feminine" character. But the concepts of "masculine" and "feminine" are of no use in psychology and we do better, in view of the findings of the psychology of the neuroses, to employ the concepts of libido and repression. (*Minutes*, 2:432)

A year later Freud was condemning Adler's rival theories as "sterile," "reactionary," and "retrogressive" and insisting that they could only do great harm to psychoanalysis as a scientific discipline. "Instead of psychology," Freud chided Adler before the Psychoanalytic Society in February 1911, "it [Adler's theory] presents, in large part, biology; instead of the psychology of the unconscious, it presents surface ego psychology. Lastly, instead of the psychology of the libido, of sexuality, it offers general psychology" (*Minutes*, 3:147).

Shortly after this last rebuke, Adler and Wilhelm Stekel (1868–1940) resigned their offices as president and vice-president of the Vienna Psychoanalytic Society, respectively, citing the basic incompatibility of their scientific views with those of Freud. Two months later, in May 1911, Adler resigned from the Vienna society altogether after Freud asked that he step down as editor of the newly founded *Zentralblatt für Psychoanalyse*. Nine Adlerian adherents (approximately one-fourth of the society's membership) also resigned with Adler in order to join the latter's own Society for Free Psychoanalysis. Wilhelm Stekel remained with the Vienna society for eighteen months more before he, too, resigned in a dispute over editorial control of the *Zentralblatt* (which Stekel retained).

Adler's school of *individual psychology* subsequently grew out of his conceptual alternative to Freudian theory. In later works Adler gave increasing emphasis to social factors; he developed the notion of sibling rivalry and treated sexuality in more symbolic terms (Adler 1912, 1920, 1927a); and in many important respects, he developed *ego psychology* ahead of its time. Moreover, he was not duped by what he perceived as Freud's biological double standard. As he responded to Freud's reprimands in 1910, "he [Adler] was less biological than if he had pursued [like Freud] the vicissitudes of the libido and of the innate sexual constitution" (*Minutes*, 2:434). Mirroring his opponent's tactics during their joint debates, Adler blamed Freud's theoretical errors upon his unwarranted biological assumptions concerning organic repression (*Minutes*, 3:142; meeting of 1 February 1911; see also Freud 1914d, S.E., 14:56–57). Freud was not swayed by Adler's counterattacks. In later years he continued to lump Adler's notion of masculine protest together with the biological conception of repression and neurosis developed by Wilhelm Fliess, and rejected both theories with the words: "I decline to sexualize repression in this way—that is, to explain it on biological grounds instead of on purely psychological ones" (1937c, S.E., 23:251).

CARL GUSTAV JUNG (1876–1961)

If Freud thought Alfred Adler's ideas were biologically unsound, Carl Gustav Jung had begun to think the same thing about Freud's. When he initiated his regular correspondence with Freud in 1906, Jung had still been unable to endorse Freud's universal sexual etiology. Freud believed he would eventually win Jung over on this point, but Jung's subsequent work at the Burghölzli Mental Hospital in Zurich only served to confirm his initial reservations about Freud's views. The debates between Adler and Freud also played an important role in Jung's growing heterodoxy. Jung's well-known fascination with "psychological typologies" was apparently first aroused when he tried to understand how Adler and Freud could hold such divergent but mutually plausible theories. Freud, preoccupied by the individual's relationship to the sexual object, manifested what Jung later called an *extroverted* attitude toward the world, while Adler, with his absorption in the individual's strivings for superiority, displayed a more *introverted* point of view. "The extroverted theory holds good," Jung later maintained in *Psychological Types*, "for the extroverted type, the introverted theory for the introverted type" (1921, *C.W.*, 6:62; see also Storr 1973:57–59).

Of principal concern to us here, however, is how Jung, too, adeptly drew upon key biological and especially biogenetic arguments in his own efforts to undermine Freud's doctrines. Freud, for his own part, had already warned Jung about the need for keeping psychoanalysis free from biological hypotheses. When Jung's colleague Sabina Spielrein delivered an overly biological paper before the Vienna Psychoanalytic Society in November 1911, Freud had responded to Jung with the anxious comment: "What troubles me most is that Fräulein Spielrein wants to subordinate the psychological material to *bio*logical considerations; this dependency is no more acceptable than a dependency on philosophy, physiology, or brain anatomy. ψA *farà da se* ['Psychoanalysis goes by itself']" (*Freud/Jung Letters*, p. 469, letter of 30 November 1911). Freud's admonition was to no avail. Just two weeks later, Jung hinted apologetically at the basic psychobiological differences that were about to come between himself and Freud. "The essential point," Jung reported in a letter, "is that I try to replace the descriptive concept of libido by a *genetic* one. Such a concept covers not only the recent-sexual libido but all those forms of it which have long since split off [phylogenetically] into organized activities. A wee bit of biology was unavoidable here" (*Freud/Jung Letters*, p. 471, letter of 11 December 1911).

Jung's dissatisfaction with Freud's libido theory ultimately centered upon three key psychoanalytic notions: infantile sexuality, the assumption of a latency period, and Freud's emphasis upon childhood experiences as the essential cause of neurosis. Jung briefly announced the biological underpinnings of his objections in the second part of his *Transformations and Symbols of the Libido* (1911–12). Then, with a personal break appearing all but inevitable, he expanded these objections toward the end of 1912. Jung's longer critique, formulated in a lecture series at Fordham University, New York, was later published as *The Theory of Psychoanalysis* (1913).

Infantile sexuality as "inadmissible biologically." Freud's "extended"

Carl Gustav Jung
in 1912 (age 37),
the year of
his break with Freud.

conception of sexuality, Jung believed, was totally unwarranted for
human infancy. *"Obtaining pleasure is by no means identical with
sexuality,"* Jung emphasized in connection with Freud's well-known
views on infantile sucking and the oral erogenous zone (1913, *C.W.*,
4:107). Freud's opinions were premised upon the erroneous genetic assumption that the instincts of hunger and sexuality develop side by
side from birth onward:

> If we judge by what we see [in biology], we must take into consideration
> the fact that in the whole realm of organic nature the life-process con-
> sists for a long time only in the functions of nutrition and growth. We
> can observe this very clearly indeed in many organisms, for instance in
> butterflies, which as caterpillars first pass through an asexual stage of
> nutrition and growth only. The intra-uterine period of human beings, as
> well as the extra-uterine period of infancy, belong to this [asexual] stage
> of the life process. (1913, *C.W.*, 4:105)

In short, Freud's conception of infantile sexuality was "inadmissible
biologically," Jung strenuously proclaimed.

Jung's criticisms on this theme, just like Freud's controversial conception of the libido, were drawn primarily from the domain of phylog-

eny. Although he avidly endorsed the same general biogenetic outlook
that had proved so useful to Freud's conception of infantile sexuality,
Jung was in sharp disagreement with Freud's own biogenetic timetable
for child development. Where Freud repeatedly compared infancy and
early childhood to hominid man during the achievement of upright
posture, Jung envisioned the child as recapitulating a far more remote
and totally asexual period in man's prehistory. To Jung, the first stages of
psychical energy in human beings coincided with the primary, undifferentiated, and asexual nutritive instinct that originally subserved
propagation among our ancestors (through cell-budding or free-floating
gamete dispersal). "In early childhood, it [the libido or psychical energy]
appears at first wholly in the form of the nutritive instinct which builds
up the body. . . . [O]ne has only to think of the influence of nutritional
factors on propagation in the lower animals and plants" (1913, *C.W.*,
4:125). In addition, Jung believed that portions of the libido had become
phylogenetically "desexualized" through secondary functions like caring
for offspring. He considered this nonsexual libido to be a major adult
source of psychical energy, an energy that independently manifests itself
in neurotic symptoms (1913, *C.W.*, 4:121, 125–26).

Latency period as a biological impossibility. Jung's heterodox biogenetic logic fostered yet another major criticism of Freud's libido theory, this one centered around the notion of *sexual latency.* Latency
period, the interruption of sexual development between the ages of five
and puberty, provides Freudian theory with a crucial developmental occasion for pathological repressions. Latency, or rather the diphasic
onset of sexuality that latency entails, is likewise instrumental in explaining why neurosis and sexuality are so intimately linked in man
(Chapter 10). Jung found major biological fault with this whole scheme:
"Such a process of development would be biologically unique. In conformity with this theory we would have to assume, for instance, that
when a plant forms a bud from which a blossom begins to unfold, the
blossom is taken back again before it is fully developed, and is again
hidden within the bud, to reappear later on in a similar form" (1913,
C.W., 4:164). Dismissing Freud's notion of sexual latency as an "impossible supposition," Jung affirmed instead this doctrine's opposite:
that the usual beginning of sexual development coincides precisely with
the onset of Freud's latency period (around the age of six or seven).

Jung's de-emphasis of childhood etiology. Freud's failure to understand the true developmental course of sexuality, Jung observed, had
prevented him from giving full etiological weight to libidinal regressions.
"The point is that the *regression of libido abolishes to a very large extent
the aetiological significance of childhood experiences.* . . . Looked at from
this point of view, childhood experiences have a significance for neurosis
only when they are made significant by a regression of libido" (1913,
C.W., 4:168). Thus, like Janet and Adler, Jung now endorsed a theory
of neurosis emphasizing current psychical conflicts, not childhood ones;
the infantile-sexual component of neurosis was almost always referable
to a later regression.

An additional phylogenetic assumption, this one tied to Jung's famous conception of the "collective unconscious," allowed him to subordinate infantile determinants even further, in favor of inborn dispositions or "archetypes" common to the human race. According to Jung's theoretical scheme, activation of the collective unconscious is achieved through psychical regressions during adulthood. Such regressions were thought to play a major role in mental disorders like dementia praecox. It is the individual's inability to assimilate the contents of this collective unconscious, Jung insisted, that leads to psychoneurosis through a "splitting of the mind" (1911–12, C.W., 5:158, 408).

To summarize Jung's theory of neurosis, libido, in significant part nonsexual, is forced by current conflicts to express itself regressively, producing symptoms with infantile as well as archetypal associations. Both infancy and sexuality therefore lose their paramount Freudian status in Jung's revision of psychoanalytic theory.

Freud's response to Jung's defection. Freud's *Totem and Taboo* (1912–13) may be seen as a calculated reply to Jung's tripartite critique of psychoanalytic theory. In this and subsequent works, Freud's formerly implicit endorsement of the biogenetic law became an increasingly explicit and detailed means of countering Jung's challenge. The polymorphous perversity of childhood sexuality (Jung's first point of contention) as well as the diphasic onset of human sexual life (Jung's second) were both bolstered by Freud's strategic appeal to phylogenetic considerations (see Chapters 7 and 10). Such phylogenetic arguments in turn vindicated, through Freud's recapitulatory logic, the importance of human infancy (Jung's third point of contention). Lest his support for phylogenetic considerations seem inconsistent, however, with his psychological emphasis upon childhood, Freud was careful to insist once again that psychoanalysis must not be subordinated to biology:

> I fully agree with Jung [1917] in recognizing the existence of this phylogenetic heritage; but I regard it as a methodological error to seize on a phylogenetic explanation before the ontogenetic possibilities have been exhausted. I cannot see any reason for obstinately disputing [like Jung] the importance of infantile prehistory while at the same time freely acknowledging the importance of ancestral prehistory. Nor can I overlook the fact that phylogenetic motives and productions themselves stand in need of elucidation, and that in quite a number of instances this is afforded by factors in the childhood of the individual. And, finally, I cannot feel surprised that what was originally produced by certain circumstances in prehistoric times and was then transmitted in the shape of a predisposition to its re-acquirement should, since the same circumstances persist, emerge in the experience of the individual. (1918b, S.E., 17:97)

In short, ontogeny should not be subordinated to phylogeny, Freud warned, any more than psychoanalysis should be subordinated to biological points of view.

G. STANLEY HALL (1844–1924)

The defections of Jung and Adler soon drew other psychoanalytic enthusiasts away from the Freudian camp, including G. Stanley Hall,

G. Stanley Hall and group at Worcester, Massachusetts, September 1909. *Left to right, standing*: A. A. Brill, Ernest Jones, Sándor Ferenczi. *Sitting*: Freud, Hall, C. G. Jung.

professor of psychology and pedagogics at Clark University, and its president as well. Hall, as I have already said, had initially been attracted to Freud's ideas owing to their pervasive ties with his own geneticism. Although Hall continued to praise what he saw as "the immense genetic significance" of psychoanalysis, he increasingly diverged from Freud on important phylogenetic grounds. Hall hinted at these biological reservations, especially concerning Freud's overemphasis of sexual matters, in a 26 September 1913 letter to his Viennese colleague. "I cannot but feel that sooner or later psychologists must break into the big open field of phylogeny and postulate many rather specific influences of the development of the race upon that of the individual, as Stekel seems to have gone far in doing in some respects" (quoted in Ross 1972:405).[5] Hall was already at work, as he further apprised Freud, on a study of childhood fears and anger, two emotions that he

5. Hall's reference to Stekel is actually a circuitous reference back to himself. Stekel (1912) had roused Hall's interest by citing the latter's own "A Study of Fears" (1897), about which Stekel had made the following remarks in a chapter entitled "General Psychology of Fear": "*The kernel of truth in his* [Hall's] *doctrine is the fact that fear is in part inherited.* It is, of course, unthinkable that fear should not be inherited through the flight of ages. Millions of years of fear certainly do not remain without influence on the brain" (1923 trans.:384).

considered to be just as susceptible to Freudian repression as the sexual ones so emphasized by Freud. A year later Hall reiterated this divergent position in his "A Synthetic Genetic Study of Fear" (1914). And the following year, in a paper entitled "Anger as a Primary Emotion, and the Application of Freudian Mechanisms to Its Phenomena," Hall insisted that fear, anger, and hunger are all "just as primary, aboriginal and independent as sex" itself (1915:82). Freud's response to Hall's show of autonomy was to label him "whimsical" and "unreliable"; and in 1914, reacting to the news that Hall had invited Alfred Adler to lecture in America, he sarcastically proclaimed to Ferenczi, "Presumably the object is to save the world from sexuality and base it on aggression" (cited by Jones 1955:134, 205).

Six years later, a new edition of *Three Essays on the Theory of Sexuality* (1920) surveyed the problematic relationship that had prevailed between psychoanalysis and biology for more than two decades. Freud observed that the progress of psychoanalytic studies displayed two sides—a psychological one and a biological one—which had unfortunately not enjoyed the same fate:

> The purely psychological theses and findings of psycho-analysis on the unconscious, repression, conflict as a cause of illness, the advantage accruing from illness, the mechanisms of the formation of symptoms, etc., have come to enjoy increasing recognition and have won notice even from those who are in general opposed to our views. That part of the theory, however, which lies on the frontiers of biology and the foundations of which are contained in this little work is still faced with undiminished contradiction. It has even led some who for a time took a very active interest in psycho-analysis to abandon it and to adopt fresh views which were intended to restrict once more the part played by the factor of sexuality in normal and pathological mental life. (1905d [1920], S.E., 7:133)

Indeed, Fliess, Adler, Jung, Stekel, Hall, and others had all been among Freud's most ardent supporters until biological assumptions finally came between them and the master. But the problem was not in psychoanalysis, Freud still insisted. Resistance to his discoveries, and the ever-present temptations of a priori biological counterarguments, were both too great, he believed, to prevent such defections (1914d, S.E., 14:19, 23–24, 55–56).

THE GENERAL RECEPTION OF FREUDIANISM:
FREUD REINTERPRETED

It is a singular fact in connection with Freud's theories that they have been received as a predominantly environmentalist doctrine. Thus they have generally been taken for something they are not, namely, a refutation of the role of heredity (and hence biological determinants) in mental illness. The reception of Freud's doctrines has therefore proceeded hand in hand with their distortion and reinterpretation as a "pure psychology." Why has this been so?

From the very outset, the fashionable mystique that grew up around analytic psychotherapy derived largely from the accidental, experiential considerations that were communicated about Freudian childhood. Patients and analysts alike were captivated by the environmental component of Freud's theories. Gone were the days of the hopeless diagnoses that had been so natural under the theory of hereditary degeneration. With Freudian psychoanalysis, a totally new era in the treatment of mental diseases had apparently arrived. Even though Freud himself had ruled out curing the acute psychoneuroses, many younger psychoanalysts were considerably more optimistic than the master. This optimistic reaction was especially true of Americans, who, more than any other nationality, flocked to Vienna to learn about Freud's new science of the mind.[6]

Even Freud's European followers were, with the principal exception of Jung, more environmentally predisposed than Freud. Freud's initial impression upon meeting Ernest Jones, conveyed in a letter to Jung of 3 May 1908, is relevant in this connection: "Jones is undoubtedly a very interesting and worthy man, but he gives me a feeling of, I was almost going to say racial strangeness. He is a fanatic. . . . He denies all heredity; to his mind even I am a reactionary. How, with your moderation, were you able to get on with him?" (*Freud/Jung Letters*, p. 145). Filled with the youthful spirit of revolutionary liberalism, Freud's followers reenacted the same revolt against biological determinism that Freud himself had championed during the 1890s. But where he had been forced to reevaluate his initial zealousness after the collapse of his seduction theory, his followers met with no such restraining influence. Fritz Wittels later recalled of the movement's earliest members how "they [had] hoped a psychoanalytic revolution would transmute the Victorian Era into a Golden Age. Freud . . . remained the most sober and cautious of them all" (Hale 1971:351; Wittels 1948:397–98).

Thus Freud, already in his fifties by the time the psychoanalytic movement had become a reality, found himself separated from his disciples by a classic generation gap in scientific thought (cf. Feuer 1974). Indeed, Freud's followers encountered him at a time when his environmentalist leanings, together with his therapeutic optimism, were in decided retreat. To Jung, Freud confessed as early as 6 December 1906: "I should not even claim that every case of hysteria can be cured by it [the psychoanalytic method], let alone all the states that go by that name. . . . It is not possible to explain anything to a hostile public; accordingly I have kept certain things that might be said

6. On the American environmentalist reception of Freud, see Nathan Hale's valuable in-depth study *Freud and the Americans* (1971:332–433, especially 349–52), Shakow and Rapaport (1964), and Burnham (1967).

concerning the limits of therapy and its mechanism to myself, or spoken of them in a way that is intelligible only to the initiate" (*Freud/ Jung Letters*, p. 12). Paralleling his sober clinical persuasions, Freud's theories took on a more constitutionalist cast with time. "Constitution is everything," he remarked on his eightieth birthday to a much surprised Ludwig Binswanger (1957:21 n.). "My discoveries are not primarily a heal-all," he told another student during the 1930s. "My discoveries are a basis for a very grave philosophy. There are very few who understand this, *there are very few who are capable of understanding this*" (H. D[oolittle] 1956:25). Freud was right. Very few people *have* understood his grave philosophy. Hence it also is that his controversial notion of a death instinct, which gave theoretical expression to his therapeutic pessimism, was equally unacceptable even to his own followers. In short, between Freud, his followers, and the public more generally there remained a major gap of communication and understanding about the nature/nurture issue.

Ironically, it was Freud himself who laid the crucial groundwork for an environmentalist and purely psychological reinterpretation of his thinking. Knowing that his innovative and far-reaching paradigm of mind needed considerable time to be tested, Freud actively sought to limit his followers to the safer domain of pure psychology. Those who did not heed his warnings were banished, as we have seen, from the psychoanalytic movement. Once, when prompted to define his attitude toward the organic approach to mental illness that Adler and Stekel had termed *organ language*, Freud unhesitatingly replied: "I had to restrain the analysts from investigations of this kind for educational reasons. Innervations, enlargements of blood vessels, and nervous paths would have been too dangerous a temptation for them. *They had to learn to limit themselves to psychological ways of thought*" (Weizsaecker 1957:68, letter of 16 October 1932; italics added). Inasmuch as the loyal followers indeed turned out, just as Freud had hoped, to be model "psychological" ones, it is hardly surprising that they lost little time after Freud's death in proclaiming a "new environmentalism" within the orthodox branch of the movement. (The expression "the new environmentalism" is from Hartmann [1956:435], who refers back to Kris [1950*b*].) "It was they," Burnham similarly notes of Freud's followers, "who particularly . . . saw in his [Freud's] writings the 'purely psychological' level of discourse. Those born later than Freud were more at ease than he with [psychical] 'fictions' . . . , that is, hypothetical models . . ." (1974:197, n. 6).

The more psychological orientation of Freud's followers also made it all the easier for them to accept his doctrines independently of the biogenetic and Lamarckian assumptions that had helped to inspire these views. Both the Lamarckian and recapitulation theories had come under mounting attack during the 1920s as biologists became more skeptical about acquired characteristics being transmitted to subsequent generations. "Freud's Lamarckian propensities [were] much regretted by many of us . . . ," Ernst Kris (1956:632) later frankly commented.

Certain of Freud's followers, most notably Ernest Jones, actually sought to dissuade Freud from endorsing such controversial views in his later years. Jones recounts:

> How immovable he was in the matter I discovered during a talk I had with him in the last year of his life over a sentence I wished him to alter in the Moses book in which he expressed the Lamarckian view in universal terms. I told him he had of course the right to hold any opinion he liked in his own field of psychology, even if it ran counter to all biological principles, but begged him to omit the passage where he applied it to the whole field of biological evolution, since no responsible biologist regarded it as tenable any longer. All he would say was that they were all wrong and the passage must stay. And he documented his recalcitrance in the book with the following words: "This state of affairs is made more difficult, it is true, by the present attitude of biological science, which rejects the idea of acquired qualities being transmitted to descendants. I admit, in all modesty, that in spite of this I cannot picture biological development proceeding without taking this factor into account." (1957:313; see also Freud 1939a, S.E., 23:100)

"But we can't bother with the [objecting] biologists," Freud just as dauntlessly informed Joseph Wortis during a 1930s discussion about Lamarckism, adding, "We have our own science" (Wortis 1954:84, analytic session of 23 November 1934).

What characterized the younger analysts' reinterpretation of Freudian doctrine also characterized their historical perception of Freud the man. In particular, a strictly psychological conception of the origins of psychoanalysis allowed Freud's followers to envision his Lamarckian and biogenetic assumptions as "late" and "peripheral" additions to his theoretical repertoire. Freud was generally seen as having been spurred on in this respect by the more speculative tendencies of Ferenczi and Jung, who became convenient scapegoats for explaining Freud's own endorsement of these biological principles.[7] In his biography of Freud, Ernest Jones later psychoanalyzed Freud's Lamarckian gullibility away by attributing it to his having heard, as a young child,

___

7. Wittels (1924b:168) writes, for example: "Prior to 1910, hardly any mention of phylogenesis can be found in Freudian teaching. When some of the Freudians, and especially Jung, began to lay stress on phylogenetic considerations, Freud became uneasy." But theoretical difficulties, Wittels adds, eventually forced Freud to follow suit. See also Jones (1957:324, 329) and Robert Fliess (1956:9) on the late arrival of phylogenetic thinking to Freudian theory and the roles of Jung and Ferenczi in this connection. Concerning the supposedly minimal impact of such ideas upon Freud, Shakow and Rapaport (1964:32, n. 37) have spoken of Freud's "credulous [Lamarckian] streak" and have argued that he "kept such notions in a distinct compartment, well separated from his real work." Glover (1950:43) likewise insists: "The whole structure of Freudian metapsychology is unaffected by his incursion into the region of phylogenetic speculation." Similarly, Ritvo (1974:187–88) concludes: "Fortunately Freud's use of the now discredited ideas of recapitulation and the inheritance of acquired characteristics were not crucial to his scientific theory. They were used almost exclusively in connection with his speculations in applied psychoanalysis." See further Kris (1950a:112), Schur and Ritvo (1970:610), and Burnham (1974:210) for additional historical judgments along these lines. As a corrective, see Heyman 1977.

Freud about 1935.

the Bible story in which God punishes the iniquity of the fathers in the children of successive generations. "For, according to Freud, it was, above all, guilt and fear that were transmitted in this fateful manner" (1957:313–14).

If Freud's biogenetic and Lamarckian propensities have provided ample motive for recasting the history of his discoveries, they are only part of the reason why his disciples have so eagerly made him into a crypto-biologist. In this connection, one must appreciate precisely what it is about Freud's ties to biology that his followers have considered so dangerous. Many analysts, particularly those with psychosomatic interests, have long recognized that Freud's theories are in large part biological. And in the period when Freud's quantitative conception of the libido and his theories of *Trieb* ("drive"), abreaction, actual neurosis, and so forth were in greater favor than they are today, those who shared Freud's economic and biophysical views were especially proud to acknowledge their own intellectual ties to biology.[8] But the views of those analysts with a biological orientation were not the decisive ones when, after Freud's death, his loyal adherents created a formalized biographical tradition. The chief aim of psychoanalyst-historians such as Ernest Jones, Ernst Kris, James Strachey, and others was to show that psychoanalysis emerged in a manner that, above all, was consistent with psychoanalytic theory itself. Thus the crucial issue for these psychoanalyst-historians was not whether psychoanalysis partook of biological points of view; that was undeniable. Rather, it was precisely *how* and *when* did Freud's theories acquire these biological points of view—*inductively* and later, through purely psychoanalytic research; or as original foundations of the psychology that was then largely and *deductively* derived from them (see pp. 18–20). What for Ernest Jones had once been a small bit of useful propaganda—namely, the strenuous claim that psychoanalysis, though containing biological implications, "does not . . . [involve] any deductive application of biological principles" to mind (1930:604)—became a far more elaborate dogma when bolstered by the psychohistorical interpretations of his Freud biography. Of the various dilemmas inherent in Freud's manifest biological persuasions, Jones solved the majority when he organized his "Biology" chapter in the Freud biography around the theme of Freud's contributions *to* biology. "Freud had thus in his purely psychological studies lighted on biological laws of the widest validity" (1957:305). "All in all," that chapter ends, "we may say that Freud's contributions to biology, though incidental to his work rather than deliberate, will prove to be increasingly valuable [to biologists]" (p. 314). As I shall show in my next chapter, this blatant reversal of historical cause and effect has also required a sophisticated substitute history—a "myth of the hero"—to portray the origins of psychoanalysis in thoroughly psychoanalytic terms.

8. See, for example, Brun 1926; Weiss and English 1943:iv, 17; Fenichel 1945: 5–6; Alexander 1950:33, 75–76; and Dunbar 1954: passim, especially pp. 32–37, where Brun's (1926) outspoken views are summarized.

SUMMARY AND CONCLUSION

In the final analysis, Freud, his opponents, his followers, and his public have all joined forces in turning his doctrines into a crypto-biology. This elaborate process has been determined by at least five distinct influences:

1. Throughout his productive life, Freud found himself caught between the Scylla of critical opposition, which repeatedly accused him of excessive speculation, and the Charybdis of his unsolved psychobiological problems. As is often the case in science, he consequently sought to portray his discoveries as rooted in empiricism and, in so doing, emphasized his debt to his clinical materials and to the psychoanalytic method, not to theoretical (and often biological) inspirations.

2. Freud, in perhaps the bulk of his psychological theories, was reacting against the extreme somatic and hereditary traditions of medicine that had immediately preceded him. Seeing himself as the discoverer of a new psychology, he continually brought biologically inspired ideas into line with his "psychological" self-identity.

3. Freud frequently failed to appreciate how extensively biological, Darwinian, and particularly biogenetic assumptions pervaded his psychoanalytic thinking. The influence of biology upon Freud and his post-Darwinian generation was so remarkably widespread as to be generally unrecognized in its totality. We are all Freudians today in this same invisible sense.

4. Freud feared disagreement and defections over the biological premises of his psychology—a fear that was repeatedly realized during his lifetime. He also feared oversimplification from the uncritical use of biology. Thus, when he objected to those who would introduce "a priori" biological assumptions into psychoanalysis, he was really objecting to the possible installation of "unfriendly" biological assumptions. At the same time, Freud firmly believed that his magnificent paradigm of mind needed considerable time to be tested before deviation could fruitfully be allowed. He therefore sought independence from those neighboring disciplines that possessed greater ontological clout, and that threatened to dictate to his young and impressionable discipline. "I try in general," he characteristically proclaimed, "to keep psychology clear from everything that is different in nature from it, even biological lines of thought" (1914c, S.E., *14*:78–79).

5. Freud's theories have consistently been reinterpreted, especially by an optimistic America, in a more purely environmentalist, and hence more psychological, vein than Freud ever intended. Furthermore, his own followers—taught by him to "think psychologically"—did just that when they, too, reinterpreted the essential nature and historical origins of his teachings. As a consequence, those initial adherents who broke from the orthodox ranks of the psychoanalytic movement (Adler, Jung, Stekel, Hall, and numerous Neo-Freudians) have generally better

understood the biological assumptions of psychoanalysis than those who remained loyal to Freud.

"What will they do with my theory after my death?" Freud once pondered in the presence of a student, adding, "Will it still resemble my basic thoughts?" (Choisy 1963:5). In terms of its present crypto-biological status, it would not be too much to say that Freudian theory, as Freud himself feared, indeed became greatly distorted after his death. Such distortions in the content of Freudian theory are not unlike the neurotic processes of repression, condensation, displacement, compromise formation, and so forth that Freud himself seized upon in a clinical context when he created the whole science of psychoanalysis. But we should not be too surprised by such striking parallels, since Freud and his movement have passed through a quasi "obsessional neurosis" of their own during their long and conflict-ridden quest for recognition as an independent branch of modern science. It is to this wider pattern of myth and distortion in the history of psychoanalysis that I now turn.

13

The Myth of the Hero
in the Psychoanalytic
Movement

Few scientific figures, if any, are as shrouded by legend as is Freud. How and why has this legend become so well developed? And what does the Freud legend tell us about the man and his psychoanalytic movement?

Above all, the traditional account of Freud's achievements has acquired its mythological proportions at the expense of historical context. Indeed, historical "decontextualization" is a prerequisite for good myths, which invariably seek to deny history. This denial process has followed two main tendencies in psychoanalytic history—namely, the extreme reluctance of Freud and his loyal followers to acknowledge the biological roots of psychoanalysis, thus transforming Freud into a crypto-biologist (Chapter 12); and the creation and elaboration of the "myth of the hero" in the psychoanalytic movement. Virtually all the major legends and misconceptions of traditional Freud scholarship have sprung from one or the other of these tendencies.

In this chapter I shall explore the second of these sources of distortion in psychoanalytic history—the myth of the hero. I shall also attempt to show how the two great myths of Freud as hero and Freud as pure psychologist have achieved their elaborate development by serving highly strategic functions in the psychoanalytic movement as counteractions to the external forces that have long opposed it. In short, it is my contention that the expedient denial and refashioning of history has been an indispensable part of the psychoanalytic revolution. Perhaps more remarkable still is the degree to which this whole process

of historical censorship, distortion, embellishment, and propaganda
has been effected with the cooperation of psychoanalysts who would
instantly proclaim such phenomena as "neurotic" if they spotted them
in anyone else.

THE MYTH OF THE HERO IN PSYCHOANALYTIC HISTORY

As Henri Ellenberger has pointed out, two main features characterize
the myth of the hero in psychoanalytic history. The first of these features emphasizes Freud's intellectual isolation during his crucial years
of discovery and exaggerates the hostile reception given to his theories
by an "unprepared" world. The second feature of the hero legend depicts Freud's "absolute originality" as a man of science and credits him
with the discoveries of his predecessors, contemporaries, rivals, and
followers (Ellenberger 1970:547).

Such myths about Freud the psychoanalytic hero are far from
being just a casual by-product of his highly charismatic personality or
eventful life. Nor are these myths merely random distortions of the
biographical facts. Rather, Freud's life history has lent itself to an
archetypal pattern shared by almost all hero myths, and his biography
has often been remolded to fit this archetypal pattern whenever suggestive biographical details have first pointed the way.

Joseph Campbell, who has surveyed hundreds of examples of hero
myths in *The Hero with a Thousand Faces* (1968), has described the
archetypal hero in detail. Although Campbell does not discuss the Freud
case, his model of the classical hero's life-path can fruitfully be applied to the Freud legend. What is significant historically in the heroic
parallels that follow is not so much the events themselves—which
might easily seem fortuitous to an outsider—but rather that precisely
these coincidental points were eagerly seized upon by Freud's biographers and made central to the Freud legend. Nor does the aura of
heroic myth about Freud invalidate its frequent kernel of biographical
truth; for it is the bona fide heroes, of which Freud was certainly one,
who inspire the best hero myths. It is in this general sense that the
classical myth of the hero seems so suggestive to the thoughtful student
of Freud's life.

According to Campbell's survey, symbolic "rites of passage" and
the theme of a "perilous journey" are typical in such stories. The dangerous journey itself has three common motifs: isolation, initiation,
and return, all of which appear prominently in the Freud legend.[1]
Take the theme of the perilous journey. The initial call to adventure,

1. These and other parallels with the classical hero will be reviewed only briefly
here since they are all documented elsewhere in the text; see especially the Supplement to this chapter, "Catalogue of Major Freud Myths," which serves as a synopsis
not only of this chapter but also of much of this book.

Campbell notes, is usually precipitated by a "chance" circumstance (cf. the remarkable case of Anna O., which antihero Josef Breuer, "intimidated" by his own momentous discovery, would not publish but happened to discuss with the more persistent Freud). A temporary refusal of the call (in Freud's case for some six years) may then occur; if so, its later acceptance may be assisted by another protective figure or guide (cf. Charcot, who subsequently convinced Freud of the lawlike nature of hysterical phenomena and thus led him to return to the whole subject). The hero must now survive a succession of difficult trials, and he may be misled in the process by women who act as temptresses (cf. the blunder of Freud's seduction theory, which temporarily diverted him from discovering infantile sexuality and the Oedipus complex). But a secret helper continues to aid the hero (viz., Fliess in his supposedly invaluable role as a "transference" figure during Freud's courageous self-analysis). At this stage along the "hero-path," atonement with the father is another frequent theme (cf. Freud's coming to terms with his own Oedipus complex following his father's death in 1896).

The most dangerous part of the journey may be overland or on water, but, as Campbell emphasizes, "fundamentally it is inward—into the depths where obscure resistances are overcome, and long lost, forgotten powers are revivified, to be made available for the transformation of the world" (1968:29). The story of Freud's heroic self-analysis follows this last archetypal subpattern in many essential respects and may be compared with such equally heroic episodes as Aeneas' descent into the underworld to learn his destiny or Moses' leadership of the Hebrews during the Exodus from Egypt. Of this "first" self-analysis, Eissler writes, for example: "The heroism—one is inclined to describe it so—that was necessary to carry out such an undertaking has not yet been sufficiently appreciated. But anyone who has ever undergone a personal analysis will know how strong the impulse is to take flight from insight into the unconscious and the repressed. . . . Freud's self-analysis will one day take a place of eminence in the history of ideas, just as the fact that it took place at all will remain, possibly for ever, a problem that is baffling to the psychologist" (1971:279–80). Similarly, another biographer calls the self-analysis "the boldest measure a man has ever tried on himself" (Robert 1966:91). It is said to have been truly "herculean," Freud's "most heroic feat," and so forth (Jones 1953:319; 1955:4). Joseph Campbell, himself a Jung devotee, compares the journey of the archetypal hero to a temporary loss of "ego control" upon entering the forbidding world of the personal unconscious—a journey whose return, he adds, culminates with the victory of the ego over the forces of the unconscious (1968:217).

Having undergone his superhuman ordeal, the archetypal hero now emerges as a person transformed, possessing the power to bestow great benefits upon his fellow man (Campbell 1968:30). Upon his return home, however, the hero usually finds himself faced by nonunderstanding opposition to his new vision of the world. Finally, after a long struggle, the hero's teachings are accepted, and he receives his due reward and fame (cf. Freud's "emergence from isolation" into international recognition [Jones 1955:3]).

Certain aspects of the archetypal hero myth are more developed than others in Freud's life. But the general motif of a journey, with its substages of adventure, isolation, initiation, and return, followed by hostile rejection and then fame, is unmistakable.[2] The analogy of a heroic journey was not lost upon Freud himself, who chose as his motto for *The Interpretation of Dreams* (1900a) the following line from Vergil's *Aeneid*: "*Flectere si nequeo superos, Acheronta movebo* [If Heaven I can not bend, then Hell I will arouse!]"—an allusion to the underworld, that is, the unconscious and its dark forces (*Aeneid* 7. 312; *Virgil*, Loeb Classical Library). Similarly, the theme of a journey is aptly captured by Freud's famous statement that "*The interpretation of dreams is the royal road to a knowledge of the unconscious activities of the mind*" (1900a, S.E., 5:608).

The two subthemes of isolation and rejection have been embellished perhaps more than any other aspects of the Freud legend. I shall therefore discuss these themes in detail, comparing them with the historical reality behind them.

THE RECEPTION OF FREUD'S THEORIES:
MYTH AND ACTUALITY

One of the most well-entrenched legends associated with the traditional account of Freud's life concerns the "hostile" and even "outraged" manner in which the publication of his psychoanalytic ideas was supposedly received. At first, so goes this traditional story, Freud's more creative discoveries, such as his theory of dreams, were "simply ignored." We are told by Ernest Jones (1953:360–61), for instance, that *The Interpretation of Dreams* had yet to be reviewed by a scientific periodical as late as eighteen months after its publication. Jones adds that only five reviews of *The Interpretation of Dreams* ever appeared, and three of them were definitely unfavorable. "Seldom," Jones (1953:361) remarks, "has [such] an important book produced no echo whatever."

But this initial conspiracy of silence did not last long, Jones goes on to assert. When *Three Essays on the Theory of Sexuality* appeared in 1905, Freud's questioning of the sexual innocence of childhood set

2. In an article entitled "Our Attitude towards Greatness," Ernest Jones (1956b) was particularly struck by the "friendly-guide" subtheme of this myth-complex. He mentions in this connection that certain misunderstanding reviewers of his Freud biography lost no time in adding the following three myths to the collection already surrounding Freud's life: (1) that Breuer actually initiated Freud's researches in neuroanatomy; (2) that Freud investigated the case of Anna O. with Breuer; and (3) that Breuer subsequently accompanied Freud to Paris in order to meet Charcot.

off a storm of Victorian protest against his "indecent" theories. "*The Interpretation of Dreams* had been hailed as fantastic and ridiculous," Jones comments, "but the *Three Essays* were shockingly wicked. Freud was a man with an evil and obscene mind. . . . This assault on the pristine innocence of childhood was unforgivable" (1955:12).

Freud has provided a similar impression of the "vacuum" that surrounded him as a result of his novel and increasingly unwelcome theories. "For more than ten years after my separation from Breuer," he wrote in his *Autobiography,* "I had no followers. I was completely isolated. In Vienna I was shunned; abroad no notice was taken of me. My *Interpretation of Dreams,* published in 1900, was scarcely reviewed in the technical journals" (1925d, S.E., 20:48). Freud soon came to recognize, as he tells us in "On the History of the Psycho-Analytic Movement," that "I was one of those who have 'disturbed the sleep of the world,' . . . and that I could not reckon upon objectivity and tolerance." These were the days of Freud's "splendid isolation," as he nostalgically recalled these early years while describing the gloomy prospects that he had then envisioned:

> I pictured the future as follows:—I should probably succeed in maintaining myself by means of the therapeutic success of the new procedure, but science would ignore me entirely during my lifetime; some decades later, someone else would infallibly come upon the same things—for which the time was not now ripe—would achieve recognition for them and bring me honour as a forerunner whose failure had been inevitable. Meanwhile, like Robinson Crusoe, I settled down as comfortably as possible on my desert island. When I look back to those lonely years, away from the pressures and confusions of to-day, it seems like a glorious heroic age. My "splendid isolation" was not without its advantages and charms. . . . My publications, which I was able to place with a little trouble, could always lag far behind my knowledge, and could be postponed as long as I pleased, since there was no doubtful "priority" to be defended. (1914d S.E., 14:22)

This traditional historical scenario of isolation and rejection has served as a congenial model for most subsequent Freud biographers.[3]

If we turn to the actual historical record, following the systematic researches of Bry and Rifkin (1962), Ellenberger (1970), and Decker (1971, 1975, 1977), we find that the initial reception of Freud's theories was quite different indeed from this traditional account. According to Bry and Rifkin, Freud's book on dreams was by no means ignored:

> . . . *The Interpretation of Dreams* was initially reviewed in at least eleven general magazines and subject journals, including seven in the fields of philosophy and theology, psychology, neuropsychiatry, psychic research, and criminal anthropology. The reviews are individualized presentations, not just routine notices, and together amount to more than 7,500 words.

3. See, for example, Wells 1960:187; Robert 1966:119, 190; Costigan 1967: 115; Balogh 1971:47, 65; Duke 1972:33; Fine 1973:77–78; and Mannoni 1974:66, 91.

The interval between publication and review averages about a year, which was not bad at all. For the essay, *On Dreams* [1901a], we have found nineteen reviews, all of which appeared in medical and psychiatric journals, with a total of some 9,500 words and an average time interval of eight months. It appears that Freud's books on dreams were widely and promptly reviewed in recognized journals which included the outstanding ones in their respective fields.

Furthermore, the editors of international annual bibliographies in psychology and philosophy selected Freud's books on dreams for inclusion. In this country [America], *The Psychological Index* listed *The Interpretation of Dreams* within four months of publication. Roughly by the end of 1901, Freud's contribution had been brought to the attention of medical, psychiatric, psychological, and generally educated circles on an international scale.

. . . Some of the reviews are thorough and highly competent, several are written by authors of major research on the subject, all are respectful. Criticism appears after a fair summary of the book's main contents. (1962:20–21)

Thus in contrast to the picture painted by Freud, Jones, and Freud's biographers more generally, Freud's two books on dreams received at least thirty separate reviews totaling some seventeen thousand words (an average of 570 words per review).[4]

Nor were these reviews predominantly hostile to Freud's new theory of dreams. The very first notice to appear—three thousand words in the December 1899 issue of *Die Gegenwart* (Berlin)—described *The Interpretation of Dreams* as an "epoch-making" (*epochalen*) work (Metzentin 1899:389). The psychologist William Stern, whose review Jones (1953:361) characterized along with several others as "almost as annihilating as complete silence would have been," offered the following words of praise for Freud's researches:

> What appears to me valuable above all is [the author's] endeavor not to confine himself, in the explanation of the dream life, to the sphere of imagination, the play of associations, phantasy activity, [and] somatic relationships, but to point out the manifold, so little known threads that lead down to the more nuclear world of the affects and that will perhaps indeed make understandable the formation and selection of the material of the imagination. In other respects, too, the book contains many details of high stimulative value, fine observations and theoretical vistas; but above all [it contains] extraordinarily rich material of very exactly recorded dreams, which must be highly welcome to every worker in this field. (1901:131)

Similarly, Paul Näcke, a psychiatrist of international reputation and a veteran reviewer in the German-speaking medical world, proclaimed of *Interpretation* that "*the book is psychologically the most profound that*

4. When one includes the reviews subsequently located by Ellenberger (1970: 783–86) and Decker (1975, 1977), the aggregate number of notices now stands closer to forty. Not included in this total are additional references to Freud's dream theory that appeared in contemporary textbooks of psychopathology (see Ellenberger and Decker for these additional textbook references).

dream psychology has produced thus far" (1901a:168; Näcke's italics).
Although Näcke, like many other reviewers, disagreed with certain of
Freud's specific dream interpretations, he concluded that "in its entirety
the work is forged as a unified whole and thought through with genius
[*genial durchdacht*]" (p. 168).

Other reviewers were equally impressed by Freud's masterwork.
Wilhelm Weygandt, who was later to oppose psychoanalysis after its
emergence as an organized movement, declared that "the book offers
well-observed, rich material and goes further in effort toward the
analysis of . . . [dreams] than anyone has yet tried" (1901:548–49).
In Geneva, Théodore Flournoy praised Freud's "sagacious penetration
and subtle ingenuity" in laying bare the psychology of the dream life
(1903:73). Additional laudatory opinions could be cited from other
reviews. In short, the general reception of Freud's researches on dreams
may be characterized as favorable and repeatedly offering the judgment
that they were quite remarkable.

As for *Three Essays on the Theory of Sexuality* (1905d)—that
"shockingly wicked" work from which Freud's contemporaries supposedly recoiled—it, too, was well received by the scientific world. "In
the ten reviews we have been able to examine," Bry and Rifkin (1962:
27) report, "certain of Freud's views were questioned, but the more
eminent reviewers welcomed his contribution." The remarks of Albert
Eulenburg, the well-known Berlin neuropathologist, were typical:

> The insightful [*geistvolle*] Viennese neuropathologist, whose psycho-
> analytic researches have proven to be so significant for the understand-
> ing of hysteria, dream life, and . . . the theory of wit, has recently again
> presented us with a ripe fruit of his studies. . . . [The work] throws a
> wealth of new ideas and often arresting and dazzling aperçus into the
> still unilluminated, nocturnal darkness of sexual life—[views] which one
> cannot cursorily pass over regardless of how one takes a stand on them
> in detail. . . . (1906:740)

Paul Näcke, who had earlier praised Freud's *Interpretation of
Dreams,* reaffirmed his admiration for the author of *Three Essays*:

> The reviewer would know of no other work that treats important
> sexual problems in so brief, so ingenious, and so brilliant a manner. To
> the reader and even to the expert, entirely new horizons are opened up,
> and teachers and parents receive new doctrines for the understanding
> of sexuality of children. . . . Admittedly, the author certainly generalizes
> his theses too much. . . . Just as everyone especially loves his own chil-
> dren, so does the author love his theories. If we are not able to follow
> him here and in so many other matters, this detracts very little from the
> value of the whole. . . . The reader alone can form a correct idea of the
> enormous richness of the contents. *Few publications might be so worth
> their money as this one!* (1906:166; Näcke's italics)

Echoing Näcke's words, Numa Praetorius concluded in his annual
review of the sexology literature for Magnus Hirschfeld's prestigious
Jahrbuch für sexuelle Zwischenstufen that no work published in 1905

had equaled Freud's for its insight into the problems of human sexuality (1906:748).

Of particular historical significance is that not one reviewer criticized Freud for his discussion of infantile sexual life, although some did question in this connection his more specific assertions about oral and anal erotogenic zones. "Nothing is more remote from the truth," Ellenberger reminds us, "than the usual assumption that Freud was the first to introduce novel sexual theories at a time when anything sexual was 'taboo'" (1970:545). And as Johnston cogently sums up the growing historical consensus: "Whatever else may have isolated Freud in Vienna, it was not his scrutiny of sex. In a city where Sacher-Masoch, Krafft-Ebing, and Weininger were read with nonchalance, Freud's pansexualism hardly shocked anyone" (1972:249). (See also Chapter 8 for my own documentation of this general historical conclusion, which I am nevertheless about to qualify.)

Origins of the "Hostile-Reception" Myth

In the light of such blatant contradictions between the actual historical facts and the traditional account of Freud's reception, one is naturally curious to understand what could have initiated such a myth. Although Freud indeed complained genuinely in his letters to Fliess, bemoaning the unappreciative and inadequate reception given to his book on dreams, he was both incompletely aware of the actual attention given it (especially outside Vienna) and peculiarly jaundiced toward even the most favorable reviews that came to his attention.[5] Thus he considered that first review in *Die Gegenwart* to be "empty" and "inadequate," although he still managed to "forgive it" on account of "the one word 'epoch-making'" (*Origins*, p. 306; Metzentin 1899). Several months later, Freud reported to Fliess that the *Umschau* had carried "a short, friendly and uncomprehending review." That was the notice by Oppenheimer concluding that Freud's theories were "very ingenious and the whole book very much worth reading" (1900:219; *Origins*, p. 320). Similarly, Freud was "astonished to find a really friendly *feuilleton* article in a newspaper, the *Wiener Fremdenblatt*," a statement that follows Freud's despondent claim that "not a leaf has stirred to show that the interpretation of dreams meant anything to anyone" (*Origins*, p. 311; H. K. 1900).

What Freud evidently wanted—and had fully expected—was a series of lengthy articles in the more technical medical weeklies in Vienna, Berlin, and other major European cities. When these were not forthcoming (for reasons that I shall treat in a moment), he despaired

5. Freud definitely knew of seven reviews—those by Metzentin (1899), Burkhardt (1900), David (1900), Oppenheimer (1900), Karell (1900), Leyen (1901), and a review (by H. K.) in the *Wiener Fremden-Blatt* (1900). He probably also knew of others, since he reported to Fliess in 1901 that the father of one of his patients had "taken zealously" to sending him cuttings of every newspaper and magazine article in which either Freud's name or his dream book was mentioned (*Origins*, p. 332, letter of 4 July 1901).

of receiving scientific recognition even within his own lifetime and became more than ever convinced that he was "isolated," and that his
theories were "shunned" (*Origins*, p. 307, 318; Decker 1975:140).

Freud's disillusionment was apparently compounded by a series of
misapprehensions on his part. In addition to his incomplete picture of
the actual reception of his book, he failed to appreciate that his work
had fallen between normal disciplinary divisions as they then existed
in the fields of psychology and medicine. The study of dreams, being
part of psychology, was then considered to fall under the formal aus-
pices of philosophy, not medicine. "*The Interpretation of Dreams* was
reviewed in nonmedical journals," Bry and Rifkin (1962:23) explain,
"because the topic was not suitable for the medical review literature.
The essay *On Dreams*, however, was reviewed in medical and psychiatric journals because it appeared in a series [Leopold Löwenfeld's *Grenzfragen des Nerven- und Seelenlebens*] with the word 'nervous' in its
title." As for the favorable impression that *Interpretation* made in the
popular and literary press, this apparently meant little to Freud. "It
seems clear that Freud's ability to convince people with literary interests," Decker (1975:134) observes, "was never in doubt. But for a number of years Freud was not particularly interested in the lay reaction;
it was medical acceptance that he at first craved." [6]

All of this is not to say that Freud and his theories met with no
significant opposition whatsoever, for they did indeed, especially as the
psychoanalytic movement gained organized momentum. The point I
wish to make here is that strong opposition was not the initial reaction
to Freud's theories; nor was any opposition premised upon the purported triumvirate of sexual prudery, hostility to innovation, and anti-
Semitism that dominates the traditional historical scenario on this
subject. Furthermore, it is important to distinguish Freud's theories
of dreams and sexual development, which were both well received at
first, from his theories of the neuroses, which provoked increasingly
lively opposition owing to his predominantly single-factor (sexual) explanation. Opposition to Freud's etiological theories dates from the
mid-1890s, but even here the objections raised by Freud's contemporaries were far more rational—and justified—than psychoanalyst-
historians have been willing to admit (Chapter 3).

Sources of Opposition to Freud's Theories

If we look at the scientific opposition to Freud's psychoanalytic
theories in specific terms, we see that there were four principal foci
of criticism that characterized such debate during the first decade of
the twentieth century: (1) Freud's controversial views on etiology;

---

6. It is significant in this connection, as Decker (1975:141) also notes, that
many of those who later became Freud's followers had at one time possessed strong
literary interests that received reinforcement from reading Freud. See, for instance,
Sachs (1944:39-40). Similarly, Otto Rank first presented himself to Freud carrying
a manuscript copy of his *Art and Artist* (Jones 1955:8).

(2) Freud's innovative psychoanalytic methodology, which was seen by some as unscientific; (3) the revolutionary boldness and frank language with which Freud championed his various theories; and (4) the rise of psychoanalysis as an organized movement. To show just how far removed the controversies over psychoanalysis actually were from a simple clash between "the hero" and his "tradition-bound" opposition, I shall briefly review each of these sources of contention.

Freud's controversial views on sexual etiology. As previously mentioned, perhaps the major source of medical opposition to Freud was neither his conception of the dream process nor his doctrine of sexuality, but rather his etiological interpretation of the neuroses. What is more, Freud's opponents saw him not so much as a "depraved revolutionary" on this subject as they did a misguided reactionary who was harking back to the superstitions of the past. The psychiatrist Konrad Rieger (1896) was apparently the first to object to Freud's theories on such grounds. After reading Freud's (1896b) exposition on the seduction theory, Rieger concluded that Freud's attempt to unite hysteria with paranoia under the common rubric of sexual etiology threatened to destroy one of the most important distinctions in all of psychiatry. Such a confusion of etiologies, Rieger insisted, "can lead to nothing else but to a simply horrible old wives' psychiatry" (1896:196).

To appreciate Rieger's criticisms, it must be understood that hysteria, as an often sporadic and curable disorder, was thought to have little in common with the predominantly organic and incurable affliction of paranoia. Rieger's apprehensions become even more understandable when one turns to his autobiography (1929), where he explains that he and his contemporaries had been trained in a period when mystical tendencies, including attempted exorcisms of sexual demons from the body of the hysteric, were still remembered in psychiatric circles. Rieger and his generation had effected a break from such superstitions, especially in connection with organically classified diseases like paranoia. It is for this reason that the derogatory phrase "old wives' psychiatry" became such a common epithet among psychiatrists in referring to Freud's seemingly antiquated theories. As Bry and Rifkin have summed up this whole episode:

> The trend of the time was to try to establish a scientific, somatically oriented psychiatry in place of the older theory, which related mental and nervous disorders to disturbances of the affects and emotions, often to sexual disturbances. A theory of the sexual etiology of neuroses could only appear to be, as Möbius put it, "a regrettable backsliding into the popular superstition." [7] Freud [1926e] himself became aware of this background and later called it an excessive reaction to a conquered phase in medicine. The phrase "old wives' psychiatry" implied that Freud was opposed by some of his contemporaries not as a revolutionary, but as a re-

7. Möbius's (1898:214) comments were made in his review of Felix Gattel's (1898) clinical study, in which Gattel had ascribed an exclusive role to sexual factors in neurasthenia and anxiety neurosis. Gattel's views had in turn been inspired by Freud; see Appendix C on Gattel's scientific collaboration with Freud.

actionary, who threatened to undermine a hard-won and precarious discipline in the still young fields of psychiatry and psychology. (1962:14; see also Decker 1971:479–80)

The fact that Freud's medical colleagues remained in the dark until 1905 concerning his important decision, reached eight years earlier, to abandon his seduction theory of psychoneurosis, only added to the reactionary image Freud had already acquired around the turn of the century. In contrast to him, sexologists Havelock Ellis and Albert Moll were conspicuously active at this time in arguing that sexual feelings are normal in childhood, and that they should not, per se, be considered a cause of later sexual pathology (see Chapter 8). When one also recalls that it was precisely such information (along with Ellis's publication of 1903) that Freud later cited in his *Three Essays on the Theory of Sexuality* (1905d) to justify his abandonment of the seduction theory, then one must also respect Freud's infamous Viennese opponent Emil Raimann for having published the same counterargument a year earlier than Freud (Raimann 1904:216). Thus, unlike the myth, certain of Freud's opponents, even prior to 1905, were using the existence of childhood sexuality to refute Freud's own reactionary theories of the psychoneuroses![8]

The findings of the sexologists had likewise been influential in turning the tide against the predominantly environmentalist explanation of sexual pathology that had temporarily gained vogue during the 1890s (Chapter 8). Although Freud (1906a), too, later conceded the need for a more hereditary viewpoint in his work, he still encountered continued opposition from those neuropathologists and psychiatrists who held to the even more organic and hereditary theories of the day (Decker 1971:475–80).

Freud's psychoanalytic methodology. Freud's innovative method of free association elicited criticism on two principal levels. After reading *The Interpretation of Dreams* (1900a), many reviewers judged certain of Freud's specific dream interpretations as arbitrary, unconvincing, and even far-fetched. Several reviewers were also dubious about his new methodology as a whole, considering it unscientific and mentioning their concern over proper disciplinary standards in the young science of psychology. Once again Freud seemed like a reactionary, not a revolutionary, to some of his medical colleagues owing to his retreat into self-observation, symbolic interpretations, and the

8. Ellenberger (1970:873, n. 145) writes of Raimann's (1904) publication that "it is indeed extraordinary that Jones [1953:361] could consider this book a vitriolic attack against Freud." There can be no question, however, as Eissler (1971:362–63) has shown, that Raimann's *Die hysterischen Geistesstörungen* (Hysterical Disturbances of the Mind, 1904) was highly anti-Freudian on the whole subject of hysteria and its treatment. In his Introduction, Raimann declared: "From Vienna a theory went out into the world which proclaims the exclusively sexual root of hysteria. . . . Universally, [a] more or less decided protest was lodged against it. It therefore seemed appropriate to [conduct a] check-up at the same place with similar clinical material and to take a stand on this theory" (1904:iv). That Raimann's stand was clearly negative is demonstrated by the rest of his book (pp. 212–18, 347–48).

sometimes dubious proofs afforded by an overly "free" association of ideas. Thus, William Stern, who had otherwise found many good things to say about Freud's dream researches, commented: "The inadmissibility of this game of dream interpretation [*Traumdeuterei*] as a scientific method had to be emphasized with all trenchancy; because the danger is great that uncritical minds might like this interesting play of ideas and that we would thereby pass into a complete mysticism and chaotic arbitrariness. One can then prove everything with anything" (1901:133). Another reviewer, Hugo Liepmann, reiterated this same general criticism when he stated that "the ingenious artist of thoughts triumphs over the scientific investigator" (1901:239).

Symbolic interpretations were a further source of skepticism about Freud's methodology. Wilhelm Weygandt, who had praised Freud for going deeper into the analysis of dreams than anyone had done before, singled out the special dangers of symbolic interpretations: "But there is often too much of a good thing, and the false paths of an unfruitful symbolism are not avoided" (1901:549).

The same sorts of criticism recurred in psychiatric circles when it came to assessing the reliability of Freud's clinical interpretations. And here the previous doubts about his method of dream interpretation, which Freud was also using to substantiate his clinical theories, only compounded the misgivings of fellow psychotherapists. "I detect the principal source of fallacy," Albert Moll contended of Freud's etiological theories, "in this arbitrary interpretation of alleged [dream] symbols" (1909; 1912a trans.:191).

Still, in spite of such objections it is surprising to learn how many of Freud's later opponents initially accepted and even employed his new clinical methods (Decker 1971). As late as 1905, Hermann Oppenheim called Freud's clinical work "original," "significant," and "ingenious" before changing his tune on psychoanalysis a few years later. Freud's study of obsessional neurosis, Oppenheim acknowledged in this earlier period, was "a very interesting attempt by a gifted physician to grasp a stubborn disease by its roots." Oppenheim also accepted Freud's childhood sexual etiology for the phobias of adult neurotics as being "valid for a large number of cases" (1905:1152, 1158, 1161). Another influential psychiatrist who initially supported Freud's new methods, together with the frequent diagnosis of sexual neurosis, was Theodor Ziehen (1902b:499, 505–7). Between 1898 and 1907, Ziehen accepted eleven different psychoanalytic papers for publication in his journal, *Monatsschrift für Psychiatrie und Neurologie*, including four by Freud. "In remembering Ziehen only as an enemy of psychoanalysis," Decker points out, "one leaves out almost ten years of his professional career during which he occasionally practiced psychoanalysis himself, never condemned it, and reported its efficacy in certain situations" (1971:466). Finally, Ziehen's early attitude toward Freud, which showed admiration for Freud's works while reserving judgment on certain issues, was typical of the medical profession more generally in the period from 1895 to 1907.

Freud's revolutionary style. Freud's style as a thinker and writer could not have failed to strike his readers as that of a revolutionary personality in science. On the subject of sex, this circumstance attached a stigma to Freud's name, especially after his views had begun to circulate outside professional circles. Freud was definitely not one to retreat into veiled allusions or, like Krafft-Ebing, to employ the Latin language when discussing sexual matters. Havelock Ellis later testified to the novelty of Freud's written approach, emphasizing that "in the matter of expression and speech his attitude was completely revolutionary. . . . In a simple, precise, and detailed manner he described the sexual phenomena presented by his patients, without attenuation or apology, but as a matter of course. This had never been done before in medical literature" (1939a:310). It was especially in his discussions of infantile sexuality, Ellis further remarks, that Freud exhibited the unmistakable stamp of his revolutionary boldness by using such deliberately startling terms as "incest" and "Oedipus complex":

> Various medical authorities before Freud had recognized the importance of sex as well as its aptitude to appear in childhood. But they had been careful to make their statements with moderation and to express them temperately, so that they might be accepted without arousing either enthusiasm or hostility. Freud's outspoken and even extravagant presentation of the subject, fortified by a literary skill which has not always been recognized, was, on the one hand, warmly welcomed by those who had never dared to reveal a secret sense of the importance of sexual phenomena, and, on the other hand, indignantly rejected by those who cherished all the ancient traditions of the mingled sacredness and obscenity of sex. (1939a:310–11)

Seen in these terms, it was not only *what* Freud said but *how he said it* that alienated many of his professional colleagues. (Still, the specialists in sexual pathology were generally unfazed by Freud's publications in this sphere and welcomed his outspokenness in contrast to the often dry nature of such publications.) In lay circles the situation was especially divisive; and when Freud's reputation began to achieve notoriety in this domain, his matter-of-fact attitude toward sexuality only served to further polarize the reception of his ideas. In Vienna this polarization occurred earlier than elsewhere, since Freud's unorthodox theories soon became widely known through the reports of patients and fellow physicians (cf. Raimann 1904:217).

One incident in 1901 along these lines illustrates the sort of atmosphere in Vienna that led Freud to consider himself isolated from his contemporaries. At Breuer's urging, Freud was invited to give a lecture on his theories before the Philosophical Society. Freud explained to his hosts that all sorts of intimate and sexual matters would have to be mentioned, and that the lecture would not therefore be suitable for a "mixed" audience. Thereupon two members of the society came to hear the lecture at Freud's home and, having done so, called it "wonderful" and told Freud that "their audience would take no exception to it." A date for the lecture was accordingly set, but at the last minute Freud received an express letter from the society telling him that "some

members had objected after 'all" and asking him, as Freud recounted to
Fliess, "to be kind enough to start by illustrating my theory with in-
offensive examples and then announce that I was coming to objectionable matter and make a pause, during which the ladies could leave the
hall. . . . Such is scientific life in Vienna!" (*Origins*, p. 329). Naturally
Freud was not one to go along with such a scheme, so the lecture had
to be canceled.

G. Stanley Hall encountered much the same problem in America
owing to his own unrestrained manner of writing about sex. "To realize
the material presented," Edward Thorndike wrote in a review of Hall's
Adolescence (1904), "one must combine his memories of medical textbooks, erotic poetry and inspirational preaching" (1904:144). Thorndike had nothing but praise, however, for the staid and dignified treatment of the sexual life of the child by Albert Moll (1909; trans. 1912a).
In an Introduction to the English-language edition of Moll's book,
Thorndike later contrasted Moll with certain other unnamed sensation-
alists (Hall and Freud?) writing on the subject of childhood sex:

> In the case of any exciting movement in advance of traditional custom,
> the forerunners are likely to combine a certain one-sidedness and lack
> of balance with their really valuable progressive ideas. The greater sagac-
> ity and critical power are more often found amongst the men of science
> who avoid public discussion of exciting social or moral reforms, and are
> suspicious of startling and revolutionary doctrines or practices. It is there-
> fore fortunate that a book on the sexual life during childhood should
> have been written by a man of critical, matter-of-fact mind, of long ex-
> perience as a medical specialist, and of wide scholarship, who has no
> private interest in any exciting psychological doctrine [like Freud] or
> educational panacea [like Hall]. (1912:v–vi)

In short, once it appeared to sober scientists such as Thorndike that
Sigmund Freud—like Hall (but unlike their German analogue Albert
Moll)—was a fanatic leading a medical crusade, and that he was unfortunately supported in his endeavors by a growing number of zealous
followers, opposition to Freud's doctrines inevitably increased. Thus we
come to the fourth and last basic source of opposition to psychoanalysis.

The rise of psychoanalysis as a movement. After Jung, Bleuler,
and their Zurich group established contact with Freud in 1906, psychoanalysis reached a certain critical mass as a movement. By the end
of that year, Freud's Psychological Wednesday Society boasted some
twenty members, including Adler, Stekel, Sadger, Federn, Hitschmann,
and Rank. These early followers were a proud and arrogant lot. They
idolized Freud as the first person to have done truly scientific work on
each of the major subjects upon which psychoanalysis had made its
mark—on dreams, the unconscious, child development, and sexual
theory, not to mention the more traditional medical topics of hysteria,
paranoia, neurosis, and the like (Bry and Rifkin 1962:28). Freud himself frequently encouraged this attitude, as when he wrote Jung on
1 January 1907, in the early stages of their relationship: "The 'leading
lights' of psychiatry really don't amount to much; the future belongs

to us and our views, and the younger men—everywhere most likely—side actively with us" (*Freud/Jung Letters,* p. 18). Other prominent members of the medical profession naturally took offense at such blatant disregard for their own work.

Furthermore, since Freud had little time or inclination to answer all the critiques of psychoanalysis that increasingly began to appear in the medical literature, he left this task to his eager and highly combative disciples. These followers resented that psychoanalysis was not better received in medical circles, and in their polemical writings and public statements a spiteful attitude was generally evident. The effect of their pronouncements was to alienate many of those medical men who had at first supported Freud's work. As Shakow and Rapaport observe, many neuropathologists, such as Janet in France and Prince and Sidis in America, "had initially partially accepted Freud's ideas, but this recognition was withdrawn when they later encountered the disregard and acrimony of Freud's pupils. Priority issues came to the fore, disregard was matched by disregard, and argument took the place of any earlier wish for understanding" (1964:107). Some idea of the polemical atmosphere surrounding the rise of the psychoanalytic movement can be gathered from the discussions at the International Congress of Medical Psychology held in Brussels during August 1910. Ellenberger provides a summary of the lively exchanges that took place at this Brussels Congress:

> At times it was as though the young [Freudians] would reply with a massive attack to anything the old would say. An example was Ernst Trömner's paper on "The Process of Falling Asleep" and hypnagogic phenomena. Foremost in the discussion of this paper was Seif, who took exception with the author because he had not quoted Freud and Silberer, adding that "the material was ripe for a psychoanalytic working-through." Forel rose to protest, whereupon Muthmann, Jones, and Graeter energetically supported Seif. De Montet undertook to contradict Freud's theory, and then Trömner reminded the audience that his paper had been on the subject of falling asleep, rather than on dreams. In the discussion of one of the next papers, Vogt protested against Seif's pretention in forbidding him to speak of dreams and the unconscious: "I object that a man like myself who has collected his own dreams since the age of sixteen and has investigated the problems under discussion here since 1894, that is, almost as long as Freud has done and longer than any of his disciples, should be refused the right to discuss these questions by any Freudian!" (Ellenberger 1970:805–6)

The rise of psychoanalysis as a movement thus served to embroil the reception of Freud's ideas even further. Neuropathologists like Oppenheim, Ziehen, Weygandt, Eulenburg, and others, who had originally held a respectful and even friendly attitude toward psychoanalysis, now felt compelled to take a negative public stance on it.[9]

9. But even after Oppenheim had become publicly critical of psychoanalysis around 1908, he was still sending suitable patients for treatment to Karl Abraham. It was only in 1910 that he called, as Jones (1955:109) reminds us, for a boycott of all sanatoria utilizing psychoanalysis. See *Freud/Abraham Letters,* pp. 60, 93.

In addition to the criticisms that had already been raised before Freud acquired a substantial following, common objections against psychoanalysis now began to include: (1) that psychoanalysts were continually introducing their assertions with the statement, "We know from psychoanalytic experience that . . . ," and then leaving the burden of proof to others; (2) that Freud's disciples refused to listen to opinions that did not coincide with their own; (3) that they never published statistics on the success of their method; (4) that they persisted in claiming that only those who had used the psychoanalytic method had the right to challenge Freud; (5) that they saw all criticism as a form of "neurotic resistance"; (6) that psychoanalysts tended to ignore all work that had been done before them and then proceeded to make unwarranted claims about their own originality; (7) that they frequently addressed themselves to the wider lay audience as if their theories were already a proven fact, thus making their opponents seem narrow-minded and ignorant; (8) that so-called wild analysts, or individuals without proper training, were analyzing patients in irresponsible ways; and (9) that Freud's followers were becoming a sect, with all of the prominent features of one, including a fanatical degree of faith, a special jargon, a sense of moral superiority, and a predilection for marked intolerance of opponents.[10] In their contemporary context, such criticisms were considerably more rational and had far more merit than traditional psychoanalytic historians have been willing to admit.

The English Context

It was this *later* opposition to psychoanalysis that Ernest Jones mistakenly confused with the earlier reception of Freud's ideas when he described how psychoanalysis met with icy silence and then with angry derision, and how Freud himself became seen as "a man with an evil and obscene mind." In addition, Jones apparently allowed his own peculiar experiences in England, where scientific discussion of sexual matters was far more restricted than on the Continent, to color his assumptions about how Freud's own sexual theories were generally received. This story is revealing.

In 1908 Jones investigated a case of hysterical paralysis at the West End Hospital in London. He was able to trace the symptoms of his patient, a ten-year-old girl, back to a sexual scene with a slightly older boy. Unfortunately, the girl later boasted to others in the hospital ward that a doctor had been asking her intimate sexual questions. This news got back to the child's parents, whereupon Jones was obliged to resign from his post. As a result of this incident, he was forced to seek a position in faraway Toronto, where he remained for four years (Jones 1959:150–51).

How different the situation in England was from that on the Con-

10. See, for example, Friedländer 1907, 1909; Weygandt 1907; Hoche 1910; and Ellenberger 1970:796–806, 814–15.

Freud in 1919, with his future biographer Ernest Jones.

tinent may be gauged by the reaction of German criminologist Hans Kurella, a decade earlier, to the famous Bedborough trial associated with Havelock Ellis's *Sexual Inversion* (1897). To his friend Ellis, Kurella wrote at the time: "For us on the Continent such a proceeding is altogether incomprehensible. What would become of science and of its practical applications if the pathology of the sexual life were put on the Index?" (cited by Peterson 1928:247). Krafft-Ebing, it will also be recalled, had published the first edition of *Psychopathia Sexualis* in 1886 and had encountered little opposition on the Continent. The reaction in England, however, was once again quite different. Moritz Benedikt (1906:163) reports in his autobiography that when Krafft-Ebing's book was published, he had to dissuade the British Medico-Psychological Association from repealing Krafft-Ebing's honorary membership. In short, what truth there is to Ernest Jones's later reconstruction of the reception of Freud's ideas is largely autobiographical truth peculiar to Jones and to sexual science in England.

The Viennese Context

Just as Ernest Jones's English experience constituted something of a special case from which he later misconstrued the overall reception of Freud's theories, so Freud's Vienna seems to have given an unrepresentative perspective to Freud himself. This circumstance is important because it helps to explain Freud's feelings of isolation around the turn of the century, while it controverts the usual assumption that this isolation was peculiar to him, or that it characterized the whole of his relationship to the scientific world.

In *Wittgenstein's Vienna*, Janik and Toulmin (1973) have shown that Viennese society exerted a pervasive influence upon a whole generation of intellectuals, including both Freud and the philosopher Ludwig Wittgenstein (1889–1951), who grew up in Vienna during the waning years of the Hapsburg Empire. From 1848, when Emperor Franz Josef began his sixty-eight-year rule of Austria-Hungary, the Hapsburg House governed from Vienna with a single guiding philosophy, which was that change, especially revolutionary change, was to be prevented at all costs. According to Janik and Toulmin, Franz Josef was so petrified by the possibility of change that "he refused to replace civil servants appointed by his predecessor, the 'revolutionary' Emperor, Joseph II, even though they were opposed to his policies, insisting that the status quo be preserved in the most literal sense" (1973:37). In this conservative and aristocratic society, which had become increasingly anomalous during the late nineteenth century compared with its more adaptable European neighbors, conformity to the system ruled supreme. Unlimited patriarchal authority and typical Viennese bourgeois values came to reflect the Hapsburgs' own fetish of stability.

Symbolic of Viennese society's display of "false consciousness" was its prevailing conspiracy of silence about sexuality, which served to make the subject a considerable, but covert, preoccupation of the

Viennese. Given a manifest double standard between the sexes, women suffered most from this prevailing moral attitude; and hysteria and frigidity were often the psychological consequences (Janik and Toulmin 1973:46–48; Johnston 1972:240).

It is hardly a matter of coincidence that Freud, whose professional livelihood involved unmasking the forces of social hypocrisy and sexual repression that brought him so many of his patients, should have repeatedly avowed his dislike for Viennese society. As Hanns Sachs, who also grew up in Vienna, has commented, "Freud's personality, his way of thinking as well as living, represents the diametrical opposite of everything that has been described . . . as typical of Vienna" (1944:36). But whereas Jones (1953:293–94) later attributed Freud's hatred of Vienna to Viennese anti-Semitism and to the community's hostile reception of his theories, Freud's feelings must actually be understood in a less personal vein. For as Janik and Toulmin have convincingly argued, Freud was part of a whole generation of alienated Viennese intellectuals who, by virtue of their own moral integrity, stood ipso facto apart from the decadent society in which they lived. Karl Kraus, the witty satirist who attacked the Viennese underbelly with his periodical *Die Fackel* (The Torch); Arnold Schönberg, the composer and conductor; Ludwig Wittgenstein, the philosopher; and Freud himself were all among those who resisted Viennese double-think and generally perceived themselves as morally and spiritually isolated from the society whose values they did not share.

Freud's intense feelings of personal isolation must therefore be seen in this peculiar Viennese light. He cultivated a personal animosity toward Vienna and assumed that the feeling must be mutual. When he came to believe that he had discovered the key to all the psycho-neuroses in repressed sexuality, he imagined himself as a martyr in science who had dared to disturb the Viennese "compact of silence" on this subject. But unlike the situation in England or the experiences reported by Havelock Ellis and Ernest Jones, Freud was never inhibited in his scientific research or in the publication of his results. The extent to which sexuality lay at the root of hysteria and other neuroses may have been hotly contested in the 1890s, but open discussion of such important scientific issues was perfectly acceptable in Viennese medical circles. Freud, however, insisted upon taking scientific criticisms of his theories as an incontrovertible sign of the Victorian morality that he knew to prevail in Viennese society. If repressed sexuality was really the true cause of all neurosis, then refusal to accept this fact had to be taken, he concluded, as a sign of a universal unconscious resistance to his discoveries. Just as Ernest Jones confused the early reception of Freud's theories both with the later period of more heated debate and with his own peculiar English experience, so Freud lumped together the prejudiced with the unprejudiced reactions to his psychoanalytic doctrines. He rationalized his critics, Viennese and otherwise, with the same psychoanalytic mythology that he had fostered about Josef Breuer's defection from his cause (Chapter 3). Thus Freud may indeed have felt isolated in

Vienna, but just how severe or externally imposed this isolation really was is a matter of considerable difference of historical opinion.[11]

As for Freud's autobiographical assertion that "for more than ten years after my separation from Breuer I had no followers," this is an overstatement to say the least (1925d, S.E., 20:48). Aside from Wilhelm Fliess, who, in spite of his fifteen years of intimate intellectual contact with Freud, goes totally unmentioned in Freud's *Autobiography*, Freud's students and sympathizers in this period of "heroic isolation" included Felix Gattel in 1897/98; the first Austrian Nobel Prize winner Robert Bárány in 1897/98;[12] Hermann Swoboda in 1900; Wilhelm Stekel in 1901; and, in 1902, the founding members of the Psychological Wednesday Evenings circle (Stekel, Adler, Kahane, and Reitler). In addition, Freud had begun exchanging letters and publications with Havelock Ellis as early as 1898. By 1906 Freud's reputation as a student of neuroanatomy, hysteria, dreams, the psychopathology of everyday life, and sexuality was worldwide. It is only the later rise of the psychoanalytic movement (together with Freud's destruction of most of his pre-1907 correspondence) that has made this early period seem like a state of heroic isolation.

Freud's Professorial Appointment

I must consider at this point, if only briefly, why Freud was made to wait the unusually long span of seventeen years for his promotion from *Privatdozent* (or Assistant Professor) to *Extraordinarius* (or Associate Professor) at the University of Vienna. Like other purported signs of Freud's scandalous treatment at the hands of official medicine, this episode has lent convincing support to the heroic nature of Freud's early struggles. There is considerable basis for such an interpretation, although not so much as the myth would have it.

In the spring of 1897, Freud had finally been nominated by Krafft-Ebing and Nothnagel for promotion to Extraordinary Professor. As Eissler (1966:183) has shown, the average wait between appointment as *Privatdozent* and promotion to *Extraordinarius* was about eight years in the Medical Faculty. Thus Freud's nomination after eleven and a half years of service was overdue, although not excessively so. Roughly

11. Cf. Ellenberger (1970:448): "There is no evidence that Freud was really isolated, and still less that he was ill-treated by his colleagues during those years [the 1890s]." Roazen (1975:195–97) and Decker (1971, 1977) agree with this judgment. On the other hand, Eissler (1971:351–64) disputes it, citing many instances of Victorian-like attitudes toward the sexual researches of Freud and others. Although Eissler's views provide a healthy corrective to the inevitable swing of the historical pendulum, it is my opinion that he does not sufficiently distinguish the English context of reception from the Continental (and Viennese), the scientific context from the lay, and the justified criticisms of Freud's theories from the unjustified.

12. Bárány won his Nobel Prize in 1914. A year later, Freud told Ferenczi that he had refused to keep Bárány on as a pupil "because he seemed to be too abnormal." Abnormal or not, Bárány never lost his admiration for Freud, and he exercised his coveted privilege as a Nobel Prize winner by nominating Freud for the next Prize. See Jones (1955:189–90) and, for Bárány's study under Freud in 1897 and 1898, Gicklhorn and Gicklhorn (1960:187).

three candidates in ten experienced waits as long or longer; and Freud, who supported himself through private practice, was less closely involved with university affairs than many other *Privatdozenten*. What is particularly unusual about Freud's wait is the additional five-year delay following his nomination. This story is curious and controversial.

Freud's nomination was approved by the Medical Faculty in June of 1897 by a vote of 22 to 10.[13] Freud and his fellow nine candidates were ignored, however, in the annual ratifications by the Minister of Education in 1898 and 1899. Then, in 1900, all the nominees in Freud's group were approved with the sole exception of Freud! Freud did not receive his promotion until 1902, and then it came through the intervention of two grateful patients, Frau Elise Gomperz and Baroness von Ferstel, who both knew the Minister of Education personally and who would not rest until Freud's appointment was confirmed through their considerable influence.[14]

The highly implausible contention of Josef and Renée Gicklhorn (1960) that Freud's promotion was delayed by his excessive preoccupation with making money in his private practice and by his consequent neglect of his teaching duties at the university has convincingly been refuted by Kurt Eissler (1966). The common assumption that Freud's promotion was opposed for anti-Semitic reasons is also not supported by the facts. Seven of the ten nominees in Freud's original 1897 group appear to have been Jewish, while the Minister of Education, von Hartel, had himself publicly condemned anti-Semitism before the Austrian Parliament (Gicklhorn and Gicklhorn 1960:38; Eissler 1966:84; Ellenberger 1970:454).

What *does* appear relevant to Freud's five-year delay is the issuing in early 1898 of a "secret" ministerial decree, which was subsequently discovered in the Austrian state archives and published by the Gicklhorns (1960:104–6).[15] The decree in question had sought to reduce the number of promotions from Assistant to Extraordinary Professor, partly for financial reasons and partly because recent promotions had created an imbalance in the Medical Faculty between the numbers of Ordinary (or Full) Professors (then 25) and the number of Extraordinary (or Associate) Professors (37) eventually supposed to succeed them (Gicklhorn and Gicklhorn 1960:116). For several years, appointments were held up by this decree until a compromise between the Ministry and the Medical Faculty was finally worked out.

13. Only one other candidate among the ten approved, Conrad Clar, received more affirmative votes than Freud, and Clar had been waiting twenty-seven years for his promotion! See Gicklhorn and Gicklhorn 1960:110–15.

14. The Baroness von Ferstel is said by Jones (1953:340) and Sachs (1944:78) to have bribed the Minister by donating an Arnold Böcklin painting that he was eager to have for the Modern Gallery. Actually, as Eissler (1971:350, n. 4) has shown, the painting concerned was a much less valuable piece by Emil Orlik and would hardly have been considered a bribe by Viennese standards.

15. The Gicklhorns (1960) published an unsigned draft of this document. Eissler (1966:20–26) subsequently found the signed version, which differs somewhat from the document published by the Gicklhorns, and his general account of Freud's delayed promotion is considerably more reliable on this and other points.

Yet why Freud alone was passed over in 1900, when all the other nominees in his group were granted their promotions, has remained something of a mystery. One possibility, as his old teacher Sigmund Exner suggested to him in 1902, is that "personal influences" were working against him in the Ministry of Education. It was at Exner's advice, in fact, that Freud then sought a "counter-influence" (Frau Gomperz) in the matter (*Origins*, pp. 342–43). Eissler (1966, 1971), who places considerable weight on Exner's testimony, has also shown that Freud's nomination actually had to be *renewed* in 1902 because the Minister claimed never to have received it (an almost unimaginable circumstance in the Austrian bureaucracy)! That Freud's controversial views on sexual etiology, added to his prior reputation as a fanatic who had defended dubious causes like Charcot and cocaine, might have annoyed someone with influence in the Ministry is certainly not implausible. Nonetheless, it is equally noteworthy that Krafft-Ebing and Nothnagel, Freud's scientific sponsors, as well as two-thirds of the Medical Faculty, unswervingly supported Freud's candidacy throughout the whole affair. Considering that Freud's nomination came at a time when many of his colleagues correctly suspected that his zealous emphasis upon childhood seductions was in error ("a scientific fairy-tale," as Krafft-Ebing dubbed it [*Origins*, p. 167 n.]), the loyal support of the Medical Faculty is all the more impressive.[16] The charitable remarks of Krafft-Ebing (in a handwritten report to the Ministry also signed by Nothnagel and four other professors) are relevant in this regard: "The novelty of these [clinical] researches and the difficulty of their verification allow no hasty judgment at the present time concerning their import. It is possible that Freud overrates these [findings] and generalizes his discoveries too far. In any event, his researches in this field are evidence of unusual talent and [the] ability to direct scientific investigations into new pathways" (Gicklhorn and Gicklhorn 1960:96–97, document dated 10 May 1897).

Above all, the enigmatic episode of Freud's delayed appointment suggests as much about the widespread operation of protection and influence in Viennese life as it does about his irrational rejection by orthodox medicine. In Vienna it was considered customary to seek influences in gaining appointments and promotions; those who did not do so were automatically at a disadvantage (see Stricker 1894:195; and Eissler 1971:349). Freud initially refused to lower himself to such a crude tactical level, and only later did he realize how much needless irritation he might have saved himself had he done a little politicking on his own behalf. As he commented to Fliess at the end of this episode: "In the whole affair there is one person with very long ears . . . ,

16. In contrast to this interpretation, Eissler (1966:168) suggests that the high regard of Krafft-Ebing and Nothnagel for Freud was probably not shared by a majority of the Medical Faculty, and that Freud's nomination was approved primarily through the influence of these two professors, who would have taken a negative vote as a personal defeat. Still, if Eissler's contention is true, one might have expected a much closer vote on Freud's nomination, as was actually the case with six of the other nine candidates in Freud's group.

and that is myself. If I had taken those few steps three years ago I should have been appointed three years earlier, and should have spared myself much. Others are just as clever, without having to go to Rome first" (*Origins,* p. 344).

SCIENTIFIC PRIORITY AS REVOLUTIONARY PROPAGANDA

I turn now to the second aspect of the myth of the hero in psychoanalytic history: the absolute originality that has so often been ascribed to Freud's achievements.

There are many prominent myths associated with the topics of originality and scientific priority in relation to Freud's achievements. One of these is the belief that Freud himself was totally unconcerned about priority issues. As Jones writes, for example, "Although Freud was never interested in questions of priority, which he found merely boring, he was fond of exploring the source of what appeared to be original ideas, particularly his own" (1957:100). In contrast to this statement, Robert Merton (1976) has found from a systematic survey of his writings that Freud expressed a personal concern over priorities on more than 150 separate occasions. He was continually reassessing his relationship to his forerunners, rivals, disciples, and posterity in terms of such priority issues. Characteristically, he even dreamt about priority matters. From Freud's various manifestations of personal concern about priority, Merton concludes: "That Freud was ambivalent toward priority, true; that he was pained by conflicts over priority, indisputable; that he was concerned to establish the priority of others as of himself, beyond doubt; but to describe him as 'never interested' in the question and as 'bored' by it requires the extraordinary feat of denying . . . [the] scores of occasions on which Freud exhibited profound interest in the question, many of those being occasions which Jones himself has detailed with the loving care of a genuine scholar" (1976:39).

Freud's attitude toward Schopenhauer and Nietzsche, whose philosophies so closely resemble the leading tenets of psychoanalysis, is particularly revealing in this regard. Like Freud, both philosophers described the unconscious and irrational sources of human behavior and stressed the self-deluding character of the intellect. But whereas Schopenhauer and Freud considered sexuality as the most important instinct, Nietzsche emphasized the aggressive and self-destructive drives of man. Nietzsche, however, preceded Freud in the use of the terms *sublimation* and *id* (*das Es*) as well as in the idea that civilization is founded upon a renunciation of instinct.

In his *Autobiography,* Freud made a special point of insisting that he had never read Schopenhauer until his own ideas were long since formulated. And to this assertion he added: "Nietzsche, another phi-

losopher whose guesses and intuitions often agree in the most astonishing way with the laborious findings of psycho-analysis, was for a
long time avoided by me on that very account. . . ." Freud's accompanying disclaimer that he was "less concerned with the question of
priority than with keeping my mind unembarrassed," contrasts vividly
with his complaints to Fliess in the 1890s upon finding himself anticipated by someone else (1925d, S.E., 20:59–60; Origins, pp. 126, 135,
231, 262). In point of fact, both Schopenhauer's and Nietzsche's ideas
were so widely discussed within late-nineteenth-century intellectual circles that Freud could not possibly have escaped a reasonably general
education in their doctrines (Ellenberger 1970:277). As has been shown
by McGrath (1967), Freud belonged as a university student to the
Leseverein der deutschen Studenten Wiens (Reading Society of the
German Students of Vienna), a radical, pan-German organization in
which the views of Schopenhauer, Wagner, and Nietzsche were avidly
discussed. The members of this reading society even corresponded
with Nietzsche, telling him of their extreme devotion to his philosophy
and vowing "to strive like you with the strongest will, selflessly and
truthfully, for the realization of those ideals which you have presented
in your writings—specifically, in your Schopenhauer as Educator"
(letter of 18 October 1877, cited by McGrath 1967:193). It is simply
inconceivable that Freud, who was a member of the Reading Society
for five years, was as totally uninfluenced by Schopenhauer and
Nietzsche as he liked to think. The point to be emphasized here, however, is not so much that these two philosophers did influence Freud—
especially since that influence is difficult to trace in any detail—but
rather that Freud was so vehement in repeatedly denying that he could
possibly have drawn anything from their work. How revealing it is to
hear him say, for example, that his occasional attempts at reading
Nietzsche were always "smothered by an excess of interest" (Minutes,
1:359)!

The other side to the ambivalence that Freud and his followers
have so typically exhibited toward priorities in their work is the list of
mythical ones that have repeatedly been claimed on Freud's behalf.
Two specific claims stand out from all the rest. The first is that Freud
discovered the unconscious (Jones 1940a:13), an assertion that was
more common in the early years of the psychoanalytic movement than
it is today. Actually the notion that Freud discovered the unconscious
is historically unfounded and was repeatedly seen as such in his own
day (e.g., Moll 1936:70–71). As Lancelot Whyte (1960:168–69) points
out in The Unconscious before Freud, "the general conception of unconscious mental processes was conceivable . . . around 1700, topical
around 1800, and fashionable around 1870–1880."

There is considerably more historical merit to a related and less
pretentious claim, namely, that what Freud really discovered was the
essential psychical laws and contents of the unconscious mind (see
Jones [1953:397–98], who championed this more limited claim in his
biography of Freud). Closely associated with this modified claim of

priority is another much more dubious but interesting one: that Freud was the first person to recognize the sexual life of the child. For above all, it was repressed childhood sexual complexes that Freud believed to be the core of every adult's unconscious mind. "Why was it that no one, before Freud, noticed," Fritz Wittels (1924b:105) asks, "that infants have erections and that they masturbate . . . ?" Similarly, Ernest Jones (1955:284) states about Freud, "He was certainly the first not only to assert that infants normally experience sexual sensations, but to give a complete description of their variety." [17]

In contrast to these traditional priority claims, I have already shown in Chapter 8 that Freud was preceded by many individuals who recognized both the normalcy and the widespread nature of childhood sexual phenomena, not the least of whom was Freud's friend Wilhelm Fliess (see Chapter 6). Ellenberger sums up the late-nineteenth-century knowledge of this topic with the assertion, "The existence of childhood sexuality was no doubt ignored by many, or considered a rare and abnormal occurrence, but there were those who knew better" (1970: 504–5). What is therefore of considerable interest to the historian of science is why Freud, who certainly knew of many of his own precursors, nevertheless felt justified on more than one occasion in claiming this discovery for himself.[18] Even more puzzling, however, is the question of why Freud later accused none other than Albert Moll, who as early as 1897 had set forth his own views on childhood sexuality in a book read closely by Freud, of *plagiarizing* Freud's (1905d) subsequent discoveries on this subject (*Minutes* 2:48).

When scientists find themselves faced with the fact of multiple independent discovery, acrimonious claims of priority and plagiarism commonly arise owing to the extreme emphasis that science generally places upon "being the first" (Merton 1976:35–42). Freud had a particularly important reason for wanting to be seen as the discoverer of infantile sexuality. He knew that this discovery constituted a prime piece of scientific propaganda in favor of the importance and efficacy of his new method of exploring the mind. Since he considered infantile sexual life to be heavily repressed in unanalyzed individuals, even direct observations, Freud claimed, had previously failed to effect

17. See also Costigan (1967:49) and Eissler (1971:175–76), who ranks Freud's discovery in importance with that of Christopher Columbus.
18. In the *Three Essays* Freud writes under the heading "Neglect of the Infantile Factor": "So far as I know, not a single author has clearly recognized the regular existence of a sexual instinct in childhood; and in the writings that have become so numerous on the development of children, the chapter on 'Sexual Development' is as a rule omitted" (1905d, S.E., 7:173). To this statement Freud appends a long footnote, reading in part: "The assertion made in the text has since struck me myself as being so bold that I have undertaken the task of testing its validity by looking through the literature once more. The outcome of this is that I have allowed my statement to stand unaltered." This same footnote goes on to review a list of works Freud consulted. The list includes Bell (1902), Groos (1899), and Pérez (1886), whose discussions of infantile sexuality Freud apparently considered too brief and superficial to alter his statement. The list does not include either Moll (1897b) or Fliess (1897). See also *Minutes* (2:48), where Freud clearly states that he was the first to discover infantile sexuality; and Jones 1953:350.

this discovery owing to their easy dismissal as "pathological" exceptions. As he later boasted in the fourth edition of *Three Essays on the Theory of Sexuality*, "None, however, but physicians who practise psycho-analysis can have any access whatever to this sphere of knowledge or any possibility of forming a judgement that is uninfluenced by their own dislikes and prejudices. If mankind had been able to learn from a direct observation of children, these three essays could have remained unwritten" (1905d [1920], *S.E.*, 7:133). In short, Freud's claim of priority had symbolic status not only for his new psychological methods but also for his personal courage in applying them to the unconscious and for the controversial conclusions derived from them.

Freud's accusation of plagiarism against Albert Moll must be seen in this light. This charge must also be understood in the context of a considerable mutual rivalry between Moll and Freud, a rivalry that had become greatly aggravated by Moll's vehement opposition to psychoanalysis.

In 1908, the year Freud made his plagiarism charge against Moll, the latter had published a new book entitled *The Sexual Life of the Child* (1909 [1908]). Freud had been eager for his paper "On the Sexual Theories of Children" (1908c) to appear before Moll's book—of whose impending publication Freud had been hearing announcements "everywhere" (Roazen 1975:193). In many ways Moll's book was simply a more up-to-date restatement of the various views on human sexual development that he had presented ten years earlier in *Investigations into the Libido Sexualis* (1897b). But Moll had also taken the opportunity in this new book to present a sharp critique of Freud's own views on the subject. Sexuality, said Moll, had received "an undue extension" in Freud's hands (1909; 1912a trans.:93). Although Moll fully acknowledged the existence of childhood erotogenic zones, including the region of the anus, he was particularly adamant in denying that sucking movements or the voluntary retention of feces had anything to do with sexuality in young children (1912a trans.:91). It was this aspect of Freud's work that led Moll to chide that Freud's ideas had "very little true relationship to the sexual life of the child" (1912a trans.:14).

Moll's criticisms of Freud's *Three Essays* (1905d) were but part of a much wider assault upon psychoanalysis itself. Having employed the psychoanalytic method with some limited success, Moll nevertheless contested whether cures were really achieved by abreaction instead of by suggestion effected through the physician's extreme devotion of time and energy to the patient concerned (1912a trans.:278–79). In any event, Moll believed that suggestive questioning, together with Freud's failure to investigate the sexual life of the child *directly* instead of through retrospective analyses of adults, was the cause of Freud's unjustified extremism about childhood sexual etiology. "The impression produced in my mind," Moll went so far as to assert, "is that the theory of Freud and his followers suffices to account for the clinical histories, not that the clinical histories suffice to prove the truth of the theory.

Freud endeavors to establish his theory by the aid of psycho-analysis. But this involves so many arbitrary interpretations, that it is impossible to speak of proof in any strict sense of the term" (1912a trans.:190).

Shortly after reading Moll's book (and particularly this passage on how Freud's psychoanalytic theories were sufficient to account for his clinical histories but not vice versa), Freud wrote to Abraham in Berlin that "several passages in the *Sexual Life of the Child* really merit a charge of libel"—although he concluded by saying that "prudence and silence" were really the best answer (*Freud/Abraham Letters*, pp. 73–74, letter of 18 February 1909). Freud's considerable antipathy toward Moll vented itself more fully during a group discussion of the latter's book at the Vienna Psychoanalytic Society (meeting of 11 November 1908). After Freud's longtime friend Oskar Rie had presented a review of the book, Freud is recorded as saying:

> PROF. FREUD stresses first that he had expected something from this book, but since listening [to the report], he must now term it an inadequate, inferior, and above all dishonest book. There are two evidences of its dishonesty. Dr. Rie has already pointed out one of them. Strange as it may sound, infantile sexuality was really discovered by him—Freud; before that, no hint of it existed in the literature. . . . Moll gleaned the importance of infantile sexuality from the *Three Essays*, and then proceeded to write his book. For that reason, Moll's whole book is permeated by the desire to deny Freud's influence.
>
> The second evidence has to do with the question of whether Moll read Freud's *Theory of Sexuality*, and in what way he may have read it. He apparently read it selectively, with the result that he failed to draw from it its most important parts. (*Minutes*, 2:48)

"It is a great misfortune," Freud caustically added about Moll's two key notions of detumescence and contrectation, "when a man who is destitute, as Moll is, of original ideas, nevertheless does have an idea for once." Finally, Freud did not hesitate to attribute Moll's scientific failings to a thoroughly objectionable personal nature: "Moll's character is only too well known. Hirschfeld has complained bitterly about him. He is a petty, malicious, narrow-minded individual. He never expresses a firm opinion . . ." (p. 49)—except, evidently, on psychoanalysis.[19]

Freud's peculiar belief that Moll had actually plagiarized Freud's own discovery of infantile sexuality makes considerably more sense if one interprets his accusation in terms of a plagiarism of influence. Freud evidently saw Moll, who was endorsing a "watered-down" version of infantile sexuality, as availing himself of the very psychoanalytic research that Moll appeared in public to be denying. Moll had thereby imputed to himself, Freud thought, a misleading and unwarranted degree of originality at Freud's own expense (Eissler 1971:

19. On the subject of Moll's personality, Freud's remarks were by no means unjustified. Magnus Hirschfeld's complaints about Moll are corroborated by the negative portrait of Moll's character later provided by Moll's friend and scientific associate Max Dessoir (1947:128–29).

176). Furthermore, it was Freud, not Moll, who for years had sacrificed his popularity as a physician by insisting upon the pathogenic significance of premature sexual experiences.[20] Now along came Moll with a book that had virtually nothing favorable to say about Freud,[21] but that owed its success, Freud felt, to an all too "selective" reading of his *Three Essays*.

At the same time, the wrath directed at Moll by Freud and his followers should be understood in terms of Moll's unique and rather disconcerting qualifications as an opponent of psychoanalysis. Unlike other critics, Moll was not so easily dismissed by the usual "repression-resistance" formula of psychoanalytic devotees, for he was a foremost sexologist who claimed to know all about infantile sexuality, and yet who still chose to reject Freud and psychoanalysis on scientific grounds. To make matters worse, Moll was not unaware of his unique and influential qualifications as a Freud critic. "If . . . it is maintained by Freudians," Moll later emphasized, "that the nonrecognition of sexual processes in childhood essentially separates the opponents of psychoanalysis from its adherents, then this is false. Even the opponents do not deny that there are sexual processes in childhood. . . . What the critics deny is that much of what Freud interprets as sexual has anything whatever to do with sexuality" (1926a:277). With an argument like that, Moll was indeed a dangerous threat to the psychoanalytic movement.

Freudians adopted two different strategies in dealing with so bothersome a critic. First, Moll's opposition was privately attributed to his being unequal to the psychoanalytic method (see Alfred Bass's remarks to this effect in *Minutes*, 2:46). Freud, however, adopted a more expedient manner of negating Moll's credibility by adding a footnote to his *Three Essays* portraying Moll as a backward opponent of infantile sexuality (1905d [1910], S.E., 7:174 n.; see also Jones 1955: 114). So Moll achieved the unique, if also contradictory, honor in psychoanalytic circles of being designated the plagiarist of a discovery that he supposedly refused to recognize, and for which his own priority over Freud was well established by almost a decade.

20. Here Freud apparently confused his priority for having insisted upon the importance of sexual events *in* childhood—beginning with the seduction theory, for which Freud's originality was indisputable—with the discovery of *spontaneous* infantile sexuality (see Freud 1905d, S.E., 7:176). In addition, a considerable degree of personal cryptomnesia was involved in Freud's plagiarism charges against Moll. Compare Freud's accusation with his annotations of Moll's (1897b) own prior discussions of childhood sexuality (see Chapter 8). Also relevant is Freud's statement to Fliess in November 1897 that privately he "would not concede priority in the idea [of abandoned childhood erotogenic zones] to anyone" in spite of having found the same idea in Moll's book (*Origins*, p. 231). Indeed, Freud never did publicly recognize Moll's prior contribution to this important aspect of human psychosexual evolution.

21. Moll did manage one compliment in the midst of all his negative judgments about Freud's researches: "The value of Freud's work appears to me to consist chiefly in this, that he has insisted more definitely than other writers upon the reality of subconscious processes." Moll also alluded to certain clinical "advantages of the psycho-analytic method" (1912a trans.:278).

Moll visited Freud at his home in 1909, and both men subsequently provided colorful descriptions of this encounter. "The unpleasant thing about Freud was his great sensitivity," Moll (1936:54–55) recalled about his visit. "He did not like being contradicted. The opposition that I offered to his doctrine, or rather to his fantasies, was taken quite personally by him. . . . I sent in my card. Freud, however, received me with the words: 'No one has attacked me as you have. You accuse us of falsifying our case histories.' In order to demonstrate this, he fetched my book on *The Sexual Life of the Child* [1909] and excitedly showed me a passage from the book (p. 172 [1912a trans.: 190])." Freud's version of this meeting was relayed in a letter to Jung written shortly afterward:

> Moll's visit provided a contrast staged by fate. To put it bluntly, he is a brute; he is not really a physician but has the intellectual and moral constitution of a pettifogging lawyer. I was amazed to discover that he regards himself as a kind of patron of our movement. I let him have it; I attacked the passage in his notorious book where he says that we compose our case histories to support our theories rather than the other way round, and had the pleasure of listening to his oily excuses: his statement was not meant as an insult, every observer is influenced by his preconceived ideas, etc. Then he complained that I was too sensitive, that I must learn to accept justified criticism; when I asked him if he had read "Little Hans" [Freud 1909b], he wound himself up into several spirals, became more and more venomous, and finally, to my great joy, jumped up and prepared to take flight. . . . [A]ll the same I wasn't fully satisfied as I saw him go. He had stunk up the room like the devil himself, and partly for lack of practice and partly because he was my guest I hadn't lambasted him enough. Now of course we can expect all sorts of dirty tricks from him. (*Freud/Jung Letters*, p. 223, letter of 16 May 1909)

The mutual antagonism between Moll and Freud continued unabated to the end of their lives. In his autobiographical *Ein Leben als Arzt der Seele* (1936), Moll later assessed his opposition to psychoanalysis, along with his criticisms of the occult sciences, as one of the major achievements of his life. There he also recalled the amusing story of how he once trained a psychoanalyst for public service. During the First World War, Moll had received a call from the German Colonial Office requesting that he prepare a certain intelligent soldier for immediate medical duty. After learning that he was to be given just four days to complete the man's training, Moll decided the only medical discipline that could possibly be learned in such a brief period was psychoanalysis! Moll therefore asked the soldier if he possessed a good imagination, which the soldier claimed he did. The soldier was then instructed in a few technical terms, like *conversion, repression,* and *the subconscious*, and introduced to a few key dream symbols. Throughout the allotted four days, Moll assiduously rehearsed his pupil, who afterward had to pass a special examination administered by Moll. Accord-

ing to Moll, his "psychoanalyst" served the Fatherland in a commendable fashion, analyzing fellow soldiers for the duration of the war
(1936:192–93).

Years later, when Moll organized and, as a capstone to his career,
was elected president of the First International Congress for Sexual
Research in 1926, Freud ordered a psychoanalytic boycott of the congress owing to Moll's continued opposition to his theories (Jones 1957:
127). In spite of the boycott, the congress was an immense success, and
a second one, this time attended by psychoanalysts, was held four
years later in London.

Priority and Transformations in Ideas

I have treated the relationship between Freud and Albert Moll at
some length because it illuminates several features that were common
to Freud's priority disputes with other important figures in his life (e.g.,
Janet and Fliess). The whole issue of priority disputes in science may be
fruitfully elucidated in terms of *transformations* in scientific ideas. As
Cohen maintains from the vantage point of the intellectual historian:
"It is my belief that all revolutionary advances in science may consist
less of sudden and dramatic revelations than a series of transformations, of which the revolutionary significance can not be seen (except
afterwards, and in retrospect, by historians) until the last great final
step. In many cases the potentiality and force of a most radical step in
such a sequence of transformations may not even be manifest to its
author" (1979: Chapter 4, §2). It follows from Cohen's assertion that
identification with tradition and one's historical predecessors or, alternatively, with innovative causes must exert a powerful influence upon
how the participants of history perceive scientific priority during such
transformations. We should expect a self-declared group of "revolution-
ists" in science, for example, to claim far more novelty for its various
transformational achievements than may appear warranted either to
other contemporary scientists or to historians in retrospect. Moreover,
claims of priority are a natural concomitant of most scientific revolutions, since priority constitutes an important means of bolstering a
movement's revolutionary image. Such claims may well be justified,
but often their legitimacy turns out to lie in a professional, or sociological, rather than in a strictly intellectual aspect of the revolution. Janik
and Toulmin have described an instance of this sort in the birth
of the analytic philosophy movement in England, which arose shortly
after Freud's own movement became a reality:

> If we look carefully enough at the writings of Moore and Russell's im-
> mediate predecessors . . . , it begins to be somewhat mysterious how
> these younger men could present their own philosophical positions as
> such great *intellectual* novelties.
>   . . . Looking back . . . from the present day, however, we can see
> how far the "revolution" . . . was sociological rather than intellectual—
> insisting on the right of academic philosophers to operate as an auton-

omous subprofession, with a specialized set of problems, methods and techniques. (1973:209, 259)

Like the inflated claims of the analytic philosophers, then, the often dubious declarations of priority by psychoanalysts must be appreciated as part of their professional rebellion—one that sought to establish Freud's doctrines outside of official medicine as a new and "independent" science of mind.

Yet once the more extravagant of these numerous priority claims have been discounted, there were few notions that Freud took up and brought to widespread attention that he did not actually transform in *some* novel manner. In the case of such general notions as the unconscious or infantile sexuality, Freud's conceptual transformations supplied convincing corroboration for his supposed priority in "discovering" these phenomena. Shakow and Rapaport have given just such an appraisal of Freud's scientific relationship to Pierre Janet in France and to Morton Prince in America: "If we try to make a balance sheet of Janet and Prince in relation to Freud [and the study of the unconscious], we find that they did have priority over Freud in certain respects. But they cannot be said to have influenced Freud in a specific way, because the essential part of his discoveries lies in precisely the place where he went beyond them. It might be said that by the time their priority [over Freud] was well established, the substance of their claims had vanished" (1964:105).

Similarly, the discovery of infantile sexuality, together with the contemporary difference of opinion as to who actually made it, must also be understood in terms of the multifaceted intellectual transformation of which it was a part. Freud, owing to the whole nature of his psychoanalytic doctrines (but especially the theory of repression), felt his title to a discovery to be self-evident in this connection. By contrast, colleagues like Havelock Ellis and Albert Moll, whose own work on childhood sexuality had sought to discount the "pathological" consequences of such everyday phenomena, saw Freud's discoveries (and his etiological formulas) as more dubious and his priority claims as unjustified. Thus what Moll, and later Ellis, appraised as "an undue extension" of childhood sexual theory by Freud, Freud deemed as the essential justification of his scientific priority over them.[22] Hence it also was that Moll could later proclaim, "In actuality, so many instances of sexuality among children had already been written about before him that Freud's alleged priority in this matter is totally out of the question" (1936:71; also see Ellis's [1939a:310] similar verdict).

In short, depending upon one's position within the extensive intellectual transformation pioneered by Charcot, Breuer, Freud, Janet, Krafft-Ebing, Moll, Ellis, Fliess, and numerous others, the issue of

22. See, for instance, Ellis and Moll's (1912:618–19) joint survey of contemporary theories of sexual pathology, which includes a critical discussion of Freud's own views. Behind this difference of opinion lies Freud's crucial endorsement of the biogenetic law, which both Moll and Ellis failed to make use of in their own scientific writings.

scientific priority for various insights and discoveries often drew sharply differing reactions from those concerned. Additionally, for Freud and his movement, scientific priority was revolutionary propaganda, just as the denial of such priority has continued to provide an effective counterpropaganda for those who oppose Freud's theories (e.g., Eysenck and Wilson 1973:390–91).

Thus far in this chapter we have seen that Freud's most creative ideas were initially well received, and that they represented contributions to fields already well established before he began his researches. The component myths of Freud's hostile reception, of his intellectual isolation, and of his absolute originality are therefore functionally interrelated, reinforcing one another as part of the more comprehensive myth of the hero in the psychoanalytic movement. This myth-complex has exaggerated its motifs of isolation, opposition, originality, and heroism out of all proportion to the historical record and has thus distorted the true legitimacy of these themes for the ever-greedy sake of the cause (cf. Coser 1974).

Now that I have sketched out the general proportions of this hero myth within psychoanalytic lore, I shall devote the remainder of this chapter to analyzing this myth in relation to Freud personally, and to his movement collectively, in order to show how this mythology has come to monopolize the biographical tradition in Freud studies to such a remarkable degree.

Freud's Personal Myth of the Hero

Freud's entire life followed the classic hero-path so closely as to suggest his conscious (or unconscious) living out of heroic expectations. A perusal of his childhood, as well as of his Jewish family background, shows that this heroic pattern was indeed ingrained in Freud at an early age, and that he cultivated it as a highly effective life-strategy in later years. "Freud was lapped in the myth of the hero . . . ," Iago Galdston concurs. "There can be little doubt that Freud felt himself heroically predestined and convinced that it was up to him to eventuate this heroic destiny" (1956:492).

As is typical of heroes, both in myth and in actuality, the reasons for Freud's high expectations of himself date from events connected with his birth. Freud was born with a caul, a circumstance that people over the centuries have taken as a portent of later fame. Also at the time, an old peasant woman announced to the proud mother that with her firstborn child she had just delivered an important man into the world (Freud 1900a, S.E., 4:192). These prophecies, in which Freud's mother evidently placed great faith, were frequently repeated to young Freud. Yet another prediction was made when he was eleven or twelve. The family was sitting one evening at a restaurant in the Prater, a famous Viennese park, when their attention was attracted by a man who, for a small fee, was improvising verse on any chosen subject. Freud was sent to fetch the poet, who began by dedicating a few lines to his young emissary, declaring that the boy would grow up to be a cabinet minister. At that time the liberal *Bürger* ("Middle-class") Ministry included a number of Jews, whose names and portraits were all well known to Jewish schoolboys. Freud was so impressed by this prediction that he decided to study law. Only at the last moment before entering the university did he change his career plans to medicine (1900a, S.E., 4:193).

Amidst all these expectations concerning Freud's impending fame —expectations that were greatly reinforced by the extreme pride and love that his mother extended to her favorite child—it is no wonder that he felt destined for greatness. The entire family revolved around his well-being. To cite one amusing and representative anecdote, when Freud found that a sister's piano practicing was disturbing his studies, both the piano lessons and the piano had to go (Anna Freud Bernays 1940:337). Freud later acknowledged the considerable psychological benefits of his favored position within his family when he commented that "people who know that they are preferred or favoured by their mother give evidence in their lives of a peculiar self-reliance and an unshakeable optimism which often seem like heroic attributes and bring actual success to their possessors" (1900a, S.E., 5:398 n.).

Freud's youthful ambitions were not just limited to those of a would-be cabinet minister. Paul Roazen (1975:29) speaks of Freud's "profound urge to become a mighty warrior"—another of Freud's childhood dreams. His principal boyhood heroes were Hannibal, the Semitic general who crossed the Alps with his Carthaginian forces and outwitted the Roman legions; Cromwell, the Parliamentarian who allowed the Jews to return to England; and Napoleon, also an emancipator of the Jews (Freud 1900a, S.E., 4:196–98; 5:447–48). Freud's identification with such military heroes was hardly evanescent, as is evident in his statement to his fiancée at the age of twenty-nine: "I have often felt as though I had inherited all the defiance and all the passions with which our ancestors defended their temple and could gladly sacrifice my life for one great moment in history" (*Letters*, p. 202).

In his role as a neurologist and later as a psychoanalyst, Freud continued to live out these heroic identifications with great warriors and leaders of the downtrodden. Declining to envision himself as a brilliant thinker in the mold of Newton, Galileo, or Goethe, Freud instead emphasized his affinity with men of boldness and courage. "For I am actually not at all a man of science," he once told his friend Fliess, "not an observer, not an experimenter, not a thinker. I am by temperament nothing but a *conquistador*, an adventurer, if you wish to translate this term—with all the inquisitiveness, daring, and tenacity characteristic of such a man" (quoted in Schur 1972:201). Later on, as leader of the psychoanalytic movement, Freud increasingly identified himself with another fabled hero, Moses. "[I]f I am Moses," he told his "son and heir" Carl Jung in 1909, "then you are Joshua and will take possession of the promised land of psychiatry, which I shall only be able to glimpse from afar" (*Freud/Jung Letters*, pp. 196–97; Jones 1955:33). Freud's fascination with the Moses parallel led to his last book, *Moses and Monotheism* (1939*a*), in which he sought to explain the unique characteristics of the Jewish people—their tenacity, intellectuality, and high self-esteem—in terms of the unconventional hypothesis that Moses was an Egyptian high official who took the Jewish people under his wing and taught them monotheism. While working on the *Moses* book in 1935, Freud confessed to Lou Andreas-Salomé that the problem of the Jewish character "has pursued me throughout the whole of my life" (*Freud/Andreas-Salomé Letters*, p. 205).

Kurt Eissler (1971:253–55) has suggested another striking example of a self-fulfilling identification dating from Freud's youth. According to Eissler, Freud identified strongly as a child with the biblical Joseph (both were their mother's first and favorite son but had older brothers by another marriage). Thus when Freud later became famous like Joseph as a dream interpreter, he was merely fulfilling his childhood veneration for this biblical hero (cf. Jones 1953:4).

It is partly through this series of hero-identifications that one must seek to understand Freud's repeated references to his isolation throughout life. As a hero, Freud thrived on opposition and the feelings of isolation that such opposition entailed. These conditions were actually important to his creative work as well as to his conviction that he was fulfilling a heroic destiny. To Fliess, Freud had spoken openly of his "zest for martyrdom" (*Origins*, p. 342). In a similar vein, Hacker has contrasted Freud "the non-joiner" with "the gregarious Vienna of his day. . . . It seems as if Freud almost insisted on his isolation, from which he suffered so bitterly. . . . More and more, he remained aloof . . ." (1956:106). Indeed he did, and Fliess, who possessed a similar sense of heroic destiny, actively encouraged Freud's increasingly self-imposed isolation during the 1890s.[23] Such withdrawn behavior seems to have served a certain anticipatory function by which Freud "assigned to himself the role of an outsider before finding out if such a role was [actually to be] imposed upon him by the powers in being" (Sherwood 1962:235–36).

Although in accordance with the established myth, we usually think of Freud's years of "splendid isolation" as coming to a close some five or six years after the turn of the century, Freud never stopped feeling isolated, no matter how famous he later became. "Long after his work had won widespread recognition, Freud continued to act like a man who daily faced the dangerous fire of the enemy" (Puner 1947:212; see also Sachs 1944:20). As late as 1914, Freud wrote to Ferenczi that he felt "more isolated from the world than ever. . . ." With the

---

23. The Fliess correspondence clearly documents the partially self-imposed nature of Freud's isolation, as well as Fliess's role in it, in a letter of 16 April 1896: "Following your suggestion [literally: invitation] I have started to isolate myself completely and find it easier to bear. However, there is still one prior commitment I have to honor—a lecture at the Psychiatric Society on Tuesday" (unpublished Fliess correspondence, quoted in Schur 1972:97).

outbreak of the First World War, Freud could console himself about his continued feelings of isolation in colorfully militaristic terms. Again to Ferenczi, he described himself as living in a "primitive trench": "I speculate and write and after severe battles have got through the first series of riddles and difficulties. Anxiety, Hysteria and Paranoia have capitulated" (letter of 15 December 1914; quoted in Jones 1955:177). When, a year later, Freud heard that his compatriot and former pupil Robert Bárány had won the Nobel Prize for physiology and medicine, he dramatically proclaimed that it would be "ridiculous" for *him* "to expect [such] a sign of recognition when one has seven-eighths of the world against one" (quoted in Jones 1955:190). Freud was, in sum, an archetypal example of what Bruce Mazlish (1976) has called the "revolutionary ascetic"—that breed of dedicated fanatics who willingly shun all mundane pleasures, including the need for group contact and group reinforcement, in order to fulfill their revolutionary mission in life.

Freud's highly ambivalent attitude toward autobiographical history was also a significant derivative of his personal hero-complex. Twice, in 1885 and 1907, he ruthlessly blotted out the past by destroying most of his personal papers. As he revealed to his fiancée on the first of these occasions—in which letters, notebooks, private diaries, and manuscripts all perished—the holocaust was necessary so that the hero's past could be properly shrouded in mystery:

> . . . I couldn't have matured or died without worrying about who would get hold of these old papers. . . . As for the biographers, let them worry, we have no desire to make it too easy for them. Each one of them will be right in his opinion of "The Development of the Hero," and I am already looking forward to seeing them go astray. (*Letters*, p. 141)

Thus to Freud, the denial of history was a prerequisite part of being and, above all, of *remaining* a full-fledged hero in the eyes of posterity. By destroying his past, he actively sought to cultivate the "unknowable" about himself and thereby to set himself apart from the more transparent nonheroes of humanity.

One last indication of Freud's sense of heroic destiny is particularly worth mentioning here. As a young medical student at the University of Vienna, he used to stroll through the great arcaded court amidst the busts of all the famous professors who had taught there. According to Jones (1955:14), not only did Freud imagine, as many other students must have imagined of themselves, that he would one day be figured among these busts, but he even envisioned the precise inscription—in Greek from Sophocles' *Oedipus Rex*—that his own statue would bear: "Who divined the famed riddle [of the Sphinx] and was a man most mighty." According to Greek legend, as immortalized by Sophocles' drama, the Theban Sphinx was a monster half-human and half-lion that posed a riddle to everyone who happened to pass near in his travels, and that devoured those who failed to answer it. The famed riddle was: What is it that possesses but one voice and yet is sometimes four-

Medallion made for Freud's fiftieth birthday (1906).

footed, sometimes two-footed, and sometimes three-footed? The answer is man, who crawls on all fours as an infant, walks when grown, and supports himself with a cane in old age. As recounted by legend, Oedipus solved the riddle, and the Sphinx thereupon killed herself. The Thebans were so grateful to Oedipus that they made him their king.

Like the solution to the Sphinx's famous riddle, Freud's novel insights into the enigmas of the human mind required a developmental conception of man in which the dramatic story of Oedipus himself came to play a significant part. Thus Freud's psychoanalytic discoveries were indeed an uncanny fulfillment of his youthful phantasy in the university arcade. It therefore came as a considerable shock to Freud when in 1906 his followers secretly had a medallion prepared in honor of his fiftieth birthday and coincidentally chose for it the same inscription from Sophocles' *Oedipus Rex*. "When Freud read the inscription," Jones reports, "he became pale and agitated and in a strangled voice demanded to know who had thought of it. He behaved as if he had encountered a *revenant*, and so he had" (1955:14).

Today, as a result of Ernest Jones's instigation, a bust of Freud, carrying the fated inscription from Sophocles, stands in the very court where Freud had imagined it. Such was the remarkable self-fulfilling power of Freud's personal myth of the hero!

THE RISE OF THE MOVEMENT
AS A REVOLUTIONARY ORGANIZATION

Few theories in science have spawned a following that can compare with the psychoanalytic movement in its cultlike manifestations, in its militancy, and in the aura of a religion that has permeated it. Not only the opponents but even the movement's adherents were struck by the analogy with a religious sect. Hanns Sachs, who, as Roazen (1975:323) remarks, accepted psychoanalysis "as a revealed religion," has described in his autobiography how, upon reading Freud's *Interpretation of Dreams*, he "found the one thing worth while for me to live for; many years later I discovered that it was the only thing I could live by" (1944:3–4). Of the small band of early followers who attended Freud's Saturday evening lectures at the University of Vienna, Fritz Wittels has reported that they used to accompany Freud "in triumph" as he left the lecture hall, deliberately seeking to make themselves "as conspicuous as possible." They knew all Freud's works by heart, Wittels adds—even the footnotes—and "were as proud . . . [of themselves] as the pupils of Aristotle in the days before that philosopher's works had become widely known" (1924b:130–31).

Similarly, Wilhelm Stekel tells of how he became "the apostle of Freud who was my Christ!" and how the Psychological Wednesday Society meetings at Freud's home were "like a revelation" to him and others (1950:106, 116). Among his followers, Freud's spoken words took on "undreamed-of significance," Theodor Reik recalls, and even Freud's casual remarks "echoed in our minds for years afterwards" (1940:27).

Another early member of the society, music critic Max Graf (father of the famous "little Hans"), wrote of these weekly gatherings: "There was an atmosphere of the foundation of a religion in that room. Freud himself was its new prophet who made the theretofore prevailing methods of psychological investigation appear superficial. Freud's pupils—all inspired and convinced—were his apostles" (1942:471). Gradually the religion became a church, Graf recalls, and heresy was dealt with by excommunication: "Freud—as the head of a church—banished Adler; he ejected him from the official church. Within the space of a few years, I lived through the whole development of a church history . . ." (p. 473).

For those followers who remained loyal to Freud's doctrines, the rewards of the church could be considerable. "Freud played the role of personal analyst, father figure, and ego ideal" to his church members (Weisz 1975:356). His disciples served him in turn by internalizing his heroic sense of mission, by adopting his values and personal mannerisms, and by spreading his gospel.

The psychoanalytic movement's sectlike characteristics were many and varied. "Among the most prominent," a sociological student of this subject writes, "were the group's elitism and sense of exclusiveness, combined with an extreme mistrust of and hostility toward the outside world; an eschatological vision of reality which made adherence to the group an experience approaching religious conversion; and, more important, an exaggerated reverence for the founder which transcended the normal bounds of scientific authoritarianism . . ." (Weisz 1975:354). This same commentator points to four principal catalysts of the sectarian characteristics common to psychoanalysis and other cultlike schools.

First, the nature of the doctrine often plays an instrumental role. If the system of knowledge being promoted is suited to a religion or a sweeping political ideology by virtue of answering fundamental questions about life and death, then it may develop sectlike attributes. Second, sectarianism is favored when the members of a school possess only marginal status in society, as was the position of psychoanalysts vis-à-vis orthodox medicine. Under such conditions, Weisz points out, individuals may use their ideology, as psychoanalysts did, to interpret their position as outcasts, a circumstance that can only foster even greater mistrust toward outsiders and hence an increasing sense of uniqueness among the group's adherents. Psychoanalysis, furthermore, attracted many disciples who had already had marginal status before joining the movement. Besides being predominantly Jewish, Freud's early followers were often "lonely and highly neurotic men" (Weisz 1975:356). A surprising number eventually committed suicide (Stekel, Federn, Kahane, Tausk, Silberer, Honegger, Schrötter; and there were others).

A third common inducement of sectarian behavior is the response of the outside world. Greater militancy and belligerence are natural in a revolutionary movement once its teachings fail to be accepted and approved. "The members, then, increasingly view the world as hostile and threatening, and themselves as an enlightened, if embattled elite" (Weisz 1975:357).

Finally, the nature of the school's leadership, which in Freud's case was paternal and authoritarian and involved the limited but financially important power of patronage through patient referrals, supplemented the previous three considerations in promoting an atypical level of scientific obedience among early Freudians. Naturally, the more independent-minded analysts found it increasingly difficult to develop their own ideas under such conditions. "The goody-goodys are no good," Freud wistfully remarked to a patient in the late 1920s, "and the naughty ones go away" (Eva Rosenfeld, quoted in Roazen 1975:303).

These subsequent defections from orthodox psychoanalysis only served to heighten the movement's sectarian features. Freud spoke of its being an act of "treason" when Wilhelm Stekel broke with him in 1912; and worse vilifications were the fate of others who left the flock (Roazen 1975:188, 217, 224, 262). The stories of these defections became legendary, reinforcing the heroic cast of the movement as a whole. After reading the colorful account of these internal dissensions as presented in Ernest Jones's (1955:126–51) biography of her father, Anna Freud responded that this period was a wonderful testimony to the fierce "resistance" so ubiquitously generated by her father's ideas (letter of 6 June 1954, Jones archives; cited by Roazen 1975:454).

It was as a direct result of the defections of Adler, Jung, and Stekel that Ernest Jones proposed the institution in 1912 of a "strictly secret" committee of loyal adherents who could be charged with safeguarding the future of psychoanalysis. The principal inspiration for this idea, as Jones tells us in his biography of Freud, was his acquaintance with "stories of Charlemagne's paladins from boyhood, and many secret societies from literature" (1955:152). The committee's appointed tasks were to share the burden of replying to Freud's critics; to direct the ever-widening movement according to a "preconcerted plan" (which included controlling the International Association and its publishing house); and, in Freud's own words, to "defend the cause against personalities and accidents when I am no more" (Jones 1955:153; 1959: 227–28). Besides Freud, the original six members comprised Jones, Abraham, Ferenczi, Sachs, and Rank. They were joined by a seventh member, Max Eitingon, in 1919. Freud presented each committee member with a special gold ring upon which was mounted an antique Greek intaglio from his private collection. The committee remained a secret organization until 1927, when it was merged with the official board of the International Association (Jones 1957:135).

Sigmund Freud with the committee (1922). *Left to right, standing:* Rank, Abraham, Eitingon, and Jones. *Sitting:* Freud, Ferenczi, and Sachs.

Freud's Followers-Turned-Biographers

In the context of the sectarian politics of the psychoanalytic movement, it becomes easier to see why psychoanalytic history is so remarkably rich in mythology. As loyal adherents to the cause, Freud's followers were an integral part of Freud's personal myth of the hero. Their history, like his, became modeled on "the heroic." Among Freud's followers-turned-biographers, the movement's belligerent, black-and-white attitude toward the world later translated itself into an equally black-and-white conception of history and thus contributed in large part to the various myths portraying Freud's absolute originality, his isolation, and his rejection by orthodox medicine.

It is with these myth-making forces in mind that one must understand and appraise Ernest Jones's monumental three-volume biography of Freud. If Jones's work may be said to be perhaps the fullest expression of the Freud legend, one must also marvel at how remarkably good this biography really is, given Jones's own intimate involvement in the cause. Jones saw himself in relation to Freud as T. H. Huxley—"Darwin's bulldog"—had stood to the embattled Darwin a half century earlier. "There was an almost Promethean revolt in Jones," Veszy-Wagner commented about him after his death, "against persons (in society, private life, or in the battle of old versus new tendencies in the realm of scientific progress) who 'cannot suffer the existence of any other God' " (1966:119). When writing his biography of Freud, Jones was reliving the countless personal battles associated with his efforts during the pioneering days of psychoanalysis. Veszy-Wagner, who was in close contact with Jones during his composition of the Freud volumes, particularly noted his undiminished virulence toward all the old opponents of Freud and psychoanalysis. "When writing Freud's biography," she recalls, "Jones carefully checked whether (and how many) of these bugbears were still alive. I had expressed doubts about the death of one individual, and in a letter to me dated December 13, 1954, Jones could scarcely conceal his pique when he wrote: 'I don't care when he died so long as I can be sure he is thoroughly dead now, since I am libelling him severely' " (1966:119). "In a way," Veszy-Wagner concludes, "he regarded the Freud biography as part of his autobiography" (1966:120)—so much so, in fact, that Jones postponed writing his own autobiography (1959) in favor of the Freud work even though he knew he might die, as he did, before completing them both. If he frequently confused fact with legendary fiction, one must still respect the immense task that Jones undertook—one to which students of Freud will always be greatly indebted. Above all, we must also appreciate that what appears to us as myth today was generally an incontestable form of "psychological reality" to Jones and the movement. In giving expression to these myths, as well as to his own subjective perceptions of Freud, Jones has told us something very essential indeed about the psychoanalytic revolution in which he took part (cf. Eissler 1966:10).

Freud Myths and the Sociology of Knowledge

By way of conclusion to this chapter, I shall draw together the themes of myth and historical reality in Freud's life by placing them within a more abstract sociological model, and in so doing, shall seek to answer two basic questions touching upon the sociology of knowledge. First, is there a "natural history" to the politics of the psychoanalytic revolution? And, if there is, what general patterns of myth formation and propaganda production can be discerned in it?

The various principles governing the politics of knowledge, especially insofar as these politics relate to propaganda and legend, have not been studied systematically in the history of science. These principles have been dealt with, however, in a more general context by students of the sociology of knowledge.[24] According to Berger and Luckmann (1966:144–50), the ideological machinery found in most revolutionary movements has crucial "didactic" and "policing" functions to perform in order to sustain the new world view. Such machinery typically includes three strategic components: *legitimation*, *nihilation*, and *therapeutics*.

The first of these mechanisms, legitimation, helps to promulgate the leader's teachings as part of a ready-made tradition of belief. Through legitimation, a movement seeks to explain the superiority of its new conceptual order by presenting a convincing history of how this new order came to detect the basic flaws of its predecessor. In psychoanalytic lore, the stories of Anna O.'s remarkable illness and "cure" by Breuer, of the revolutionary discoveries that ensued when Freud turned his new methods inward upon himself, and of Freud's lonely years of scientific isolation before finally emerging into world fame—these stories and many others have all legitimated the heroic superiority of Freud's achievements.

The technique of legitimation nevertheless fails to explain why a particular new reality is the *only* possible one, why, that is, this new reality should not someday be supplanted by another, as was the fate of the prevailing dogma before it. This is where nihilation (a negative version of legitimation) and therapeutics come in. To guard against such challenges to a movement's credibility, the line between the legitimate and the illegitimate must be made as unambiguous as possible. Two common forms of nihilation are employed toward this end: a sharp contrast is introduced between preconversion existence and the world of the initiated, and a reinterpretation of past events and individuals is often required so that they harmonize with the present reality. Often, discrepant events or persons are replaced by substitutes that serve the new dogma's purposes more effectively. Yet the rewriting of history that nihilation always entails need not be wholly premeditated. Such "invented" versions of history may be introduced quite unintentionally out of a desire to bring the past into line with the present (Butterfield 1931).

So successful has the process of nihilation been in psychoanalytic history that even Freud's own disciples were long at a loss to imagine

24. For an introduction to the sociology of knowledge, see Mannheim 1936, 1952; Stark 1958; Douglas 1966, 1970; and Borhek and Curtis 1975. The sociology of science has long been closely associated with the work of Robert Merton and his school. For a useful review of this literature, see Norman Storer's Introduction to Merton's (1973) collected essays on the sociology of science; and Barnes 1974.

any other derivation for his discoveries than a sort of intellectual "spontaneous generation." "Strangely enough," Erik Erikson confessed in the late 1950s, "we students [of Freud] knew little of his beginnings, nothing of that mysterious self-analysis which he alluded to in his writings. We knew people whom Freud had introduced into psychoanalysis, but psychoanalysis itself had, to all appearances, sprung from his head like Athena from the head of Zeus" (1957:80; cf. 1955:15). As a particularly strategic tool in this nihilation process, the story of Freud's "mysterious self-analysis" grew in importance with the years, filling in historical gaps here and there, while serving all the time as a key mechanism in the denial of history. As early as the 1920s, Fritz Wittels tentatively attributed Freud's discovery of infantile sexuality to this famous self-analysis, even though Freud had never said as much himself (1924b:107). Other biographers followed suit, and with the help of the Fliess correspondence, published in 1950, the self-analysis seemed truly limitless in its marvelous powers of historical explanation. "Psychoanalysis proper is essentially a product of Freud's self-analysis," claims one such spokesman for the forces of historical nihilation (Wells 1960:189).

If Freud's self-analysis provided the psychoanalytic movement with a major vehicle of historical nihilation, the training analysis soon became a more everyday means of reinforcing the nihilation process. Hanns Sachs, one of the first training analysts, was fully cognizant of the tripart initiation/nihilation/conversion pattern inherent in such didactic analyses. "Religions," he once wrote, "have always demanded a trial period, a novitiate, of those among their devotees who desired to give their entire life into the service [of the Church]. . . . It can be seen that analysis needs something corresponding to the novitiate of the Church" (quoted in Roazen 1975:323). Edward Glover, after sixteen years as Director of Research at the London Institute of Psycho-Analysis, had the following critical words to say about the indoctrinating influence of training analyses:

> It is scarcely to be expected that a student who has spent some years under the artificial and sometimes hothouse conditions of a training analysis and whose professional career depends on overcoming "resistance" to the satisfaction of his training analyst, can be in a favourable position to defend his scientific integrity against his analyst's theory and practice. And the longer he remains in training analysis, the less likely he is to do so. For according to his analyst the candidate's objections to interpretations rate as "resistances." In short there is a tendency inherent in the training situation to perpetuate error. (1952:403)

To sum up the repercussions of nihilation in psychoanalysis, between the parable of Freud's self-analytic path to discovery and the more everyday influences of training analysis, several generations of psychoanalysts have successfully learned to overcome "conscious" doubts about psychoanalytic propositions and to accept Freud's theories as the sole source of psychological truth.

One last principle from our politics-of-knowledge trichotomy remains to be considered. Great revolutionary movements need not only legitimating and nihilating procedures but also therapeutic ones, which help to keep the new order pure by placing the whole burden of blame for deviance upon those who defect. The notorious "repression-resistance" argument of psychoanalysts became a most effective propaganda mechanism in this connection. Indeed, the protective function of therapeutics was intimately bound up with the whole conception of Freudian "therapy." Had not Freud himself explicitly instructed his followers to treat all their scientific critics as they would an unanalyzed patient offering "resistance" (*Freud/Jung Letters*, p. 18)? On the eve of his break with Freud, Jung spoke bitterly of just such propaganda pressures, now being directed against himself, when he complained to Freud that far too many psychoanalysts were misusing psychoanalysis "for the purpose of devaluing others. . . . Anything that might make them think is written off as a complex. This protective function of ΨA [psychoanalysis] badly . . . [needs] unmasking" (*Freud/Jung Letters*, pp. 526–27, letter of 3 December 1912). But Jung and other dissidents were expecting too much when they sought exemption from a polemical technique that they themselves had advantageously applied—with great relish—to Freud's nonanalytic critics.

OVERVIEW AND CONCLUSION

With its characteristic emphasis upon Freud's absolute originality, his lonely years of intellectual isolation, and his hostile reception by the scientific world, the psychoanalytic movement's myth of the hero has made ample use of the three general principles I have just reviewed. By *legitimating* the special and hard-wrought nature of psychoanalytic truth; by *nihilating* the achievements and credibility of Freud's critics; and by offering a built-in *therapy* to explain defections from the movement—this powerful ideological machinery, together with the commanding hero myth that lies behind it, has inspired and sustained countless students of Freud's teachings. There is, in fact, no other theory in the history of scientific thought that can rival psychoanalysis for such an elaborate system of self-reinforcing defenses.

It is now possible to unite the last two chapters of this book under a common rubric. The myth of the hero and the myth of Freud as pure psychologist stand as the two great pillars around which traditional psychoanalytic history has long cultivated its inspiring image of Freud. Through legitimation, nihilation, and therapeutics, the psychoanalytic movement has sought to control the future by controlling (and recasting) the myth-laden past. In systematic amplification of this point, I have collected in a Supplement to this chapter a chronological listing of twenty-six major myths and misconceptions about Freud.

Each myth is related back to one or the other of the two great myth-complexes in psychoanalytic history, and each is further explained as an expression of legitimation, nihilation, or therapeutics in the service of the cause.

Although independent of one another in many respects, the two great myth-complexes of Freud the hero and Freud as pure psychologist have repeatedly converged in their far-reaching defense of what is essential to the cause, namely, the theory of psychoanalysis. Biological psychology (including the prevailing doctrines of hereditary taint, degeneration theory, somatic and localization doctrines, physiological reductionism, and biological determinism more generally) was expediently seen by Freud and his followers as part of the faulty scientific reality that Freud—the pure psychologist—had overthrown. Furthermore, as the principal source of criticisms against, and defections from, psychoanalytic propositions, biological points of view supplied the single most important target for nihilation and therapeutics in the history of the movement (Chapter 12). Freud himself summed up this anti-biological rationale when, in the wake of all the dissensions and defections, he proclaimed of his loyal followers, "They had to learn to limit themselves to psychological ways of thought" (Weizsaecker 1957:68).

Above all, one must appreciate the remarkably complementary nature of the movement's two great myth-complexes. Wherever the myth of the pure psychologist has nihilated an unwanted portion of Freud's life, that of the psychoanalytic hero has created a plausible substitute history. Indeed, the successful denial of history would be impossible without the simultaneous creation of alternative scenarios to plug the historical gaps. Perhaps nowhere can one see more clearly how these sister mythologies have dedicated themselves to the same protective end than in their influential unification within the heroic theme of self-analysis. "It was his analysis of himself," asserts one typical biographer, "that brought about the decisive change in his interest from neurology to psychology, and created a whole new science, psycho-analysis" (Fine 1963:31). And just as Freud's heroic self-analysis supplied the crucial historical paradigm for a purely psychological explanation of his discoveries, the general features of traditional Freud history evolved from the repeated application of psychoanalytic theory to the lives of the hero, his predecessors, his enemies, and his disciples. Under such circumstances, a fundamentally psychological account of Freud's discoveries became the only possible one, and the more psychological that account became, the more heroic and unprecedented Freud's achievements seemed.

In short, the myths of the hero and of Freud as pure psychologist are the heart of the epistemological politics that have pervaded the entire psychoanalytic revolution. This interlocking web of legend has been absolutely essential to the strategy of revolution employed by Freud and his loyal followers. Indeed, their efforts would have been sorely deficient without a keen eye to Freud's potential value as a mythological being. And precisely because he and his followers were so personally caught up by the mythical history they sought to invent for themselves, they actually lived this history as subjective reality and allowed it to become powerfully prescriptive of revolutionary deeds.

Finally, for Freud, who likened the myths of nations to the inevitable distortions that individuals create about their early childhood, man's insatiable need for historical falsifications was a fundamental tenet of his science (1910c, *S.E.*, *11*:83–84). Is it not understandable, then, that he and his disciples should have availed themselves of such a splendid mythology of their own collective making?

SUPPLEMENT TO CHAPTER 13

Catalogue of Major Freud Myths

Specific Myths (1–22)		
Myth	Function	Sources
1. That Freud's "novel" ideas on male hysteria (1886d) were rudely rejected, thus marking the beginning of his "isolation" from Viennese scientific life.	As a legitimation of the myth of the hero; as a legitimation of "psychological" theory (Charcot's French point of view) over the "sterile" somatic doctrines of German medicine.	*Myth*: Freud 1925d, *S.E.*, 20:15–16; Wittels 1924b: 32–35; Bernfeld and Bernfeld 1952:39–44. *Rebuttal*: Jones 1953: 230–32; Bry and Rifkin 1962:9–12; Ellenberger 1970:437–42; this book, Chapter 2, pp. 35–42. But in counterrebuttal, see Eissler 1971:351–55.
2. That Anna O. was completely cured of her hysteria by Breuer; that hers was a "classic" case of hysteria.	As a legitimation of the miraclelike efficacy of the psychoanalytic method in its first, and most paradigmatic, case history.	*Myth*: Freud (and Breuer) 1895d, *S.E.*, 2:40–41; Freud 1925d, *S.E.*, 20:20; Wittels 1924b:37; Puner 1947:97. *Rebuttal*: Jones 1953: 225; Ellenberger 1970: 483–84; Ellenberger 1972; Hirschmüller 1978: 153–57; this book, Chapter 2, p. 57.

SUPPLEMENT TO CHAPTER 13 (Continued)

Myth	Function	Sources
3. That the cause of Anna O.'s illness was finally perceived by Breuer as sexual in nature—as dramatically revealed to him by Anna O.'s phantom pregnancy and hence her "transference relationship" with him; that Breuer ceased to study the subject for this reason and later concealed this aspect of his findings from Freud. (This myth is a mixture of partial truth, unconfirmed hearsay, ex post facto inference, and highly mythical embellishment of the details.)	As a legitimation of the sexual nature of hysteria; as a therapy for Breuer's later break with Freud. See also Myth 5.	*Myth*: Freud 1925*d*, *S.E.*, 20:26; Jones 1953:224–25; Robert 1966:83–86; Costigan 1967:35; many other authors. *Rebuttal*: Ellenberger 1970:483–84; Ellenberger 1972; Hirschmüller 1978:170–78, 266; this book, Chapter 3, pp. 78–80, 83–85.
4. That Josef Breuer's ideas on hysteria were more strictly "physiological" than Freud's.	As a legitimation of Freud's growing identity as a "pure psychologist"; as a nihilation of Breuer's rational (philosophical) differences with Freud on the mind-body problem and on the theory of hysteria; as a therapy against the introduction of biological premises in psychoanalysis.	*Myth*: Wittels 1924*b*:37, 42; Jones 1953:275. *Rebuttal*: Stewart 1967: 17–18; Strachey, *S.E.*, 2:xxiv; Hirschmüller 1978:195, 218, 267–68; this book, Appendix B.
5. That "timid" Breuer broke with Freud when Breuer found it impossible to accept the sexual etiology of neurosis.	As a nihilation of Freud's fanaticism and Breuer's own open-mindedness on this issue; as a therapy for Breuer's otherwise surprising defection from the cause. See also Myth 3.	*Myth*: Freud 1925*d*, *S.E.*, 20:26–27; Jones 1953: 224–25, 254; Robert 1966:86; Fine 1973:24; many other authors. *Rebuttal*: Galdston 1956: 493–94; Cranefield 1958; Ackerknecht 1963:129; Stewart 1967:17–18; Hirschmüller 1978:176, 185–89, 218, 225–36, 267–68; this book, Chapter 3, pp. 78–80, 87–89, 99–100; Appendix A.
6. That Freud was initially part of the Helmholtz school of medicine and later retracted that allegiance in favor of a "purely psychological" outlook.	As a straw-man argument to legitimate Freud's supposedly revolutionary break from his biological past; as a legitimation of psychoanalysis as a "pure psychology"; and, hence, as a nihilation of biological influences upon Freud's thinking. See also Myth 12.	*Myth*: Bernfeld 1944, 1949; Puner 1947:62–63; Jones 1953: passim—see index under "Helmholtz School"; Natenberg 1955: 119; Brome 1967:2–3; many other authors. *Rebuttal*: Shakow and Rapaport 1964:33–35, 41–46; Cranefield 1966*a*, 1966*b*, 1970*b*; this book, Chapter 2, pp. 65–66.

SUPPLEMENT TO CHAPTER 13 *(Continued)*

Myth	Function	Sources
7. That Freud's *Project for a Scientific Psychology* (1895) was only a "neurological" document and was "abandoned" by him shortly after being written; that Freud's subsequent theory of mind represents a "pure psychology."	As a legitimation of Freud's supposed break with neurophysiological reductionism; as a nihilation of the presence of biological assumptions in psychoanalysis.	*Myth*: Jones 1953:381–82, 395; Kris 1954:27, 350–51; Erikson 1955; Bernfeld 1955; Strachey, *S.E.*, 1:293. *Rebuttal*: Holt 1965a, 1968a; Amacher 1965; Kanzer 1973; Pribram and Gill 1976; this book, Chapter 4, pp. 120–26, 130–31.
8. That Wilhelm Fliess's value to Freud was that of a friend and a "listener," and occasionally that of a "proofreader" and "a censor," during Freud's lonely period of isolation; that their scientific communications were "duologues rather than dialogues."	As a nihilation of Fliess's intellectual (and biological) influence upon Freud.	*Myth*: Jones 1953:297–303; Kris 1954:13–14, 43; Robert 1966:98–99; Costigan 1967:58; many other authors. *Rebuttal*: Galdston 1956; Eissler 1971:169; this book, Chapters 5 and 6.
9. That Fliess, applying his own theories, predicted Freud would die at 51; that the interval of 51 *years* had any significance whatsoever in Fliessian periodicity theory; that Freud's preoccupation with death was the reason for his interest in Fliess's theories.	As a nihilation of the rationality of Fliess's theories; as a nihilation of biologically deterministic views more generally; as a nihilation of the compatibility of Fliess's theories with, and their possible influence upon, Freudian psychoanalysis.	*Myth*: Jones 1953:310, 348, 357; Bakan 1958:308; Lauzon 1963:47; Gardner 1966:109; Costigan 1967:52; Schur 1972:95, 187; Mannoni 1974:38, 79. *Rebuttal*: This book, Chapter 5, p. 166.
10. That Fliess's theories were predominantly derived from a (Jewish) mystical tradition and/or from German *Naturphilosophie*.	As a nihiliation of the rational, biological premises of Fliess's thinking, together with their considerable evolutionary and physiological plausibility.	*Myth*: Jones 1953:296–97; Erikson 1955:13; Galdston 1956; Bakan 1958:63; Robert 1966:92; Costigan 1967:59; Holt 1968b; Ellenberger 1970:545. *Rebuttal*: This book, Chapter 5.
11. That Fliess's biological theories were totally "pseudoscientific" and led to his break with Freud; that Fliess's work could only have "hindered" Freud's progress in the 1890s.	As a nihilation of Freud's intimate, collaborative association with the now-discredited Fliess; as a nihilation of the compatibility between biological and psychological points of view within psychoanalytic theory.	*Myth*: Jones 1953:297–304; Kris 1954:14, 35, 45–46; Lauzon 1963:46; Robert 1966:92–99; Gardner 1966; Brome 1967:3–5; Costigan 1967:59; many other authors. *Rebuttal*: Galdston 1956;

SUPPLEMENT TO CHAPTER 13 *(Continued)*

Myth	Function	Sources
		Rebuttal (continued): this book, Chapter 5, pp. 147–70; Chapter 6, pp. 171–213, 235–37.
12. That the break with Fliess was symbolic of Freud's break with the Helmholtz school of medicine as well as being indicative of his decision to make psychoanalysis into a "pure psychology."	As a nihilation of biological assumptions in psychoanalysis. See also Myth 6.	*Myth:* Kris 1950*a*:115; Kris 1954:35, 45–46; Shakow and Rapaport 1964:46; Robert 1966:98. *Rebuttal:* This book, Chapter 6, pp. 214–37.
13. That Freud's need for a "transference figure" during his self-analysis accounts for "the unaccountable" in his relationship with Fliess; hence, when the self-analysis came to an end, so did the relationship with Fliess.	As a legitimation of Freud's otherwise "peculiar" admiration for Fliess; as a legitimation of Freud's heroic, self-analytic path of discovery; as a nihilation of Fliess's real intellectual influence upon Freud.	*Myth:* Jones 1953:307; Shakow and Rapaport 1964:44; Robert 1966:91; Costigan 1967:53–54, 60–61; Fine 1973:242. *Rebuttal:* This book, Chapter 6.
14. That psychoanalysis is essentially the product of Freud's self-analysis; that the self-analysis was a "herculean" and totally "unprecedented" feat.	As a legitimation (1) of the myth of the hero, (2) of psychoanalysis as an *independent* science, (3) of the unique methodology of psychoanalysis, and (4) of didactic analyses and a closed teaching organization as prerequisites for (*a*) psychoanalytic competency and (*b*) the right to criticize psychoanalytic propositions; as a nihilation of Freud's debt to biology and other intellectual sources.	*Myth:* Jones 1953:319; Jones 1955:4; Erikson 1955:15; Wells 1960:189; Fine 1963:31–32. *Rebuttal:* This book, Chapter 1, pp. 18–19; Chapter 6, pp. 207–10; Chapter 13, pp. 485–86.
15. That Freud's self-analysis led to his abandonment of the seduction theory and to his discovery of infantile sexuality.	As a legitimation of Freud's heroic, self-analytic path to discovery (Myth 14); as a legitimation of the importance of psychical reality; as a legitimation of Freud's earlier blunder (the seduction theory) in terms of the Oedipus complex.	*Myth:* Wittels 1924*b*:107; Kris 1950*a*:113; Kris 1954:33; Loewenstein 1951:633; Jones 1953:265, 325; Anzieu 1959:59–65; Fine 1963:218; Stewart 1967:22; Duke 1972:29; many other authors; Huston's film *Freud* (1962). *Rebuttal:* This book, Chapter 6, pp. 207–10.

SUPPLEMENT TO CHAPTER 13 *(Continued)*

Myth	Function	Sources
16. That Freud discovered infantile sexuality and the unconscious.	As a legitimation of the hero myth (i.e., Freud's absolute originality); as a legitimation of the necessity of using Freud's new methodology of psychological inquiry.	*Myth*: Freud 1905*d*, *S.E.*, 7:173; and *Minutes*, 2:48; Wittels 1924*b*:105; Jones 1940*a*:13; Jones 1955:284; Costigan 1967:49; Eissler 1971:175–76. *Rebuttal*: Ellenberger 1970:502–5; Kern 1973; Whyte 1960:168–69; this book, Chapter 6, pp. 117–210; Chapter 8; Chapter 13, pp. 468–69.
17. That Freud's sexual theories grew out of his self-analysis and *The Interpretation of Dreams*.	As a legitimation of Myths 14, 15, and 16; as a nihilation of the influence of Fliess and the contemporary sexology movement upon Freud.	*Myth*: Jones 1955:6, 285; Fine 1963:218; Robert 1966:178. *Rebuttal*: This book, Chapter 6, pp. 171–213; Chapter 8.
18. That Freud was scientifically isolated from about 1894 to about 1906.	As a legitimation of the lonely and heroic nature of Freud's discoveries; as a nihilation of his considerable intellectual debts to his contemporaries; as a rationalization of his friendship with Fliess (Myth 8).	*Myth*: Freud 1914*d*, *S.E.*, 14:22; Freud 1925*d*, *S.E.*, 20:48; Puner 1947:131–33, 136–37; Jones 1955:6–7; Natenberg 1955: Chap. 8; Robert 1966:151–52; many other authors. *Rebuttal*: Hacker 1956:106; Ellenberger 1970:448, 455, 468; Decker 1971:480–81; Roazen 1975:195–97, 288; this book, Chapter 13, pp. 462–64, 478–79; Appendix C.
19. That Freud's promotion to Extraordinary Professor was delayed by anti-Semitism (untrue) and by Freud's sexual theories (quite possibly true, but the theories at issue, nota bene, were then in considerable error); that the appointment was only secured when a grateful patient bribed the Minister of Education with a Böcklin painting.	As a legitimation of the lonely and heroic nature of Freud's achievements; as a nihilation of the rational basis upon which many of Freud's scientific claims were criticized by his peers.	*Myth*: Sachs 1944:78; Jones 1953:339–40; Robert 1966:141, 148–49; Costigan 1967:81. *Rebuttal*: Gicklhorn and Gicklhorn 1960; Ellenberger 1970:452–54; this book, Chapter 13, pp. 464–67; but see in counterrebuttal of certain revisionist extremes in this connection, Eissler 1966, and 1971:343–50.

SUPPLEMENT TO CHAPTER 13 *(Continued)*

Myth	Function	Sources
20. That Freud broke with Adler and Jung when these two disciples, unlike Freud, began to subordinate psychology to a priori biological assumptions.	As a legitimation of psychoanalysis as a "pure psychology"; as a therapy against further defections.	*Myth*: Freud, *Minutes*, 2:432; 3:147; Freud 1914d, S.E., 14:19; Freud 1905d [1920], S.E., 7:133; Freud 1937c, S.E., 23:251. *Rebuttal*: This book, Chapter 12, pp. 425–37, 443.
21. That Freud's biogenetic and Lamarckian propensities were "late" and "peripheral" additions to his psychoanalytic thinking; that such additions were spurred on by the more speculative tendencies of Ferenczi, Jung, and Abraham.	As a nihilation of the possible influence of these discredited biological doctrines upon psychoanalysis; as a scapegoat therapy against known defectors.	*Myth*: Wittels 1924b:168; Glover 1950:43; Flugel 1955:130–31; Robert Fliess 1956:9; Jones 1957:324, 329; Shakow and Rapaport 1964:32, n. 37; Yazmajian 1967:204; Ritvo 1974:187–89. *Rebuttal*: This book, Chapter 3, pp. 93–94; Chapter 6, pp. 198–204; Chapter 12, pp. 439–42.
22. That Freud's death-instinct theory was subjectively determined.	As a nihilation of an unpopular, biological aspect of Freud's thinking among his fellow psychoanalysts; as a nihilation of biogenetic assumptions in Freud's doctrines.	*Myth*: Wittels 1924b:251; Puner 1947:297–99; Ekstein 1949; Jones 1957:278; Robert 1966:329; Costigan 1967:229–30; Schur 1972:328–33; Andreski 1972:138; Fine 1973:178. *Rebuttal*: This book, Chapter 11.

General Myths (23–26)

Myth	Function	Sources
23. That Freud's theories were given an inadequate, hostile, and irrational reception by his contemporaries.	As a legitimation of the myth of the hero, together with the revolutionary nature of Freud's discoveries; as a legitimation of the theories of repression and resistance; by purporting Freud's absolute originality, as a nihilation of the work of his contemporaries; as a nihilation of Freud's extremism and fanaticism as a theorist.	*Myth*: Freud 1914d, S.E., 14:22–23; Freud 1925d, S.E., 20:48–50; Puner 1947:129–31, 134; Jones 1953:252, 360–61; Jones 1955:12, 107–25; Robert 1966:119, 190; Brome 1967: 31–34; Balogh 1971:47, 65; Mannoni 1974:66, 91; many other authors; Huston's film *Freud* (1962). *Rebuttal*: Bry and Rifkin 1962; Ellenberger 1970: 450, 486, 783–86, 792–93;

SUPPLEMENT TO CHAPTER 13 *(Continued)*

Myth	Function	Sources
		Rebuttal (continued): Decker 1971, 1975, 1977; this book, Chapter 3, pp. 80–83; Chapter 9, pp. 347–50; Chapter 13, pp. 448–64.
24. That Freud was unconcerned about priorities in science and considered the whole issue "a bore."	As a legitimation of Freud's noble and heroic image as a man of science; as a nihilation of the degree to which psychoanalytic ideas were "in the air" and, hence, were not original to Freud.	*Myth:* Freud 1914d, S.E., 14:22; Jones 1957:100. *Rebuttal:* Ellenberger 1970:448–49; Roazen 1975:70, 93–94, 109, 190–202; Merton 1976: 37–39; this book, Chapter 3, pp. 86–87; Chapter 13, pp. 467–72.
25. That Freud's theories are primarily an environmentalist interpretation of mental illness.	As a nihilation of the role of biological assumptions in psychoanalysis.	*Myth:* Spawned by Freud's more optimistic followers (especially the American ones); see Chapter 12, pp. 437–44. *Rebuttal:* Freud 1906a, S.E., 7:275; Freud 1916–17, S.E., 16:361–62; Hale 1971:349–52; Johnston 1972:229; this book, Chapter 10, pp. 364–92; Chapter 12, pp. 437–44.
26. That biological influences upon psychoanalysis extend only to its terminology, not to its basic concepts; that the biological impact of Freud's theories was derived from purely clinico-psychological observation.	As a nihilation of the influence of a priori biological influences upon psychoanalytic theory.	*Myth:* Jones 1930:604; Kris 1950a:116; Kris 1954:47; Jones 1957: 314; Marx 1970:369. *Rebuttal:* Amacher 1965; Holt 1965a, 1968a; Ritvo 1965, 1972, 1974; Yazmajian 1967; McCarley and Hobson 1977; this book, Chapters 2–12.

14

Epilogue and Conclusion

This study grew out of two principal ambitions: to produce a comprehensive intellectual biography of Freud and to resolve the key historical questions inherent in his transformation from neuroanatomist to psychoanalyst. In the process of this undertaking, we have seen how traditional Freud historiography has consistently masked Freud's path to discovery by portraying him as a heroically isolated figure who drew his findings predominantly from the forbidding depths of his own unconscious. It was as a major consequence of this distortion that Freud became a crypto-biologist even in his own lifetime—with all of the problems that this circumstance has created for the subsequent understanding of his ideas.

In place of this traditional historical scenario, I have documented here a Freud who was anything but isolated from the intellectual currents of his age. Although the influences upon Freud were multifarious, one grand theme—the abiding psychobiological vision that I have throughout attributed to his conceptions—united them all within psychoanalytic theory. Having begun his career as a biologist and having pursued that career for more than two decades before psychoanalysis emerged to take its place, Freud necessarily carried with him the fundamental tenets of his previous scientific training. As he himself once conceded in his sixty-eighth year, "It is making severe demands on the unity of the personality to try and make me identify myself with the author of the paper on the spinal ganglia of the petromyzon [Freud 1878a]. Nevertheless I must be he, and I think I was happier about that discovery than about others since" (Freud/Abraham Letters, p. 369). In short, what traditional psychoanalytic historians would see as Freud's heroic and ultimately triumphant struggle to cut himself off from his biological past ranks as mythical propaganda in one of its most well-developed forms.

Yet this is not to deny that substantial conflict arose in Freud's mind over the proper relationship between psychological and biological levels of scientific analysis. What has generally been misunderstood is the precise nature of this reductionistic conflict. During his scientific career, Freud indeed underwent a major struggle concerning the biological basis of human behavior, just as he subscribed to two separate forms of biological reductionism: neurophysiological and evolutionary-historical. As we have seen, the evolutionary-historical form ultimately won out over the neurophysiological during the crucial period that inaugurated Freud's psychobiological theory of mind.

The sequence of intellectual development that I have documented in Freud's work mirrored changes that were occurring in medical psychology in general throughout the last two decades of the nineteenth century. And therein lies the great interest that Freud's intellectual transformation holds for the historian of ideas. For thirty years, the intellectual influence of Darwin and evolutionary theory laid the groundwork for a sophisticated new paradigm of human behavior; and by the 1890s, the decade of Freud's most creative achievements, that influence was at its peak in medical psychology. But few thinkers took the step from a physiological to an evolutionary theory of mind more ardently than did Sigmund Freud, with his conceptual syntheses of the biogenetic law; the unconscious as the phylogenetically archaic in man; the primacy of early experience and the power of fixation, regression, and the inherited past; the theory of psychosexual stages; the dichotomy between primary (impulsive) and secondary (inhibitory) psychical systems; and, above all, evolutionary solutions to his three great psychoanalytic problems (pathological repression, the choice of neurosis, and Why sex?). Seen in proper historical perspective, Freud's theory of mind is the embodiment of a scientific age imbued with the rising tide of Darwinism, a tide that had induced the enrapt young Freud to alter his career plans from law to medicine during his last year at the Gymnasium (*Autobiography*, 1925d, S.E., 20:8). "With neurotics it is as though we were in a prehistoric landscape—for instance, in the Jurassic. The great saurians are still running about; the horse-tails grow as high as palms (?)" (1941f [1938], S.E., 23:299). With this one poetic statement, jotted down the year before his death, Freud summed up a lifetime of psychoanalytic thought about the causes of human behavior. Perhaps no one synthesized the biological assumptions of his scientific generation more boldly than did Freud. His theories—right or wrong—stand as an epitome of the late-nineteenth-century vision of man put forth by so many of his forgotten contemporaries.

Psychophysics, Psycho–Lamarckism, and the Biogenetic Law in Psychoanalysis

Acceptance of Freud's historical debt to biology requires a rather uncongenial conclusion for most psychoanalytic practitioners, namely, that Freud's theories reflect the faulty logic of outmoded nineteenth-century biological assumptions, particularly those of a psychophysicalist, Lamarckian, and biogenetic nature.[1] As we have seen, these assumptions were eminently plausible in Freud's day. Indeed, so plausible were they that Freud was not always aware of how much faith he placed in them or of how much his clinical observations absorbed from them "empirical" meaning. Yet because he pursued such a bold and relentless logic in the world of scientific ideas, his thinking illuminates the power of his theoretical preconceptions in a particularly dramatic fashion. "If any of his theories are unacceptable," Ramzy (1956:120) has similarly insisted about Freud's logic, "this is not due to the way he argued it, but to the premises he started with. . . ." Thus, such "clinical" discoveries as the abreaction of trauma seemed to Freud a direct corroboration of the bioenergetic principles that pervaded his theory of mind. Similarly, the child does appear to recapitulate the history of the race in many essential respects, but it recapitulates the embryonic, not the adult stages, as Freud and other biogeneticists had mistakenly thought. Plausible enough as they may have seemed to Freud, such assumptions were nevertheless wrong; and much that is wrong with orthodox psychoanalysis may be traced directly back to them. To cite a prime example, Freud claimed that no one, looking at a nursing infant, could possibly dispute the sexual nature of oral gratification in infancy—a claim that indeed can be disputed if one does not equate infantile forms of pleasure, as he did on biogenetic grounds, with animallike sex.[2] Time and time again, Freud saw in his patients what psychoanalytic theory led him to look for and then to interpret the way he did; and when the theory changed, so did the clinical findings.

Nor were Freud's fundamental biological assumptions a "late" or "peripheral" addition to his psychoanalytic thinking, as has so often been claimed about the phylogenetic ones. From the discovery of spontaneous infantile sexuality (1896/97) to the very end of his life, Freud's endorsement of biogenetic and Lamarckian viewpoints inspired many of his most controversial psychoanalytic conceptions. More especially, these premises bolstered the heart of his developmental theories, legitimating their controversial claim to universality amidst a storm of skeptical opposition. Furthermore, these assumptions prevented Freud from accepting negative evidence and alternative explanations for his views. All in all, it is easy to see why Freud's erroneous biological assumptions prompted such elaborate steps by his followers to deny their importance in Freudian theory (Chapter 12).

1. See Chapter 2, pp. 61–67; Chapter 3, pp. 89–98; Chapter 4; Chapter 6, pp. 198–204; Chapter 7, pp. 258–75; Chapter 8, pp. 290–97, 318–19; Chapter 10; Chapter 11, pp. 398–409, 415; and Chapter 12.
2. Cf. Chodoff (1966), who likewise comments about Freud's theory-laden expectations in this regard.

FREUD'S PLACE IN THE HISTORY OF IDEAS

"The opinion is gaining ground," Peter Medawar has declared, "that doctrinaire psychoanalytic theory is the most stupendous intellectual confidence trick of the twentieth century: and a terminal product as well—something akin to a dinosaur or a zeppelin in the history of ideas, a vast structure of radically unsound design and with no posterity" (1975:17). No doubt, there are many individuals sharing such a negative persuasion about psychoanalysis who might easily seize upon the substance of this book in order to bolster their arguments about the folly of Freud's theories. Although the problem of what is right and what is wrong with psychoanalysis goes far beyond my scope here, I do not deny that various unconfirmed aspects of Freud's theories may be correlated almost point by point with his erroneous premises.[3] But even if his theories *are* misguided in many important respects, are we to conclude that Freud has been overestimated by history? Is Freud really, as some would consider him today, one of the most overrated figures of the twentieth century (Heller 1977)?

I believe that such a historical verdict misjudges both the merits of Freud's influence and the nature of his scientific greatness. A scientist necessarily works with the instruments, the information, and the theories that are available to him in his time. The mark of capability in science is to make do with what one has and, in the process, to reach fruitful insights, often with less than perfect theory or corroborating information. Even though those who abide by the accepted rules of scientific method are reluctant to acknowledge it, the most creative minds in science have always been guided by a priori and extrascientific beliefs, daring to make inferences from these assumptions that more critical minds have known to be unwarranted at the time (Holton 1973). Freud was a thinker from this exceptional mold—a self-styled conquistador in science, whose bold theoretical scope and intellectual daring transformed the field of psychology as it existed in his time.

Nor should Freud be judged against the higher standards of certainty that generally prevail for research and discovery in the physical

3. Along these lines, see Stewart (1967:151) and Holt (1965a). Kline (1972) and Eysenck and Wilson (1973) have exhaustively surveyed the experimental status of Freudian theory, albeit with contrasting conclusions. The work by Eysenck and Wilson reprints, with critical commentary, many of the most definitive studies on this topic. A similar survey of objective studies is offered by Fischer and Greenberg (1977), who have reached the following three conclusions, among others: (1) that Freud's basic notion of dreams as highly disguised wish-fulfillments, together with his distinction between latent and manifest dream-content, is much too narrow, and particularly neglects the anticipatory function of dreams; (2) that certain Freudian clinical syndromes, such as Freud's "oral" and "anal" character types, *do* exist, but that his specific explanations of their childhood origins are not substantiated; and (3) that orthodox psychoanalysis is no better as a mode of therapy than many other psychotherapeutic alternatives. Yazmajian (1967) has discussed several revisions in the theory of psychosexual development that are necessitated in the light of Freud's erroneous biogenetic logic.

sciences. Once, too, these sciences were young like psychology and were beset by similar epistemological problems. Thus, to borrow Kuhn's (1962) useful terminology, history is inevitably harsh in its assessment of those individuals who have sought to transform "preparadigmatic" into "paradigmatic" sciences. Such was the nature of Freud's endeavor. If he was only partially successful, one must still acknowledge that his synthetic approach and his theoretical daring were highly appropriate to the particular historical context in which he expressed them. Perhaps only Aristotle and Darwin have equaled Freud's marriage of theory and observation in the broad realm of the life sciences.

Still, what remains today of Freud's insights and influence is remarkable indeed and provides ample testimony to his greatness. "What is accepted," Shakow and Rapaport conclude in a survey of Freud's influence, "is Freud's new view of man and his pioneering in new areas for psychological study. There has been a slow realization that Freud awakened interest in human nature, in infancy and childhood, in the irrational in man; that he is the fountainhead of dynamic psychology in general, and of psychology's present-day conceptions of motivation and of the unconscious in particular" (1964:10). To those who share Freud's goal of uniting psychology with biology, Freud must likewise be considered, with Darwin, as a founding father of the psychobiological conception of man. An exciting question for the future is to what extent Freud's psychobiological vision of man and of social behavior may be further developed under currently accepted Darwinian theory. This is a challenge that has already been accepted by the sociobiologists, who, in the synthetic spirit of Freud, have called once more for a closer interchange of ideas between psychiatrists, psychoanalysts, and evolutionary biologists (Wilson 1977:135–36).[4]

Above and beyond all these contributions, Freud's writings may be said to contain a richness of thought and observation about human behavior that will continue to outlive the particular theoretical constructs he championed. In Freud's own lifetime, amidst the storm of controversy over his psychoanalytic claims, Havelock Ellis summed up this timeless quality to Freud's insights: "But if . . . Freud sometimes selects a very thin thread [in tying together his theoretical arguments], he seldom fails to string pearls on it, and these have their value whether the thread snaps or not" (1910b:523).

---

4. Although much is truly novel and revolutionary in the new discipline of sociobiology, sociobiologists such as Edward O. Wilson are also independently rediscovering many notions that were first proposed, and even became commonplace, during the late nineteenth century. One may cite in this connection the biological nature of incest taboos, with their intimate relationship to the genetics of outbreeding; the adaptive and hereditary nature of childhood phobias; the role of man's constitutional bisexuality in homosexuality; the importance of facial expressions in the biology of social behavior; and the theory that myth and religion are mass "illusions" helping to cement the loyalties of the group (see Wilson's *On Human Nature*, 1978). In Freudian language, sociobiology represents a dramatic "return of the repressed." For this reason, sociobiologists may find within the Freudian corpus, with its underlying biological rationale and its numerous anticipations of sociobiological doctrine, a stimulating source of future ideas.

Freud in 1938 (age 82).

THE INDELIBLE NATURE OF MYTH

The ideological forces that govern the creation of myth during major revolutions do not just dissipate once their task has been accomplished; rather, they continue to inhere within the structure of myth they have created. As the revolution becomes dogma, myth increasingly assumes the role of its conservative guardian in order to continue to mediate between stability and change long after the revolutionary phase has passed away. "This static quality," John Marcus has observed of such myth-laden ideologies, "has been fully evident in the mystiques of revolution which reject with particular violence heterodox interpretations of their mystique-ideal. Hence while the mystique, like every element in history, is always undergoing change, it does so reluctantly and often with violent convulsions" (1960:227).

We are accustomed to such myths, mystiques, and cults of personality in major social and political movements; but their manifestation in the objective world of science is more surprising. Since the evolution of myth has been particularly pronounced in the history of the psychoanalytic movement, we may well ask whether psychoanalysis is perhaps unique among the sciences in having sought so strenuously to shroud its origins in myth.

At first glance, psychoanalysis indeed seems exceptional by virtue of being the first theory in science to hold within itself a necessary historical vision of how it arose. No doubt the ever-present temptation to bring history into line with psychoanalytic theory contributed much to the mythology created by Freud and his followers. The mythical features that have long surrounded Freud's self-analysis are perhaps the most prominent instance of such distortion effected in the name of psychoanalytic theory.

Still, psychoanalysis may have exceptional features in this respect, but it is hardly exceptional within science for the general *trend* of its myths. Like psychoanalysts, all scientists hold a theory, however unspoken and implicit, about the proper route to scientific discovery; and that theory mythologizes the memory of every great achievement in science. In their most general terms, the great myths of scientific discovery seek to portray the scientific investigator as a "pure empiricist" who happily comes upon the truth, often in some serendipitous manner, through hard-nosed attention to "the facts." The mythology of science goes to great lengths to mask both the theory-laden nature of its achievements and the role that creative inspiration so often plays in them. Above all, such myths (among which rank Galileo's famous experiments at the Leaning Tower of Pisa, Newton and the celebrated apple, Darwin's fateful visit to the Galapagos Islands, and Einstein's inspiration by the Michelson-Morley experiment) are stories that have long proven themselves superior to the historical truth in their role as exemplars of orthodox scientific methodology (Cohen 1974:363, 366;

Holton 1969; Kuhn 1970a:136–43; Brush 1974). It would be most fruitful to trace these famous myths in more detail, to study their historical origins and their political functions in each particular instance of "discovery," and to demonstrate the pervasive grip they have exerted upon historical belief. But this is a matter for future inquiry. For the present I must be content with insisting how fully the history of psychoanalysis illuminates this myth-making process, providing us in microcosm with a brilliant reflection of the politics of knowledge that pervades all of science.

From this wider perspective, the recent disparities between traditional and revisionist histories of psychoanalysis appear to be part of an inevitable phase in Freud scholarship. Nevertheless, the advantage still remains with the Freudians and with their traditional historical scenario; and in many respects the advantage will always remain with them. Good historical myths are generally far more exciting, significantly more teachable, and more readily remembered than the real thing. By telescoping history around heroic and critical moments that always lead to the inevitable present, myths surpass all but the most exceptional historical truth in their appeal to human interest. It is this inherent credibility of myth that allows its historical creations to spring back unperturbed from the onslaughts of the specialists (cf. Butterfield 1931:5–7). Great "origins" myths are too much of a cultural art form, too good at conveying the "lesson of history," to die out simply because they are not true. Thus Ernst Kris was probably right when he proclaimed, "The story of Freud's self-analysis will, I believe, become part of that great store of accounts which in the history of science plays a peculiarly inspiring part—accounts which report how in sacrifice and loneliness the great scientist works" (1956:633). In more ways than we acknowledge, myth rules history with an iron grip, dictating the preservation of mythical fact and the destruction of antimyth long before the historian can even begin to reverse this relentless process. Mankind, it would seem, will not tolerate the critical assaults upon its heroes and the charitable reassessments of its villains that mythless history requires.

In many respects, then, Freud will always remain a crypto-biologist, his self-analysis will always be seen as heroic and unprecedented, and his years of discovery will always partake of a "splendid isolation" and an inscrutable genius. After all, Freud really was a hero. The myths are merely his historical due, and they shall continue to live on, protecting his brilliant legacy to mankind, as long as this legacy remains a powerful part of human consciousness.

APPENDICES

BIBLIOGRAPHY

INDEX

APPENDIX A

Two Published Accounts Detailing
Josef Breuer's 4 November 1895
Defense of Freud's Views on
Sexuality and Neurosis

On 14, 21, and 28 October 1895, Freud delivered three lectures, entitled "On Hysteria," before the Vienna College of Physicians. These lectures were widely followed by the German-language medical weeklies, five of which also reported, in varying detail, the lively discussion about Freud's lectures that followed on 4 and 11 November.[1] Among the commentators was Josef Breuer, who strenuously supported Freud's findings. I have translated here in full the two longest accounts of Breuer's remarks, which were evidently taken down in shorthand as he spoke. The first and longer of these two transcriptions is from the *Wiener medizinische Presse*:

> J. Breuer remarked by way of introduction that even though he has laid the cornerstone for the structure built by Freud, the structure itself is exclusively Freud's intellectual property; indeed, he initially faced the development of Freud's tenets and theories skeptically and with reservations. To be sure, he was countered step by step in his objections and is now converted and convinced.
>
> If Freud's theories at first give the impression of being ingenious psychological theorems, linked to the facts, but essentially aprioristically constructed, then the speaker can insist that it is actually a matter of

1. *Wiener medizinische Presse*, 36 (1895):1717–18, 1757–58; *Wiener medizinische Blätter*, 18 (1895):716–17; *Wiener klinische Rundschau*, 9 (1895):711, 728; *Wiener medizinische Wochenschrift*, 45 (1895):1995–97; *Münchener medicinische Wochenschrift*, 42 (1895):1092–93. Only the first and third of these medical journals carried a report of the 11 November discussion.

facts and interpretations that have grown out of observations. As against the suspicion that the recollections of patients might be artificial products suggested by the physician, Breuer can assert from his own observations that it is enormously and especially difficult to force something upon, or put something over on, this sort of patient. Besides, this point can hardly play a role with regard to the vast quantity of facts that constitute the foundation of Freud's theory. A third objection concerns the overvaluation of sexuality. One can perhaps say in this connection that, to be sure, not every symptom of hysteria is sexual, but that the original root of the same probably is. Neurasthenia is certainly an illness that is sexual in root. Breuer is indebted to these views [of Freud's] for hints as to practical, everyday treatment in matters that he previously never understood. Thus, in the case of a young girl, for example, it is really not right because she is pale and easily exhaustible—in short, in a condition that would immediately lead us to think of masturbation and pollutions in the case of a boy—that we should overlook the sexual factor merely on account of the fact that we are dealing with a girl, and prescribe iron. It would only be a step forward if we would think more frequently in practical life of that which belongs, after all, to the fundamentals of human existence. The adult human being is, of course, only sexual in small part; but who does not know the extent to which sexuality plays a role [in neurosis] at the time of puberty? We assume and know this for boys, but not for girls. We know very little whatsoever about the sexuality of young girls and are also not able to transpose our own [male] sexuality into that of women. Nevertheless, we are dealing with conditions [prevailing] in half of mankind that are of the utmost concern. Now for this reason the things that Freud is finding are the most important human documents. Even though the reported theories still appear to be forced here and there, we are also dealing here with only a provisional conclusion, insofar as it corresponds to the discovered facts. (*Wiener medizinische Presse*, 36 [1895]:1717–18)

The second account, although shorter than the first by some forty words, seems to be slightly more faithful to Breuer's original language as reflected in the other still briefer accounts (listed in note 1); it is from the *Wiener medizinische Blätter*:[2]

Breuer explains right from the beginning of his presentation, which was received with lively applause, that one would be mistaken if one expected that he would speak here as coauthor, because the entire theory of repression is essentially Freud's property. He is acquainted with a large portion of the cases that constitute the foundation of Freud's theory. To be precise, he witnessed the birth of the theory at first hand and, indeed, not without some opposition to it; but he now stands, as a result of Freud's illuminating explanations, as a convert before the assembly.

If one supposes that his [Freud's] theories are an a priori construction, then this would be a mistake. Much work and a great quantity of observations are contained in Freud's lectures. One might also suppose that the patients are under the pressuring influence of the physician, that

2. Throughout this translation I have rendered the subjunctive mode, which is used in German for indirect discourse, in the less cumbersome mode of direct discourse.

the physician suggests to his patients everything that he wants to hear. This just isn't so. The speaker has found it enormously difficult to force something upon patients. One point on which the speaker is not in agreement with Freud is the overvaluation of sexuality. Freud probably did not intend to say that every hysterical symptom has a sexual background, but rather that the original root of hysteria is sexual. We still see unclearly [in these matters]. It is left only to the future, to the masses of observations, to bring full clarification to this question; in any case, one must be thankful to Freud for the theoretical hints he has given us.

In the case of the female sex the complaint about the underestimation of the sexual factor is especially justified. It is not right, for example, that one should simply prescribe iron against anemia in young girls who suffer from insomnia, etc.—without even thinking of masturbation—while we im....ediately look for pollutions in the case of young men. We find ourselves in the state of a hysteria with regard to this matter; we repress this feeling which is unpleasant to us. We simply know nothing about the sexuality of young girls and women. No physician has any idea what sort of symptoms an erection calls forth in women, because the young women refuse to speak of the matter and the old ones have already forgotten about it.

The objection might also perhaps have been raised that a lack of coherence makes itself felt in Freud's explanations; now there is something to this, for one ought not to forget that we have provisional conclusions before us and that every theory is a temporary structure. (*Wiener medizinische Blätter, 18* [1895]:717)

Both of these accounts show that by the fall of 1895 Breuer had come to agree wholeheartedly with Freud that sexuality was a very important, and a generally underrated, factor in the etiology of hysteria and other neuroses (see Chapter 3). At the same time, Breuer's comments make it equally clear that he was still reserving final judgment on certain of Freud's theoretical formulations, and that he did not regard the sexual etiology as extending to *every* symptom of hysteria.

One also receives the impression from Breuer's remarks that, in an effort to get Freud's views accepted, he was intentionally portraying Freud's theories as being more moderate on the issue of sexuality than in fact he, Breuer, knew them to be. This impression is reinforced by a third account of Breuer's 4 November 1895 comments, which reads in part, "Regarding a possible overvaluation of the sexual factor in the formation of hysteria, he [Breuer] would like to believe [*möchte er glauben*] that Freud does not attribute every hysterical symptom to the sexual sphere; rather, that his assertions on this matter go only so far as to claim that the root of hysteria arises from this sphere" (*Wiener klinische Rundschau, 9* [1895]:711).

In conclusion, contrary to the traditional psychoanalytic portrayal of Breuer as refusing to accept sexuality's important role in neurosis, his scientific stand may be characterized as one of strong partisan support for Freud, tempered by a reasonable apprehension that Freud might, out of revolutionary zeal, be promulgating his findings within a prematurely rigid theoretical system.

APPENDIX B

Josef Breuer's Metapsychology: The Matter of the "Remarkable Paradox"

Notwithstanding Breuer and Freud's collaborative development of a psychophysicalist model for hysterical symptom formation, their respective approaches to the mind-body problem in the 1890s were actually somewhat antagonistic. Not only have these philosophical differences been little appreciated by Freud scholars, but, when mentioned at all, such differences are generally reversed. It is important to clarify these two positions if we are to understand precisely why Breuer found it impossible to endorse certain of Freud's more controversial theoretical conclusions.

Specifically, Breuer's emphasis upon hypnoid states in the causation of hysteria (that is, as a presumably congenital tendency toward dissociated states of consciousness) has generally been considered by historians of psychoanalysis as a purely *physiological* account of that affliction. On the other hand, Freud, with his notion of psychic defense against incompatible (sexual) ideas, has been judged as preferring a more *psychological* theory of mental illness.[1]

It should not be forgotten, however, that it was Josef Breuer who, in the opening portion of his "Theoretical" contribution to *Studies on Hysteria*, vigorously defended the priority of purely psychological modes of explanation over more physiological ones. "In what follows," Breuer forewarned his readers, "little mention will be made of the brain and none whatever of molecules. Psychical processes will be dealt with in the language of psychology; and, indeed, it cannot possibly be otherwise. If instead of 'idea' we chose to speak of 'excitation of the cortex,' the latter term would only have any meaning for us in so far as we recognized an old friend under the cloak and tacitly reinstated the 'idea.' . . . Accordingly, I may perhaps be forgiven if I make almost exclusive

---

1. See, for example, Jones (1953:275), who calls Breuer's approach "plainly a physiological one," in contrast to Freud's.

use of psychological terms" (1895d, S.E., 2:185). Thus, contrary to the usual characterization of Breuer's theoretical approach to psychopathology, it would appear that he actually preferred a more exclusively psychological conception of mental illness than Freud himself was advocating at this same time. Indeed, Freud, as we know from his posthumously published *Project for a Scientific Psychology*, was already engrossed by mid-1895 in an incredibly ambitious attempt to place psychopathology within a rigorous neurological and physicochemical explanatory framework (see Chapter 4).

I have raised this general issue because, as James Strachey has commented in connection with Breuer's approach to the mental apparatus, "A remarkable paradox is thus revealed" (S.E., 2:xxiv). Herein lies the paradox. Breuer, for his own part, had vowed in the *Studies* to explain hysteria along purely psychological lines; and yet, as the "Theoretical" chapter so plainly reveals, the dual physicalistic notions of "intracerebral excitation" and "the tendency to keep intracerebral excitation constant" (both involving repeated comparisons of the nervous system with an electrical apparatus) had dominated that chapter. In fact, these notions also underlay the essential metapsychological basis of the whole Breuer-Freud theory of unconscious trauma, catharsis, abreaction, and cure. The theoretical essence of this collaboration, then, appears to be intimately associated with Breuer's curious disregard for his own formal insistence that psychological processes should be treated solely in "the language of psychology."

This "remarkable paradox" of which Strachey has spoken sheds considerable light upon why Breuer and Freud agreed only partially on the issue of sexual etiology. Freud took his psychophysicalist model literally and accordingly understood the noxious influence of sexuality in organic as well as in psychological terms (see Chapters 3 and 4). Freud's dualist conception of the matter thus made sexuality (unlike, say, "fright") seem etiologically special to him (i.e., chemically tangible and hence potentially toxic). Breuer, on the other hand, continued to give more eclectic psychological recognition to the adverse etiological effects of *all* affects (sexuality, fright, anxiety, anger, revenge, and so forth). It is not surprising, then, that he questioned Freud's purely toxicological theory of the neurotic effects stemming from coitus interruptus and ejaculatio praecox and preferred instead a more psychodynamic explanation of this problem (*Studies*, 1895d, S.E., 2:246).

At the same time, the "remarkable paradox" presented by Breuer's "Theoretical" contribution to the *Studies* holds the principal key to his supposed chagrin at the public reception of the book. I base this assertion upon what turns out to have been Breuer's undeniable dismay over just one specific review of the *Studies*: that by Adolf Strümpell, a distinguished German neurologist whose similar views on hysteria Breuer and Freud had cited (1895d, S.E., 2:7–8, n. 3).

Although the bulk of this review was a balanced mixture of appreciative praise and reasoned criticism, Strümpell had gone on to castigate Josef Breuer's own "Theoretical" contribution to the *Studies* and had highlighted, furthermore, the "remarkable paradox" about which James Strachey has commented. "Instead of starting from plain medical experience and staying on the ground of factual observation," Strümpell objected, "Breuer begins with the 'intracerebral tonic excitation,' stating as a 'matter of fact' that 'there exists a tendency in the organism to the conservation of intracerebral excitation,' and then discusses the affect-reactions and explains certain hysterical symptoms . . ." (1896:159). The result of all this deductive analysis, Strümpell further complained, was a series of strange and all-too-generalized terms like "discharge," "abnormal reflex," "hysterical conversion," "abreacted" and "nonabreacted" ideas, the "principle of least resistance," "determination in a symbolic manner," "strangulated affect," "hysterical retention-phenomena," and so forth—terms which in his opinion were more scientifically pretentious than medically illuminating. "It seems to me," Strümpell concluded, "that most of this could have been said much more simply, more naturally, and more intelligibly. If it is certainly proper, as Breuer himself emphasizes, that psychological subjects should be discussed in the language of psychology, then the language used throughout cannot attain clarity by continually using a multitude of unnecessary foreign expressions . . . which perhaps evoke the appearance of scientific profundity, but which in reality only make more difficult and more obscure the simple, clear grasp of the actual processes of consciousness" (pp. 159–60).

Of all the reviewers of *Studies on Hysteria*, Adolf Strümpell was the only one who challenged the reductionistic "pretensions" upon which Breuer and Freud had based their whole metapsychological analysis of the problem.[2] Naturally it was Breuer, as author of the "Theoretical" chapter, who bore the brunt of this criticism. When we recall, moreover, that it was Breuer (1895d, S.E., 2:185) who had dubbed as "no more than a pointless disguise" the attempt to substitute the certainty of physicochemical terms for the obvious mysteries of purely psychological ones, it is not too hard to see why he might have been dismayed by Strümpell's trenchant criticisms.

To conclude, it is possible to see from the "remarkable paradox" inherent in Breuer's collaborative relationship with Freud that these two investigators converged on the problem of hysteria with conflicting explanatory (and reductionistic) allegiances during the 1890s. Where Breuer saw the appeal to physicalistic analogies as largely heuristic, Freud took these analogies literally and continually attempted to generalize from them—especially on the issue of sexual etiology (see Chapters 3 and 4).

2. Strümpell's 1896 critique of Breuer's "Theoretical" chapter is not much different, however, from that of a more recent and equally faultfinding judgment by a group of psychoanalyst-trainees. In articles that are hardly convincing, Gedo et al. (1964) and Schlessinger et al. (1967) have sought to attribute Breuer's unusually "speculative" bent in the "Theoretical" chapter to his insufficient "reality-testing" capabilities in the sphere of psychology.

APPENDIX C

Dr. Felix Gattel's Scientific

Collaboration with Freud (1897/98)

I offer here a brief statement of frank speculation as to what influence, if any, Dr. Felix Gattel (d. 1904) may have exerted upon Freud during the summer of 1897. Half-American by birth, Gattel came to Freud from Berlin as a professional pupil in mid-May 1897 (*Origins*, pp. 201–2).[1] Gattel remained in Vienna for precisely six months while also undertaking a systematic examination of one hundred consecutive cases of anxiety neurosis and neurasthenia from Krafft-Ebing's Psychiatric Clinic at the Vienna General Hospital (Gattel 1898).

Of particular historical interest is the fact that Gattel's study was undertaken for the sole purpose of testing Freud's own theories on the actual neuroses. In this endeavor Gattel was most successful, confirming Freud's sexual etiology in virtually every case that he examined.[2] In a letter to Fliess of 7 July 1897, Freud reported of Gattel that he "is becoming much attached to me and my theories, . . ." (*Origins*, p. 213).[3]

Gattel's most interesting discovery (at least as far as Freud was probably concerned) was not, however, the many sexual abnormalities he was able to correlate with the choice of actual neurosis according

1. Ernest Jones (1953:334) identifies Gattel as a pupil sent to Freud by Wilhelm Fliess. The published Fliess correspondence, from which references to Gattel have been partially excised, does not bear out this assertion, since Freud expressed his eagerness for Fliess to meet Gattel when the latter *returned* to Berlin (*Origins*, p. 213, letter of 7 July 1897).

2. For a critical review of Gattel's (1898) monograph, see Möbius (1898), who disagreed with Gattel's exclusive etiological emphasis upon sexuality; if one looked deep enough, Möbius countered, one could always find disturbances of a sexual nature in highly nervous or neurotic individuals. For a similar but somewhat more positive discussion of Gattel's monograph, see Havelock Ellis 1900a:213.

3. Unfortunately, further discussion of Gattel is omitted in mid-sentence from the published version of this letter; see *Anfänge*, p. 227, where the ellipsis points and punctuation make this deletion clear.

to Freud's own theories. Rather, a much more surprising finding emerged from this study. Gattel had initially attempted to exclude all cases of hysteria from his clinical sample, owing to the greater time generally required to confirm a childhood etiology using the psychoanalytic method (1898:11–12). Yet he still ended up with seventeen cases (or 17 percent of his sample) that displayed mild hysteria in either a pure form or in combination with an actual neurosis.

Given Gattel's purposeful exclusion of severe hysterias from his overall one-hundred-patient sample, the number that remained must be considered unusually high for anyone who was also prepared to endorse Freud's traumatic and "seductionist" theory of that disorder. Were childhood sexual assaults really one-third or even one-half as common as cases of chronic adolescent masturbation leading to neurasthenia? Gattel's statistics pointed to this remarkable conclusion, and, if anything, they actually underestimated the frequency of hysteria relative to other neurotic disorders. Freud, it must also be remembered, tended to see and to treat by psychoanalysis only the more severe cases of hysteria, for which his seduction etiology, he claimed, seemed perfectly plausible (Freud 1896c, S.E., 3:208). Nor was the high proportion of hysterics among Freud's patients upsetting to his theories, since he, unlike Gattel, was a known specialist in the treatment of this disorder. But the surprising frequency of hysterics in Gattel's *random* sample of nervous disorders was another matter entirely.

It is therefore of considerable relevance that Freud, in his letter of 21 September 1897 to Fliess announcing his abandonment of the seduction theory, specifically referred to his apparently recent "realization of the unexpected frequency of hysteria, in every case of which the same thing [a childhood seduction] applied . . ." (*Origins*, p. 215). Also of interest is the fact that Gattel, when he published his findings, ascribed most of his seventeen cases of hysteria to spontaneous sexual activity in childhood.[4] In only two cases (nos. 37 and 43) did Gattel find definite evidence of seduction in childhood by an older person, and neither case involved the father.

The supposition that Freud and Gattel were on close intellectual terms throughout the summer of 1897 is reinforced by Freud's invitation to Gattel to accompany him and his family on a three-week tour of Italy in early September 1897 (Jones 1953:334). Had Gattel completed his clinical work by the time he made this tour with Freud? It would seem likely that he had, given his relatively short stay in Vienna and his use of consecutively admitted patients at Krafft-Ebing's Psychiatric Clinic. Unfortunately, the available internal evidence from Gattel's monograph (that is, the dates he recorded in connection with individual case histories) does not allow us to be at all certain on this point. For example, the latest date recorded in any of the case histories (no. 93) refers to a patient whose anxiety attacks occurred "throughout the summer" of 1897 ("*den ganzen Sommer hindurch*" [1898:47]). Thus

4. See cases 23, 34, 35, 44, 56, 64, 68, 80, 87, and 90, where Gattel reports evidence of early masturbation and of "sex play" with other children.

Gattel seems to have had contact with patients as late as the end of September, when he and Freud had returned to Vienna. The formal number of the case history, however, suggests that this was one of Gattel's last patients. Thus he may have actually completed his study before traveling with Freud to Italy and then reinterviewed a few patients who were still in residence at Krafft-Ebing's clinic when he returned. Or, Gattel may have compiled the bulk of his case histories before traveling to Italy and then added a few more apparently consecutive cases to his total sample before returning to Berlin in mid-November.

In any event, it cannot be disputed that Freud and Gattel worked closely on this study and discussed the results with each other. Wilhelm Fliess later reported in 1906 that Freud eventually came to consider Gattel as his plagiarist—apparently for not offering him coauthorship in Gattel's publication! Fliess quoted the following remark by Freud from an unpublished portion of their correspondence: "It is embarrassing to me to say to him [Gattel] that he cannot publish these things as his own property even if he has pursued them further [than I]" (Fliess 1906a:18, letter of unknown date). Freud was also sufficiently impressed by Gattel's findings that in 1901 he contemplated publishing a similar clinical study of his own. "I have begun collecting my notes," Freud informed Fliess on 15 February, "of things told me by neurotics in my consulting room for the purpose of demonstrating the connection between sexual life and neurosis revealed even by such necessarily fleeting observation, and of adding my own comments. In other words I am doing roughly the same sort of thing as Gattl [sic] did when he made himself so unpopular in Vienna" (Origins, pp. 328–29).

In conclusion, the fact that Gattel's scientific collaboration with Freud has hitherto received no consideration from students of Freud's life reflects the considerable power that the myth of Freud's intellectual isolation has exerted over Freud scholarship.[5] Whether Gattel's researches, conducted with Freud's guidance, actually helped to undermine Freud's seduction etiology in the fall of 1897 is impossible to say for certain; but it is likely that they did, and, in any event, the collaboration was assuredly not without a more general influence upon Freud.

---

5. Decker's (1977:5, 95, 135) valuable monograph, which has appeared since I drafted this appendix, briefly treats Gattel's association with Freud, but only in terms of the latter's influence upon Gattel.

APPENDIX D

The Dating of Freud's Reading

of Albert Moll's *Untersuchungen*

über die Libido sexualis

I have argued in Chapter 8 that Albert Moll's *Untersuchungen über die Libido sexualis* (1897*b*) probably influenced Freud's crucial decision in the fall of 1897 to abandon the seduction theory of neurosis. It is therefore incumbent upon me to establish that Freud had actually read this work prior to 21 September 1897, when he announced his decision to Wilhelm Fliess (*Origins*, p. 215). I shall take up this issue under three separate headings: the evidence suggested by Freud's personal copy of the *Libido Sexualis*; the evidence relating to the actual availability of Moll's book in 1897; and the critical evidence provided by a passing reference to Moll's ideas in Freud's correspondence with Fliess.

Freud's copy of Moll's work. Freud's personal copy of Moll's *Libido Sexualis* bears an 1898 imprint, by which date of imprint Freud himself always referred to this work in his own publications. Such evidence seems inconsistent with my historical hypothesis. There can be no question, however, that Moll's book was originally issued, in two separate parts, in the spring and summer of 1897. When first issued, Part One of the *Libido Sexualis* carried a paper cover and title page, both dated 1897, while Part Two carried a similar paper cover dated 1898 and a second title page dated 1897.

How, then, did Freud acquire a copy of the *Libido Sexualis* carrying an 1898 imprint at the *head* of the volume? Did he perhaps acquire a second printing of the work in 1898—a possibility that would invalidate my historical conclusions in this connection? Comparison of Freud's personal copy of Moll's work with numerous other copies in American and European libraries reveals that Freud's is atypical in certain respects, and that it must have passed through the following history. First, Freud's copy was originally read by him in soft-cover form, as issued in 1897, and was then bound in leather at a later date. (Freud's marginal comment *"ubw Ph"* ["unconscious phantasies"] on page 13 has been slightly cut off by the binder's subsequent trimming of the pages.) Freud was in the habit of having his books bound whenever he acquired them in soft-cover form, and numerous volumes in his London library—the Moll volume included—possess identical or near-identical leather bindings. It is the process of binding that explains the atypical nature of Freud's copy, with its 1898 imprint at the head of the volume. Part Two had been issued with a separate sixteen-page signature containing a half-title page, yet another title page (with an 1898 imprint), a Preface, and a Table of Contents for the entire work (Kalischer 1897b). This separate signature was meant to be placed at the head of the volume, as it doubtless was for all new copies issued by the publisher, and as it also was by Freud's binder, who discarded all the additional preliminary pages, and hence all evidence of the 1897 imprint.

The availability of Moll's book. We have it on Moll's (1897a: 161 n.) own testimony that Part One of the *Libido Sexualis* was already on sale in April 1897 when he published an article on homosexuality. Part Two, according to this article, was scheduled to appear "in a few days." The second part had already been printed by this date, since Moll was able to refer to specific paginations in the installment about to be issued (1897a: 161 n., 162 n.).

Moll's testimony regarding the publication dates of his book is corroborated by the subsequent reviews of Kalischer (1897a, 1897b). The first of these reviews, treating Part One of the *Libido Sexualis*, appeared in the *Zeitschrift für Medizinalbeamte* on 15 June 1897. It was followed by a second review, devoted to Part Two of the *Libido Sexualis*, in the 15 November 1897 issue of this same periodical. In this second notice, Kalischer mentions that Part Two of Moll's book had indeed appeared "a short time after the appearance of the first part" (1897b: 812).

Also of relevance is the fact that Moll's Preface, bound in the same signature containing the Table of Contents issued with Part Two, is dated "July 1897." Judging from this July date and from Kalischer's November comment that Part Two had appeared "a short time after" Part One, it is probable that the entire work was available toward the end of July or the beginning of August.

That Freud would have known about the appearance of this work almost as soon as it became available seems likely owing to his close professional contact with Richard von Krafft-Ebing. Krafft-Ebing, the most cited authority in Moll's work, would very likely have received a complimentary copy from Moll, whose *Libido Sexualis* he later lauded in subsequent editions of the *Psychopathia Sexualis*. The appearance of Moll's book also coincides with the period in which Krafft-Ebing was busy writing a report on Freud in connection with the latter's nomination for a professorship (*Origins*, p. 193, letter of 6 April 1897; Gickl-horn and Gicklhorn 1960:95–98, document dated 10 May 1897). Dubious as he was about Freud's seduction theory, Krafft-Ebing may well have discussed with him the considerable relevance that Moll's latest clinical findings possessed on this controversial issue. In any event, Krafft-Ebing continued to praise Moll's researches for having demonstrated "very clearly and convincingly" that childhood seductions and sexual play among members of the same sex do not lead to homosexuality (*Psychopathia Sexualis*, 1892:193–94 n.; 1899 trans.:276 n.).

Freud's reference to Moll in the Fliess correspondence. A single reference to Albert Moll appears in Freud's correspondence with Wilhelm Fliess in a letter dated 14 November 1897: "I have often supected that something organic played a part in repression; I have told you before that it is a question of the attitude adopted to former sexual zones, and I added that I had been pleased to come across the same idea in Moll. Privately, I would not concede priority in the idea to anyone; in my case the suggestion was linked to the changed part played by sensations of smell . . ." (*Origins*, p. 231). The context of Freud's reference suggests that Freud was thinking of Moll's similar treatment, in Part Two of the *Libido Sexualis* (1897b:376–99), of the various phylogenetic changes that have served to differentiate human sexuality from animal sexuality (loss of the sense of smell, adoption of clothing, etc.). None of Moll's previous publications, including a brief synopsis of the *Libido Sexualis* published earlier that year (1897a), had discussed this same point. Thus Freud had evidently read Part Two of Moll's *Libido Sexualis* by November 1897. Freud's marginal annotations of Moll's book (mostly scorings of noteworthy passages, including several in the rele-vant portion of Part Two [pp. 386–87, 399]) are unfortunately of no help in dating his reading of it.

This November 1897 mention of Moll also makes it clear that Freud had previously discussed Moll's ideas on sexual evolution with Fliess. No such discussion appears in the published Fliess correspondence, and, in any event, Freud's November reference to the subject sug-gests that the earlier communication was an oral one. Freud's most recent meeting with Fliess had taken place immediately after Freud re-turned from his summer holiday and announced his abandonment of the seduction theory (*Origins*, p. 217). Thus, unless Freud read Part Two of Moll's *Libido Sexualis* during the four or five days before leaving for Berlin to meet with Fliess, he must have already been familiar with Moll's work during the period immediately preceding his decision to abandon the seduction theory.

BIBLIOGRAPHY

NOTE: Where both American and British editions of the same publication date are listed and pagination differs, I have cited the American edition. The established alphabetical subscripts for Freud's works within individual years have been retained from the Bibliography of Freud's publications assembled in the final volume of *The Standard Edition of the Complete Psychological Works of Sigmund Freud* (1953–74, 24:47–82). The *Standard Edition*'s practice of modernizing spelling for journal and publication titles has not, however, been followed here. For full bibliographical information on the *Standard Edition*, see Freud 1953–74.

ABRAHAM, KARL

1924. *Versuch einer Entwicklungsgeschichte der Libido auf Grund der Psychoanalyse seelischer Störungen*. Leipzig, Vienna, Zurich: Internationaler Psychoanalytischer Verlag.
Trans.: "A Short Study of the Development of the Libido, Viewed in the Light of Mental Disorders" (Abraham 1953:418–501).

1927. *Selected Papers of Karl Abraham*. With an Introductory Memoir by Ernest Jones. Translated by Douglas Bryan and Alix Strachey. London: Hogarth Press and The Institute of Psycho-Analysis.

1953. *Selected Papers*. Vol. 1: *Selected Papers on Psychoanalysis*. With an Introductory Memoir by Ernest Jones. Translated by Douglas Bryan and Alix Strachey. New York: Basic Books; London: Hogarth Press, 1954.

1955. *Selected Papers*. Vol. 2: *Selected Papers: Clinical Papers and Essays on Psychoanalysis*. Edited by Hilda Abraham. Translated by Hilda Abraham and D. R. Ellison. New York: Basic Books; London: Hogarth Press.

ABRAHAMSEN, DAVID

1946. *The Mind and Death of a Genius*. New York: Columbia University Press.

ACKERKNECHT, ERWIN H.

1963. "Josef Breuer (1842–1925)." *Neue Österreichische Biographie ab 1815*, 15:126–30.

ADAMS, MARK B.

1973. "Aleksandr Onufrievich Kovalevsky." *Dictionary of Scientific Biography*, 7:474–77.

ADLER, ALFRED

1907. *Studie über Minderwertigkeit von Organen*. Berlin: Urban & Schwarzenberg.
Trans.: Adler (1917a).

1910. "Der psychische Hermaphroditismus im Leben und in der Neurose." *Fortschritte der Medizin*, 38:486–93.

ADLER, ALFRED *(continued)*

1912. *Ueber den nervösen Charakter: Grundzüge einer vergleichenden Individual-Psychologie und Psychotherapie.* Wiesbaden: J. F. Bergmann.
   Trans.: Adler (1917*b*).
1917*a.* *Study of Organ Inferiority and Its Psychical Compensation.* Translated by Smith Ely Jelliffe. New York: Nervous and Mental Disease Publishing Co.
   German Text: Adler (1907).
1917*b.* *The Neurotic Constitution: Outlines of a Comparative Individualistic Psychology and Psychotherapy.* Translated by Bernard Glueck and John E. Lind. New York: Moffat, Yard & Co.
   German Text: Adler (1912).
1920. *Praxis und Theorie der Individual-Psychologie: Vorträge zur Einführung in die Psychotherapie für Ärzte, Psychologen und Lehrer.* Munich and Wiesbaden: J. F. Bergmann.
   Trans.: Adler (1924).
1924. *The Practice and Theory of Individual Psychology.* Translated by P. Radin. London: Kegan Paul, Trench, Trubner & Co.
   German Text: Adler (1920).
1927*a.* *Menschenkenntnis.* Leipzig: S. Hirzel.
   Trans.: Adler (1927*b*).
1927*b.* *Understanding Human Nature.* Translated by Walter Béran Wolfe. New York: Greenberg; London: George Allen & Unwin, 1928.
   German Text: Adler (1927*a*).
1931. *What Life Should Mean to You.* Edited by Alan Porter. Boston: Little, Brown & Co.; London: George Allen & Unwin, 1932.
1956. *The Individual Psychology of Alfred Adler: A Systematic Presentation in Selections from His Writings.* Edited and annotated by Heinz L. Ansbacher and Rowena R. Ansbacher. New York: Basic Books; London: George Allen & Unwin, 1958.

AEBLY, JAKOB

1928. *Die Fliess'sche Periodenlehre im Lichte biologischer und mathematischer Kritik: Ein Beitrag zur Geschichte der Zahlenmystik im XX. Jahrhundert.* Stuttgart: Hippokrates-Verlag.

ALEXANDER, FRANZ

1921. "Metapsychologische Betrachtungen." *Internationale Zeitschrift für Psychoanalyse,* 6:270–85.
1950. *Psychosomatic Medicine: Its Principles and Applications.* New York: W. W. Norton & Co.; London: George Allen & Unwin, 1952.

ALLERS, RUDOLF

1940. *The Successful Error: A Critical Study of Freudian Psychoanalysis.* New York: Sheed & Ward.

ALTHAUS, JULIUS

1882. "Beiträge zur Physiologie und Pathologie des N. Olfactorius." *Archiv für Psychiatrie und Nervenkrankheiten,* 12:122–40.

ALTHUSSER, LOUIS

1969. *For Marx.* Translated from the French by Ben Brewster. London: Allen Lane.

AMACHER, PETER

1965. *Freud's Neurological Education and Its Influence on Psychoanalytic Theory. Psychological Issues,* 4, no. 4 (Monograph 16).
1972. "Sigmund Freud." *Dictionary of Scientific Biography,* 5:171–81.
1974. "The Concepts of the Pleasure Principle and Infantile Erogenous Zones Shaped by Freud's Neurological Education." *The Psychoanalytic Quarterly,* 43:218–23.

The American Journal of Neurology and Psychiatry

1882. Review of "Zur 'conträren Sexualempfindung' in klinisch-forensischer Hinsicht," by Richard von Krafft-Ebing (1882). 1:323–25.

ANDERSSON, OLA

1962. *Studies in the Prehistory of Psychoanalysis: The Etiology of Psychoneuroses and Some Related Themes in Sigmund Freud's Scientific Writings and Letters, 1886–1896.* Stockholm: Svenska Bokförlaget.

ANDREAS-SALOMÉ, LOU

1958 [1912–13]. *In der Schule bei Freud: Tagebuch eines Jahres,* 1912/1913. Edited by Ernst Pfeiffer. Zurich: M. Niehans.
  Trans.: Andreas-Salomé (1964 [1912–13]).
1964 [1912–13]. *The Freud Journal of Lou Andreas-Salomé.* Translated and with an Introduction by Stanley A. Leavy. New York: Basic Books.
  German Text: Andreas-Salomé (1958 [1912–13]).

ANDRESKI, STANISLAV

1972. *Social Sciences as Sorcery.* London: André Deutsch; New York: St. Martin's Press, 1973.

ANSBACHER, HEINZ L.

1959. "The Significance of the Socio-Economic Status of the Patients of Freud and of Adler." *American Journal of Psychotherapy, 13*:376–82.

ANZIEU, DIDIER

1959. *L'Auto-analyse: Son Rôle dans la découverte de la psychanalyse par Freud, sa fonction en psychanalyse.* Paris: Presses Universitaires de France.

ARDUIN

1900. "Die Frauenfrage und die sexuellen Zwischenstufen." *Jahrbuch für sexuelle Zwischenstufen, 2*:211–23.

ARRHENIUS, SVANTE

1898. "Die Einwirkung kosmischer Einflüsse auf physiologische Verhältnisse." *Skandinavisches Archiv für Physiologie, 8*:367–416.

ASCHENBRANDT, THEODOR

1883. "Die physiologische Wirkung und Bedeutung des Cocain. muriat. auf den menschlichen Organismus." *Deutsche medizinische Wochenschrift, 9*:730–32.

ATKINSON, JAMES JASPER

1903. *Primal Law.* Published with Andrew Lang, *Social Origins,* pp. 209–94. London: Longmans, Green, and Co.

BAILEY, PERCIVAL

1965. *Sigmund the Unserene: A Tragedy in Three Acts.* Springfield, Ill.: Charles C. Thomas.

BAKAN, DAVID

1958. *Sigmund Freud and the Jewish Mystical Tradition.* Princeton: D. Van Nostrand Co.

BALDWIN, JAMES MARK

1895. *Mental Development in the Child and the Race: Methods and Processes.* New York and London: Macmillan and Co.

BALOGH, PENELOPE

   1971.   *Freud: A Biographical Introduction.* New York: Charles Scribner's Sons.

BALTZER, FRIEDRICH [FRITZ]

   1967.   *Theodor Boveri: Life and Work of a Great Biologist, 1862–1915.* Translated
            from the German by Dorothea Rudnick. Berkeley: University of California
            Press.

BARNES, BARRY

   1974.   *Scientific Knowledge and Sociological Theory.* Monographs in Social Theory.
            London and Boston: Routledge & Kegan Paul.

BEARD, JOHN

   1896.   *On Certain Problems of Vertebrate Embryology.* Jena: Gustav Fischer.
   1897.   *The Span of Gestation and the Cause of Birth: A Study of the Critical
            Period and Its Effects in Mammalia.* Jena: Gustav Fischer.

BECKER, ERNEST

   1973.   *The Denial of Death.* New York: Free Press.

BELL, SANFORD

   1902.   "A Preliminary Study of the Emotion of Love between the Sexes." *The
            American Journal of Psychology, 13*:325–54.

BENEDIKT, MORITZ

   1868.   *Elektrotherapie.* Vienna: Tendler & Co.
   1889.   "Aus der Pariser Kongresszeit. Erinnerungen und Betrachtungen." *Inter-
            nationale klinische Rundschau, 3*:1611–14, 1657–59.
   1894.   *Hypnotismus und Suggestion: Eine klinisch-psychologische Studie.* Leipzig
            and Vienna: M. Breitenstein.
   1901.   "Die Nasen-Messiade von Fliess." *Wiener medizinische Wochenschrift, 51*:
            361–65.
   1906.   *Aus meinem Leben: Erinnerungen und Erörterungen.* Vienna: Carl Konegen.

BERGER, ALFRED VON

   1896.   "Chirurgie der Seele." Review of *Studien über Hysterie,* by Josef Breuer
            and Sigmund Freud (1895). *Neue Freie Presse,* 2 February. Partially re-
            printed in *Almanach der Psychoanalyse,* pp. 285–89. Vienna: Internation-
            aler Psychoanalytischer Verlag, 1933.
   1897.   "Wahrheit und Irrtum in der Katharsis-Theorie des Aristoteles." In *Aris-
            toteles' Poetik übersetzt und eingeleitet von Theodor Gomperz,* pp. 69–98.
            Leipzig: Von Veit.

BERGER, PETER L., AND LUCKMANN, THOMAS

   1966.   *The Social Construction of Reality: A Treatise in the Sociology of Knowl-
            edge.* Garden City, N.Y.: Doubleday & Co.; London: Allen Lane, 1967.

BERNAYS, ANNA FREUD

   1940.   "My Brother, Sigmund Freud." *The American Mercury, 51*:335–42.

BERNAYS, JACOB

   1857.   *Grundzüge der verlorenen Abhandlung des Aristoteles über Wirkung der
            Tragödie.* Breslau: E. Trewendt.
   1880.   *Zwei Abhandlungen über die Aristotelische Theorie des Drama.* Berlin:
            Wilhelm Hertz.

BERNFELD, SIEGFRIED

1944. "Freud's Earliest Theories and the School of Helmholtz." *The Psychoanalytic Quarterly*, 13:341–62.
1949. "Freud's Scientific Beginnings." *The American Imago*, 6:163–96.
1951. "Sigmund Freud, M.D., 1882–1885." *The International Journal of Psycho-Analysis*, 32:204–17.
1953. "Freud's Studies on Cocaine, 1884–1887." *Journal of the American Psychoanalytic Association*, 1:581–613.

BERNFELD, SIEGFRIED, AND BERNFELD, SUZANNE CASSIRER

1952. "Freud's First Year in Practice, 1886–1887." *Bulletin of the Menninger Clinic*, 16:37–49.

BERNFELD, SIEGFRIED, AND FEITELBERG, SERGEI

1930. "Der Entropiesatz und der Todestrieb." *Imago*, 16:187–206.

BERNFELD, SUZANNE CASSIRER

1955. "Sigmund Freud: The Origins of Psychoanalysis; a Book Review." *The Psychoanalytic Quarterly*, 24:384–91.

BERNHEIM, HIPPOLYTE

1884. *De la Suggestion dans l'état hypnotique et dans l'état de veille.* Paris: Octave Doin.
1886. *De la Suggestion et de ses applications à la thérapeutique.* Paris: Octave Doin.
        Trans.: Bernheim (1897).
1891. *Hypnotisme, suggestion, psychothérapie: Études nouvelles.* Paris: Octave Doin.
1897. *Suggestive Therapeutics: A Treatise on the Nature and Uses of Hypnotism.* Translated from the 2nd rev. ed. by Christian Herter. New York: G. P. Putnam's Sons.
        French Text: Bernheim (1886).

BIBRING, EDWARD

1941. "The Development and Problems of the Theory of the Instincts." *The International Journal of Psycho-Analysis*, 22:102–31.

BILLINSKY, JOHN M.

1969. "Jung and Freud (The End of a Romance)." *Andover Newton Quarterly*, 10:39–43.

BINET, ALFRED

1887. "Le Fétichisme dans l'amour." *Revue Philosophique*, 24:143–67, 252–74.
1892. *Les Altérations de la personnalité.* Paris: Félix Alcan.

BINET, ALFRED, AND FÉRÉ, CHARLES

1887. *Le Magnétisme animal.* Paris: Félix Alcan.

BINSWANGER, LUDWIG

1957. *Sigmund Freud: Reminiscences of a Friendship.* Translated by Norbert Guterman. New York and London: Grune & Stratton.

BINZ, CARL

1878. *Über den Traum: Nach einem 1876 gehaltenen öffentlichen Vortrag.* Bonn: Adolph Marcus.

BLANTON, SMILEY

1971.   *Diary of My Analysis with Sigmund Freud*. With biographical notes and
        comments by Margaret Gray Blanton. Introduction by Iago Galdston. New
        York: Hawthorn Books.

BLEULER, EUGEN

1896.   Review of *Studien über Hysterie*, by Josef Breuer and Sigmund Freud
        (1895). *Münchener medicinische Wochenschrift*, 43:524–25.

BLOCH, IWAN

1902–3. *Beiträge zur Aetiologie der Psychopathia sexualis*. 2 vols. Foreword by
         Albert Eulenburg. Dresden: H. R. Dohrn.
            Trans.: Bloch (1933, 1935).
1907.   *Das Sexualleben unserer Zeit in seinen Beziehungen zur modernen Kultur*.
         Berlin: Louis Marcus.
            Trans.: Bloch (1910).
1910.   *The Sexual Life of Our Time in Its Relations to Modern Civilization*. Trans-
         lated from the 6th ed. by M. Eden Paul. London: Rebman.
            German Text: Bloch (1907).
1914.   "Aufgaben und Ziele der Sexualwissenschaft." *Zeitschrift für Sexualwis-
         senschaft*, 1:2–11.
1916.   "Über die Freudsche Lehre." *Zeitschrift für Sexualwissenschaft*, 3:57–63.
1917.   "Worte der Erinnerung an Albert Eulenburg." *Zeitschrift für Sexualwis-
         senschaft*, 4:240–43.
1933.   *Anthropological Studies in the Strange Sexual Practices of All Races in
         All Ages, Ancient and Modern, Oriental and Occidental, Primitive and
         Civilized*. Translated by Keene Wallis. New York: Anthropological Press.
            German Text: Bloch (1902–3, 1).
1935.   *Anthropological and Ethnological Studies in the Strangest Sex Acts in
         Modes of Love of All Races Illustrated, Oriental, Occidental, Savage, Civil-
         ized*. Translated by Ernst Vogel. New York: Falstaff Press.
            German Text: Bloch (1902–3, 2).

BLUMENFELD, FELIX

1926.   "Allgemeine Pathologie und Symptomatologie." In *Handbuch der Hals-,
        Nasen-, und Ohren-Heilkunde*. Vol. 2: *Die Krankheiten der Luftwege und
        der Mundhöhle*, pp. 28–64. Edited by A. Denker and O. Kahler. Berlin:
        Julius Springer; Munich: J. F. Bergmann.

BOLK, LOUIS

1926.   *Das Problem der Menschwerdung*. Jena: Gustav Fischer.

BÖLSCHE, WILHELM

1898.   *Charles Darwin: Ein Lebensbild*. Leipzig: R. Voigtländer.
1898–1903. *Das Liebesleben in der Natur: Eine Entwickelungsgeschichte der
         Liebe*. 3 vols. Berlin and Leipzig: Eugen Diederichs.
            Trans.: Bölsche (1931).
1900.   *Ernst Haeckel: Ein Lebensbild*. Dresden and Leipzig: H. Seemann.
            Trans.: Bölsche (1906).
1904.   *Die Abstammung des Menschen*. 20th ed. Stuttgart: Kosmos, Gesellschaft
         der Naturfreunde.
            Trans.: Bölsche (1905).
1905.   *The Evolution of Man*. Translated by Ernest Untermann. Chicago: C. H.
         Kerr & Co.
            German Text: Bölsche (1904).
1906.   *Haeckel: His Life and Work*. Translated by Joseph McCabe. London:
         T. Fisher Unwin.
            German Text: Bölsche (1900).
1911–13. *Das Liebesleben in der Natur: Eine Entwickelungsgeschichte der Liebe*.
         2 vols. [5th (?) ed.]. Jena: Eugen Diederichs.
            Trans.: Bölsche (1931).

BÖLSCHE, WILHELM (continued)

1931. Love-Life in Nature: The Story of the Evolution of Love. Edited by Nor-
       man Haire. Translated by Cyril Brown. London: Jonathan Cape.
       German Text: Bölsche (1898–1903 and later eds.).

BOLLE, FRITZ

1955. "Wilhelm Bölsche." Neue Deutsche Biographie, 2:400.

BORHEK, JAMES T., AND CURTIS, RICHARD F.

1975. A Sociology of Belief. New York: John Wiley & Sons.

BORING, EDWIN G.

1950. A History of Experimental Psychology. 2nd ed. New York: Appleton-
       Century-Crofts.

BOTTOME, PHYLLIS

1939. Alfred Adler: A Biography. New York: G. P. Putnam's Sons.

BOURKE, JOHN GREGORY

1891. Scatalogic Rites of All Nations. Washington, D. C.: W. H. Lowdermilk
       & Co.

BOWLBY, JOHN

1969. Attachment and Loss. Vol. 1: Attachment. New York: Basic Books; Lon-
       don: Hogarth Press and The Institute of Psycho-Analysis.

BRAGG, B. W., AND ALLEN, V. L.

1970. ·"Ordinal Position and Conformity: A Role Theory Analysis." Sociometry,
       33:371–81.

BRAMWELL, J. MILNE

1896. "On the Evolution of Hypnotic Theory." Brain, 19:459–568.

BRESSLER, JOHANN

1896–97. "Culturhistorischer Beitrag zur Hysterie." Allgemeine Zeitschrift für
       Psychiatrie, 53:333–76.

BREUER, JOSEF

1868. "Die Selbststeuerung der Athmung durch den Nervus vagus." Sitzungs-
       berichte der kaiserlichen Akademie der Wissenschaften [Wien].
       Mathematisch-Naturwissenschaftliche Classe, 58, II. Abtheilung:909–37.
1874. "Ueber die Funktion der Bogengänge des Ohrlabyrinths." Medizinische
       Jahrbücher, 2nd series, 4:72–124.
1875. "Beiträge zur Lehre vom statischen Sinne (Gleichgewichtsorgan, Vesti-
       bularapparat des Ohrlabyrinths)." Medizinische Jahrbücher, 2nd series,
       5:87–156.
1895a. 4 November discussion of "Über Hysterie," three lectures delivered by
       Sigmund Freud (1895g) before the Wiener medicinische Doctorencol-
       legium on 14, 21, and 28 October 1895. Wiener medizinische Presse, 36:
       1717–18.
1895b. 4 November discussion of "Über Hysterie," three lectures delivered by
       Sigmund Freud (1895g) before the Wiener medicinische Doctorencol-
       legium on 14, 21, and 28 October 1895. Wiener medizinische Blätter, 18:
       717.
1895c. 4 November discussion of "Über Hysterie," three lectures delivered by
       Sigmund Freud (1895g) before the Wiener medicinische Doctorencol-
       legium on 14, 21, and 28 October 1895. Wiener klinische Rundschau,
       9:711.

BREUER, JOSEF *(continued)*

1895*d*. 4 November discussion of "Über Hysterie," three lectures delivered by Sigmund Freud (1895*g*) before the Wiener medicinische Doctorencollegium on 14, 21, and 28 October 1895. *Wiener medizinische Wochenschrift*, 45:1996–97.

1895*e*. 4 November discussion of "Über Hysterie," three lectures delivered by Sigmund Freud (1895*g*) before the Wiener medicinische Doctorencollegium on 14, 21, and 28 October 1895. *Münchener medicinische Wochenschrift*, 42:1092–93.

1907. "Über das Gehörorgan der Vögel." *Sitzungsberichte der kaiserlichen Akademie der Wissenschaften [Wien]*. Mathematisch-Naturwissenschaftliche Klasse, 116, III. Abteilung:249–92.

[1925]. *Curriculum vitae*. [Vienna].
Partial Trans.: Oberndorf (1953).

BREUER, JOSEF, AND FREUD, SIGMUND

1895. *Studien über Hysterie*. Leipzig and Vienna: Franz Deuticke.
Trans.: Freud (1895*d*).

BRIERLEY, MARJORIE

1967. Review of *The Standard Edition of the Complete Psychological Works of Sigmund Freud*, vol. 1, by Sigmund Freud (1953–74, 1 [1966]). *The International Journal of Psycho-Analysis*, 48:323–26.

BRIQUET, PIERRE

1859. *Traité clinique et thérapeutique de l'hystérie*. Paris: J. B. Baillière.

The British Medical Journal

1893. Review of *Psychopathia Sexualis*, by Richard von Krafft-Ebing (1886; 1892 trans.). 24 June, pp. 1325–26.

BROME, VINCENT

1967. *Freud and His Early Circle: The Struggles of Psycho-Analysis*. London: Heinemann; New York: William Morrow & Co., 1968.

BROSIN, HENRY W.

1960. "Evolution and Understanding of Diseases of the Mind." In *Evolution After Darwin*. Edited by Sol Tax. Vol. 2: *The Evolution of Man, Mind, Culture and Society*, pp. 373–422. Chicago: University of Chicago Press.

BROWN, JAMES A. C.

1961. *Freud and the Post-Freudians*. Middlesex, England: Penguin Books.

BRUN, RUDOLF

1926. "Experimentelle Beiträge zur Dynamik und Oekonomie des Triebkonflikts (Biologische Parallelen zu Freuds Trieblehre)." *Imago*, 12:147–70.

1936. "Sigmund Freuds Leistungen auf dem Gebiete der organischen Neurologie." *Schweizer Archiv für Neurologie und Psychiatrie*, 37:200–207.

1953. "Über Freuds Hypothese vom Todestrieb." *Psyche*, 7:81–111.

1954. "Biologie, Psychologie und Psychoanalyse." *Wiener Zeitschrift für Nervenheilkunde und deren Grenzgebiete*, 9:333–58.

BRUSH, STEPHEN G.

1974. "Should the History of Science be Rated X?" *Science*, 183:1164–72.

BRY, ILSE, AND RIFKIN, ALFRED H.

1962. "Freud and the History of Ideas: Primary Sources, 1886–1910." In *Science and Psychoanalysis*. Edited by Jules H. Masserman. Vol. 5: *Psychoanalytic Education*, pp. 6–36. New York: Grune & Stratton.

BUELENS, JAN

1971. *Sigmund Freud, Kind van zijn Tijd: Evolutie en Achtergronden van zijn Werk tot 1900.* Meppel: Boom.

BURCKHARDT, MAX

1900. "Ein modernes Traumbuch." Review of *Die Traumdeutung,* by Sigmund Freud (1900a). *Die Zeit,* 22, no. 275 (6 January):911; no. 276 (13 January):25–27.

BURNHAM, JOHN CHYNOWETH

1967. *Psychoanalysis and American Medicine, 1894–1918: Medicine, Science, and Culture. Psychological Issues,* 5 (Monograph 20).
1974. "The Medical Origins and Cultural Use of Freud's Instinctual Drive Theory." *The Psychoanalytic Quarterly,* 43:193–217.

BUTLER, SAMUEL

1880. *Unconscious Memory: A Comparison between the Theory of Dr. Ewald Hering . . . and the "Philosophy of the Unconscious" of Dr. Edward von Hartmann; with Translations from These Authors.* London: David Bogue.

BUTTERFIELD, HERBERT

1931. *The Whig Interpretation of History.* London: G. Bell and Sons.

BUXBAUM, E.

1951. "Freud's Dream Interpretation in the Light of His Letters to Fliess." *Bulletin of the Menninger Clinic,* 15:197–212.

CALOGERAS, ROY C., AND SCHUPPER, FABIAN X.

1972. "Origins and Early Formulations of the Oedipus Complex." *Journal of the American Psychoanalytic Association,* 20:751–75.

CAMPBELL, JOSEPH

1968. *The Hero with a Thousand Faces.* 2nd ed. Princeton: Princeton University Press. First ed., 1949.

CANT, REGINALD

1965. *Freud.* London: S.P.C.K.

CASPER, JOHANN LUDWIG

1863. *Klinische Novellen zur gerichtlichen Medicin: Nach eignen Erfahrungen.* Berlin: A. Hirschwald.
1881. *Practisches Handbuch der gerichtlichen Medicin.* 2 vols. 7th ed. Berlin: A. Hirschwald. First ed., 1857–58.

CASSIRER, ERNST

1950. *The Problem of Knowledge: Philosophy, Science, and History since Hegel.* Translated by William H. Woglom and Charles W. Hendel. New Haven: Yale University Press.

CHAMBARD, ERNEST

1881. *Du Somnambulisme en général: Analogies, signification nosologique et étiologie.* Paris: Parent.

CHAMBERLAIN, ALEXANDER FRANCIS

1900. *The Child: A Study in the Evolution of Man.* The Contemporary Science Series, vol. 39. London: Walter Scott Publishing Co.; New York: Charles Scribner's Sons.

CHARCOT, JEAN-MARTIN

1882. "Sur les divers états nerveux déterminés par l'hypnotisation chez les hystériques." *Comptes Rendus Hebdomadaires des Séances de l'Académie des Sciences*, 94:403–5.
1887. *Leçons sur les maladies du système nerveux, faites à la Salpêtrière, III.* In *Œuvres complètes* (1888–94, 3).
1887–89. *Leçons du mardi à la Salpêtrière: Policliniques, 1887–[1889].* 2 vols. Paris: Bureaux du Progrès Médical.
1888–94. *Œuvres complètes.* 9 vols. Paris: Bureaux du Progrès Médical, A. Delahaye & E. Lecrosnier.
1893. "La Foi qui guérit." *Archives de Neurologie*, 25:72–87.

CHARCOT, JEAN-MARTIN, AND MAGNAN, VALENTIN

1882. "Inversion du sens génital." *Archives de Neurologie*, 3:53–60; 4:296–322.

CHEVALIER, JULIEN

1885. *De L'Inversion de l'instinct sexuel au point de vue médico-légal.* Paris: Octave Doin.
1893. *Une Maladie de la personnalité: L'Inversion sexuelle; psycho-physiologie, sociologie, tératologie, aliénation mentale, psychologie morbide, anthropologie, médecine judiciaire.* Preface by A. Lacassagne. Lyon and Paris: A. Storck.

CHODOFF, PAUL

1966. "A Critique of Freud's Theory of Infantile Sexuality." *The American Journal of Psychiatry*, 123:507–18.

CHOISY, MARYSE

1963. *Sigmund Freud: A New Appraisal.* New York: Philosophical Library.

CHURCHILL, FREDERICK BARTON

1966. "Wilhelm Roux and a Program for Embryology." Ph.D. dissertation, Harvard University.

CLARKE, J. MICHELL

1896. Review of *Studien über Hysterie,* by Josef Breuer and Sigmund Freud (1895). *Brain,* 19:401–14.

CLAUS, CARL

1868. *Grundzüge der Zoologie, zum Gebrauche an Universitäten und höhern Lehranstalten: Leitfaden zur Einführung in das wissenschaftliche Studium der Zoologie.* Marburg and Leipzig: N. G. Elwert.
1874. *Die Typenlehre und E. Haeckel's sog. Gastraea-Theorie.* Vienna: G. F. Manz.
1891. *Lehrbuch der Zoologie.* 5th ed. Marburg: N. G. Elwert. First ed., 1880.

CLEVENGER, SHOBAL VAIL

1881. "Hunger the Primitive Desire." *Science: A Weekly Journal of Scientific Progress,* 2:14.
1884. "Disadvantages of the Upright Position." *The American Naturalist,* 18:1–9.
1885. *Comparative Physiology and Psychology: A Discussion of the Evolution and Relations of the Mind and Body of Man and Animals.* Chicago: Jansen, McClurg, & Co.
1889. *Spinal Concussion.* Philadelphia: F. A. Davis Co.
1903. *The Evolution of Man and His Mind.* Chicago: Evolution Publishing Co.

CLOUSTON, THOMAS SMITH

1883. *Clinical Lectures on Mental Diseases.* London: J. & A. Churchill. 3rd ed., 1892.
1891. *The Neuroses of Development: Being the Morison Lectures for 1890.* Edinburgh: Oliver and Boyd.

COHEN, I. BERNARD

1966. "Transformations of Scientific Ideas." The Wiles Lectures, held at Queens University, Belfast, 17–20 May.
1974. "History and the Philosopher of Science." In The Structure of Scientific Theories, pp. 308–73. Edited by Frederick Suppe. Urbana, Ill.: University of Illinois Press.
1979. The Newtonian Revolution in Science, with Illustrations of the Transformation of Scientific Ideas. Cambridge: Cambridge University Press.

COMFORT, ALEX

1960. "Darwin and Freud." The Lancet, 16 July, pp. 107–11.

COPE, EDWARD DRINKER

1887. The Origin of the Fittest: Essays on Evolution. New York: D. Appleton and Co.
1896. The Primary Factors of Organic Evolution. Chicago and London: Open Court Publishing Co.

COSER, LEWIS A.

1974. Greedy Institutions: Patterns of Undivided Commitment. New York: Free Press.

COSTIGAN, GIOVANNI

1967. Sigmund Freud: A Short Biography. London: Robert Hale; New York: Macmillan Co., 1965.

CRAMER, AUGUST

1897. "Die conträre Sexualempfindung in ihren Beziehungen zum §175 des Strafgesetzbuches." Berliner klinischer Wochenschrift, 34:934–36, 962–65.

CRANEFIELD, PAUL F.

1957. "The Organic Physics of 1847 and the Biophysics of Today." Journal of the History of Medicine and Allied Sciences, 12:407–23.
1958. "Josef Breuer's Evaluation of His Contribution to Psycho-Analysis." The International Journal of Psycho-Analysis, 39:319–22.
1959. "The Nineteenth-Century Prelude to Modern Biophysics." In Proceedings of the First National Biophysics Conference (Columbus, Ohio, March 4–6, 1957), pp. 19–26. Edited by Henry Quastler and Harold J. Morowitz. New Haven: Yale University Press.
1966a. "The Philosophical and Cultural Interests of the Biophysics Movement of 1847." Journal of the History of Medicine and Allied Sciences, 21:1–7.
1966b. "Freud and the 'School of Helmholtz.'" Gesnerus, 23:35–39.
1970a. "Josef Breuer." Dictionary of Scientific Biography, 2:445–50.
1970b. "Some Problems in Writing the History of Psychoanalysis." In Psychiatry and Its History: Methodological Problems in Research, pp. 41–55. Edited by George Moria and Jeanne L. Brand. Springfield, Ill.: Charles C. Thomas.

DALLEMAGNE, JULES

1894. Dégénérés et déséquilibrés. Brussels: Henri Lamertin; Paris: Félix Alcan, 1895.

DALMA, JUAN

1963. "La Catarsis en Aristoteles, Bernays y Freud." Revista de Psiquiatría y Psicología Medical, 6:253–69.
1964. "Reminiscencias culturales clásicas en algunas corrientes de psicología moderna." Revista de la Facultad de Medicina de Tucumán, 5:301–32.

DARNTON, ROBERT

1968. Mesmerism and the End of the Enlightenment in France. Cambridge: Harvard University Press.

DARWIN, CHARLES ROBERT

1859.   *On the Origin of Species by means of Natural Selection, or, The Preserva-
        tion of Favoured Races in the Struggle for Life.* London: John Murray.
1868.   *The Variation of Animals and Plants under Domestication.* 2 vols. London:
        John Murray.
1871.   *The Descent of Man, and Selection in Relation to Sex.* 2 vols. London:
        John Murray.
1872.   *The Expression of the Emotions in Man and Animals.* London: John
        Murray.
1874.   *The Descent of Man, and Selection in Relation to Sex.* 2nd ed., rev. & enl.
        London: John Murray.
1877.   "A Biographical Sketch of an Infant." *Mind*, 2:285–94.
1883.   "A Posthumous Essay on Instinct." In *Mental Evolution in Animals*,
        pp. 355–84. By George John Romanes. London: Kegan Paul, Trench & Co.
1887.   *The Life and Letters of Charles Darwin, Including an Autobiographical
        Chapter.* 3 vols. 2nd ed. Edited by Francis Darwin. London: John Murray.
        First ed., 1887.
1958 [1876]. *Autobiography: With Original Omissions Restored.* Edited with
        Appendix and Notes by his grand-daughter, Nora Barlow. London: Collins.

DARWIN, ERASMUS

1794–96. *Zoonomia; or, The Laws of Organic Life.* 2 vols. London: J. Johnson.
1801.   *Zoonomia; or, The Laws of Organic Life.* 2 vols. 3rd ed. London:
          J. Johnson.

DAVID, JACOB JULIUS

1900.   "Die Traumdeutung." Review of *Die Traumdeutung*, by Sigmund Freud
        (*1900a*). *Die Nation*, 17:238–39.

DAWKINS, RICHARD

1976.   *The Selfish Gene.* New York and Oxford: Oxford University Press.

DE BEER, GAVIN

1960–61. Ed. "Darwin's Notebooks on Transmutation of Species. Parts I–V."
          Bulletin of the British Museum (Natural History), Historical Series, 2,
          nos. 2–6.
1964.   *Charles Darwin: Evolution by Natural Selection.* Garden City, N.Y.:
          Doubleday & Co.; London: Thomas Nelson & Sons, 1963.

DE BEER, GAVIN; ROWLANDS, M. J.; AND SKRAMOVSKY, B. M., EDS.

1967.   "Darwin's Notebooks on Transmutation of Species. Part VI: Pages Excised
        by Darwin." *Bulletin of the British Museum (Natural History)*, Historical
        Series, 3, no. 5.

DECKER, HANNAH S.

1971.   "The Medical Reception of Psychoanalysis in Germany, 1894–1907: Three
        Brief Studies." *Bulletin of the History of Medicine*, 45:461–81.
1975.   "*The Interpretation of Dreams*: Early Reception by the Educated German
        Public." *Journal of the History of the Behavioral Sciences*, 11:129–41.
1977.   *Freud in Germany: Revolution and Reaction in Science, 1893–1907.*
        Psychological Issues, 11, no. 1 (Monograph 41).

DELAGE, YVES

1891.   "Essai sur la théorie du rêve." *Revue Scientifique*, 48:40–48.

DELAVAN, D. BRYSON

1933.   "John Noland Mackenzie (1853–1925)." *Dictionary of American Biog-
        raphy*, 12:93–94.

DELBOEUF, JOSEPH

1886. "De l'Influence de l'éducation et de l'imitation dans le somnambulisme provoqué." *Revue Philosophique*, 22:146–71.
1889. *Le Magnétisme animal: À propos d'une visite à l'École de Nancy.* Paris: Félix Alcan.

DESSOIR, MAX

1888. *Bibliographie des modernen Hypnotismus.* Berlin: Carl Duncker.
1890. *Das Doppel-Ich.* Leipzig: E. Günther.
1894. "Zur Psychologie der Vita sexualis." *Allgemeine Zeitschrift für Psychiatrie,* 50:941–75.
1947. *Buch der Erinnerung.* 2nd ed. Stuttgart: Ferdinand Enke.

D[OOLITTLE], H[ILDA]

1956. *Tribute to Freud.* New York: Pantheon Books; London: Carcanet Press, n.d.

DORER, MARIA

1932. *Historische Grundlagen der Psychoanalyse.* Leipzig: Felix Meiner.

DOUGLAS, MARY

1966. *Purity and Danger: An Analysis of Concepts of Pollution and Taboo.* London: Routledge & Kegan Paul.
1970. *Natural Symbols: Explorations in Cosmology.* New York: Pantheon Books; London: Barrie & Jenkins, 1973.

DRUMONT, ÉDOUARD

1886. *La France juive: Essai d'histoire contemporaine.* 2 vols. Paris: C. Marpon & E. Flammarion.

DU BOIS-REYMOND, ÉMIL

1918. *Jugendbriefe, von Émil du Bois-Reymond an Eduard Hallmann.* Edited by Estelle du Bois-Reymond. Berlin: D. Reimer.

DUKE, MICHAEL HARE

1972. *Sigmund Freud.* Makers of Modern Thought. London: Lutterworth Press.

DUNBAR, HELEN FLANDERS

1954. *Emotions and Bodily Changes: A Survey of Literature on Psychosomatic Interrelationships, 1910–1953.* 4th ed. New York: Columbia University Press.

DUNCAN, DAVID

1908. *Life and Letters of Herbert Spencer.* 2 vols. New York: D. Appleton and Co.

DÜSING, KARL

1884. *Die Regulierung des Geschlechtsverhältnisses bei der Vermehrung der Menschen, Tiere und Pflanzen.* Foreword by W. Preyer. Jena: Gustav Fischer.

EDINGER, DORA

1963. *Bertha Pappenheim: Leben und Schriften.* Frankfurt am Main: Ner-Tamid-Verlag.
    Trans.: Edinger (1968).
1968. *Bertha Pappenheim: Freud's Anna O.* Highland Park, Ill.: Congregation Solel.
    German Text: Edinger (1963).

EISSLER, KURT R.

1965. *Medical Orthodoxy and the Future of Psychoanalysis.* New York: International Universities Press.
1966. *Sigmund Freud und die Wiener Universität: Über die Pseudo-Wissenschaftlichkeit der jüngsten Wiener Freud-Biographik.* Bern and Stuttgart: Hans Huber.
1971. *Talent and Genius: The Fictitious Case of Tausk contra Freud.* New York: Quadrangle Books.

EISSLER, KURT R.; FREUD, SIGMUND; GOEPPERT, SEBASTIAN; AND

SCHRÖTTER, KLAUS

1974. *Aus Sigmund Freuds Sprachwelt und andere Beiträge.* Bern, Stuttgart, Vienna: Hans Huber.

EKMAN, PAUL, ED.

1973. *Darwin and Facial Expression: A Century of Research in Review.* New York and London: Academic Press.

EKSTEIN, RUDOLF

1949. "A Biographical Comment on Freud's Dual Instinct Theory." *The American Imago,* 6:211–16.

ELLENBERGER, HENRI F.

1956. "Fechner and Freud." *Bulletin of the Menninger Clinic,* 20:201–14.
1970. *The Discovery of the Unconscious: The History and Evolution of Dynamic Psychiatry.* New York: Basic Books; London: Allen Lane.
1972. "The Story of 'Anna O': A Critical Review with New Data." *Journal of the History of the Behavioral Sciences,* 8:267–79.
1977. "L'Histoire d' 'Emmy von N.' " *L'Evolution Psychiatrique,* 42:519–40.

ELLIS, HAVELOCK

1890. *The Criminal.* Contemporary Science Series, vol. 7. London: Walter Scott; New York: Charles Scribner's Sons.
1894. *Man and Woman: A Study of Human Secondary Sexual Characteristics.* Contemporary Science Series, vol. 24. London: Walter Scott; New York: Charles Scribner's Sons.
1896a. "Die Theorie der conträren Sexualempfindung." *Centralblatt für Nervenheilkunde und Psychiatrie,* n.s., 7:57–63.
1896b. With Symonds, J. A. *Das konträre Geschlechtsgefühl.* Translated by Hans Kurella. Leipzig: Georg H. Wigand.
        English Text: Ellis (1897).
1897. [With Symonds, J. A.] *Studies in the Psychology of Sex.* Vol. 1: *Sexual Inversion.* London: The University Press [i.e., George Ferdinand Springmuhl von Weissenfeld].
        German Text: Ellis (1896b).
1898a. "Auto-Erotism: A Psychological Study." *The Alienist and Neurologist,* 19: 260–99.
1898b. "Hysteria in Relation to the Sexual Emotions." *The Alienist and Neurologist,* 19:599–615.
1898c. *A Note on the Bedborough Trial.* London: The University Press [i.e., George Ferdinand Springmuhl von Weissenfeld].
1899. "The Stuff that Dreams are Made Of." *Appleton's Popular Science Monthly,* 54:721–35.
1900a. *Studies in the Psychology of Sex.* Vol. 2: *The Evolution of Modesty. The Phenomena of Sexual Periodicity. Auto-Erotism.* Philadelphia: F. A. Davis Co.
1900b. "The Analysis of the Sexual Impulse." *The Alienist and Neurologist,* 21: 247–62.
1901a. Review of *Ueber den Traum,* by Sigmund Freud (1901a). *The Journal of Mental Science,* 47:370–71.

ELLIS, HAVELOCK *(continued)*

1901*b*. "The Development of the Sexual Instinct." *The Alienist and Neurologist*, 22:500–21, 615–23.

1903. *Studies in the Psychology of Sex*. Vol. 3: *Analysis of the Sexual Impulse. Love and Pain. The Sexual Impulse in Women*. Philadelphia: F. A. Davis Co.

1905. *Studies in the Psychology of Sex*. Vol. 4: *Sexual Selection in Man: I. Touch. II. Smell. III. Hearing. IV. Vision*. Philadelphia: F. A. Davis Co.

1906. *Studies in the Psychology of Sex*. Vol. 5: *Erotic Symbolism. The Mechanism of Detumescence. The Psychic State in Pregnancy*. Philadelphia: F. A. Davis Co.

1910*a*. *Studies in the Psychology of Sex*. Vol. 6: *Sex in Relation to Society*. Philadelphia: F. A. Davis Co.

1910*b*. Review of *A Psycho-analytic Study of Leonardo da Vinci [Eine Kindheitserinnerung des Leonardo da Vinci]*, by Sigmund Freud (1910*c*). *The Journal of Mental Science*, 56:522–23.

1928. *Studies in the Psychology of Sex*. 7 vols. 3rd ed., rev. and enl. Philadelphia: F. A. Davis Co.

1933. *Psychology of Sex: A Manual for Students*. New York: Emerson Books.

1936. Foreword to *Studies in the Psychology of Sex*, by Havelock Ellis. 2 vols. New York: Random House.

1939*a*. "Freud's Influence on the Changed Attitude toward Sex." *The American Journal of Sociology*, 45:309–17.

1939*b*. *My Life: Autobiography of Havelock Ellis*. Boston: Houghton Mifflin Co.

ELLIS, HAVELOCK, AND MOLL, ALBERT

1912. "Die Funktionsstörungen des Sexuallebens." In *Handbuch der Sexualwissenschaften: Mit besonderer Berücksichtigung der kulturgeschichtlichen Beziehungen*, pp. 605–740. Edited by Albert Moll (1912*b*). Leipzig: F. C. W. Vogel.

ENGELMAN, EDMUND

1976. *Berggasse 19: Sigmund Freud's Home and Offices, Vienna 1938; The Photographs of Edmund Engelman*. With an Introduction by Peter Gay. Captions by Rita Ransohoff. New York: Basic Books.

ERIKSON, ERIK HOMBURGER

1955. "Freud's 'The Origins of Psychoanalysis.'" Review of Freud (1950*a*; 1954*e* trans.). *The International Journal of Psycho-Analysis*, 36:1–15.

1957. "The First Psychoanalyst." In *Freud and the 20th Century*, pp. 79–101. Edited and selected by Benjamin Nelson. New York: Meridian Books.

1977. "Themes of Adult Conflict in Freud's Correspondence with Fliess and Jung." *Bulletin of The American Academy of Arts and Sciences*, 31 (October):32–44.

ERLENMEYER, ALBRECHT

1885. "Ueber die Wirkung des Cocaïn bei der Morphiumentziehung." *Centralblatt für Nervenheilkunde, Psychiatrie und gerichtliche Psychopathologie*, 8: 289–99.

ERNST, MORRIS L.

1936. Foreword to *Studies in the Psychology of Sex*, by Havelock Ellis. 2 vols. New York: Random House.

EULENBURG, ALBERT

1895. *Sexuale Neuropathie: Genitale Neurosen und Neuropsychosen der Männer und Frauen*. Leipzig: F. C. W. Vogel.

1902. *Sadismus und Masochismus*. Wiesbaden: J. F. Bergmann. *Trans.*: Eulenburg (1934).

1906. Review of *Drei Abhandlungen zur Sexualtheorie*, by Sigmund Freud (1905*d*). *Medizinische Klinik*, 2:740.

EULENBURG, ALBERT *(continued)*

1907. "Geschlechtsleben und Nervensystem." *Mitteilungen der Deutschen Gesell-schaft zur Bekämpfung der Geschlechtskrankheiten*, 5:35–43, 105–10.

1914. 20 February discussion of "Über 'erogene Zonen,' " a lecture delivered by Hans Liebermann before the Ärztliche Gesellschaft für Sexualwissenschaft und Eugenik in Berlin on 19 December 1913. *Zeitschrift für Sexualwissenschaft*, 1:34.

1934. *"Sadism and Masochism": Algolagnia; The Psychology, Neurology and Physiology of Sadistic Love and Masochism.* Translated by Harold Kent. New York: New Era Press.
    German Text: Eulenburg (1902).

EXNER, SIGMUND

1894. *Entwurf zu einer physiologischen Erklärung der psychischen Erscheinungen.* Leipzig and Vienna: Franz Deuticke.

EYSENCK, HANS J., AND WILSON, GLENN D.

1973. *The Experimental Study of Freudian Theories.* London: Methuen & Co.

FANCHER, RAYMOND E.

1973. *Psychoanalytic Psychology: The Development of Freud's Thought.* New York: W. W. Norton & Co.

FECHNER, GUSTAV THEODOR

1873. *Einige Ideen zur Schöpfungs- und Entwickelungsgeschichte der Organismen.* Leipzig: Breitkopf und Härtel.

FENICHEL, OTTO

1945. *The Psychoanalytic Theory of Neurosis.* New York: W. W. Norton & Co.

FÉRÉ, CHARLES

1883. "Les Hypnotiques hystériques considérées comme sujets d'expérience en médecine mentale. (Illusions, hallucinations, impulsions irrésistibles provoquées; leur importance au point de vue médico-légal.)." *Archives de Neurologie*, 6:122–35.

1896. "La Descendance d'un inverti." *Revue Générale de Clinique et de Thérapeutique*, 2nd series, 10:561–65.

1899. *L'Instinct sexuel: Évolution et dissolution.* Paris: Félix Alcan.

FERENCZI, SÁNDOR

1913. "Stages in the Development of the Sense of Reality." In *First Contributions to Psycho-Analysis* (1952:213–39).

1914. "The Ontogenesis of the Interest in Money." In *First Contributions to Psycho-Analysis* (1952:319–31).

1924. *Versuch einer Genitaltheorie.* Leipzig: Internationaler Psychoanalytischer Verlag.
    Trans.: Ferenczi (1968).

1952. *First Contributions to Psycho-Analysis.* The International Psycho-Analytical Library. Translated by Ernest Jones. London: Hogarth Press and The Institute of Psycho-Analysis.

1968. *Thalassa: A Theory of Genitality.* Translated by Henry Alden Bunker. New York: W. W. Norton & Co.
    German Text: Ferenczi (1924).

FEUER, LOUIS S.

1974. *Einstein and the Generations of Science.* New York: Basic Books.

FICK, ADOLF

1874. "Die Methoden und Richtungen der physiologischen Forschung." Reprinted in *Gesammelte Schriften von Adolf Fick*, 4 (1906):386–94. Edited by Rudolf Fick. Würzburg: Oscar Stahel, 1903–6.

FINE, REUBEN

1963. *Freud: A Critical Re-Evaluation of His Theories.* London: George Allen & Unwin.
1973. *The Development of Freud's Thought: From the Beginnings (1886–1900) through Id Psychology (1900–1914) to Ego Psychology (1914–1939).* New York: Jason Aronson.

FISHER, RONALD A.

1936. "Has Mendel's Work Been Rediscovered?" *Annals of Science,* 1:115–37.

FISHER, SEYMOUR, AND GREENBERG, ROGER P.

1977. *The Scientific Credibility of Freud's Theories and Therapy.* New York: Basic Books; Hassocks, Sussex: Harvester Press.

FISKE, JOHN

1874. *Outlines of Cosmic Philosophy, Based on the Doctrine of Evolution, with Criticisms on the Positive Philosophy.* 2 vols. London: Macmillan and Co.
1884. *Excursions of an Evolutionist.* Boston: Houghton Mifflin and Co.

FLIESS, ELENORE

1974. *Robert Fliess: The Making of a Psychoanalyst.* Croydon, England: Roffey & Clark.

FLIESS, ROBERT

1956. *Erogeneity and Libido: Addenda to the Theory of the Psychosexual Development of the Human.* Psychoanalytic Series, vol. 1. New York: International Universities Press.

FLIESS, WILHELM

1893a. *Neue Beiträge zur Klinik und Therapie der nasalen Reflexneurose.* Leipzig and Vienna: Franz Deuticke.
1893b. "Die nasale Reflexneurose." *Verhandlungen des Kongresses für Innere Medizin,* pp. 384–94. Wiesbaden: J. F. Bergmann.
1893c. "Les Réflexes d'origine nasale." *Archives Internationales de Laryngologie,* 6:266–69.
1895. "Magenschmerz und Dysmenorrhoe in einem neuen Zusammenhang." *Wiener klinische Rundschau,* 9:4–6, 20–22, 37–39, 65–67, 115–17, 131–33, 150–52.
1897. *Die Beziehungen zwischen Nase und weiblichen Geschlechtsorganen: In ihrer biologischen Bedeutung dargestellt.* Leipzig and Vienna: Franz Deuticke.
1902. *Über den ursächlichen Zusammenhang von Nase und Geschlechtsorgan: Zugleich ein Beitrag zur Nervenphysiologie.* Halle a. S.: Carl Marhold. 2nd ed., 1910. 3rd ed., 1926 (as *Nasale Fernleiden* [Leipzig and Vienna: Franz Deuticke]).
1906a. *In eigener Sache: Gegen Otto Weininger und Hermann Swoboda.* Berlin: Emil Goldschmidt.
1906b. *Der Ablauf des Lebens: Grundlegung zur exakten Biologie.* Leipzig and Vienna: Franz Deuticke. 2nd ed., 1923.
1907. "Zum Ablauf des Lebens." *Annalen der Naturphilosophie,* 6:121–38.
1908. "Knabenüberschuss." *Morgan,* 6 April.
1909. *Vom Leben und Tod: Biologische Vorträge.* Jena: Eugen Diederichs. 2nd ed., 1914; 3rd ed., 1916; 4th ed., 1919; 5th ed., 1924.
1911. "Der Ablauf des Lebens und seine Kritiker." *Annalen der Naturphilosophie,* 10:314–50.
1914. "Männlich und Weiblich." *Zeitschrift für Sexualwissenschaft,* 1:15–20.
1918a. "Innere Sekretion." *Zeitschrift für Sexualwissenschaft,* 5:129–35.
1918b. "Sexualität und Symmetrie: Entgegnung auf den gleichnamigen Aufsatz v. Paul Kammerer." *Zeitschrift für Sexualwissenschaft,* 5:249–61, 281–94.
1918c. *Das Jahr im Lebendigen.* Jena: Eugen Diederichs. 2nd ed., 1924.
1925. *Zur Periodenlehre: Gesammelte Aufsätze.* Jena: Eugen Diederichs.

FLOURNOY, THÉODORE

1903. Review of *Die Traumdeutung*, by Sigmund Freud (1900*a*). *Archives de Psychologie*, 2:72–73.

FLUGEL, JOHN CARL

1955. *Studies in Feeling and Desire*. London: Gerald Duckworth & Co.

FOREL, AUGUST

1889. *Der Hypnotismus, seine Bedeutung und seine Handhabung, in kurzgefasster Darstellung*. Stuttgart: Ferdinand Enke.
1905. *Die sexuelle Frage: Eine naturwissenschaftliche, psychologische, hygienische und soziologische Studie für Gebildete*. Munich: E. Reinhardt. *Trans.*: Forel (1911).
1911. *The Sexual Question: A Scientific, Psychological, Hygienic and Sociological Study*. Translated by C. F. Marshall. New York: Rebman Co. *German Text*: Forel (1905).

FOUCAULT, MICHEL

1978. *The History of Sexuality*. Vol. 1: *An Introduction*. Translated from the French by Robert Hurley. New York: Pantheon Books.

FRANK, EMANUEL

1886. Account of 15 October 1886 lecture by Sigmund Freud, "Ueber männliche Hysterie," delivered at the K. k. Gesellschaft der Ärzte, and of the discussion that followed. *Allgemeine Wiener medizinische Zeitung*, 31:506–7.

FRAZER, JAMES G.

1910. *Totemism and Exogamy, a Treatise on Certain Early Forms of Superstition and Society*. 4 vols. London: Macmillan and Co.

FREEMAN, LUCY

1972. *The Story of Anna O*. With an Introduction by Karl A. Menninger. New York: Walker & Co.

FREUD, SIGMUND

1877*a*. "Über den Ursprung der hinteren Nervenwurzeln im Rückenmark von Ammocoetes (Petromyzon Planeri)." *Sitzungsberichte der kaiserlichen Akademie der Wissenschaften [Wien]*. Mathematisch-Naturwissenschaftliche Classe, 75, III. Abtheilung:15–27.
1877*b*. "Beobachtungen über Gestaltung und feineren Bau der als Hoden beschriebenen Lappenorgane des Aals." *Sitzungsberichte der kaiserlichen Akademie der Wissenschaften [Wien]*. Mathematisch-Naturwissenschaftliche Classe, 75, I. Abtheilung:419–30.
1878*a*. "Über Spinalganglien und Rückenmark des Petromyzon." *Sitzungsberichte der kaiserlichen Akademie der Wissenschaften [Wien]*. Mathematisch-Naturwissenschaftliche Classe, 78, III. Abtheilung:81–167.
1879*a*. "Notiz über eine Methode zur anatomischen Präparation des Nervensystems." *Centralblatt für die medicinischen Wissenschaften*, 17:468–69.
1882*a*. "Über den Bau der Nervenfasern und Nervenzellen beim Flusskrebs." *Sitzungsberichte der kaiserlichen Akademie der Wissenschaften [Wien]*. Mathematisch-Naturwissenschaftliche Classe, 85, III. Abtheilung:9–46.
1884*a*. "Ein Fall von Hirnblutung mit indirekten basalen Herdsymptomen bei Skorbut." *Wiener medizinische Wochenschrift*, 34:244–46, 276–79.
1884*b*. "Eine neue Methode zum Studium des Faserverlaufs im Centralnervensystem." *Centralblatt für die medicinischen Wissenschaften*, 22:161–63.
1884*c*. "A New Histological Method for the Study of Nerve-Tracts in the Brain and Spinal Chord." *Brain*, 7:86–88.
1884*d*. "Eine neue Methode zum Studium des Faserverlaufs im Centralnervensystem." *Archiv für Anatomie und Physiologie, Anatomische Abtheilung*, pp. 453–60.

FREUD, SIGMUND (*continued*)

1884*e.* "Ueber Coca." *Centralblatt für die gesammte Therapie*, 2:289–314.
    Trans.: "On Coca" (Freud 1974*a*:49–73).
1884*f* [1882]. "Die Struktur der Elemente des Nervensystems." *Jahrbücher für Psychiatrie*, 5:221–29.
1885*a.* "Beitrag zur Kenntniss der Cocawirkung." *Wiener medizinische Wochenschrift*, 35:129–33.
    Trans.: "Contribution to the Knowledge of the Effect of Cocaine" (Freud 1974*a*:97–104).
1885*b.* "Über die Allgemeinwirkung des Cocaïns." *Medicinisch-chirurgisches Centralblatt*, 20:374–75.
    Trans.: "On the General Effect of Cocaine" (Freud 1974*a*:113–18).
1885*d.* "Zur Kenntniss der Olivenzwischenschicht." *Neurologisches Centralblatt*, 4:268–70.
1885*e.* "Gutachten über das Parke Cocaïn." In "Neue Arzneimittel und Heilmethoden. Über die verschiedenen Cocaïn-Präparate und deren Wirkung," by [Hermann] Gutt[macher]. *Wiener medizinische Presse*, 26:1036.
    Trans.: "New Medications and Therapeutic Techniques. Concerning the Different Cocaine Preparations and Their Effect" (Freud 1974*a*:121–25).
1885*f.* "Nachträge über Coca." In reprint of Freud (1884*e*). Vienna: Moritz Perles.
    Trans.: "Addenda to 'On Coca'" (Freud 1974*a*:107–9).
1886*b.* With Darkschewitsch, L. O. von. "Ueber die Beziehung des Strickkörpers zum Hinterstrang und Hinterstrangskern nebst Bemerkungen über zwei Felder der Oblongata." *Neurologisches Centralblatt*, 5:121–29.
1886*c.* "Über den Ursprung des Nervus acusticus." *Monatsschrift für Ohrenheilkunde*, n.s., 20:245–51, 277–82.
1886*d.* "Observation of a Severe Case of Hemi-Anaesthesia in a Hysterical Male." In *Standard Edition*, 1:24–31.
1886*f.* "Preface to the Translation of Charcot's *Lectures on the Diseases of the Nervous System*." In *Standard Edition*, 1:19–22.
1887*d.* "Beiträge über die Anwendung des Cocaïn. Zweite Serie. I. Bemerkungen über Cocaïnsucht und Cocaïnfurcht mit Beziehung auf einen Vortrag W. A. Hammond's." *Wiener medizinische Wochenschrift*, 37:929–32.
    Trans.: "Contributions about the Applications of Cocaine. Second Series. I. Remarks on Craving for and Fear of Cocaine with Reference to a Lecture by W. A. Hammond" (Freud 1974*a*:171–76).
1888*a.* "Ueber Hemianopsie im frühesten Kindesalter." *Wiener medizinische Wochenschrift*, 38:1081–86, 1116–21.
1888*b.* "Aphasia," "Gehirn," "Hysterie," and "Hysteroepilepsie." In *Handwörterbuch der gesamten Medizin*, 1. Edited by Albert Villaret. Stuttgart: Ferdinand Enke. (Unsigned; authorship uncertain.)
    Trans.: "Hysteria" and "Hystero-Epilepsy," *Standard Edition*, 1:39–57, 58–59. (The other two articles have not been translated.)
1888–89. "Preface to the Translation of Bernheim's *Suggestion*." In *Standard Edition*, 1:73–85.
1889*a.* "Review of August Forel's *Hypnotism*." In *Standard Edition*, 1:90–102.
1891*a.* With Rie, Oskar. *Klinische Studie über die halbseitige Cerebrallähmung der Kinder*. Heft III of *Beiträge zur Kinderheilkunde*. Edited by Max Kassowitz. Vienna: Moritz Perles.
1891*b.* *Zur Auffassung der Aphasien: Eine kritische Studie*. Leipzig and Vienna: Franz Deuticke.
    Trans:. Freud (1953*a*).
1891*c.* "Kinderlähmung" and "Lähmung." In *Handwörterbuch der gesamten Medizin*, 2. Edited by Albert Villaret. Stuttgart: Ferdinand Enke. (Unsigned; authorship uncertain.)
1891*d.* "Hypnosis." In *Standard Edition*, 1:104–14.
1892*a.* Translation of *Hypnotisme, suggestion, psychothérapie: Études nouvelles*, by Hippolyte Bernheim (1891), under the title *Neue Studien über Hypnotismus, Suggestion und Psychotherapie*. Leipzig and Vienna: Franz Deuticke.
1892–93. "A Case of Successful Treatment by Hypnotism: With Some Remarks on the Origin of Hysterical Symptoms through 'Counter-Will.'" In *Standard Edition*, 1:116–28.
1892–94. "Preface and Footnotes to the Translation of Charcot's *Tuesday Lectures*." In *Standard Edition*, 1:131–43.

FREUD, SIGMUND (continued)

1893a. With Breuer, Josef. "On the Psychical Mechanism of Hysterical Phenom-
        ena: Preliminary Communication." In Standard Edition, 2:3–17.
1893b. Zur Kenntniss der cerebralen Diplegien des Kindesalters (im Anschluss an
        die Little'sche Krankheit). Heft III, Neue Folge, of Beiträge zur Kinderheil-
        kunde. Edited by Max Kassowitz. Vienna: Moritz Perles.
1893c. "Some Points for a Comparative Study of Organic and Hysterical Motor
        Paralyses." In Standard Edition, 1:157–72.
1893d. "Über familiäre Formen von cerebralen Diplegien." Neurologisches Cen-
        tralblatt, 12:512–15, 542–47.
1893e. "Les Diplégies cérébrales infantiles." Revue Neurologique, 1:177–83.
1893f. "Charcot." In Standard Edition, 3:9–23.
1894a. "The Neuro-Psychoses of Defence: (An Attempt at a Psychological Theory
        of Acquired Hysteria, of Many Phobias and Obsessions and of Certain Hal-
        lucinatory Psychoses)." In Standard Edition, 3:43–61.
1895a. Review of "Eine neue Theorie über die Ursachen einiger Nervenkrank-
        heiten, insbesondere der Neuritis und der Tabes," by L. Edinger. Wiener
        klinische Rundschau, 9:27–28.
1895b. [1894]. "On the Grounds for Detaching a Particular Syndrome from Neu-
        rasthenia under the Description 'Anxiety Neurosis.'" In Standard Edition,
        3:87–115.
1895c. [1894]. "Obsessions and Phobias: Their Psychical Mechanism and Their
        Aetiology." In Standard Edition, 3:71–82.
1895d. With Breuer, Josef. Studies on Hysteria. In Standard Edition, 2.
        German Text: Breuer and Freud (1895).
1895f. "A Reply to Criticisms of My Paper on Anxiety Neurosis." In Standard
        Edition, 3:121–39.
1895g. "Ueber Hysterie." Three lectures by Freud abstracted in Wiener klinische
        Rundschau, 9:662–63, 679–80, 696–97.
1895h. "Mechanismus der Zwangsvorstellungen und Phobien." Author's abstract.
        Wiener klinische Wochenschrift, 8:496.
1896a. "Heredity and the Aetiology of the Neuroses." In Standard Edition, 3:
        142–56.
1896b. "Further Remarks on the Neuro-Psychoses of Defence." In Standard Edi-
        tion, 3:159–85.
1896c. "The Aetiology of Hysteria." In Standard Edition, 3:189–221.
1896d. "Preface to the Second German Edition of Bernheim's Suggestion." In
        Standard Edition, 1:86–87.
1897a. Die infantile Cerebrallähmung. In Specielle Pathologie und Therapie, 9,
        II. Theil, II. Abtheilung. Edited by Hermann Nothnagel. Vienna: Alfred
        Hölder.
        Trans.: Freud (1968b).
1897b. Abstracts of the Scientific Writings of Dr. Sigm. Freud 1877–1897. In
        Standard Edition, 3:225–57.
1898a. "Sexuality in the Aetiology of the Neuroses." In Standard Edition, 3:261–85.
1898b. "The Psychical Mechanism of Forgetfulness." In Standard Edition, 3:
        288–97.
1898c. "Cerebrale Kinderlähmung [I]." (29 reviews and abstracts.) Jahresbericht
        über die Leistungen und Fortschritte auf dem Gebiete der Neurologie und
        Psychiatrie, 1 (1897):613–32.
1899a. "Screen Memories." In Standard Edition, 3:301–22.
1899b. "Cerebrale Kinderlähmung [II]." (29 reviews and abstracts.) Jahresbericht
        über die Leistungen und Fortschritte auf dem Gebiete der Neurologie und
        Psychiatrie, 2 (1898):632–42.
1900a. The Interpretation of Dreams. In Standard Edition, 4–5.
1900b. "Cerebrale Kinderlähmung [III]." (18 reviews and abstracts.) Jahresbe-
        richt über die Leistungen und Fortschritte auf dem Gebiete der Neurologie
        und Psychiatrie, 3 (1899):611–18.
1901a. On Dreams. In Standard Edition, 5:631–86.
1901b. The Psychopathology of Everyday Life. In Standard Edition, 6.
1905c. Jokes and Their Relation to the Unconscious. In Standard Edition, 8.
1905d. Three Essays on the Theory of Sexuality. In Standard Edition, 7:125–243.
1905e. [1901]. "Fragment of an Analysis of a Case of Hysteria." In Standard
        Edition, 7:3–122.
1906a. "My Views on the Part Played by Sexuality in the Aetiology of the Neu-
        roses." In Standard Edition, 7:270–79.

FREUD, SIGMUND (*continued*)

1906*d*. Two Letters to Magnus Hirschfeld. In *Monatsbericht des wissenschaftlich-humanitären Komitees*, 5:30. (First letter incomplete.)

1906*e* [1904]. Two Letters to Wilhelm Fliess. In *Wilhelm Fliess und seine Nachentdecker*, by Richard Pfennig (1906:26–27, 30–31), and *In Eigener Sache*, by Wilhelm Fliess (1906*a*:19–20, 22–23).

1907*b*. "Obsessive Actions and Religious Practices." In *Standard Edition*, 9:116–27.

1908*a*. "Hysterical Phantasies and Their Relation to Bisexuality." In *Standard Edition*, 9:157–66.

1908*c*. "On the Sexual Theories of Children." In *Standard Edition*, 9:207–26.

1908*d*. "'Civilized' Sexual Morality and Modern Nervous Illness." In *Standard Edition*, 9:179–204.

1908*f*. "Preface to Wilhelm Stekel's *Nervous Anxiety-States and Their Treatment*." In *Standard Edition*, 9:250–51.

1909*b*. "Analysis of a Phobia in a Five-Year-Old Boy." In *Standard Edition*, 10:3–147.

1909*d*. "Notes upon a Case of Obsessional Neurosis." In *Standard Edition*, 10:153–318.

1910*a* [1909]. "Five Lectures on Psycho-Analysis." In *Standard Edition*, 11:3–55.

1910*c*. *Leonardo da Vinci and a Memory of His Childhood*. In *Standard Edition*, 11:59–137.

1910*e*. "The Antithetical Meaning of Primal Words." In *Standard Edition*, 11:154–61.

1910*f*. "Letter to Dr. Friedrich S. Krauss on *Anthropophyteia*." In *Standard Edition*, 11:233–35.

1910*i*. "The Psycho-Analytic View of Psychogenic Disturbance of Vision." In *Standard Edition*, 11:210–18.

1911*b*. "Formulations on the Two Principles of Mental Functioning." In *Standard Edition*, 12:215–26.

1911*c* [1910]. "Psycho-Analytic Notes on an Autobiographical Account of a Case of Paranoia (Dementia Paranoides)." In *Standard Edition*, 12:3–79.

1912*a*. Postscript (1912 [1911]) to "Psycho-Analytic Notes on an Autobiographical Account of a Case of Paranoia (Dementia Paranoides) [1911*c*]." In *Standard Edition*, 12:80–82.

1912*c*. "Types of Onset of Neurosis." In *Standard Edition*, 12:229–38.

1912*d*. "On the Universal Tendency to Debasement in the Sphere of Love (Contributions to the Psychology of Love II)." In *Standard Edition*, 11:178–90.

1912*e*. "Recommendations to Physicians Practising Psycho-Analysis." In *Standard Edition*, 12:110–20.

1912*f*. "Contributions to a Discussion on Masturbation." In *Standard Edition*, 12:241–54.

1912–13. *Totem and Taboo*. In *Standard Edition*, 13:1–161.

1913*a*. "An Evidential Dream." In *Standard Edition*, 12:268–77.

1913*c*. "On Beginning the Treatment (Further Recommendations on the Technique of Psycho-Analysis, I)." In *Standard Edition*, 12:122–44.

1913*i*. "The Disposition to Obsessional Neurosis: A Contribution to the Problem of Choice of Neurosis." In *Standard Edition*, 12:313–26.

1913*j*. "The Claims of Psycho-Analysis to Scientific Interest." In *Standard Edition*, 13:164–90.

1913*k*. "Preface to Bourke's *Scatalogic Rites of All Nations*." In *Standard Edition*, 12:334–37.

1914*c*. "On Narcissism: An Introduction." In *Standard Edition*, 14:69–102.

1914*d*. "On the History of the Psycho-Analytic Movement." In *Standard Edition*, 14:3–66.

1915*c*. "Instincts and Their Vicissitudes." In *Standard Edition*, 14:111–40.

1915*d*. "Repression." In *Standard Edition*, 14:143–58.

1915*e*. "The Unconscious." In *Standard Edition*, 14:161–204.

1915*f*. "A Case of Paranoia Running Counter to the Psycho-Analytic Theory of the Disease." In *Standard Edition*, 14:262–72.

1916–17. *Introductory Lectures on Psycho-Analysis*. In *Standard Edition*, 15–16.

1917*a*. "A Difficulty in the Path of Psycho-Analysis." In *Standard Edition*, 17:136–44.

1918*b* [1914]. "From the History of an Infantile Neurosis." In *Standard Edition*, 17:3–122.

1919*d*. "Introduction to *Psycho-Analysis and the War Neuroses*." In *Standard Edition*, 17:206–10.

FREUD, SIGMUND (continued)

1919e. "'A Child is Being Beaten': A Contribution to the Study of the Origin of Sexual Perversions." In Standard Edition, 17:177–204.

1920a. "The Psychogenesis of a Case of Homosexuality in a Woman." In Standard Edition, 18:146–72.

1920g. Beyond the Pleasure Principle. In Standard Edition, 18:3–64.

1921c. Group Psychology and the Analysis of the Ego. In Standard Edition, 18:67–143.

1923a [1922]. "Two Encyclopedia Articles." In Standard Edition, 18:234–59.

1923b. The Ego and the Id. In Standard Edition, 19:3–59.

1923f. "Josef Popper-Lynkeus and the Theory of Dreams." In Standard Edition, 19:260–63.

1924c. "The Economic Problem of Masochism." In Standard Edition, 19:157–70.

1924d. "The Dissolution of the Oedipus Complex." In Standard Edition, 19:172–79.

1924f [1923]. "A Short Account of Psycho-Analysis." In Standard Edition, 19:190–209.

1925d [1924]. An Autobiographical Study. In Standard Edition, 20:3–70.

1925e [1924]. "The Resistance to Psycho-Analysis." In Standard Edition, 19:212–22.

1925g. "Josef Breuer." In Standard Edition, 19:278–80.

1925i. "Some Additional Notes on Dream-Interpretation as a Whole." In Standard Edition, 19:125–38.

1925j. "Some Psychical Consequences of the Anatomical Distinction between the Sexes." In Standard Edition, 19:243–58.

1926d [1925]. Inhibitions, Symptoms and Anxiety. In Standard Edition, 20:77–172.

1926e. The Question of Lay Analysis: Conversations with an Impartial Person. In Standard Edition, 20:179–250.

1926f. "Psycho-Analysis." In Standard Edition, 20:261–70.

1926g. Translation, with Footnote, of The Unconscious (Part I, Section 13: "Samuel Butler"), by Israel Levine (London: L. Parsons, 1923), under the title Das Unbewusste. Leipzig and Vienna: Internationaler Psychoanalytischer Verlag.
        Trans.: In "Appendix A: Freud and Ewald Hering," Standard Edition, 14:205.

1927a. Postscript (1927) to The Question of Lay Analysis [1926e]. In Standard Edition, 20:251–58.

1927c. The Future of an Illusion. In Standard Edition, 21:3–56.

1930a. Civilization and Its Discontents. In Standard Edition, 21:59–145.

1931b. "Female Sexuality." In Standard Edition, 21:223–43.

1932a. "The Acquisition and Control of Fire." In Standard Edition, 22:185–93.

1932c. "My Contact with Josef Popper-Lynkeus." In Standard Edition, 22:218–24.

1933a. New Introductory Lectures on Psycho-Analysis. In Standard Edition, 22:3–182.

1933b. Why War? In Standard Edition, 22:197–215.

1933c. "Sándor Ferenczi." In Standard Edition, 22:226–29.

1935a. Postscript (1935) to An Autobiographical Study [1925d; 2nd ed., 1935]. In Standard Edition, 20:71–74.

1937c. "Analysis Terminable and Interminable." In Standard Edition, 23:211–53.

1938. The Basic Writings of Sigmund Freud. Translated by A. A. Brill. New York: Random House, The Modern Library.

1939a [1937–39]. Moses and Monotheism: Three Essays. In Standard Edition, 23:3–137.

1940a [1938]. An Outline of Psycho-Analysis. In Standard Edition, 23:141–207.

1940d [1892]. With Breuer, Josef. "On the Theory of Hysterical Attacks." In Standard Edition, 1:151–54.

1940–68. Gesammelte Werke. 18 vols. Edited by Anna Freud with the collaboration of Marie Bonaparte (and others). Vols. 1–17, London: Imago Publishing Co., 1940–52; vol. 18, Frankfurt am Main: S. Fischer, 1968.

1941a [1892]. "Letter to Josef Breuer." In Standard Edition, 1:147–48.

1941b [1892]. "III." In Standard Edition, 1:149–50.

1941d [1921]. "Psycho-Analysis and Telepathy." In Standard Edition, 18:175–93.

1941e [1926]. "Address to the Society of B'nai B'rith." In Standard Edition, 20:272–74.

1941f [1938]. "Findings, Ideas, Problems." In Standard Edition, 23:299–300.

FREUD, SIGMUND *(continued)*

1950a [1887–1902]. *Aus den Anfängen der Psychoanalyse: Briefe an Wilhelm Fliess, Abhandlungen und Notizen aus den Jahren 1887–1902.* Introduction by Ernst Kris. Edited by Marie Bonaparte, Anna Freud, and Ernst Kris. London: Imago Publishing Co.
   Trans.: Freud (1954e).

1953a. *On Aphasia: A Critical Study.* Translated and with an Introduction by E. Stengel. London: Imago Publishing Co.; New York: International Universities Press.
   German Text: Freud (1891b).

1953–74. *The Standard Edition of the Complete Psychological Works of Sigmund Freud.* 24 vols. Translated from the German under the General Editorship of James Strachey. In collaboration with Anna Freud. Assisted by Alix Strachey and Alan Tyson. London: Hogarth Press and The Institute of Psycho-Analysis.

1954e [1887–1902]. *The Origins of Psycho-Analysis, Letters to Wilhelm Fliess, Drafts and Notes: 1887–1902.* Introduction by Ernst Kris. Edited by Marie Bonaparte, Anna Freud, and Ernst Kris. Translated by Eric Mosbacher and James Strachey. New York: Basic Books; London: Imago Publishing Co.
   German Text: Freud (1950a).

1955d [1876]. Two Applications for Grants for Biological Research. In Josef Gicklhorn, "Wissenschaftsgeschichtliche Notizen zu den Studien von S. Syrski (1874) und S. Freud (1877) über männliche Flußaale." *Sitzungsberichte der Österreichischen Akademie der Wissenschaften [Wien].* Mathematisch-Naturwissenschaftliche Klasse, 164, I. Abteilung:1–24.

1956a [1886]. "Report on My Studies in Paris and Berlin: Carried Out with the Assistance of a Travelling Bursary Granted from the University Jubilee Fund (October, 1885–End of March, 1886)." In *Standard Edition,* 1:3–15.

1960a. *Briefe 1873–1939.* Edited by Ernst L. Freud. Frankfurt am Main: S. Fischer. 2nd enl. ed., 1968.
   Trans.: Freud (1960b).

1960b. *Letters of Sigmund Freud.* Selected and edited by Ernst L. Freud. Translated by Tania and James Stern. New York: Basic Books; London: Hogarth Press, 1961.
   German Text: Freud (1960a).

1963a. *Sigmund Freud/Oskar Pfister: Briefe 1909 bis 1939.* Edited by Ernst L. Freud and Heinrich Meng. Frankfurt am Main: S. Fischer.
   Trans.: Freud (1963b).

1963b. *Psycho-Analysis and Faith: The Letters of Sigmund Freud and Oskar Pfister.* Edited by Ernst L. Freud and Heinrich Meng. Translated by Eric Mosbacher. New York: Basic Books; London: Hogarth Press and The Institute of Psycho-Analysis.
   German Text: Freud (1963a).

1965a. *Sigmund Freud/Karl Abraham: Briefe 1907 bis 1926.* Edited by Hilda C. Abraham and Ernst L. Freud. Frankfurt am Main: S. Fischer.
   Trans.: Freud (1965b).

1965b. *A Psycho-Analytic Dialogue: The Letters of Sigmund Freud and Karl Abraham 1907–1926.* Edited by Hilda C. Abraham and Ernst L. Freud. Translated by Bernard Marsh and Hilda C. Abraham. New York: Basic Books; London: Hogarth Press and The Institute of Psycho-Analysis.
   German Text: Freud (1965a).

1966a. *Sigmund Freud/Lou Andreas-Salomé: Briefwechsel.* Edited by Ernst Pfeiffer. Frankfurt am Main: S. Fischer.
   Trans.: Freud (1972a).

1968b. *Infantile Cerebral Paralysis.* Translated by Lester A. Russin. Miami, Fla.: University of Miami Press.
   German Text: Freud (1897a).

1972a. *Sigmund Freud and Lou Andreas-Salomé: Letters.* Edited by Ernst Pfeiffer. Translated by William and Elaine Robson-Scott. New York: Harcourt Brace Jovanovich; London: Hogarth Press and The Institute of Psycho-Analysis.
   German Text: Freud (1966a).

1974a. *Cocaine Papers.* Edited and with an Introduction by Robert Byck. Notes by Anna Freud. New York: Stonehill Publishing Co.
   Partial German Text: Freud (1884e, 1885a, 1885b, 1885e, 1885f, 1887d).

FREUD, SIGMUND (*continued*)

1974b. *The Freud/Jung Letters: The Correspondence between Sigmund Freud and C. G. Jung.* Edited by William McGuire. Translated by Ralph Manheim and R. F. C. Hull. Bollingen Series XCIV. Princeton: Princeton University Press; London: Routledge & Kegan Paul.
　　　　German Text: Freud (1974c).
1974c. *Briefwechsel: Sigmund Freud, C. G. Jung.* Edited by William McGuire and Wolfgang Sauerländer. Frankfurt am Main: S. Fischer.
　　　　Trans.: Freud (1974b).
Forthcoming.　*The Pre-Analytic Works of Sigmund Freud.* 3 vols. General Editor, Erwin Stengel. London: Hogarth Press and The Institute of Psycho-Analysis.

FRIEDLÄNDER, ADOLF

1907.　　"Ueber Hysterie und die Freudsche psychoanalytische Behandlung derselben." *Monatsschrift für Psychiatrie und Neurologie,* 22 (Ergänzungsheft): 45–54.
1909.　　"Hysterie und moderne Psychoanalyse." XVIᵉ *Congrès international de médecine,* Budapest: *Compte-rendu.* Vol. 12: *Psychiatrie,* pp. 146–72. Budapest.

FROMM, ERICH

1932.　　"Psychoanalytic Characterology and Its Relevance for Social Psychology." Reprinted in *The Crisis of Psychoanalysis* (Fromm 1970c:164–87).
1959.　　*Sigmund Freud's Mission: An Analysis of His Personality and Influence.* New York: Harper & Brothers.
1970a.　"Freud's Model of Man and Its Social Determinants." In *The Crisis of Psychoanalysis* (Fromm 1970c:44–60).
1970b.　"The Crisis of Psychoanalysis." In *The Crisis of Psychoanalysis* (Fromm 1970c:12–41).
1970c.　*The Crisis of Psychoanalysis.* Greenwich, Conn.: Fawcett Publications; London: Jonathan Cape, 1971.

GALDSTON, IAGO

1956.　　"Freud and Romantic Medicine." *Bulletin of the History of Medicine,* 30: 489–507.

GARDNER, MARTIN

1957.　　*Fads and Fallacies in the Name of Science.* New York: Dover Publications. Originally published as *In the Name of Science.* New York: G. P. Putnam's Sons, 1952.
1966.　　"Freud's Friend Wilhelm Fliess and His Theory of Male and Female Life Cycles." *Scientific American,* 215 (July):108–12.

GATTEL, FELIX

1898.　　*Ueber die sexuellen Ursachen der Neurasthenie und Angstneurose.* Berlin: August Hirschwald.

GAY, PETER

1978.　　*Freud, Jews and Other Germans: Masters and Victims in Modernist Culture.* New York: Oxford University Press.

GEDDES, PATRICK, AND THOMSON, J. ARTHUR

1889.　　*The Evolution of Sex.* The Contemporary Science Series, vol. 1. London: Walter Scott. [2nd] rev. ed., 1901.
1914.　　*Sex.* New York: Henry Holt and Co.; London: Williams and Norgate.

GEDO, JOHN E., AND POLLOCK, GEORGE H.

1975.　　*Freud: The Fusion of Science and Humanism: The Intellectual History of Psychoanalysis. Psychological Issues,* 9 (Monographs 34–35).

GEDO, JOHN E.; SABSHIN, MELVIN; SADOW, LEO; AND
       SCHLESSINGER, NATHAN
   1964. " 'Studies on Hysteria': A Methodological Evaluation." *Journal of the American Psychoanalytic Association, 12*:734–51.

GHISELIN, MICHAEL T.
   1969. *The Triumph of the Darwinian Method.* Berkeley: University of California Press.
   1973. "Darwin and Evolutionary Psychology." *Science, 179*:964–68.

GICKLHORN, JOSEF, AND GICKLHORN, RENÉE
   1960. *Sigmund Freuds akademische Laufbahn im Lichte der Dokumente.* Vienna and Innsbruck: Urban & Schwarzenberg.

GIESSLER, CARL MAX
   1902. Review of *Ueber den Traum,* by Sigmund Freud (1901a). *Zeitschrift für Psychologie und Physiologie der Sinnesorgane, 29*:228–31.

GITTELSON, BERNARD
   1977. *Biorhythm Sports Forecasting.* New York: Arco Publishing Co.

GLEY, E.
   1884. "Les Aberrations de l'instinct sexuel d'après des travaux récents." *Revue Philosophique, 17*:66–92.

GLOVER, EDWARD
   1950. *Freud or Jung.* London: George Allen & Unwin.
   1952. "Research Methods in Psycho-Analysis." *The International Journal of Psycho-Analysis, 33*:403–9.

GOLDBERG, ISAAC
   1926. *Havelock Ellis: A Biographical and Critical Survey.* New York: Simon and Schuster.

GOULD, STEPHEN JAY
   1977. *Ontogeny and Phylogeny.* Cambridge and London: Harvard University Press, Belknap Press.

GRAF, MAX
   1942. "Reminiscences of Professor Sigmund Freud." *The Psychoanalytic Quarterly, 11*:465–76.

GREEN, H. L.
   1897. "Periodicity, a Physiological Law in the Male Sex as well as in the Female." *Journal of the American Medical Association, 28*:723–26.

GREENBLATT, S. H.
   1965. "The Major Influences on the Early Life and Work of John Hughlings Jackson." *Bulletin of the History of Medicine, 39*:346–76.

GREENE, JOHN C.
   1975. "Reflections on the Progress of Darwin Studies." *Journal of the History of Biology, 8*:243–73.

GRIESINGER, WILHELM

1861. *Die Pathologie und Therapie der psychischen Krankheiten für Aerzte und Studirende.* 2nd ed. Stuttgart: Adolph Krabbe. First ed., 1845.

GRINSTEIN, ALEXANDER

1968. *On Sigmund Freud's Dreams.* Detroit: Wayne State University Press.

GROOS, KARL

1896. *Die Spiele der Thiere.* Jena: Gustav Fischer.
    Trans.: Groos (1898).
1898. *The Play of Animals: A Study of Animal Life and Instinct.* Preface by J. Mark Baldwin. Translated by Elizabeth L. Baldwin. London: Chapman and Hall; New York: D. Appleton and Co.
    German Text: Groos (1896).
1899. *Die Spiele der Menschen.* Jena: Gustav Fischer.
    Trans.: Groos (1901).
1901. *The Play of Man.* Preface by J. Mark Baldwin. Translated by Elizabeth L. Baldwin. New York: D. Appleton and Co.
    German Text: Groos (1899).

GRUBER, HOWARD E.

1974. *Darwin on Man: A Psychological Study of Scientific Creativity.* Together with *Darwin's Early and Unpublished Notebooks.* Transcribed and annotated by Paul H. Barrett. With a Foreword by Jean Piaget. New York: E. P. Dutton & Co.; London: Wildwood House.

GUILLAIN, GEORGES

1955. *J.-M. Charcot, 1825–1893: Sa Vie, son œuvre.* Paris: Masson et Cie.
    Trans.: Guillain (1959).
1959. *J.-M. Charcot, 1825–1893: His Life—His Work.* Edited and translated by Pearce Bailey. New York: Paul B. Hoeber.
    French Text: Guillain (1955).

HACK, WILHELM

1884. *Ueber eine operative Radical-Behandlung bestimmter Formen von Migräne, Asthma, Heufieber, sowie zahlreicher verwandter Erscheinungen: Erfahrungen auf dem Gebiete der Nasenkrankheiten.* Wiesbaden: J. F. Bergmann.

HACKER, FREDERICK J.

1956. "The Living Image of Freud." *Bulletin of the Menninger Clinic,* 20: 103–11.

HAECKEL, ERNST

1866. *Generelle Morphologie der Organismen: Allgemeine Grundzüge der organischen Formen-Wissenschaft, mechanisch begründet durch die von Charles Darwin reformirte Descendenztheorie.* 2 vols. Berlin: Georg Reimer.
1868. *Natürliche Schöpfungsgeschichte.* Berlin: Georg Reimer.
1874a. *Anthropogenie oder Entwickelungsgeschichte des Menschen: Keimes- und Stammes-Geschichte.* Leipzig: Wilhelm Engelmann.
    Trans.: Haeckel [1874c].
1874b. "Die Gastraea-Theorie, die phylogenetische Classification des Thierreichs und die Homologie der Keimblätter." *Jenische Zeitschrift für Naturwissenschaft,* 8:1–57.
[1874c]. *The Evolution of Man: A Popular Exposition of the Principal Points of Human Ontogeny and Phylogeny.* 2 vols. International Science Library. New York: A. L. Fowle.
    German Text: Haeckel (1874a).
1875. "Die Gastrula und die Eifurchung der Thiere." *Jenische Zeitschrift für Naturwissenschaft,* 9:402–508.

HAECKEL, ERNST *(continued)*

1876. *Die Perigenesis der Plastidule oder die Wellenzeugung der Lebenstheilchen.*
       Berlin: Georg Reimer.
1877. *Anthropogenie oder Entwickelungsgeschichte des Menschen: Gemeinver-*
       ständliche wissenschaftliche Vorträge über die Grundzüge der mensch-
       lichen Keimes- und Stammes-Geschichte. Leipzig: Wilhelm Engelmann.
1891. *Anthropogenie oder Entwickelungsgeschichte des Menschen: Gemeinver-*
       ständliche wissenschaftliche Vorträge. 2 vols. 4th ed. Leipzig: Wilhelm
       Engelmann.
1899. *Die Welträthsel: Gemeinverständliche Studien über monistische Philoso-*
       phie. Bonn: Emil Strauss.
       Trans.: Haeckel (1900).
1900. *The Riddle of the Universe at the Close of the Nineteenth Century.*
       Translated by Joseph McCabe. New York and London: Harper & Brothers.
       German Text: Haeckel (1899).
1913. "Gonochorismus und Hermaphrodismus: Ein Beitrag zur Lehre von den
       Geschlechts-Umwandlungen (Metaptosen)." *Jahrbuch für sexuelle Zwi-*
       schenstufen, 14:259–87.

HAECKEL, WALTHER, ED.

1914. *Ernst Haeckel im Bilde: Eine phijsiognomische Studie zu seinem 80.*
       Geburtstage. With an Introduction by Wilhelm Bölsche. Berlin: Georg
       Reimer.

HALE, NATHAN G., JR.

1971. *Freud and the Americans.* Vol. 1: *The Beginnings of Psychoanalysis in*
       the United States, 1876–1917. New York: Oxford University Press.
1978. "From Berggasse XIX to Central Park West: The Americanization of
       Psychoanalysis, 1919–1940." *Journal of the History of the Behavioral*
       Sciences, 14:299–315.

HALL, G. STANLEY

1897. "A Study of Fears." *The American Journal of Psychology,* 8:147–249.
1904. *Adolescence: Its Psychology and Its Relations to Physiology, Anthropology,*
       Sociology, Sex, Crime, Religion and Education. 2 vols. New York: D. Ap-
       pleton and Co.
1914. "A Synthetic Genetic Study of Fear." *The American Journal of Psychology,*
       25:149–200, 321–92.
1915. "Anger as a Primary Emotion, and the Application of Freudian Mecha-
       nisms to Its Phenomena." *The Journal of Abnormal Psychology,* 10:81–87.
1918. "A Medium in the Bud." *The American Journal of Psychology,* 29:144–58.
1923. *Life and Confessions of a Psychologist.* New York and London: D. Apple-
       ton and Co.

HAMBURGER, VICTOR

1969. "Hans Spemann and the Organizer Concept." *Experientia,* 25:1121–25.

HARTMANN, EDUARD VON

1869. *Philosophie des Unbewussten: Versuch einer Weltanschauung.* Berlin:
       Carl Duncker.
       Trans.: Hartmann (1884).
1872. *Das Unbewusste vom Standpunkt der Physiologie und Descendenztheorie:*
       Eine kritische Beleuchtung des Naturphilosophischen Theils der Philoso-
       phie des Unbewussten aus naturwissenschaftlichen Gesichtspunkten. Ber-
       lin: Carl Duncker.
1875. *Wahrheit und Irrtum in Darwinismus: Eine kritische Darstellung der*
       organischen Entwickelungstheorie. Berlin: Carl Duncker.
1884. *Philosophy of the Unconscious: Speculative Results according to the In-*
       ductive Method of Physical Science. 3 vols. Translated by William Chatter-
       ton Coupland. London: Trübner & Co.
       German Text: Hartmann (1869).

HARTMANN, HEINZ

1939. "Ich-Psychologie und Anpassungsproblem." *Internationale Zeitschrift für Psychoanalyse und Imago*, 24:62–135.
   Trans.: Hartmann (1958).
1956. "The Development of the Ego Concept in Freud's Work." *The International Journal of Psycho-Analysis*, 37:425–38.
1958. *Ego Psychology and the Problem of Adaptation.* Translated by David Rapaport. New York: International Universities Press.
   German Text: Hartmann (1939).

HARTMANN, HEINZ, AND KRIS, ERNST

1945. "The Genetic Approach in Psychoanalysis." *The Psychoanalytic Study of the Child*, 1:11–30.

HARTMANN, HEINZ; KRIS, ERNST; AND LOEWENSTEIN, RUDOLPH M.

1964. *Papers on Psychoanalytic Psychology. Psychological Issues*, 4 (Monograph 14).

HEINE, MAURICE, ED.

1936. *Recueil de confessions et observations psycho-sexuelles tirées de la littérature médicale.* Paris: Jean Crès.

HELLER, ERICH

1977. "Reputations Revisited." *Times Literary Supplement*, 21 January, pp. 67–68.

HENDERSON, ROBERT L., AND JOHNS, MICHAEL E.

1977. "The Clinical Use of Cocaine." *Drug Therapy*, February, pp. 31–41.

HENNING, HANS

1910. "Neupythagoräer." *Annalen der Naturphilosophie*, 9:217–36.

HERING, EWALD

1870. *Über das Gedächtniss als eine allgemeine Function der organisirten Materie.* Vienna: K. K. Hof- und Staatsdruckerei.

HERMAN, G.

1903. "Genesis." *Das Gesetz der Zeugung.* Vol. 5: *Libido und Manie.* Leipzig: Arwed Strauch.

HERVEY DE SAINT-DENYS, MARIE JEAN LÉON

1867. *Les Rêves et les moyens de les diriger: Observations pratiques.* Paris: Amyot.

HEYMAN, STEVEN R.

1977. "Freud and the Concept of Inherited Racial Memories." *The Psychoanalytic Review*, 64:461–64.

HILDEBRANDT, F. W.

[1875]. *Der Traum und seine Verwertung für's Leben: Eine psychologische Studie.* Leipzig: Reinboth.

HILGARD, ERNEST R.

1960. "Psychology after Darwin." In *Evolution After Darwin.* Edited by Sol Tax. Vol. 2: *The Evolution of Man, Mind, Culture and Society*, pp. 269–87. Chicago: University of Chicago Press.

HINRICHSEN

1914.   Review of *Drei Abhandlungen zur Sexualtheorie*, by Sigmund Freud (1905d;
        2nd ed., 1910). *Zeitschrift für Psychologie und Physiologie der Sinnesor-
        gane (I. Abteilung. Zeitschrift für Psychologie)*, 69:142.

HIRSCH, MAX

1928.   "Nachruf auf Wilhelm Fliess." *Archiv für Frauenkunde und Konstitutions-
        forschung*, 14:422–24.

HIRSCHFELD, MAGNUS

1898.   Foreword to *Forschungen über das Rätsel der mannmännlichen Liebe*, by
        Carl Heinrich Ulrichs (1898). 12 vols. Leipzig: Max Spohr.
1899.   "Die objektive Diagnose der Homosexualität." *Jahrbuch für sexuelle Zwi-
        schenstufen*, 1:4–35.
1906.   *Vom Wesen der Liebe: Zugleich ein Beitrag zur Lösung der Frage der Bi-
        sexualität*. Leipzig: Max Spohr.
1912.   *Naturgesetze der Liebe: Eine gemeinverständliche Untersuchung über den
        Liebes-Eindruck, Liebes-Drang und Liebes-Ausdruck*. Berlin: A. Pulver-
        macher & Co.
1914.   *Die Homosexualität des Mannes und des Weibes*. Berlin: Louis Marcus.
1948.   *Sexual Anomalies: The Origins, Nature and Treatment of Sexual Disorders;
        A Summary of the Works of Magnus Hirschfeld*. Rev. ed. New York: Emer-
        son Books.

HIRSCHMÜLLER, ALBRECHT

1978.   *Physiologie und Psychoanalyse in Leben und Werk Josef Breuers*. Bern:
        Hans Huber.

HOCHE, ALFRED

1896.   "Zur Frage der forensischen Beurtheilung sexueller Vergehen." *Neurolo-
        gisches Centralblatt*, 15:57–68.
1910.   "Eine psychische Epidemie unter Aerzten." *Medizinische Klinik*, 6:1007–10.

HOFFER, ERIC

1951.   *The True Believer: Thoughts on the Nature of Mass Movements*. New York:
        Harper & Brothers.

HOLT, ROBERT R.

1962.   "A Critical Examination of Freud's Concept of Bound vs. Free Cathexis."
        Journal of the American Psychoanalytic Association, 10:475–525.
1963.   "Two Influences on Freud's Scientific Thought: A Fragment of Intellectual
        Biography." In *The Study of Lives: Essays on Personality in Honor of
        Henry A. Murray*, pp. 364–87. Edited by Robert W. White. New York:
        Atherton Press.
1965a. "A Review of Some of Freud's Biological Assumptions and Their Influence
        on His Theories." In *Psychoanalysis and Current Biological Thought*, pp.
        93–124. Edited by Norman S. Greenfield and William C. Lewis. Madison
        and Milwaukee: University of Wisconsin Press.
1965b. "Freud's Cognitive Style." *The American Imago*, 22:163–79.
1968a. "Beyond Vitalism and Mechanism: Freud's Concept of Psychic Energy."
        In *Historical Roots of Contemporary Psychology*, pp. 196–226. Edited by
        Benjamin B. Wolman. New York: Harper & Row.
1968b. "Sigmund Freud." *International Encyclopedia of the Social Sciences*, 6:1–12.
1972.   "Freud's Mechanistic and Humanistic Images of Man." In *Psychoanalysis
        and Contemporary Science*, 1:3–24. Edited by Robert R. Holt and Emanuel
        Peterfreund. New York: Macmillan Co.; London: Collier-Macmillan.
1974.   "On Reading Freud." Introduction to *Abstracts of the Standard Edition of
        Freud*. New York: Jason Aronson.
1975.   "Drive or Wish? A Reconsideration of the Psychoanalytic Theory of Moti-
        vation." In *Psychology versus Metapsychology: Psychoanalytic Essays in*

HOLT, ROBERT R. *(continued)*

        Memory of George S. Klein, pp. 158–97. Edited by M. M. Gill and P. S. Holzman. *Psychological Issues*, 9 (Monograph 36).

1976.   "Freud's Theory of the Primary Process—Present Status." In *Psychoanalysis and Contemporary Science*, 5:61–99. Edited by Theodore Shapiro. New York: International Universities Press.

HOLTON, GERALD

1969.   "Einstein, Michelson, and the 'Crucial' Experiment." *Isis*, 60:133–97.
1973.   *The Thematic Origins of Scientific Thought: Kepler to Einstein*. Cambridge: Harvard University Press.

HORNEY, KAREN

1939.   *New Ways in Psychoanalysis*. New York: W. W. Norton & Co.

HUSTON, JOHN

1962.   Director. *Freud—The Secret Passion*. (A motion picture depicting the early career of Sigmund Freud, played by Montgomery Clift.) Universal Pictures Co.

JACKSON, JOHN HUGHLINGS

1875.   "On the Anatomical and Physiological Localization of Movements in the Brain." Reprinted in *Selected Writings of John Hughlings Jackson* (1931, 1:37–76).
1879.   "On Affections of Speech from Disease of the Brain." *Brain*, 1:304–30; 2:203–22, 323–56. Partially reprinted in *Selected Writings of John Hughlings Jackson* (1931, 2:155–204).
1884.   "Evolution and Dissolution of the Nervous System." Reprinted in *Selected Writings of John Hughlings Jackson* (1931, 2:45–75).
1894.   "The Factors of Insanities." Reprinted in *Selected Writings of John Hughlings Jackson* (1931, 2:411–21).
1925.   *Neurological Fragments*. With a Biographical Memoir by James Taylor. Including "Recollections" of Sir Jonathan Hutchinson and Dr. Charles Mercier. Oxford Medical Publications. London: Humphrey Milford, Oxford University Press.
1931.   *Selected Writings of John Hughlings Jackson*. 2 vols. Edited by James Taylor. London: Hodder and Stoughton; reprint edition, New York: Basic Books, 1958.

JACKSON, STANLEY W.

1969.   "The History of Freud's Concepts of Regression." *Journal of the American Psychoanalytic Association*, 17:743–84.

JAMES, WILLIAM

1890.   *The Principles of Psychology*. 2 vols. New York: Henry Holt and Co.

JANET, JULES

1888.   "L'Hystérie et l'hypnotisme, d'après la théorie de la double personnalité." *Revue Scientifique (Revue Rose)*, 3rd series, 15:616–23.

JANET, PIERRE

1889.   *L'Automatisme psychologique: Essai de psychologie expérimentale sur les formes inférieures de l'activité humaine*. Paris: Félix Alcan.
1893a. "Quelques définitions récents de l'hystérie." *Archives de Neurologie*, 25: 417–38; 26:1–29.
1893b. *Contribution à l'étude des accidents mentaux chez les hystériques*. Thèse méd. Paris, 1892–93, no. 432. Paris: Rueff.
1894.   *État mental des hystériques*. Vol. 2: *Les Accidents mentaux*. Paris: Rueff.
1898.   *Névroses et idées fixes*. 2 vols. Paris: Félix Alcan.
1914–15. "Psychoanalysis." *The Journal of Abnormal Psychology*, 9:1–35, 153–87.

JANIK, ALLAN, AND TOULMIN, STEPHEN

   1973. *Wittgenstein's Vienna*. New York: Simon and Schuster.

JELLIFFE, SMITH ELY

   1937. "Sigmund Freud as a Neurologist: Some Notes on His Earlier Neurobiological and Clinical Neurological Studies." *Journal of Nervous and Mental Disease*, 85:696–711.
   1939. "Sigmund Freud and Psychiatry: A Partial Appraisal." *The American Journal of Sociology*, 45:326–40.

JOHNSTON, WILLIAM M.

   1972. *The Austrian Mind: An Intellectual and Social History 1848–1938*. Berkeley: University of California Press.

JONES, ERNEST

   1911. "The Psychopathology of Everyday Life." *The American Journal of Psychology*, 22:477–527.
   1913. *Papers on Psycho-Analysis*. London: Baillière, Tindall and Cox; New York: William Wood and Co.
   1914–15. "Professor Janet on Psychoanalysis: A Rejoinder." *The Journal of Abnormal Psychology*, 9:400–10.
   1930. "Psycho-Analysis and Biology." *Proceedings of the Second International Congress for Sex Research, London 1930*, pp. 601–23. Edited by A. W. Greenwood. Edinburgh and London: Oliver and Boyd.
   1932. "The Phallic Phase." Reprinted in *Papers on Psycho-Analysis* (Jones 1961: 452–84).
   1935. "Early Female Sexuality." Reprinted in *Papers on Psycho-Analysis* (Jones 1961:485–95).
   1940a. "Sigmund Freud." *The International Journal of Psycho-Analysis*, 21:2–26.
   1940b. Review of *Der Mann Moses und die monotheistische Religion*, by Sigmund Freud (1939a). *The International Journal of Psycho-Analysis*, 21:230–40.
   1953. *The Life and Work of Sigmund Freud*. Vol. 1: *The Formative Years and the Great Discoveries, 1856–1900*. New York: Basic Books; London: Hogarth Press.
   1955. *The Life and Work of Sigmund Freud*. Vol. 2: *Years of Maturity, 1901–1919*. New York: Basic Books; London: Hogarth Press.
   1956a. "The Inception of 'Totem and Taboo.'" *The International Journal of Psycho-Analysis*, 37:34–35.
   1956b. "Our Attitude towards Greatness." *Journal of the American Psychoanalytic Association*, 4:626–43.
   1956c. "The Achievement of Sigmund Freud." *The Listener*, 55:589–91.
   1956d. *Sigmund Freud: Four Centenary Addresses*. New York: Basic Books.
   1957. *The Life and Work of Sigmund Freud*. Vol. 3: *The Last Phase, 1919–1939*. New York: Basic Books; London: Hogarth Press.
   1959. *Free Associations: Memories of a Psycho-Analyst*. London: Hogarth Press; New York: Basic Books.
   1961. *Papers on Psycho-Analysis*. 5th ed. Boston: Beacon Press.

JOSEPH, ALFRED

   1931. "Rheumatoide Erscheinungen und ihre seelische Beeinflussung: Eine experimentell-psychologische Untersuchung über 100 Fälle von Lumbago und Torticollis rheumatoides." *Zeitschrift für ärztliche Fortbildung*, 28:119–21.

JUNG, CARL GUSTAV

   1907. *The Psychology of Dementia Praecox*. In *Collected Works* (1953– , 3:3–151).
   1911–12. *Symbols of Transformation: An Analysis of the Prelude to a Case of Schizophrenia*. In *Collected Works* (1953– , 5).
   1913. *The Theory of Psychoanalysis*. In *Collected Works* (1953– , 4:83–226).
   1917. *The Psychology of the Unconscious*. In *Collected Works* (1953– , 7:3–117).
   1921. *Psychological Types*. In *Collected Works* (1953– , 6:xi–495).

JUNG, CARL GUSTAV *(continued)*

1939. "In Memory of Sigmund Freud." In *Collected Works* (1953— , 15:41–49).
1953—   *The Collected Works of C. G. Jung.* Edited by Gerhard Adler, Michael
        Fordham, and Herbert Read. William McGuire, Executive Editor. Trans-
        lated by R. F. C. Hull. Bollingen Series XX. Vols. 1, 3–5, 7–12, and 15–17,
        New York: Pantheon Books, 1953–66; vols. 2, 6, 13–14, and 18, Princeton:
        Princeton University Press, 1967–76; London: Routledge & Kegan Paul.
1963.   *Memories, Dreams, Reflections.* Recorded and edited by Aniela Jaffé. Trans-
        lated by Richard and Clara Winston. New York: Pantheon Books; London:
        Collins & Routledge & Kegan Paul.

K., H.

1900.   "Träume und Traumdeutung." Review of *Die Traumdeutung*, by Sigmund
        Freud (1900a). *Wiener Fremden-Blatt*, 54, no. 67 (10 March):13–14.

KALISCHER, S.

1897a. Review of *Untersuchungen über die Libido sexualis* (Part One), by Albert
        Moll (1897b). *Zeitschrift für Medizinalbeamte*, 10:453–54.
1897b. Review of *Untersuchungen über die Libido sexualis* (Part Two), by Albert
        Moll (1897b). *Zeitschrift für Medizinalbeamte*, 10:812–14.

KANZER, MARK

1973.   "Two Prevalent Misconceptions about Freud's 'Project.'" In *The Annual of
        Psychoanalysis*, 1:88–103. New York: Quadrangle/New York Times Book
        Co.

KAPP, REGINALD O.

1931.   "Comments on Bernfeld and Feitelberg's 'The Principle of Entropy and the
        Death Instinct.'" *The International Journal of Psycho-Analysis*, 12:82–86.

KARELL, LUDWIG

1900.   "Träume." Review of *Die Traumdeutungen (sic)*, by Sigmund Freud (1900a).
        Beilage zur Allgemeinen Zeitung, Munich, no. 234, 12 October, pp. 4–5.

KAUTZNER, KARL

1899.   "Homosexualität: Erläutert an einem einschlägigen Falle." *Archiv für
        Kriminal-Anthropologie und Kriminalistik*, 2:153–62.

KAZIN, ALFRED

1962.   *Contemporaries.* Boston: Little, Brown & Co.

KERN, STEPHEN

1973.   "Freud and the Discovery of Child Sexuality." *History of Childhood Quar-
        terly*, 1:117–41.
1975.   *Anatomy and Destiny: A Cultural History of the Human Body.* Indian-
        apolis and New York: Bobbs-Merrill Co.

KIERNAN, JAMES G.

1884.   "Insanity: Lecture XXVI.—Sexual Perversion." *Detroit Lancet*, 7:481–84.
1888.   "Sexual Perversion, and the Whitechapel Murders." *The Medical Standard*,
        4 (November):129–30; (December):170–72.
1891.   "Psychological Aspects of the Sexual Appetite." *The Alienist and Neu-
        rologist*, 12:188–219.

KING, A. F. A.

1891.   "Hysteria." *The American Journal of Obstetrics*, 24:513–32.

KLINE, PAUL

1972.   *Fact and Fantasy in Freudian Theory.* London: Methuen & Co.

KOBLANCK, ALFRED

1914. 20 March discussion of "Die Nase in ihren Beziehungen zu den Sexual-
       organen," a lecture delivered by Max Senator (1914) before the Ärztliche
       Gesellschaft für Sexualwissenschaft und Eugenik in Berlin on 20 February.
       Zeitschrift für Sexualwissenschaft, 1:76.

KOENIGSBERGER, LEO

1902-3. *Hermann von Helmholtz.* 3 vols. Braunschweig: F. Vieweg und Sohn.

KOHNSTAMM, OSKAR

1902. Review of *Ueber den Traum,* by Sigmund Freud (1901a). *Fortschritte der
       Medicin,* 22:45–46.

KORNFELD, HERMANN

1901. Review of *Ueber den Traum,* by Sigmund Freud (1901a). *Psychiatrische
       Wochenschrift,* 2:430–31.

KOVALEVSKY, ALEKSANDR

1866. "Entwickelungsgeschichte der einfachen Ascidien." *Mémoires de l'Acadé-
       mie Impériale des Sciences de St.-Pétersbourg,* 7th series, 10, no. 15.
1868. "Beitrag zur Entwickelungsgeschichte der Tunikaten." *Nachrichten von
       der G. A. Universität und der Königlichen Gesellschaft der Wissenschaften
       zu Göttingen,* no. 19, pp. 401–15.

KOYRÉ, ALEXANDRE

1937. "Galilée et l'expérience de Pise: à propos d'une légende." *Annales de l'Uni-
       versité de Paris,* pp. 441–53.
1943. "Traduttore-traditore, à propos de Copernic et de Galilée." *Isis,* 34:209–10.

KRAFFT-EBING, RICHARD VON

1875. *Lehrbuch der gerichtlichen Psychopathologie, mit Berücksichtigung der
       Gesetzgebung von Österreich, Deutschland und Frankreich.* Stuttgart: Fer-
       dinand Enke.
1877. "Ueber gewisse Anomalien des Geschlechtstriebs und die klinisch-foren-
       sische Verwerthung derselben als eines wahrscheinlich functionellen De-
       generationszeichens des centralen Nerven-Systems." *Archiv für Psychiatrie,*
       7:291–312.
1879-80. *Lehrbuch der Psychiatrie auf klinischer Grundlage für practische Ärzte
          und Studirende.* 3 vols. Stuttgart: Ferdinand Enke.
          Trans.: Krafft-Ebing (1904).
1882. "Zur 'conträren Sexualempfindung' in klinisch-forensischer Hinsicht." *All-
       gemeine Zeitschrift für Psychiatrie und psychisch-gerichtliche Medicin,*
       38:211–27.
1886. *Psychopathia sexualis: Eine klinisch-forensische Studie.* Stuttgart: Ferdi-
       nand Enke.
       Trans.: Krafft-Ebing (1899).
1889. "Ueber Neurosen und Psychosen durch sexuelle Abstinenz." *Jahrbuch für
       Psychiatrie,* 8:1–6.
1889-90a. "Angeborene konträre Sexualempfindung: Erfolgreiche hypnotische
           Absuggerierung homosexualer Empfindungen." *Internationales Centralblatt
           für die Physiologie und Pathologie der Harn- und Sexual-Organe,* 1:7–11.
1889-90b. "Über psychosexuales Zwittertum." *Internationales Centralblatt für
           die Physiologie und Pathologie der Harn- und Sexual-Organe,* 1:55–65.
1892. *Psychopathia sexualis, mit besonderer Berücksichtigung der conträren Sex-
       ualempfindung: Eine klinisch-forensische Studie.* 7th ed. Stuttgart: Ferdi-
       nand Enke.
1893. *Psychopathia sexualis, mit besonderer Berücksichtigung der conträren Sex-
       ualempfindung: Eine klinisch-forensische Studie.* 8th ed. Stuttgart: Ferdi-
       nand Enke.
1894. *Psychopathia sexualis, mit besonderer Berücksichtigung der conträren Sex-
       ualempfindung: Eine klinisch-forensische Studie.* 9th ed. Stuttgart: Ferdi-
       nand Enke.

KRAFFT-EBING, RICHARD VON (*continued*)

1895.   "Zur Erklärung der conträren Sexualempfindung." *Jahrbücher für Psychiatrie und Nervenheilkunde*, 13:98–112.

1896.   "Zur Suggestivbehandlung der Hysteria Gravis." *Zeitschrift für Hypnotismus*, 4:27–31.

1897–99.   *Arbeiten aus dem Gesammtgebiet der Psychiatrie und Neuropathologie.* 4 vols. Leipzig: J. A. Barth.

1899.   *Psychopathia Sexualis, with Especial Reference to Antipathic Sexual Instinct: A Medico-Forensic Study.* Translated from the 10th [1898] German edition [by F. J. Rebman]. London: Rebman.
                  German Text: Krafft-Ebing (1886 and later eds.).

1901*a*.   "Des Perversions sexuelles obsédantes et impulsives au point de vue médico-légal." In *XIIIe Congrès international de médecine. Paris 1900: Comptes rendus.* Vol. 8: *Section de Psychiatrie,* pp. 418–27. Paris: Masson et Cie.

1901*b*.   "Neue Studien auf dem Gebiete der Homosexualität." *Jahrbuch für sexuelle Zwischenstufen*, 3:1–36.

1902.   *Psychosis menstrualis: Eine klinisch-forensische Studie.* Stuttgart: Ferdinand Enke.

1904.   *Text-Book of Insanity, Based on Clinical Observations: For Practitioners and Students of Medicine.* Translated from the German by Charles Gilbert Chaddock. Philadelphia: F. A. Davis Co.
                  German Text: Krafft-Ebing (1879–80 and later eds.).

KRIS, ERNST

1950*a*.   "The Significance of Freud's Earliest Discoveries." *The International Journal of Psycho-Analysis*, 31:108–16.

1950*b*.   "Notes on the Development and on Some Current Problems of Psychoanalytic Child Psychology." *The Psychoanalytic Study of the Child*, 5:24–46.

1954.   Introduction to *The Origins of Psychoanalysis, Letters to Wilhelm Fliess, Drafts and Notes: 1887–1902,* by Sigmund Freud (1954*e*). Edited by Marie Bonaparte, Anna Freud, and Ernst Kris. Translated by Eric Mosbacher and James Strachey. New York: Basic Books; London: Imago Publishing Co.

1956.   "Freud in the History of Science." *The Listener*, 55:631–33; London BBC, May 1956.

KUHN, THOMAS

1962.   *The Structure of Scientific Revolutions.* Chicago: University of Chicago Press.

1970*a*.   *The Structure of Scientific Revolutions.* 2nd ed., with a "Postscript, 1969." Chicago: University of Chicago Press.

1970*b*.   "Reflections on my Critics." In *Criticism and the Growth of Knowledge*, pp. 231–78. Edited by Imre Lakatos and Alan Musgrave. Cambridge: Cambridge University Press.

1974.   "Second Thoughts on Paradigms." In *The Structure of Scientific Theory*, pp. 459–99. Edited with a Critical Introduction by Frederick Suppe. Urbana, Ill.: University of Illinois Press.

KURELLA, HANS

1896.   "Zum biologischen Verständniss der somatischen und psychischen Bisexualität." *Centralblatt für Nervenheilkunde und Psychiatrie*, 19:234–41.

1899.   "Zur Psychologie der Grausamkeit." (Abstract.) *Zeitschrift für Pädagogische Psychologie*, 1:100–102.

1911.   *Cesare Lombroso: A Modern Man of Science.* Translated from the German by M. Eden Paul. London: Rebman Co.

LACAN, JACQUES

1978.   *The Four Fundamental Concepts of Psycho-Analysis.* Edited by Jacques-Alain Miller. Translated from the French by Alan Sheridan. New York: W. W. Norton & Co.

LAMPL, HANS

1953. "The Influence of Biological and Psychological Factors upon the Development of the Latency Period." In *Drives, Affects, Behavior*, pp. 380–87. Edited by Rudolph M. Loewenstein. New York: International Universities Press.

LANG, ANDREW

1903. *Social Origins.* Published with J. J. Atkinson, *Primal Law.* London: Longmans, Green, and Co.

LAUZON, GÉRARD

1963. *Sigmund Freud: The Man and His Theories.* Translated from the French by Patrick Evans. Edited by Jacques Ahrweiler. London: Souvenir Press.

LAYCOCK, THOMAS

1840. *A Treatise on the Nervous Diseases of Women: Comprising an Inquiry into the Nature, Causes, and Treatment of Spinal and Hysterical Disorders.* London: Longman, Orme, Brown, Green, and Longmans.

1842a. "Evidence and Arguments in Proof of the Existence of a General Law of Periodicity in the Phenomena of Life." *The Lancet,* 22 October, pp. 124–29; 29 October, pp. 160–64.

1842b. "Further Development of a General Law of Vital Periodicity; Being a Contribution to Proleptics." *The Lancet,* 17 December, pp. 423–27.

1843a. [1842]. "On a General Law of Vital Periodicity." *Report of the Twelfth Meeting of the British Association for the Advancement of Science.* Part II: *Miscellaneous Communications to the Sections,* pp. 81–82. London: John Murray.

1843b. "On Some of the Causes which Determine the Minor Periods of Vital Movements." *The Lancet,* 25 March, pp. 929–33.

1843c. "On Lunar Influence; Being a Fourth Contribution to Proleptics." *The Lancet,* 24 June, pp. 438–44.

1843d. "On the Influence of the Moon and the Atmosphere of the Earth, and on the Pathological Influence of the Seasons." *The Lancet,* 9 September, pp. 826–30.

1843e. "On Annual Vital Periods, Being a Fifth Contribution to Vital Proleptics." *The Lancet,* 21 October, pp. 85–89.

1843f. "On the Major Periods of Development in Man, Being a Sixth Contribution to Proleptics." *The Lancet,* 25 November, pp. 253–58.

1843g. "On the Periods of Years, Being a Seventh Contribution to Proleptics." *The Lancet,* 30 December, pp. 430–32.

1844. "The Periods Regulating the Recurrence of Vital Phenomena; Being a General Summary of Previous Contributions to Proleptical Science." *The Lancet,* 20 July, pp. 523–24.

1860. *Mind and Brain: or, The Correlations of Consciousness and Organization. . . .* 2 vols. Edinburgh: Sutherland and Knox. 2nd ed., London: Simpkin and Marshall, 1869.

LESKY, ERNA

1965. *Die Wiener medizinische Schule in 19. Jahrhundert.* Graz and Cologne: Verlag Hermann Böhlaus Nachf.

LEVIN, KENNETH

1978. *Freud's Early Psychology of the Neuroses: A Historical Perspective.* Pittsburgh: University of Pittsburgh Press.

LEWIS, BERNARD

1975. *History—Remembered, Recovered, Invented.* Princeton: Princeton University Press.

LEWIS, NOLAN D. C., AND LANDIS, CARNEY

1957. "Freud's Library." *The Psychoanalytic Review,* 44:327–54.

LEYEN, FRIEDRICH VON DER

  1901. "Traum und Märchen." *Der Lotse,* 1:382–90.

LICHTENSTEIN, HEINZ

  1935. "Zur Phänomenologie des Wiederholungszwanges und des Todestriebes."
    Imago, 21:466–80.

LIÉBEAULT, AMBROISE AUGUSTE

  1866. *Du Sommeil et des états analogues, considérés surtout au point de vue de
    l'action du moral sur le physique.* Paris: V. Masson et fils; Nancy: N.
    Grosjean.

LIEPMANN, HUGO

  1901. Review of *Ueber den Traum,* by Sigmund Freud (1901*a*). *Monatsschrift
    für Psychiatrie und Neurologie,* 10:237–39.

LIFTON, ROBERT JAY

  1976. *The Life of the Self: Toward a New Psychology.* New York: Simon and
    Schuster.

LINDNER, GUSTAV ADOLF

  1858. *Lehrbuch der empirischen Psychologie nach genetischer Methode.* Graz:
    Wiesner.

LINDNER, S.

  1879. "Das Saugen an den Fingern, Lippen etc. bei den Kindern. (Ludeln.).
    Eine Studie." *Jahrbuch für Kinderheilkunde und physische Erziehung,* n.s.,
    14:68–91.

LIPPS, THEODOR

  1883. *Grundtatsachen des Seelenlebens.* Bonn: M. Cohen & Sohn.
  1897. "Der Begriff des Unbewussten in der Psychologie." III. *Internationaler
    Congress für Psychologie in München vom 4. bis 7. August 1896,* pp. 146–
    64. Munich: J. F. Lehmann.
  1898. *Komik und Humor: Eine psychologisch-ästhetische Untersuchung.* Ham-
    burg and Leipzig: L. Voss.

LOEWENSTEIN, RUDOLPH M.

  1951. "Freud: Man and Scientist." *Bulletin of the N.Y. Academy of Medicine,*
    27:623–37.

LOMBROSO, CESARE

  1876. *L'Uomo delinquente: Studiato in rapporto alla antropologia, alla medicina
    legale ed alle discipline carcerarie.* Milan: Heopli.
  1881. "L'Amore nei pazzi." *Archivio di psichiatria, scienze penali ed antropologia
    criminale,* 2:1–32.
  1882. *Genio e follia, in rapporto alla medicina legale, alle critica ed all storia.*
    4th ed. Rome: Fratelli Bocca.
  1894. "La Nevrosi in Dante e Michelangelo." *Archivio di psichiatria, scienze
    penali ed antropologia criminale,* 15:126–32.
  1911. Introduction to *Criminal Man: According to the Classification of Cesare
    Lombroso,* by Gina Lombroso-Ferrero (1911). New York and London:
    G. P. Putnam's Sons.

LOMBROSO, CESARE, AND FERRERO, GUGLIELMO

  1893. *La Donna delinquente: La Prostituta e la donna normale.* Turin: Roux.

LOMBROSO-FERRERO, GINA

  1911. *Criminal Man: According to the Classification of Cesare Lombroso, Briefly
    Summarized by his Daughter Gina Lombroso-Ferrero.* With an Introduction
    by Cesare Lombroso. New York and London: G. P. Putnam's Sons.

LOVEJOY, ARTHUR O.

1959. "Schopenhauer as an Evolutionist." In *Forerunners of Darwinism 1745–1859*, pp. 415–37. Edited by Bentley Glass, Owsei Temkin, and William L. Straus, Jr. Baltimore: Johns Hopkins Press.

LÖWENFELD, LEOPOLD

1895. "Über die Verknüpfung neurasthenischer und hysterischer Symptome in Anfallsform nebst Bemerkungen über die Freudsche Angstneurose." *Münchener medicinische Wochenschrift*, 42:282–85.

1914. *Sexualleben und Nervenleiden: Nebst einem Anhang über Prophylaxe und Behandlung der sexuellen Neurasthenie.* 5th ed. Wiesbaden: J. F. Bergmann. First ed. published as *Die nervösen Störungen sexuellen Ursprungs.* Wiesbaden: J. F. Bergmann, 1891.

LUDWIG, CARL

1852–56. *Lehrbuch der Physiologie des Menschen.* 2 vols. Heidelberg: C. F. Winter.

LUZENBERGER, A. V.

1886. "Ueber einem Fall von Dyschromatopsie bei einem hysterischen Manne." *Wiener medizinische Blätter*, 9:1113–26.

LYDSTON, G. FRANK

1889. "Sexual Perversion, Satyriasis and Nymphomania." *Medical and Surgical Reporter*, 61:253–58, 281–85.

MACALPINE, IDA, AND HUNTER, RICHARD A.

1953. "The Schreber Case." *The Psychoanalytic Quarterly*, 22:328–71.

1956. *Schizophrenia, 1677: A Psychiatric Study of an Illustrated Autobiographical Record of Demoniacal Possession.* London: Wm. Dawson and Sons.

McCARLEY, ROBERT W., AND HOBSON, J. ALLAN

1977. "The Neurobiological Origins of Psychoanalytic Dream Theory." *The American Journal of Psychiatry*, 134:1211–21.

McDOUGALL, WILLIAM

1936. *Psycho-Analysis and Social Psychology.* London: Methuen & Co.

McGRATH, WILLIAM J.

1967. "Student Radicalism in Vienna." *Journal of Contemporary History*, 2:183–201.

MACKENZIE, JOHN NOLAND

1884. "Irritation of the Sexual Apparatus as an Etiological Factor in the Production of Nasal Disease." *The American Journal of the Medical Sciences*, n.s., 88:360–65.

1898. "The Physiological and Pathological Relations between the Nose and the Sexual Apparatus of Man." *The Journal of Laryngology, Rhinology, and Otology*, 13:109–23.

MACMILLAN, M. B.

1976. "Beard's Concept of Neurasthenia and Freud's Concept of the Actual Neuroses." *Journal of the History of the Behavioral Sciences*, 12:376–90.

1977a. "The Cathartic Method and the Expectancies of Breuer and Anna O." *The International Journal of Clinical and Experimental Hypnosis*, 25:106–18.

1977b. "Freud's Expectations and the Childhood Seduction Theory." *Australian Journal of Psychology*, 29:223–36.

MADISON, PETER

1961. *Freud's Concept of Repression and Defense, Its Theoretical and Observational Language.* Minneapolis: University of Minnesota Press.

MAGOUN, H. W.

1960. "Evolutionary Concepts of Brain Function Following Darwin and Spencer."
In *Evolution After Darwin*. Edited by Sol Tax. Vol. 2: *The Evolution of
Man, Mind, Culture and Society*, pp. 187–209. Chicago: University of Chi-
cago Press.

MALTHUS, THOMAS ROBERT

1798. *An Essay on the Principle of Population, as It Affects the Future Improvement of Society. With Remarks on the Speculations of Mr. Godwin, M.
Condorcet, and Other Writers*. London: J. Johnson.
1826. *An Essay on the Principle of Population: Or, a View of Its Past and Present Effects on Human Happiness; with an Inquiry into our Prospects re-
specting the Future Removal or Mitigation of the Evils which It Occasions.*
2 vols. 6th ed. London: John Murray.

MANNHEIM, KARL

1936. *Ideology and Utopia: An Introduction to the Sociology of Knowledge*. Pref-
ace by Louis Wirth. Translated from the German by Louis Wirth and
Edward Shils. London: Kegan Paul, Trench, Trubner & Co.; New York:
Harcourt, Brace and Co.
1952. *Essays on the Sociology of Knowledge*. Edited by Paul Kecskemeti. New
York: Oxford University Press; London: Routledge & Kegan Paul.

MANNONI, OCTAVE

1974. *Freud*. Translated from the French by Renaud Bruce. New York: Vintage
Books; London: New Left Books, 1972.

MARCINOWSKI, JOHANNES

1902. Review of *Ueber den Traum*, by Sigmund Freud (1901a). *Aerztliche Sach-
verständigen-Zeitung*, 8:125.

MARCUS, JOHN T.

1960. "The World Impact of the West: The Mystique and the Sense of Participation in History." In *Myth and Mythmaking*, pp. 221–39. Edited and with
an Introduction by Henry A. Murray. New York: George Braziller; reprint
ed., Boston: Beacon Press, 1968.

MARCUS, STEVEN

1974. *The Other Victorians: A Study of Sexuality and Pornography in Mid-
Nineteenth-Century England*. 2nd ed. New York: Basic Books.

MARX, OTTO M.

1966. "Aphasia Studies and Language Theory in the 19th Century." *Bulletin of
the History of Medicine*, 4:328–49.
1970. "Nineteenth-Century Medical Psychology: Theoretical Problems in the
Work of Griesinger, Meynert, and Wernicke." *Isis*, 61:355–70.

MAUDSLEY, HENRY

1867. *The Physiology and Pathology of the Mind*. London: Macmillan and Co.;
New York: D. Appleton and Co.
1872. "An Address on Medical Psychology." *The British Medical Journal*, 10
August, pp. 163–67.

MAURY, ALFRED

1861. *Le Sommeil et les rêves: Études psychologiques sur ces phénomènes*. Paris:
Didier. 2nd ed., 1862; 3rd ed., 1865; 4th ed., 1878.

MAYR, ERNST

1961. "Cause and Effect in Biology." *Science*, 134:1501–6.

MAZLISH, BRUCE

1976. *The Revolutionary Ascetic: Evolution of a Political Type.* New York: Basic Books.

MEDAWAR, PETER B.

1957. *The Uniqueness of the Individual.* London: Methuen & Co.; New York: Basic Books.
1975. "Victims of Psychiatry." Review of *The Victim Is Always the Same*, by I. S. Cooper. *The New York Review of Books*, January 23, p. 17.

MENTZ, PAUL

1901. Review of *Die Traumdeutung*, by Sigmund Freud (1900a). *Vierteljahrsschrift für wissenschaftliche Philosophie und Soziologie*, 25:112–13.

MERINGER, RUDOLF, AND MAYER, KARL

1895. *Versprechen und Verlesen: Eine psychologisch-linguistische Studie.* Stuttgart: G. J. Göschen.

MERTON, ROBERT K.

1973. *The Sociology of Science: Theoretical and Empirical Investigations.* Edited and with an Introduction by Norman W. Storer. Chicago and London: University of Chicago Press.
1976. "The Ambivalence of Scientists." In *Sociological Ambivalence and Other Essays*, pp. 32–55. New York: Free Press.

METZENTIN, CARL

1899. "Ueber wissenschaftliche Traumdeutung." Review of *Die Traumdeutung*, by Sigmund Freud (1900a). *Die Gegenwart*, 56:386–89.

MEYER, ADOLPH

1906. "Interpretation of Obsessions." Review of *Drei Abhandlungen zur Sexualtheorie* and "Bruchstück einer Hysterie-Analyse," by Sigmund Freud (1905d, 1905e [1901]). *Psychological Bulletin*, 3:280–83.

MEYER, ERNST

1906. Review of *Drei Abhandlungen zur Sexualtheorie*, by Sigmund Freud (1905d). *Monatsschrift für Psychiatrie und Neurologie*, 20:92–93.

MEYER, HANS HORST

1928. "Josef Breuer 1842–1925." *Neue Österreichische Biographie 1815–1918*, 5:30–47.

MEYJES, WILLEM

1898. "On the Etiology of Some Nasal Reflex Neuroses." *The Journal of Laryngology, Rhinology, and Otology*, 13:580–83.

MEYNERT, THEODOR

1884. *Psychiatrie: Klinik der Erkrankungen des Vorderhirns begründet auf dessen Bau, Leistungen und Ernährung.* Vienna: Wilhelm Braumüller.
    Trans.: Meynert (1885).
1885. *Psychiatry: A Clinical Treatise on Diseases of the Fore-Brain Based upon a Study of Its Structure, Functions, and Nutrition.* Translated by B. Sachs. New York and London: G. P. Putnam's Sons.
    German Text: Meynert (1884).
1888. "Über hypnotische Erscheinungen." *Wiener klinische Wochenschrift*, 1: 451–53, 473–76, 495–98.
1889a. "Zum Verständnisse der traumatischen Neurosen im Gegensatze zu ihrer hypnotischen Entstehungstheorie." *Wiener medizinische Wochenschrift*, 39:686–87.

MEYNERT, THEODOR *(continued)*

1889b. "Beitrag zum Verständniss der traumatischen Neurose." *Wiener klinische Wochenschrift*, 2:475–76, 498–503, 522–24.
1889c. 7 June discussion of "Elektrischer Beleuchtungsapparat zum Taschengebrauch," a lecture delivered by Vohwinkel before the K. k. Gesellschaft der Ärzte on 7 June 1889. *Wiener klinische Wochenschrift*, 2:490.
1890.   *Klinische Vorlesungen über Psychiatrie aus wissenschaftlichen Grundlagen für Studirende und Aerzte.* Vienna: Wilhelm Braumüller.

MITTWOCH, URSULA

1977.   "To Be Born Right Is to Be Born Male." *New Scientist*, 73:74–76.

MÖBIUS, PAUL J.

1888.   "Über den Begriff der Hysterie." *Centralblatt für Nervenheilkunde*, 11: 66–71. Reprinted in *Neurologische Beiträge* (1894–98, 1:1–7).
1894.   "Über Astasie-Abasie." In *Neurologische Beiträge* (1894–98, 1:8–19).
1894–98. *Neurologische Beiträge.* 5 vols. Leipzig: Ambr. Abel (Arthur Meiner).
1895.   "Über die gegenwärtige Auffassung der Hysterie." *Monatsschrift für Geburtshülfe und Gynaekologie*, 1:12–21.
1898.   Review of *Ueber die sexuellen Ursachen der Neurasthenie und Angstneurose*, by Felix Gattel (1898). *Schmidt's Jahrbücher der in- und ausländischen gesammten Medicin*, 259:214.
1901.   Review of *Ueber den Traum*, by Sigmund Freud (1901a). *Schmidt's Jahrbücher der in- und ausländischen gesammten Medicin*, 269:271.
1906.   Review of *Sammlung kleiner Schriften zur Neurosenlehre aus den Jahren 1893–1906*, by Sigmund Freud. *Schmidt's Jahrbücher der in- und ausländischen gesammten Medicin*, 292:270.

MOLL, ALBERT

1889.   *Der Hypnotismus.* Berlin: Fischer's Medicinische Buchhandlung, H. Kornfeld.
        Trans.: Moll (1913).
1890.   *Der Hypnotismus.* 2nd ed. Berlin: Fischer's Medicinische Buchhandlung, H. Kornfeld.
1891.   *Die conträre Sexualempfindung.* Foreword by Richard von Krafft-Ebing. Berlin: Fischer's Medicinische Buchhandlung, H. Kornfeld.
        Trans.: Moll (1931).
1897a. "Probleme in der Homosexualität." *Zeitschrift für Criminal-Anthropologie, Gefängnis-Wissenschaft und Prostitution*, 1:157–89.
1897b. *Untersuchungen über die Libido sexualis.* Berlin: Fischer's Medicinische Buchhandlung, H. Kornfeld.
        Partial Trans.: Moll (1933).
1901.   "Ueber eine wenig beachtete Gefahr der Prügelstrafe bei Kindern." *Zeitschrift für Pädagogische Psychologie*, 3:215–19.
1907.   "Hysterie." In *Encyclopädische Jahrbücher der gesamten Heilkunde*, 14 (n.s., 5):268–85. Edited by Albert Eulenburg. Berlin and Vienna: Urban & Schwarzenberg.
1909.   *Das Sexualleben des Kindes.* Berlin: H. Walther.
        Trans.: Moll (1912a).
1912a. *The Sexual Life of the Child.* Translated by Eden Paul. Introduction by Edward L. Thorndike. New York: Macmillan Co.
        German Text: Moll (1909).
1912b. Ed. *Handbuch der Sexualwissenschaften: Mit besonderer Berücksichtigung der kulturgeschichtlichen Beziehungen.* Leipzig: F. C. W. Vogel.
1912c. "Sexuelle Hygiene." In *Handbuch der Sexualwissenschaften*, pp. 879–922. Edited by Albert Moll (1912b). Leipzig: F. C. W. Vogel.
1913.   *Hypnotism: Including a Study of the Chief Points of Psychotherapeutics and Occultism.* The Contemporary Science Series, vol. 9. Translated from the 4th German ed. by Arthur F. Hopkirk. London: Walter Scott. First English ed., 1890.
        German Text: Moll (1889 and later eds.).
1926a. "Die Psychologie des normalen Geschlechtstriebes." In *Handbuch der Sexualwissenschaften: Mit besonderer Berücksichtigung der kulturgeschichtlichen Beziehungen*, 1:235–300. 3rd ed. Edited by Albert Moll. Leipzig: F. C. W. Vogel.

MOLL, ALBERT *(continued)*

1926b. "Sexuelle Hygiene." (Expanded version of Moll 1912c.) In *Handbuch der Sexualwissenschaften: Mit besonderer Berücksichtigung der kulturgeschichtlichen Beziehungen,* 2:1069–1157. 3rd ed. Edited by Albert Moll. Leipzig: F. C. W. Vogel.

1931. *Perversions of the Sex Instinct: A Study of Sexual Inversion Based on Clinical Data and Official Documents.* Translated by Maurice Popkin. Newark, N.J.: Julian Press.
German Text: Moll (1891).

1933. *Libido Sexualis: Studies in the Psychosexual Laws of Love Verified by Clinical Sexual Case Histories.* Translated by David Berger. New York: American Ethnological Press.
German Text: Moll (1897b).

1936. *Ein Leben als Arzt der Seele: Erinnerungen.* Dresden: Carl Reissner.

MOREAU (DE TOURS), JACQUES-JOSEPH

1845. *Du Hachisch et de l'aliénation mentale: Études psychologiques.* Paris: Fortin, Masson et Cie.

MOREL, BÉNÉDICT AUGUSTE

1857. *Traité des dégénérescences physiques, intellectuelles et morales de l'espèce humaine et des causes qui produisent ces variétés maladives.* Paris: J. B. Baillière; New York: H. Baillière.

MÜLLER, FRIEDRICH MAX

1902. *The Life and Letters of the Right Honourable Friedrich Max Müller.* 2 vols. Edited by his wife. London and New York: Longmans, Green, and Co.

MÜLLER, ROBERT

1907. *Sexualbiologie: Vergleichend-entwickelungsgeschichtliche Studien über das Geschlechtsleben des Menschen und der höheren Tiere.* Berlin: Louis Marcus.

MÜLLER-LYER, FRANZ

1912. *Die Entwicklungsstufen der Menschheit.* Vol. 4: *Die Familie.* Munich: J. F. Lehmann.

1913. *Die Entwicklungsstufen der Menschheit.* Vol. 5: *Phasen der Liebe: Eine Soziologie des Verhältnisses der Geschlechter.* Munich: Albert Langen. 2nd ed., 1917.
Trans.: Müller-Lyer (1930).

1930. *The Evolution of Modern Marriage: A Sociology of Sexual Relations.* Translated by Isabella C. Wigglesworth. New York: Alfred A. Knopf.
German Text: Müller-Lyer (1913).

MYERS, FREDERIC W. H.

1897. "Hysteria and Genius." *Journal of the Society for Psychical Research,* 8:50–59, 69–71.

NÄCKE, PAUL

1899a. Review of *Untersuchungen über die Libido sexualis,* by Albert Moll (1897b). *Archiv für Kriminal-Anthropologie und Kriminalistik,* 2:170–73.

1899b. "Kritisches zum Kapitel der normalen und pathologischen Sexualität." *Archiv für Psychiatrie,* 32:356–86.

1901a. Review of *Die Traumdeutung,* by Sigmund Freud (1900a). *Archiv für Kriminal-Anthropologie und Kriminalistik,* 7:168.

1901b. Review of *Ueber den Traum,* by Sigmund Freud (1901a). *Archiv für Kriminal-Anthropologie und Kriminalistik,* 7:169.

1903. Review of *Beiträge zur Aetiologie der Psychopathia sexualis,* by Iwan Bloch (1902–3). *Archiv für Kriminal-Anthropologie und Kriminalistik,* 11:276–77.

1906. Review of *Drei Abhandlungen zur Sexualtheorie,* by Sigmund Freud (1905d). *Archiv für Kriminal-Anthropologie und Kriminalistik,* 24:166.

NAGERA, HUMBERTO; BAKER, S.; COLONNA, A.; FIRST, E.; GAVSHON, A.;
    HOLDER, A.; JONES, G.; KOCH, E.; LAUFER, M.; MEERS, D.;
    NEURATH, L.; AND REES, K.

    1969a. *Basic Psychoanalytic Concepts on the Libido Theory.* The Hampstead
    Clinic Psychoanalytic Library, vol. 1. Edited by Humberto Nagera. Lon-
    don: George Allen & Unwin.

NAGERA, HUMBERTO; BAKER, S.; COLONNA, A.; EDGCUMBE, R.;
    HOLDER, A.; KEARNEY, L.; KAWENOKA, M.; LEGG, C.;
    MEERS, D.; NEURATH, L.; AND REES, K.

    1969b. *Basic Psychoanalytic Concepts on the Theory of Dreams.* The Hampstead
    Clinic Psychoanalytic Library, vol. 2. Edited by Humberto Nagera. Lon-
    don: George Allen & Unwin.

NAGERA, HUMBERTO; BAKER, S.; EDGCUMBE, R.; HOLDER, A.;
    LAUFER, M.; MEERS, D.; AND REES, K.

    1970a. *Basic Psychoanalytic Concepts on the Theory of Instincts.* The Hampstead
    Clinic Psychoanalytic Library, vol. 3. Edited by Humberto Nagera. Lon-
    don: George Allen & Unwin.

NAGERA, HUMBERTO; COLONNA, A.; DANSKY, E.; FIRST, E.;
    GAVSHON, A.; HOLDER, A.; KEARNEY, L.; AND RADFORD, P.

    1970b. *Basic Psychoanalytic Concepts on Metapsychology, Conflicts, Anxiety, and
    Other Subjects.* The Hampstead Clinic Psychoanalytic Library, vol. 4.
    Edited by Humberto Nagera. London: George Allen & Unwin.

NATENBERG, MAURICE

    1955. *The Case History of Sigmund Freud: A Psycho-Biography.* Chicago:
    Regent House.

NIEDERLAND, WILLIAM G.

    1959a. "The 'Miracled-Up' World of Schreber's Childhood." *The Psychoanalytic
    Study of the Child,* 14:383–413.
    1959b. "Schreber: Father and Son." *The Psychoanalytic Quarterly,* 28:151–69.
    1963. "Further Data and Memorabilia Pertaining to the Schreber Case." *The
    International Journal of Psycho-Analysis,* 44:201–7.
    1974. *The Schreber Case: Psychoanalytic Profile of a Paranoid Personality.* New
    York: Quadrangle/New York Times Book Co.

NUNBERG, HERMAN

    1932. *Allgemeine Neurosenlehre auf psychoanalytischer Grundlage.* Foreword
    by Sigmund Freud. Bern: Hans Huber Verlag.
    Trans.: Nunberg (1955).
    1955. *Principles of Psychoanalysis: Their Application to the Neuroses.* Foreword
    by Sigmund Freud. Translated by Madlyn Kahr and Sidney Kahr. New
    York: International Universities Press.
    German Text: Nunberg (1932).

NUNBERG, HERMAN, AND FEDERN, ERNST, EDS.

    1962–75. *Minutes of the Vienna Psychoanalytic Society.* 4 vols. Translated by
    M. Nunberg in collaboration with Harold Collins. New York: International
    Universities Press.

OBERNDORF, C. P.
1953. "Autobiography of Josef Breuer (1842–1925)." *The International Journal of Psycho-Analysis*, 34:64–67.
German Text: Breuer [1925].

OBERSTEINER, HEINRICH
1893. *Die Lehre vom Hypnotismus: Eine kurzgefasste Darstellung.* Leipzig and Vienna: M. Breitenstein.

OPPENHEIM, HERMANN
1905. *Lehrbuch der Nervenkrankheiten für Ärzte und Studirende.* 2 vols. 4th ed. Berlin: S. Karger. First ed., 1894.

OPPENHEIMER, CARL
1900. Review of *Die Traumdeutung*, by Sigmund Freud (1900a). *Die Umschau*, 4:218–19.

ORWELL, GEORGE
1949. *Nineteen Eighty-Four, a Novel.* London: Secker & Warburg.

OSTWALD, WILHELM
1907. Review of *Der Ablauf des Lebens*, by Wilhelm Fliess (1906b). *Annalen der Naturphilosophie*, 6:94–96.

OWEN, ALAN R. G.
1971. *Hysteria, Hypnosis and Healing: The Work of J.-M. Charcot.* London: Dobson; New York: Garrett Publications.

PAGE, HERBERT
1883. *Injuries of the Spine and Spinal Chord without Apparent Mechanical Lesions, and Nervous Shock, in Their Surgical and Medico-Legal Aspects.* London: J. & A. Churchill.

PAGEL, WALTER
1954. "The Speculative Basis of Modern Pathology." *Bulletin of the History of Medicine, 18:1–43.*

PAULY, AUGUST
1905. *Darwinismus und Lamarckismus: Entwurf einer psychophysischen Teleologie.* Munich: E. Reinhardt.

PENROSE, L. S.
1931. "Freud's Theory of Instinct and Other Psycho-Biological Theories." *The International Journal of Psycho-Analysis, 12:87–97.*

PENTA, PASQUALE
1893. *I Pervertimenti sessuali nell' uomo e Vincenzo Verzeni, strangolatore di donne: Studio biologico.* Naples: L. Pierro.

PÉREZ, BERNARD
1886. *L'Enfant de trois à sept ans.* Paris: Félix Alcan.

PETERSON, FREDERICK
1904. Introduction to *Text-Book of Insanity, Based on Clinical Observations: For Practitioners and Students of Medicine*, by Richard von Krafft-Ebing. Translated by Charles Gilbert Chaddock. Philadelphia: F. A. Davis Co.

PETERSON, HOUSTON

    1928.   *Havelock Ellis, Philosopher of Love.* Boston and New York: Houghton
           Mifflin Co.

PEYER, ALEXANDER

    1890.   *Der unvollständige Beischlaf (Congressus interruptus, Onanismus con-
           jugalis) und seine Folgen beim männlichen Geschlechte.* Stuttgart: Ferdi-
           nand Enke.

PFENNIG, RICHARD

    1906.   *Wilhelm Fliess und seine Nachentdecker: O. Weininger und H. Swoboda.*
           Berlin: Emil Goldschmidt.
    1912.   "Eine neuer Einwand gegen Fließ' Periodenlehre?" *Annalen der Natur-
           philosophie, 11*:373–82.
    1918.   *Grundzüge der Fließschen Periodenrechnung.* Leipzig and Vienna: Franz
           Deuticke.

PHALEN, JAMES M.

    1933.   "George Frank Lydston." *Dictionary of American Biography, 11*:513–14.
    1935.   "Edward Charles Spitzka." *Dictionary of American Biography, 17*:461–62.

PICK, ARNOLD

    1901.   Review of *Ueber den Traum,* by Sigmund Freud (1901a). *Prager me-
           dicinische Wochenschrift,* 26:145.

PILCZ, ALEXANDER

    1902.   Review of *Ueber den Traum,* by Sigmund Freud (1901a). *Wiener klinische
           Rundschau,* 16:962.

PLOSS, HERMANN HEINRICH

    1885.   *Das Weib in der Natur- und Völkerkunde: Anthropologische Studien.* 2
           vols. Leipzig: T. Grieben.

POLLOCK, GEORGE H.

    1968.   "The Possible Significance of Childhood Object Loss in the Josef Breuer-
           Bertha Pappenheim (Anna O.)-Sigmund Freud Relationship. I. Josef
           Breuer." *Journal of the American Psychoanalytic Association,* 16:711–39.
    1972.   "Bertha Pappenheim's Pathological Mourning: Possible Effects of Child-
           hood Sibling Loss." *Journal of the American Psychoanalytic Association,*
           20:476–93.

POPPER, JOSEF [LYNKEUS]

    1899.   *Phantasien eines Realisten.* 2 vols. Dresden and Leipzig: C. Reissner.

PRAETORIUS, NUMA

    1906.   Review of *Drei Abhandlungen zur Sexualtheorie,* by Sigmund Freud
           (1905d). *Jahrbuch für sexuelle Zwischenstufen,* 8:729–48.

PRATT, JOHN SHEALS

    1958.   "Epilegomena to the Study of Freudian Instinct Theory." *The International
           Journal of Psycho-Analysis,* 39:17–24.

PREBLE, EDWARD

    1930.   "Shobal Vail Clevenger." *Dictionary of American Biography,* 4:213–14.

PREYER, WILLIAM

1882.   *Die Seele des Kindes: Beobachtungen über die geistige Entwicklung des Menschen in den ersten Lebensjahren.* Leipzig: T. Grieben.
        Trans.: Preyer (1888–89).
1888–89. *The Mind of the Child: Observations concerning the Mental Development of the Human Being in the First Years of Life.* 2 vols. Translated by H. W. Brown. New York: D. Appleton & Co.
        German Text: Preyer (1882).

PRIBRAM, KARL H.

1962.   "The Neuropsychology of Sigmund Freud." In *Experimental Foundations of Clinical Psychology,* pp. 442–68. Edited by A. J. Bachrach. New York: Basic Books.
1965.   "Freud's *Project:* An Open, Biologically Based Model for Psychoanalysis." In *Psychoanalysis and Current Biological Thought,* pp. 81–92. Edited by Norman S. Greenfield and William C. Lewis. Madison and Milwaukee: University of Wisconsin Press.

PRIBRAM, KARL H., AND GILL, MERTON M.

1976.   *Freud's 'Project' Re-Assessed: Preface to Contemporary Cognitive Theory and Neuropsychology.* New York: Basic Books; London: Hutchinson Publishing Group.

PUNER, HELEN WALKER

1947.   *Freud: His Life and His Mind, a Biography.* New York: Howell, Soskin; London: Grey Walls Press, 1949.

PUTNAM, JAMES J.

1883.   "Recent Investigations into the Pathology of So-called Concussion of the Spine." *Boston Medical and Surgical Journal,* 109:217–20.

RAFFALOVICH, MARC-ANDRÉ

1896.   *Uranisme et unisexualité: Étude sur différentes manifestations de l'instinct sexuel.* Lyon: A. Storck.

RAIMANN, EMIL

1904.   *Die hysterischen Geistesstörungen: Eine klinische Studie.* Leipzig and Vienna: Franz Deuticke.
1905.   Review of *Drei Abhandlungen zur Sexualtheorie,* by Sigmund Freud (1905d). *Wiener klinische Wochenschrift,* 18:1016–17.

RAMZY, ISHAK

1956.   "From Aristotle to Freud: A Few Notes on the Roots of Psychoanalysis." *Bulletin of the Menninger Clinic,* 20:112–23.

RAPAPORT, DAVID

1960a. *The Structure of Psychoanalytic Theory: A Systematizing Attempt. Psychological Issues,* 2, no. 2 (Monograph 6).
1960b. "Psychoanalysis as a Developmental Psychology." In *Perspectives in Psychological Theory: Essays in Honor of Heinz Werner,* pp. 209–55. Edited by Bernard Kaplan and Seymour Wapner. New York: International Universities Press.

RAPAPORT, DAVID, AND GILL, MERTON M.

1959.   "The Points of View and Assumptions of Metapsychology." *The International Journal of Psycho-Analysis,* 40:153–62.

REIK, THEODOR

   1940. *From Thirty Years with Freud.* Translated by Richard Winston. New York: Farrar & Rinehart.

RENTERGHEM, ALBERT WILLEM VAN

   1898. *Liébeault en zijne School.* Amsterdam: F. van Rossen.

RIBOT, THÉODULE

   1881. *Les Maladies de la mémoire.* Paris: Germer Baillière et Cie.
   1896. *La Psychologie des sentiments.* Paris: Félix Alcan.
       Trans.: Ribot (1897).
   1897. *The Psychology of the Emotions.* The Contemporary Science Series. London: Walter Scott; New York: Charles Scribner's Sons.
       French Text: Ribot (1896).

RICOEUR, PAUL

   1970. *Freud and Philosophy: An Essay on Interpretation.* Translated by Denis Savage. New Haven and London: Yale University Press.

RIEBOLD, GEORG

   1908. "Der Nachweis des Vorhandenseins somatischer Perioden im weiblichen Organismus und ihrer Abhängigkeit von kosmischen Perioden." *Archiv für Gynaekologie,* 84:182–97.
   1942. *Einblick in den periodischen Ablauf des Lebens, mit besonderer Berücksichtigung des Menstruationsvorganges.* Stuttgart: Hippokrates-Verlag, Marquardt & Cie.

RIEFF, PHILIP

   1959. *Freud: The Mind of a Moralist.* New York: Viking Press; Garden City, N.Y.: Doubleday & Co., 1961.

RIEGER, KONRAD

   1896. "Über die Behandlung 'Nervenkranker.'" *Schmidt's Jahrbücher der in- und ausländischen gesammten Medicin,* 251:193–98, 273–76.
   1929. "Konrad Rieger." In *Die Medizin der Gegenwart in Selbstdarstellungen,* 8:125–74. Edited by L. R. Grote. Leipzig: Felix Meiner.

RIES, EMIL

   1903. "A New Treatment for Dysmenorrhea." *American Gynecology,* 3:375–79.

RITVO, LUCILLE B.

   1965. "Darwin as the Source of Freud's Neo-Lamarckianism." *Journal of the American Psychoanalytic Association,* 13:499–517.
   1972. "Carl Claus as Freud's Professor of the New Darwinian Biology." *The International Journal of Psycho-Analysis,* 53:277–83.
   1974. "The Impact of Darwin on Freud." *The Psychoanalytic Quarterly,* 43:177–92.

ROAZEN, PAUL

   1968. *Freud: Political and Social Thought.* New York: Alfred A. Knopf.
   1969. *Brother Animal: The Story of Freud and Tausk.* New York: Alfred A. Knopf; London: Allen Lane, 1970.
   1975. *Freud and His Followers.* New York: Alfred A. Knopf; London: Allen Lane, 1976.

ROBERT, MARTHE

   1966. *The Psychoanalytic Revolution: Sigmund Freud's Life and Achievement.* Translated by Kenneth Morgan. London: George Allen & Unwin; New York: Harcourt, Brace & World.

ROBERT, W.

1886. *Der Traum als Naturnothwendigkeit erklärt.* 2nd ed. Hamburg: Hermann
       Seippel.

ROBINSON, VICTOR

1919. *The Don Quixote of Psychiatry.* New York: Historico-Medical Press.
1953. Introduction to *Psychopathia Sexualis: A Medico-Forensic Study,* by
       Richard von Krafft-Ebing. New York: Pioneer Publications.

ROEDER, H.

1914. 20 March discussion of "Die Nase in ihren Beziehungen zu den Sexual-
       organen," a lecture delivered by Max Senator (1914) before the Ärzt-
       liche Gesellschaft für Sexualwissenschaft und Eugenik in Berlin on 20
       February. *Zeitschrift für Sexualwissenschaft,* 1:76–77.

ROEMER, AUGUST

1891. "Ueber psychopathische Minderwerthigkeiten des Säuglingsalters." *Me-
       dicinisches Correspondenz-Blatt des Württembergischen ärztlichen Landes-
       vereins,* 61:265–269, 273–79, 281–85, 289–92.

ROGER, JACQUES

1963. *Les Sciences de la vie dans la pensée française du XVIIIe siècle: La
       Génération des animaux de Descartes à l'Encyclopédie.* Paris: Armand
       Colin.

ROHLEDER, HERMANN

1899. *Die Masturbation: Eine Monographie für Ärzte und Pädagogen.* Berlin:
       Fischer's Medicinische Buchhandlung, H. Kornfeld.
1901. *Vorlesungen über Sexualtrieb und Sexualleben des Menschen.* Berlin:
       Fischer's Medicinische Buchhandlung, H. Kornfeld.
1907. *Vorlesungen über Geschlechtstrieb und gesamtes Geschlechtsleben des
       Menschen.* 2 vols. 2nd ed. Berlin: Fischer's Medicinische Buchhandlung,
       H. Kornfeld. First ed. published as Rohleder (1901).

ROMANES, MRS. ETHEL, ED.

1896. *The Life and Letters of George John Romanes Written and Edited by His
       Wife.* London and New York: Longmans, Green, and Co.

ROMANES, GEORGE JOHN

1873. "Permanent Variation of Colour in Fish." (Letter to the Editor.) *Nature,*
       8:101.
1881. "The Struggle of Parts in the Organism." Review of *Der Kampf der
       Theile im Organismus,* by Wilhelm Roux (1881). *Nature,* 24:505–6.
1883. *Mental Evolution in Animals. With a Posthumous Essay on Instinct by
       Charles Darwin.* London: Kegan Paul, Trench & Co.
1888. *Mental Evolution in Man: Origin of Human Faculty.* London: Kegan Paul,
       Trench & Co.
1892–97. *Darwin and After Darwin: An Exposition of the Darwinian Theory
       and a Discussion of Post-Darwinian Questions.* 3 vols. London: Longmans,
       Green, and Co.

ROSENTHAL, MORITZ

1870. *Handbuch der Diagnostik und Therapie der Nervenkrankheiten.* Erlangen:
       Ferdinand Enke.
1875. *Klinik der Nervenkrankheiten nach seiner an der Wiener Universität
       gehaltenen Vorträgen.* 2nd ed. Stuttgart: Ferdinand Enke. First ed. pub-
       lished as Rosenthal (1870).

ROSS, DOROTHY

1972. *G. Stanley Hall: The Psychologist as Prophet.* Chicago and London: Uni-
       versity of Chicago Press.

ROUX, WILHELM

1881. *Der Kampf der Theile im Organismus: Ein Beitrag zur Vervollständigung der mechanischen Zweckmässigkeitslehre.* Leipzig: Wilhelm Engelmann.

RUBLE, DIANE N.

1977. "Premenstrual Symptoms: A Reinterpretation." *Science, 197*:291–92.

RUNKLE, ERWIN W.

1899. Review of *Studien über Hysterie,* by Josef Breuer and Sigmund Freud (1895). *The American Journal of Psychology, 10*:592–94.

RUSSELL, EDWARD STUART

1916. *Form and Function: A Contribution to the History of Animal Morphology.* London: John Murray.

1930. *The Interpretation of Development and Heredity: A Study in Biological Method.* Oxford: Clarendon Press.

RY. [DR. BENJAMIN RISCHAWY?]

1898. Review of *Die Beziehungen zwischen Nase und weiblichen Geschlechtsorganen,* by Wilhelm Fliess (1897). *Wiener klinische Rundschau, 12*: 240.

SAALER, BRUNO

1912. "Eine Hysterie-Analyse und ihre Lehren." *Allgemeine Zeitschrift für Psychiatrie und psychisch-gerichtliche Medizin, 69*:866–911.

1914. "Die Fliess'sche Periodizitätslehre und ihre Bedeutung für die Sexualbiologie." *Zentralblatt für Psychoanalyse und Psychotherapie, 4*:337–46.

1921. "Neue Wege der Familienforschung: Die Fließschen Periodizitätslehre." *Zeitschrift für Sexualwissenschaft, 7*:353–60, 369–79.

SABLIK, K.

1968. "Sigmund Freud und die Gesellschaft der Ärzte in Wien." *Wiener klinische Wochenschrift, 80*:107–10.

SACHS, HANNS

1944. *Freud, Master and Friend.* Cambridge: Harvard University Press; London: Imago Publishing Co., 1945.

SADGER, ISIDOR

1907. "Die Bedeutung der psychoanalytischen Methode nach Freud." *Centralblatt für Nervenheilkunde und Psychiatrie,* n.s., *18*:41–52.

SAMPSON, E. E.

1962. "Birth Order, Need Achievement, and Conformity." *Journal of Abnormal and Social Psychology, 64*:155–59.

SAUL, LEON J.

1958. "Freud's Death Instinct and the Second Law of Thermodynamics." *The International Journal of Psycho-Analysis, 39*:323–25.

SCHAEFER

1891. Review of "Ein Beitrag zur Lehre von der konträren Sexualempfindung," by A. Peyer. *Zeitschrift für Psychologie, 2*:128.

SCHATZ, FRIEDRICH

1904–6. "Wann tritt die Geburt an? (Vorausbestimmung des Geburtstages)." *Archiv für Gynaekologie, 72*:168–260; *80*:558–680.

SCHATZMANN, MORTON

1973. "Paranoia or Persecution: The Case of Schreber." *History of Childhood Quarterly*, 1:62–88.

SCHERNER, KARL ALBERT

1861. *Das Leben des Traums*. Berlin: Heinrich Schindler.

SCHIFF, ARTHUR

1901. "Über die Beziehungen zwischen Nase und weiblichen Sexualorganen." A lecture delivered before the K. k. Gesellschaft der Ärtze in Vienna on 11 January 1901. *Deutsche Medizinal-Zeitung*, 22:128. For the ensuing discussion, see pp. 152–53, 177, and 202.

SCHLESSINGER, NATHAN; GEDO, JOHN E.; MILLER, JULIAN; POLLOCK, GEORGE H.; SABSHIN, MELVIN; AND SADOW, LEO

1967. "The Scientific Style of Breuer and Freud in the Origins of Psychoanalysis." *Journal of the American Psychoanalytic Association*, 15:404–22.

SCHLIEPER, HANS

1909. *Der Rhythmus des Lebendigen: Zur Entdeckung von W. Fliess*. Jena: Eugen Diederichs.
1928. "Wilhelm Fliess." *Vossische Zeitung*, 14 October, [p. 32].

SCHNITZLER, ARTHUR

1886. Account of 15 October 1886 lecture by Sigmund Freud, "Ueber männliche Hysterie," delivered at the K. k. Gesellschaft der Ärtze, and of the discussion that followed. *Wiener medizinische Presse*, 27:1407–9.

SCHOENWALD, RICHARD L.

1955. "Recent Studies of the Younger Freud." *Bulletin of the History of Medicine*, 29:261–68.
1956. *Freud, the Man, and His Mind, 1856–1956*. New York: Alfred A. Knopf.

SCHOLZ, FRIEDRICH

1891. *Die Charakterfehler des Kindes: Eine Erziehungslehre für Haus und Schule*. Leipzig: E. H. Mayer.

SCHOPENHAUER, ARTHUR

1844. *Die Welt als Wille und Vorstellung*. 2nd ed. Reprinted in *Sämmtliche Werke*, 1–2. Edited by Julius Frauenstädt. Leipzig: F. A. Brockhaus, 1873–74. First ed., 1819.

SCHOPF, THOMAS J. M.

1976. "Paleontological Clocks." Review of *Growth Rhythms and the History of the Earth's Rotation*, G. D. Rosenberg and S. K. Runcorn, eds. *Science*, 191:375–76.

SCHORSKE, CARL E.

1973. "Politics and Patricide in Freud's *Interpretation of Dreams*." *The American Historical Review*, 78:328–47.

SCHREBER, DANIEL PAUL

1903. *Denkwürdigkeiten eines Nervenkranken*. Leipzig: Oswald Mutze. *Trans.*: Schreber (1955).
1955. *Memoirs of My Nervous Illness*. Translated and edited, with Introduction, notes and discussion, by Ida Macalpine and Richard A. Hunter. London: Wm. Dawson and Sons. *German Text*: Schreber (1903).

SCHRENCK-NOTZING, ALBERT VON

1889. "Un Cas d'inversion sexuelle amélioré par la suggestion hypnotique." In *Premier congrès international de l'hypnotisme expérimental et thérapeutique: Comptes rendus*, pp. 319–22. Edited by Edgar Bérillon. Paris: Octave Doin.

1892. *Die Suggestions-Therapie bei krankhaften Erscheinungen des Geschlechtssinnes: Mit besonderer Berücksichtigung der conträren Sexualempfindung.* Stuttgart: Ferdinand Enke.
 Trans.: Schrenck-Notzing (1895).

1895. *Therapeutic Suggestion in Psychopathia Sexualis (Pathological Manifestations of the Sexual Sense), with Especial Reference to Contrary Sexual Instinct.* Translated by Charles Gilbert Chaddock. Philadelphia: F. A. Davis Co.
 German Text: Schrenck-Notzing (1892).

1898–99. "Beiträge zur forensischen Beurtheilung von Sittlichkeitsvergehen mit besonderer Berücksichtigung der Pathogenese psychosexueller Anomalien." *Archiv für Kriminal-Anthropologie und Kriminalistik, 1*:5–25, 137–82.

1899. "Literaturzusammenstellung über die Psychologie und Psychopathologie der vita sexualis." *Zeitschrift für Hypnotismus, 8*:40–53, 275–91.

SCHUR, MAX

1965. Introduction to *Drives, Affects, Behavior*. Vol. 2. Edited by Max Schur. New York: International Universities Press.

1972. *Freud: Living and Dying.* The International Psycho-Analytic Library. London: Hogarth Press and The Institute of Psycho-Analysis; New York: International Universities Press.

SCHUR, MAX, AND RITVO, LUCILLE B.

1970. "The Concept of Development and Evolution in Psychoanalysis." In *Development and Evolution of Behavior: Essays in Memory of T. C. Schneirla*, pp. 600–619. Edited by Lester R. Aronson et al. San Francisco: W. H. Freeman and Co.

SEMON, FELIX

1900. "A Lecture on Nasal Reflex-Neuroses." *The Clinical Journal, 15*:241–47.

SENATOR, MAX

1914. "Die Nase in ihren Beziehungen zu den Sexualorganen." A lecture delivered before the Ärztliche Gesellschaft für Sexualwissenschaft und Eugenik in Berlin on 20 February. *Zeitschrift für Sexualwissenschaft, 1*: 37–38.

SHAKOW, DAVID, AND RAPAPORT, DAVID

1964. *The Influence of Freud on American Psychology. Psychological Issues, 4*, no. 1 (Monograph 13).

SHERWOOD, STEPHEN L.

1962. Review of *Sigmund Freuds Akademische Laufbahn im Lichte der Dokumente*, by Josef Gicklhorn and Renée Gicklhorn (1960). *Diseases of the Nervous System, 23*:235–37.

SIEGMUND, A.

1914. 20 March discussion of "Die Nase in ihren Beziehungen zu den Sexualorganen," a lecture delivered by Max Senator (1914) before the Ärztliche Gesellschaft für Sexualwissenschaft und Eugenik in Berlin on 20 February. *Zeitschrift für Sexualwissenschaft, 1*:77.

SIMPSON, GEORGE GAYLORD

1974. "Darwin's Crucial Years." Review of *Darwin on Man*, by Howard E. Gruber and Paul H. Barrett (1974). *Science, 186*:133–34.

SMITH, W. ROBERTSON

1894.   *Lectures on the Religion of the Semites.* New [2nd] ed. London: A. and C.
         Block. First ed., 1889.

SMITH-ROSENBERG, CARROLL

1972.   "The Hysterical Woman: Sex Roles and Role Conflict in 19th-Century
         America." *Social Research,* 39:652–78.

SNYDER, FREDERICK

1966.   "Toward an Evolutionary Theory of Dreaming." *The American Journal of
         Psychiatry,* 123:121–36.

SOLLIER, PAUL

1891.   *Psychologie de l'idiot et de l'imbécile.* Paris: Félix Alcan.
1900.   *Le Problème de la mémoire: Essai de psycho-mécanique.* Paris: Félix Alcan.

SOYKA, OTTO

1905.   "Zwei Bücher." Review of *Drei Abhandlungen zur Sexualtheorie,* by Sig-
         mund Freud (1905d). *Die Fackel,* 21 December, pp. 6–11.

SPALDING, DOUGLAS A.

1873.   "Instinct: With Original Observations on Young Animals." *Macmillan's
         Magazine,* 27:282–93.

SPEHLMANN, RAINER

1953.   *Sigmund Freuds neurologische Schriften: Eine Untersuchung zur Vorge-
         schichte der Psychoanalyse.* Berlin: Springer.

SPEMANN, FRIEDRICH WILHELM, ED.

1948.   *Hans Spemann, Forschung und Leben.* Stuttgart: Verlag Ad. Spemann.

SPENCER, HERBERT

1855.   *The Principles of Psychology.* London: Longmans, Brown, Green, and
         Longmans.
1862.   *First Principles.* London: Williams and Norgate.
1864–67. *The Principles of Biology.* 2 vols. London: Williams and Norgate.
1870–72. *The Principles of Psychology.* 2 vols. 2nd ed. London: Williams and
         Norgate.

SPERBER, HANS

1912.   "Über den Einfluss sexueller Momente auf Entstehung und Entwicklung
         der Sprache." *Imago,* 1:405–53.

SPERBER, MANÈS

1970.   *Alfred Adler, oder das Elend der Psychologie.* Translated from the French
         by Wolfgang Kraus, Reinhard Urbach, and Hans Weigel. Vienna, Munich,
         and Zurich: Fritz Molden.

SPIEGEL, LEO A.

1976.   Letter to the Editor. *The New York Review of Books,* 14 October, p. 54.

SPITZKA, EDWARD CHARLES

1881.   "Note in Regard to 'Primitive Desires.'" *Science: A Weekly Journal of
         Scientific Progress,* 2:302.

STARK, WERNER

    1958.   *The Sociology of Knowledge: An Essay in Aid of a Deeper Understanding of the History of Ideas.* London: Routledge and Kegan Paul; Glencoe, Ill.: Free Press.

STEKEL, WILHELM

    1895.   "Ueber Coitus im Kindesalter: Eine hygienische Studie." *Wiener medizinische Blätter, 18*:247–49.

    1902.   Review of *Die Traumdeutung,* by Sigmund Freud (1900a). *Neues Wiener Tagblatt,* 29 and 30 January.

    1908.   *Nervöse Angstzustände und ihre Behandlung.* Foreword by Sigmund Freud (1908f). Berlin and Vienna: Urban & Schwarzenberg.
           Trans.: Stekel (1923).

    1911.   *Die Sprache des Traumes: Eine Darstellung der Symbolik und Deutung des Traumes in ihren Beziehungen zur kranken und gesunden Seele, für Ärzte und Psychologen.* Wiesbaden: J. F. Bergmann.

    1912.   *Nervöse Angstzustände und ihre Behandlung.* 2nd ed. Berlin and Vienna: Urban & Schwarzenberg.
           Trans.: Stekel (1923).

    1923.   *Conditions of Nervous Anxiety and Their Treatment.* Translated by Rosalie Gabler. London: Kegan Paul, Trench, Trubner & Co.
           German Text: Stekel (1908 and later eds.).

    1950.   *The Autobiography of Wilhelm Stekel: The Life Story of a Pioneer Psychoanalyst.* Edited by Emil A. Gutheil. New York: Liveright Publishing Co.

STENGEL, ERWIN

    1953.   Introduction to *On Aphasia: A Critical Study,* by Sigmund Freud (1953a). Translated by Erwin Stengel. London: Imago Publishing Co.; New York: International Universities Press.

    1954.   "A Re-Evaluation of Freud's Book 'On Aphasia': Its Significance for Psycho-Analysis." *The International Journal of Psycho-Analysis, 35*:85–89.

    1963.   "Hughlings Jackson's Influence in Psychiatry." *British Journal of Psychiatry, 109*:348–55.

STERN, WILLIAM

    1901.   Review of *Die Traumdeutung,* by Sigmund Freud (1900a). *Zeitschrift für Psychologie und Physiologie der Sinnesorgane, 26*:130–33.

STEWART, LARRY

    1977.   "Freud before Oedipus: Race and Heredity in the Origins of Psychoanalysis." *Journal of the History of Biology, 9*:215–28.

STEWART, WALTER A.

    1967.   *Psychoanalysis: The First Ten Years, 1888–1898.* New York: Macmillan Co.; London: George Allen & Unwin, 1969.

STOCKERT-MEYNERT, DORA

    1930.   *Theodor Meynert und seine Zeit.* Vienna and Leipzig: Oesterreichischer Bundesverlag.

STOODLEY, BARTLETT H.

    1959.   *The Concepts of Sigmund Freud.* Glencoe, Ill.: Free Press.

STORR, ANTHONY

    1973.   *C. G. Jung.* Modern Masters Series. New York: Viking Press; London: Fontana Books.

    1977.   "Checking Out Freud's Ideas." Review of *The Scientific Credibility of Freud's Theories and Therapy,* by Seymour Fisher and Roger P. Greenberg (1977). *The New York Review of Books,* 22 May, pp. 10, 30.

STRICKER, SALOMON

1894. "Über das medicinische Unterrichtswesen." *Wiener klinische Wochenschrift*, 7:86–88, 105–8, 143–45, 161–63, 198–200.

STRÜMPELL, ADOLF VON

1892. *Ueber die Entstehung und die Heilung von Krankheiten durch Vorstellungen*. Erlangen: Junge & Sohn.
1896. Review of *Studien über Hysterie*, by Josef Breuer and Sigmund Freud (1895). *Deutsche Zeitschrift für Nervenheilkunde*, 8:159–61.

STRÜMPELL, LUDWIG

1877. *Die Natur und Entstehung der Träume*. Leipzig: Von Veit & Co.

SULLY, JAMES

1884. *Outlines of Psychology: With Special Reference to the Theory of Education*. London: Longmans, Green, and Co.
1892. *The Human Mind: A Text-book of Psychology*. 2 vols. New York: D. Appleton and Co.
1893. "The Dream as a Revelation." *Fortnightly Review*, 59:354–65.
1896. *Studies of Childhood*. New York: D. Appleton and Co.
1918. *My Life and Friends: A Psychologist's Memories*. London: T. Fisher Unwin.

SUTTON-SMITH, BRIAN, AND ROSENBERG, B. G.

1970. *The Sibling*. New York: Holt, Rinehart, and Winston.

SWOBODA, HERMANN

1904. *Die Periode des menschlichen Organismus in ihrer psychologischen und biologischen Bedeutung*. Leipzig and Vienna: Franz Deuticke.
1905. *Studien zur Grundlegung der Psychologie*. Leipzig and Vienna: Franz Deuticke.
1906. *Die gemeinnützige Forschung und der eigennützige Forscher*. Vienna and Leipzig: Wilhelm Braumüller.
1909. *Die kritischen Tage des Menschen und ihre Berechnung mit dem Periodenschieber*. Leipzig: Franz Deuticke.
1917. *Das Siebenjahr: Untersuchungen über die zeitliche Gesetzmässigkeit des Menschenlebens*. Vienna and Leipzig: Orion-Verlag.

TAINE, HIPPOLYTE

1876. "Note sur l'acquisition du langage chez les enfants et dans l'espèce humaine." *Revue Philosophique*, 1:5–23.
      Partial Trans.: Taine (1877).
1877. "M. Taine on the Acquisition of Language by Children." *Mind*, 2:252–59.
      French Text: Taine (1876).

TARNOWSKY, BENJAMIN

1886. *Die krankhaften Erscheinungen des Geschlechtssinnes: Eine forensisch-psychiatrische Studie*. Berlin: August Hirschwald.
      Trans.: Tarnowsky (1898).
1898. *The Sexual Instinct and Its Morbid Manifestations from the Double Standpoint of Jurisprudence and Psychiatry*. Translated by W. C. Costello and Alfred Allinson. Paris: Charles Carrington.
      German Text: Tarnowsky (1886).

TELEKY, [LUDWIG?]

1895. 11 November discussion of "Über Hysterie," three lectures delivered by Sigmund Freud (1895g) before the Wiener medicinische Doctorencollegium on 14, 21, and 28 October 1895. *Wiener medizinische Presse*, 36:1757–58; *Wiener klinische Rundschau*, 9:728.

TERMAN, LEWIS M.

1905. "A Study in Precocity and Prematuration." *The American Journal of Psychology*, 16:145–83.

THACKRAY, ARNOLD

1972. *John Dalton: Critical Assessments of His Life and Science.* Harvard Monographs in the History of Science. Cambridge: Harvard University Press.

THOMMEN, GEORGE S.

1964. *Is This Your Day?: How Biorhythm Helps You Determine Your Life Cycles.* New York: Crown Publishers.
1973. *Is This Your Day?: How Biorhythm Helps You Determine Your Life Cycles.* New rev. ed. New York: Crown Publishers.

THOMSEN, R., AND OPPENHEIM, H.

1884. "Ueber das Vorkommen und die Bedeutung der sensorischen Anästhesie bei Erkrankungen des centralen Nervensystems." *Archiv für Psychiatrie*, 15:559–83, 633–80.

THORNDIKE, EDWARD L.

1904. Review of *Adolescence,* by G. Stanley Hall (1904). *Science,* n.s., 20:144.
1912. Introduction to *The Sexual Life of the Child,* by Albert Moll (1912a). New York: Macmillan Co.

TRIVERS, ROBERT L., AND WILLARD, DAN E.

1973. "Natural Selection of Parental Ability to Vary the Sex Ratio of Offspring." *Science,* 179:90–92.

TROSMAN, HARRY, AND SIMMONS, ROGER DENNIS

1973. "The Freud Library." *Journal of the American Psychoanalytic Association,* 21:646–87.

TURKLE, SHERRY

1978. *Psychoanalytic Politics: Freud's French Revolution.* New York: Basic Books.

ULRICHS, CARL HEINRICH [NUMA NUMANTIUS]

1864a. *"Vindex": Sozial-juristische Studien über mannmännliche Geschlechtsliebe.* Leipzig: Otto und Kadler. Reprinted in *Forschungen* (1898, 1).
1864b. *"Inclusa": Anthropologische Studien über mannmännliche Geschlechtsliebe.* Leipzig: Otto und Kadler. Reprinted in *Forschungen* (1898, 2).
1868. *"Memnon": Die Geschlechtsnatur des mannliebenden Urnings.* Schleiz. Reprinted in *Forschungen* (1898, 7).
1898. *Forschungen über das Rätsel der mannmännlichen Liebe.* 12 vols. Leipzig: Max Spohr.

VENTURI, SILVIO

1892. *Le Degenerazioni psico-sessuali nella vita degli individui e nella storia delle società.* Turin: Fratelli Bocca.
        Trans.: Venturi (1899).
1899. *Corrélations psycho-sexuelles.* Paris: A. Maloine.
        Italian Text: Venturi (1892).

VESZY-WAGNER, LILLA

1966. "Ernest Jones (1879–1958)." In *Psychoanalytic Pioneers,* pp. 87–141. Edited by Franz Alexander, Samuel Eisenstein, and Martin Grotjahn. New York: Basic Books.

VOSS, GEORG

1901. Review of *Ueber den Traum,* by Sigmund Freud (1901a). *St. Petersburger medicinische Wochenschrift,* n.s., 18:325.

WAGNER-JAUREGG, JULIUS

1950. *Lebenserinnerungen.* Edited by L. Schönbauer and M. Jantsch. Vienna: Springer.

WALDEYER, WILHELM

1891. "Ueber einige neuere Forschungen im Gebiete der Anatomie des Central-nervensystems." *Berliner klinische Wochenschrift, 28:691.*

WALTON, G. L.

1883. "Case of Typical Hysterical Hemianesthesia in a Man Following Injury." *Archives of Medicine, 10:88–95.*
1884. "Case of Hysterical Hemianaesthesia, Convulsions and Motor Paralysis Brought on by a Fall." *Boston Medical and Surgical Journal, 111:558–59.*

WASSERMANN, IZYDOR

1958. Letter to the Editor. *American Journal of Psychotherapy, 12:623–27.*

WATSON, ANDREW S.

1958. "Freud the Translator: Some Contacts with Philosophy." *The International Journal of Psycho-Analysis, 39:326–27.*

WEBER, LUDWIG WILHELM

1907. Review of *Drei Abhandlungen zur Sexualtheorie,* by Sigmund Freud (1905d). *Deutsche medizinische Wochenschrift, 33:276–77.*

WEININGER, OTTO

1903. *Geschlecht und Charakter: Eine prinzipielle Untersuchung.* Vienna: Wilhelm Braumüller.
         Trans.: Weininger (1906).
1906. *Sex and Character.* Translated from the 6th German ed. London: W. Heinemann; New York: G. P. Putnam's Sons.
         German Text: Weininger (1903).

WEISMANN, AUGUST

1892. *Das Keimplasma: Eine Theorie der Vererbung.* Jena: Gustav Fischer.

WEISS, EDWARD, AND ENGLISH, O. SPURGEON

1943. *Psychosomatic Medicine: The Clinical Application of Psychopathology to General Medical Problems.* Philadelphia and London: W. B. Saunders Co.

WEISS, HEINRICH

1895. 11 November discussion of "Über Hysterie," three lectures by Sigmund Freud (1895g) before the Wiener medicinische Doctorencollegium on 14, 21, and 28 October 1895. *Wiener medizinische Presse, 36:1757–58; Wiener klinische Rundschau, 9:728.*

WEISZ, GEORGE

1975. "Scientists and Sectarians: The Case of Psychoanalysis." *Journal of the History of the Behavioral Sciences, 11:350–64.*

WEIZSAECKER, VIKTOR VON

1957. "Reminiscences of Freud and Jung." In *Freud and the 20th Century,* pp. 59–75. Edited and selected by Benjamin Nelson. New York: Meridian Books.

WELLS, HARRY K.

1960. *Pavlov and Freud.* Vol. 2: *Sigmund Freud: A Pavlovian Critique.* New York: International Publishers.

WERNLI, HANS J.

[1959]. *Biorhythmisch Leben.* Zurich: Bio-Rit-Verlag.
        Trans.: Wernli, (1961).
1961.   *Biorhythm: A Scientific Exploration into the Life Cycles of the Indi-
        vidual.* Translated by Rosemary Colmers. Technical supervisor, George S.
        Thommen. New York: Crown Publishers.
        German Text: Wernli (1959).

WESTPHAL, CARL

1870.   "Die conträre Sexualempfindung: Symptom eines neuropathischen (psy-
        chopathischen) Zustandes." *Archiv für Psychiatrie,* 2:73–108.
1876.   "Zur conträren Sexualempfindung." *Archiv für Psychiatrie,* 6:620–21.

WETTLEY, ANNEMARIE, AND LEIBBRAND, W.

1959.   *Von der 'Psychopathia sexualis' zur Sexualwissenschaft.* Stuttgart: Ferdi-
        nand Enke.

WEYGANDT, WILHELM

1901.   Review of *Die Traumdeutung,* by Sigmund Freud (1900a). *Centralblatt
        für Nervenheilkunde und Psychiatrie,* n.s., 12:548–49.
1907.   "Kritische Bemerkungen zur Psychologie der Dementia Praecox." *Monats-
        schrift für Psychiatrie und Neurologie,* 22:289–302.

WHEELER, WILLIAM MORTON

1920–21 [1917]. "On Instincts." *The Journal of Abnormal Psychology,* 15:295–
        318.

WHYTE, LANCELOT LAW

1960.   *The Unconscious before Freud.* New York: Basic Books; London: Tavi-
        stock Publications, 1962.

WILSON, EDWARD O.

1975.   *Sociobiology: The New Synthesis.* Cambridge and London: Harvard Uni-
        versity Press, Belknap Press.
1977.   "Biology and the Social Sciences." *Dædalus,* Fall, pp. 127–40.
1978.   *On Human Nature.* Cambridge and London: Harvard University Press.

WINNICOTT, D. W.

1958.   "Ernest Jones." *The International Journal of Psycho-Analysis,* 39:298–302.

WITTELS, FRITZ

1912.   *Alles um Liebe: Eine Urweltdichtung.* Berlin: E. Fleischel & Co.
1924a. *Sigmund Freud: Der Mann, die Lehre, die Schule.* Leipzig: E. P. Tal & Co.
        Trans.: Wittels (1924b).
1924b. *Sigmund Freud: His Personality, His Teaching, and His School.* Translated
        by Eden and Ceder Paul. London: George Allen & Unwin.
        German Text: Wittels (1924a).
1933.   "Revision of a Biography." *The Psychoanalytic Review,* 20:361–74.
1948.   "Brill—the Pioneer." *The Psychoanalytic Review,* 35:394–98.

WOLLHEIM, RICHARD

1971.   *Sigmund Freud.* Modern Masters Series. New York: Viking Press; London:
        Fontana Books.

WORTIS, JOSEPH

1954.   *Fragments of an Analysis with Freud.* New York: Simon and Schuster.

WRIGHT, SEWALL

1966.   "Mendel's Ratios." In *The Origin of Genetics: A Mendel Source Book*, pp.
         173–75. Edited by Curt Stern and Eva R. Sherwood. San Francisco: W. H.
         Freeman and Co.

WYSS, WALTER VON

1958.   *Charles Darwin: Ein Forscherleben*. Zurich and Stuttgart: Artemis-Verlag.

YAZMAJIAN, RICHARD V.

1967.   "Biological Aspects of Infantile Sexuality and the Latency Period." *The
         Psychoanalytic Quarterly*, 36:203–29.

YOUNG, ROBERT M.

1970.   *Mind, Brain and Adaptation in the Nineteenth Century: Cerebral Localiza-
         tion and Its Biological Context from Gall to Ferrier*. Oxford: Clarendon
         Press.

ZETZEL, ELIZABETH R.

1958.   "Ernest Jones: His Contribution to Theory." *The International Journal of
         Psycho-Analysis*, 39:311–18.

ZIEHEN, THEODOR

1902a.   Review of *Ueber den Traum*, by Sigmund Freud (1901a). *Jahresbericht
         über die Leistungen und Fortschritte auf dem Gebiete der Neurologie und
         Psychiatrie*, 5 (1901):829.
1902b.   *Psychiatrie für Ärzte und Studierende bearbeitet*. 2nd ed. Leipzig: S. Hirzel.

ZILBOORG, GREGORY

1951.   *Sigmund Freud: His Exploration of the Mind of Man*. New York: Charles
         Scribner's Sons.

INDEX

Index

587

fetishism:
  Adler on, 430
  Binet on, 285–87
  classified by Krafft-Ebing, 283
  puberty and, 304
  religion and, 316
Feuer, Louis S., 438
Fichte, Johann Gottlieb, 146
Fick, Adolf, 66
Finch, Kiernan on, 293
Fine, Reuben, 18n, 19, 203n, 207, 329n, 395n, 449n, 488, 490, 492–94
First International Congress for Sexual Research (1926), 474
First International Congress of Hypnotism (1889), 286–87
Fisher, Ronald A., 168, 420n
Fisher, Seymour, 499
Fiske, John, 378
fixation, 180, 184, 211–12, 236; see also development, arrested or inhibited; instinctual fixation; libido
  biological bases of 388–90
  choice of neurosis and, 211, 383, 388–89, 391
  Darwin on, 265
  Freud on, 180, 211–12, 267–68, 297, 383–84, 388–89, 391, 396–97
  Freud's use of term, 264n
  in homosexuality, 184
  instinct and, 264–68
  origins of concept, 264–65
  periodicity theory (Fliess) and, 388–89
  petromyzon and, 267–68
  regression and, 398
  to traumas, 396–97
Fleischl von Marxow, Ernst, 15, 25, 26
Fliess, Elenore (Mrs. Robert), 191n
Fliess, Ida (Fliess's wife), 163n, 181, 191n
Fliess, Robert (son of Wilhelm Fliess), 181, 190, 191, 412, 440n, 494
  career, 191n, 233
  on his father, 191n
  infantile sexual life of, 191, 209
  supports periodicity theory, 191n
Fliess, Wilhelm, 135–237, 256, 263n, 278n, 297, 319, 333, 426, 430, 437, 469n, 474, 475, 515; see also Fliess correspondence; Freud, Fliess and; Freud–Fliess estrangement; Freud legend, Myths 8–13, 17–18; Origins of Psycho-Analysis
  Abraham and, 233
  on actual neuroses, 140, 142, 192
  on anxiety neurosis in children, 172, 173–74, 178, 192
  on astronomical conditions, 141, 169, 402
  on bilaterality and handedness, 146n, 170n, 230n, 427
  bioenergetic ideas of, 163, 177, 186
  on birth intervals, 141, 181, 182
  on bisexuality, 140, 172, 183–84, 219, 230
  bisexuality theory developed independently of, 297
  on bisexual complementarity, 183n, 224, 230
  on bisexual periodicities, 159, 168, 171–72
  Bloch on, 316
  on child development, 141, 172, 176–83, 186, 195
  on childhood seduction, 192
  cocaine therapy, 149n, 152
  compared with: Kepler, 144; Mendel, 169
  congresses with Freud, 114, 130, 137–38, 184, 196, 200, 205, 220–21
  on conservation of energy, 141

criticisms of, 141–47, 151, 165–66
on disease acquisition, 141
encourages writing of Project, 138
Entwicklungsschubmechanik, 141, 176–77, 180, 236, 388–89
etymological interests, 174, 178
evolutionary theory and, 170, 237, 276; see also bisexuality; nasogenital link; periodicity
family background, 231–32
as a father, 191n
Freud offers coauthorship to, 187, 223
Freud's identification with, 144
Freud's regard for, 138, 142, 143, 165, 170, 189, 194, 195, 196, 205, 219, 220, 221, 233, 402, 427
Freud's theory of paranoia and, 233
on hemorrhoids, 175
on homosexuality, 183, 184
on human sexual development, 163, 177, 195
on infantile sexuality, 171–88, 190, 191, 236, 318, 333
influence, current, 187, 232–33
influenced by: Darwin, 237; Hack, 149; Helmholtz, 139, 147, 163, 235; Naturphilosophie, 146; see also Freud legend, Myth 10
influence on: Ellis, 178n; Eulenburg, 169; Freud, 138, 144–47, 163, 170, 171–206, 234, 235–37, 402; Krafft-Ebing, 149; otolaryngologists, 152; outside Germany, 165n, 187
as intellectual catalyst for Freud, 189
on Interpretation of Dreams (Freud), 218
as Kepler of biology, 144
on left-handedness, see Fliess, on bilaterality and handedness
on life-span, 141, 143, 166
meets Freud, 135
on menstruation, 139–40, 167–68
myths about, see Freud legend, Myths 8–13, 17–18
omitted from Freud's autobiography, 463
operates on Freud's nose, 143
and organology, 173–75
on pavor nocturnus, 178, 333
personality, 135
on primary sexual ratio, 164–65
priority disputes: with Freud, 222–23; with Swoboda, 226–29; with Weininger, 223–32
professional career, 135
reaction formation and, 175–79
reductionist aims, 138, 139, 147, 163, 169–70, 177
on repression, 183–84, 230, 426, 431
researches on: his children, 190–91; sexuality, 138–41, 172–88
scientific interests, 138–41
scientific rivalry with Freud, 215–23
as "secret helper" in Freud legend, 447
on seduction theory, 192
on sex determination, 140–41, 164, 172
on sexual latency, 175–77
on shame, 178
speculative tendencies of, 135
sublimation and, 177–79
theories: biomedical context of, 147–65; genital spots of nose, 140; nasal reflex neurosis, 139–40; nasogenital link, 139–40, 152n; periodicity, see periodicity theory; vital periodicity, 167–69
on 33-day cycle, 142
on 28-day cycle, 140–41, 143, 163–65, 166–68, 182